1996

Classic Readings
in American Politics

CLASSIC READINGS
IN AMERICAN POLITICS

EDITED BY

Pietro S. Nivola
University of Vermont

David H. Rosenbloom
Syracuse University

ST. MARTIN'S PRESS   NEW YORK

For our sons and daughters, Adrian, Alessandro, Joshua, Sarah, and Leah

Library of Congress Catalog Card Number: 85-61249
Manufactured in the United States of America.
09876
fedcba
For information, write St. Martin's Press, Inc.
175 Fifth Avenue, New York, N.Y. 10010

ISBN: 0-312-14258-7

Cover design: Darby Downey
Cover photograph: Paul S. Conklin
Book design: Levavi & Levavi

Acknowledgments

Graham T. Allison, "Conceptual Models and the Cuban Missile Crisis," *American Political Science Review* (September 1969), vol. 63, pp. 689–718. Copyright © 1969 by the American Political Science Association. Used with permission of the American Political Science Association and the author.

Peter Bachrach and Morton S. Baratz, "Two Faces of Power," *American Political Science Review* (December 1962), vol. 56, pp. 947–952. Reprinted by permission of the American Political Science Association and the authors.

Edward C. Banfield, "Influence and the Public Interest." Reprinted with permission of The Free Press, a division of Macmillan, Inc., from *Political Influence* by Edward C. Banfield. Copyright © 1961 by The Free Press.

James D. Barber, "The Presidency: What Americans Want," *Center Magazine*, January 1971. Reprinted with permission from *The Center Magazine*, a publication of the Center for the Study of Democratic Institutions.

Raymond A. Bauer, Ithiel de Sola Pool, Lewis Anthony Dexter, "American Business and Public Policy." From Raymond A. Bauer, Ithiel de Sola Pool, Lewis Anthony Dexter, *American Business and Public Policy: The Politics of Foreign Trade*, second edition (New York: Aldine Publishing Company). Copyright © 1963, 1972 by Massachusetts Institute of Technology. Used by permission.

Acknowledgments and copyrights continue at the back of the book on pages 611–612, which constitute an extension of the copyright page.

CONTENTS

Whereas Dahl and the "pluralist" theorists describe political power in America as widely distributed, C. Wright Mills in his well-known book *The Power Elite* views power as narrowly concentrated. This article is an abbreviated version of that thesis.

Political influence is often exerted in subtle and barely visible ways. The interests that shape a political system's underlying "mobilization of bias" can be more important than the explicit "decisions" of formal political actors.

IV. POLITICAL PARTIES AND ELECTIONS 153

In this early statistical study of voting behavior, party identification in the electorate was viewed as highly stable and durable. Major shifts in party affiliations do occur, but only under extraordinary political circumstances.

American voters have become more issue conscious than they were in the immediate postwar period. Party identification exerts a looser influence on individual voting behavior than it did in the past.

Is the electorate undergoing a partisan realignment, or perhaps a "dealignment"? The consequences of declining voter participation and growing voter apathy are examined in Burnham's article.

V. INTEREST GROUPS 207

In this popular version of his ground-breaking essay, "The Logic of Collective Action," Mancur Olson argues that although organizations are expected to further the interests of their members, they may also further the interests of broad categories of nonmembers in the process. Consequently, large organizations must develop incentives to induce individuals to join.

This article analyzes the increased fragmentation of power in Congress, but finds that attending this development are enlarged incentives for congressionally inspired policy innovation. Increasingly, Congress "incubates" the policy initiatives that presidents advance.

A chapter from Sundquist's broad study, *The Decline and Resurgence of Congress,* this excerpt reviews continuing shortcomings in Congress's policymaking capabilities.

Congress conducts most of its work in committees. The committees, however, differ widely according to the goals of their members, the kinds of audiences they address, and the operating procedures they rely on. Diverse legislative orientations emerge.

Increasingly, incumbent members of the House of Representatives are safely reelected time after time. Why? This essay is an analysis of the causes and consequences of prolonged incumbency in Congress.

VII. THE PRESIDENCY 387

Americans seek reassurance, a sense of progress and action, and a sense of legitimacy from the presidency.

Writing in the 1880s, Bryce concludes that American presidents tend to be "commonplace" for a number of reasons that may be familiar to the contemporary reader.

PREFACE

The American political system has fascinated observers since the eighteenth century. No other Western democracy has inspired more scholarly debate and analysis that attempt to explain its governmental institutions and processes. Out of this intellectual ferment have emerged certain works of enduring value; they continue to provide particularly salient insights and frequently define the terms in which social scientists discuss American politics. Many of these classics are incorporated, some in their entirety, some in abridged form, in the following anthology. This collection of seminal essays, articles, cases, and excerpts from books written by a broad spectrum of authors is intended for readers who seek an accessible, reasonably comprehensive introduction to such classics.

Students at both introductory and advanced levels will find this book helpful in identifying the central questions addressed in college courses on American government. Instructors will discover that the book is a useful teaching tool—pulling together in one place mainstays of "the literature," thereby avoiding the use of inconvenient library reserve assignments for students. (For example, instead of having to hunt down the pivotal Supreme Court cases, *Marbury v. Madison* and *McCulloch v. Maryland,* plus the key Federalist papers, and, say, Woodrow Wilson's treatise on Congress or Mancur Olson's indispensable analysis of collective action, students who own this book will have the cases, papers, treatises, and analyses here at their fingertips.)

Through years of experience teaching large undergraduate courses in political science at several institutions, including the University of Vermont, the University of Kansas, and Harvard College, we found that, as in other fields, students had come to appreciate and expect a more rigorous exposure to "the basics." Amid the welter of textbooks and readers on the market, precious few seemed to satisfy this need. Too often they offered merely topical or entertaining material, at the expense of more scholarly, time-tested selections. Therefore, students were not adequately introduced to a serious cross-section of the literature in the discipline they were supposed to be studying.

Incorporated into our book are readings from writers who rank among the most distinguished scholars of politics and government in the United States, past and present. Thus, the volume is a rich sourcebook of important original writings that can be used independently, or as a complement to standard texts in the field.

Although each selection in the compendium represents an authoritative treatment of an aspect of the American political experience, we have chosen these readings with an additional consideration in mind. They are organized so as to stress the main themes or arguments of the section of the book in which they appear. There are ten sections, corresponding to the topics and institutional dimensions on which the study of U.S. politics has traditionally focused: the nation's political culture; federalism; the nature and meaning of power; political parties and elections; interest groups; the Congress; the presidency; the federal bureaucracy; the judiciary; and the policy-making process.

We begin each part with an introduction that highlights the central points of interest and sketches the contribution of each reading to an understanding of the main issues. For example, in Part Three (Political Power) we first compare the leading theories on the distribution of power in the United States—pluralism and elitism—by noting how the writings of Robert A. Dahl and C. Wright Mills enunciate those theories. Then we bring in a third perspective (the argument advanced by Peter Bachrach and Morton S. Baratz), which suggests that it is usually difficult to determine with certainty "who governs" because power is often exercised in subtle, barely visible ways. Selected readings illustrating the three views are then presented. As consistently as possible throughout the book, materials are arranged in this fashion, offering competing interpretations of the topic in question.

Inevitably, this volume comprises only a modest sample of classic readings in American politics. Many other celebrated works could have been added. To include them all, however, would have produced a book of encyclopedic proportions.

Pietro S. Nivola
Burlington, Vermont

David H. Rosenbloom
Syracuse, New York

FOREWORD

BY

THEODORE J. LOWl

In music, the term classic refers to the age of Haydn and Mozart because that was the period when musical forms, instruments, and ensembles became standardized, providing the framework for most subsequent Western musical composition and performance. Classic was not intended to refer to superior results; nor was it intended to distinguish between serious music and popular music. As one music historian put it, "To group all music which does not come under the head of popular music as classical is a mark of lack of cultivation."

This musical usage is consistent with the *Oxford English Dictionary*, where, although the primary definition identifies classic as referring to things of the highest quality, the brief history of its usage affirms that the meaning of classic arises out of references to "classes of colleges or schools." It is probable that this notion influenced the extension of the word to the ancient authors themselves, as studied in school or college. It is also probable that "the transference of the epithet from the first-class or standard writers in Greek and Latin to these languages themselves has been partly owing to the notion that the latter are intrinsically excellent or of the first order, in comparison to the modern tongues." Thus, a musical composition or an essay is referred to as classic if it is thought to perform as the model or standard for other works in a school of thought or a discipline.

But here's the rub. If a work qualifies as classic only when it is loyally imitated by all successors, then not even the masterpieces of the great Haydn or Mozart would fit the definition because significant departures from their model occurred even before they were cold in the grave. The classical era of music was rather quickly replaced by the romantic era. What we can say, however, is that the works of Haydn and Mozart were classic because, as the models, they set the terms of discourse, even for the dissenters and the innovators.

How are the essays in this volume classics? Each is considered something of a classic because it has helped shape the terms of discourse in political science. Each has served as a kind of jumping off point for other scholars. Actually, I should say jumping *on* point, since many scholars have found it useful to criticize one or more of these works as a way of distinguishing their own. In other words, a work can become a classic regardless of its weaknesses. The hundreds of citations of these works in the footnotes of others indicate how influential they have been. To cite another author's work does not mean it is being used as the authority to clinch the argument. More often, a work is cited because it has been integrated into the thought on that subject. Even a cursory reading of the essays in this volume shows that the authors were seeking to be part of a discourse outside the confines of their own research by saying something lasting about the conditions of political life—especially about the conditions of that most delicate of all political specimens, institutionalized democracy.

In the introduction to his own classic work, *American Capitalism*, John Kenneth Galbraith characterized the U.S. economy by observing that "such are the aerodynamics and wing-loading of the bumblebee that, in principle, it cannot fly. It does, and the knowledge that it defies the august authority of Isaac Newton and Orville Wright must keep the bee in constant fear of a crack-up."[1] Such a comparison is more appropriate for the American polity, because it has been relatively stable for over two hundred years despite the fact that American society and the American economy have been unstable. To add to the mystery, American democracy itself was built on contradictions: How is it possible to balance free thought and free choice with the requirements of public order? In a representative legislature? But is it possible to set up a legislature that gives equality of access to policymaking and still makes important decisions in time to meet the collective needs of an immensely complex society? And how can we have intelligent policymakers if a very substantial fraction of the American electorate is ignorant of the issues? Or an accountable bureaucracy without giving its leader, the president, powers far in excess of what a legislature can oversee or the people or the courts will accept?

Political scientists address themselves to these difficult issues with one hand tied behind their backs; that is, they are trying to study with scientific precision matters as complex and ever-changing as the institutions of government. Science requires analysis, it has its own language—that of variables and hypotheses—and it holds to its own standards of truth, which presume strict canons of evidence and demonstration, and an attitude of utmost objectivity. Few political scientists want to reject the scientific method, but they use it at a heavy cost. While being scientific, political scientists sacrifice at least some concern for the questions of history, context, and value, which attend all political issues. Does this mean that we yield to others the joy of confrontation with big questions, even when our findings may bear on them?

The authors in this collection have indicated an unwillingness to yield. But this does not mean they have abandoned their discipline. An outstanding characteristic of these selections, especially those drawn from the professional

---

[1] John Kenneth Galbraith, *American Capitalism*, second edition, revised (Boston: Houghton Mifflin, 1956), p. 1.

political science of the twentieth century, is that each started on a fairly solid evidentiary base and each *lifted the discourse* from that base to an entirely different language—from a language of variables to a language of argument, from a language of causes to a language of consequences. That, to me, is the secret of a classic, whether it succeeds or whether it fails; and that is the only way to make political science interesting.

Lifting the discourse toward the larger consequences that are of concern to the whole political community also makes authors more vulnerable than if they stayed within the confines of what has been carefully studied. As Woodrow Wilson said in 1911 in his address as president of the American Political Science Association, "There is no such thing as an expert in human relationships."[2] Inevitably, those who seek to engage in the larger, continuing discourse concerning human—and political—relationships must go a considerable distance beyond their professional competence.

Not everyone wants to take such a risk, but those who do have something in common: They are both teachers and scholars. Although four of the six pre-twentieth century authors represented here—Madison, Hamilton, Chief Justice Marshall, and de Tocqueville—were not academicians, they were, in their own way teachers of politics. For example, Madison and Hamilton addressed their arguments in *Federalist* #10 and #78 to the New York voters and the members of the New York State Assembly who were polarized over whether to ratify the new Constitution. Alexis de Tocqueville wrote about democracy in the America of the 1830s but aimed his argument at the French public. All the others, including the late nineteenth-century authors Woodrow Wilson and Lord Bryce, were card-carrying academic political scientists (with the exception of a half dozen who took Ph.D.s in some related academic field but addressed a large number of their writings to political scientists); and all but one had a career in college teaching.

Is this dominance by teacher-scholars merely a reflection of editorial bias? I doubt it, because the primary interest of the editors is to provide selections, regardless of the source or author, most likely to be considered essential reading by the largest segment of the relevant market, namely, the professors who select books and students who are assigned to purchase and read them. I think the explanation is to be found in the creative contradiction faced by college teachers who embrace their discipline by carrying on a parallel career in research and writing. Writing for the discipline of political science subjects the author to the anonymous, professional peer review process of scholarly journals and book publishing. The college classroom subjects the teacher to the contrary pressure of trying to transcend the methods and results of research in the discipline by explaining its value to students. College students require of their teachers at least some concern for consequential argument as well as causal analysis. They want to know "So what?" In the classroom, professors rarely can talk down to their

---

[2] Raymond Seidelman, with the assistance of Edward J. Harpham, *Disenchanted Realists: Political Science and the American Crisis* (Albany: State University of New York Press, 1985).

students; generally they have to talk *up* to their students because they have the difficult task of bringing specialized research and unspecialized students to a community of common concern: how we govern ourselves.

A teacher's attempt to be memorable by being consequential is the important bridge between the down-to-earth science of our research and the more elevated argument of our teaching. The contradiction between the stringencies of science and the goal of a higher, more consequence-oriented level of discourse is not only creative, it is also invaluable. If in the process we reveal our incompetence, that is in itself good teaching, because it encourages students to join the process as bona fide participants.

In the preface to his intellectual history of political science (*The Tragedy of Political Science*, 1984) David Ricci observes that with the rise of academic political science, "The line of first-rate thinkers in the Western tradition came to an end." Those whose writings form the basis for the history of political science—from Plato and Aristotle to Marx and Mill—were not the product of an academic environment, though some of them did teach for a living. As Ricci put it, "The longer I thought about the declining number of great thinkers and the growing prominence of universities, the more I was convinced that these two trends must be significantly related."[3] It is difficult to disagree with Ricci's contention that the twentieth century has yet to produce a single political thinker of the stature of a Marx or Mill, the last of the great thinkers before political writing and teaching became organized into the discipline of political science. But it would be equally difficult for him to disagree with the contention that in the 2,000-plus years between Plato and Mill, *no* country or century—not even the Greece of classical antiquity—could lay claim to many great thinkers. Great thinkers just don't come along very often. And it's even possible that their appearance may drop still further because of the tendency of both democracy and science to reduce issues to manageable proportions, while thinkers tend to magnify issues. America's greatest thinkers all appeared at the time of our founding, with the possible exception of Abraham Lincoln and a half dozen members of the U.S. Supreme Court—and all for the same reason: They confronted issues too big to trivialize, and they crafted their responses accordingly.

Modern academic political scientists from Woodrow Wilson to the present, including all the contemporary authors in this volume, have overcome many of the constraints of science and democracy, and although there are still no Aristotles or Rousseaus, we can consider ourselves keepers of the flame. If enough political scientists can transcend the discipline without unsciencing it, we can maintain a discourse worthy of the great thinkers to come—who may be in our classrooms at this very moment. We cannot yet know who they are, and we cannot create them. But we can encourage them by exposing them to the best thinking our field of study can offer.

[3] David Ricci, *The Tragedy of Political Science: Politics, Scholarship, and Democracy* (New Haven: Yale University Press, 1984).

CLASSIC READINGS
IN AMERICAN POLITICS

PART ONE

POLITICAL CULTURE AND TRADITIONS

American and foreign observers have long considered government and politics in the United States to be unique. This uniqueness is suggested by structural features such as a written constitution, a two-party system, an elaborate separation of powers, a bicameral legislature, federalism, and judicial review—features that are not found together in other political systems. But the unique qualities of the American polity reach well beyond structures and institutions; they go to the very core of the United States' political culture.

Political culture involves the ways in which the members of a political community think, feel, and evaluate their government and politics. This is a broad concern upon which almost all general theories of the American political experience dwell. Although different scholars have stressed various keys to understanding the United States' political culture, the classic interpretations tend to stress two related elements—equality and constitutionalism.

The first selection on political culture is drawn from the seminal work of Alexis de Tocqueville, whom some consider still the keenest observer of the American political community. In *Democracy in America* (Vol. I, 1838; Vol. II, 1840), this visitor from France not only identified equality as the fundamental aspect of the developing American political culture, but he also addressed the very breaches of equality that still confound the political system today. Thus, in perhaps his best-known words, Tocqueville wrote, "The great advantage of the Americans is that they have arrived at a state of democracy without having to endure a democratic revolution; and that they are born equal, instead of becoming so." But in a lesser-known passage, he commented that "in no country has such constant care been taken as in America to trace two clearly distinct lines of action for the two sexes, and to make them keep pace one with the other, but in two pathways which are always different." Moreover, he referred to the existence of three distinct races within the United States polity as one of the "dangers which menace that confederation," as these groups might almost be termed "hostile to each other" and "do not amalgamate," but rather "each race fulfils its destiny apart." Consequently, although we have titled the selections from Tocqueville "Equality," his understanding of the fundamental social cleavages facing the nation is also stressed.

Although Tocqueville presents a sound beginning for the student of American political culture, Louis Hartz is correct in pointing out that "no school of American historians has ever come out of the well known work of the greatest foreign critic America ever had—Tocqueville." Hence, while frequently rooted in Tocqueville's work, intellectual traditions concerning American political culture have frequently moved beyond his formulations in addressing additional dimensions.

In his *Liberal Tradition in America* (1955), Hartz argues that what sets America apart from other countries is its liberal consensus. Although "liberalism" eludes a precise definition, Hartz uses it to refer to a democratic ethos stressing individual rights, political equality, and limited government. In his view, this liberalism developed naturally from the absence of a feudal past in America. Essentially, a nonfeudal society lacks both a genuine revolutionary tradition and a tradition of reaction; this makes it possible for what would be revolutionary elsewhere (liberalism) to be a matter of consensus in a political community such as the United States.

Seymour Martin Lipset also addresses the unique qualities of the American political experience. In *The First New Nation* (1963), he compares the emergence of the United States as an independent state in the eighteenth century to the experiences of new nations in the twentieth century. He finds some fundamental similarities in the challenges facing all states upon gaining independence. However, several elements set the newly formed United States apart. Perhaps most important, in Lipset's view, was "the fact that the weight of ancient tradition which is present in almost all of the contemporary new states was largely absent. It was not only a new nation, it was a new society, much less bound to the customs and values of the past than any nation of Europe." Lipset believes that the values of the new society were proclaimed in the preeminent document of the American Revolution—the Declaration of Independence—and that these values have continuously influenced American social and political behavior.

The Constitution is another document of enduring importance in U.S. government and politics. An early recognition of the role the Constitution could play, or a "constitutionalist" approach, was manifested in the writings of "Publius," the pseudonym Alexander Hamilton, James Madison, and John Jay used in writing *The Federalist Papers* (1787–1788). Regardless of the particular topic under discussion, Publius' basic assumption is that a written constitution can serve to structure both the operation of a nation's government and the nature of its politics. *The Federalist Papers* included here state what can be taken as the Founders' general theory of government and politics. They deal with republicanism, the separation of powers, and the nature of executive power.

Aside from the *The Federalist Papers*, Charles Beard's *Economic Interpretation of the Constitution of the United States* (1913) is considered to be the most important effort to understand the American political culture through a constitutionalist approach. Beard's argument, based on an analysis of the economic holdings and activities of those who attended the Constitutional Convention of 1787, is influential because it was the first to propose that the Founders had common economic interests that they sought to protect through the Constitution. "These are the great powers conferred on the new government: taxation, war, commercial control, and disposition of western lands," Beard writes. "Through them public creditors may be paid in full, domestic peace maintained, advantages obtained in dealing with foreign nations, manufactures protected, and the development of the territories go forward with full swing." Moreover, he points out, "None of the powers conferred by the Constitution on Congress permits a direct attack on property." Although Beard's controversial thesis has been criticized for overstating the Founders' economic motives, his argument still retains much of its original insight. Its contemporary relevance lies primarily in the fact that, whatever their exact motives, the Founders sought to construct a government that was based on popular support but not immediately or highly responsive to shifts in public opinion. For instance, fixed and staggered terms for elected officials and bicameralism were intended as checks on the people to protect the Founders, an upper-class minority, from popular pressures for greater equality. Thus, the constitutionalist approach reminds us that American government was not designed to translate every majoritarian impulse into public policy. Rather, it was intended to reflect the long-term values and policy objectives embodied in the political culture.

1

ALEXIS DE TOCQUEVILLE

EQUALITY

Amongst the novel objects that attracted my attention during my stay in the United States, nothing struck me more forcibly than the general equality of conditions. I readily discovered the prodigious influence which this primary fact exercises on the whole course of society, by giving a certain direction to public opinion, and a certain tenor to the laws; by imparting new maxims to the governing powers, and peculiar habits to the governed.

I speedily perceived that the influence of this fact extends far beyond the political character and the laws of the country, and that it has no less empire over civil society than over the Government; it creates opinions, engenders sentiments, suggests the ordinary practices of life, and modifies whatever it does not produce.

The more I advanced in the study of American society, the more I perceived that the equality of conditions is the fundamental fact from which all others seem to be derived, and the central point at which all my observations constantly terminated. . . .

INDIVIDUALISM STRONGER
AT THE CLOSE OF A DEMOCRATIC REVOLUTION
THAN AT OTHER PERIODS

The period when the construction of democratic society upon the ruins of an aristocracy has just been completed, is especially that at which this separation of men from one another, and the egotism resulting from it, most forcibly strike the observation. Democratic communities not only contain a large number of independent citizens, but they are constantly filled with men who, having entered but yesterday upon their independent condition, are intoxicated with their new power. They entertain a presumptuous confidence in their strength, and as they do not suppose that they can henceforward ever have occasion to claim the assistance of their fellow-creatures, they do not scruple to show that they care for nobody but themselves.

An aristocracy seldom yields without a protracted struggle, in the course of which implacable animosities are kindled between the different classes of society.

These passions survive the victory, and traces of them may be observed in the midst of the democratic confusion which ensues.

Those members of the community who were at the top of the late gradations of rank cannot immediately forget their former greatness; they will long regard themselves as aliens in the midst of the newly composed society. They look upon all those whom this state of society has made their equals as oppressors, whose destiny can excite no sympathy; they have lost sight of their former equals, and feel no longer bound by a common interest to their fate: each of them, standing aloof, thinks that he is reduced to care for himself alone. Those, on the contrary, who were formerly at the foot of the social scale, and who have been brought up to the common level by a sudden revolution, cannot enjoy their newly acquired independence without secret uneasiness; and if they meet with some of their former superiors on the same footing as themselves, they stand aloof from them with an expression of triumph and of fear.

It is, then, commonly at the outset of democratic society that citizens are most disposed to live apart. Democracy leads men not to draw near to their fellow-creatures; but democratic revolutions lead them to shun each other, and perpetuate in a state of equality the animosities which the state of inequality engendered.

The great advantage of the Americans is that they have arrived at a state of democracy without having to endure a democratic revolution; and that they are born equal, instead of becoming so. . . .

HOW THE AMERICANS UNDERSTAND
THE EQUALITY OF THE SEXES

I have shown how democracy destroys or modifies the different inequalities which originate in society: but is this all? or does it not ultimately affect that great inequality of man and woman which has seemed, up to the present day, to be eternally based in human nature? I believe that the social changes which bring nearer to the same level the father and son, the master and servant, and superiors and inferiors generally speaking, will raise woman and make her more and more the equal of man. But here, more than ever, I feel the necessity of making myself clearly understood; for there is no subject on which the coarse and lawless fancies of our age have taken a freer range.

There are people in Europe who, confounding together the different characteristics of the sexes, would make of man and woman beings not only equal but alike. They would give to both the same functions, impose on both the same duties, and grant to both the same rights: they would mix them in all things— their occupations, their pleasures, their business. It may readily be conceived, that by thus attempting to make one sex equal to the other, both are degraded; and from so preposterous a medley of the works of nature, nothing could ever result but weak men and disorderly women.

It is not thus that the Americans understand that species of democratic equality which may be established between the sexes. They admit, that as nature has appointed such wide differences between the physical and moral constitutions of man and woman, her manifest design was to give a distinct employment to their various faculties; and they hold that improvement does not consist in making beings so dissimilar do pretty nearly the same things, but in getting each of them to fulfil their respective tasks in the best possible manner. The Americans have applied to the sexes the great principle of political economy which governs the manufactures of our age, by carefully dividing the duties of man from those of woman, in order that the great work of society may be the better carried on.

In no country had such constant care been taken as in America to trace two clearly distinct lines of action for the two sexes, and to make them keep pace one with the other, but in two pathways which are always different. American women never manage the outward concerns of the family, or conduct a business, or take a part in political life; nor are they, on the other hand, ever compelled to perform the rough labor of the fields, or to make any of those laborious exertions which demand the exertion of physical strength. No families are so poor as to form an exception to this rule. If on the one hand an American woman cannot escape from the quiet circle of domestic employments, on the other hand she is never forced to go beyond it. Hence it is that the women of America, who often exhibit a masculine strength of understanding and a manly energy, generally preserve great delicacy of personal appearance and always retain the manners of women, although they sometimes show that they have the hearts and minds of men.

Nor have the Americans ever supposed that one consequence of democratic principles is the subversion of marital power, or the confusion of the natural authorities in families. They hold that every association must have a head in order to accomplish its object, and that the natural head of the conjugal association is man. They do not therefore deny him the right of directing his partner; and they maintain, that in the smaller association of husband and wife, as well as in the great social community, the object of democracy is to regulate and legalize the powers which are necessary, not to subvert all power.

This opinion is not peculiar to one sex, and contested by the other: I never observed that the women of America consider conjugal authority as a fortunate usurpation of their rights, nor that they thought themselves degraded by submitting to it. It appeared to me, on the contrary, that they attach a sort of pride to the voluntary surrender of their own will, and make it their boast to bend themselves to the yoke, not to shake it off. Such at least is the feeling expressed by the most virtuous of their sex; the others are silent; and in the United States it is not the practice for a guilty wife to clamour for the rights of woman, while she is trampling on her holiest duties.

It has often been remarked that in Europe a certain degree of contempt lurks even in the flattery which men lavish upon women: although a European frequently affects to be the slave of woman, it may be seen that he never sincerely thinks her his equal. In the United States men seldom compliment women, but they daily show how much they esteem them. They constantly display an entire confidence in the understanding of a wife, and a profound respect for her freedom; they have decided that her mind is just as fitted as that of a man to discover the plain truth, and her heart as firm to embrace it; and they have never sought to place her virtue, any more than his, under the shelter of prejudice, ignorance, and fear.

It would seem that in Europe, where man so easily submits to the despotic sway of women, they are nevertheless curtailed of some of the greatest qualities of the human species, and considered as seductive but imperfect beings; and (what may well provoke astonishment) women ultimately look upon themselves in the same light, and almost consider it as a privilege that they are entitled to show themselves futile, feeble, and timid. The women of America claim no such privileges.

Again, it may be said, that in our morals we have reserved strange immunities to man; so that there is, as it were, one virtue for his use, and another for the guidance of his partner; and that, according to the opinion of the public, the very same act may be punished alternately as a crime or only as a fault. The Americans know not this iniquitous division of duties and rights; among them the seducer is as much dishonoured as his victim.

It is true that the Americans rarely lavish upon women those eager attentions which are commonly paid them in Europe; but their conduct to women always implies that they suppose them to be virtuous and refined; and such is the respect entertained for the moral freedom of the sex, that in the presence of a woman the most guarded language is used, lest her ear should be offended by an expression. In America a young unmarried woman may, alone and without fear, undertake a long journey.

The legislators of the United States, who have mitigated almost all the penalties of criminal law, still make rape a capital offence, and no crime, is visited with more inexorable severity by public opinion. This may be accounted for; as the Americans can conceive nothing more precious than a woman's honour, and nothing which ought so much to be respected as her independence, they hold that no punishment is too severe for the man who deprives her of them against her will. In France, where the same offence is visited with far milder penalties, it is frequently difficult to get a verdict from a jury against the prisoner. Is this a consequence of contempt of decency or contempt of woman? I cannot but believe that it is a contempt of one and of the other.

Thus the Americans do not think that man and woman have either the duty or the right to perform the same offices, but they show an equal regard for both their respective parts; and though their lot is different, they consider both of them as beings of equal value. They do not give to the courage of woman the same form or the same direction as to that of man; but they never doubt her courage: and if they hold that man and his partner ought not always to exercise their intellect and understanding in the same manner, they at least believe the understanding of the one to be as sound as that of the other, and her intellect to be as clear. Thus, then, while they have allowed the social inferiority of woman to subsist, they have done all they could to raise her morally and intellectually to the level of man; and in this respect they appear to me to have excellently understood the true principle of democratic improvement.

As for myself, I do not hesitate to avow, that, although the women of the United States are confined within the narrow circle of domestic life, and their situation is in some respects one of extreme dependance, I have nowhere seen women occupying a loftier position; and if I were asked, now that I am drawing to the close of this work, in which I have spoken of so many important things done by the Americans, to what the singular prosperity and growing strength of that people ought mainly to be attributed, I should reply—to the superiority of their women. . . .

THE PRESENT, AND PROBABLE FUTURE CONDITION OF THE THREE RACES WHICH INHABIT THE TERRITORY OF THE UNITED STATES

The principal part of the task which I had imposed upon myself is now performed: I have shown, as far as I was able, the laws and the manners of the American democracy. Here I might stop; but the reader would perhaps feel that I had not satisfied his expectations.

The absolute supremacy of democracy is not all that we meet with in America; the inhabitants of the New World may be considered from more than one point of view. In the course of this work my subject has often led me to speak of the Indians and the Negroes; but I have never been able to stop in order to show what place these two races occupy, in the midst of the democratic people whom I was engaged in describing. I have mentioned in what spirit, and according to what laws, the Anglo-American Union was formed; but I could only glance at the dangers which menace that confederation, whilst it was equally impossible for me to give a detailed account of its chances of duration, independently of its laws and manners. When speaking of the United republican States, I hazarded no conjectures upon the permanence of republican forms in the New World; and when making frequent allusion to the commercial activity which reigns in the Union, I was unable to inquire into the future condition of the Americans as a commercial people.

These topics are collaterally connected with my subject, without forming a part of it; they are American, without being democratic; and to portray democracy has been my principal aim. It was therefore necessary to postpone these questions, which I now take up as the proper termination of my work.

The territory now occupied or claimed by the American Union spreads from the shores of the Atlantic to those of the Pacific Ocean. On the East and West its limits are those of the continent itself. On the South it advances nearly to the Tropic, and it extends upwards to the icy regions of the North.

The human beings who are scattered over this space do not form, as in Europe, so many branches of the same stock. Three races naturally distinct, and I might almost say hostile to each other, are discoverable amongst them at the first glance. Almost insurmountable barriers had been raised between them by education and by law, as well as by their origin and outward characteristics; but fortune has brought them together on the same soil, where, although they are mixed, they do not amalgamate, and each race fulfils its destiny apart.

Amongst these widely differing families of men, the first which attracts attention, the superior in intelligence, in power and in enjoyment, is the White or European, the MAN pre-eminent; and in subordinate grades, the Negro and the Indian. These two unhappy races have nothing in common; neither birth, nor features, nor language, nor habits. Their only resemblance lies in their misfortunes. Both of them occupy an inferior rank in the country they inhabit; both suffer from tyranny; and if their wrongs are not the same, they originate at any rate with the same authors.

If we reasoned from what passes in the world, we should almost say that the European is to the other races of mankind, what man is to the lower animals;— he makes them subservient to his use; and when he cannot subdue, he destroys them. Oppression has at one stroke deprived the descendants of the Africans of almost all the privileges of humanity. The Negro of the United States has lost all remembrance of his country; the language which his forefathers spoke is never heard around him; he adjured their religion and forgot their customs when he ceased to belong to Africa, without acquiring any claim to European privileges. But he remains half-way between the two communities; sold by the one, repulsed by the other; finding not a spot in the universe to call by the name of country, except the faint image of a home which the shelter of his master's roof affords.

The Negro has no family; woman is merely the temporary companion of his pleasures, and his children are upon an equality with himself from the moment of their birth. Am I to call it a proof of God's mercy, or a visitation of his wrath, that man in certain states appears to be insensible to his extreme wretchedness, and almost affects with a depraved taste the cause of his misfortunes? The Negro, who is plunged in this abyss of evils, scarcely feels his own calamitous situation. Violence made him a slave, and the habit of servitude gives him the thoughts and desires of a slave; he admires his tyrants more than he hates them, and finds his joy and his pride in the servile imitation of those who oppress him: his understanding is degraded to the level of his soul.

The Negro enters upon slavery as soon as he is born; nay, he may have been purchased in the womb, and have begun his slavery before he began his existence. Equally devoid of wants and of enjoyment, and useless to himself, he learns, with his first notions of existence, that he is the property of another who has an interest in preserving his life, and that the care of it does not devolve upon himself; even the power of thought appears to him a useless gift of Providence, and he quietly enjoys the privileges of his debasement.

If he becomes free, independence is often felt by him to be a heavier burden than slavery; for having learned, in the course of his life, to submit to everything except reason, he is too much unacquainted with her dictates to obey them. A thousand new desires beset him, and he is destitute of the knowledge and energy necessary to resist them: these are masters which it is necessary to contend with, and he has learnt only to submit and obey. In short, he sinks to such a depth of wretchedness, that while servitude brutalizes, liberty destroys him.

Oppression has been no less fatal to the Indian than to the Negro race, but its effects are different. Before the arrival of white men in the New World, the inhabitants of North America lived quietly in their woods, enduring the vicissitudes and practising the virtues and vices common to savage nations. The Europeans, having dispersed the Indian tribes and driven them into the deserts, condemned them to a wandering life full of inexpressible sufferings.

Savage nations are only controlled by opinion and by custom. When the North American Indians had lost the sentiment of attachment to their country; when their families were dispersed, their traditions obscured, and the chain of their recollections broken; when all their habits were changed, and their wants increased beyond measure, European tyranny rendered them more disorderly and less civilized than they were before. The moral and physical condition of these tribes continually grew worse, and they became more barbarous as they became more wretched. Nevertheless the Europeans have not been able to metamorphose the character of the Indians; and though they have had power to destroy them, they have never been able to make them submit to the rules of civilized society.

The lot of the Negro is placed on the extreme limit of servitude, while that of the Indian lies on the uttermost verge of liberty; and slavery does not produce more fatal effects upon the first, than independence upon the second. The Negro has lost all property in his own person, and he cannot dispose of his existence without committing a sort of fraud: but the savage is his own master as soon as he is able to act; parental authority is scarcely known to him; he has never bent his will to that of any of his kind, nor learned the difference between voluntary obedience and a shameful subjection; and the very name of law is unknown to him. To be free, with him, signifies to escape from all the shackles of society. As he delights in this barbarous independence, and would rather perish than sacrifice the least part of it, civilization has little power over him.

The Negro makes a thousand fruitless efforts to insinuate himself amongst men who repulse him; he conforms to the tastes of his oppressors, adopts their opinions, and hopes by imitating them to form a part of their community. Having been told from infancy that his race is naturally inferior to that of the Whites, he assents to the proposition, and is ashamed of his own nature. In each of his features he discovers a trace of slavery, and, if it were in his power, he would willingly rid himself of everything that makes him what he is.

The Indian, on the contrary, has his imagination inflated with the pretended nobility of his origin, and lives and dies in the midst of these dreams of pride. Far from desiring to conform his habits to ours, he loves his savage life as the distinguishing mark of his race, and he repels every advance to civilization, less perhaps from the hatred which he entertains for it, than from a dread of resembling the Europeans. While he has nothing to oppose to our perfection in the arts but the resources of the desert, to our tactics nothing but undisciplined courage; whilst our well-digested plans are met by the spontaneous instincts of savage life, who can wonder if he fails in this unequal contest?

The Negro, who earnestly desires to mingle his race with that of the European, cannot effect it; while the Indian, who might succeed to a certain extent, disdains to make the attempt. The servility of the one dooms him to slavery, the pride of the other to death.

I remember that while I was travelling through the forests which still cover the State of Alabama, I arrived one day at the log-house of a pioneer. I did not wish to penetrate into the dwelling of the American, but retired to rest myself for a while on the margin of a spring, which was not far off, in the woods. While I was in this place, (which was in the neighborhood of the Creek territory,) an Indian woman appeared, followed by a negress, and holding by the hand a little white girl of five or six years old, whom I took to be the daughter of the pioneer. A sort of barbarous luxury set off the costume of the Indian; rings of metal were hanging from her nostrils and ears; her hair, which was adorned with glass beads, fell loosely upon her shoulders; and I saw that she was not married, for she still wore that necklace of shells which the bride always deposits on the nuptial couch. The negress was clad in squalid European garments.

They all three came and seated themselves upon the banks of the fountain; and the young Indian, taking the child in her arms, lavished upon her such fond caresses as mothers give; while the negress endeavored by various little artifices to attract the attention of the young creole. The child displayed in her slightest gestures a consciousness of superiority which formed a strange contrast with her infantine weakness; as if she received the attentions of her companions with a sort of condescension.

The negress was seated on the ground before her mistress, watching her smallest desires, and apparently divided between strong affection for the child and servile fear; whilst the savage displayed, in the midst of her tenderness, an air of freedom and of pride which was almost ferocious. I had approached the group, and I contemplated them in silence; but my curiosity was probably displeasing to the Indian woman, for she suddenly rose, pushed the child roughly from her, and giving me an angry look plunged into the thicket.

I had often chanced to see individuals met together in the same place, who belonged to the three races of men which people North America. I had perceived from many different results the preponderance of the Whites. But in the picture which I have just been describing there was something peculiarly touching; a bond of affection here united the oppressors with the oppressed, and the effort of Nature to bring them together rendered still more striking the immense distance placed between them by prejudice and by law.

2

LOUIS HARTZ

THE CONCEPT
OF A LIBERAL SOCIETY

1. AMERICA AND EUROPE

The analysis which this book contains is based on what might be called the storybook truth about American history: that America was settled by men who fled from the feudal and clerical oppressions of the Old World. If there is anything in this view, as old as the national folklore itself, then the outstanding thing about the American community in Western history ought to be the nonexistence of those oppressions, or since the reaction against them was in the broadest sense liberal, that the American community is a liberal community. We are confronted, as it were, with a kind of inverted Trotskyite law of combined development, America skipping the feudal stage of history as Russia presumably skipped the liberal stage. I know that I am using broad terms broadly here. "Feudalism" refers technically to the institutions of the medieval era, and it is well known that aspects of the decadent feudalism of the later period, such as primogeniture, entail, and quitrents, were present in America even in the eighteenth century.[1] "Liberalism" is an even vaguer term, clouded as it is by all sorts of modern social reform connotations, and even when one insists on using it in the classic Lockian sense, as I shall insist here, there are aspects of our original life in the Puritan colonies and the South which hardly fit its meaning. But these are the liabilities of any large generalization, danger points but not insuperable barriers. What in the end is more interesting is the curious failure of American historians, after repeating endlessly that America was grounded in escape from the European past, to interpret our history in the light of that fact. There are a number of reasons for this which we shall encounter before we are through, but one is obvious at the outset: the separation of the study of American from European history and politics. Any attempt to uncover the nature of an American society without feudalism can only be accomplished by studying it in conjunction with a European society where the feudal structure and the feudal ethos did in fact survive. This is not to deny our national uniqueness, one of the reasons curiously given for studying America alone, but actually to affirm it. How can we know the uniqueness of anything except by contrasting it with what is not unique? The rationale for a separate American study, once you begin to think about it, explodes the study itself.

In the end, however, it is not logic but experience, to use a Holmesian phrase, which exposes the traditional approach. We could use our uniqueness as an excuse for evading its study so long as our world position did not really require us to know much about it. Now that a whole series of alien cultures have crashed in upon the American world, shattering the peaceful landscape of Bancroft and Beard, the old non sequitur simply will not do. When we need desperately to know the idiosyncrasies which interfere with our understanding of Europe, we can hardly break away from "European schemes" of analysis, as J. Franklin Jameson urged American historians to do in 1891 (not that they ever really used them in the first place) on the ground that we are idiosyncratic. But the issue is deeper than foreign policy, for the world involvement has also brought to the surface of American life great new domestic forces which must remain inexplicable without comparative study. It has redefined, as Communism shows, the issue of our internal freedom in terms of our external life. So in fact it is the entire crisis of our time which compels us to make that journey to Europe and back which ends in the discovery of the American liberal world.

2. "NATURAL LIBERALISM": THE FRAME OF MIND

One of the central characteristics of a nonfeudal society is that it lacks a genuine revolutionary tradition, the tradition which in Europe has been linked with the Puritan and French revolutions: that it is "born equal," as Tocqueville said. And this being the case, it lacks also a tradition of reaction: lacking Robespierre it lacks Maistre, lacking Sydney it lacks Charles II. Its liberalism is what Santayana called, referring to American democracy, a "natural" phenomenon. But the matter is curiously broader than this, for a society which begins with Locke, and thus transforms him, stays with Locke, by virtue of an absolute and irrational attachment it develops for him, and becomes as indifferent to the challenge of socialism in the later era as it was unfamiliar with the heritage of feudalism in the earlier one. It has within it, as it were, a kind of self-completing mechanism, which insures the universality of the liberal idea. Here, we shall see, is one of the places where Marx went wrong in his historical analysis, attributing as he did the emergence of the socialist ideology to the objective movement of economic forces. Actually socialism is largely an ideological phenomenon, arising out of the principles of class and the revolutionary liberal revolt against them which the old European order inspired. It is not accidental that America which has uniquely lacked a feudal tradition has uniquely lacked also a socialist tradition. The hidden origin of socialist thought everywhere in the West is to be found in the feudal ethos. The ancien régime inspires Rousseau; both inspire Marx.

Which brings us to the substantive quality of the natural liberal mind. And this poses no easy problem. For when the words of Locke are used and a prior Filmer is absent, how are we to delineate the significance of the latter fact? In politics men who make speeches do not go out of their way to explain how differently they would speak if the enemies they had were larger in size or different in character. On the contrary whatever enemies they fight they paint in satanic terms, so that a problem sufficiently difficult to begin with in a liberal society becomes complicated further by the inevitable perspectives of political battle. Take the American Revolution. With John Adams identifying the Stamp Act with the worst of the historic European oppressions, how can we distinguish the man from Lilburne or the philosophers of the French Enlightenment? And yet if we study the American liberal language in terms of intensity and emphasis, if we look for silent omissions as well as explicit inclusions, we begin to see a pattern emerging that smacks distinctively of the New World. It has a quiet, matter of fact quality, it does not understand the meaning of sovereign power, the bourgeois class passion is scarcely present, the sense of the past is altered, and there is about it all, as compared with the European pattern, a vast and almost charming innocence of mind. Twain's "Innocents Abroad" is a pretty relevant concept, for the psyche that springs from social war and social revolution is given to far suspicions and sidelong glances that the American liberal cannot easily understand. Possibly this is what people mean when they say that European thought is "deeper" than American, though anyone who tries to grapple with America in Western terms will wonder whether the term "depth" is the proper one to use. There can be an appalling complexity to innocence, especially if your point of departure is guilt.

Now if the *ancien régime* is not present to begin with, one thing follows automatically: it does not return in a blaze of glory. It does not flower in the nineteenth century in a Disraeli or a Ballanche, however different from each other these men may be. I do not mean to imply that no trace of the feudal urge, no shadow whatsoever of Sir Walter Scott, has been found on the hills and plains of the New World. One can get into a lot of useless argument if he affirms the liberalness of a liberal society in absolute mathematical fashion. The top strata of the American community, from the time of Peggy Hutchinson to the time of Margaret Kennedy, have yearned for the aristocratic ethos. But instead of exemplifying the typical Western situation, these yearnings represent an inversion of it. America has presented the world with the peculiar phenomenon, not of a frustrated middle class, but of a "frustrated aristocracy"—of men, Aristotelian-like, trying to break out of the egalitarian confines of middle class life but suffering guilt and failure in the process. The South before the Civil War is the case par excellence of this, though New England of course exemplifies it also. Driven away from Jefferson by abolitionism, the Fitzhughs of the ante-bellum era actually dared to ape the doctrinal patterns of the Western reaction, of Disraeli and Bonald. But when Jefferson is traditional, European traditionalism is a curious thing indeed. The Southerners were thrown into fantastic contradictions by their iconoclastic conservatism, by what I have called the "Reactionary Enlightenment," and after the Civil War for good historical reasons they fell quickly into oblivion. The South, as John Crowe Ransom has said, has been the part of America closest to Old World Europe, but it has never really been Europe. It has been an alien child in a liberal family, tortured and confused, driven to a fantasy life which, instead of disproving the power of Locke in America, portrays more poignantly than anything else the tyranny he has had.

But is not the problem of Fitzhugh at once the problem of De Leon? Here we have one of the great and neglected relationships in American history: the common fecklessness of the Southern "feudalists" and the modern socialists. It is not accidental, but something rooted in the logic of all of Western history, that they should fail alike to leave a dent in the American liberal intelligence. For if the concept of class was meaningless in its Disraelian form, and if American liberalism had never acquired it in its bourgeois form, why should it be any more meaningful in its Marxian form? This secret process of ideological transmission is not, however, the only thing involved. Socialism arises not only to fight capitalism but remnants of feudalism itself, so that the failure of the Southern Filmerians, in addition to setting the pattern for the failure of the later Marxists, robbed them in the process of a normal ground for growth. Could De Leon take over the liberal goal of extended suffrage as Lasalle did in Germany or the crusade against the House of Lords as the Labor Party did in England? Marx himself noted the absence of an American feudalism, but since he misinterpreted the complex origins of European socialism in the European *ancien régime*, he did not grasp the significance of it.

Surely, then, it is a remarkable force: this fixed, dogmatic liberalism of a liberal way of life. It is the secret root from which have sprung many of the most puzzling of American cultural phenomena. Take the unusual power of the Supreme Court and the cult of constitution worship on which it rests. Federal factors apart, judicial review as it has worked in America would be inconceivable without the national acceptance of the Lockian creed, ultimately enshrined in the Constitution, since the removal of high policy to the realm of adjudication implies a prior recognition of the principles to be legally interpreted. At the very moment that Senator Benton was hailing the rise of America's constitutional fetishism, in France Royer Collard and the Doctrinaires were desperately trying to build precisely the same atmosphere around the Restoration Charter of 1814, but being a patchwork of Maistre and Rousseau, that constitutional document exploded in their faces in the July Revolution. *Inter arma leges silent*. If in England a marvelous organic cohesion has held together the feudal, liberal, and socialist ideas, it would still be unthinkable there that the largest issues of public policy should be put before nine Talmudic judges examining a single text. But this is merely another way of saying that law has flourished on the corpse of philosophy in America, for the settlement of the ultimate moral question is the end of speculation upon it. Pragmatism, interestingly enough America's great contribution to the philosophic tradition, does not alter this, since it feeds itself on the Lockian settlement. It is only when you take your ethics for granted that all problems emerge as problems of technique. Not that this is a bar in America to institutional innovations of highly non-Lockian kind. Indeed, as the New Deal shows, when you simply "solve problems" on the basis of a submerged and absolute liberal faith, you can depart from Locke with a kind of inventive freedom that European Liberal reformers and even European socialists, dominated by ideological systems, cannot duplicate. But the main point remains: if

Fitzhugh and De Leon were crucified by the American general will, John Marshall and John Dewey flourished in consequence of their crucifixion. The moral unanimity of a liberal society reaches out in many directions.

At bottom it is riddled with paradox. Here is a Lockian doctrine which in the West as a whole is the symbol of rationalism, yet in America the devotion to it has been so irrational that it has not even been recognized for what it is: liberalism. There has never been a "liberal movement" or a real "liberal party" in America: we have only had the American Way of Life, a nationalist articulation of Locke which usually does not know that Locke himself is involved; and we did not even get that until after the Civil War when the Whigs of the nation, deserting the Hamiltonian tradition, saw the capital that could be made out of it. This is why even critics who have noticed America's moral unity have usually missed its substance. Ironically, "liberalism" is a stranger in the land of its greatest realization and fulfillment. But this is not all. Here is a doctrine which everywhere in the West has been a glorious symbol of individual liberty, yet in America its compulsive power has been so great that it has posed a threat to liberty itself. Actually Locke has a hidden conformitarian germ to begin with, since natural law tells equal people equal things, but when this germ is fed by the explosive power of modern nationalism, it mushrooms into something pretty remarkable. One can reasonably wonder about the liberty one finds in Burke.

I believe that this is the basic ethical problem of a liberal society: not the danger of the majority which has been its conscious fear, but the danger of unanimity, which has slumbered unconsciously behind it: the "tyranny of opinion" that Tocqueville saw unfolding as even the pathetic social distinctions of the Federalist era collapsed before his eyes. But in recent times this manifestation of irrational Lockianism, or of "Americanism," to use a favorite term of the American Legion, one of the best expounders of the national spirit that Whiggery discovered after the Civil War, has neither slumbered nor been unconscious. It has been very much awake in a red scare hysteria which no other nation in the West has really been able to understand. And this suggests a very significant principle: that when a liberal community faces military and ideological pressure from without it transforms eccentricity into sin, and the irritating figure of the bourgeois gossip flowers into the frightening figure of an A. Mitchell Palmer or a Senator McCarthy. Do we not find here, hidden away at the base of the American mind, one of the reasons why its legalism has been so imperfect a barrier against the violent moods of its mass Lockianism? If the latter is nourished by the former, how can we expect it to be strong? We say of the Supreme Court that it is courageous when it challenges Jefferson, but since in a liberal society the individualism of Hamilton is also a secret part of the Jeffersonian psyche, we make too much of this. The real test of the Court is when it faces the excitement both of Jefferson and Hamilton, when the Talmudic text is itself at stake, when the general will on which it feeds rises to the surface in anger. And here, brave as the Court has been at moments, its record has been no more heroic than the logic of the situation would suggest.

The decisive domestic issue of our time may well lie in the counter resources a liberal society can muster against this deep and unwritten tyrannical compulsion it contains. They exist. Given the individualist nature of the Lockian doctrine, there is always a logical impulse within it to transcend the very conformitarian spirit it breeds in a Lockian society: witness the spirit of Holmes and Hand. Given the fact, which we shall study at length later, that "Americanism" oddly disadvantages the Progressive despite the fact that he shares it to the full, there is always a strategic impulse within him to transcend it: witness the spirit of Brandeis, Roosevelt, and Stevenson. In some sense the tragedy of these movements has lain in the imperfect knowledge they have had of the enemy they face, above all in their failure to see their own unwitting contribution to his strength. The record of Brandeis was good on civil liberties, but anyone who studies his Progressive thought will see that he was, for good or bad, on that score a vital part of the compulsive "Americanism" which bred the hysteria he fought. The Progressive tradition, if it is to transcend the national general will, has got to realize, as it has not yet done, how deeply its own Jacksonian heroes have been rooted in it.

But the most powerful force working to shatter the American absolutism is, paradoxically enough, the very international involvement which tensifies it. This involvement is complex in its implications. If in the context of the Russian Revolution it elicits a domestic red scare, in the context of diplomacy it elicits an impulse to impose Locke everywhere. The way in which "Americanism" brings McCarthy together with Wilson is of great significance and it is, needless to say, another one of Progressivism's neglected roots in the Rousseauean tide it often seeks to stem. Thus to say that world politics shatters "Americanism" at the moment it intensifies it is to say a lot: it is to say that the basic horizons of the nation both at home and abroad are drastically widened by it. But has this not been the obvious experience of the recent past? Along with the fetish that has been made of Locke at peace conferences and at Congressional investigations has not Locke suffered a relativistic beating at the same time? You can turn the issue of Wilsonianism upside down: when has the nation appreciated more keenly the limits of its own cultural pattern as applied to the rest of the world? You can turn the issue of McCarthyism upside down: when has the meaning of civil liberties been more ardently understood than now? A dialectic process is at work, evil eliciting the challenge of a conscious good, so that in difficult moments progress is made. The outcome of the battle between intensified "Americanism" and new enlightenment is still an open question.

Historically the issue here is one for which we have little precedent. It raises the question of whether a nation can compensate for the uniformity of its domestic life by contact with alien cultures outside it. It asks whether American liberalism can acquire through external experience that sense of relativity, that spark of philosophy which European liberalism acquired through an internal experience of social diversity and social conflict. But if the final problem posed by the American liberal community is bizarre, this is merely a continuation of its historic record. That community has always been a place where the common issues of the West have taken strange and singular shape. . . .

NOTE

[1] There is no precise term for feudal institutions and feudal ideas as they persisted into the modern period amid the national states and economic movements which progressively undermined them. The phrases "quasi-feudal" and "ancien régime" are nebulous enough. Some historians speak of "corporate society," but since a good deal more is involved than a congeries of associational units and since "corporate" is often used to describe current fascist states, the term has disadvantages. Under the circumstances it seems best to retain the simple word "feudal," realizing that its technical meaning is stretched when one applies it in the modern era.

3

SEYMOUR MARTIN LIPSET

FORMULATING A NATIONAL IDENTITY

All states that have recently gained independence are faced with two interrelated problems, legitimating the use of political power and establishing national identity. And if it is a democratic polity they seek to establish, they must develop institutional and normative constraints upon efforts to inhibit organized opposition or to deny civil liberties to individual critics of those in power.

. . . National identity was formed under the aegis, first of a charismatic authority figure, and later under the leadership of a dominant "left wing" or revolutionary party led successively by three Founding Fathers. The pressures in new nations to outlaw opposition movements were reduced in America by the rapid decline of the conservative opposition. The revolutionary, democratic values that thus became part of the national self-image, and the basis for its authority structure, gained legitimacy as they proved effective—that is, as the nation prospered.

The need to establish stable authority and a sense of identity led the leaders of the United States to resist efforts by "old states" to involve the young nation in their quarrels. But at the same time that Americans rejected "foreign entanglements," they clearly used the Old World as both a negative and a positive point of reference, rejecting its political and class structures as backward, but nevertheless viewing its cultural and economic achievements as worthy of emulation. The intellectuals in particular expressed this ambivalence, since they played a major role in establishing and defining the state; but they then found that the task of operating and even living in it required them to conform to vulgar populist and provincial values.

In specifying those processes in the evolution of the first new nation that are comparable to what has been taking place in the societies of Asia and Africa in our own time, I am relying upon analogy. It ought to go without saying that: "We cannot assume that because conditions in one century led to certain effects, even roughly parallel conditions in another century would lead to similar effects. Neither can we be sure, of course, that the conditions were even roughly parallel."[1] It is fairly obvious that conditions in the early United States were quite different from those faced by most of the new nations of today. Many of the internal conditions that hamper the evolution of stable authority and a unifying sense of national identity in the new nations of the twentieth century were much less acute in the early United States. But the evidence suggests that despite its advantages, the United States came very close to failing in its effort to establish a unified legitimate authority. The first attempt to do so in 1783, following on Independence, was a failure. The second and successful effort was endangered by frequent threats of secession and the open flaunting of central authority until the Civil War. The advantages which the early United States possessed, as compared with most of the contemporary new states, then, only show more strongly how significant the similarities are.

There were other American advantages that should be mentioned. Although internal conflicts stemming from attitudes toward the French Revolution disrupted the young American polity, there was no worldwide totalitarian conspiracy seeking to upset political and economic development from within, and holding up an alternative model of seemingly successful economic growth through the use of authoritarian methods. Also the absence of rapid mass communication systems meant that Americans were relatively isolated, and hence did not immediately compare their conditions with those in the more developed countries. The United States did not so urgently face a "revolution of rising expectations" based on the knowledge that life is much better elsewhere. The accepted concepts of natural or appropriate rights did not include a justification of the lower classes' organized participation in the polity to gain higher income, welfare support from the state, and the like. And whatever the exaggeration in the effects frequently attributed to the existence of an open land frontier, there can be little doubt that it contributed to social stability.

Internal value cleavages, which frustrate contemporary new nations, were comparatively less significant in young America. Shils points out that in today's new nations "the parochialism of kinship, caste and locality makes it difficult to create stable and coherent nation-wide parties."[2] None of these parochialisms was as strong in the United States which was formed by a relatively homogeneous population with a common language, a relatively similar religious background (although denominational differences did cause some problems), and a common cultural and political tradition.

American social structure did not possess those great "gaps" which, in the contemporary new states, "conspire to separate the ordinary people from their government."[3] The culture with which the educated identified contrasted less strongly with that of the uneducated. The ideology in the name of which America made its revolution was less alien to prevailing modes of thought than some of today's revolutionary creeds. Perhaps most important, the class structure of America, even before the establishment of the new nation, came closer to meeting the conditions for a stable democracy than do those of the new nations of our time—or, indeed, than those of the Old World at that time. Writing shortly before Independence was finally attained, Crèvecoeur, though sympathetic to the Tory cause, pointed up the egalitarianism of American society:

> The rich and the poor are not so far removed from each other as they are in
> Europe. . . . A pleasing uniformity of decent competence appears throughout our
> habitations. . . . It must take some time ere he [the foreign traveler] can reconcile

himself to our dictionary, which is but short in words of dignity, and names of honor. . . . Here man is as free as he ought to be; nor is this pleasing equality so transitory as many others are.[4]

The ability to work the institutions of a democratic nation requires sophistication both at the elite level and the level of the citizenry at large. And as Carl Bridenbaugh has well demonstrated, the America of revolutionary times was not a colonial backwater.[5] Philadelphia was the second largest English city—only London surpassed it in numbers. Philadelphia and other colonial American capitals were centers of relatively high culture at this time: they had universities and learned societies, and their elite was in touch with, and contributed to, the intellectual and scientific life of Britain.

In this respect, the political traditions that the American colonists held in common, were of particular importance since they included the concept of the rule of law, and even of constitutionalism. Each colony operated under a charter which defined and limited governmental powers. Although colonial subjects, Americans were also Englishmen and were thus accustomed to the rights and privileges of Englishmen. Through their local governments they actually possessed more rights than did most of the residents of Britain itself. In a sense, even before independence, Americans met a basic condition for democratic government, the ability to operate its fundamental institutions.[6]

> It requires, not only efficient administration, but an independent judiciary with high professional standards and, in all branches of government, a scrupulous respect for rules, written and unwritten, governing the exercise of power. What these rules are must be known to more people than those who actually have the power supposed to be limited by these rules, and it must be possible to lodge effective complaints against those people who are suspected of breaking the rules. This means that there must be, in the broad sense, constitutional government.[7]

In many contemporary new nations, a potentially politically powerful military class, who have a patriotic, national outlook, may use the army to seize power if it becomes impatient with civilian leadership.[8] When the United States was seeking to establish a national authority, it was not bedeviled by such a class. The entire army in 1789 consisted of 672 men; and even after a decade of threats of war, there were only 3,429 soldiers in 1800. The potential military strength was, of course, much larger, for it included various state militia reserves. The latter, however, were simply the citizenry, and as long as the government had the loyalty of the general population, it had no need to fear its professional soldiers.[9]

Of great significance in facilitating America's development as a nation, both politically and economically, was the fact that the weight of ancient tradition which is present in almost all of the contemporary new states was largely absent. It was not only a new nation, it was a new society, much less bound to the customs and values of the past than any nation of Europe. Crèvecoeur well described the American as a "new man," the likes of which had never been seen before.[10]

Religion, of course, may be viewed as a "traditional" institution which played an important role in the United States. But in the first half-decade of the American Republic, as we have seen, the defenders of religious traditionalism were seriously weakened, as the various state churches—Anglican in the South and Congregationalist in New England—were gradually disestablished. Moreover, the new United States was particularly fortunate in the religious traditions which it did inherit. Calvinistic Puritanism, which was stronger in the colonies than in the mother country, was not as "uncongenial to modernity" as are some of the traditional beliefs inherited by new nations today. A positive orientation toward savings and hard work, and the strong motivation to achieve high positions that derives from this religious tradition, have been seen as causes of the remarkable economic expansion that made possible the legitimation of equalitarian values and democratic government. Max Weber, the most prominent exponent of the thesis that ascetic Protestantism played a major role in the development of capitalism in the Western world, argued that "one must never overlook that without the universal diffusion of these qualities and principles of a methodical way of life, qualities which were maintained through these [Calvinist] religious communities, capitalism, today, even in America, would not be what it is. . . ."[11] Calvinism's "insistence that one's works were signs of eternal grace or damnation" has been transformed into a secular emphasis upon achievement.[12]

Other Puritan influences on American development have perhaps not been sufficiently emphasized. As Richard Schlatter has pointed out in a recent summary of the researches on this subject, the Puritan tradition involved a respect for learning which led to the establishment of schools and universities on a scale that surpassed England.[13] The opportunities for learning thus created, and the pressures for widespread education that equalitarian values implied,[14] led to a wide distribution of literacy. The census of 1840 reported only 9 per cent of the white population twenty years old and over as illiterate.[15]

The Puritan tradition may also have made it easier to legitimize American democracy as the rule of law. Tocqueville saw the special need of an egalitarian and democratic society for a self-restraining value system that would inhibit the tyranny of the majority, a function supposedly once fulfilled in the European societies by a secure and sophisticated aristocratic elite. In a democracy only religion could play this role, and therefore the less coercive the political institutions of such a society, the more it has need for a system of common belief to help restrict the actions of the rulers and the electorate. As he put it:

> But the revolutionists of America are obliged to profess an ostensible respect for Christian morality and equity, which does not permit them to violate wantonly the laws that oppose their designs; nor would they find it easy to surmount the scruples of their partisans even if they were able to get over their own. . . . Thus while the law permits Americans to do what they please, religion prevents them from conceiving, and forbids them to commit, what is rash or unjust.[16]

While Tocqueville pointed out that Catholicism was not necessarily incompatible with democratic or egalitarian values, since "it confounds all the distinctions of society at the foot of the same altar," he describes the "form of Christianity" in early America as "a democratic and republican religion."[17] It would indeed seem that the Calvinistic-Puritan tradition was particularly valuable in training men to the sort of self-restraint that Tocqueville felt was necessary for democracy. By making every man God's agent, ascetic Protestantism made each individual responsible for the state of morality in the society; and by making the congregation a disciplinary agent it helped to prevent any one individual from assuming that his brand of morality was better than others.[18]

Puritanism had been associated with the movement of the squirearchy for political recognition in England. As Trevelyan has put it:

> Under Elizabeth the increasing Puritanism of the squires introduced a new element. The fear and love of God began to strive with the fear and love of the Queen in the breast of the Parliament men. . . . Protestantism and Parliamentary privilege were already closely connected, before even the first Stuart came to trouble [the] still further seething waters [of Cromwell's rebellion].[19]

So that, as Schlatter has pointed out, the Puritan tradition implied a concern for "constitutionalism and limited government," as well as a belief "that they are a peculiar people, destined by Providence to live in a more perfect community than any known in the Old World. . . ."[20]

In establishing its identity, the new America quickly came to see itself, and to be perceived by others, as a radical society in which conservatism and traditionalism had no proper place. The religious traditions on which it drew stressed that it was to be different from European nations. But its really radical character derived from its revolutionary origins.

The political scientist Clinton Rossiter has described the effects of the revolution on the political ideologies of the nation in explaining why conservatism as a doctrine is weak in America:

> The reason the American Right is not Conservative today is that it has not been Conservative for more than a hundred years. . . .
> Conservatism first emerged to meet the challenge of democracy. In countries like England it was able to survive the rise of this new way of life by giving way a little at a time under its relentless pounding, but in America the triumph of democracy was too sudden and complete. It came to society as well as to politics; it came early in the history of the Republic and found the opposition only half dug in. . . . The result was a disaster for genuine, old-country Conservatism. Nowhere in the world did the progressive, optimistic, egalitarian mode of thinking invade so completely the mind of an entire people. Nowhere was the Right forced so abruptly into such an untenable position. If there is any single quality that the Right seems always and everywhere to cultivate, it is unquestioning patriotism, and this, in turn, calls for unquestioning devotion to the nation's ideals. The long-standing merger of "America" and "democracy" has meant that to profess Conservatism is to be something less than "one hundred per cent American"; indeed, it is to question the nation's destiny. Worse than that, this merger has doomed outspoken Conservatism to political failure.[21]

From Tocqueville and Martineau in the 1830's to Gunnar Myrdal in more recent times, foreign visitors have been impressed by the extent to which the values proclaimed in the Declaration of Independence have operated to prescribe social and political behavior. And the legitimacy which the American authority structure ultimately attained has been based on the assumption that as a nation it is dedicated to equality and to liberty, to the fulfillment of its original political objectives.

As Frank Thistlethwaite put it a few years ago:

> In the mid-twentieth century the American people still pursue their Revolutionary ideal: a Republic established in the belief that men of good will could voluntarily come together in the sanctuary of an American wilderness to order their common affairs according to rational principles; a dedicated association in which men participate not by virtue of being born into it as heirs of immemorial custom, but by virtue of free choice, of the will to affirm certain sacred principles; a community of the uprooted, of migrants who have turned their back on the past in which they were born; . . . a society fluid and experimental, uncommitted to rigid values, cherishing freedom of will and choice and bestowing all the promise of the future on those with the manhood to reject the past.[22]

NOTES

[1] Karl W. Deutsch, S. A. Burrell, R. A. Kann, M. Lee, Jr., M. Lichterman, R. E. Lindgren, F. L. Loewenheim, R. W. Van Wagenen, *Political Community and the North Atlantic Area* (Princeton, N.J.: Princeton University Press, 1957), p. 11.

[2] Edward Shils, "The Military in the Political Development of the New States" in John J. Johnson, *The Role of the Military in Underdeveloped Countries* (Princeton, N.J.: Princeton University Press, 1962), p. 14.

[3] *Ibid.*, p. 29.

[4] J. Hector St. John Crèvecoeur, *Letters from an American Farmer* (New York: Dolphin Books, n. d.), pp. 46–47.

[5] Carl Bridenbaugh, *Rebels and Gentlemen, Philadelphia in the Age of Franklin* (New York: Reynal and Hitchcock, 1942).

[6] See John Plamenatz, *On Alien Rule and Self Government* (New York: Longman's, Green, 1960), pp. 47–48.

[7] *Ibid.*, p. 51.

[8] Shils, "The Military . . . ," *op cit.*, p. 40.

[9] James R. Jacobs, *The Beginning of the U.S. Army, 1783–1812* (Princeton, N.J.: Princeton University Press, 1947); see also Deutsch, *et al.*, *Political Community and the North Atlantic Area*, p. 26.

[10] "What then is the American, this new man . . . ? He is an American, who leaving behind him all his ancient prejudices and manners, receives new ones from the new mode of life he has embraced. . . . He becomes an American by being received in the broad lap of our great *Alma Mater*. The American is a new man, who acts upon new principles; he must therefore entertain new ideas and form new opinions." J. Hector St. John Crèvecoeur, *Letters from an American Farmer* (New York: Dolphin Books), pp. 49–50.

[11] Max Weber, "The Protestant Sects and the Spirit of Capitalism," in *Essays in Sociology*, translated by Hans Gerth and C. W. Mills (New York: Oxford University Press, 1946), pp. 309, 313.

[12] Robin Williams, *American Society* (New York: Alfred A. Knopf, 1957), p. 313.

[13] Richard Schlatter, "The Puritan Strain," in John Higham, ed., *The Reconstruction of American History* (New York: Harper & Bros., 1962), pp. 39–42. See also Bernard Bailyn, *Education in the Forming of American Society* (Chapel Hill: The University of North Carolina Press, 1960), for a discussion of the influence which the multiplication of numerous sects by the eve of the Revolution had upon the spread of education. The promotional and propagandizing possibilities of education made it an instrument of survival among competing sects. "Sectarian groups, without regard to the intellectual complexity of their doctrine or to their views on the value of learning to religion, became dynamic elements in the spread of education, spawning schools of all sorts, continuously, competitively in all their settlements; carrying education into the remote frontiers." Bailyn, pp. 40–41.

[14] "What strikes one most forcibly about the Puritans' efforts in education is the expectation of uniformity. Every family, without regard to its fortunes and the accomplishment of its head, and every town, without regard to its condition or resources, was expected to provide an equal minimum of education—for who, in what place, should be exempt from the essential work of life? . . . the quest for salvation . . . this was an occupation without limit, in the proper training for which all were expected to join equally, without regard to natural ability and worldly circumstance." Bailyn, *ibid.*, p. 81.

[15] Bureau of the Census, A *Statistical Abstract Supplement, Historical Statistics of the U.S. Colonial Times to 1957* (Washington: 1957), p. 214. The census of 1840 was the first to report literacy.

[16] Tocqueville, *Democracy in America*, Vol. I, p. 316.

[17] *Ibid.*, p. 311.

[18] Williams, *American Society*, p. 312.

[19] G. M. Trevelyan, *History of England* (Garden City, N.Y.: Doubleday Anchor Books, 1954), Vol. II, pp. 143–144.

[20] Schlatter, "The Puritan Strain," *op. cit.*, p. 42.

[21] Clinton Rossiter, *Conservatism in America* (New York: Vintage Books, 1962), pp. 201–202.

[22] Frank Thistlethwaite, *The Great Experiment* (New York: Cambridge University Press, 1955), pp. 319–320.

4

"PUBLIUS" (ALEXANDER HAMILTON, JAMES MADISON, AND JOHN JAY)

THE FEDERALIST PAPERS

NUMBER 10

Among the numerous advantages promised by a well-constructed Union, none deserves to be more accurately developed than its tendency to break and control the violence of faction. The friend of popular governments never finds himself so much alarmed for their character and fate as when he contemplates their propensity to this dangerous vice. He will not fail, therefore, to set a due value on any plan which, without violating the principles to which he is attached, provides a proper cure for it. The instability, injustice, and confusion introduced into the public councils have, in truth, been the mortal diseases under which popular governments have everywhere perished, as they continue to be the favorite and fruitful topics from which the adversaries to liberty derive their most specious declamations. The valuable improvements made by the American constitutions on the popular models, both ancient and modern, cannot certainly be too much admired; but it would be an unwarrantable partiality to contend that they have as effectually obviated the danger on this side, as was wished and expected. Complaints are everywhere heard from our most considerate and virtuous citizens, equally the friends of public and private faith and of public and personal liberty, that our governments are too unstable, that the public good is disregarded in the conflicts of rival parties, and that measures are too often decided, not according to the rules of justice and the rights of the minor party, but by the superior force of an interested and overbearing majority. However anxiously we may wish that these complaints had no foundation, the evidence of known facts will not permit us to deny that they are in some degree true. It will be found, indeed, on a candid review of our situation, that some of the distresses under which we labor have been erroneously charged on the operation of our governments; but it will be found, at the same time, that other causes will not alone account for many of our heaviest misfortunes; and, particularly, for that prevailing and increasing distrust of public engagements and alarm for private rights which are echoed from one end of the continent to the other. These must be chiefly, if not wholly, effects of the unsteadiness and injustice with which a factious spirit has tainted our public administration.

By a faction I understand a number of citizens, whether amounting to a majority or minority of the whole, who are united and actuated by some common impulse of passion, or of interest, adverse to the rights of other citizens, or to the permanent and aggregate interests of the community.

There are two methods of curing the mischiefs of faction: the one, by removing its causes; the other, by controlling its effects.

There are again two methods of removing the causes of faction: the one, by destroying the liberty which is essential to its existence; the other, by giving to every citizen the same opinions, the same passions, and the same interests.

It could never be more truly said than of the first remedy that it was worse than the disease. Liberty is to faction what air is to fire, an aliment without which it instantly expires. But it could not be a less folly to abolish liberty, which is essential to political life, because it nourishes faction than it would be to wish the annihilation of air, which is essential to animal life, because it imparts to fire its destructive agency.

The second expedient is as impracticable as the first would be unwise. As long as the reason of man continues fallible, and he is at liberty to exercise it, different opinions will be formed. As long as the connection subsists between his reason and his self-love, his opinions and his passions will have a reciprocal influence on each other; and the former will be objects to which the latter will attach themselves. The diversity in the faculties of men, from which the rights of property originate, is not less an insuperable obstacle to a uniformity of interests. The protection of these faculties is the first object of government. From the protection of different and unequal faculties of acquiring property, the possession of different degrees and kinds of property immediately results; and from the influence of these on the sentiments and views of the respective proprietors ensues a division of the society into different interests and parties.

The latent causes of faction are thus sown in the nature of man; and we see them everywhere brought into different degrees of activity, according to the different circumstances of civil society. A zeal for different opinions concerning religion, concerning government, and many other points, as well of speculation as of practice; an attachment to different leaders ambitiously contending for pre-eminence and power; or to persons of other descriptions whose fortunes have been interesting to the human passions, have, in turn, divided mankind into parties, inflamed them with mutual animosity, and rendered them much more disposed to vex and oppress each other than to co-operate for their common good. So strong is this propensity of mankind to fall into mutual animosities that where no substantial occasion presents itself the most frivolous and fanciful distinctions have been sufficient to kindle their unfriendly passions and excite their most violent conflicts. But the most common and durable source of factions has been the various and unequal distribution of property. Those who hold and those who are without property have ever formed distinct interests in society. Those who are creditors, and those who are debtors, fall under a like discrimination. A landed interest, a manufacturing interest, a mercantile interest, a moneyed interest, with many lesser interests, grow up of necessity in civilized nations, and divide them into different classes, actuated by different sentiments and views. The regulation of these various and interfering interests forms the principal task of modern legislation and involves the spirit of party and faction in the necessary and ordinary operations of government.

No man is allowed to be a judge in his own cause, because his interest would certainly bias his judgment, and, not improbably, corrupt his integrity. With equal, nay with greater reason, a body of men are unfit to be both judges and parties at the same time; yet what are many of the most important acts of legislation but so many judicial determinations, not indeed concerning the rights of single persons, but concerning the rights of large bodies of citizens? And what are the different classes of legislators but advocates and parties to the causes which they determine? Is a law proposed concerning private debts? It is a question to which the creditors are parties on one side and the debtors on the other. Justice ought to hold the balance between them. Yet the parties are, and must be, themselves the judges; and the most numerous party, or in other words, the most powerful faction must be expected to prevail. Shall domestic manufacturers be encouraged, and in what degree, by restrictions on foreign manufacturers? are questions which would be differently decided by the landed and the manufacturing classes, and probably by neither with a sole regard to justice and the public good. The apportionment of taxes on the various descriptions of property is an act which seems to require the most exact impartiality; yet there is, perhaps, no legislative act in which greater opportunity and temptation are given to a predominant party to trample on the rules of justice. Every shilling with which they overburden the inferior number is a shilling saved to their own pockets.

It is in vain to say that enlightened statesmen will be able to adjust these clashing interests and render them all subservient to the public good. Enlightened statesmen will not always be at the helm. Nor, in many cases, can such an adjustment be made at all without taking into view indirect and remote considerations, which will rarely prevail over the immediate interest which one party may find in disregarding the rights of another or the good of the whole.

The inference to which we are brought is that the *causes* of faction cannot be removed and that relief is only to be sought in the means of controlling its *effects*.

If a faction consists of less than a majority, relief is supplied by the republican principle, which enables the majority to defeat its sinister views by regular vote. It may clog the administration, it may convulse the society; but it will be unable to execute and mask its violence under the forms of the Constitution. When a majority is included in a faction, the form of popular government, on the other hand, enables it to sacrifice to its ruling passion or interest both the public good and the rights of other citizens. To secure the public good and private rights against the danger of such a faction, and at the same time to preserve the spirit and the form of popular government, is then the great object to which our inquiries are directed. Let me add that it is the great desideratum by which alone this form of government can be rescued from the opprobrium under which it has so long labored and be recommended to the esteem and adoption of mankind.

By what means is this object attainable? Evidently by one of two only. Either the existence of the same passion or interest in a majority at the same time must be prevented, or the majority, having such coexistent passion or interest, must be rendered, by their number and local situation, unable to concert and carry into effect schemes of oppression. If the impulse and the opportunity be suffered to coincide, we well know that neither moral nor religious motives can be relied on as an adequate control. They are not found to be such on the injustice and violence of individuals, and lose their efficacy in proportion to the number combined together, that is, in proportion as their efficacy becomes needful.

From this view of the subject it may be concluded that a pure democracy, by which I mean a society consisting of a small number of citizens, who assemble and administer the government in person, can admit of no cure for the mischiefs of faction. A common passion or interest will, in almost every case, be felt by a majority of the whole; a communication and concert results from the form of government itself; and there is nothing to check the inducements to sacrifice the weaker party or an obnoxious individual. Hence it is that such democracies have ever been spectacles of turbulence and contention; have ever been found incompatible with personal security or the rights of property; and have in general been as short in their lives as they have been violent in their deaths. Theoretic politicians, who have patronized this species of government, have erroneously supposed that by reducing mankind to a perfect equality in their political rights, they would at the same time be perfectly equalized and assimilated in their possessions, their opinions, and their passions.

A republic, by which I mean a government in which the scheme of representation takes place, opens a different prospect and promises the cure for which we are seeking. Let us examine the points in which it varies from pure democracy, and we shall comprehend both the nature of the cure and the efficacy which it must derive from the Union.

The two great points of difference between a democracy and a republic are: first, the delegation of the government, in the latter, to a small number of citizens elected by the rest; secondly, the greater number of citizens and greater sphere of country over which the latter may be extended.

The effect of the first difference is, on the one hand, to refine and enlarge the public views by passing them through the medium of a chosen body of citizens, whose wisdom may best discern the true interest of their country and whose patriotism and love of justice will be least likely to sacrifice it to temporary or partial considerations. Under such a regulation it may well happen that the public voice, pronounced by the representatives of the people, will be more consonant to the public good than if pronounced by the people themselves, convened for the purpose. On the other hand, the effect may be inverted. Men of factious tempers, of local prejudices, or of sinister designs, may, by intrigue, by corruption, or by other means, first obtain the suffrages, and then betray the interests of the people. The question resulting is, whether small or extensive republics are most favorable to the election of proper guardians of the public weal; and it is clearly decided in favor of the latter by two obvious considerations.

In the first place it is to be remarked that however small the republic may be the representatives must be raised to a certain number in order to guard against the cabals of a few; and that however large it may be they must be limited to a certain number in order to guard against the confusion of a multitude. Hence, the number of representatives in the two cases not being in proportion to that of the constituents, and being proportionally greatest in the small republic, it follows that if the proportion of fit characters be not less in the large than in the small republic, the former will present a greater option, and consequently a greater probability of a fit choice.

In the next place, as each representative will be chosen by a greater number of citizens in the large than in the small republic, it will be more difficult for unworthy candidates to practise with success the vicious arts by which elections are too often carried; and the suffrages of the people being more free, will be more likely to center on men who possess the most attractive merit and the most diffusive and established characters.

It must be confessed that in this, as in most other cases, there is a mean, on both sides of which inconveniencies will be found to lie. By enlarging too much the number of electors, you render the representative too little acquainted with all their local circumstances and lesser interests; as by reducing it too much, you render him unduly attached to these, and too little fit to comprehend and pursue great and national objects. The federal Constitution forms a happy combination in this respect; the great and aggregate interests being referred to the national, the local and particular to the State legislatures.

The other point of difference is the greater number of citizens and extent of territory which may be brought within the compass of republican than of democratic government; and it is this circumstance principally which renders factious combinations less to be dreaded in the former than in the latter. The smaller the society, the fewer probably will be the distinct parties and interests composing it; the fewer the distinct parties and interests, the more frequently will a majority be found of the same party; and the smaller the number of individuals composing a majority, and the smaller the compass within which they are placed, the more easily will they concert and execute their plans of oppression. Extend the sphere and you take in a greater variety of parties and interests; you make it less probable that a majority of the whole will have a common motive to invade the rights of other citizens; or if such a common motive exists, it will be more difficult for all who feel it to discover their own strength and to act in unison with each other. Besides other impediments, it may be remarked that, where there is a consciousness of unjust or dishonorable purposes, communication is always checked by distrust in proportion to the number whose concurrence is necessary.

Hence, it clearly appears that the same advantage which a republic has over a democracy in controlling the effects of faction is enjoyed by a large over a small republic—is enjoyed by the Union over the States composing it. Does this advantage consist in the substitution of representatives whose enlightened views and virtuous sentiments render them superior to local prejudices and to schemes of injustice? It will not be denied that the representation of the Union will be most likely to possess these requisite endowments. Does it consist in the greater security afforded by a greater variety of parties, against the event of any one party being able to outnumber and oppress the rest? In an equal degree does the increased variety of parties comprised within the Union increase this security. Does it, in fine, consist in the greater obstacles opposed to the concert and accomplishment of the secret wishes of an unjust and interested majority? Here again the extent of the Union gives it the most palpable advantage.

The influence of factious leaders may kindle a flame within their particular States but will be unable to spread a general conflagration through the other States. A religious sect may degenerate into a political faction in a part of the Confederacy; but the variety of sects dispersed over the entire face of it must secure the national councils against any danger from that source. A rage for paper money, for an abolition of debts, for an equal division of property, or for any other improper or wicked project, will be less apt to pervade the whole body of the Union than a particular member of it, in the same proportion as such a malady is more likely to taint a particular county or district than an entire State.

In the extent and proper structure of the Union, therefore, we behold a republican remedy for the diseases most incident to republican government. And according to the degree of pleasure and pride we feel in being republicans ought to be our zeal in cherishing the spirit and supporting the character of federalists.

Publius
(James Madison)

NUMBER 39

The last paper having concluded the observations which were meant to introduce a candid survey of the plan of government reported by the convention, we now proceed to the execution of that part of our undertaking.

The first question that offers itself is whether the general form and aspect of the government be strictly republican. It is evident that no other form would be reconcilable with the genius of the people of America; with the fundamental principles of the Revolution; or with that honorable determination which animates every votary of freedom to rest all our political experiments on the capacity of mankind for self-government. If the plan of the convention, therefore, be found to depart from the republican character, its advocates must abandon it as no longer defensible.

What, then, are the distinctive characters of the republican form? Were an answer to this question to be sought, not by recurring to principles but in the application of the term by political writers to the constitutions of different States, no satisfactory one would ever be found. Holland, in which no particle of the supreme authority is derived from the people, has passed almost universally under the denomination of a republic. The same title has been bestowed on Venice, where absolute power over the great body of the people is exercised in the most absolute manner by a small body of hereditary nobles. Poland, which is a mixture of aristocracy and of monarchy in their worst forms, has been dignified with the same appellation. The government of England, which has one republican branch only, combined with an hereditary aristocracy and monarchy, has with equal impropriety been frequently placed on the list of republics. These examples, which are nearly as dissimilar to each other as to a genuine republic, show the extreme inaccuracy with which the term has been used in political disquisitions.

If we resort for a criterion to the different principles on which different forms of government are established, we may define a republic to be, or at least may bestow that name on, a government which derives all its powers directly or indirectly from the great body of the people, and is administered by persons holding their offices during pleasure for a limited period, or during good behavior. It is *essential* to such a government that it be derived from the great body of the society, not from an inconsiderable proportion or a favored class of it; otherwise a handful of tyrannical nobles, exercising their oppressions by a delegation of their powers, might aspire to the rank of republicans and claim for their government the honorable title of republic. It is *sufficient* for such a government that the persons administering it be appointed, either directly or indirectly, by the people; and that they hold their appointments by either of the tenures just specified; otherwise every government in the United States, as well as every other popular government that has been or can be well organized or well executed, would be degraded from the republican character. According to the constitution of every State in the Union, some or other of the officers of government are appointed indirectly only by the people. According to most of them, the chief magistrate himself is so appointed. And according to one, this mode of appointment is extended to one of the co-ordinate branches of the legislature. According to all the constitutions, also, the tenure of the highest offices is extended to a definite period, and in many instances, both within the legislative and executive departments, to a period of years. According to the provisions of most of the constitutions, again, as well as according to the most respectable and received opinions on the subject, the members of the judiciary department are to retain their offices by the firm tenure of good behavior.

On comparing the Constitution planned by the convention with the standard here fixed, we perceived at once that it is, in the most rigid sense, conformable to it. The House of Representatives, like that of one branch at least of all the State legislatures, is elected immediately by the great body of the people. The Senate, like the present Congress and the Senate of Maryland, derives its appointment indirectly from the people. The President is indirectly derived from the choice of the people, according to the example in most of the States. Even the judges, with all other officers of the Union, will, as in the several States, be the choice, though a remote choice, of the people themselves. The duration of the appointments is equally conformable to the republican standard and to the model of State constitutions. The House of Representatives is periodically elective, as in all the States; and for the period of two years, as in the State of South Carolina. The Senate is elective for the period of six years, which is but one year more than the period of the Senate of Maryland, and but two more than that of the Senates of New York and Virginia. The President is to continue in office for the period of four years; as in New York and Delaware the chief magistrate is elected for three years, and in South Carolina for two years. In the other States the election is annual. In several of the States, however, no explicit provision is made for the impeachment of the chief magistrate. And in Delaware and Virginia he is not impeachable till out of office. The President of the United States is impeachable at any time during his continuance in office. The tenure by which the judges are to hold their places is, as it unquestionably ought to be, that of good behavior. The tenure of the ministerial offices generally will be a subject of legal regulation, conformably to the reason of the case and the example of the State constitutions.

Could any further proof be required of the republican complexion of this system, the most decisive one might be found in its absolute prohibition of titles of nobility, both under the federal and the State governments; and in its express guaranty of the republican form to each of the latter.

"But it was not sufficient," say the adversaries of the proposed Constitution, "for the convention to adhere to the republican form. They ought with equal care to have preserved the *federal* form, which regards the Union as a *Confederacy* of sovereign states; instead of which they have framed a *national* government, which regards the Union as a *consolidation* of the States." And it is asked by what authority this bold and radical innovation was undertaken? The handle which has been made of this objection requires that it should be examined with some precision.

Without inquiring into the accuracy of the distinction on which the objection is founded, it will be necessary to a just estimate of its force, first, to ascertain the real character of the government in question; secondly, to inquire how far the convention were authorized to propose such a government; and thirdly, how far the duty they owed to their country could supply any defect of regular authority.

First.—In order to ascertain the real character of the government, it may be considered in relation to the foundation on which it is to be established; to the sources from which its ordinary powers are to be drawn; to the operation of those powers; to the extent of them; and to the authority by which future changes in the government are to be introduced.

On examining the first relation, it appears, on one hand, that the Constitution is to be founded on the assent and ratification of the people of America, given by deputies elected for the special purpose; but, on the other, that this assent and ratification is to be given by the people, not as individuals composing one entire nation, but as composing the distinct and independent States to which they respectively belong. It is to be the assent and ratification of the several States, derived from the supreme authority in each State—the authority of the people themselves. The act, therefore, establishing the Constitution will not be a *national* but a *federal* act.

That it will be a federal and not a national act, as these terms are understood by the objectors—the act of the people, as forming so many independent States, not as forming one aggregate nation—is obvious from the single consideration: that it is to result neither from the decision of a *majority* of the people of the Union, nor from that of a *majority* of the States. It must result from the *unanimous* assent of the several States that are parties to it, differing no otherwise from their ordinary assent than in its being expressed, not by the legislative authority, but by that of the people themselves. Were the people regarded in this transaction as forming one nation, the will of the majority of the whole people of the United States would bind the minority, in the same manner as the majority in each State must bind the minority; and the will of the majority must be determined either by a comparison of the individual votes, or by considering the will of the majority of the States as evidence of the will of a majority of the people of the United States. Neither of these rules has been adopted. Each State, in ratifying the Constitution, is considered as a sovereign body independent of all others, and only to be bound by its own voluntary act. In this relation, then, the new Constitution will, if established, be a *federal* and not a *national* constitution.

The next relation is to the sources from which the ordinary powers of government are to be derived. The House of Representatives will derive its powers from the people of America; and the people will be represented in the same proportion and on the same principle as they are in the legislature of a particular State. So far the government is *national*, not *federal*. The Senate, on the other hand, will derive its powers from the States as political and coequal societies; and these will be represented on the principle of equality in the Senate, as they now are in the existing Congress. So far the government is *federal*, not *national*. The executive power will be derived from a very compound source. The immediate election of the President is to be made by the States in their political characters. The votes allotted to them are in a compound ratio, which considers them partly as distinct and coequal societies, partly as unequal members of the same society. The eventual election, again, is to be made by that branch of the legislature which consists of the national representatives; but in this particular act they are to be thrown into the form of individual delegations from so many distinct and coequal bodies politic. From this aspect of the government it appears to be of a mixed character, presenting at least as many *federal* as *national* features.

The difference between a federal and national government, as it relates to the *operation of the government*, is by the adversaries of the plan of the convention supposed to consist in this, that in the former the powers operate on the political bodies composing the Confederacy in their political capacities; in the latter, on the individual citizens composing the nation in their individual capacities. On trying the Constitution by this criterion, it falls under the *national* not the *federal* character; though perhaps not so completely as has been understood. In several cases, and particularly in the trial of controversies to which States may be parties, they must be viewed and proceeded against in their collective and political capacities only. But the operation of the government on the people in their individual capacities, in its ordinary and most essential proceedings, will, in the sense of its opponents, on the whole, designate it, in this relation, a *national* government.

But if the government be national with regard to the *operation* of its powers, it changes its aspect again when we contemplate it in relation to the extent of its powers. The idea of a national government involves in it not only an authority over the individual citizens, but an indefinite supremacy over all persons and things, so far as they are objects of lawful government. Among a people consolidated into one nation, this supremacy is completely vested in the national legislature. Among communities united for particular purposes, it is vested partly in the general and partly in the municipal legislatures. In the former case, all local authorities are subordinate to the supreme; and may be controlled, directed, or abolished by it at pleasure. In the latter, the local or municipal authorities form distinct and independent portions of the supremacy, no more subject, within their respective spheres, to the general authority than the general authority is subject to them, within its own sphere. In this relation, then, the proposed government cannot be deemed a *national* one; since its jurisdiction extends to certain enumerated objects only, and leaves to the several States a residuary and inviolable sovereignty over all other objects. It is true that in controversies relating to the boundary between the two jurisdictions, the tribunal which is ultimately to decide is to be established under the general government. But this does not change the principle of the case. The decision is to be impartially made, according to the rules of the Constitution; and all the usual and most effectual precautions are taken to secure this impartiality. Some such tribunal is clearly essential to prevent an appeal to the sword and a dissolution of the compact; and that it ought to be established under the general rather than under the local governments, or, to speak more properly, that it could be safely established under the first alone, is a position not likely to be combated.

If we try the Constitution by its last relation to the authority by which amendments are to be made, we find it neither wholly *national* nor wholly *federal*. Were it wholly national, the supreme and ultimate authority would reside in the *majority* of the people of the Union; and this authority would be competent at all times, like that of a majority of every national society to alter or abolish its established government. Were it wholly federal, on the other hand, the concurrence of each State in the Union would be essential to every alteration that would be binding on all. The mode provided by the plan of the convention is not founded on either of these principles. In requiring more than a majority, and particularly in computing the proportion by *States*, not by *citizens*, it departs from the national and advances towards the *federal* character; in rendering the concurrence of less than the whole number of States sufficient, it loses again the *federal* and partakes of the *national* character.

The proposed Constitution, therefore, even when tested by the rules laid down by its antagonists, is, in strictness, neither a national nor a federal Constitution, but a composition of both. In its foundation it is federal, not national; in the sources from which the ordinary powers of the government are drawn, it is partly federal and partly national; in the operation of these powers, it is national, not federal; in the extent of them, again, it is federal, not national; and, finally in the authoritative mode of introducing amendments, it is neither wholly federal nor wholly national.

Publius
(James Madison)

NUMBER 46

Resuming the subject of the last paper, I proceed to inquire whether the federal government or the State governments will have the advantage with regard to the predilection and support of the people. Notwithstanding the different modes in which they are appointed, we must consider both of them as substantially dependent on the great body of the citizens of the United States. I assume this position here as it respects the first, reserving the proofs for another place. The federal and State governments are in fact but different agents and trustees of the people, constituted with different powers and designed for different purposes. The adversaries of the Constitution seem to have lost sight of the people altogether in their reasonings on this subject; and to have viewed these different establishments not only as mutual rivals and enemies, but as uncontrolled by any common superior in their efforts to usurp the authorities of each other. These gentlemen must here be reminded of their error. They must be told that the ultimate authority, wherever the derivative may be found, resides in the people alone, and that it will not depend merely on the comparative ambition or address of the different governments whether either, or which of them, will be able to enlarge its sphere of jurisdiction at the expense of the other. Truth, no less than decency, requires that the event in every case should be supposed to depend on the sentiments and sanction of their common constituents.

Many considerations, besides those suggested on a former occasion, seem to place it beyond doubt that the first and most natural attachment of the people will be to the governments of their respective States. Into the administration of these a greater number of individuals will expect to rise. From the gift of these a greater number of offices and emoluments will flow. By the superintending care of these, all the more domestic and personal interests of the people will be regulated and provided for. With the affairs of these, the people will be more familiarly and minutely conversant. And with the members of these will a greater proportion of the people have the ties of personal acquaintance and friendship, and of family and party attachments; on the side of these, therefore, the popular bias may well be expected most strongly to incline.

Experience speaks the same language in this case. The federal administration, though hitherto very defective in comparison with what may be hoped under a better system, had, during the war, and particularly whilst the independent fund of paper emissions was in credit, an activity and importance as great as it can well have in any future circumstances whatever. It was engaged, too, in a course of measures which had for their object the protection of everything that was dear, and the acquisition of everything that could be desirable to the people at large. It was, nevertheless, invariably found, after the transient enthusiasm for the early Congresses was over, that the attention and attachment of the people were turned anew to their own particular governments; that the federal council was at no time the idol of popular favor; and that opposition to proposed enlargements of its powers and importance was the side usually taken by the men who wished to build their political consequence on the prepossessions of their fellow-citizens.

If, therefore, as has been elsewhere remarked, the people should in future become more partial to the federal than to the State governments, the change can only result from such manifest and irresistible proofs of a better administration as will overcome all their antecedent propensities. And in that case, the people ought not surely to be precluded from giving most of their confidence where they may discover it to be most due; but even in that case the State governments could have little to apprehend, because it is only within a certain sphere that the federal power can, in the nature of things, be advantageously administered.

The remaining points on which I propose to compare the federal and State governments are the disposition and the faculty they may respectively possess to resist and frustrate the measures of each other.

It has been already proved that the members of the federal will be more dependent on the members of the State governments than the latter will be on the former. It has appeared also that the prepossessions of the people, on whom both will depend, will be more on the side of the State governments than of the federal government. So far as the disposition of each towards the other may be influenced by these causes, the State governments must clearly have the advantage. But in a distinct and very important point of view, the advantage will lie on the same side. The prepossessions, which the members themselves will carry into the federal government, will generally be favorable to the States; whilst it will rarely happen that the members of the State governments will carry into the public councils a bias in favor of the general government. A local spirit will infallibly prevail much more in the members of Congress than a national spirit will prevail in the legislatures of the particular States. Everyone knows that a great proportion of the errors committed by the State legislatures proceeds from the disposition of the members to sacrifice the comprehensive and permanent interest of the State to the particular and separate views of the counties or districts in which they reside. And if they do not sufficiently enlarge their policy to embrace the collective welfare of their particular State, how can it be imagined that they will make the aggregate prosperity of the Union, and the dignity and respectability of its government, the objects of their affections and consultations? For the same reason that the members of the State legislatures will be unlikely to attach themselves sufficiently to national objects, the members of the federal legislature will be likely to attach themselves too much to local objects. The States will be to the latter what counties and towns are to the former. Measures will too often be decided according to their probable effect, not on the national prosperity and happiness, but on the prejudices, interests, and pursuits of the governments and people of the individual States. What is the spirit that has in general characterized the proceedings of Congress? A perusal of their journals, as well as the candid acknowledgments of such as have had a seat in that assembly, will inform us that the members have but too frequently displayed the character rather of partisans of their respective States than of impartial guardians of a common interest; that where on one occasion improper sacrifices have been made of local considerations to the aggrandizement of the federal government, the great interests of the nation have suffered on a hundred from an undue attention to the local prejudices, interests, and views of the particular States. I mean not by these reflections to insinuate that the new federal government will not embrace a more enlarged plan of policy than the existing government may have pursued; much less that its views will be as confined as those of the State legislatures; but only that it will partake sufficiently of the spirit of both to be disinclined to invade the rights of the individual States, or the prerogatives of their governments. The motives on the part of the State governments to augment their prerogatives by defalcations from the federal government will be overruled by no reciprocal predispositions in the members.

Were it admitted, however, that the federal government may feel an equal disposition with the State governments to extend its power beyond the due limits, the latter would still have the advantage in the means of defeating such encroachments. If an act of a particular State, though unfriendly to the national government, be generally popular in that State, and should not too grossly violate the oaths of the State officers, it is executed immediately and, of course, by means on the spot and depending on the State alone. The opposition of the federal government, or the interposition of federal officers, would but inflame the zeal of all parties on the side of the State, and the evil could not be prevented or repaired, if at all, without the employment of means which must always be resorted to with reluctance and difficulty. On the other hand, should an unwarrantable measure of the federal government be unpopular in particular States, which would seldom fail to be the case, or even a warrantable measure be so, which may sometimes be the case, the means of opposition to it are powerful and at hand. The disquietude of the people; their repugnance and, perhaps, refusal to co-operate with the officers of the Union; the frowns of the executive magistracy of the State; the embarrassments created by legislative devices, which would often be added on such occasions, would oppose, in any State, difficulties not to be despised; would form, in a large State, very serious impediments; and where the sentiments of several adjoining States happened to be in unison, would present obstructions which the federal government would hardly be willing to encounter.

But ambitious encroachments of the federal government on the authority of the State governments would not excite the opposition of a single State, or of a few States only. They would be signals of general alarm. Every government would espouse the common cause. A correspondence would be opened. Plans of resistance would be concerted. One spirit would animate and conduct the whole. The same combinations, in short, would result from an apprehension of the federal, as was produced by the dread of a foreign, yoke; and unless the projected innovations should be voluntarily renounced, the same appeal to a trial of force would be made in the one case as was made in the other. But what degree of madness could ever drive the federal government to such an extremity? In the contest with Great Britain, one part of the empire was employed against the other. The more numerous part invaded the rights of the less numerous part. The attempt was unjust and unwise; but it was not in speculation absolutely chimerical. But what would be the contest in the case we are supposing? Who would be the parties? A few representatives of the people would be opposed to the people themselves; or rather one set of representatives would be contending against thirteen sets of representatives, with the whole body of their common constituents on the side of the latter.

The only refuge left for those who prophesy the downfall of the State governments is the visionary supposition that the federal government may previously accumulate a military force for the projects of ambition. The reasonings contained in these papers must have been employed to little purpose indeed, if it could be necessary now to disprove the reality of this danger. That the people and the States should, for a sufficient period of time, elect an uninterrupted succession of men ready to betray both; that the traitors should, throughout this period, uniformly and systematically pursue some fixed plan for the extension of the military establishment; that the governments and the people of the States should silently and patiently behold the gathering storm and continue to supply the materials until it should be prepared to burst on their own heads must appear to everyone more like the incoherent dreams of a delirious jealousy, or the misjudged exaggerations of a counterfeit zeal, than like the sober apprehensions of genuine patriotism. Extravagant as the supposition is, let it, however, be made. Let a regular army, fully equal to the resources of the country, be formed; and let it be entirely at the devotion of the federal government: still it would not be going too far to say that the State governments with the people on their side would be able to repel the danger. The highest number to which, according to the best computation, a standing army can be carried in any country does not exceed one hundredth part of the whole number of souls; or one twenty-fifth part of the number able to bear arms. This proportion would not yield, in the United States, an army of more than twenty-five or thirty thousand men. To these would be opposed a militia amounting to near half a million of citizens with arms in their hands, officered by men chosen from among themselves, fighting for their common liberties and united and conducted by governments possessing their affections and confidence. It may well be doubted whether a militia thus circumstanced could ever be conquered by such a proportion of regular troops. Those who are best acquainted with the late successful resistance of this country against the British arms will be most inclined to deny the possibility of it. Besides the advantage of being armed, which the Americans possess over the people of almost every other nation, the existence of subordinate governments, to which the people are attached and by which the militia officers are appointed, forms a barrier against the enterprises of ambition, more insurmountable than any which a simple government of any form can admit of. Notwithstanding the military establishments in the several kingdoms of Europe, which are carried as far as the public resources will bear, the governments are afraid to trust the people with arms. And it is not certain that with this aid alone they would not be able to shake off their yokes. But were the people to possess the additional advantages of local governments chosen by themselves, who could collect the national will and direct the national force, and of officers appointed out of the militia by these governments and attached both to them and to the militia, it may be affirmed with the greatest assurance that the throne of every tyranny in Europe would be speedily overturned in spite of the legions which surround it. Let us not insult the free and gallant citizens of America with the suspicion that they would be less able to defend the rights of which they would be in actual possession than the debased subjects of arbitrary power would be to rescue theirs from the hands of their oppressors. Let us rather no longer insult them with the supposition that they can ever reduce themselves to the necessity of making the experiment by a blind and tame submission to the long train of insidious measures which must precede and produce it.

The argument under the present head may be put into a very concise form, which appears altogether conclusive. Either the mode in which the federal government is to be constructed will render it sufficiently dependent on the people, or it will not. On the first supposition, it will be restrained by that dependence from forming schemes obnoxious to their constituents. On the other supposition, it will not possess the confidence of the people, and its schemes of usurpation will be easily defeated by the State governments, who will be supported by the people.

On summing up the considerations stated in this and the last paper, they seem to amount to the most convincing evidence that the powers proposed to be lodged in the federal government are as little formidable to those reserved to the individual States as they are indispensably necessary to accomplish the purposes of the Union; and that all those alarms which have been sounded of a meditated and consequential annihilation of the State governments must, on the most favorable interpretation, be ascribed to the chimerical fears of the authors of them.

Publius
(James Madison)

NUMBER 47

Having reviewed the general form of the proposed government and the general mass of power allotted to it, I proceed to examine the particular structure of this government, and the distribution of this mass of power among its constituent parts.

One of the principal objections inculcated by the more respectable adversaries to the Constitution is its supposed violation of the political maxim that the legislative, executive, and judiciary departments ought to be separate and distinct. In the structure of the federal government no regard, it is said, seems to have been paid to this essential precaution in favor of liberty. The several departments of power are distributed and blended in such a manner as at once to destroy all symmetry and beauty of form, and to expose some of the essential parts of the edifice to the danger of being crushed by the disproportionate weight of other parts.

No political truth is certainly of greater intrinsic value, or is stamped with the authority of more enlightened patrons of liberty than that on which the objection is founded. The accumulation of all powers, legislative, executive, and judiciary, in the same hands, whether of one, a few, or many, and whether hereditary, self-appointed, or elective, may justly be pronounced the very definition of tyranny. Were the federal Constitution, therefore, really chargeable with this accumulation of power, or with a mixture of powers, having a dangerous tendency to such an accumulation, no further arguments would be necessary to inspire a universal reprobation of the system. I persuade myself, however, that it will be made apparent to everyone that the charge cannot be supported, and that the maxim on which it relies has been totally misconceived and misapplied. In order to form correct ideas on this important subject it will be proper to investigate the sense in which the preservation of liberty requires that the three great departments of power should be separate and distinct.

The oracle who is always consulted and cited on this subject is the celebrated Montesquieu. If he be not the author of this invaluable precept in the science of politics, he has the merit at least of displaying and recommending it most effectually to the attention of mankind. Let us endeavor, in the first place, to ascertain his meaning on this point.

The British Constitution was to Montesquieu what Homer has been to the didactic writers on epic poetry. As the latter have considered the work of the immortal bard as the perfect model from which the principles and rules of the epic art were to be drawn, and by which all similar works were to be judged, so this great political critic appears to have viewed the Constitution of England as the standard, or to use his own expression, as the mirror of political liberty; and to have delivered, in the form of elementary truths, the several characteristic principles of that particular system. That we may be sure, then, not to mistake his meaning in this case, let us recur to the source from which the maxim was drawn.

On the slightest view of the British Constitution, we must perceive that the legislative, executive, and judiciary departments are by no means totally separate and distinct from each other. The executive magistrate forms an integral part of the legislative authority. He alone has the prerogative of making treaties with foreign sovereigns which, when made, have, under certain limitations, the force of legislative acts. All the members of the judiciary department are appointed by him, can be removed by him on the address of the two Houses of Parliament, and form, when he pleases to consult them, one of his constitutional councils. One branch of the legislative department forms also a great constitutional council to the executive chief, as, on another hand, it is the sole depositary of judicial power in cases of impeachment, and is invested with the supreme appellate jurisdiction in all other cases. The judges, again, are so far connected with the legislative department as often to attend and participate in its deliberations, though not admitted to a legislative vote.

From these facts, by which Montesquieu was guided, it may clearly be inferred that in saying "There can be no liberty where the legislative and executive powers are united in the same person, or body of magistrates," or, "if the power of judging be not separated from the legislative and executive powers," he did not mean that these departments ought to have no *partial agency* in, or no *control* over, the acts of each other. His meaning, as his own words import, and still more conclusively as illustrated by the example in his eye, can amount to no more than this, that where the *whole* power of one department is exercised by the same hands which possess the *whole* power of another department, the fundamental principles of a free constitution are subverted. This would have been the case in the constitution examined by him, if the king, who is the sole executive magistrate, had possessed also the complete legislative power, or the supreme administration of justice; or if the entire legislative body had possessed the supreme judiciary, or the supreme executive authority. This, however, is not among the vices of that constitution. The magistrate in whom the whole executive power resides cannot of himself make a law, though he can put a negative on every law; nor administer justice in person, though he has the appointment of those who do administer it. The judges can exercise no executive prerogative, though they are shoots from the executive stock; nor any legislative function, though they may be advised by the legislative councils. The entire legislature can perform no judiciary act, though by the joint act of two of its branches the judges may be removed from their offices, and though one of its branches is possessed of the judicial power in the last resort. The entire legislature, again, can exercise no executive prerogative, though one of its branches constitutes the supreme executive magistracy, and another, on the impeachment of a third, can try and condemn all the subordinate officers in the executive department.

The reasons on which Montesquieu grounds his maxim are a further demonstration of his meaning. "When the legislative and executive powers are united in the same person or body," says he, "there can be no liberty, because apprehensions may arise lest *the same* monarch or senate should *enact* tyrannical laws to *execute* them in a tyrannical manner." Again: "Were the power of judging joined with the legislative, the life and liberty of the subject would be exposed to arbitrary control, for *the judge* would then be *the legislator*. Were it joined to the executive power, *the judge* might behave with all the violence of *an oppressor*." Some of these reasons are more fully explained in other passages; but briefly stated as they are here they sufficiently establish the meaning which we have put on this celebrated maxim of this celebrated author.

If we look into the constitutions of the several States we find that, notwithstanding the emphatical and, in some instances, the unqualified terms in which this axiom has been laid down, there is not a single instance in which the several departments of power have been kept absolutely separate and distinct. New Hampshire, whose constitution was the last formed, seems to have been fully aware of the impossibility and inexpediency of avoiding any mixture whatever of these departments, and has qualified the doctrine by declaring "that the legislative, executive, and judiciary powers ought to be kept as separate from, and independent of, each other *as the nature of a free government will admit; or as is consistent with that chain of connection that binds the whole fabric of the constitution in one indissoluble bond of unity and amity.*" Her constitution accordingly mixes these departments in several respects. The Senate, which is a branch of the legislative department, is also a judicial tribunal for the trial of impeachments. The President, who is the head of the executive department, is the presiding member also of the Senate; and, besides an equal vote in all cases, has a casting vote in case of a tie. The executive head is himself eventually elective every year by the legislative department, and his council is every year chosen by and from the members of the same department. Several of the officers of state are also appointed by the legislature. And the members of the judiciary department are appointed by the executive department.

The constitution of Massachusetts has observed a sufficient though less pointed caution in expressing this fundamental article of liberty. It declares "that the legislative department shall never exercise the executive and judicial powers, or either of them; the executive shall never exercise the legislative and judicial powers, or either of them; the judicial shall never exercise the legislative and executive powers, or either of them." This declaration corresponds precisely with the doctrine of Montesquieu, as it has been explained, and is not in a single point violated by the plan of the convention. It goes no farther than to prohibit any one of the entire departments from exercising the powers of another department. In the very Constitution to which it is prefixed, a partial mixture of powers has been admitted. The executive magistrate has a qualified negative on the legislative body, and the Senate, which is a part of the legislature, is a court of impeachment for members both of the executive and judiciary departments. The members of the judiciary department, again, are appointable by the executive department, and removable by the same authority on the address of the two legislative branches. Lastly, a number of the officers of government are annually appointed by the legislative department. As the appointment to offices, particularly executive offices, is in its nature an executive function, the compilers of the Constitution have, in this last point at least, violated the rule established by themselves.

I pass over the constitutions of Rhode Island and Connecticut, because they were formed prior to the Revolution and even before the principle under examination had become an object of political attention.

The constitution of New York contains no declaration on this subject, but appears very clearly to have been framed with an eye to the danger of improperly blending the different departments. It gives, nevertheless, to the executive magistrate, a partial control over the legislative department; and, what is more, gives a like control to the judiciary department; and even blends the executive and judiciary departments in the exercise of this control. In its council of appointment members of the legislative are associated with the executive authority, in the appointment of officers, both executive and judiciary. And its court for the trial of impeachments and correction of errors is to consist of one branch of the legislature and the principal members of the judiciary department.

The constitution of New Jersey has blended the different powers of government more than any of the preceding. The governor, who is the executive magistrate, is appointed by the legislature; is chancellor and ordinary, or surrogate of the State; is a member of the Supreme Court of Appeals, and president, with a casting vote, of one of the legislative branches. The same legislative branch acts again as executive council to the governor, and with him constitutes the Court of Appeals. The members of the judiciary department are appointed by the legislative department, and removable by one branch of it, on the impeachment of the other.

According to the constitution of Pennsylvania, the president, who is the head of the executive department, is annually elected by a vote in which the legislative department predominates. In conjunction with an executive council, he appoints the members of the judiciary department and forms a court of impeachment for trial of all officers, judiciary as well as executive. The judges of the Supreme Court and justices of the peace seem also to be removable by the legislature; and the executive power of pardoning, in certain cases, to be referred to the same department. The members of the executive council are made EX OFFICIO justices of peace throughout the State.

In Delaware, the chief executive magistrate is annually elected by the legislative department. The speakers of the two legislative branches are vice-presidents in the executive department. The executive chief, with six others appointed, three by each of the legislative branches, constitutes the Supreme Court of Appeals; he is joined with the legislative department in the appointment of the other judges. Throughout the States it appears that the members of the legislature may at the same time be justices of the peace; in this State, the members of one branch of it are EX OFFICIO justices of the peace; as are also the members of the executive council. The principal officers of the executive department are appointed by the legislative; and one branch of the latter forms a court of impeachments. All officers may be removed on address of the legislature.

Maryland has adopted the maxim in the most unqualified terms; declaring that the legislative, executive, and judicial powers of government ought to be forever separate and distinct from each other. Her constitution, notwithstanding, makes the executive magistrate appointable by the legislative department; and the members of the judiciary by the executive department.

The language of Virginia is still more pointed on this subject. Her constitution declares "that the legislative, executive, and judiciary departments shall be separate and distinct; so that neither exercises the powers properly belonging to the other; nor shall any person exercise the powers of more than one of them at the same time, except that the justices of county courts shall be eligible to either House of Assembly." Yet we find not only this express exception with respect to the members of the inferior courts, but that the chief magistrate, with his executive council, are appointable by the legislature; that two members of the latter are triennially displaced at the pleasure of the legislature; and that all the principal offices, both executive and judiciary, are filled by the same department. The executive prerogative of pardon, also, is in one case vested in the legislative department.

The constitution of North Carolina, which declares "that the legislative, executive, and supreme judicial powers of government ought to be forever separate and distinct from each other," refers, at the same time, to the legislative department, the appointment not only of the executive chief, but all the principal officers within both that and the judiciary department.

In South Carolina, the constitution makes the executive magistracy eligible by the legislative department. It gives to the latter, also, the appointment of the members of the judiciary department, including even justices of the peace and sheriffs; and the appointment of officers in the executive department, down to captains in the army and navy of the State.

In the constitution of Georgia where it is declared "that the legislative, executive, and judiciary departments shall be separate and distinct, so that neither exercise the powers properly belonging to the other," we find that the executive department is to be filled by appointments of the legislature; and the executive prerogative of pardon to be finally exercised by the same authority. Even justices of the peace are to be appointed by the legislature.

In citing these cases, in which the legislative, executive, and judiciary departments have not been kept totally separate and distinct, I wish not to be regarded as an advocate for the particular organizations of the several State governments. I am fully aware that among the many excellent principles which they exemplify they carry strong marks of the haste, and still stronger of the inexperience, under which they were framed. It is but too obvious that in some instances the fundamental principle under consideration has been violated by too great a mixture, and even an actual consolidation of the different powers; and that in no instance has a competent provision been made for maintaining in practice the separation delineated on paper. What I have wished to evince is that the charge brought against the proposed Constitution of violating the sacred maxim of free government is warranted neither by the real meaning annexed to that maxim by its author, nor by the sense in which it has hitherto been understood in America. This interesting subject will be resumed in the ensuing paper.

Publius
(James Madison)

NUMBER 51

To what expedient, then, shall we finally resort, for maintaining in practice the necessary partition of power among the several departments as laid down in the Constitution? The only answer that can be given is that as all these exterior provisions are found to be inadequate the defect must be supplied, by so contriving the interior structure of the government as that its several constituent parts may, by their mutual relations, be the means of keeping each other in their proper places. Without presuming to undertake a full development of this important idea I will hazard a few general observations which may perhaps place it in a clearer light, and enable us to form a more correct judgment of the principles and structure of the government planned by the convention.

In order to lay a due foundation for that separate and distinct exercise of the different powers of government, which to a certain extent is admitted on all hands to be essential to the preservation of liberty, it is evident that each department should have a will of its own; and consequently should be so constituted that the members of each should have as little agency as possible in the appointment of the members of the others. Were this principle rigorously adhered to, it would require that all the appointments for the supreme executive, legislative, and judiciary magistracies should be drawn from the same fountain of authority, the people, through channels having no communication whatever with one another. Perhaps such a plan of constructing the several departments would be less difficult in practice than it may in contemplation appear. Some difficulties, however, and some additional expense would attend the execution of it. Some deviations, therefore, from the principle must be admitted. In the constitution of the judiciary department in particular, it might be inexpedient to insist rigorously on the principle: first, because peculiar qualifications being essential in the members, the primary consideration ought to be to select that mode of choice which best secures these qualifications; second, because the permanent tenure by which the appointments are held in that department must soon destroy all sense of dependence on the authority conferring them.

It is equally evident that the members of each department should be as little dependent as possible on those of the others for the emoluments annexed to their offices. Were the executive magistrate, or the judges, not independent of the legislature in this particular, their independence in every other would be merely nominal.

But the great security against a gradual concentration of the several powers in the same department consists in giving to those who administer each department the necessary constitutional means and personal motives to resist encroachments of the others. The provision for defense must in this, as in all other cases, be made commensurate to the danger of attack. Ambition must be made to counteract ambition. The interest of the man must be connected with the constitutional rights of the place. It may be a reflection on human nature that such devices should be necessary to control the abuses of government. But what is government itself but the greatest of all reflections on human nature? If men were angels, no government would be necessary. If angels were to govern men, neither external nor internal controls on government would be necessary. In framing a government which is to be administered by men over men, the great difficulty lies in this: you must first enable the government to control the governed; and in the next place oblige it to control itself. A dependence on the people is, no doubt, the primary control on the government; but experience has taught mankind the necessity of auxiliary precautions.

This policy of supplying, by opposite and rival interests, the defect of better motives, might be traced through the whole system of human affairs, private as well as public. We see it particularly displayed in all the subordinate distributions of power, where the constant aim is to divide and arrange the several offices in such a manner as that each may be a check on the other—that the private interest of every individual may be a sentinel over the public rights. These inventions of prudence cannot be less requisite in the distribution of the supreme powers of the State.

But it is not possible to give to each department an equal power of self-defense. In republican government, the legislative authority necessarily predominates.

The remedy for this inconveniency is to divide the legislature into different branches; and to render them, by different modes of election and different principles of action, as little connected with each other as the nature of their common functions and their common dependence on the society will admit. It may even be necessary to guard against dangerous encroachments by still further precautions. As the weight of the legislative authority requires that it should be thus divided, the weakness of the executive may require, on the other hand, that it should be fortified. An absolute negative on the legislature appears, at first view, to be the natural defense with which the executive magistrate should be armed. But perhaps it would be neither altogether safe nor alone sufficient. On ordinary occasions it might not be exerted with the requisite firmness, and on extraordinary occasions it might be perfidiously abused. May not this defect of an absolute negative be supplied by some qualified connection between this weaker department and the weaker branch of the stronger department, by which the latter may be led to support the constitutional rights of the former, without being too much detached from the rights of its own department?

If the principles on which these observations are founded be just, as I persuade myself they are, and they be applied as a criterion to the several State constitutions, and to the federal Constitution, it will be found that if the latter does not perfectly correspond with them, the former are infinitely less able to bear such a test.

There are, moreover, two considerations particularly applicable to the federal system of America, which place that system in a very interesting point of view.

First. In a single republic, all the power surrendered by the people is submitted to the administration of a single government; and the usurpations are guarded against by a division of the government into distinct and separate departments. In the compound republic of America, the power surrendered by the people is first divided between two distinct governments, and then the portion allotted to each subdivided among distinct and separate departments. Hence a double security arises to the rights of the people. The different governments will control each other, at the same time that each will be controlled by itself.

Second. It is of great importance in a republic not only to guard the society against the oppression of its rulers, but to guard one part of the society against the injustice of the other part. Different interests necessarily exist in different classes of citizens. If a majority be united by a common interest, the rights of the minority will be insecure. There are but two methods of providing against this evil: the one by creating a will in the community independent of the majority— that is, of the society itself; the other, by comprehending in the society so many separate descriptions of citizens as will render an unjust combination of a majority of the whole very improbable, if not impracticable. The first method prevails in all governments possessing an hereditary or self-appointed authority. This, at best, is but a precarious security; because a power independent of the society may as well espouse the unjust views of the major as the rightful interests of the minor party, and may possibly be turned against both parties. The second method will be exemplified in the federal republic of the United States. Whilst all authority in it will be derived from and dependent on the society, the society itself will be broken into so many parts, interests and classes of citizens, that the rights of individuals, or of the minority, will be in little danger from interested combinations of the majority. In a free government the security for civil rights must be the same as that for religious rights. It consists in the one case in the multiplicity of interests, and in the other in the multiplicity of sects. The degree of security in both cases will depend on the number of interests and sects; and this may be presumed to depend on the extent of country and number of people comprehended under the same government. This view of the subject must particularly recommend a proper federal system to all the sincere and considerate friends of republican government, since it shows that in exact proportion as the territory of the Union may be formed into more circumscribed Confederacies, or States, oppressive combinations of a majority will be facilitated; the best security, under the republican forms, for the rights of every class of citizen, will be diminished; and consequently the stability and independence of some member of the government, the only other security, must be proportionally increased. Justice is the end of government. It is the end of civil society. It ever has been and ever will be pursued until it be obtained, or until liberty be lost in the pursuit. In a society under the forms of which the stronger faction can readily unite and oppress the weaker, anarchy may as truly be said to reign as in a state of nature, where the weaker individual is not secured against the violence of the stronger; and as, in the latter state, even the stronger individuals are prompted, by the uncertainty of their condition, to submit to a government which may protect the weak as well as themselves; so, in the former state, will the more powerful factions or parties be gradually induced, by a like motive, to wish for a government which will protect all parties, the weaker as well as the more powerful. It can be little doubted that if the State of Rhode Island was separated from the Confederacy and left to itself, the insecurity of rights under the popular form of government within such narrow limits would be displayed by such reiterated oppressions of factious majorities that some power altogether independent of the people would soon be called for by the voice of the very factions whose misrule had proved the necessity of it. In the extended republic of the United States, and among the great variety of interests, parties, and sects which it embraces, a coalition of a majority of the whole society could seldom take place on any other principles than those of justice and the general good; whilst there being thus less danger to a minor from the will of a major party, there must be less pretext, also, to provide for the security of the former, by introducing into the government a will not dependent on the latter, or, in other words, a will independent of the society itself. It is no less certain than it is important, notwithstanding the contrary opinions which have been entertained, that the larger the society, provided it lie within a practicable sphere, the more duly capable it will be of self-government. And happily for the *republican cause*, the practicable sphere may be carried to a very great extent by a judicious modification and mixture of the *federal principle*.

Publius
(James Madison)

NUMBER 69

I proceed now to trace the real characters of the proposed executive, as they are marked out in the plan of the convention. This will serve to place in a strong light the unfairness of the representations which have been made in regard to it.

The first thing which strikes our attention is that the executive authority, with few exceptions, is to be vested in a single magistrate. This will scarcely, however, be considered as a point upon which any comparison can be grounded; for if, in this particular, there be a resemblance to the king of Great Britain, there is not less a resemblance to the Grand Seignior, to the khan of Tartary, to the Man of the Seven Mountains, or to the governor of New York.

That magistrate is to be elected for *four* years; and is to be re-eligible as often as the people of the United States shall think him worthy of their confidence. In these circumstances there is a total dissimilitude between *him* and a king of Great Britain, who is an *hereditary* monarch, possessing the crown as a patrimony descendible to his heirs forever; but there is a close analogy between *him* and a governor of New York, who is elected for *three* years, and is re-eligible without limitation or intermission. If we consider how much less time would be requisite for establishing a dangerous influence in a single State than for establishing a like influence throughout the United States, we must conclude that a duration of *four* years for the Chief Magistrate of the Union is a degree of permanency far less to be dreaded in that office, than a duration of *three* years for a corresponding office in a single State.

The President of the United States would be liable to be impeached, tried, and, upon conviction of treason, bribery, or other high crimes or misdemeanors, removed from office; and would afterwards be liable to prosecution and punishment in the ordinary course of law. The person of the King of Great Britain is sacred and inviolable; there is no constitutional tribunal to which he is amenable; no punishment to which he can be subjected without involving the crisis of a national revolution. In this delicate and important circumstance of personal responsibility, the President of Confederated America would stand upon no better ground than a governor of New York, and upon worse ground than the governors of Virginia and Delaware.

The President of the United States is to have power to return a bill, which shall have passed the two branches of the legislature, for reconsideration; but the bill so returned is not to become a law unless, upon that reconsideration, it be approved by two thirds of both houses. The king of Great Britain, on his part, has an absolute negative upon the acts of the two houses of Parliament. The disuse of that power for a considerable time past does not affect the reality of its existence and is to be ascribed wholly to the crown's having found the means of substituting influence to authority, or the art of gaining a majority in one or the other of the two houses, to the necessity of exerting a prerogative which could seldom be exerted without hazarding some degree of national agitation. The qualified negative of the President differs widely from this absolute negative of the British sovereign and tallies exactly with the revisionary authority of the council of revision of this State, of which the governor is a constituent part. In this respect the power of the President would exceed that of the governor of New York, because the former would possess, singly, what the latter shares with the chancellor and judges; but it would be precisely the same with that of the governor of Massachusetts, whose constitution, as to this article, seems to have been the original from which the convention have copied.

The President is to be the "commander-in-chief of the army and navy of the United States, and of the militia of the several States, when called into the actual service of the United States. He is to have power to grant reprieves and pardons for offenses against the United States, *except in cases of impeachment*; to recommend to the consideration of Congress such measures as he shall judge necessary and expedient; to convene, on extraordinary occasions, both houses of the legislature, or either of them, and, in case of disagreement between them *with respect to the time of adjournment*, to adjourn them to such time as he shall think proper; to take care that the laws be faithfully executed; and to commission all officers of the United States." In most of these particulars, the power of the President will resemble equally that of the king of Great Britain and of the governor of New York. The most material points of difference are these:—*First*. The President will have only the occasional command of such part of the militia of the nation as by legislative provision may be called into the actual service of the Union. The king of Great Britain and the governor of New York have at all times the entire command of all the militia within their several jurisdictions. In this article, therefore, the power of the President would be inferior to that of either the monarch or the governor. *Second*. The President is to be commander-in-chief of the army and navy of the United States. In this respect his authority would be nominally the same with that of the king of Great Britain, but in substance much inferior to it. It would amount to nothing more than the supreme command and direction of the military and naval forces, as first general and admiral of the Confederacy; while that of the British king extends to the *declaring* of war and to the *raising* and *regulating* of fleets and armies—all which, by the Constitution under consideration, would appertain to the legislature.[1] The governor of New York, on the other hand, is by the constitution of the State vested only with the command of its militia and navy. But the constitutions of several of the States expressly declare their governors to be commanders-in-chief, as well of the army as navy; and it may well be a question whether those of New Hampshire and Massachusetts, in particular, do not, in this instance, confer larger powers upon their respective governors than could be claimed by a President of the United States. *Third*. The power of the President, in respect to pardons, would extend to all cases, *except those of impeachment*. The governor of New York may pardon in all cases, even in those of impeachment, except for treason and murder. Is not the power of the governor, in this article, on a calculation of political consequences, greater than that of the President? All conspiracies and plots against the government which have not been matured into actual treason may be screened from punishment of every kind by the interposition of the prerogative of pardoning. If a governor of New York, therefore, should be at the head of any such conspiracy, until the design had been ripened into actual hostility he could insure his accomplices and adherents an entire impunity. A President of the Union, on the other hand, though he may even pardon treason, when prosecuted in the ordinary course of law, could shelter no offender, in any degree, from the effects of impeachment and conviction. Would not the prospect of a total indemnity for all the preliminary steps be a greater temptation to undertake and persevere in an enterprise against the public liberty, than the mere prospect of an exemption from death and confiscation, if the final execution of the design, upon an actual appeal to arms, should miscarry? Would this last expectation have any influence at all, when the probability was computed that the person who was to afford that exemption might himself be involved in the consequences of the measure, and might be incapacitated by his agency in it from affording the desired impunity? The better to judge of this matter, it will be necessary to recollect that, by the proposed Constitution, the offense of treason is limited "to levying war upon the United States, and adhering to their enemies, giving them aid and comfort"; and that by the laws of New York it is confined within similar bounds. *Fourth.* The President can only adjourn the national legislature in the single case of disagreement about the time of adjournment. The British monarch may prorogue or even dissolve the Parliament. The governor of New York may also prorogue the legislature of this State for a limited time; a power which, in certain situations, may be employed to very important purposes.

The President is to have power, with the advice and consent of the Senate, to make treaties, provided two thirds of the senators present concur. The king of Great Britain is the sole and absolute representative of the nation in all foreign transactions. He can of his own accord make treaties of peace, commerce, alliance, and of every other description. It has been insinuated that his authority in this respect is not conclusive, and that his conventions with foreign powers are subject to the revision, and stand in need of the ratification, of Parliament. But I believe this doctrine was never heard of until it was broached upon the present occasion. Every jurist[2] of that kingdom, and every other man acquainted with its Constitution knows, as an established fact, that the prerogative of making treaties exists in the crown in its utmost plenitude; and that the compacts entered into by the royal authority have the most complete legal validity and perfection, independent of any other sanction. The Parliament, it is true, is sometimes seen employing itself in altering the existing laws to conform them to the stipulations in a new treaty; and this may have possibly given birth to the imagination that its co-operation was necessary to the obligatory efficacy of the treaty. But this parliamentary interposition proceeds from a different cause: from the necessity of adjusting a most artificial and intricate system of revenue and commercial laws, to the changes made in them by the operation of the treaty; and of adapting new provisions and precautions to the new state of things, to keep the machine from running into disorder. In this respect, therefore, there is no comparison between the intended power of the President and the actual power of the British sovereign. The one can perform alone what the other can only do with the concurrence of a branch of the legislature. It must be admitted that in this instance the power of the federal executive would exceed that of any State executive. But this arises naturally from the exclusive possession by the Union of that part of the sovereign power which relates to treaties. If the Confederacy were to be dissolved, it would become a question whether the executives of the several States were not solely invested with that delicate and important prerogative.

The President is also to be authorized to receive ambassadors and other public ministers. This, though it has been a rich theme of declamation, is more a matter of dignity than of authority. It is a circumstance which will be without consequence in the administration of the government; and it was far more convenient that it should be arranged in this manner than that there should be a necessity of convening the legislature, or one of its branches, upon every arrival of a foreign minister, though it were merely to take the place of a departed predecessor.

The President is to nominate, and, *with the advice and consent of the Senate*, to appoint ambassadors and other public ministers, judges of the Supreme Court, and in general all officers of the United States established by law, and whose appointments are not otherwise provided for by the Constitution. The king of Great Britain is emphatically and truly styled the fountain of honor. He not only appoints to all offices, but can create offices. He can confer titles of nobility at pleasure, and has the disposal of an immense number of church preferments. There is evidently a great inferiority in the power of the President, in this particular, to that of the British king; nor is it equal to that of the governor of New York, if we are to interpret the meaning of the constitution of the State by the practice which has obtained under it. The power of appointment is with us lodged in a council, composed of the governor and four members of the Senate, chosen by the Assembly. The governor *claims*, and has frequently *exercised*, the right of nomination, and is *entitled* to a casting vote in the appointment. If he really has the right of nominating, his authority is in this respect equal to that of the President, and exceeds it in the article of the casting vote. In the national government, if the Senate should be divided, no appointment could be made; in the government of New York, if the council should be divided, the governor can turn the scale and confirm his own nomination.[3] If we compare the publicity which must necessarily attend the mode of appointment by the President and an entire branch of the national legislature, with the privacy in the mode of appointment by the governor of New York, closeted in a secret apartment with at most four, and frequently with only two persons; and if we at the same time consider how much more easy it must be to influence the small number of which a council of appointment consists than the considerable number of which the national Senate would consist, we cannot hesitate to pronounce that the power of the chief magistrate of this State, in the disposition of offices, must, in practice, be greatly superior to that of the Chief Magistrate of the Union.

Hence it appears that, except as to the concurrent authority of the President in the article of treaties, it would be difficult to determine whether that magistrate would, in the aggregate, possess more or less power than the governor of New York. And it appears yet more unequivocally that there is no pretense for the parallel which has been attempted between him and the king of Great Britain.

But to render the contrast in this respect still more striking, it may be of use to throw the principal circumstances of dissimilitude into a closer group.

The President of the United States would be an officer elected by the people for *four* years; the king of Great Britain is a perpetual and *hereditary* prince. The one would be amenable to personal punishment and disgrace; the person of the other is sacred and inviolable. The one would have a *qualified* negative upon the acts of the legislative body; the other has an *absolute* negative. The one would have a right to command the military and naval forces of the nation; the other, in addition to this right, possesses that of *declaring* war, and of *raising* and *regulating* fleets and armies by his own authority. The one would have a concurrent power with a branch of the legislature in the formation of treaties; the other is the *sole possessor* of the power of making treaties. The one would have a like concurrent authority in appointing to offices; the other is the sole author of all appointments. The one can confer no privileges whatever; the other can make denizens of aliens, noblemen of commoners; can erect corporations with all the rights incident to corporate bodies. The one can prescribe no rules concerning the commerce or currency of the nation; the other is in several respects the arbiter of commerce, and in this capacity can establish markets and fairs, can regulate weights and measures, can lay embargoes for a limited time, can coin money, can authorize or prohibit the circulation of foreign coin. The one has no particle of spiritual jurisdiction; the other is the supreme head and governor of the national church! What answer shall we give to those who would persuade us that things so unlike resemble each other? The same that ought to be given to those who tell us that a government, the whole power of which would be in the hands of the elective and periodical servants of the people, is an aristocracy, a monarchy, and a despotism.

Publius
(Alexander Hamilton)

NOTES

[1] A writer in a Pennsylvania paper, under the signature of Tamony, has asserted that the king of Great Britain owes his prerogative as commander-in-chief to an annual mutiny bill. The truth is, on the contrary, that his prerogative in this respect is immemorial, and was only disputed "contrary to all reason and precedent," as Blackstone, vol. i, page 262, expresses it, by the Long Parliament of Charles I; but by the statute the 13th of Charles II, chap. 6, it was declared to be in the king alone, for that the sole supreme government and command of the militia within his Majesty's realms and dominions, and of all forces by sea and land, and of all forts and places of strength, EVER WAS AND IS the undoubted right of his Majesty and his royal predecessors, kings and queens of England, and that both or either house of Parliament cannot nor ought to pretend to the same.

[2] *Vide* Blackstone's *Commentaries*, Vol. I., p. 257.

[3] Candor, however, demands an acknowledgment that I do not think the claim of the governor to a right of nomination well founded. Yet it is always justifiable to reason from the practice of a government till its propriety has been constitutionally questioned. And independent of this claim, when we take into view the other considerations and pursue them through all their consequences, we shall be inclined to draw much the same conclusion.

5

CHARLES A. BEARD

THE CONSTITUTION
AS AN ECONOMIC DOCUMENT

It is difficult for the superficial student of the Constitution, who has read only the commentaries of the legists, to conceive of that instrument as an economic document. It places no property qualifications on voters or officers; it gives no outward recognition of any economic groups in society; it mentions no special privileges to be conferred upon any class. It betrays no feeling, such as vibrates through the French constitution of 1791; its language is cold, formal, and severe.

The true inwardness of the Constitution is not revealed by an examination of its provisions as simple propositions of law; but by a long and careful study of the voluminous correspondence of the period, contemporary newspapers and pamphlets, the records of the debates in the Convention at Philadelphia and in the several state conventions, and particularly, *The Federalist*, which was widely circulated during the struggle over ratification. The correspondence shows the exact character of the evils which the Constitution was intended to remedy; the records of the proceedings in the Philadelphia Convention reveal the successive steps in the building of the framework of the government under the pressure of economic interests; the pamphlets and newspapers disclose the ideas of the contestants over the ratification; and *The Federalist* presents the political science of the new system as conceived by three of the profoundest thinkers of the period, Hamilton, Madison, and Jay. . . .

THE POWERS CONFERRED
UPON THE FEDERAL GOVERNMENT

1. The powers for positive action conferred upon the new government were few, but they were adequate to the purposes of the framers. They included, first, the power to lay and collect taxes; but here the rural interests were conciliated by the provision that direct taxes must be apportioned among the states according to population, counting three-fifths of the slaves. This, in the opinion of contemporaries eminently qualified to speak, was designed to prevent the populations of the manufacturing states from shifting the burdens of taxation to the sparsely settled agricultural regions.

In a letter to the governor of their state, three delegates from North Carolina, Blount, Spaight, and Williamson, explained the advantage of this safeguard on taxation to the southern planters and farmers: "We had many things to hope from a National Government and the chief thing we had to fear from such a Government was the risque of unequal or heavy Taxation, but we hope you will believe as we do that the Southern states in general and North Carolina in particular are well secured on that head by the proposed system. It is provided in the 9th section of article the first that no Capitation or direct Tax shall be laid except in proportion to the number of inhabitants, in which number five blacks are only counted as three. If a land tax is laid, we are to pay the same rate; for example, fifty citizens of North Carolina can be taxed no more for all their Lands than fifty Citizens in one of the Eastern States. This must be greatly in our favour, for as most of their farms are small and many of them live in Towns we certainly have, one with another, land of twice the value that they possess. When it is also considered that five Negroes are only to be charged the same Poll Tax as three whites, the advantage must be considerably increased under the proposed Form of Government. The Southern states have also a better security for the return of slaves who might endeavour to escape than they had under the original Confederation."

The taxing power was the basis of all other positive powers, and it afforded the revenues that were to discharge the public debt in full. Provision was made for this discharge in Article VI to the effect that "All debts contracted and engagements entered into before the adoption of this Constitution shall be valid against the United States under this Constitution as under the Confederation."

But the cautious student of public economy, remembering the difficulties which Congress encountered under the Articles of Confederation in its attempts to raise the money to meet the interest on the debt, may ask how the framers of the Constitution could expect to overcome the hostile economic forces which had hitherto blocked the payment of the requisitions. The answer is short. Under the Articles, Congress had no power to lay and collect taxes immediately; it could only make requisitions on the state legislatures. Inasmuch as most of the states relied largely on direct taxes for their revenues, the demands of Congress were keenly felt and stoutly resisted. Under the new system, however, Congress is authorized to lay taxes on its own account, but it is evident that the framers contemplated placing practically all of the national burden on the consumer. The provision requiring the apportionment of direct taxes on a basis of population obviously implied that such taxes were to be viewed as a last resort when indirect taxes failed to provide the required revenue.

With his usual acumen, Hamilton conciliates the freeholders and property owners in general by pointing out that they will not be called upon to support the national government by payments proportioned to their wealth. Experience has demonstrated that it is impracticable to raise any considerable sums by direct taxation. Even where the government is strong, as in Great Britain, resort must be had chiefly to indirect taxation. The pockets of the farmers "will reluctantly yield but scanty supplies, in the unwelcome shape of impositions on their houses and lands; and personal property is too precarious and invisible a fund to be laid hold of in any other way than by the imperceptible agency of taxes on consumption." Real and personal property are thus assured a generous immunity from such burdens as Congress had attempted to impose under the Articles; taxes under the new system will, therefore, be less troublesome than under the old.

2. Congress was given, in the second place, plenary power to raise and support military and naval forces, for the defence of the country against foreign and domestic foes. These forces were to be at the disposal of the President in the execution of national laws; and to guard the states against renewed attempts of "desperate debtors" like Shays, the United States guaranteed to every common-wealth a republican form of government and promised to aid in quelling internal disorder on call of the proper authorities.

The army and navy are considered by the authors of *The Federalist* as genuine economic instrumentalities. As will be pointed out below, they regarded trade and commerce as the fundamental cause of wars between nations; and the source of domestic insurrection they traced to class conflicts within society. "Nations in general," says Jay, "will make war whenever they have a prospect of getting anything by it"; and it is obvious that the United States dissevered and discordant will be the easy prey to the commercial ambitions of their neighbors and rivals.

The material gains to be made by other nations at the expense of the United States are so apparent that the former cannot restrain themselves from aggression. France and Great Britain feel the pressure of our rivalry in the fisheries; they and other European nations are our competitors in navigation and the carrying trade; our independent voyages to China interfere with the monopolies enjoyed by other countries there; Spain would like to shut the Mississippi against us on one side and Great Britain fain would close the St. Lawrence on the other. The cheapness and excellence of our productions will excite their jealousy, and the enterprise and address of our merchants will not be consistent with the wishes or policy of the sovereigns of Europe. But, adds the commentator, by way of clinching the argument, "if they see that our national government is efficient and well administered, our trade prudently regulated, our militia properly organized and disciplined, our resources and finances discreetly managed, our credit re-established, our people free, contented, and united, they will be much more disposed to cultivate our friendship than provoke our resentment."

All the powers of Europe could not prevail against us. "Under a vigorous national government the natural strength and resources of the country, directed to a common interest, would baffle all the combinations of European jealousy to restrain our growth. . . . An active commerce, an extensive navigation, and a flourishing marine would then be the offspring of moral and physical necessity. We might defy the little arts of the little politicians to control or vary the irresistible and unchangeable course of nature." In the present state of disunion the profits of trade are snatched from us; our commerce languishes; and poverty threatens to overspread a country which might outrival the world in riches.

The army and navy are to be not only instruments of defence in protecting the United States against the commercial and territorial ambitions of other countries; but they may be used also in forcing open foreign markets. What discriminatory tariffs and navigation laws may not accomplish the sword may achieve. The authors of *The Federalist* do not contemplate that policy of mild and innocuous isolation which was later made famous by Washington's farewell address. On the contrary—they do not expect the United States to change human nature and make our commercial classes less ambitious than those of other countries to extend their spheres of trade. A strong navy will command the respect of European states. "There can be no doubt that the continuance of the Union under an efficient government would put it within our power, at a period not very distant, to create a navy which, if it could not vie with those of the great maritime powers, would at least be of respectable weight if thrown into the scale of either of two contending parties. . . . A few ships of the line sent opportunely to the reinforcement of either side, would often be sufficient to decide the fate of a campaign, on the event of which interests of the greatest magnitude were suspended. Our position is, in this respect, a most commanding one. And if to this consideration we add that of the usefulness of supplies from this country, in the prosecution of military operations in the West Indies, it will be readily perceived that a situation so favorable would enable us to bargain with great advantage for commercial privileges. A price would be set not only upon our friendship, but upon our neutrality. By a steady adherence to the Union, we may hope, ere long, to become the arbiter of Europe in America, and to be able to incline the balance of European competitions in this part of the world as our interest may dictate."

As to dangers from class wars within particular states, the authors of *The Federalist* did not deem it necessary to make extended remarks: the recent events in New England were only too vividly impressed upon the public mind. "The tempestuous situation from which Massachusetts has scarcely emerged," says Hamilton, "evinces that dangers of this kind are not merely speculative. Who can determine what might have been the issue of her late convulsions, if the malcontents had been headed by a Caesar or by a Cromwell." The strong arm of the Union must be available in such crises.

In considering the importance of defence against domestic insurrection, the authors of *The Federalist* do not overlook an appeal to the slave-holders' instinctive fear of a servile revolt. Naturally, it is Madison whose interest catches this point and drives it home, by appearing to discount it. In dealing with the dangers of insurrection, he says: "I take no notice of an unhappy species of population abounding in some of the states who, during the calm of regular government are sunk below the level of men; but who, in the tempestuous scenes of civil violence, may emerge into human character and give a superiority of strength to any party with which they may associate themselves."

3. In addition to the power to lay and collect taxes and raise and maintain armed forces on land and sea, the Constitution vests in Congress plenary control over foreign and interstate commerce, and thus authorizes it to institute protective and discriminatory laws in favor of American interests, and to create a wide sweep for free trade throughout the whole American empire. A single clause thus reflects the strong impulse of economic forces in the towns and young manufacturing centres. In a few simple words the mercantile and

manufacturing interests wrote their *Zweck im Recht*; and they paid for their victory by large concessions to the slave-owning planters of the south.

While dealing with commerce in *The Federalist* Hamilton does not neglect the subject of interstate traffic and intercourse. He shows how free trade over a wide range will be to reciprocal advantage, will give great diversity to commercial enterprise, and will render stagnation less liable by offering more distant markets when local demands fall off. "The speculative trader," he concludes, "will at once perceive the force of these observations and will acknowledge that the aggregate balance of the commerce of the United States would bid fair to be much more favorable than that of the thirteen states without union or with partial unions."

4. Another great economic antagonism found its expression in the clause conferring upon Congress the power to dispose of the territories and make rules and regulations for their government and admission to the Union. In this contest, the interests of the states which held territories came prominently to the front; and the ambiguity of the language used in the Constitution on this point may be attributed to the inability of the contestants to reach precise conclusions. The leaders were willing to risk the proper management of the land problem after the new government was safely launched; and they were correct in their estimate of their future political prowess. . . .

RESTRICTIONS LAID UPON STATE LEGISLATURES

Equally important to personalty as the positive powers conferred upon Congress to tax, support armies, and regulate commerce were the restrictions imposed on the states. Indeed, we have the high authority of Madison for the statement that of the forces which created the Constitution, those property interests seeking protection against omnipotent legislatures were the most active.

In a letter to Jefferson, written in October, 1787, Madison elaborates the principle of federal judicial control over state legislation, and explains the importance of this new institution in connection with the restrictions laid down in the Constitution on laws affecting private rights. "The mutability of the laws of the States," he says, "is found to be a serious evil. The injustice of them has been so frequent and so flagrant as to alarm the most steadfast friends of Republicanism. I am persuaded I do not err in saying that the evils issuing from these sources contributed more to that uneasiness which produced the Convention, and prepared the public mind for a general reform, than those which accrued to our national character and interest from the inadequacy of the Confederation to its immediate objects. A reform, therefore, which does not make provision for private rights must be materially defective."

Two small clauses embody the chief demands of personalty against agrarianism: the emission of paper money is prohibited and the states are forbidden to impair the obligation of contract. The first of these means a return to a specie basis—when coupled with the requirement that the gold and silver coin of the United States shall be the legal tender. The Shays and their paper money legions, who assaulted the vested rights of personalty by the process of legislative depreciation, are now subdued forever, and money lenders and security holders may be sure of their operations. Contracts are to be safe, and whoever engages in a financial operation, public or private, may know that state legislatures cannot destroy overnight the rules by which the game is played. . . .

PART TWO

FEDERALISM

Relations between the national and state governments have been perhaps the single most persistent source of conflict in American politics. The protracted struggles over such issues as slavery and civil rights, government regulation of business, and the provision of social welfare programs all reflect in one manner or another the underlying tension of the federal system: the conflict between national interests and states' rights. While other nations such as Great Britain have debated how to extend basic rights (such as the right to vote) to certain groups, or to provide forms of social insurance, or to nationalize the railroads, the United States has debated a different question—whether the central government *had the right* to do such things.[1] Even now, after many of these disputes have been resolved—usually with the national government successfully asserting its right to intervene—the states have retained leverage over the final administration of federal programs, ensuring that the distribution of power between levels of government remains in flux.

Complicating American intergovernmental relations is the fact that the Constitution does not always state clearly where federal authority begins and state sovereignty ends. In part, the framers, faced with the difficult task of winning ratification of the document, often found it inexpedient to be precise. But in part, also, it was hard to be precise when creating a novel form of government that, unlike the known models of the past, was to be neither a confederation of loosely allied provinces nor a strictly unitary regime, but rather an unfamiliar admixture of both.

The question of exactly what the framers had in mind by "federalism" is the subject of a famous essay, the first selection in this section, by the late Martin Diamond. After analyzing carefully the contents of *The Federalist Papers*, Diamond concludes that the concept of federalism at the time of the founding conventionally signified a mere compact among independent states, or a "confederal" arrangement, such as the Articles of Confederation. The intent of the American federalists was not to adopt such a limited arrangement, or even to make a modest modification thereof, but to establish instead a relatively strong *national* government that integrated the states into its framework. "The great teaching of *The Federalist*," Diamond notes, "is not how to be federal in a better way, but how to be better by being less federal."

That the original design provided the basis for a solid union of the separate states is also a theme in Samuel H. Beer's article "Federalism, Nationalism, and Democracy in America." But Beer's analysis is primarily concerned with the philosophical underpinnings of the federal structure. He argues that the Founders espoused a new conception of political representation that would combine *territorial* pluralism as a defense against the hegemony of national

[1] James Q. Wilson, *American Government: Institution and Policies* (Lexington, Mass.: D.C. Heath and Company, 1980), pp. 42–44.

majorities with *social* pluralism as a protection against factional dominance of the states.

Another question Beer raises is whether the growth of government generally has tended to centralize the federal system or has continued to diffuse power. The massive expansion of federal grants-in-aid to local governments, for instance, would seem to imply the former. In reality, however, he who pays the piper does not necessarily call the tune. State and local authorities continue to shape federal programs, to exert substantial control over their implementation, and to lobby actively and use political parties to influence the direction of public policy.

This interpretation of American federalism as a system characterized by *mutual* influence among levels of government is not new. The view was first advanced in 1960 by Morton Grodzins, who expressed it by way of a now-famous analogy: contrary to what the old doctrine of dual federalism suggested, the federal system is not a "layer cake," in which clear functional distinctions can be drawn between the national and subordinate governments, but a "marble cake." "As colors are mixed in the marble cake," Grodzins writes, "so functions are mixed in the American federal system." Moreover, in the article reprinted here, Grodzins affirms that the marble cake model is not a recent development, but a suitable description of federal-state relations from the start: "Relative to what governments did, intergovernmental cooperation during the last century was comparable with that existing today."

The final excerpt is from William Riker's important 1964 work on federalism entitled *Federalism: Origin, Operation, Significance*. The contrast between Riker's perspective and that of Samuel Beer is striking. While Beer stresses the role of ideas and theory in the foundation of a free federal union, Riker asserts that federalism is seldom, if ever, devised to guarantee freedom. Independent states tend to federate, Riker insists, only when the political leaders in one or more states seek to expand their territorial control: "federalism is the only feasible means to accomplish a desired expansion without the use of force." What do the member states gain from the federal bargain? Protection against external threats, as well as opportunities to share the benefits of the federation.

6

MARTIN DIAMOND

THE FEDERALIST'S VIEW
OF FEDERALISM

The American Republic has been regarded by nearly all modern observers as *the* example of a federal government. Indeed the various modern definitions of federalism are little more than slightly generalized descriptions of the American way of governing.

> Federalism may be defined as the division of political power between a central government, with authority over the entire territory of a nation, and a series of local governments, called 'states' in America . . .

> A federation is a *single* state in which the powers and functions of government are divided between a central government and several 'local' governments, each having a sphere of jurisdiction within which it is supreme.

> The essential relationship involves a division of activities between the autonomous parts and the common or central organs of a composite whole.

According to these typical definitions, the essential federal characteristic is the "division of political power," a division of supremacy (sovereignty, as used to be said) between member states and a central government, each having the final say regarding matters belonging to its sphere. There is a corollary to this sort of definition which has also come to be generally accepted. All college students are now taught that, in this respect, there are three kinds of government—confederal, federal, and unitary (national)—and that the United States exemplifies the middle term. This familiar distinction illuminates the definitions of federalism. In this view, a confederacy and a nation are seen as the extremes. The defining characteristic of a confederacy is that the associated states retain all the sovereign power, with the central body entirely dependent legally upon their will; the defining characteristic of a nation is that the central body has all the sovereign power, with the localities entirely dependent legally upon the will of

I have been helped in the work of which the present essay is a part, by many people in many ways. At the risk of displaying ingratitude, I use this opportunity to acknowledge only my great indebtedness to Professors Marvin Meyers and Herbert Storing of the University of Chicago.

the nation. In this view, then, federalism is truly the middle term for *its* defining characteristic is that it modifies and then combines the defining characteristics of the other two forms. A *federal* system combines states which *confederally* retain sovereignty within a certain sphere, with a central body that *nationally* possesses sovereignty within another sphere; the combination creates a new and different thing to which is given the name federal. To this statement of the modern view of federalism—that the United States is the example of the federal division of sovereignty, a form lying between and combining the confederal and national extremes—must be added only the following. It is further thought that the invention of federal government was the great contribution of the Founding Fathers to the art of government.

Now what is strange is this. *The Federalist*, the great contemporary exposition of the Constitution, emphatically does *not* regard the Constitution as establishing a typically federal, perhaps not even a primarily federal system of government. *The Federalist* regards the new American Union as departing significantly from the essentially federal character. The decisive statement is: "The proposed Constitution, therefore, is, in strictness, neither a national nor a federal Constitution, but a composition of both." As will become clear, our now familiar tripartite distinction was completely unknown to the men who made the Constitution. For them, there were but two possible modes: confederal or federal as opposed to unitary or national. In short, they had a very different understanding than we do of what federalism is. They had, therefore, in strictness, to regard their Constitution as a composition of federal and national features. We now give the single word federal to the system the framers regarded as possessing both federal and national features. This means we now deem as a unique principle what *The Federalist* regarded as a mere compound.

A careful reading of *The Federalist*, therefore, is to encounter a view which raises questions about the adequacy of the modern understanding of federalism. But the intention here is not primarily to judge of these two views of federalism. The aim is primarily to state fully *The Federalist*'s view of federalism. The differing modern view has been stated to remind the reader what preconceptions about federalism must at least temporarily be set aside in order to let *The Federalist* state its own case.

I

How *The Federalist* speaks of federalism must be understood in the light of its task and its audience. It sought to influence the ratification of the Constitution. It chose to do so by means of a careful commentary on the Constitution which would emphasize the error or irrelevance of the criticisms being made against it. Foremost among those criticisms was the charge that the Constitution had departed grievously from the true federal form, indeed was "calculated ultimately to make the states one consolidated government." The author of that phrase has come to be identified as one of the leading *anti-federalists*. But it must be remembered that in the article quoted from he signed himself "Letters of a Federal Farmer." The men we have come to call the *anti*-federalists regarded themselves as the true federalists. And we must remember that the choice of *The Federalist* as the title of the essays was regarded by many as a shrewd and unwarranted usurpation of that term. As the issue was fought in 1787–89, *The Federalist* (and the Constitution it defended) was attacked as covertly consolidationist, while the opponents of the Constitution fought as the true defenders of the federal principle. Everything that *The Federalist* says about the federal aspects of the Constitution must be understood, therefore, in the light of its great necessity: the demonstration that the Constitution should not be rejected on the grounds of inadequate regard for the federal principle.

It will be seen that it was not accidental that, as compared with its use of other important terms and concepts, *The Federalist* is rather inexplicit and ambiguous in its treatment of federalism. The only explicit definition of federalism occurs in *Federalist* 9 by Hamilton. His definition, it will be seen, is similar and leads easily to the modern definition of federalism. Indeed it could be argued that the modern understanding of federalism results largely from the effort of *The Federalist* to allay the fears of the "true federalists." However well *The Federalist* succeeded with its contemporaries, it succeeded surpassingly with modern political science. But I propose to show that Hamilton's definition and discussion of federalism in Number 9 is, at least, incomplete, and consequently is misleading, perhaps deliberately misleading.

Federalist 9 is the very important paper that discusses the improvements in "the science of politics" which have made it possible for "the enlightened friends to liberty" to accept and defend republican government. Hamilton deals especially with the improvement he calls the "enlargement of the orbit" within which popular systems may revolve. He is led of necessity to rebut the then familiar view that republics must be small and he seeks to show that Montesquieu, the authority usually cited in support of that view, in fact recommends confederation "as the proper expedient for extending the sphere of popular government . . . ." This leads to a consideration of what may be done by way of enlargement which is yet consonant with the idea of confederation. Hamilton's statement must be quoted at length.

> A distinction, more subtle than accurate, has been raised between a *confederacy* and a *consolidation* of the States. The essential characteristic of the first is said to be the restriction of its authority to the members in their collective capacities . . . . It is [also] contended that the national council ought to have no concern with any object of internal administration. An exact equality of suffrage between the members has also been insisted upon as a leading feature of a confederate government. These positions are, in the main, arbitrary; they are supported neither by principle nor precedent. It has indeed happened, that governments of this kind have generally operated in the manner which the distinction, taken notice of, supposes to be inherent in their nature; but there have been in most of them extensive exceptions to the practice, which serve to prove, as far as example will go, that there is no absolute rule on the subject. And it will be clearly shown, in the course of this investigation, that as far as the principle contended for has prevailed, it has been the cause of incurable disorder and imbecility in the government.
>
> The definition of a *confederate republic* seems simply to be, 'an assemblage of

societies,' or an association of two or more states into one state. The extent, modifications, and objects of the federal authority are mere matters of discretion. So long as the separate organization of the members be not abolished; so long as it exists, by a constitutional necessity, for local purposes; though it should be in perfect subordination to the general authority of the union, it would still be, in fact and in theory, an association of states, or a confederacy. The proposed Constitution, so far from implying an abolition of the State governments, makes them constituent parts of the national sovereignty, by allowing them a direct representation in the Senate, and leaves in their possession certain exclusive and very important portions of sovereign power. This fully corresponds, in every rational import of the terms, with the idea of a federal government.

Before examining this passage closely, it will be well to make clear the view that Hamilton is attacking. Those who made the impugned distinction between a confederacy and a consolidation, and who assign to a confederacy the three features which Hamilton denies are essential, were simply employing what was then the common and traditional view of federalism. That traditional view is made perfectly clear in the dictionaries Hamilton and Madison and their readers used.

> Federal . . . from foedus (faith) . . . Relating to a league or contract.
> Federary . . . A confederate.
> Federation . . . A League.
> Federative . . . Having power to make a league or a contract.

Dr. Johnson makes clear that the then common understanding of federalism involved no distinction between confederation and federalism. *The Federalist* similarly makes no such distinction. This is evident in the long passage from Hamilton and is true of the entire work; federal and confederal are used as completely interchangeable terms. *The Federalist* agrees fully with the then common usage at least in seeing but one kind of federal mode. In a moment I shall argue that *The Federalist* further agrees with the traditional view—despite the way Hamilton in *Federalist* 9 obscures the extent and significance of that agreement—that the federal mode is characterized by a contractual, voluntary relationship of States and has, therefore, the status of a league. In any event it is because this was the then universal understanding of federalism that the Articles of Confederation plainly refers to what it establishes as a "firm league of friendship."[1] This is the sense in which Locke used the word federative to refer to that power or function of government which makes arrangements with other nations. This is why Jefferson spoke of "foreign relations" when describing the proper jurisdiction of the central government, apparently including in this term the relations among the states, as well as of the whole Union with other nations.

We may now begin to consider what Hamilton is doing in the long passage quoted. The men he is attacking were employing the traditional understanding of federalism. From that traditional understanding, these men had inferred three characteristics as traditionally belonging to a federal system, and thus distinguishing such a system from a consolidated (national) system. Now the Constitution was substantially lacking in these three characteristics. *The Federalist* was seeking to win the votes of Americans, the generality of whom were committed to the position that the problems of the Union should be solved only by federal means; that is, there was a very general abhorrence of "consolidation." If federalism was admitted to require the three things which, it had to be admitted, the Constitution substantially lacked, then the adoption of the Constitution was gravely imperiled. Therefore, Hamilton had great reason to impugn the traditional distinction between a confederacy and a consolidation as being "more subtle than accurate." He does not, and of course could not, deny that there is some difference between the two. But he wishes to have the difference understood so that the new Constitution could be deemed to belong to the federal class. This meant that the difference had to be understood in such a way that a confederacy did *not* require the three characteristics. In general, it will be seen that Hamilton is trying mightily to accomplish a narrowing of the difference seen between confederacy and consolidation. He is trying to reduce the difference so that certain features of the Constitution will seem a sufficient fulfillment of the requirements of a federal system. The question then becomes: has Hamilton satisfactorily exorcised the three characteristics from the idea of federalism, and thereby rendered sufficient the single requirement to which he reduces the idea of federalism?

In my opinion, Hamilton does not make his case satisfactorily. The three characteristics his opponents claim for federalism are ("the essential characteristic") government over collectivities, abstinence from internal administration, and equal suffrage of the members. Hamilton says that "these positions are, in the main, arbitrary; they are supported neither by principle nor precedent." "Principle" here means according to theory or the nature of the thing; "precedent" means historical practice. Thus, Hamilton is claiming that neither the nature nor the history of confederacies supports the view that the three characteristics belong to federalism.

Regarding history, notice that Hamilton admits that "it has indeed *happened*" that confederacies have generally possessed the claimed characteristics. He only argues that there have been "extensive exceptions" to the way he admits that confederacies have "generally operated." These extensive exceptions "serve to prove, as far as example will go, that there is no absolute rule on the subject." Since no one could deny the existence of those exceptions, Hamilton presumes thus to have disposed of any support his opponents find in the history of confederacies. But, it can be suggested that history *is* on the side of his opponents. "As far as example will go," Hamilton says, we can discern no "*absolute* rule." But neither Hamilton nor his opponents ever considered that history ("example") settled difficult questions absolutely. Hamilton's opponents would have seen support in the history of confederacies in a more intelligent way than he suggests. They would have regarded history not as itself *settling* the question of what federalism is, but rather as *supporting* their view of the nature of federalism, a view which would have to rest upon theoretical considerations. Consider a query that they could address to Hamilton: *why* has it "happened" that confederacies "have generally operated in the manner . . . [our view] supposes to be inherent in their nature?" They themselves would answer, and rightly in my opinion, in the following way. History need not and does not always display single principles in their pure form. Actual confederacies therefore can include characteristics belonging to other principles, which become mixed in practice with the federal principle. To support a theoretical view, history need only typically or preponderantly display the things the theory supposes. It is admitted that actual confederacies preponderantly display what the theory supposes; hence example supports, in the only way example can support, the theoretical view that federalism requires the three characteristics. Or to state it still more forcefully for Hamilton's opponents: federalism is such a thing that it requires these three characteristics; *accordingly*, actual confederacies typically display them throughout history. If pressed, Hamilton himself, I am convinced, would have agreed with this rejoinder. That is, he may very well have been aware that he had not met the real issue; he may very well have known that his argument could with effort be refuted. Yet his refutable argument well served *The Federalist*'s purposes.

Hamilton *claimed* that his opponents had no *support* in history, but he *proved* only that history supplies no *absolute rule* on the subject. As has been suggested, Hamilton would have to admit that his reasoning is, strictly speaking, fallacious; but it is at first blush persuasive. He manages to leave the reader with the impression that history leaves the question entirely open. His fallacious but persuasive argument accomplishes a great deal for the political object of *The Federalist*. He accomplishes nothing with the thoughtful "anti-federalists," for they would know the difference between finding support in history and finding an absolute rule in history. But he accomplishes a great deal with their less thoughtful supporters who may well have been fortified by a simple conviction that history unambiguously and absolutely condemned the Constitution as departing from the federal principle. By unexceptionably proving that history supplies no absolute rule, and by even seeming to have proved that history leaves the question entirely open, Hamilton forcefully upsets the simple conviction and thereby weakens the opposition to the Constitution. To hold their followers, the thoughtful "anti-federalists" would now have to make a much more compli-cated, and hence less politically persuasive, argument. However much *The Federalist* may wish later to appeal to other portions of its audience, paradoxi-cally, on the grounds of the novelty of the Constitution, Hamilton has here managed to weaken the force of that opposition to the Constitution which spoke in the name of tradition.

Hamilton claimed that his opponents' view had no support in principle or precedent. He failed to sustain the claim regarding precedent. He again only seems to sustain but does not actually sustain his claim regarding the principle of the thing. Before proceeding to the second paragraph of the long quotation given above, where he asserts his own view of the nature and hence the requirements of federalism, Hamilton makes only one statement to prove that his opponents are wrong about the principle of federalism.

It will clearly be shown, in the course of this investigation, that as far as the principle contended for has prevailed, it has been the cause of incurable disorder and imbecility in the government.

This clearly tells us nothing about what the principle of federalism is, about what it requires. Although that is precisely what he must do to show how his opponents err regarding the principle of federalism, Hamilton abruptly alters the thrust of the argument. Notice the shift in the way he now uses the word "principle." "Principle," which first meant according to theory or nature, now becomes "the principle contended for" by his opponents. That is, "principle" now refers to the *position* of his opponents, which position Hamilton denounces as having always "been the cause of incurable disorder and imbecility in the government." As it were, Hamilton sets up the question, "are these three things required by the nature of federalism?" But he answers, "they are very bad things for society," which is not to have answered the question at all. In short, to this point, it is Hamilton's refutation of his opponents' view which is "arbitrary," having been vindicated "neither by principle nor precedent."

With his opponents' view skillfully impugned but perfectly intact, Hamilton proceeds to supply his own definition of federalism, one which permits him to derive only a single characteristic, which the Constitution possesses, as necessary to the federal mode. "The definition of a *confederate republic*," Hamilton says, "seems simply to be 'an assemblage of societies' . . . ." There are a number of reasons why we must regard as questionable the status of Hamilton's explicit definition of federalism. It occurs in a passage where, as has been shown, Hamilton's argument has been very weak, uncharacteristically weak, albeit rhetorically effective. Notice that Hamilton does not say what federalism is but rather what it *seems* to be. His definition belies, as I shall show, the way *The Federalist* more profoundly and more soberly understands federalism. He does not speak primarily in his own name, but rather relies on Montesquieu. There is something slightly odd in the quotation from Montesquieu. And Montesquieu properly understood supports not Hamilton's view but rather that of his opponents. Above all the whole statement is little more than a mere assertion.

Consider how Hamilton uses Montesquieu. He quotes the key phrase twice in *Federalist* 9. What is slightly odd is that the second time he quotes Montesquieu he varies the wording slightly. The first time Hamilton gives the passage as "*a kind of* assemblage of societies." This is an exact rendering of the English translation of Montesquieu used in America at the time. The second time it becomes merely "*an* assemblage of societies." What is interesting is that Hamilton's slight variation from the English translation further obscures what the translation had already made unclear. Had Montesquieu's meaning not been obscured in the English translation, Hamilton never could have used Montesquieu's definition of a confederal republic against his opponents; and Hamilton's slight variation made it even easier for him to use the already garbled Montesquieu. Montesquieu's meaning and its significance here become clear when the relevant passage is translated accurately, if ungracefully.

> This form of government [république fédérative] is a convention by which *several bodies politic* consent to become *citizens* of a larger State that they want to form. This is a *society of societies* who form a new one, which can enlarge itself through new associates who join up. (Italics supplied)

Clearly the "anti-federalists" would greatly welcome the proper statement of Montesquieu's definition. It strengthens their case and weakens Hamilton's. It is the *bodies politic* which become the *citizens* of the larger State. It is in this precise sense that it is a *society of societies* rather than a society of persons; hence Montesquieu's play on the words. When one compares Hamilton with Montesquieu, perhaps especially when one's attention is alerted by the way Hamilton twice quoted Montesquieu, it becomes apparent that Hamilton has introduced a novel content into Montesquieu's original explicit statement about federal republics. Consider only that for Hamilton, decisively, the "citizens" of the proposed Union are not "bodies politic," but individual persons, as in national governments. From Montesquieu's "society of societies," in which the associating bodies politic are the citizens of the larger body, it is reasonable to infer, as Hamilton's opponents did, that a federal system must govern over collectivities, abstain from internal affairs, and that the member societies must have an equal suffrage. But with Nugent's "a kind of assemblage of societies," and even more with Hamilton's "an assemblage of societies," one can begin to escape the inferences drawn by the "anti-federalists," and to prepare men to accept that much less is required for a system to be deemed fully federal.

Despite the obscurity of the English translation, the "anti-federalists" had correctly understood this passage in Montesquieu. They knew what *kind* of an assemblage of societies he meant, and what traditionally was supposed to be the standing of the member states within it. In this respect, they rightly regarded themselves as having the authority of Montesquieu; Hamilton was using the passage in a novel way. It is apparently not known whether Hamilton, who was proficient in French, read Montesquieu in the original. Had he, it would follow that he supported his novel understanding of federalism by a deliberate misuse of Montesquieu. Without that knowledge, it can at least be claimed that, contrary to the general understanding of the passage, Hamilton without further ado employed it for his own purposes.

Having brought the discussion down to the vague statement about "an assemblage of societies," Hamilton proceeds to claim that there are no necessary limits to the power of the "federal authority."

> So long as the separate organization of the members be not abolished; so long as it exists, by a constitutional necessity, for local purposes; though it should be in perfect subordination to the general authority of the union, it would still be, in fact and theory, an association of states, or a confederacy.

The existence of the States by "constitutional necessity," then, Hamilton declares to be the essential and sole federal element. His opponents would of course agree that it is *a* federal element. And this element the Constitution of course possessed. But on what ground may we agree with Hamilton, against his opponents, that this is all that federalism requires? Saving one argument, Hamilton's crucial statement is a mere assertion, in the form of an arbitrarily stated inference from what was in fact a garbled Montesquieu.

The one argument involves again a reference to Montesquieu. In the last paragraph of the ninth paper, Hamilton quotes Montesquieu: "Were I to give a model of an excellent Confederate Republic, it would be that of Lycia." Drawing upon Montesquieu, Hamilton emphasizes that the Lycian confederacy had an unequal suffrage of members and intervened in an extremely important internal matter. Notice that Lycia *did* comply with one of the three alleged requirements, and that the one deemed by the "anti-federalists" to be "the essential characteristic": the Lycian confederacy apparently governed only over collectivities. Remember also that this was for Hamilton the requirement most necessary to deny; but Lycia apparently supports his opponents on this one. In any event, Montesquieu is shown thus to have regarded with the greatest favor a confederacy which did not display two of the three characteristics claimed for the federal form. We have here then a massive "exception" to the way confederacies "generally operated." The question is: does Lycia prove the "anti-federalists" wrong because it lacked what they claimed to be necessary, or was Lycia "wrong," that is, less federal in that it lacked what the "anti-federalists" claimed to be necessary to federalism? All that Hamilton offers to answer this question, which must be raised, is that Lycia was for Montesquieu, so respected by the "anti-federalists," the "model of an excellent Confederate Republic."

It must suffice here to observe only the following. Until Montesquieu made it his "model," the Lycian confederacy had traditionally been regarded as the least federal of all the famous confederacies. What Montesquieu had in mind must be left for another discussion. But one can understand what Hamilton found attractive in a confederacy the fame of which rested on the extent to which it departed from the federal form. That Hamilton relied so emphatically on so dubious a confederal example only casts further doubt on the extent to which *The Federalist* means to settle the federal question with the attrited understanding supplied by Hamilton in Number 9.

II

Hamilton narrowed or truncated the understanding of federalism, creating thereby a federal test which the Constitution could easily pass. In the course of his argument he was able to claim that tradition and even the venerated Montesquieu, if not unequivocally on the side of the Constitution, were at least not the enemies of the Constitution. He was enabled thus to assuage or at least confuse those whose great fear was the "consolidating" tendency of the Constitution. But the uncharacteristic weakness and other peculiarities of his argument suggest strongly that he may not have regarded the proposed Constitution as nearly so federal as he makes it seem; that he in fact gives more credence than seems at first to the traditional view of federalism; and that, therefore, we may expect *The Federalist* later to disclose a more deeply considered view of federalism and one which acknowledges the extent to which the Constitution departs from the federal character.

The fuller and more revealing discussion occurs primarily in *Federalist* 39. After dealing with the charge that the Constitution is inadequately republican, Madison turns to the federal question.

> "But it was not sufficient," say the adversaries of the proposed Constitution, "for the convention to adhere to the republican form. They ought, with equal care, to have preserved the *federal* form, which regards the Union as a *Confederacy* of sovereign states; instead of which, they have framed a *national* government, which regards the Union as a consolidation of the States."

Madison begins his defense, interestingly, with a statement like Hamilton's: "Without inquiring into the accuracy of the distinction on which the objection is founded . . ." Thus both Hamilton and Madison begin by casting doubt upon the way their opponents see the distinction between a confederacy and a consolidation, which way of seeing the distinction (that is, way of defining federalism) leads to a rejection of the Constitution. But then Madison and Hamilton handle the matter differently.[2] Hamilton so narrowed down the traditional definition of federalism that the Constitution could be deemed unqualifiedly federal. Madison, however, after entering a demurrer to the distinction, proceeds to employ the definition of federalism it involves. Early in the argument, Madison specifically reminds the reader of his demurrer. He says of an aspect of the Constitution that "it will be a federal and not a national act, *as these terms are understood by the objectors* . . ." (Italics supplied.) The style of his argument is therefore: even if your understanding of federalism is granted, the Constitution is still *sufficiently* federal to satisfy you. By not plainly accepting his opponents' understanding of the terms federal and national, Madison is able to retain for *The Federalist* any rhetorical advantage gained by Hamilton in Number 9. Yet only once more in Number 39 does Madison thus hold himself aloof from the objector's use of the term. By the end of the paper, and in other papers, Madison drops even the demurrer, and in effect accepts that, strictly speaking, federalism is what his opponents understand it to be. Thus by the end of the paper, he says, without cavil, that the Constitution is "in strictness" a compound of federal and national features.

To estimate justly the force of the criticism that the Constitution "framed a national government,"[3] Madison says, at the outset, that it will be necessary "to ascertain the real character of the government in question."

> In order to ascertain the real character of the government, it may be considered in relation [1] to the foundation on which it is to be established; [2] to the sources from which its ordinary powers are to be drawn; [3] to the operation of those powers; [4] to the extent of them; and [5] to the authority by which future changes in the government are to be introduced.

Madison examines these five ways of determining whether the proposed government is a confederacy or a national government. First, as to its mode of establishment: "The Constitution is to be founded on the assent and ratification of the people of America . . . ; [however] not as individuals composing one entire nation, but as composing the distinct and independent States to which they respectively belong." "The act, therefore, establishing the Constitution, will not be a *national*, but a *federal act*." He emphasizes this by pointing out that neither a majority of people, nor a majority of States can ratify the Constitution. Hence, "each State, in ratifying the Constitution, is considered as a sovereign body, independent of all others, and only to be bound by its own voluntary act. In this relation, then, the new Constitution will, if established, be a *federal*, and not a *national* constitution." The mode of ratification, then, is deemed federal by virtue of its conformity with the traditional idea of federalism: the States are the "citizens" ratifying the Constitution (albeit, crucially, not mere organs of existing state government, but the *people* of the States acting in their constitutive capacity); these "societies" are forming the larger society. The "distinctness and independence of States" is what constitutes the federal.

Second, he deals with "the sources from which the ordinary powers of government are to be derived." Madison styles the House of Representatives unequivocally national because it derives "its powers from the people of America . . . in the same proportion, and on the same principle, as they are in the legislature of a particular State." Contrarily, the Senate is a federal institution because it "will derive its powers from the States; as political and *co-equal* societies. . . ." Madison judges the Presidency to be "compound," "presenting at least as many *federal* as *national* features." The criterion for what is federal is the extent to which the States, in the election of the president, function as "distinct and co-equal bodies politic."

As to the operation of the ordinary powers of government, Madison prefaces his judgment with a reference to the view of his opponents.

> The difference between a federal and national government, as it relates to the *operation of the government*, is supposed to consist in this, that in the former the powers operate on the political bodies, composing the Confederacy, in their political capacities; in the latter, on the individual citizens composing the nation, in their individual capacities. On trying the Constitution by this criterion, it falls under the *national*, not the *federal* character . . .

But it is crucial to see that Madison does not in the least attempt to invalidate this view, and indeed implicitly accepts it. He offers no argument whatsoever that would support any other view than that in this respect the government is national.

Fourth, regarding "extent of powers":

> The idea of a national government involves in it, not only an authority over the individual citizens, but an indefinite supremacy over all persons and things, so far as they are objects of lawful government. Among a people consolidated into one nation, this supremacy is completely vested in the national legislature.

Madison concludes that, with regard to extent of powers,

> the proposed government cannot be deemed a national one; since its jurisdiction extends to certain enumerated objects only, and leaves to the several States a residuary and inviolable sovereignty over all other objects.

Interestingly, he does not say that it is, therefore, on this count a federal system; he says only that it "cannot be deemed a national one." This passage differs strikingly from the other four comparable passages in that the words federal or confederal never appear; whereas in the other four cases, Madison sums up his judgment by saying that the feature is either "national, not federal," or "federal, not national." However, it must be noted that in the short summarizing paragraph which concludes *Federalist* 39, Madison does explicitly refer to this aspect of the government as "federal." I believe that Madison, on the standard of judgment he is using, is not entitled to go so far; "compound" would be more accurate. What Madison does not say but clearly implies, I think, is the following. Insofar as some portion of the whole governing power remains with the states, the system is federal; insofar as some portion of the governing power belongs to a *national* central government, the system is national. It is thus more accurate to say that the system, with regard to extent of powers, is compound. We shall be led soon to speculate on *The Federalist*'s view of what will be the future of this compound system, whether it will be stable or whether the one or the other principle will predominate.

Finally fifth, as to the "authority by which amendments are to be made," Madison finds it neither wholly national nor wholly federal.

> Were it wholly national, the supreme and ultimate authority would reside in the *majority* of the people of the Union; and this authority would be competent at all times, like that of a majority of every national society, to alter or abolish its established government. Were it wholly federal, on the other hand, the concurrence of each State in the Union would be essential to every alteration that would be binding on all . . . .
> In requiring more than a majority, and particularly in computing the proportion by *States*, not by *citizens*, it departs from the *national* and advances towards the *federal* character; in rendering the concurrence of less than the whole number of States sufficient, it loses again the federal and partakes of the national character.

Again, Madison is lucidly employing the traditional understanding of federalism. Indeed, at the very end of the passage, in making federalism require unanimity, he outdoes his opponents in the strictness with which he understands the federal principle. *The Federalist* wants a new and looser meaning to be attributed to federalism; it wants to have the Constitution considered satisfactorily federal. It employs rhetoric to exonerate the Constitution, whenever it can, from the stain of consolidationism. But when *The Federalist* speaks strictly what emerges is the traditional understanding of the federal principle. According to the accepted meaning in 1787, and perhaps in all earlier political discussions, federalism was that which related "to a league or contract"; it was a relationship of "bodies politic," linked as the etymology of the word tells us, by the obligations of faith (*foedus,* cognate with *fides*); its operating principles derived from its contractual nature and its dependence on good faith.[4] What I have tried to establish is that *The Federalist* implicitly but utterly accepts this as the strict, that is, proper understanding of federalism. *The Federalist* had no novel understanding of what is federal, it only departed from others in regarding the simply federal as radically inadequate for the purposes of the Union it has in mind. It did have a novel understanding of a new thing, not a simply federal thing, but a compound which it was happy to have men call by the old name federal. Only when we see *The Federalist's* implicit understanding of federalism may we understand the full force of the statement: "The proposed Constitution, therefore, is, in strictness, neither a national nor a federal Constitution, but a composition of both."

A passage from Hamilton, in which I believe Madison fully concurs, makes clear the extent to which *The Federalist* regards the simply federal as inadequate.

> There is nothing absurd or impracticable in the idea of a league or alliance between independent nations for certain defined purposes precisely stated in a treaty . . . and depending for its execution on the good faith of the parties. . . . If the particular States in this country are disposed to stand in a similar relation to each other, and to drop the project of a general DISCRETIONARY SUPERINTENDENCE, the scheme would indeed be pernicious . . . but it would have the merit of being, at least, consistent and practicable. Abandoning all views towards a confederate *government,* this would bring us to a simple alliance offensive and defensive. . . . But if . . . we still will adhere to the design of a *national government,* or, which is the same thing, of a superintending power, under the direction of a common council, we must resolve to incorporate into our plan those ingredients which may be considered as forming the characteristic difference between a league and a government; we must extend the authority of the Union to the persons of the citizens—the only proper objects of government.

This passage is from the famous *Federalist* 15, the theme of which is the denunciation of legislation for states in their collective capacities, as under the Articles, and a defense of the "idea of government" as displayed in the "augmentation of federal authority" under the proposed Constitution. Hamilton is striking hard and brilliantly at perhaps the weakest point in the "anti-federalist" view. The "anti-federalists," he claims, want "things repugnant and irreconcilable"; they want to augment the federal authority "without a diminution of State authority." They want a "political monster": "sovereignty in the Union, and complete independence in the members." Hamilton says one must choose between a league and a government. But this choice, I argue, is in the strict sense ultimately the choice between the federal and the national principles. I have sought to show that *The Federalist* and its opponents agree that the federal is "the idea of a league . . . for certain defined purposes . . . depending . . . on the good faith of the parties." When Hamilton denounces that arrangement as totally incapable of bringing the blessings of Union which all want, he is implicitly denouncing and rejecting a decisively federal arrangement for America. The blessings of Union require *government,* and that means "*national* government." The underlying problem is whether there can be "confederate government," that is, whether the confederal principle is ultimately incompatible with the governing principle. Governing directly over individual citizens is what Hamilton contends for, and that is exactly what Madison had to characterize as national when he examined the "operation of the government." In short, the "characteristic difference between a league and a government" is essentially the difference between the federal and the national. The "characteristic difference" Hamilton is insisting upon is what distinguished the proposed American Union from what was regarded by all contemporary men, including *The Federalist*'s authors, as the essentially federal.

Let me indicate now the extent of *The Federalist*'s awareness of the novel things it is doing to the federal idea. In *Federalist* 37, Madison defends the Federal Convention and urges that "many allowances ought to be made for the difficulties inherent in the very nature of the undertaking referred to the convention." The very first difficulty concerns the problem of federalism.

> The novelty of the undertaking immediately strikes us. It has been shown in the course of these papers, that the existing Confederation is founded on principles which are fallacious. . . . It has been shown, that the other confederacies which could be consulted as precedents have been vitiated by the same erroneous principles, and can therefore furnish no other light than that of beacons, which give warning of the course to be shunned, without pointing out that which ought to be pursued.

The proposed Union, thus, is a very novel confederacy indeed; for the Convention did, as *The Federalist* makes clear, shun the errors of all past confederacies. But, as is also clear, it avoided past confederal errors by creating a Union which was radically less federal. *The Federalist*, it must be understood, does not argue that the "other confederacies" perished because they used federal principles fallaciously or erroneously. What was wrong with the Articles and the other confederacies were the essential federal principles themselves. The great teaching of *The Federalist* is not how to be federal in a better way, but how to be better by being less federal.

This conclusion would be supported by a close examination of *The Federalist*'s extended analysis of all earlier confederacies. The indictment of the earlier confederacies is savage. The heart of the indictment is that these confederacies perished miserably, or live contemptibly, precisely because of their fidelity to the whole of the federal principle. The "novelty" of the Constitution is again, in this context, indicated curiously. Long after the lengthy descriptions of former confederacies, and of the miseries that resulted from their essential principles, the whole purpose of which recitation is to serve as a warning for the formation of the American Union, we are casually informed in passing that the proposed Union is "so dissimilar" from "most" of the earlier confederacies "as greatly to weaken any inference" concerning the former from the latter. Again, it is a very novel confederacy indeed for which inferences cannot well be drawn from the experience of other confederacies.

I summarize my argument to this point. In opposing *The Federalist*'s idea of federalism to the modern understanding, I emphasize *The Federalist*'s view that the federal consists not only in residual state jurisdictions, but in the nature of the central government. *The Federalist* admits, indeed in its subtle rhetoric, claims that the proposed central government is varyingly federal and national. I have shown further that this accords with the traditional understanding of federalism. It is possible then to understand the contribution which the Constitution, and *The Federalist* as the great argument expounding it, made to the "art of federal government." The contribution consists in this: they altered the traditional federal form, by subtracting from it certain decisively federal features and adding to it certain decisively national features. In short, the contribution of *The Federalist* is the presentation and justification of a new form of government, neither federal nor national, but an admixture of both characters. . . .

NOTES

[1] This is not to suggest that the Confederacy under the Articles was only a league. The Confederacy was not, as is often said, a weak league; on the contrary, it was a very strong league as far as leagues go. Because Americans sought so much from them, the Articles indeed pushed in the direction of national government. But that is not the point here; all that is emphasized is that the language of the Articles reveals what men then understood to be the necessities of the federal form.

[2] I do not mean that Madison in Number 39 is inconsistent with or contradictory to Hamilton in Number 9. Contrary to a common view, I regard *The Federalist* to be what it claims to be, the consistent and comprehensive work of a single author, *Publius* by name. I emphasize therefore that when I refer to the difference between Hamilton and Madison, I mean only that kind of a difference one could find in the work of a single author, a difference in the way the author's meaning is stated as his work unfolds.

[3] Note how Madison states the criticism in the way most susceptible of rejoinder. The "anti-federalists" did not typically charge that the Constitution straightforwardly "framed a national government," rather that its compound of federal and national features was spurious, i.e., was calculated to become a simple national government. As will be seen, *The Federalist* has some curious things to say about the future of the compound.

[4] It may be useful at this point to be reminded of the modern view of federalism. On behalf of that view Professor A. W. Macmahon has claimed that "the etymological kinship of the word (from Latin *foedus*) with ideas of treaty and of contract illuminates but no longer fixes the meaning of a protean and widely applicable principle. The essential relationship involves a division of activities between the autonomous parts and the common or central organs of a composite whole." (*Encyclopedia of the Social Sciences*, VI, 173.) I insist in this essay only that we must see the older meaning in our reading of *The Federalist*. But it may be an error to treat federalism as quite so "protean and widely applicable" a principle. Perhaps *The Federalist* is wiser, in regarding the Constitution as a "compound" of two principles, than the modern usage which makes that compound a thing in itself, a single principle. The answer would depend in good part upon which usage contributed most to analytical clarity. But that is a matter beyond the scope of the present essay.

7

SAMUEL H. BEER

FEDERALISM, NATIONALISM, AND DEMOCRACY IN AMERICA

During the 1960s in the United States, as in most advanced countries, there was a large and sudden surge upward in the growth of the public sector, largely under the impetus of the central government. Supporters of this new phase of centralization sometimes see it as one more, and perhaps the final, stage in the transformation of the American polity into virtually a unitary system. Critics, on the other hand, seek to revive federalism, frequently proposing a reallocation of functions between levels of government. Some find evidence of such a revival in the decentralization accomplished by recent less restrictive schemes of federal aid.

I should like to present a third position. My thesis is that more important than any shifts of power or function between levels of government has been the emergence of new arenas of mutual influence among levels of government. Within the field of intergovernmental relations a new and powerful system of representation has arisen, as the federal government has made a vast new use of state and local governments and these governments in turn have asserted a new direct influence on the federal government. What is interesting about American federalism today is not its particular allocation of functions or powers between levels of government, but rather what it is adding to our national system of representation.

Moreover, I should say that these developments, while new, are in harmony with the original design of the federal system. Federalism as the mutually exclusive allocation of powers between the general and the state governments—dual federalism, it may be called—belongs to the past. Dual federalism was indeed a feature of the original design and, broadly speaking, characterized our system of multilevel government until the New Deal. Federalism in this sense does not apply, and given the realities of our times, could not be made to apply, to that system today.

But dual federalism was only one and a secondary feature of the original design. The theory governing that design made its territorial allocation of powers

I wish to dedicate this paper to the memory of Martin Diamond from whom over the years I have learned much about American federalism and especially about the importance of theory to its original design.

an instrument of a far more important purpose. That purpose was so to divide and organize power as to avert the evils and realize the benefits of free government. Within this general scheme, the federal division of powers served a representative function by creating a structure of mutual balance and influence between the two main levels of government. In this manner, dual federalism was a means to representational federalism.

In the first part of this article I shall, therefore, be talking about the original federal design, in order, in the second part, to direct attention to the way that representational federalism has been reconstituted by recent developments in intergovernmental relations. Since these developments have parallels in other countries, I shall conclude with a few questions for comparative study suggested by American experience.

THE ORIGINAL FEDERAL DESIGN

The Democratic Purpose

To see the original federal design as the solution to a problem of representation links it directly and intimately to the great cause that led to the American Revolution. That cause was liberty. To the colonial dissidents liberty meant certain personal rights, such as freedom of conscience, but above all political liberty, the right to government by "the consent of the governed." And by "consent" they meant not some presumed agreement to a form of government delivered by social contract in the distant past, but rather a consent that closely and actively joined voter and representative. Ambiguities in this idea permitted various degrees of control by voters over representatives, ranging from strict delegation to a fiduciary relationship subject to frequent accountability. Sometimes the two tendencies were mixed, as when the town meeting of Boston in May 1764 at the height of the Stamp Act crisis delegated to their representatives in the provincial assembly "the power of acting in their public concerns in general as your own prudence shall direct you, always reserving to themselves the constitutional right of expressing their mind and giving you such instruction upon particular matters as they at any time shall judge proper." One part of the charge leads toward legislative discretion, the other toward popular sovereignty. Either makes government crucially dependent on the will of the voters.

Whether in a more or a less radical form, government by consent as understood by the colonial dissidents was fundamentally and irreconcilably in conflict with the theory and practice of British government in the eighteenth century. The Old Whig constitution had emerged from a medieval past and, although the philosophical and sociological foundations of the polity had been transformed by modernity, John Adams was quite right to see in it powerful remnants of the canon and feudal laws. This polity was hierarchical and corporatist and its hierarchy and corporatism did not depend, and were not believed to depend, upon the will of the voters. From the premises of the system virtual representation and parliamentary sovereignty followed logically. The polity included a great variety of corporate groupings, functional and territorial, often of unequal value and authority. Representation in the House of Commons was adjusted to this ordering. For the individual to be represented, it was not necessary that he actually have a vote for a member of Parliament, but only that persons belonging to his rank or order and residing in his sort of community should have a vote. Indeed, according to these beliefs, if all the people had been enfranchised and grouped in constituencies that would give their votes equal weight, essential differentiations of value and authority would be destroyed. For the same reason, the sovereign authority could not be located in the people, but only in that complex body, the Parliament, which, including King, Lords and Commons, brought all elements of the polity into a common deliberation in their proper ordering. The American dissidents, seized with a different ideology, which descended from that failed democratic revolution of the English seventeenth century, the Commonwealth, were impelled into fundamental conflict with this Old Whig regime and its rulers. The polemic in the decade or so before the Revolution rightly focused this conflict between hierarchy and democracy on the question of representation.

To give such emphasis to the democratic character of the American Revolution is to play down its national character. One could argue the opposite case, saying, for instance, as Schumpeter did, that by the middle of the eighteenth century most Americans had come to regard the British rulers as foreigners who were interfering with American interests, but that, perhaps because the ideology of nationalism had not yet appeared, the Americans sought to legitimate with democratic principles what was really a national uprising. This hypothesis may gain some plausibility because of the primacy of nationalism over democracy in the creation of many new states in recent decades. It does not, however, fit the facts of the American case. Given the depth of the conflict one might well conclude that an ultimate decision for independence was inevitable. Some of the colonial leaders came to that conclusion rather sooner than others. But there is no reason to doubt the sincerity of the dissidents as a whole when through a decade of bitter debate they steadfastly claimed that they sought only freedom within the British empire, not freedom from it. For months after Washington took command of the Continental Army in 1775 he and his officers daily drank the king's health.

The federal question did not arise until independence had been chosen. Naturally. One could not seriously consider how or why to allocate powers between a central government and various provincial governments in an American polity until it had been decided to have an American polity. The prerevolutionary debate, therefore, although much concerned with the specific powers that Parliament might exercise in comparison with those of the colonial assemblies, showed no preference for a federal arrangement. Indeed, the first major proposal put forward by a colonial spokesman embodied a unitary, not a federal solution to the problem of imperial government, when James Otis in 1764, echoing an idea favored by Franklin ten years earlier, proposed "an American representation in Parliament." In his scheme, which was said to have been "universally approved" of in the colonies, although insisting that the colonial legislatures be maintained, he conceded parliamentary sovereignty and granted that the provincial legislatures were unquestionably subordinate to that of Great Britain.

In the following years, various plans were offered for a division of powers between the imperial and the colonial legislatures. These efforts to "draw a line" were based on such rationales as the distinction between internal and external taxation or between the power to regulate the trade of the colonies and the power to tax them. If one may call these schemes federal, one must, on the other hand, recognize that on the eve of independence they succumbed to a proposal which was once again unitary insofar as it denied any and all authority to Parliament over the colonies. This was the idea—of what much later came to be known as "dominion status"—that the colonies and Britain were "distinct states" within the empire connected with one another only by having the same king. This view of the juridical status of Parliament was carried over into the Declaration of Independence which, turning its full attention to justifying a break with the king, dismissed Parliament as never having exercised legitimate authority over the colonies. No one of the many and various schemes for imperial reorganization had solved the conflict for the simple reason that the conflict was not about the territorial allocation of powers, but about the democratic basis of power.

The National Question

When this failure had led to independence, the national question came suddenly and urgently to the fore. What was the source of the authority of the new government? Obviously, the consent of the people—that and nothing more. But was this consent given by one people or by several peoples, by the nation or by the states? The Declaration of Independence described itself in Jefferson's words as the act of "one people" and eleven years later the Constitution similarly declared that it was ordained and established by "We, the people." According to Abraham Lincoln, the unity of the nation asserted in these documents dated back to the time of the Continental Congress when the colonists chose to form the Union, which is, in his words, "older than any of the States, and, in fact . . . created the States" and "produced their independence and liberty."

This version of events provides the historical basis for the national theory of American federalism. According to that theory, a single sovereign power, the people of the United States, created both the federal and state governments, delegating to each a certain limited authority. In this theory of the juridical basis of the American polity popular sovereignty appears as a single national will acting as the constituent power. The compact theory, on the other hand, takes a different view of the same events and arrives at a different view of the Constitution and of federalism. According to this view, the colonies became separate, independent polities when they cast loose from Britain and only thereafter entered into an agreement to have a general government for certain limited purposes. From this theory justifications have been deduced for secession, interposition, or at least extensive "states' rights."

The national theory, I should say, is a superior interpretation of what actually happened, an interpretation incidentally which has been given further powerful support by recent historical research. The important thing, however, for the present inquiry into the original design of American federalism, is that the men who conceived and elaborated that design worked from the premises of the national theory. Their federalism presupposes their nationalism. In their view the constituent power was one people, the nation. What they sought to produce in the constitution of the new polity was a scheme by which that nation would act not only as the constituent power, but also as the continuous controlling and directing influence in the political life of the new polity. In seeking to give such effect to this idea of national democracy, they were consistently carrying out the belief in government by consent that had rationalized and impelled the resistance to Great Britain in prerevolutionary days. The problem of representation which had preoccupied the energies of that long struggle continued to be central to the shaping of the federal structure.

The Framers' Theory

Theory had powerfully directed their labors of resistance and theory powerfully directed their labors of construction. In the later as in the earlier phase, the orienting ideology consisted of those same liberal democratic ideas that had come down from the seventeenth century. In their work of construction, however, the Americans also made wide use of "the new science of politics" which had blossomed in the early eighteenth century. This new study was by no means conceived as value-free, but was dominated by the new hope of the time, free government. Its main concern was how to protect liberty by dividing and balancing power within a polity. The premise of this concern and of its consequent technique was a certain distrust of human nature. Although many of these authors, as in the case of the Americans, had had a Protestant upbringing, I would not say that this distrust was Calvinist—it did not approach that black despair—nor even that it was distinctively Christian or biblical. It was more modern, more secular, a workable pessimism which saw a love of power in all men and feared any monopoly of the instruments of power, but which held that if control over these instruments were properly divided and balanced, power could be made to check power so that it would be used only for the common good. One technique was a separation of powers according to the "natural" functions of government or according to the ranks and orders of society. Another consisted in a division of powers between a general government and a number of provincial governments. It was, of course, this latter sort of balancing that the framers sought to achieve in their federal design.

That design was unique. At Philadelphia in 1787, it is generally recognized, the Americans invented federalism as it has come to be understood since that time. The scheme had no precedent. Its authors were not, as some have claimed, attempting to restore an allocation of powers between central and provincial governments like that the colonists had experienced in the days of "benign and salutary neglect" under the old empire before the Sugar Act. They were surely not trying to imitate the Dutch, Swiss or German regimes, a type of polity which they regarded as "the cause of incurable disorder and imbecility."

Their new creation was theory-based. Yet even in drawing generously on the political science of their time, they did not follow their authorities slavishly. Indeed, their inventiveness consisted precisely in combining elements taken from two incompatible constructions of, respectively, Montesquieu and Hume.

Montesquieu's contribution came principally from his famous discussion of the confederate republic in Books VIII and IX of *The Spirit of the Laws*. There he was trying to reconcile the conflicting conditions conducive respectively to liberty and to security. In conformity with the conventional view, he held that "republican government" could flourish only in a small state where "the public good" is "more obvious, better understood, and more within the reach of every citizen." In an extensive republic, on the other hand, although its defensive posture would be stronger, the public good would be "sacrificed to a thousand private views" and encroachments on liberty would be able to grow without arousing general resistance. Distance, size or—more properly—scale would present the man of ambition with his opportunity and his temptation. Montesquieu proposed to realize the respective advantages of smallness and largeness of scale without introducing their disadvantages by means of a confederate republic. Formed by "a convention" among a number of small republics, such a polity could amass defensive power without making itself vulnerable to the internal corruption of despotism, because the member states would retain the independent force to prevent the abuse of power by the general government. The territorial pluralism of these continuing small governments would counteract tendencies toward corruption in the wider polity.

Montesquieu's confederate republic alone was clearly not the model for the constitution makers at Philadelphia. It was rather the sort of regime which in their eyes had proved to be both inefficient and dangerous to liberty under the Articles of Confederation. Their radical transformation was to impose on it certain features of a unitary regime. For the sake of "stability and energy" they gave the general government a new instrument of power by enabling it to act directly on individuals. But their main concern was to add a further protection of "republican liberty" by providing for the representation of individuals in the federal legislature.

The significance of this new scheme of representation was given its classical exposition in Madison's Tenth Federalist. His idea is an adaptation of a proposal put forward by Hume in his essay on the "Idea of a Perfect Commonwealth." In that essay, first published in 1752, Hume sketched an elaborate system of representative government and against this background attacked the "common opinion" that republican government is more likely to survive in a small than a large polity. On the contrary, he argued, the "near habitation" of the citizens of a small polity will make even their division into small parties vulnerable to "the force of popular tides and currents." In the large representative republic, however, not only will the "higher magistrates" "refine" the opinions of the voters, but also the various parts will be less likely to unite against "the public interest." Madison improves on this model by stressing the diversity of social and economic interests that will be embraced in the more extensive republic. Thanks to the greater differentiation that goes with larger scale, the social pluralism of the general government will counteract tendencies toward a factional abuse of power in the subordinate governments.

The invention at Philadelphia transformed Montesquieu's model by integrating with it this Humean construction. The new unitary features meant that now the social pluralism of the nation as a whole would be represented in the general government, which, within limits, would be able to avert the dangers of faction within the states, while the continued existence of the states meant that, as in Montesquieu's model, territorial pluralism would constitute a safeguard against encroachments by the general government. It was a unified, internally coherent and highly original model of a new kind of government. This invention resulted from compromise, to be sure—not the compromise of stalemate, however, but of social learning.

Federalism as Representational

In the *Federalist* papers and the ratification debates, the new model was set forth and defended. It had a military version in which the possession of instruments of coercive force by each level held the balance for free government. "Power being almost always the rival of power," wrote Hamilton, "the general government will at all times stand ready to check the usurpations of the state governments, and these will have the same disposition towards the general government." His next sentence revealed the motor in the mechanism: "The people, by throwing themselves into either scale, will infallibly make it preponderate. If their rights are invaded by either, they can make use of the other as the instrument of redress." In short, the same force which, according to the national theory, had brought the Constitution into existence and formed its juridical foundation, the sovereign people, would continue to guarantee its free operation.

This military version of how the federal design would operate is hardly more than an historical curiosity today. But its authors were, of course, also thinking in larger terms and of a more political application. They expected the social pluralism of the general government to operate not only in emergencies, but also in day-to-day decision making. Nor did they see this function as merely negative—to prevent narrow and oppressive majorities from forming or acting. Their political science taught them that "the larger the society . . . the more duly capable it will be of self-government." They therefore expected that the majority coalitions which did form within the general government not only would respect "the rights of every class of citizens," but also would positively express "principles . . . of justice and the general good." The framers were not some sort of early-day laissez-fairists. Indeed, Turgot gave them a famous scolding for their interventionism. They lived in an age of state-building and mercantilism and fully recognized the need for active government in their developing economy. They saw no need, however, to trade off liberty for development and, although by no means utopians, they had high hopes for their political engineering, believing that its processes of mutual balance and influence would not only break the violence of faction, but also produce decisions worthy of general assent.

In the *Federalist* papers and the ratification debates, discussion of the military aspects of the federal balance shade off into a more political version, which tells us a good deal about how the American system has actually worked and which is still vividly relevant to its operation today. "Notwithstanding the different modes in which [the federal and state governments] are appointed," Madison wrote in the 46th *Federalist*, "we must consider both of them as substantially dependent on the great body of the citizens of the United States. . . . The federal and the State governments are in fact but different agents and trustees of the people, constituted with different powers, and designed for different purposes." "The people" is "the ultimate authority," the "common superior" of both. Nor does he mean this only in the sense of juridical foundation or military balance. He is also concerned to show how the people, acting as the common electorate of all levels of government, bring state perspectives to bear on federal decisions and federal perspectives to bear on state decisions. The three main propositions in his analysis are that these perspectives will not merely reflect the immediate wishes of the voters, but will be shaped by the processes of self-government in which the voters take part; that the influence between levels will pass from state to general government, but also from general government to state government; and finally that the medium through which this influence will be transmitted will be the common electorate of the two sets of governments.

The essence of the invention of 1787 was the use of the same electorate to choose two sets of governments, each with constitutional protection. As in the military version of the new federal system, where the people were to maintain the balance for free government by casting their weight in one or the other scale, in this political version the medium of interaction was the common electorate. Governing himself through two different governments, the voter views the political world from two perspectives, one shaped by the social pluralism of the general government, the other shaped by the territorial pluralism of state government. In his political life, as a member of one nation, he does not separate from one another the two perspectives and the interests each elicits in him. His state perspective affects his choices and decisions in federal politics as his federal perspective affects his choices and decisions in state politics. One may call this process "representational federalism" because it gives representation in the general government to the territorial pluralism of the states and representation in the state governments to the social pluralism of the general government.

In framing and debating the new federal structure, Americans of the time were concerned with the same central problem that had stirred them to criticism, resistance and rebellion a generation before: the problem of representation. Now as then their interest in the allocation of specific powers between levels of government was secondary to this overriding concern. They did believe that certain government functions were more effectively exercised at one rather than the other level. Defense, for instance, was more properly a function of the general government. Yet, guided by their primary concern for liberty, they did not hesitate to divide authority over this function, giving important military powers to the states.

Federalism has often been advocated primarily as a means of accommodating levels of government to territorial diversity. The compact theory would lead one to expect this to be the major subject of debate during the framing and ratification of the Constitution. Supporters as well as critics did recognize that the "sentiments, habits, and customs" of the states were diverse and that, therefore, "a government which might be very suitable for one might not be agreeable to the other." Yet the great mass of utterance at Philadelphia and the ratifying conventions displays remarkably little concern with this fact. Even the most ardent champions of greater powers for the states gave little or no weight to the argument from territorial diversity. Luther Martin, for instance, did not ground his advocacy of state power in his identification with Maryland as a distinctive community or in its need for authority commensurate with its special values or way of life. When he attacked the new powers of the federal government, he, as much as Madison or Hamilton, saw liberty as his goal and the new science of politics as the means for reaching that goal. He differed from them only in clinging to the conventional wisdom of the time as put forward in an unalloyed version of Montesquieu's theory of the confederate republic. It is consistent with this ground of the differences among Americans of that day over the Constitution that a bill of rights, which protected the liberties most valued by their common ideology and which was, as John Hancock said, "in no wise local, but calculated to give security and ease alike to all the states," served to win over critics and produce the quick subsidence of opposition that followed ratification.

NEW STRUCTURES OF REPRESENTATIONAL FEDERALISM

In summary, my historical thesis is: that in making a democratic revolution, the American rebels created a nation and invented representational federalism as a means of governing their new national democracy.

A Rationale for the States

The reason for looking at this history and especially at its theoretical component is that they tell us something important about how the American polity has actually worked and continues to work. This perspective, in the first place, throws light on what we can and cannot expect of the states today. Any modern polity will have one or more levels of government. The smaller governments may be designed simply as administrative districts under the central authority. They may be set up for an economic purpose, and, accordingly, endowed with powers and boundaries suited to a distinctive complex of agricultural, commercial or industrial activity. They may be so laid out as to match patterns of cultural differentiation, as in the case of linguistic boundaries or other indicators of diversity in community values.

None of these rationales, administrative, economic or cultural, makes sense of the American states, except occasionally and accidentally. Look at the map. It must make you wonder whether there could have been a United States, if the rectangle had not been invented. Typically, those boundaries were not laid out to fit some pre-existing community of value or complex of interests, nor has it been possible to adapt them to territorial diversities as these have emerged. Most of the boundaries were dictated by Act of Congress, usually when the area was sparsely populated and had only the status of a territory. If the purpose of the states had been to provide a level of self-government functional to territorial diversity, then it would have been imperative, in this rapidly growing and developing society, that their boundaries be changed from time to time. On the contrary, however, our national policy toward federalism has been to freeze the boundaries of the states into a virtually unchangeable form by giving them constitutional protection.

Michael Reagan observes that the constitutional meaning of federalism still has importance in only one respect: the guarantee of the independent existence of the states. This may be so, but it does not mean that federalism is dead. Such a guarantee, to be sure, is dysfunctional to an administrative, economic or cultural role for the states. It is, however, highly functional and, I should say, indispensable to their political role in representational federalism. Even if state and federal power were completely overlapping, even if our society were perfectly homogeneous, it would still be necessary, in the light of the original design, that state government have its constitutionally protected existence. The rigidities of our federal system may often frustrate the purposes of public administration, economic efficiency and community living, but they make political sense as the foundation of a major and distinctive element of our representative system.

The Dual Role of Party

Over the course of time, both state and general governments have performed in various ways the roles assigned them in this system by representational federalism. When one asks what specific forms these processes have taken, the answer, until very recently, I suggest, would be found mainly in the mode of operation of the major political parties. The original federal design endowed the voter with two basic roles, a federal role and a state role. Typically, any major American party has reflected this dualism. The territorial pluralism of the federal structure has had such great and obvious effect as to lead us often to speak of the parties as coalitions of state and local organizations. At the same time, we recognize that their participation in the politics of the general government draws them into a competition which addresses problems and appeals to group interests transcending state and local boundaries. In spite of the resulting territorial and social pluralism, each party is also national, as a body of voters possessing at all levels of government common symbols which focus sentiments of party identification and ideas of party principle. This affectual and cognitive identification is a bond of cohesion that helps make each party a forum within which federal and state perspectives mutually influence one another, instead of merely finding expression in separate spheres.

The politics of civil rights during the past generation provides striking illustration of how the Madisonian mechanism may work through the medium of party. I will merely suggest the outlines of this very complicated process. After World War II, the movement of southern blacks to Northern cities admitted them for the first time to effective political participation in the social pluralism of the more extensive republic. The competition of Republicans and Democrats for this vote led to intervention by the federal government to remedy the denial by state governments of rights generally enjoyed by American citizens. At the same time, within the Democratic party an interaction between federal and state levels was producing political changes tending toward the same result. Action by the national party organs supported and stimulated within some southern state parties the rise of loyalist groups favorable to civil rights. These groups fought the old leadership, won power in state parties and influence on state government and so were able in some degree to ease the acceptance of federal initiatives. Thanks to the party system the pluralism of the more extensive republic helped bring about a universalistic result.

Public Sector Politics

I have made this brief reference to the way that representational federalism has worked through the medium of the party system in order by contrast to bring out the significance of a recent and major change. The party system operates outside government to bring influence to bear on government. Recently, however, powerful new centers of influence on what government does have arisen within government itself. These new centers of influence arise and act within what one may call the public sector of the polity. For the polity like the economy has a public sector. The private sector of the polity consists of people in their private capacities trying to influence government action. This includes their activity as individuals, as members of organized groups, as adherents of political parties. The character of the public sector of the polity is evident by contrast. It consists of people in their public capacities trying to influence government action: a chief executive vetoing a bill, legislators logrolling appropriations, bureaucratic experts developing new programs, mayors lobbying Congress for more federal aid.

Within this public sector of the polity two types of influence have been on the rise during the past decade or so. One results from functional specialization in the modern state. I call it the professional bureaucratic complex. The other results from territorial specialization and I call it the intergovernmental lobby. The action and interaction of the professional bureaucratic complex and the intergovernmental lobby constitute the new form taken by representational federalism.

The growing role of professionalism in government is so well recognized as to need only a few words to show its relevance to the present discussion. People with scientific and technical training have been important to the modern state from its very beginnings. But during the past generation or so scientific advance has proceeded at such a vastly increased rate as to give "professional specialisms" a new role in policy making. The term "professional bureaucratic complex" is singular: the examples are many. One is the "military industrial complex," from which I adapted the name. A similar structure is shared by the "health syndicate," the "educational establishment," the "highway lobby." The main component in any such complex is a core of officials with scientific or professional training. This bureaucratic core also normally works closely with two other components: certain interested legislators, especially the chairmen of the relevant specialized subcommittees, and the spokesmen for the group that benefits from the program. Such a tripartite complex or subsystem is [called an] "iron triangle."

The intellectual history of federal domestic programs since the days of the Great Society is deeply marked by the influence of such complexes of professional expertise. I do not mean to exclude the continuing influence of more familiar political agents, such as an activist president responsive to problems and to the suggestion of problems. But I would remark how rarely additions to the public sector have been *initiated* by the demands of voters or the advocacy of pressure groups or the platforms of political parties. On the contrary, in the fields of health, housing, urban renewal, transportation, welfare, education, poverty, and energy, it has been, in very great measure, people in government service, or closely associated with it, acting on the basis of their specialized and technical knowledge, who first perceived the problem, conceived the program, initially urged it on president and Congress, went on to help lobby it through to enactment, and then saw to its administration. Scientific and technical knowledge by its nature is specialized and the prodigious increase in the number of categorical grants-in-aid to state and local governments is an indication of the rising influence of professionalism. In 1962 there were some 160 separate categorical programs. The catalog of federal grants in aid for 1976 lists 1,030. The amount of aid rose in proportion from $7 billion in 1960 to $60 billion in 1976.

This expansion of the public sector was accomplished by an unprecedented use of the federal structure. With few exceptions the new specialized programs were not administered directly by the federal government, but by means of state and local governments. One might expect such attempts to join bureaucratic agents at different levels of government in the administration of specialized programs would create awkward inter-level conflicts. Actually, among similarly trained professionals their common discipline has facilitated cooperation, helping them stand off the claims of rival disciplines and the directives of coordinating authorities. Vertical bureaucratic hierarchies cutting across different levels of government have become a main feature of the present phase of American federalism.

Technocracy and Topocracy

The general term which suggests the decision-making power based on technical expertise of the new professionals is "technocratic." By using it I do not mean to raise fears of a dictatorship of men in white coats. On the contrary, one of the more interesting features of this new influence is the way in which it has promoted the rise of a countervailing power in the form of the intergovernmental lobby. By the intergovernmental lobby I mean the governors, mayors, county supervisors and other officeholders, usually elective, who exercise general responsibilities in state and local governments.

Like the new professionalism the intergovernmental lobby in some form can be found in other advanced countries. A term suitable for comparative use is needed. I propose the word "topocrat," from the Greek *topos*, meaning "place" or "locality," and *kratos*, meaning "authority"—and herewith thank its author, Roy Macridis, who responded to my request for a single, general and non-American term that would save me from having to say "state and local government officials" and the equivalent mouth-filling phrase when speaking of other countries.

In the United States these topocrats act in a representative capacity through their organizations, the National Governors Conference, the Council of State Governments, the United States Conference of Mayors, the National League of Cities, the National Association of Counties, the International City Management Association, and the National Legislative Conference, and through alliances of them, such as the "Big Six" during the initial enactment of general revenue sharing. But their most important front lies along the continual, almost day-to-day activity of individual officeholders and their agents, offering advice and pressing requests before the executive and legislative branches of the federal government.

To appreciate the significance of this activity we must remind ourselves how very recently state and local officeholders began to take an interest of this kind and degree in what goes on in Washington. Their sudden surge of activity dates from the mid-sixties and came as a response to the increase in federal programs spawned by the new professionalism. As the mayors and other executives of the governments through which these programs were carried out became aware of their value—their political value and their problem-solving promise—they developed a heightened interest in and increasing contact with federal policy making and administration. Their Washington activities grew and their national organizations headquartered there expanded in members, budgets and staffs. In this sense it was not the lobby that created the programs but the programs of the professional bureaucratic complex that created the intergovernmental lobby.

In time the intergovernmental lobby acquired sufficient political influence to initiate demands more closely reflecting its members' political interests. A major demand was for fewer federal strings on more federal money. Accordingly, in the past few years the mayors, governors, county executives and others have played a major role in bringing about a shift in the character of federal aid. In 1966 categorical aid accounted for 98 percent of federal aid. By 1975 it was down to 75 percent as a result of general revenue sharing and block grants.

In brief, then, I am saying that over the past generation and especially since the early sixties the technocratic tendencies of the new professionalism have called forth the topocratic tendencies of the intergovernmental lobby. If one asks whether the process has been centralizing or decentralizing the answer must be a bit complicated. It has been strongly centralizing insofar as the new programs have carried the technocratic perspectives formed at the federal level into the daily thought and action of state and local governments. It has been decentralizing in that these governments, as the administrative agents of the new programs, have often been able to adapt them to their own local purposes, an option that has been deliberately expanded by some loosening of federal strings. The process was centralizing in that it drew state and local office holders into direct contact with the federal government and decentralizing in that it has brought their topocratic perspectives to bear on federal policy making. The trend is not toward a centralized unitary system. Neither is there much sign of significantly greater autonomy for state or local governments. But whatever that balance may be, the interesting and important thing, it seems to me, is the way in which the polarity of representational federalism has been reasserted. The impact of technocrat and topocrat upon opposing levels of government is adding a new dimension in an old pattern to our system of national representation.

CONCLUSION

. . . Professionalism extends its domains in all advanced countries and surely will continue to do so. The modern state at this late date is not likely to turn its back on science and technology. In these countries, as in the United States, there has been a surge of social spending since the 1960s. Professional, centrally directed hierarchies are the normal agencies of the programs financed by this spending.

But whom or what do these agencies represent? In their dealings with their local authorities they represent their central governments. To what extent do they also represent social and economic interests within the society and outside the public sector? In many welfare states, beginning as far back as the interwar years, organized interests developed relations with government departments so close and institutionalized as to constitute a system of functional representation. How far are the professional hierarchies of recent years dependencies of these corporatistic arrangements? How far are they veritably technocratic in the sense of generating their own initiatives from within the public sector and independently of outside interests? In what ways, if any, is the social pluralism of modern society transmitted to the professional bureaucratic complex?

. . . In spite of overpowering forces making for centralization, the modern state seems to be unable to do without territorial subunits. Nor are these mere branch offices of administration, but rather governmental units with a political capacity. Much has been said, but little done in any country about decentralizing power to them or enlarging their autonomy. They have been widely used, however, as vehicles for carrying out the programs of central governments and, at the same time, have taken an increasingly active role as agents of representation before, and indeed, within those central governments. In other countries, both unitary and federal, the equivalent of the American intergovernmental lobby has appeared and flourishes. These varieties of topocratic representation are many and complex and light up major contrasts among the different versions of the modern state.

As we will want to look into the relation of technocratic representation to older processes of pressure group politics and functional representation, we shall also ask what are the conflicts and connections between topocratic representation and the older structures of territorial representation. In the U.S., for instance, the political relations of mayors and members of Congress are one of the great unexplored mysteries.

Moreover, whom does the topocrat represent when he formulates the presumed needs of his government before central authorities? He will commonly speak on behalf of groups among his constituents. He may know and be responsive to them. He might even have been chosen by them in part because he was expected to be a good lobbyist in the national capital. Yet he is subject not only to their wishes, but also to an array of influences proceeding from his position as the agent of a bureaucratic and political body. This governmental position will affect and may dominate his representative role.

I can communicate my unease at these technocratic and topocratic dilutions of the popular will by saying that the new structures have a strong connotation of corporate rather than personal representation. They do add real strengths to the modern state. But this may be at some cost to free government.

8

MORTON GRODZINS

THE FEDERAL SYSTEM

Federalism is a device for dividing decisions and functions of government. As the constitutional fathers well understood, the federal structure is a means, not an end. The pages that follow are therefore not concerned with an exposition of American federalism as a formal, legal set of relationships. The focus, rather, is on the purpose of federalism, that is to say, on the distribution of power between central and peripheral units of government.

THE SHARING OF FUNCTIONS

The American form of government is often, but erroneously, symbolized by a three-layer cake. A far more accurate image is the rainbow or marble cake, characterized by an inseparable mingling of differently colored ingredients, the colors appearing in vertical and diagonal strands and unexpected whirls. As colors are mixed in the marble cake, so functions are mixed in the American federal system. Consider the health officer, styled "sanitarian," of a rural county in a border state. He embodies the whole idea of the marble cake of government.

The sanitarian is appointed by the state under merit standards established by the federal government. His base salary comes jointly from state and federal funds, the county provides him with an office and office amenities and pays a portion of his expenses, and the largest city in the county also contributes to his salary and office by virtue of his appointment as a city plumbing inspector. It is impossible from moment to moment to tell under which governmental hat the sanitarian operates. His work of inspecting the purity of food is carried out under federal standards; but he is enforcing state laws when inspecting commodities that have not been in interstate commerce; and somewhat perversely he also acts under state authority when inspecting milk coming into the county from producing areas across the state border. He is a federal officer when impounding impure drugs shipped from a neighboring state; a federal-state officer when distributing typhoid immunization serum; a state officer when enforcing standards of industrial hygiene; a state-local officer when inspecting the city's water supply; and (to complete the circle) a local officer when insisting that the city butchers adopt more hygienic methods of handling their garbage. But he cannot and does not think of himself as acting in these separate capacities. All business in the county that concerns public health and sanitation he considers his business. Paid largely from federal funds, he does not find it strange to attend meetings of the city council to give expert advice on matters ranging from rotten apples to rabies control. He is even deputized as a member of both the city and county police forces.

The sanitarian is an extreme case, but he accurately represents an important aspect of the whole range of governmental activities in the United States. Functions are not neatly parceled out among the many governments. They are shared functions. It is difficult to find any governmental activity which does not involve all three of the so-called "levels" of the federal system. In the most local of local functions—law enforcement or education, for example—the federal and state governments play important roles. In what, a priori, may be considered the purest central government activities—the conduct of foreign affairs, for example—the state and local governments have considerable responsibilities, directly and indirectly.

The federal grant programs are only the most obvious example of shared functions. They also most clearly exhibit how sharing serves to disperse governmental powers. The grants utilize the greater wealth-gathering abilities of the central government and establish nationwide standards, yet they are "in aid" of functions carried out under state law, with considerable state and local discretion. The national supervision of such programs is largely a process of mutual accommodation. Leading state and local officials, acting through their professional organizations, are in considerable part responsible for the very standards that national officers try to persuade all state and local officers to accept.

Even in the absence of joint financing, federal-state-local collaboration is the characteristic mode of action. Federal expertise is available to aid in the building of a local jail (which may later be used to house federal prisoners), to improve a local water purification system, to step up building inspections, to provide standards for state and local personnel in protecting housewives against dishonest butchers' scales, to prevent gas explosions, or to produce a land use plan. States and localities, on the other hand, take important formal responsibilities in the development of national programs for atomic energy, civil defense, the regulation of commerce, and the protection of purity in foods and drugs; local political weight is always a factor in the operation of even a post office or a military establishment. From abattoirs and accounting through zoning and zoo administration, any governmental activity is almost certain to involve the influence, if not the formal administration, of all three planes of the federal system.

ATTEMPTS TO UNWIND THE FEDERAL SYSTEM

Within the past dozen years there have been four major attempts to reform or reorganize the federal system: the first (1947–1949) and second (1953–1955) Hoover Commissions on Executive Organization; the Kestnbaum Commission on Intergovernmental Relations (1953–1955); and the Joint Federal-State Action

Committee (1957–1959). All four of these groups have aimed to minimize federal activities. None of them has recognized the sharing of functions as the characteristic way American governments do things. Even when making recommendations for joint action, these official commissions take the view (as expressed in the Kestnbaum report) that "the main tradition of American federalism [is] the tradition of separateness." All four have, in varying degrees, worked to separate functions and tax sources.

The history of the Joint Federal-State Action Committee is especially instructive. The committee was established at the suggestion of President Eisenhower, who charged it, first of all, "to designate functions which the States are ready and willing to assume and finance that are now performed or financed wholly or in part by the Federal Government." He also gave the committee the task of recommending "Federal and State revenue adjustments required to enable the States to assume such functions."[1]

The committee subsequently established seemed most favorably situated to accomplish the task of functional separation. It was composed of distinguished and able men, including among its personnel three leading members of the President's Cabinet, the director of the Bureau of the Budget, and ten state governors. It had the full support of the President at every point, and it worked hard and conscientiously. Excellent staff studies were supplied by the Bureau of the Budget, the White House, the Treasury Department, and, from the state side, the Council of State Governments. It had available to it a large mass of research data, including the sixteen recently completed volumes of the Kestnbaum Commission. There existed no disagreements on party lines within the committee and, of course, no constitutional impediments to its mission. The President, his Cabinet members, and all the governors (with one possible exception) on the committee completely agreed on the desirability of decentralization-via-separation-of-functions-and-taxes. They were unanimous in wanting to justify the committee's name and to produce action, not just another report.

The committee worked for more than two years. It found exactly two programs to recommend for transfer from federal to state hands. One was the federal grant program for vocational education (including practical-nurse training and aid to fishery trades); the other was federal grants for municipal waste treatment plants. The programs together cost the federal government less than $80 million in 1957, slightly more than two per cent of the total federal grants for that year. To allow the states to pay for these programs, the committee recommended that they be allowed a credit against the federal tax on local telephone calls. Calculations showed that this offset device, plus an equalizing factor, would give every state at least 40 percent more from the tax than it received from the federal government in vocational education and sewage disposal grants. Some states were "equalized" to receive twice as much.

The recommendations were modest enough, and the generous financing feature seemed calculated to gain state support. The President recommended to Congress that all points of the program be legislated. None of them was, none has been since, and none is likely to be.

A POINT OF HISTORY

The American federal system has never been a system of separated governmental activities. There has never been a time when it was possible to put neat labels on discrete "federal," "state," and "local" functions. Even before the Constitution, a statute of 1785, reinforced by the Northwest Ordinance of 1787, gave grants-in-land to the states for public schools. Thus the national government was a prime force in making possible what is now taken to be the most local function of all, primary and secondary education. More important, the nation, before it was fully organized, established by this action a first principle of American federalism: the national government would use its superior resources to initiate and support national programs, principally administered by the states and localities.

The essential unity of state and federal financial systems was again recognized in the earliest constitutional days with the assumption by the federal government of the Revolutionary War debts of the states. Other points of federal-state collaboration during the Federalist period concerned the militia, law enforcement, court practices, the administration of elections, public health measures, pilot laws, and many other matters.

The nineteenth century is widely believed to have been the preeminent period of duality in the American system. Lord Bryce at the end of the century described (in *The American Commonwealth*) the federal and state government as "distinct and separate in their action." The system, he said, was "like a great factory wherein two sets of machinery are at work, their revolving wheels apparently intermixed, their bands crossing one another, yet each set doing its own work without touching or hampering the other." Great works may contain gross errors. Bryce was wrong. The nineteenth century, like the early days of the republic, was a period principally characterized by intergovernmental collaboration.

Decisions of the Supreme Court are often cited as evidence of nineteenth-century duality. In the early part of the century the Court, heavily weighted with Federalists, was intent upon enlarging the sphere of national authority; in the later years (and to the 1930s) its actions were in the direction of paring down national powers and indeed all governmental authority. Decisions referred to "areas of exclusive competence" exercised by the federal government and the states; to their powers being "separated and distinct"; and to neither being able "to intrude within the jurisdiction of the other."

Judicial rhetoric is not always consistent with judicial action, and the Court did not always adhere to separatist doctrine. Indeed, its rhetoric sometimes indicated a positive view of cooperation. In any case, the Court was rarely, if ever, directly confronted with the issue of cooperation versus separation as such. Rather it was concerned with defining permissible areas of action for the central government and the states; or with saying with respect to a point at issue whether any government could take action. The Marshall Court contributed to intergovernmental cooperation by the very act of permitting federal operations where they had not existed before. Furthermore, even Marshall was willing to allow interstate commerce to be affected by the states in their use of the police power. Later courts also upheld state laws that had an impact on interstate commerce, just as they approved the expansion of the national commerce power, as in statutes providing for the control of telegraphic communication or prohibiting the interstate transportation of lotteries, impure foods and drugs, and prostitutes. Similar room for cooperation was found outside the commerce field, notably in the Court's refusal to interfere with federal grants-in-land or cash to the states. Although research to clinch the point has not been completed, it is probably true that the Supreme Court from 1800 to 1936 allowed far more federal-state collaboration than it blocked.

Political behavior and administrative action of the nineteenth century provide positive evidence that, throughout the entire era of so-called dual federalism, the many governments in the American federal system continued the close administrative and fiscal collaboration of the earlier period. Governmental activities were not extensive. But relative to what governments did, intergovernmental cooperation during the last century was comparable with that existing today.

Occasional presidential vetoes (from Madison to Buchanan) of cash and land grants are evidence of constitutional and ideological apprehensions about the extensive expansion of federal activities which produced widespread intergovernmental collaboration. In perspective, however, the vetoes are a more important evidence of the continuous search, not least by state officials, for ways and means to involve the central government in a wide variety of joint programs. The search was successful.

Grants-in-land and grants-in-services from the national government were of first importance in virtually all the principal functions undertaken by the states and their local subsidiaries. Land grants were made to the states for, among other purposes, elementary schools, colleges, and special educational institutions; roads, canals, rivers, harbors, and railroads; reclamation of desert and swamp lands; and veterans' welfare. In fact whatever was at the focus of state attention became the recipient of national grants. (Then, as today, national grants established state emphasis as well as followed it.) If Connecticut wished to establish a program for the care and education of the deaf and dumb, federal money in the form of a land grant was found to aid that program. If higher education relating to agriculture became a pressing need, Congress could dip into the public domain and make appropriate grants to states. If the need for swamp drainage and flood control appeared, the federal government could supply both grants-in-land and, from the Army's Corps of Engineers, the services of the only trained engineers then available.

Aid also went in the other direction. The federal government, theoretically in exclusive control of the Indian population, relied continuously (and not always wisely) on the experience and resources of state and local governments. State militias were an all-important ingredient in the nation's armed forces. State governments became unofficial but real partners in federal programs for homesteading, reclamation, tree culture, law enforcement, inland waterways, the nation's internal communications system (including highway and railroad routes), and veterans' aid of various sorts. Administrative contacts were voluminous, and the whole process of interaction was lubricated, then as today, by constituent-conscious members of Congress.

The essential continuity of the collaborative system is best demonstrated by the history of the grants. The land grant tended to become a cash grant based on the calculated disposable value of the land, and the cash grant tended to become an annual grant based upon the national government's superior tax powers. In 1887, only three years before the frontier was officially closed, thus signalizing the end of the disposable public domain, Congress enacted the first continuing cash grants.

A long, extensive, and continuous experience is therefore the foundation of the present system of shared functions characteristic of the American federal system, what we have called the marble cake of government. It is a misjudgment of our history and our present situation to believe that a neat separation of governmental functions could take place without drastic alterations in our society and system of government.

DYNAMICS OF SHARING:
THE POLITICS OF THE FEDERAL SYSTEM

Many causes contribute to dispersed power in the federal system. One is the simple historical fact that the states existed before the nation. A second is in the form of creed, the traditional opinion of Americans that expresses distrust of centralized power and places great value in the strength and vitality of local units of government. Another is pride in locality and state, nurtured by the nation's size and by variations of regional and state history. Still a fourth cause of decentralization is the sheer wealth of the nation. It allows all groups, including state and local governments, to partake of the central government's largesse, supplies room for experimentation and even waste, and makes unnecessary the tight organization of political power that must follow when the support of one program necessarily means the deprivation of another.

In one important respect, the Constitution no longer operates to impede centralized government. The Supreme Court since 1937 has given Congress a relatively free hand. The federal government can build substantive programs in many areas on the taxation and commerce powers. Limitations of such central programs based on the argument, "it's unconstitutional," are no longer possible as long as Congress (in the Court's view) acts reasonably in the interest of the whole nation. The Court is unlikely to reverse this permissive view in the foreseeable future.

Nevertheless, some constitutional restraints on centralization continue to operate. The strong constitutional position of the states—for example, the assignment of two Senators to each state, the role given the states in administering even national elections, and the relatively few limitations on their lawmaking powers—establish the geographical units as natural centers of administrative and political strength. Many clauses of the Constitution are not subject to the same latitude of interpretation as the commerce and tax clauses. The simple, clearly stated, unambiguous phrases—for example, the President "shall hold his office during the term of four years"—are subject to change only through the formal amendment process. Similar provisions exist with respect to the terms of Senators and Congressmen and the amendment process. All of them have the effect of retarding or restraining centralizing action of the federal government. The fixed terms of the President and members of Congress, for example, greatly impede the development of nationwide, disciplined political parties that almost certainly would have to precede continuous large-scale expansion of federal functions.

The constitutional restraints on the expansion of national authority are less important and less direct today than they were in 1879 or in 1936. But to say that they are less important is not to say that they are unimportant.

The nation's politics reflect these decentralizing causes and add some of their own. The political parties of the United States are unique. They seldom perform the function that parties traditionally perform in other countries, the function of gathering together diverse strands of power and welding them into one. Except during the period of nominating and electing a President and for the essential but nonsubstantive business of organizing the houses of Congress, the American parties rarely coalesce power at all. Characteristically they do the reverse, serving as a canopy under which special and local interests are represented with little regard for anything that can be called a party program. National leaders are elected on a party ticket, but in Congress they must seek cross-party support if their leadership is to be effective. It is a rare President during rare periods who can produce legislation without facing the defection of substantial numbers of his own party. (Wilson could do this in the first session of the Sixty-Third Congress; but Franklin D. Roosevelt could not, even during the famous hundred days of 1933.) Presidents whose parties form the majority of the Congressional houses must still count heavily on support from the other party.

The parties provide the pivot on which the entire governmental system swings. Party operations, first of all, produce in legislation the basic division of functions between the federal government, on the one hand, and state and local governments, on the other. The Supreme Court's permissiveness with respect to the expansion of national powers has not in fact produced any considerable extension of exclusive federal functions. The body of federal law in all fields has remained, in the words of Henry M. Hart, Jr., and Herbert Wechsler, "interstitial in its nature," limited in objective and resting upon the principal body of legal relationships defined by state law. It is difficult to find any area of federal legislation that is not significantly affected by state law.

In areas of new or enlarged federal activity, legislation characteristically provides important roles for state and local governments. This is as true of Democratic as of Republican administrations and true even of functions for which arguments of efficiency would produce exclusive federal responsibility.

Thus the unemployment compensation program of the New Deal and the airport program of President Truman's administration both provided important responsibilities for state governments. In both cases attempts to eliminate state participation were defeated by a cross-party coalition of pro-state votes and influence. A large fraction of the Senate is usually made up of ex-governors, and the membership of both houses is composed of men who know that their reelection depends less upon national leaders or national party organization than upon support from their home constituencies. State and local officials are key members of these constituencies, often central figures in selecting candidates and in turning out the vote. Under such circumstances, national legislation taking state and local views heavily into account is inevitable.

Second, the undisciplined parties affect the character of the federal system as a result of Senatorial and Congressional interference in federal administrative programs on behalf of local interests. Many aspects of the legislative involvement in administrative affairs are formalized. The Legislative Reorganization Act of 1946, to take only one example, provided that each of the standing committees "shall exercise continuous watchfulness" over administration of laws within its jurisdiction. But the formal system of controls, extensive as it is, does not compare in importance with the informal and extralegal network of relationships in producing continuous legislative involvement in administrative affairs.

Senators and Congressmen spend a major fraction of their time representing problems of their constituents before administrative agencies. An even larger fraction of Congressional staff time is devoted to the same task. The total magnitude of such "case work" operations is great. In one five-month period of 1943 the Office of Price Administration received a weekly average of 842 letters from members of Congress. If phone calls and personal contacts are added, each member of Congress on the average presented the OPA with a problem involving one of his constituents twice a day in each five-day work week. Data for less vulnerable agencies during less intensive periods are also impressive. In 1958, to take only one example, the Department of Agriculture estimated (and underestimated) that it received an average of 159 Congressional letters per working day. Special Congressional liaison staffs have been created to service this mass of business, though all higher officials meet it in one form or another. The Air Force in 1958 had, under the command of a major general, 137 people (55 officers and 82 civilians) working in its liaison office.

The widespread, consistent, and in many ways unpredictable character of legislative interference in administrative affairs has many consequences for the tone and character of American administrative behavior. From the perspective of this paper, the important consequence is the comprehensive, day-to-day, even hour-by-hour, impact of local views on national programs. No point of substance or procedure is immune from Congressional scrutiny. A substantial portion of the entire weight of this impact is on behalf of the state and local governments. It is a weight than can alter procedures for screening immigration applications, divert the course of a national highway, change the tone of an international negotiation, and amend a social security law to accommodate local practices or fulfill local desires.

The party system compels administrators to take a political role. This is a third way in which the parties function to decentralize the American system. The administrator must play politics for the same reason that the politician is able to play in administration: the parties are without program and without discipline.

In response to the unprotected position in which the party situation places him, the administrator is forced to seek support where he can find it. One ever-present task is to nurse the Congress of the United States, that crucial constituency which ultimately controls his agency's budget and program. From the administrator's view, a sympathetic consideration of Congressional requests (if not downright submission to them) is the surest way to build the political support without which the administrative job could not continue. Even the completely task-oriented administrator must be sensitive to the need for Congressional support and to the relationship between case work requests, on one side, and budgetary and legislative support, on the other. "You do a good job handling the personal problems and requests of a Congressman," a White House officer said, "and you have an easier time convincing him to back your program." Thus there is an important link between the nursing of Congressional requests, requests that largely concern local matters, and the most comprehensive national programs. The administrator must accommodate to the former as a price of gaining support for the latter.

One result of administrative politics is that the administrative agency may become the captive of the nationwide interest group it serves or presumably regulates. In such cases no government may come out with effective authority: the winners are the interest groups themselves. But in a very large number of cases, states and localities also win influence. The politics of administration is a process of making peace with legislators who for the most part consider themselves the guardians of local interests. The political role of administrators therefore contributes to the power of states and localities in national programs.

Finally, the way the party system operates gives American politics their overall distinctive tone. The lack of party discipline produces an openness in the system that allows individuals, groups, and institutions (including state and local governments) to attempt to influence national policy at every step of the legislative-administrative process. This is the "multiple-crack" attribute of the American government. "Crack" has two meanings. It means not only many fissures or access points; it also means, less statically, opportunities for wallops or smacks at government.

If the parties were more disciplined, the result would not be a cessation of the process by which individuals and groups impinge themselves upon the central government. But the present state of the parties clearly allows for a far greater operation of the multiple crack than would be possible under the conditions of centralized party control. American interest groups exploit literally uncountable access points in the legislative-administrative process. If legislative lobbying, from committee stages to the conference committee, does not produce results, a Cabinet secretary is called. His immediate associates are petitioned. Bureau chiefs and their aides are hit. Field officers are put under pressure. Campaigns are instituted by which friends of the agency apply a secondary influence on behalf of the interested party. A conference with the President may be urged.

To these multiple points for bringing influence must be added the multiple voices of the influencers. Consider, for example, those in a small town who wish to have a federal action taken. The easy merging of public and private interest at the local level means that the influence attempt is made in the name of the whole community, thus removing it from political partisanship. The Rotary Club as well as the City Council, the Chamber of Commerce and the mayor, eminent citizens and political bosses—all are readily enlisted. If a conference in a Senator's office will expedite matters, someone on the local scene can be found to make such a conference possible and effective. If technical information is needed, technicians will supply it. State or national professional organizations of local officials, individual Congressmen and Senators, and not infrequently whole state delegations will make the local cause their own. Federal field officers, who service localities, often assume local views. So may elected and appointed state officers. Friendships are exploited, and political mortgages called due. Under these circumstances, national policies are molded by local action.

In summary, then, the party system functions to devolve power. The American parties, unlike any other, are highly responsive when directives move from the bottom to the top, highly unresponsive from top to bottom. Congressmen and Senators can rarely ignore concerted demands from their home constituencies; but no party leader can expect the same kind of response from those below, whether he be a President asking for Congressional support or a Congressman seeking aid from local or state leaders.

Any tightening of the party apparatus would have the effect of strengthening the central government. The four characteristics of the system, discussed above, would become less important. If control from the top were strictly applied, these hallmarks of American decentralization might entirely disappear. To be specific, if disciplined and program-oriented parties were achieved: (1) It would make far less likely legislation that takes heavily into account the desires and prejudices of the highly centralized power groups and institutions of the country, including the state and local governments. (2) It would to a large extent prevent legislators, individually and collectively, from intruding themselves on behalf of non-national interests in national administrative programs. (3) It would put an end to the administrator's search for his own political support, a search that often results in fostering state, local, and other non-national powers. (4) It would dampen the process by which individuals and groups, including state and local political leaders, take advantage of multiple cracks to steer national legislation and administration in ways congenial to them and the institutions they represent.

Alterations of this sort could only accompany basic changes in the organization and style of politics which, in turn, presuppose fundamental changes at the parties' social base. The sharing of functions is, in fact, the sharing of power. To end this sharing process would mean the destruction of whatever measure of decentralization exists in the United States today.

GOALS FOR THE SYSTEM OF SHARING

The Goal of Understanding

Our structure of government is complex, and the politics operating that structure are mildy chaotic. Circumstances are ever-changing. Old institutions mask intricate procedures. The nation's history can be read with alternative glosses, and what is nearest at hand may be furthest from comprehension. Simply to understand the federal system is therefore a difficult task. Yet without understanding there is little possibility of producing desired changes in the system. Social structures and processes are relatively impervious to purposeful change. They also exhibit intricate interrelationships so that change induced at point "A" often produces unanticipated results at point "Z." Changes introduced into an imperfectly understood system are as likely to produce reverse consequences as the desired ones.

This is counsel of neither futility nor conservation for those who seek to make our government a better servant of the people. It is only to say that the first goal for those setting goals with respect to the federal system is that of understanding it.

Two Kinds of Decentralization

The recent major efforts to reform the federal system have in large part been aimed at separating functions and tax sources, at dividing them between the federal government and the states. All of these attempts have failed. We can now add that their success would be undesirable.

It is easy to specify the conditions under which an ordered separation of functions could take place. What is principally needed is a majority political party, under firm leadership, in control of both Presidency and Congress, and, ideally but not necessarily, also in control of a number of states. The political discontinuities, or the absence of party links, (1) between the governors and their state legislatures, (2) between the President and the governors, and (3) between the President and Congress clearly account for both the picayune recommendations of the Federal-State Action Committee and for the failure of even those recommendations in Congress. If the President had been in control of Congress (that is, consistently able to direct a majority of House and Senate votes), this alone would have made possible some genuine separation and devolution of functions. The failure to decentralize by order is a measure of the decentralization of power in the political parties.

Stated positively, party centralization must precede governmental decentralization by order. But this is a slender reed on which to hang decentralization. It implies the power to centralize. A majority party powerful enough to bring about ordered decentralization is far more likely to choose in favor of ordered centralization. And a society that produced centralized national parties would, by that very fact, be a society prepared to accept centralized government.

Decentralization by order must be contrasted with the different kind of decentralization that exists today in the United States. It may be called the decentralization of mild chaos. It exists because of the existence of dispersed power centers. This form of decentralization is less visible and less neat. It rests on no discretion of central authorities. It produces at times specific acts that many citizens may consider undesirable or evil. But power sometimes wielded even for evil ends may be desirable power. To those who find value in the dispersion of power, decentralization by mild chaos is infinitely more desirable than decentralization by order. The preservation of mild chaos is an important goal for the American federal system.

Oiling the Squeak Points

In a governmental system of genuinely shared responsibilities, disagreements inevitably occur. Opinions clash over proximate ends, particular ways of doing things become the subject of public debate, innovations are contested. These are not basic defects in the system. Rather, they are the system's energy-reflecting life blood. There can be no permanent "solutions" short of changing the system itself by elevating one partner to absolute supremacy. What can be done is to attempt to produce conditions in which conflict will not fester but be turned to constructive solutions of particular problems.

A long list of specific points of difficulty in the federal system can be easily identified. No adequate congressional or administrative mechanism exists to review the patchwork of grants in terms of national needs. There is no procedure by which to judge, for example, whether the national government is justified in spending so much more for highways than for education. The working force in some states is inadequate for the effective performance of some nationwide programs, while honest and not-so-honest graft frustrates efficiency in others. Some federal aid programs distort state budgets, and some are so closely supervised as to impede state action in meeting local needs. Grants are given for programs too narrowly defined, and overall programs at the state level consequently suffer. Administrative, accounting and auditing difficulties are the consequence of the multiplicity of grant programs. City officials complain that the states are intrusive fifth wheels in housing, urban redevelopment, and airport building programs.

Some differences are so basic that only a demonstration of strength on one side or another can solve them. School desegregation illustrates such an issue. It also illustrates the correct solution (although not the most desirable method of reaching it): in policy conflicts of fundamental importance, touching the nature of democracy itself, the view of the whole nation must prevail. Such basic ends, however, are rarely at issue, and sides are rarely taken with such passion that loggerheads are reached. Modes of settlement can usually be found to lubricate the squeak points of the system.

A pressing and permanent state problem, general in its impact, is the difficulty of raising sufficient revenue without putting local industries at a competitive disadvantage or without an expansion of sales taxes that press hardest on the least wealthy. A possible way of meeting this problem is to establish a state-levied income tax that could be used as an offset for federal taxes. The maximum level of the tax which could be offset would be fixed by federal law. When levied by a state, the state collection would be deducted from federal taxes. But if a state did not levy the tax, the federal government would. An additional fraction of the total tax imposed by the states would be collected directly by the federal government and used as an equalization fund, that is, distributed among the less wealthy states. Such a tax would almost certainly be imposed by all states since not to levy it would give neither political advantage to its public leaders nor financial advantage to its citizens. The net effect would be an increase in the total personal and corporate income tax.

The offset has great promise for strengthening state governments. It would help produce a more economic distribution of industry. It would have obvious financial advantages for the vast majority of states. Since a large fraction of all state income is used to aid political subdivisions, the local governments would also profit, though not equally as long as cities are underrepresented in state legislatures. On the other hand, such a scheme will appear disadvantageous to some low-tax states which profit from the in-migration of industry (though it would by no means end all state-by-state tax differentials). It will probably excite the opposition of those concerned over governmental centralization, and they will not be assuaged by methods that suggest themselves for making both state and central governments bear the psychological impact of the tax. Although the offset would probably produce an across-the-board tax increase, wealthier persons, who are affected more by an income tax than by other levies, can be expected to join forces with those whose fear is centralization. (This is a common alliance and, in the nature of things, the philosophical issue rather than financial advantage is kept foremost.)

Those opposing such a tax would gain additional ammunition from the certain knowledge that federal participation in the scheme would lead to some federal standards governing the use of the funds. Yet the political strength of the states would keep these from becoming onerous. Indeed, inauguration of the tax offset as a means of providing funds to the states might be an occasion for dropping some of the specifications for existing federal grants. One federal standard, however, might be possible because of the greater representation of urban areas in the constituency of Congress and the President than in the constituency of state legislatures: Congress might make a state's participation in the offset scheme dependent upon a periodic reapportionment of state legislatures.

The income tax offset it only one of many ideas that can be generated to meet serious problems of closely meshed governments. The fate of all such schemes ultimately rests, as it should, with the politics of a free people. But much can be done if the primary technical effort of those concerned with improving the federal system were directed not at separating its interrelated parts but at making them work together more effectively. Temporary commissions are relatively inefficient in this effort, though they may be useful for making general assessments and for generating new ideas. The professional organizations of government workers do part of the job of continuously scrutinizing programs and ways and means of improving them. A permanent staff, established in the President's office and working closely with state and local officials, could also perform a useful and perhaps important role.

The Strength of the Parts

Whatever governmental "strength" or "vitality" may be, it does not consist of independent decision-making in legislation and administration. Federal-state interpenetration here is extensive. Indeed, a judgment of the relative domestic strength of the two planes must take heavily into account the influence of one on the other's decisions. In such an analysis the strength of the states (and localities) does not weigh lightly. The nature of the nation's politics makes federal functions more vulnerable to state influence than state offices are to federal influence. Many states, as the Kestnbaum Commission noted, live with "self-imposed constitutional limitations" that make it difficult for them to "perform all of the services that their citizens require." If this has the result of adding to federal responsibilities, the states' importance in shaping and administering federal programs eliminates much of the sting.

The geography of state boundaries, as well as many aspects of state internal organization, are the products of history and cannot be justified on any grounds of rational efficiency. Who, today, would create major governmental subdivisions the size of Maryland, Delaware, New Jersey, or Rhode Island? Who would write into Oklahoma's fundamental law an absolute state debt limit of $500,000? Who would design (to cite only the most extreme cases) Georgia's and Florida's gross underrepresentation of urban areas in both houses of the legislature?

A complete catalogue of state political and administrative horrors would fill a sizeable volume. Yet exhortations to erase them have roughly the same effect as similar exhortations to erase sin. Some of the worst inanities—for example, the boundaries of the states, themselves—are fixed in the national constitution and defy alteration for all foreseeable time. Others, such as urban underrepresentation in state legislatures, serve the overrepresented groups, including some urban ones, and the effective political organization of the deprived groups must precede reform.

Despite deficiencies of politics and organizations that are unchangeable or slowly changing, it is an error to look at the states as static anachronisms. Some of them—New York, Minnesota, and California, to take three examples spanning the country—have administrative organizations that compare favorably in many ways with the national establishment. Many more in recent years have moved rapidly towards integrated administrative departments, statewide budgeting, and central leadership. The others have models-in-existence to follow, and active professional organizations (led by the Council of State Governments) promoting their development. Slow as this change may be, the states move in the direction of greater internal effectiveness.

The pace toward more effective performance at the state level is likely to increase. Urban leaders, who generally feel themselves disadvantaged in state affairs, and suburban and rural spokesmen, who are most concerned about national centralization, have a common interest in this task. The urban dwellers want greater equality in state affairs, including a more equitable share of state financial aid; nonurban dwellers are concerned that city dissatisfactions should not be met by exclusive federal, or federal-local, programs. Antagonistic, rather than amiable, cooperation may be the consequence. But it is a cooperation that can be turned to politically effective measures for a desirable upgrading of state institutions.

If one looks closely, there is scant evidence for the fear of the federal octopus, the fear that expansion of central programs and influence threatens to reduce the states and localities to compliant administrative arms of the central government. In fact, state and local governments are touching a larger proportion of the people in more ways than ever before; and they are spending a higher fraction of the total national product than ever before. Federal programs have increased, rather than diminished, the importance of the governors; stimulated profession-alism in state agencies; increased citizen interest and participation in govern-ment; and, generally, enlarged and made more effective the scope of state action.[2] It may no longer be true in any significant sense that the states and localities are "closer" than the federal government to the people. It is true that the smaller governments remain active and powerful members of the federal system.

Central Leadership: The Need for Balance

The chaos of party processes makes difficult the task of presidential leadership. It deprives the President of ready-made Congressional majorities. It may produce, as in the chairmen of legislative committees, power-holders relatively hidden from public scrutiny and relatively protected from presidential direction. It allows the growth of administrative agencies which sometimes escape control by central officials. These are prices paid for a wide dispersion of political power. The cost is tolerable because the total results of dispersed power are themselves desirable and because, where clear national supremacy is essential, in foreign policy and military affairs, it is easiest to secure.

Moreover, in the balance of strength between the central and peripheral governments, the central government has on its side the whole secular drift towards the concentration of power. It has on its side technical developments that make central decisions easy and sometimes mandatory. It has on its side potent purse powers, the result of superior tax-gathering resources. It has potentially on its side national leadership capacities of the presidential office. The last factor is the controlling one, and national strength in the federal system has shifted with the leadership desires and capacities of the Chief Executive. As these have varied, so there has been an almost rhythmic pattern: periods of central strength put to use alternating with periods of central strength dormant.

Following a high point of federal influence during the early and middle years of the New Deal, the postwar years have been, in the weighing of central-peripheral strength, a period of light federal activity. Excepting the Supreme Court's action in favor of school desegregation, national influence by design or default has not been strong in domestic affairs. The danger now is that the central government is doing too little rather than too much. National deficiencies in education and health require the renewed attention of the national government. Steepening population and urbanization trend lines have produced metropolitan area problems that can be effectively attacked only with the aid of federal resources. New definitions of old programs in housing and urban redevelopment, and new programs to deal with air pollution, water supply, and mass transportation are necessary. The federal government's essential role in the federal system is that of organizing, and helping to finance, such nationwide programs.

The American federal system exhibits many evidences of the dispersion of power not only because of formal federalism but more importantly because our politics reflect and reinforce the nation's diversities-within-unity. Those who value the virtues of decentralization, which writ large are virtues of freedom, need not scruple at recognizing the defects of those virtues. The defects are principally the danger that parochial and private interests may not coincide with, or give way to, the nation's interest. The necessary cure for these defects is effective national leadership.

The centrifugal force of domestic politics needs to be balanced by the centripetal force of strong presidential leadership. Simultaneous strength at center and periphery exhibits the American system at its best, if also at its noisiest. The interests of both find effective spokesmen. States and localities (and private interest groups) do not lose their influence opportunities, but national policy becomes more than the simple consequence of successful, momentary concentrations of non-national pressures: it is guided by national leaders.

NOTES

[1] The President's third suggestion was that the committee "identify functions and responsibilities likely to require state or federal attention in the future and . . . recommend the level of state effort, or federal effort, or both, that will be needed to assure effective action." The committee initially devoted little attention to this problem. Upon discovering the difficulty of making separatist recommendations, i.e., for turning over federal functions and taxes to the states, it developed a series of proposals looking to greater effectiveness in intergovernmental collaboration. The committee was succeeded by a legislatively based, 26-member Advisory Commission on Intergovernmental Relations, established September 29, 1959.

[2] See the valuable report, *The Impact of Federal Grants-in-Aid on the Structure and Functions of State and Local Governments*, submitted to the Commission on Intergovernmental Relations by the Governmental Affairs Institute (Washington, 1955).

9

WILLIAM H. RIKER

FEDERALISM: ORIGIN, OPERATION, SIGNIFICANCE

THE POPULARITY OF FEDERAL CONSTITUTIONS

The recent popularity of federal constitutions is not surprising because federalism is one way to solve the problem of enlarging governments—a problem that is one of the most pressing political concerns in the modern world. Like so many other modern problems, this one is a consequence of rapid technological change. Each advance in the technology of transportation makes it possible to rule a larger geographic area from one center, to fill a treasury more abundantly, to maintain a larger bureaucracy and police, and, most important of all, to assemble a larger army. There seem to be enough ambitious politicians in the world at any one time to guarantee that at least one government will use the new technology of transport to enlarge its area of control. And, once one government enlarges itself, then its neighbors and competitors feel compelled to do likewise in order, supposedly, to forestall anticipated aggression. Hence it is that technological change and a sense of competition together guarantee that governments will expand to the full extent that technology permits.

At the dawn of written history, most governmental units were tiny, consisting typically of an urban place and a few square miles of farms and villages. But with technological advance, imperial dominions became possible. Some of these in the ancient Near East and central and south Asia were based on the domestication of the horse; others like the Egyptian and Chinese were based on the exploitation of a river system as a channel of transport. The Roman empire is especially interesting for it was first created by control of the Mediterranean (*mare nostrum*) as a channel of transportation and was expanded by the invention of the Roman roads to control western Europe. Even so, the ancient empires were small by modern standards and at its height Rome probably ruled less land and fewer people than are now ruled from any one of these cites: Washington, Ottawa, Brazilia, Moscow, New Delhi, Peking, and Canberra. A necessary condition for these numerous large governments of today is of course innovation in transportation. First came the navigational discoveries (compass, triangular sail, sextant, trigonometry, etc.) that permitted the so-called expansion of

Europe and, second, the innovations in land transportation (the steam railroad, the automotive engine, road building and earth moving, the airplane, etc.).

The initial form of most of the great modern governments was empire. That is, large territories were accumulated by conquest when the technologically sophisticated Europeans subdued the relatively primitive inhabitants of America, Asia, and Africa. Thus were created the Spanish, Portuguese, Dutch, British, French, German, Russian, and Belgian empires. Of modern empires, only the Austrian, Turkish, and Chinese involved the conquest of territory inhabited by people as technologically sophisticated as the conqueror and even in these cases the conqueror had some kind of technological superiority in transportation and military equipment.

The collapse of imperialism forces a constitutional alternative on all successful rebels: Since they necessarily rebel within the subdivisions established by the imperial power for its own convenience in governing, one alternative is to establish the freed subdivisions as independent political units. But the subdivisions, coordinated as they have been by the colonial office in the center, are not usually large enough to take advantage of the technological conditions that made the empire possible in the first place. Hence, if the newly independent subdivisions stand alone as political entities, they are highly vulnerable to yet a new imperialism. This is what happened, for example, to the Balkan rebels against the Austrian and Turkish empires. Freed from one imperial master as a result of 19th-century revolutions and World War I, and yet too small to support large armies, they fell victim in World War II to Hitler's abortive Third Reich and then to Stalin's Communist hegemony. The whole of Africa and the Near East is now Balkanized in a similar way and it is not fanciful to suggest that something of a similar future awaits these new nations. The other alternative for successful rebels is to join several former imperial subdivisions together. But if they join the subdivisions in one centralized political unit, then the rebels have merely exchanged one imperial master for a lesser one. Thereby much of the justification for rebellion is lost. The subdivisions can, however, be joined in some kind of federation, which preserves at least the semblance of political self-control for the former subdivisions and at the same time allows them (by means of the government of the federation) to make use of the technological advantages in the size of treasuries and armies and thus to compete successfully with their neighbors.

In this sense federalism is the main alternative to empire as a technique of aggregating large areas under one government. Although it probably does not so clearly assure large treasuries and armies, it does assure them to some degree— and it avoids the offensiveness of imperial control. It is this combination of attributes, I believe, that accounts for the 20th-century popularity of the federal kind of constitutional bargain and explains why today all the governments of large territories (except China) have federal constitutions at least in name.

CONDITIONS OF THE FEDERAL BARGAIN

As bargains, the acts of making federal constitutions should display the main feature of bargains generally, which is that all parties are willing to make them. Assuming that they do display this feature, one may ask what it is that predisposes the parties to favor this kind of bargain. . . . I infer the existence of at least two circumstances encouraging a willingness to strike the bargain of federalism:

1. The politicians who offer the bargain desire to expand their territorial control, usually either to meet an external military or diplomatic threat or to prepare for military or diplomatic aggression and aggrandizement. But, though they desire to expand, they are not able to do so by conquest, because of either military incapacity or ideological distaste. Hence, if they are to satisfy the desire to expand, they must offer concessions to the rulers of constituent units, which is the essence of the federal bargain. The predisposition for those who offer the bargain is, then, that federalism is the only feasible means to accomplish a desired expansion without the use of force.

2. The politicians who accept the bargain, giving up some independence for the sake of union, are willing to do so because of some external military-diplomatic threat or opportunity. Either they desire protection from an external threat or they desire to participate in the potential aggression of the federation. And furthermore the desire for either protection or participation outweighs any desire they may have for indepedence. The predisposition is the cognizance of the pressing need for the military strength or diplomatic maneuverability that comes with a larger and presumably stronger government. (It is not, of course, necessary that their assessment of the military-diplomatic circumstances be objectively correct.)

I shall briefly examine two widely asserted fallacies about the origin of federalism.

One is the ideological fallacy, which is the assertion that federal forms are adopted as a device to guarantee freedom. Numerous writers on federalism, so many that it would be invidious to pick out an example, have committed this ideological fallacy. It is true, of course, that federalism does involve a guarantee of provincial autonomy and it is easy to see how some writers have confused this guarantee with the notion of a free society. Indeed, in certain circumstances, for example by encouraging provinces to have different policies or even simply to be inefficient, federalism may provide interstices in the social order in which personal liberties can thrive. And I suppose it is the observation of this fact that leads one to the ideological fallacy.

The worst error involved in this fallacy is the simple association of (1) federalism and (2) freedom or a non-dictatorial regime. Only the most casual observation of, for example, the Soviet Union or Mexico demonstrates, however, that even though all the forms of federalism are fairly scrupulously maintained, it is possible to convert the government into a dictatorship. In the two examples mentioned, the conversion has been accomplished by a strict one-party system, which suggests that the crucial feature of freedom is not a particular constitutional form, but rather a system of more than one party. But in other countries, *e.g.*, Brazil, Argentina, imperial Germany, even federalism and a multi-party system have been unable to prevent dictatorships, so probably some even more subtle condition is necessary to maintain free government. What it is I cannot say, but I am certain that there is no simple causal relationship between federalism and freedom.

Alongside the rather crude ideological fallacy is the subtler and initially more impressive reductionist fallacy, which is the assertion that federalism is a response to certain social conditions that create some sense of a common interest. On the basis of a theory of this sort, British colonial administrators have encouraged a number of federalisms, some successful, some not. It is the fact of some failures that is interesting—for they indicate the inadequacy of the theory. Perhaps the most exhaustive statement of this kind of theory is contained in the work of Deutsch and his collaborators,[1] who produced a list of nine "essential conditions for an amalgamated security-community" of which class the class of federalisms is a sub-class:

> (1) mutual compatibility of main values; (2) a distinctive way of life; (3) expectations of stronger economic ties or gains; (4) marked increase in political and administrative capabilities of at least some participating units; (5) superior economic growth on the part of at least some participating units; (6) unbroken links of social communication, both geographically between territories and sociologically between different social strata; (7) a broadening of the political elite; (8) mobility of persons at least among the politically relevant strata; and (9) a multiplicity of ranges of communications and transactions.

There are many defects in such a list. It is apparent that these conditions are not sufficient to bring about amalgamation for, if they were, federalisms like the Central American Federation would never have broken up or a pan-Arabic movement would reunite the Arabic parts of the former Turkish empire. Nor are all these conditions necessary, for a great many successful amalgamations have violated some or even all of them, *e.g.*, the Swiss confederation seems to have violated conditions (1) and (2) during most of its history and 19th-century colonial empires violated almost all conditions. If these conditions are neither jointly necessary nor sufficient, it is hard to imagine in what sense they are "essential."

The trouble with the Deutsch list is that it attempts to reduce the explanation of the political phenomenon of joining together to an explanation of the social and economic condition of the population. In bypassing the political, in bypassing the act of bargaining itself, it leaves out the crucial condition of the predisposition to make the bargain. What this list amounts to is a set of frequently observed conditions in which politicians can develop a predisposition to unite in some way or another. But it omits any mention of the political conditions in which, given some of these and other social and economic conditions, the actual predisposition to bargain occurs. The theory I have set forth, on the other hand, is confined to the political level entirely. It assumes some sense of common interest, of course, and then asserts the invariant conditions of forming one kind of larger political association, namely, federalism. (Incidentally, by confining the theory to a specific kind of amalgamation, the theory has a political focus that Deutsch and his collaborators failed to achieve.)

THE INVENTION OF CENTRALIZED FEDERALISM

The federal relationship is centralized according to the degree to which the parties organized to operate the central government control the parties organized to operate the constituent governments. This amounts to the assertion that the proximate cause of variations in the degree of centralization (or peripheralization) in the constitutional structure of a federalism is the variation in degree of party centralization.

There are strong *a priori* arguments for the validity of this assertion of a causal connection. Suppose the officials of the central government wish to centralize to a degree greater than the formal constitution of the federalism contemplates (*i.e.*, suppose these officials wish to break the federal bargain in their favor). Suppose further that these officials are the leaders of a party that also operates constituent government through subordinate leaders. That is, suppose the parties are highly centralized. Then, it would seem that all the constitutional and institutional prohibitions guaranteeing constituent governments against revision of the federal bargain would be ineffectual. If, on the other hand, the officials of the central government do not have partisan supporters operating the constituent governments, they may expect some opposition to their breaking of the guarantees. Whether or not the opposition is strong enough to maintain the bargain depends of course on a variety of institutional circumstances. But whether or not the opposition occurs at all seems to depend initially on a partisan difference between the central and constituent leadership. There is even some empirical evidence supporting the notion that the degree of partisan unity between the constituent and central governments is closely related to changes in the federal relationship. In another place,[2] Schaps and I devised a measure of the degree of partisan disharmony between the two levels of government and, when we correlated the index of disharmony by eight recent bienniums in the United States with the absolute amount of litigation between the two levels of governments in the Supreme Court, we obtained a coefficient of correlation of about $+0.8$, which is within the 2 per cent level of confidence. This finding suggests that to a very high degree variations in the federal relationship, especially variations in the ability of constituent governments to conflict with the central government, depend on variations in partisan relationships between the two levels.

What is suggested by this finding about a barely visible feature of federalism in the United States is also suggested by a much grosser observation of other systems. Thus, consider the federalisms in which the central government is invariably able to overawe the constituent governments, *viz.* Mexico, the Soviet Union, and Yugoslavia. One other characteristic these three political systems share is the fact that one and only one political party rules all levels of government. If the theory just set forth is correct, it is the feature of one-partyism that causes the rupture of the federal bargain. At the other extreme, consider the federalisms in which constituent governments can overawe the center, whereas central officials cannot overawe them. There are relatively few governments in this category (since it verges on the complete collapse of the federal bargain), but Nigeria offers at least one contemporary example. If the theory here set forth is correct, there should be many parties in Nigeria and the national levels of these parties should have little or no influence over the constituent levels. Such in fact is the case, for the main party leaders prefer to hold office in the constituent governments rather than in the central government. Thus at both extremes of variation in the federal relationship, it appears that the variations in partisanship are causally related to variations in federalism. Since in the instance of the United States, the same causal relationship appears, one easily infers that the same causal connection is valid for all systems in all categories.

The exact nature of this causal connection can best be examined by asking how to measure the federal relationship according to the partisan variation. Once one asks this question, it is immediately apparent that there are involved two kinds of relationships between parties at the two levels: (1) the degree to which one party controls both levels of government; and (2) the degree to which each potential governing party at the national level controls its partisan associates at the level of constituent governments.

WHAT MAINTAINS FEDERALISM?

1. The division and sharing of administrative responsibilities which is often said to be at the heart of federal arrangements, has little or nothing to do with maintaining the bargain. In the United States such centralization as has occurred seems to have been occasioned by technological considerations and to have had little effect, one way or another, on the bargain. Certainly in the period most crucial for its maintenance, some functions were centralized and others peripheralized, which suggests the genuine irrelevance of this consideration. In seven other federalisms there seems to be no rhyme or reason for the degree of administrative centralization except administrative traditions and convenience. Again there seems to be no connection between centralization or peripheralization in decision making and centralization or peripheralization of administrative functions.

2. It is true that federalism is maintained by the existence of dual citizen loyalties to the two levels of government. But this assertion is almost a tautology. Federalism means the existence of two levels each to some degree able to decide questions independently. Without loyalty to each of the two levels, both could not continue to exist. Besides being tautological, this statement tells us little about the degree of centralization in federalism.

Many writers wish to utter a much stronger companion statement: Federalism is maintained by the existence of dissident provincial patriotisms. Although this sentence appears to be true in many instances (*e.g.*, the United States, where a gradual decline in provincialism seems to accompany some centralization,

Canada, Brazil, etc.), it does not appear to be true of Australia or Argentina, where provincial patriotisms seem to be relatively weak.

Hence, in a larger sense one can say the federal bargain is maintained by loyalties to both levels, but one cannot always say that it is maintained because of the need to satisfy a dissident provincialism such as that of the South in the United States or of French Canadians in Canada.

3. Whatever the general social conditions, if any, that sustain the federal bargain, there is one institutional condition that controls the nature of the bargain in all the instances here examined and in all others with which I am familiar. This is the structure of the party system, which may be regarded as the main variable intervening between the background social conditions and the specific nature of the federal bargain.

4. It is theoretically possible but practically difficult to measure the structure of the party system.

NOTES

[1] Karl Deutsch, *et al.*, *Political Community in the North Atlantic Area* (Princeton: Princeton University Press, 1957), p. 58.

[2] William H. Riker and Ronald Schaps, "Disharmony in Federal Government," *Behavioral Science*, Vol. 2 (1957), pp. 276–90.

PART THREE

POLITICAL POWER

What is the actual distribution of power in the American polity? No issue has preoccupied political scientists more or provoked greater debate among them. It is easy to see why. Democracy is predicated on the dispersion of political power. An excessive concentration of power in the hands of one individual or group implies, not democracy, but autocracy or oligarchy. Thus, to answer the question "How democratic is the American regime?" one must first ask (as Robert Dahl does in the title of his celebrated book), "Who governs?"

Over the years, those who have pondered this issue have divided themselves roughly into two schools of thought. One sees American government as characterized by elitism, the other by pluralism. The first theory was most forcefully expressed by C. Wright Mills in his book *The Power Elite*. (The article we have chosen to reprint here is essentially an abridged version of that work.) According to Mills, American society is dominated by a "triangle of power" composed of corporate leaders, top military officers, and a handful of key political leaders. Some elite theorists believe "The Establishment" is limited to fewer participants (chiefly corporate interests, for instance), while others would widen Mills' triangle to include, say, the major communications media and even the big labor leaders. But the gist of the argument is the same: government is manipulated, largely from without, by a few top leaders who possess great advantages in wealth, status, and organizational position. Other actors and institutions, such as the mass political parties and the Congress, that once provided autonomous bases of power, are now increasingly inert or subservient to the "power elite" that operates mostly in and around the national executive. Although Mills is careful not to assert that the power elite is engaged in some sort of conscious conspiracy to subvert the democratic system, he perceives subtle forces enabling its members to concert their actions. Among the conditions facilitating coordination are a coincidence of interest (as between defense contractors and the military); the interconnected patterns of recruitment between public and private institutions; and the social milieus at the highest reaches of government and business (i.e., the intermingling of men with similar social origins, educations, professional backgrounds, and life-styles).

Although the alternative pluralist theory has no single intellectual parent, Robert Dahl's work is probably the best known exposition of it. At the heart of the pluralist perspective is the notion that *political resources* are not limited to wealth and social standing, but encompass a broad range of factors that can be translated into political power. In fact, as Dahl contends in the brief excerpt that follows, political resources now tend to be so diverse and widely scattered in American politics that no single elite can have anything like a monopoly on them. Rather, the effectiveness of any given set of resources depends in large measure on the nature of the particular issue in question; the forms of influence that may prove efficient in decision making on, say, foreign policy may be quite distinct from those required to shape some domestic program. Accordingly, different groups are influential in different issue-areas. Note that Dahl does not claim that political resources are distributed equally in society, only that the distribution was more uneven in the past than it is now; control has moved, in his terms, from a system of "cumulative inequalities" to one of "dispersed inequalities." Put another way, elites continue to govern, even in the pluralist model, but there is a difference: here we have a multiplicity of elites. They are seldom in collusion with one another (though *ad hoc* coalitions or alliances often arise); instead, the elites tend to be independent and competitive. Indeed, so numerous are the conflicting groups that all, or almost all, relevant interests in society have a chance to affect government policy.

At the same time, the pluralists sometimes overstate the diffusion of power in American life. (Dahl may be right in saying that "certainly no group of more than a few individuals is entirely lacking in some influence resources." Yet, at least before the civil rights legislation of the 1960s, the influence resources of, for example, many blacks were, for all intents and purposes, trivial.) And the pluralists sometimes underemphasize the extent to which national policy is determined, not by discrete organizations, but by complex networks of public and private interests.

At bottom, the dispute between exponents of the two schools may never be resolved conclusively. To resolve it, political scientists would have to ascertain the manifestations of power and the wielders of such power in all contexts. A methodology capable of doing this perspicuously does not exist. As Peter Bachrach and Morton S. Baratz demonstrate in their brilliant article "Two Faces of Power" (1962), it is misleading to assume that persons reputed to be powerful necessarily *exercise* power. By the same token, it is not enough to observe overt instances of decision making in selected issue-areas to discern exactly who the influential actors are. Power is sometimes exerted covertly, where no external investigator can see it. At times, also, policies will be made, not in response to political pressures, but *in anticipation* of them. In such cases, no act of power can be identified; there is only an unstated *quid pro quo*. Finally, power is often exercised by confining the scope of decision making to "safe" issues—that is, by delimiting the political agenda. A given set of decision makers may appear, to the outside observer, as highly active in certain visible spheres. But behind the scenes may lie an entirely different group, one that defines the rules of the game (so to speak) and that is able to decide *what sorts* of issues can be freely ventilated. In the last analysis, with so many possible forms that political power can take, a rigorous, definitive response to the question "Who really rules?" is likely to remain elusive.

10

ROBERT A. DAHL

On *the Species* Homo Politicus

. . . Let us start with man himself: with his opportunities and resources for gaining influence and the way he exploits—or more often neglects to exploit—his political potentialities.

HOMO CIVICUS

Civic man is, at heart, simply man; man is the child grown up; the child is the human species after millions of years of evolution. In spite of ideas and ideals, the human organism still relentlessly insists on its primordial quest for gratifications and release from pain. The child and the youth learn various forms of gratifying experience; they learn of love, and food, of play, work, and rest, of the pursuit of curiosity, the perception of order and pattern, sex, friendship, self-esteem, social esteem. Throughout man's life, experiences like these channel his efforts, his energies, his attention. They represent his hungers, his needs, his wants.

The child, the budding civic man, learns all too soon that he cannot indulge himself without stint. Constraints are imposed on his liberty to gratify himself, both by nature herself in the form of physiological, mechanical, and psychological limitations and also by other individuals—his family, to begin with, then playmates, teachers, and later a host of others. The child struggles, resists, and is caught, more or less firmly, in a net woven by himself and his society.

He learns how to delay his gratifying experiences; because of the various barriers imposed on him, the routes he now chooses to his goals are frequently complex and time-consuming, sometimes boring, occasionally painful, at times dangerous.

He discovers that just as others constrain him in his efforts to achieve his primary goals, he too has resources that he can use to influence others to gain his own ends. At first these resources are closely attached to his own person and consist of simple, direct actions and reactions like affection, friendliness, anger, hostility, crying, destructiveness. But the world, as he gradually learns, contains many resources that can be used more indirectly. In our own culture, for

[This study is part of a larger study of the distribution of political power in New Haven, Connecticut.—Eds.]

example, he soon finds that money has a magical power to induce the compliance of many different people for many different purposes.

Thus *homo civicus* begins to develop strategies, ways of using his resources to achieve his goals. Even in choosing strategies, he discovers, he does not enjoy complete freedom. Some strategies are banned, some are permissible, others are encouraged, many are all but unavoidable. Schooling and a job are presented to him as compulsory strategies; it is made clear that any attempt to depart from these paths will be visited not only by a great loss in his capacity to attain his goals but possibly even by outright punishment. Schooling is considered instrumental in gaining knowledge, and knowledge is a resource of widespread applicability; a job is instrumental in acquiring income and social standing, resources that are important for a variety of ends.

Young *homo civicus* learns that his choices are constrained by laws enforced by the police, by courts, and by many other officials. He learns of clusters of institutions and men called governments, toward some of which he develops sentiments of loyalty or cynicism. He may accept the constraints on his choices flowing from the actions of these governments, or he may try to evade them, but in either case he gradually learns that the range of permissible strategies in dealing with governments is a good deal wider and includes many subtler alternatives than he had first assumed. Among his resources for influencing officials, *homo civicus* discovers the ballot. Although the prevailing public doctrine of American society places a high value on this resource, and *homo civicus* may himself give lip service to that doctrine, in fact he may doubt its value and rarely if ever employ it, or he may vote merely out of habit and sense of duty. Or he may see the ballot as a useful device for influencing politicians.

Homo civicus has other resources, too. For example, he can forego a movie or two in order to make a contribution to a political campaign; he can forego an evening of television in order to distribute propaganda for a candidate. But the chances are very great that political activity will always seem rather remote from the main focus of his life. Typically, as a source of direct gratifications political activity will appear to *homo civicus* as less attractive than a host of other activities; and, as a strategy to achieve his gratifications indirectly, political action will seem considerably less efficient than working at his job, earning more money, taking out insurance, joining a club, planning a vacation, moving to another neighborhood or city, or coping with an uncertain future in manifold other ways.

Sometimes, however, the actions or inactions of governments may threaten the primary goals of *homo civicus*. . . . Then *homo civicus* may set out deliberately to use the resources at his disposal in order to influence the actions of governments. But when the danger passes, *homo civicus* may usually be counted on to revert to his normal preoccupation with nonpolitical strategies for attaining his primary goals.

Homo civicus is not, by nature, a political animal.

HOMO POLITICUS

Despite several thousand years of richly insightful speculation, not much can be said with confidence about the factors that shape *homo politicus* out of the apolitical clay of *homo civicus*. Presumably, in the course of development some individuals find that political action is a powerful source of gratifications, both direct and indirect. If and when the primary goals that animate *homo civicus* become durably attached to political action, a new member of the genus *homo politicus* is born. Political man, unlike civic man, deliberately allocates a very sizable share of his resources to the process of gaining and maintaining control over the policies of government. Control over policies usually requires control over officials. And where, as in the United States, key officials are elected by voters, political man usually allocates an important share of his resources to the process of gaining and maintaining influence over voters. Because the acquiescence of *homo civicus* is always a necessary condition for rulership, and to gain his consent is often economical, in all political systems *homo politicus* deliberately employs some resources to influence the choices of *homo civicus*. Political man invariably seeks to influence civic man directly, but even in democratic systems civic man only occasionally seeks to influence political man directly.

Like civic man, political man develops strategies that govern the ways in which he uses the resources at his disposal. Like civic man, political man chooses his strategies from a narrowly limited set. In some political systems, the limits imposed on *homo politicus* are broad; in others the limits are relatively narrow. In pluralistic, democratic political systems with wide political consensus the range of acceptable strategies is narrowed by beliefs and habits rooted in traditions of legality, constitutionality, and legitimacy that are constantly reinforced by a great variety of social processes for generating agreement on and adherence to political norms. Whoever departs from these acceptable strategies incurs a high risk of defeat, for the resources that will be mounted against the political deviant are almost certain to be vastly greater than the resources the political deviant can himself muster. Even *homo civicus* (under the prodding of rival political leaders) can be counted on to rise briefly out of his preoccupation with apolitical goals and employ some of his resources to smite down the political man who begins to deviate noticeably in his choice of strategies from the norms prescribed in the political culture.

RESOURCES

The resources available to political man for influencing others are limited, though not permanently fixed. For our purposes in this book, a resource is anything that can be used to sway the specific choices or the strategies of another individual. Or, to use different language, whatever may be used as an inducement is a resource.

How one classifies resources is to some extent arbitrary. It would be possible to list resources in great detail, distinguishing one from the other with the utmost subtlety or to deal in very broad categories. One could search for a comprehensive and logically exhaustive classification or simply list resources according to the dictates of common sense. One could employ elaborate psychological categories derived from theories of modern psychology, or one could use more commonplace terms to classify resources. . . . it will do, I think, to use categories dictated by common sense; to do more at this stage of our knowledge would be pseudoscientific window dressing.

Some resources can be used more or less directly as inducements. Or, put another way, the kinds of effective and cognitive experiences mentioned a moment ago as peculiarly fundamental and universal depend rather directly on some kinds of resources and more indirectly on others.

A list of resources in the American political system might include an individual's own time; access to money, credit, and wealth; control over jobs; control over information; esteem or social standing; the possession of charisma, popularity, legitimacy, legality; and the rights pertaining to public office. The list might also include solidarity: the capacity of a member of one segment of society to evoke support from others who identify him as like themselves because of similarities in occupation, social standing, religion, ethnic origin, or racial stock. The list would include the right to vote, intelligence, education, and perhaps even one's energy level.

One could easily think of refinements and additions to this list; it is not intended as an exhaustive list so much as an illustration of the richness and variety of political resources. All too often, attempts to explain the distribution and patterns of influence in political systems begin with an *a priori* assumption that everything can be explained by reference to only one kind of resource. On the contrary, . . . various manifestations of influence . . . can be explained, as we shall see, only by taking into account a number of different political resources.

Although the kinds and amounts of resources available to political man are always limited and at any given moment fixed, they are not, as was pointed out a moment ago, permanently fixed as to either kind or amount. Political man can use his resources to gain influence, and he can then use his influence to gain more resources. Political resources can be pyramided in much the same way that a man who starts out in business sometimes pyramids a small investment into a large corporate empire. To the political entrepreneur who has skill and drive, the political system offers unusual opportunities for pyramiding a small amount of initial resources into a sizable political holding. . . .

HYPOTHESES

In [an earlier part of this study] we saw how the monopoly over public life enjoyed by the Congregational patrician families of New Haven was destroyed, how the entrepreneurs without inherited social position and education acquired the prerogatives of office, and how these men were in their turn displaced by ex-plebes who lacked the most salient resources of influence possessed by their predecessors: hereditary social status, wealth, business prominence, professional attainments, and frequently even formal education beyond high school. The change in the New Haven political system from the election of Elizur Goodrich in 1803 to John W. Murphy in 1931—the first a descendant of a sixteenth-century Anglican Bishop, a Yale graduate, a Congregationalist, a lawyer, a judge, congressman, Federalist; the second a descendant of Irish immigrants, a Catholic, a Democrat, and a union official in Samuel Gompers' old Cigar Makers International Union—represented nothing less than an extended and peaceful revolution that transformed the social, economic, and political institutions of New Haven.

This change in New Haven is fully consistent with three of the key hypotheses in this study. First, a number of old American cities, of which New Haven is one, have passed through a roughly similar transformation from a system in which resources of influence were highly concentrated to a system in which they are highly dispersed. Second, the present dispersion is a consequence of certain fundamental aspects of the social, economic, and political structures of New Haven. Third, the present dispersion does not represent equality of resources but fragmentation. The revolution in New Haven might be said to constitute a change from a system of *cumulative inequalities* in political resources to a system of noncumulative or *dispersed inequalities* in political resources.

This system of dispersed inequalities is, I believe, marked by the following six characteristics.

1. Many different kinds of resources for influencing officials are available to different citizens.

2. With few exceptions, these resources are unequally distributed.

3. Individuals best off in their access to one kind of resource are often badly off with respect to many other resources.

4. No one influence resource dominates all the others in all or even in most key decisions.

5. With some exceptions, an influence resource is effective in some issue-areas or in some specific decisions but not in all.

6. Virtually no one, and certainly no group of more than a few individuals, is entirely lacking in some influence resources. . . .

11

C. WRIGHT MILLS

THE STRUCTURE OF POWER
IN AMERICAN SOCIETY

I

Power has to do with whatever decisions men make about the arrangements under which they live, and about the events which make up the history of their times. Events that are beyond human decision do happen; social arrangements do change without benefit of explicit decision. But in so far as such decisions are made, the problem of who is involved in making them is the basic problem of power. In so far as they could be made but are not, the problem becomes who fails to make them?

We cannot today merely assume that in the last resort men must always be governed by their own consent. For among the means of power which now prevail is the power to manage and to manipulate the consent of men. That we do not know the limits of such power, and that we hope it does have limits, does not remove the fact that much power today is successfully employed without the sanction of the reason or the conscience of the obedient.

Surely nowadays we need not argue that, in the last resort, coercion is the 'final' form of power. But then, we are by no means constantly at the last resort. Authority (power that is justified by the beliefs of the voluntarily obedient) and manipulation (power that is wielded unbeknown to the powerless)—must also be considered, along with coercion. In fact, the three types must be sorted out whenever we think about power.

In the modern world, we must bear in mind, power is often not so authoritative as it seemed to be in the medieval epoch: ideas which justify rulers no longer seem so necessary to their exercise of power. At least for many of the great decisions of our time—especially those of an international sort—mass 'persuasion' has not been 'necessary'; the fact is simply accomplished. Furthermore, such ideas as are available to the powerful are often neither taken up nor used by them. Such ideologies usually arise as a response to an effective

A draft of this lecture was presented at a residential weekend at the Beatrice Webb House, Surrey, on 2 March 1957; and at the University of Frankfurt on 3 May 1957. A more detailed exposition of the general argument, as well as documentation, will be found in *The Power Elite* (New York City: Oxford University Press), 1956.

debunking of power; in the United States such opposition has not been effective enough recently to create the felt need for new ideologies of rule.

There has, in fact, come about a situation in which many who have lost faith in prevailing loyalties have not aquired new ones, and so pay no attention to politics of any kind. They are not radical, not liberal, not conservative, not reactionary. They are inactionary. They are out of it. If we accept the Greek's definition of the idiot as an altogether private man, then we must conclude that many American citizens are now idiots. And I should not be surprised, although I do not know, if there were not some such idiots even in Germany. This—and I use the word with care—this spiritual condition seems to me the key to many modern troubles of political intellectuals, as well as the key to much political bewilderment in modern society. Intellectual 'conviction' and moral 'belief' are not necessary, in either the rulers or the ruled, for a ruling power to persist and even to flourish. So far as the role of ideologies is concerned, their frequent absences and the prevalence of mass indifference are surely two of the major political facts about the western societies today.

How large a role any explicit decisions do play in the making of history is itself an historical problem. For how large that role may be depends very much upon the means of power that are available at any given time in any given society. In some societies, the innumerable actions of innumerable men modify their milieux, and so gradually modify the structure itself. These modifications—the course of history—go on behind the backs of men. History is drift, although in total 'men make it.' Thus, innumerable entrepreneurs and innumerable con- sumers by ten-thousand decisions per minute may shape and re-shape the free-market economy. Perhaps this was the chief kind of limitation Marx had in mind when he wrote, in *The 18th Brumaire*: that 'Men make their own history, but they do not make it just as they please; they do not make it under circumstances chosen by themselves. . . .'

But in other societies—certainly in the United States and in the Soviet Union today—a few men may be so placed within the structure that by their decisions they modify the milieux of many other men, and in fact nowadays the structural conditions under which most men live. Such elites of power also make history under circumstances not chosen altogether by themselves, yet compared with other men, and compared with other periods of world history, these circum- stances do indeed seem less limiting.

I should contend that 'men are free to make history', but that some men are indeed much freer than others. For such freedom requires access to the means of decision and of power by which history can now be made. It has not always been so made; but in the later phases of the modern epoch it is. It is with reference to this epoch that I am contending that if men do not make history, they tend increasingly to become the utensils of history-makers as well as the mere objects of indeed seem less limiting [sic].

The history of modern society may readily be understood as the story of the enlargement and the centralization of the means of power—in economic, in political, and in military institutions. The rise of industrial society has involved these developments in the means of economic production. The rise of the nation-state has involved similar developments in the means of violence and in those of political administration.

In the western societies, such transformations have generally occurred gradually, and many cultural traditions have restrained and shaped them. In most of the Soviet societies, they are happening very rapidly indeed and without the great discourse of western civilization, without the Renaissance and without the Reformation, which so greatly strengthened and gave political focus to the idea of freedom. In those societies, the enlargement and the co-ordination of all the means of power has occurred more brutally, and from the beginning under tightly centralized authority. But in both types, the means of power have now become international in scope and similar in form. To be sure, each of them has its own ups and downs; neither is as yet absolute; how they are run differs quite sharply.

Yet so great is the reach of the means of violence, and so great the economy required to produce and support them, that we have in the immediate past witnessed the consolidation of these two world centres, either of which dwarfs the power of Ancient Rome. As we pay attention to the awesome means of power now available to quite small groups of men we come to realize that Caesar could do less with Rome than Napoleon with France; Napoleon less with France than Lenin with Russia. But what was Caesar's power at its height compared with the power of the changing inner circles of Soviet Russia and the temporary administrations of the United States? We come to realize—indeed they continually remind us—how a few men have access to the means by which in a few days continents can be turned into thermonuclear wastelands. That the facilities of power are so enormously enlarged and so decisively centralized surely means that the powers of quite small groups of men, which we may call elites, are now of literally inhuman consequence.

My concern here is not with the international scene but with the United States in the middle of the twentieth century. I must emphasize 'in the middle of the twentieth century' because in our attempt to understand any society we come upon images which have been drawn from its past and which often confuse our attempt to confront its present reality. That is one minor reason why history is the shank of any social science: we must study it if only to rid ourselves of it. In the United States, there are indeed many such images and usually they have to do with the first half of the nineteenth century. At that time the economic facilities of the United States were very widely dispersed and subject to little or to no central authority.

The state watched in the night but was without decisive voice in the day.

One man meant one rifle and the militia were without centralized orders.

Any American as old-fashioned as I can only agree with R. H. Tawney that 'Whatever the future may contain, the past has shown no more excellent social order than that in which the mass of the people were the masters of the holdings which they ploughed and the tools with which they worked, and could boast . . . 'It is a quietness to a man's mind to live upon his own and to know his heir certain.'

But then we must immediately add: all that is of the past and of little relevance to our understanding of the United States today. Within this society three broad levels of power may now be distinguished. I shall begin at the top and move downward.

II

The power to make decisions of national and international consequence is now so clearly seated in political, military, and economic institutions that other areas of society seem off to the side and, on occasion, readily subordinated to these. The scattered institutions of religion, education and family are increasingly shaped by the big three, in which history-making decisions now regularly occur. Behind this fact there is all the push and drive of a fabulous technology; for these three institutional orders have incorporated this technology and now guide it, even as it shapes and paces their development.

As each has assumed its modern shape, its effects upon the other two have become greater, and the traffic between the three has increased. There is no longer, on the one hand, an economy, and, on the other, a political order, containing a military establishment unimportant to politics and to money-making. There is a political economy numerously linked with military order and decision. This triangle of power is now a structural fact, and it is the key to any understanding of the higher circles in America today. For as each of these domains has coincided with the others, as decisions in each have become broader, the leading men of each—the high military, the corporation executives, the political directorate—have tended to come together to form the power elite of America.

The political order, once composed of several dozen states with a weak federal-centre, has become an executive apparatus which has taken up into itself many powers previously scattered, legislative as well as administrative, and which now reaches into all parts of the social structure. The long-time tendency of business and government to become more closely connected has since World War II reached a new point of explicitness. Neither can now be seen clearly as a distinct world. The growth of executive government does not mean merely the 'enlargement of government' as some kind of autonomous bureaucracy: under American conditions, it has meant the ascendency of the corporation man into political eminence. Already during the New Deal, such men had joined the political directorate; as of World War II they came to dominate it. Long involved with government, now they have moved into quite full direction of the economy of the war effort and of the post-war era.

The economy, once a great scatter of small productive units in somewhat automatic balance, has become internally dominated by a few hundred corporations, administratively and politically interrelated, which together hold the keys to economic decision. This economy is at once a permanent-war economy and a private-corporation economy. The most important relations of the corporation to the state now rest on the coincidence between military and corporate interests, as defined by the military and the corporate rich, and accepted by politicians and public. Within the elite as a whole, this coincidence of military domain and corporate realm strengthens both of them and further subordinates the merely political man. Not the party politician, but the corporation executive, is now more likely to sit with the military to answer the question: what is to be done?

The military order, once a slim establishment in a context of civilian distrust, has become the largest and most expensive feature of government; behind smiling public relations, it has all the grim and clumsy efficiency of a great and sprawling bureaucracy. The high military have gained decisive political and economic relevance. The seemingly permanent military threat places a premium upon them and virtually all political and economic actions are now judged in terms of military definitions of reality: the higher military have ascended to a firm position within the power elite of our time.

In part at least this is a result of an historical fact, pivotal for the years since 1939: the attention of the elite has shifted from domestic problems—centered in the 'thirties around slump—to international problems—centered in the 'forties and 'fifties around war. By long historical usage, the government of the United States has been shaped by domestic clash and balance; it does not have suitable agencies and traditions for the democratic handling of international affairs. In considerable part, it is in this vacuum that the power elite has grown.

(i) To understand the unity of this power elite, we must pay attention to the psychology of its several members in their respective milieux. In so far as the power elite is composed of men of similar origin and education, of similar career and style of life, their unity may be said to rest upon the fact that they are of similar social type, and to lead to the fact of their easy intermingling. This kind of unity reaches its frothier apex in the sharing of that prestige which is to be had in the world of the celebrity. It achieves a more solid culmination in the fact of the interchangeability of positions between the three dominant institutional orders. It is revealed by considerable traffic of personnel within and between these three, as well as by the rise of specialized go-betweens as in the new style high-level lobbying.

(ii) Behind such psychological and social unity are the structure and the mechanics of those institutional hierarchies over which the political directorate, the corporate rich, and the high military now preside. How each of these hierarchies is shaped and what relations it has with the others determine in large part the relations of their rulers. Were these hierarchies scattered and disjointed, then their respective elites might tend to be scattered and disjointed; but if they have many interconnections and points of coinciding interest, then their elites tend to form a coherent kind of grouping. The unity of the elite is not a simple reflection of the unity of institutions, but men and institutions are always related; that is why we must understand the elite today in connection with such institutional trends as the development of a permanent-war establishment, alongside a privately incorporated economy, inside a virtual political vacuum. For the men at the top have been selected and formed by such institutional trends.

(iii) Their unity, however, does not rest solely upon psychological similarity and social intermingling, nor entirely upon the structural blending of command-

ing positions and common interests. At times it is the unity of a more explicit
co-ordination.

To say that these higher circles are increasingly co-ordinated, that this is *one*
basis of their unity, and that at times—as during open war—such co-ordination
is quite wilful, is not to say that the co-ordination is total or continuous, or even
that it is very surefooted. Much less is it to say that the power elite has emerged
as the realization of a plot. Its rise cannot be adequately explained in any
psychological terms.

Yet we must remember that institutional trends may be defined as opportunities by those who occupy the command posts. Once such opportunities are
recognized, men may avail themselves of them. Certain types of men from each
of these three areas, more far-sighted than others, have actively promoted the
liaison even before it took its truly modern shape. Now more have come to see
that their several interests can more easily be realized if they work together, in
informal as well as in formal ways, and accordingly they have done so.

The idea of the power elite is of course an interpretation. It rests upon and it
enables us to make sense of major institutional trends, the social similarities and
psychological affinities of the men at the top. But the idea is also based upon
what has been happening on the middle and lower levels of power, to which I
now turn.

III

There are of course other interpretations of the American system of power.
The most usual is that it is a moving balance of many competing interests. The
image of balance, at least in America, is derived from the idea of the economic
market: in the nineteenth century, the balance was thought to occur between a
great scatter of individuals and enterprises; in the twentieth century, it is thought
to occur between great interest blocs. In both views, the politician is the key man
of power because he is the broker of many conflicting powers.

I believe that the balance and the compromise in American society—the
'countervailing powers' and the 'veto groups', of parties and associations, of strata
and unions—must now be seen as having mainly to do with the middle levels of
power. It is these middle levels that the political journalist and the scholar of
politics are most likely to understand and to write about—if only because, being
mainly middle class themselves, they are closer to them. Moreover these levels
provide the noisy content of most 'political' news and gossip; the images of these
levels are more or less in accord with the folklore of how democracy works; and,
if the master-image of balance is accepted, many intellectuals, especially in their
current patrioteering, are readily able to satisfy such political optimism as they
wish to feel. Accordingly, liberal interpretations of what is happening in the
United States are now virtually the only interpretations that are widely distributed.

But to believe that the power system reflects a balancing society is, I think, to
confuse the present era with earlier times, and to confuse its top and bottom with
its middle levels.

By the top levels, as distinguished from the middle, I intend to refer, first of all, to the scope of the decisions that are made. At the top today, these decisions have to do with all the issues of war and peace. They have also to do with slump and poverty which are now so very much problems of international scope. I intend also to refer to whether or not the groups that struggle politically have a chance to gain the positions from which such top decisions are made, and indeed whether their members do usually hope for such top national command. Most of the competing interests which make up the clang and clash of American politics are strictly concerned with their slice of the existing pie. Labour unions, for example, certainly have no policies of an international sort other than those which given unions adopt for the strict economic protection of their members. Neither do farm organizations. The actions of such middle-level powers may indeed have consequence for top-level policy; certainly at times they hamper these policies. But they are not truly concerned with them, which means of course that their influence tends to be quite irresponsible.

The facts of the middle levels may in part be understood in terms of the rise of the power elite. The expanded and centralized and interlocked hierarchies over which the power elite preside have encroached upon the old balance and relegated it to the middle level. But there are also independent developments of the middle levels. These, it seems to me, are better understood as an affair of intrenched and provincial demands than as a centre of national decision. As such, the middle level often seems much more of a stalemate than a moving balance.

(i) The middle level of politics is not a forum in which there are debated the big decisions of national and international life. Such debate is not carried on by nationally responsible parties representing and clarifying alternative policies. There are no such parties in the United States. More and more, fundamental issues never come to any point or decision before the Congress, much less before the electorate in party campaigns. In the case of Formosa, in the spring of 1955, the Congress abdicated all debate concerning events and decisions which surely bordered on war. The same is largely true of the 1957 crisis in the Middle East. Such decisions now regularly by-pass the Congress, and are never clearly focused issues for public decision.

The American political campaign distracts attention from national and international issues, but that is not to say that there are no issues in these campaigns. In each district and state, issues are set up and watched by organized interests of sovereign local importance. The professional politician is of course a party politician, and the two parties are semi-feudal organizations: they trade patronage and other favours for votes and for protection. The differences between them, so far as national issues are concerned, are very narrow and very mixed up. Often each seems to be forty-eight parties, one to each state; and accordingly, the politician as campaigner and as Congressman is not concerned with national party lines, if any are discernible. Often he is not subject to any effective national party discipline. He speaks for the interests of his own constituency, and he is concerned with national issues only in so far as they affect the interests effectively organized there, and hence his chances of re-election. That is why, when he does speak of national matters, the result is so often such an empty rhetoric. Seated in his sovereign locality, the politician is not at the national summit. He is on and of the middle levels of power.

(ii) Politics is not an arena in which free and independent organizations truly connect the lower and middle levels of society with the top levels of decision. Such organizations are not an effective and major part of American life today. As more people are drawn into the political arena, their associations become mass in scale, and the power of the individual becomes dependent upon them; to the extent that they are effective, they have become larger, and to that extent they have become less accessible to the influence of the individual. This is a central fact about associations in any mass society: it is of most consequence for political parties and for trade unions.

In the 'thirties, it often seemed that labour would become an insurgent power independent of corporation and state. Organized labour was then emerging for the first time on an American scale, and the only political sense of direction it needed was the slogan, 'organize the unorganized'. Now without the mandate of the slump, labour remains without political direction. Instead of economic and political struggles it has become deeply entangled in administrative routines with both corporation and state. One of its major functions, as a vested interest of the new society, is the regulation of such irregular tendencies as may occur among the rank and file.

There is nothing, it seems to me, in the make-up of the current labour leadership to allow us to expect that it can or that it will lead, rather than merely react. In so far as it fights at all it fights over a share of the goods of a single way of life and not over that way of life itself. The typical labour leader in the U.S.A. today is better understood as an adaptive creature of the main business drift than as an independent actor in a truly national context.

(iii) The idea that this society is a balance of powers requires us to assume that the units in balance are of more or less equal power and that they are truly independent of one another. These assumptions have rested, it seems clear, upon the historical importance of a large and independent middle class. In the latter nineteenth century and during the Progressive Era, such a class of farmers and small businessmen fought politically—and lost—their last struggle for a paramount role in national decision. Even then, their aspirations seemed bound to their own imagined past.

This old, independent middle class has of course declined. On the most generous count, it is now 40 per cent of the total middle class (at most 20 per cent of the total labour force). Moreover, it has become politically as well as economically dependent upon the state, most notably in the case of the subsidized farmer.

The *new* middle class of white-collar employees is certainly not the political pivot of any balancing society. It is in no way politically unified. Its unions, such as they are, often serve merely to incorporate it as hanger-on of the labour interest. For a considerable period, the old middle class *was* an independent base of power; the new middle class cannot be. Political freedom and economic security *were* anchored in small and independent properties; they are not anchored in the worlds of the white-collar job. Scattered property holders were economically united by more or less free markets; the jobs of the new middle class are integrated by corporate authority. Economically, the white-collar classes are in the same condition as wage workers; politically, they are in a worse condition, for they are not organized. They are no vanguard of historic change; they are at best a rear-guard of the welfare state.

The agrarian revolt of the 'nineties, the small-business revolt that has been more or less continuous since the 'eighties, the labour revolt of the 'thirties—each of these has failed as an independent movement which could countervail against the powers that be; they have failed as politically autonomous third parties. But they have succeeded, in varying degree, as interests vested in the expanded corporation and state; they have succeeded as parochial interests seated in particular districts, in local divisions of the two parties, and in the Congress. What they would become, in short, are well-established features of the *middle* levels of balancing power, on which we may now observe all those strata and interests which in the course of American history have been defeated in their bids for top power or which have never made such bids.

Fifty years ago many observers thought of the American state as a mask behind which an invisible government operated. But nowadays, much of what was called the old lobby, visible or invisible, is part of the quite visible government. The 'governmentalization of the lobby' has proceeded in both the legislative and the executive domain, as well as between them. The executive bureaucracy becomes not only the centre of decision but also the arena within which major conflicts of power are resolved or denied resolution. 'Administration' replaces electoral politics; the manoeuvring of cliques (which include leading Senators as well as civil servants) replaces the open clash of parties.

The shift of corporation men into the political directorate has accelerated the decline of the politicians in the Congress to the middle levels of power; the formation of the power elite rests in part upon this relegation. It rests also upon the semi-organized stalemate of the interests of sovereign localities, into which the legislative function has so largely fallen; upon the virtually complete absence of a civil service that is a politically neutral but politically relevant, depository of brain-power and executive skill; and it rests upon the increased official secrecy behind which great decisions are made without benefit of public or even of Congressional debate.

IV

There is one last belief upon which liberal observers everywhere base their interpretations and rest their hopes. That is the idea of the public and the associated idea of public opinion. Conservative thinkers, since the French Revolution, have of course Viewed With Alarm the rise of the public, which they have usually called the masses, or something to that effect. 'The populace is sovereign,' wrote Gustave Le Bon, 'and the tide of barbarism mounts.' But surely those who have supposed the masses to be well on their way to triumph are mistaken. In our time, the influence of publics or of masses within political life is in fact decreasing, and such influence as on occasion they do have tends, to an unknown but increasing degree, to be guided by the means of mass communication.

In a society of publics, discussion is the ascendant means of communication, and the mass media, if they exist, simply enlarge and animate this discussion, linking one face-to-face public with the discussions of another. In a mass society, the dominant type of communication is the formal media, and publics become mere markets for these media: the 'public' of a radio programme consists of all those exposed to it. When we try to look upon the United States today as a society of publics, we realize that it has moved a considerable distance along the road to the mass society.

In official circles, the very term, 'the public', has come to have a phantom meaning, which dramatically reveals its eclipse. The deciding elite can identify some of those who clamour publicly as 'Labour', others as 'Business', still others as 'Farmer'. But these are not the public. 'The public' consists of the unidentified and the non-partisan in a world of defined and partisan interests. In this faint echo of the classic notion, the public is composed of these remnants of the old and new middle classes whose interests are not explicitly defined, organized, or clamorous. In a curious adaptation, 'the public' often becomes, in administrative fact, 'the disengaged expert', who, although ever so well informed, has never taken a clear-cut and public stand on controversial issues. He is the 'public' member of the board, the commission, the committee. What 'the public' stands for, accordingly, is often a vagueness of policy (called 'open-mindedness'), a lack of involvement in public affairs (known as 'reasonableness'), and a professional disinterest (known as 'tolerance').

All this is indeed far removed from the eighteenth-century idea of the public of public opinion. That idea parallels the economic idea of the magical market. Here is the market composed of freely competing entrepreneurs; there is the public composed of circles of people in discussion. As price is the result of anonymous, equally weighted, bargaining individuals, so public opinion is the result of each man's having thought things out for himself and then contributing his voice to the great chorus. To be sure, some may have more influence on the state of opinion than others, but no one group monopolizes the discussion, or by itself determines the opinions that prevail.

In this classic image, the people are presented with problems. They discuss them. They formulate viewpoints. These viewpoints are organized, and they compete. One viewpoint 'wins out'. Then the people act on this view, or their representatives are instructed to act it out, and this they promptly do.

Such are the images of democracy which are still used as working justifications of power in America. We must now recognize this description as more a fairy tale than a useful approximation. The issues that now shape man's fate are neither raised nor decided by any public at large. The idea of a society that is at bottom composed of publics is not a matter of fact; it is the proclamation of an ideal, and as well the assertion of a legitimation masquerading as fact.

I cannot here describe the several great forces within American society as well as elsewhere which have been at work in the debilitation of the public. I want only to remind you that publics, like free associations, can be deliberately and suddenly smashed, or they can more slowly wither away. But whether smashed in a week or withered in a generation, the demise of the public must be seen in connection with the rise of centralized organizations, with all their new means of power, including those of the mass media of distraction. These, we now know, often seem to expropriate the rationality and the will of the terrorized or—as the case may be—the voluntarily indifferent society of masses. In the more democratic process of indifference the remnants of such publics as remain may only occasionally be intimidated by fanatics in search of 'disloyalty'. But regardless of that, they lose their will for decision because they do not possess the instruments for decision; they lose their sense of political belonging because they do not belong; they lose their political will because they see no way to realize it.

The political structure of a modern democratic state requires that such a public as is projected by democratic theorists not only exist but that it be the very forum within which a politics of real issues is enacted.

It requires a civil service that is firmly linked with the world of knowledge and sensibility, and which is composed of skilled men who, in their careers and in their aspirations, are truly independent of any private, which is to say, corporation, interests.

It requires nationally responsible parties which debate openly and clearly the issues which the nation, and indeed the world, now so rigidly confronts.

It requires an intelligentsia, inside as well as outside the universities, who carry on the big discourse of the western world, and whose work is relevant to and influential among parties and movements and publics.

And it certainly requires, as a fact of power, that there be free associations standing between families and smaller communities and publics, on the one hand, and the state, the military, the corporation, on the other. For unless these do exist, there are no vehicles for reasoned opinion, no instruments for the rational exertion of public will.

Such democratic formations are not now ascendant in the power structure of the United States, and accordingly the men of decision are not men selected and formed by careers within such associations and by their performance before such publics. The top of modern American society is increasingly unified, and often seems wilfully co-ordinated: at the top there has emerged an elite whose power probably exceeds that of any small group of men in world history. The middle levels are often a drifting set of stalemated forces: the middle does not link the bottom with the top. The bottom of this society is politically fragmented, and even as a passive fact, increasingly powerless: at the bottom there is emerging a mass society.

These developments, I believe, can be correctly understood neither in terms of the liberal nor the marxian interpretation of politics and history. Both these ways of thought arose as guidelines to reflection about a type of society which does not now exist in the United States. We confront there a new kind of social structure, which embodies elements and tendencies of all modern society, but in which they have assumed a more naked and flamboyant prominence.

That does not mean that we must give up the ideals of these classic political expectations. I believe that both have been concerned with the problem of rationality and of freedom: liberalism, with freedom and rationality as supreme facts about the individual; marxism, as supreme facts about man's role in the political making of history. What I have said here, I suppose, may be taken as an attempt to make evident why the ideas of freedom and of rationality now so often seem so ambiguous in the new society of the United States of America.

12

PETER BACHRACH AND MORTON S. BARATZ

TWO FACES OF POWER

The concept of power remains elusive despite the recent and prolific outpourings of case studies on community power. Its elusiveness is dramatically demonstrated by the regularity of disagreement as to the locus of community power between the sociologists and the political scientists. Sociologically oriented researchers have consistently found that power is highly centralized, while scholars trained in political science have just as regularly concluded that in "their" communities power is widely diffused.[1] Presumably, this explains why the latter group styles itself "pluralist," its counterpart "elitist."

There seems no room for doubt that the sharply divergent findings of the two groups are the product, not of sheer coincidence, but of fundamental differences in both their underlying assumptions and research methodology. The political scientists have contended that these differences in findings can be explained by the faulty approach and presuppositions of the sociologists. We contend in this paper that the pluralists themselves have not grasped the whole truth of the matter; that while their criticisms of the elitists are sound, they, like the elitists, utilize an approach and assumptions which predetermine their conclusions. Our argument is cast within the frame of our central thesis: that there are two faces of power, neither of which the sociologists see and only one of which the political scientists see.

I

Against the elitist approach to power several criticisms may be, and have been levelled.[2] One has to do with its basic premise that in every human institution there is an ordered system of power, a "power structure" which is an integral part and the mirror image of the organization's stratification. This postulate the pluralists emphatically—and, to our mind, correctly—reject, on the ground that

> nothing categorical can be assumed about power in any community. . . . If anything, there seems to be an unspoken notion among pluralist researchers that at bottom *nobody* dominates in a town, so that their first question is not likely to be,

This paper is an outgrowth of a seminar in Problems of Power in Contemporary Society, conducted jointly by the authors for graduate students and undergraduate majors in political science and economics.

"Who runs this community?," but rather, "Does anyone at all run this community?" The first query is somewhat like, "Have you stopped beating your wife?," in that virtually any response short of total unwillingness to answer will supply the researchers with a "power elite" along the lines presupposed by the stratification theory.[3]

Equally objectionable to the pluralists—and to us—is the sociologists' hypothesis that the power structure tends to be stable over time.

Pluralists hold that power may be tied to issues, and issues can be fleeting or persistent, provoking coalitions among interested groups and citizens, ranging in their duration from momentary to semi-permanent. . . . To presume that the set of coalitions which exists in the community at any given time is a timelessly stable aspect of social structure is to introduce systematic inaccuracies into one's description of social reality.[4]

A third criticism of the elitist model is that it wrongly equates reputed with actual power:

If a man's major life work is banking, the pluralist presumes he will spend his time at the bank, and not in manipulating community decisions. This presumption holds until the banker's activities and participations indicate otherwise. . . . If we presume that the banker is "really" engaged in running the community, there is practically no way of disconfirming this notion, even if it is totally erroneous. On the other hand, it is easy to spot the banker who really *does* run community affairs when we presume he does not, because his activities will make this fact apparent.[5]

This is not an exhaustive bill of particulars; there are flaws other than these in the sociological model and methodology[6]—including some which the pluralists themselves have not noticed. But to go into this would not materially serve our current purposes. Suffice it simply to observe that whatever the merits of their own approach to power, the pluralists have effectively exposed the main weaknesses of the elitist model.

As the foregoing quotations make clear, the pluralists concentrate their attention, not upon the sources of power, but its exercise. Power to them means "participation in decision-making"[7] and can be analyzed only after "careful examination of a series of concrete decisions."[8] As a result, the pluralist researcher is uninterested in the reputedly powerful. His concerns instead are to (a) select for study a number of "key" as opposed to "routine" political decisions, (b) identify the people who took an active part in the decision-making process, (c) obtain a full account of their actual behavior while the policy conflict was being resolved, and (d) determine and analyze the specific outcome of the conflict.

The advantages of this approach, relative to the elitist alternative, need no further exposition. The same may not be said, however, about its defects—two of which seem to us to be of fundamental importance. One is that the model takes no account of the fact that power may be, and often is, exercised by confining the scope of decision-making to relatively "safe" issues. The other is that the model provides no *objective* criteria for distinguishing between "important" and "unimportant" issues arising in the political arena.

II

There is no gainsaying that an analysis grounded entirely upon what is specific and visible to the outside observer is more "scientific" than one based upon pure speculation. To put it another way,

> If we can get our social life stated in terms of activity, and of nothing else, we have not indeed succeeded in measuring it, but we have at least reached a foundation upon which a coherent system of measurements can be built up. . . . We shall cease to be blocked by the intervention of unmeasurable elements, which claim to be themselves the real causes of all that is happening, and which by their spook-like arbitrariness make impossible any progress toward dependable knowledge. [9]

The question is, however, how can one be certain in any given situation that the "unmeasurable elements" are inconsequential, are not of decisive importance? Cast in slightly different terms, can a sound concept of power be predicated on the assumption that power is totally embodied and fully reflected in "concrete decisions" or in activity bearing directly upon their making?

We think not. Of course power is exercised when A participates in the making of decisions that affect B. But power is also exercised when A devotes his energies to creating or reinforcing social and political values and institutional practices that limit the scope of the political process to public consideration of only those issues which are comparatively innocuous to A. To the extent that A succeeds in doing this, B is prevented, for all practical purposes, from bringing to the fore any issues that might in their resolution be seriously detrimented to A's set of preferences. [10]

Situations of this kind are common. Consider, for example, the case—surely not unfamiliar to this audience—of the discontented faculty member in an academic institution headed by a tradition-bound executive. Aggrieved about a long-standing policy around which a strong vested interest has developed, the professor resolves in the privacy of his office to launch an attack upon the policy at the next faculty meeting. But, when the moment of truth is at hand, he sits frozen in silence. Why? Among the many possible reasons, one or more of these could have been of crucial importance: (a) the professor was fearful that his intended action would be interpreted as an expression of his disloyalty to the institution; or (b) he decided that, given the beliefs and attitudes of his colleagues on the faculty, he would almost certainly constitute on this issue a minority of one; or (c) he concluded that, given the nature of the law-making process in the institution, his proposed remedies would be pigeonholed permanently. But whatever the case, the central point to be made is the same: to the extent that a person or group—consciously or unconsciously—creates or reinforces barriers to the public airing of policy conflicts, that person or group has power. Or, as Professor Schattschneider has so admirably put it:

All forms of political organization have a bias in favor of the exploitation of some kinds of conflict and the suppression of others because *organization is the mobilization of bias.* Some issues are organized into politics while others are organized out.[11]

Is such bias not relevant to the study of power? Should not the student be continuously alert to its possible existence in the human institution that he studies, and be ever prepared to examine the forces which brought it into being and sustain it? Can he safely ignore the possibility, for instance, that an individual or group in a community participates more vigorously in supporting the *nondecision-making* process than in participating in actual decisions within the process? Stated differently, can the researcher overlook the chance that some person or association could limit decision-making to relatively non-controversial matters, by influencing community values and political procedures and rituals, notwithstanding that there are in the community serious but latent power conflicts?[12] To do so is, in our judgment, to overlook the less apparent, but nonetheless extremely important, face of power.

III

In his critique of the "ruling-elite model," Professor Dahl argues that "the hypothesis of the existence of a ruling elite can be strictly tested only if . . . [t]here is a fair sample of cases involving key political decisions in which the preferences of the hypothetical ruling elite run counter to those of any other likely group that might be suggested."[13] With this assertion we have two complaints. One we have already discussed, viz., in erroneously assuming that power is solely reflected in concrete decisions, Dahl thereby excludes the possibility that in the community in question there is a group capable of preventing contests from arising on issues of importance to it. Beyond that, however, by ignoring the less apparent face of power Dahl and those who accept his pluralist approach are unable adequately to differentiate between a "key" and a "routine" political decision.

Nelson Polsby, for example, proposes that "by pre-selecting as issues for study those which are generally agreed to be significant, pluralist researchers can test stratification theory."[14] He is silent, however, on how the researcher is to determine *what* issues are "generally agreed to be significant," and on how the researcher is to appraise the reliability of the agreement. In fact, Polsby is guilty here of the same fault he himself has found with elitist methodology: by presupposing that in any community there are significant issues in the political arena, he takes for granted the very question which is in doubt. He accepts as issues what are reputed to be issues. As a result, his findings are fore-ordained. For even if there is no "truly" significant issue in the community under study, there is every likelihood that Polsby (or any like-minded researcher) will find one or some and, after careful study, reach the appropriate pluralistic conclusions.[15]

Dahl's definition of "key political issues" in his essay on the ruling-elite model is open to the same criticism. He states that it is "a necessary although possibly not a sufficient condition that the [key] issue should involve actual disagreement in preferences among two or more groups."[16] In our view, this is an inadequate characterization of a "key political issue," simply because groups can have disagreements in preferences on unimportant as well as on important issues. Elite preferences which border on the indifferent are certainly not significant in determining whether a monolithic or polylithic distribution of power prevails in a given community. Using Dahl's definition of "key political issues," the researcher would have little difficulty in finding such in practically any community; and it would not be surprising then if he ultimately concluded that power in the community was widely diffused.

The distinction between important and unimportant issues, we believe, cannot be made intelligently in the absence of an analysis of the "mobilization of bias" in the community; of the dominant values and the political myths, rituals, and institutions which tend to favor the vested interests of one or more groups, relative to others. Armed with this knowledge, one could conclude that any challenge to the predominant values or to the established "rules of the game" would constitute an "important" issue; all else, unimportant. To be sure, judgments of this kind cannot be entirely objective. But to avoid making them in a study of power is both to neglect a highly significant aspect of power and thereby to undermine the only sound basis for discriminating between "key" and "routine" decisions. In effect, we contend, the pluralists have made each of these mistakes; that is to say, they have done just that for which Kaufman and Jones so severely taxed Floyd Hunter: they have begun "their structure at the mezzanine without showing us a lobby or foundation,"[17] i.e., they have begun by studying the issues rather than the values and biases that are built into the political system and that, for the student of power, give real meaning to those issues which do enter the political arena.

IV

There is no better fulcrum for our critique of the pluralist model than Dahl's recent study of power in New Haven.[18]

At the outset it may be observed that Dahl does not attempt in this work to define his concept, "key political decision." In asking whether the "Notables" of New Haven are "influential overtly or covertly in the making of government decisions," he simply states that he will examine "three different 'issue-areas' in which important public decisions are made: nominations by the two political parties, urban redevelopment, and public education." These choices are justified on the grounds that "nominations determine which persons will hold public office. The New Haven redevelopment program measured by its cost—present and potential—is the largest in the country. Public education, aside from its intrinsic importance, is the costliest item in the city's budget." Therefore, Dahl concludes, "It is reasonable to expect . . . that the relative influence over public officials wielded by the . . . Notables would be revealed by an examination of their participation in these three areas of activity."[19]

The difficulty with this latter statement is that it is evident from Dahl's own account that the Notables are in fact uninterested in two of the three "key" decisions he has chosen. In regard to the public school issue, for example, Dahl points out that many of the Notables live in the suburbs and that those who do live in New Haven choose in the main to send their children to private schools. "As a consequence," he writes, "their interest in the public schools is ordinarily rather slight."[20] Nominations by the two political parties as an important "issue-area," is somewhat analogous to the public schools, in that the apparent lack of interest among the Notables in this issue is partially accounted for by their suburban residence—because of which they are disqualified from holding public office in New Haven. Indeed, Dahl himself concedes that with respect to both these issues the Notables are largely indifferent: "Business leaders might ignore the public schools or the political parties without any sharp awareness that their indifference would hurt their pocketbooks . . ." He goes on, however, to say that

> the prospect of profound changes [as a result of the urban-redevelopment program] in ownership, physical layout, and usage of property in the downtown area and the effects of these changes on the commercial and industrial prosperity of New Haven were all related in an obvious way to the daily concerns of businessmen.[21]

Thus, if one believes—as Professor Dahl did when he wrote his critique of the ruling-elite model—that an issue, to be considered as important, "should involve actual disagreement in preferences among two or more groups,"[22] then clearly he has now for all practical purposes written off public education and party nominations as key "issue-areas." But this point aside, it appears somewhat dubious at best that "the relative influence over public officials wielded by the Social Notables" can be revealed by an examination of their nonparticipation in areas in which they were not interested.

Furthermore, we would not rule out the possibility that even on those issues to which they appear indifferent, the Notables may have a significant degree of *indirect* influence. We would suggest, for example, that although they send their children to private schools, the Notables do recognize that public school expenditures have a direct bearing upon their own tax liabilities. This being so, and given their strong representation on the New Haven Board of Finance,[23] the expectation must be that it is in their direct interest to play an active role in fiscal policy-making, in the establishment of the educational budget in particular. But as to this, Dahl is silent: he inquires not at all into either the decisions made by the Board of Finance with respect to education nor into their impact upon the public schools.[24] Let it be understood clearly that in making these points we are not attempting to refute Dahl's contention that the Notables lack power in New Haven. What we *are* saying, however, is that this conclusion is not adequately supported by his analysis of the "issue-areas" of public education and party nominations.

The same may not be said of redevelopment. This issue is by any reasonable standard important for purposes of determining whether New Haven is ruled by "the hidden hand of an economic elite."[25] For the Economic Notables have taken an active interest in the program and, beyond that, the socio-economic implications of it are not necessarily in harmony with the basic interests and values of businesses and businessmen.

In an effort to assure that the redevelopment program would be acceptable to what he dubbed "the biggest muscles" in New Haven, Mayor Lee created the Citizens Action Commission (CAC) and appointed to it primarily representatives of the economic elite. It was given the function of overseeing the work of the mayor and other officials involved in redevelopment, and, as well, the responsibility for organizing and encouraging citizens' participation in the program through an extensive committee system.

In order to weigh the relative influence of the mayor, other key officials, and the members of the CAC, Dahl reconstructs "all the *important* decisions on redevelopment and renewal between 1950–58 . . . [to] determine which individuals most often initiated the proposals that were finally adopted or most often successfully vetoed the proposals of the others."[26] The results of this test indicate that the mayor and his development administrator were by far the most influential, and that the "muscles" on the Commission, excepting in a few trivial instances, "never directly initiated, opposed, vetoed, or altered any proposal brought before them. . . ."[27]

This finding is, in our view, unreliable, not so much because Dahl was compelled to make a subjective selection of what constituted *important* decisions within what he felt to be an *important* "issue-area," as because the finding was based upon an excessively narrow test of influence. To measure relative influence solely in terms of the ability to initiate and veto proposals is to ignore the possible exercise of influence or power in limiting the scope of initiation. How, that is to say, can a judgment be made as to the relative influence of Mayor Lee and the CAC without knowing (through prior study of the political and social views of all concerned) the proposals that Lee did *not* make because he anticipated that they would provoke strenuous opposition and, perhaps, sanctions on the part of the CAC?[28]

In sum, since he does not recognize *both* faces of power, Dahl is in no position to evaluate the relative influence or power of the initiator and decision-maker, on the one hand, and of those persons, on the other, who may have been indirectly instrumental in preventing potentially dangerous issues from being raised.[29] As a result, he unduly emphasizes the importance of initiating, deciding, and vetoing, and in the process casts the pluralist conclusions of his study into serious doubt.

V

We have contended in this paper that a fresh approach to the study of power is called for, an approach based upon a recognition of the two faces of power. Under this approach the researcher would begin—not, as does the sociologist who asks, "Who rules?" nor as does the pluralist who asks, "Does anyone have power?"—but by investigating the particular "mobilization of bias" in the institution under scrutiny. Then, having analyzed the dominant values, the myths and the established political procedures and rules of the game, he would make a careful inquiry into which persons or groups, if any, gain from the existing bias and which, if any, are handicapped by it. Next, he would investigate the dynamics of *nondecision-making*; that is, he would examine the extent to which and the manner in which the *status quo* oriented persons and groups influence those community values and those political institutions (as, *e.g.*, the unanimity "rule" of New York City's Board of Estimate[30]) which tend to limit the scope of actual decision-making to "safe" issues. Finally, using his knowledge of the restrictive face of power as a foundation for analysis and as a standard for distinguishing between "key" and "routine" political decisions, the researcher would, after the manner of the pluralists, analyze participation in decision-making of concrete issues.

We reject in advance as unimpressive the possible criticism that this approach to the study of power is likely to prove fruitless because it goes beyond an investigation of what is objectively measurable. In reacting against the subjective aspects of the sociological model of power, the pluralists have, we believe, made the mistake of discarding "unmeasurable elements" as unreal. It is ironical that, by so doing, they have exposed themselves to the same fundamental criticism they have so forcefully levelled against the elitists: their approach to and assumptions about power predetermine their findings and conclusions.

NOTES

[1] Compare, for example, the sociological studies of Floyd Hunter, *Community Power Structure* (Chapel Hill, 1953); Roland Pellegrini and Charles H. Coates, "Absentee-Owned Corporations and Community Power Structure," *American Journal of Sociology*, Vol. 61 (March 1956), pp. 413–19; and Robert O. Schulze, "Economic Dominants and Community Power Structure," *American Sociological Review*, Vol. 23 (February 1958), pp. 3–9; with political science studies of Wallace S. Sayre and Herbert Kaufman, *Governing New York City* (New York, 1960); Robert A. Dahl, *Who Governs?* (New Haven, 1961); and Norton E. Long and George Belknap, "A Research Program on Leadership and Decision-Making in Metropolitan Areas" (New York, Governmental Affairs Institute, 1956). See also Nelson W. Polsby, "How to Study Community Power: The Pluralist Alternative," *Journal of Politics*, Vol. 22 (August, 1960), pp. 474–84.

[2] See especially N. W. Polsby, *op. cit.*, p. 475f.

[3] *Ibid.*, pp. 476.

[4] *Ibid.*, pp. 478–79.

[5] *Ibid.*, pp. 480–81.

[6] See especially Robert A. Dahl, "A Critique of the Ruling-Elite Model," *American Political Science Review*, Vol. 52 (June 1958), pp. 463–69; and Lawrence J. R. Herson, "In the Footsteps of Community Power," *American Political Science Review*, Vol. 55 (December 1961), pp. 817–31.

[7] This definition originated with Harold D. Lasswell and Abraham Kaplan, *Power and Society* (New Haven, 1950), p. 75.

[8] Robert A. Dahl, "A Critique of the Ruling-Elite Model," *loc. cit.*, p. 466.

[9] Arthur Bentley, *The Process of Government* (Chicago, 1908), p. 202, quoted in Polsby, *op. cit.*, p. 481n.

[10] As is perhaps self-evident, there are similarities in both faces of power. In each, A participates in decisions and thereby adversely affects B. But there is an important difference between the two: in

150   PETER BACHRACH AND MORTON S. BARATZ

the one case, A openly participates; in the other, he participates only in the sense that he works to
sustain those values and rules of procedure that help him keep certain issues out of the public
domain. True enough, participation of the second kind may at times be overt; that is the case, for
instance, in cloture fights in the Congress. But the point is that it need not be. In fact, when the
maneuver is most successfully executed, it neither involves nor can be identified with decisions
arrived at on specific issues.

[11] E. E. Schattschneider, *The Semi-Sovereign People* (New York, 1960), p. 71.

[12] Dahl *partially* concedes this point when he observes ("A Critique of the Ruling-Elite Model,"
pp. 468–69) that "one could argue that even in a society like ours a ruling elite might be so influential
over ideas, attitudes, and opinions that a kind of false consensus will exist—not the phony consensus
of a terroristic totalitarian dictatorship but the manipulated and superficially self-imposed adherence
to the norms and goals of the elite by broad sections of a community. . . . This objection points to
the need to be circumspect in interpreting the evidence." But that he largely misses our point is clear
from the succeeding sentence: "Yet here, too, it seems to me that the hypothesis cannot be
satisfactorily confirmed without something equivalent to the test I have proposed," and that is "by an
examination of a series of concrete cases where key decisions are made. . . ."

[13] *Op. cit.*, p. 466.

[14] *Op. cit.*, p. 478.

[15] As he points out, the expectations of the pluralist researchers "have seldom been disappointed."
(*Ibid.*, p. 477).

[16] *Op. cit.*, p. 467.

[17] Herbert Kaufman and Victor Jones, "The Mystery of Power," *Public Administration Review*,
Vol. 14 (Summer 1954), p. 207.

[18] Robert A. Dahl, *Who Governs?* (New Haven, 1961).

[19] *Ibid.*, p. 64.

[20] *Ibid.*, p. 70.

[21] *Ibid.*, p. 71.

[22] *Op. cit.*, p. 467.

[23] *Who Governs?*, p. 82. Dahl points out that "the main policy thrust of the Economic Notables
is to oppose tax increases; this leads them to oppose expenditures for anything more than minimal
traditional city services. In this effort their two most effective weapons ordinarily are the mayor and
the Board of Finance. The policies of the Notables are most easily achieved under a strong mayor
if his policies coincide with theirs or under a weak mayor if they have the support of the Board of
Finance. . . . New Haven mayors have continued to find it expedient to create confidence in their
financial policies among businessmen by appointing them to the Board." (pp. 81–2)

[24] Dahl does discuss in general terms (pp. 79–84) changes in the level of tax rates and assessments
in past years, but not actual decisions of the Board of Finance or their effects on the public school
system.

[25] *Ibid.*, p. 124.

[26] *Ibid.* "A rough test of a person's overt or covert influence," Dahl states in the first section of the
book, "is the frequency with which he successfully initiates an important policy over the opposition
of others, or vetoes policies initiated by others, or initiates a policy where no opposition appears."
(*Ibid.*, p. 66)

[27] *Ibid.*, p. 131.

[28] Dahl is, of course, aware of the "law of anticipated reactions." In the case of the mayor's
relationship with the CAC, Dahl notes that Lee was "particularly skillful in estimating what the CAC
could be expected to support or reject." (p. 137). However, Dahl was not interested in analyzing or
appraising to what extent the CAC limited Lee's freedom of action. Because of his restricted concept
of power, Dahl did not consider that the CAC might in this respect have exercised power. That the
CAC did not initiate or veto actual proposals by the mayor was to Dahl evidence enough that the
CAC was virtually powerless; it might as plausibly be evidence that the CAC was (in itself or in what
it represented) so powerful that Lee ventured nothing it would find worth quarreling with.

[29] The fact that the initiator of decisions also refrains—because he anticipates adverse reactions—
from initiating other proposals does not obviously lessen the power of the agent who limited his
initiative powers. Dahl missed this point: "It is," he writes, "all the more improbable, then, that a

secret cabal of Notables dominates the public life of New Haven through means so clandestine that not one of the fifty prominent citizens interviewed in the course of this study—citizens who had participated extensively in various decisions—hinted at the existence of such a cabal. . ." (p. 185).

In conceiving of elite domination exclusively in the form of a conscious cabal exercising the power of decision-making and vetoing, he overlooks a more subtle form of domination; one in which those who actually dominate are not conscious of it themselves, simply because their position of dominance has never seriously been challenged.

[30] Sayre and Kaufman, *op. cit.*, p. 640. For perceptive study of the "mobilization of bias" in a rural American community, see Arthur Vidich and Joseph Bensman, *Small Town in Mass Society* (Princeton, 1958).

PART FOUR

POLITICAL PARTIES AND ELECTIONS

Elections lie at the heart of the democratic process, and because in any large democracy political parties organize electoral competition, a vital party system is essential to democratic politics. On this general proposition, few political scientists would disagree. Opinions differ, however, as to exactly what a vital party system is; whether the United States still has one; and hence, how "democratic" American national elections will be with the passage of time.

In 1950, the American Political Science Association issued a famous report that called for thorough reform of the political parties to promote a "more responsible two-party system." By "more responsible," the authors meant an arrangement analogous to the British model, that is, a system with certain attributes. The parties would offer the electorate a clear choice between alternative platforms; the party garnering a popular majority in a general election could then claim the consent of the people when adopting its announced course of action; and representatives elected to office would deliver on their campaign promises. If the voters grew disenchanted with the governing party's program, they could withdraw their mandate by voting in the opposition at the next election. Until that time, however, the minority party would mostly be in a position to criticize government policies and to articulate alternatives, but not to frustrate continually, or compromise, the policies. Finally, to make the party system dependable and accountable in this fashion, the stature of party leaders would have to improve, the national party organizations would have to be strengthened, and greater party loyalty would have to be encouraged, principally by sharpening the programmatic differences between the contenders.

It is hard to think of a time in American history when the political parties closely approximated this ideal. (To be sure, there have been periods—the election of 1896, for instance—when the ideological breach between Democrats and Republicans was particularly wide. But seldom has party discipline in Congress, for example, resembled that in most European parliaments. Nor is it likely to. The separation of powers provides Congress and the presidency with different constituencies and functions that inevitably hinder party cohesion in ways parliamentary structures do not.) Nonetheless, at least until quite recently, party played a central role in American elections. Not only did the party organizations nominate candidates, simplify the choices before the public, and actively mobilize voters, but party identification also ran deep in the electorate. The large-scale voting study conducted by Angus Campbell and his associates at the University of Michigan's Survey Research Center during the 1950s discovered that no variable better predicted voting decisions than did party affiliation. According to the Michigan researchers' findings in *The American Voter* (a key portion of which follows), party attachments are formed early in life and internalized; once established, they tend to be remarkably stable. Only the most wrenching personal experiences (such as migrations, occupational shifts, or fundamental changes in one's social milieu) or cataclysmic historical events (e.g., the Civil War, the Great Depression) could be expected to alter partisan orientations.

Yet, by the 1970s it became apparent that a dramatic change had occurred— party affiliation was no longer the decisive predictor of the vote it had been formerly. In their analysis of recent data, Norman Nie, Sidney Verba, and John Petrocik depict a pattern of voting behavior that contrasts markedly with that portrayed in the Michigan study. Reporting the results of their research in an important book titled, appropriately, *The Changing American Voter*, these writers conclude that voter preferences now seem much more closely tied to attitudes on issues than in the past. Paradoxically, the novel propensity toward "issue-voting" has not been associated with a consolidation of party constituencies or a reaffirmation of partisan attachments. On the contrary, the proportion of the electorate not identified with either party has increased strikingly, as has the proportion of people identified with a party who are willing to vote for the opposite party. These developments have been enhanced by the emerging tendency of the system to field presidential candidates whose ideological stances are relatively unambiguous. Contrary to what proponents of "responsible" parties might expect, clarifications of party postures do not appear to have bolstered the organizations, nor to have deepened their grass roots. Indeed, some observers argue that the rise of issue-conscious candidates and voters has sometimes resulted in presidential contests so unbalanced as to render the victor less accountable and the system, consequently, perhaps less democratic.

Are the political parties decaying? The conclusion that Walter Dean Burnham draws in our final selection is that they are. Burnham, however, goes further. According to him, elections since the nineteenth century have exhibited a more or less continuous drop in voter participation, a rise in ticket splitting, and an increased incidence of voter "drop off" (the tendency of voters to take an interest only in "prestige" offices, not in lesser races). To Burnham, these basic trends signify more than just the decline of partisan politics; they imply growing voter apathy. Ultimately, Burnham fears that an apathetic electorate could become increasingly vulnerable to totalitarian or quasi-totalitarian appeals.

Actually, the thesis that the electorate is more apolitical now than it once was is the subject of considerable controversy among historians. The higher turnouts of the nineteenth century, for instance, may well have been more illusory than real. Votes were much more easily manipulated then: the political parties printed the ballots and often took part in counting them; ballots were commonly cast in public, not in the privacy of voting booths; few efforts were made to determine who was eligible to vote; opportunities for fraud and for padding the totals abounded. Similarly, ticket splitting may be more an artifact of the modern "office-bloc" ballot (adopted by most states in the wake of the Progressive reform movement) than it is an indication of voter fickleness or inexorable partisan disintegration. In short, not only are forecasts about the future of American electoral politics necessarily murky, but our understanding of past electoral dynamics is often far from exact.

13

ANGUS CAMPBELL, PHILIP E. CONVERSE,
WARREN E. MILLER, DONALD E. STOKES

THE DEVELOPMENT
OF PARTY IDENTIFICATION

ORIGINS OF PARTY IDENTIFICATION

When we examine the evidence on the manner in which party attachment develops and changes during the lifetime of the individual citizen, we find a picture characterized more by stability than by change—not by rigid, immutable fixation on one party rather than the other, but by a persistent adherence and a resistance to contrary influence.

Early Politicization

At the time we meet the respondents of our surveys they have reached the minimum voting age, and most of them are considerably beyond it. The only information we can obtain about their political experience in their pre-adult years depends on their recall. Hyman's review of the literature on "political socialization" brings together the available data to extend our understanding of this important stage of political growth.[1] It is apparent from his presentation that an orientation toward political affairs typically begins before the individual attains voting age and that this orientation strongly reflects his immediate social milieu, in particular his family.

Our own data are entirely consistent with this conclusion. The high degree of correspondence between the partisan preference of our respondents with that which they report for their parents may be taken as a rough measure of the extent to which partisanship is passed from one generation to the next.[2] This correspondence is somewhat higher among those people who report one or both of their parents as having been "actively concerned" with politics than among those whose parents were not politically active. If we make the reasonable assumption that in the "active" homes the political views of the parents were more frequently and intensely cognized by the children than in the inactive homes, we should of course expect to find these views more faithfully reproduced in these children when they reach adult years. In contrast, we find that persons from inactive homes, especially those with no clear political orientation, tend strongly toward nonpartisan positions themselves. For a large proportion of the electorate the orientation toward politics expressed in our measure of party identification has its origins in the early family years. We are not able to trace the history of these families to find an explanation of why the homes of some people were politically oriented and others were not. Such homes appear to exist in all social strata, less frequently in some than in others, of course.

The Persistence of Partisanship

The extent to which pre-adult experience shapes the individual's political future may be judged from the constancy with which most people hold to the partisan orientation they have at the time they enter the electorate. When we ask people to recall their first presidential vote, for example, we discover that of those who can remember their first vote for President two thirds still identify with the same party they first voted for. A majority (56 per cent) of these presidential voters have never crossed party lines; they have always supported their party's candidate.

A direct assessment of the stability with which the average citizen holds to his political orientation may be obtained from his report on whether he has ever identified himself differently than he does at present. The picture is generally one of firm but not immovable attachment. The greatest mobility (32%) is found among those people whose party attachment is weakest; the strongly identified are least likely to have changed sides (only 7% of strong Democrats, and 15% of strong Republicans).

It is apparent from these various pieces of evidence that identification with political parties, once established, is an attachment which is not easily changed. Some members of the electorate do not form strong party attachments, however, and they make up a sufficiently large proportion of the population to permit the short-term influence of political forces associated with issues and candidates to play a significant role in determining the outcome of specific elections. Even strong identifiers are not impervious to such influences, and, as we shall see, occasional cataclysmic national events have had the power to produce substantial realignment in long-standing divisions of political sentiment.

Changes in public attitudes may be classified according to the type of stimulus that produces them. We may speak of *personal forces*, which move individuals selectively without reference to the larger social categories to which they belong, or of *social forces*, which move large sections of the population more or less simultaneously. Personal forces produce changes that vary in an uncorrelated way from individual to individual and do not have a significant impact on the prevailing pattern of attitudes, even though the total proportion of people shifting their position may be sizable. Social forces influence large numbers of people in similar ways and may produce substantial realignments of the total distribution of attitudes.[3]

Changes Produced by Personal Forces

A variety of circumstances in the life of the ordinary citizen have political significance for him as a person without having any accompanying implications for broader groups. When we examine the reports of those of our respondents who shifted parties for reasons that appear to be entirely individual, we find that their change in partisanship tended to be associated with a change in their social milieu. A marriage, a new job, or a change in neighborhood may place a person under strong social pressure to conform to political values different from his own. Close personal relationships are usually associated with common political identifications in American society, and discrepancies tend to create strain, especially if the conflicting political views are strongly held.

Of the 20 per cent of our respondents who say they have changed party affiliation during their lifetime only about one in six explains this change as a result of personal influence. Considering the high degree of mobility in American society, one might have anticipated that changes of this kind would be more numerous. The movements of large numbers of people from the farm to the city, from the city to the suburbs, from region to region, and from one employment situation to another undoubtedly result in profound differences in their manner of living. But none of these movements necessarily implies a change in one's immediate surroundings. As we know, there are large representations of both parties at virtually all social and occupational levels and it would not be surprising for a person of either political persuasion to find himself among copartisans in almost any new situation into which he moved. We would, in fact, expect him to seek out such associates. Only in certain special groups, such as labor union members in mass industry in Northern metropolitan centers or high income business owners and executives, do we find such strong consensus of political belief that a dissenter might find himself in a lonely position.

Changes Produced by Social Forces

Although the changes resulting from purely personal circumstances may be expected to occur about as often in one partisan direction as the other, changes brought about by experiences shared in common are likely to be cumulative. If these experiences are sufficiently intense and sufficiently widespread, their political consequences may be profound.

Social forces create cumulative changes, but these changes need not disturb the prevailing balance of party strength. If the stimulus to which the public is subjected strikes different segments of the electorate in ways that have contrasting political implications, the resulting shifts in partisanship may change the makeup of each party's support without altering the relative proportions supporting each party. The impact of social forces may also have quite a different character, producing systematic movements from one party to the other that are not offset by movements in the opposite direction. There are two general types of public experience that appear to have this quality: those experiences associated with great national crises and, less obviously, those associated with progress through the life cycle. There have been two occasions when national crises have shaken prevailing political loyalties so violently that they reversed the balance of party strength throughout the country.

The political upheaval associated with the Civil War imposed a regional dimension on the partisan attachments of the American electorate. The violent reaction in the East and Midwest to the passage of the Kansas-Nebraska Act in 1854 led to the creation of the Republican Party, committed to resisting the extension of the "great moral, social, and political evil" of slavery. The Free Soil movement, taken up as a major principle by the Republican Party, and the Homestead Act of 1862 created a resource of rural Republican strength throughout the Northern and Western areas. Within a short period the political contours of the nation had been drastically reshaped. The South, which in prewar years had divided its votes in proportions similar to those of the North, became the Solid South. Northern communities that had been Democratic turned Republican and remained so for decades. The distribution of partisan attachments in the nation today, a century after the Civil War, follows the same regional lines laid down at that time.

The second national crisis that reshaped the political profile of the nation took place during the lifetime of most of our respondents, and we can see directly the impact of that event in their lives. The economic collapse that befell the nation during the administration of Herbert Hoover swept out of office a party that had dominated national politics since the election of William McKinley in 1896. The scope of the reversal of the party fortunes that followed 1932 is amply documented by the election statistics. In the early years of the New Deal there was a swing to the Democratic ticket, which was felt in varying degrees throughout the country. The tide then receded, and those areas that had been centers of Republican strength returned to Republican majorities. But the Republican Party did not regain the national majority that it had obviously had prior to 1932. When we ask from what levels of society the Democratic Party drew this new strength, we find from our survey data and from the aggregative election figures that the impact of the events of that period appears to have been felt most strongly by the youth, the economically underprivileged, and the minority groups.

YOUTH Our inquiries into the political histories of our respondents lead us to believe that a larger component of the Democratic gain came from young voters entering the electorate and older people who had previously failed to vote than from Republicans who defected from their party.

A demonstration of the impact of the depression on the people reaching voting age at that time is given in Fig. 13-1. We have here arrayed our respondents by age group according to the party identification they reported at the time of our interview with them. Those members of the present electorate who came of age during the 1920's have a lower proportion of Democratic identifiers than do any of the groups that entered the electorate in later years. The sharp increase in Democratic identification among those who reached their majority at the end of

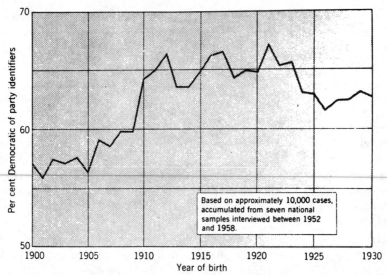

FIG. 13-1.   PARTY IDENTIFICATION OF PARTY IDENTIFIERS BORN BETWEEN 1900 AND 1930

this decade or during the early 1930's does not represent the total shift toward the Democratic Party at that time, but it does show the proportion of that shift that has persisted over the intervening years to the present time.

ECONOMIC GROUPS   The appeal of the New Deal was unquestionably strongly economic in character; it had, after all, been brought into being in the midst of the greatest economic catastrophe in American history. Mr. Roosevelt spoke about the "forgotten man" and sponsored a program of social legislation that his critics regarded as outright socialism. It is difficult to estimate how much influence all this had on the economic composition of the followings of the two parties, but it can be said with assurance that the economic and class distinctions between the two parties increased during this period. Such associations as had existed prior to the Depression between the less favored sections of the electorate and the Democratic Party were undoubtedly greatly enhanced.

On the basis of extensive analysis of the election returns from 1932 and 1936 Key offers these "educated guesses." "The policies of the New Deal brought in 1936 substantial new support from their beneficiaries. Metropolitan, industrial workers turned in heavy Democratic majorities. The unemployed, and those who feared they might become unemployed, voted Democratic in higher degree. Organized labor moved more solidly into the Democratic ranks."[4]

Our surveys do not go backward in time sufficiently for us to follow the political changes at the various economic levels during the Depression period, but the impact of the Depression is unmistakable in the images of the parties that we find in the public mind long after that tragic decade had passed. The association of the Republican Party with economic depression was one of the strongest features of the picture the public held of that party at the time of our 1952 study. Through their twenty years out of office the Republican Party could not erase the memory that lingered in many minds of the hardships of the Depression nor rid itself of the onus of responsibility for them.

MINORITY GROUPS   The impact of the Depression and the New Deal was not exclusively economic. The philosophy of the Roosevelt Administration contained a strong element of social equalitarianism, which gave it a special appeal to religious and racial minorities who had reason to feel themselves discriminated against. Catholics have had a long history of association with the Democratic Party. During the Eisenhower elections there were substantial defections among Catholics to the Republican nominee, but even at that time Catholics were more likely (5–2) to consider themselves Democrats than Republicans.

The Jewish minority comprises one of the most Democratic groups to be found in the electorate; Democratic Jews outnumber Republican Jews in the order of 4–1. During the 1920's the vote in heavily Jewish districts of the Eastern metropolises ran as high as 80 per cent Republican.[5] Although vote is not the same as party identification, it can scarcely be doubted that the orientation of this group toward the two parties was substantially altered during the 1930's. We may surmise that the rise of the Nazi dictatorship in Germany and the opposition of the Roosevelt Administration to it must have played an important role in this change. Whatever the cause, the shift of Jewish allegiances to the Democratic Party was one of the most impressive of the several group movements in political preference during the Roosevelt period.

Prior to the 1930's, so far as we can tell from election statistics, the prevailing political preference among Negroes was Republican. This was a consequence, of course, of the Civil War and the attachment of Negroes to the party of Lincoln. During the 1930's politics took on a different significance to the Negro tenth of the electorate. It is impossible to know whether the shift of Negro allegiances to the Democratic standard from the traditions inherited from earlier generations occurred as the reactions of individual Negroes to the personalities and events of the times or as a mass movement resulting largely from the mobilization of Negro sentiment by an articulate leadership. No doubt both of these circumstances were present. In any case, the conversion of Negroes to the Democratic Party was very substantial. During the Eisenhower period Democratically identified Negroes outnumbered Republican Negroes by a margin of 3–1.

We turn now to a class of changes in party identification that does not depend on the dramatic impact of national catastrophes but on the gradual and commonplace changes in life situations that occur as one grows older. The fact that the successive phases of the life cycle are associated with a certain degree of common experience for most members of our society means that we may expect to find systematic changes in attitudes and behavior associated with changes in age. Such age-related changes are clearly present in the political orientation of the American electorate.

INTENSITY OF IDENTIFICATION We find a steady increase in strong party attachments as we move through successive age levels, demonstrating the presence of age-related influences that are obviously not random. Young people, just entering the electorate, are more likely than any of the older age groups to call themselves Independents. This proportion drops among people in their late twenties and thirties and is accompanied by a proportionate increase in the number of strong identifiers. The older half of the electorate are clearly more likely to show a strong party attachment, with the most extreme position of all held by those people over 65 years old, a group that now constitutes approximately one twelfth of our adult population; 50 per cent of this age group are strong party identifiers, compared with 24 per cent of those 21 to 24 years of age.

We may now consider the way in which identification with political parties develops over the lifetime of the individual elector. Most people learn the party labels and something of what they mean during the early years when they are living with their parents. As young adults they are not overly interested in politics, they are indifferent voters, and they do not typically regard themselves as strongly attached to the political parties. As the young adult passes through the early egocentric years, however, the salience that political matters have in his life gradually increases. This happens for a variety of reasons. He is, for one thing, drawn into close association with social groups of one kind or another, some of which may have strong political orientations. He becomes aware of their political interests and he absorbs their interests as his own. It is also likely that as he becomes a more fully integrated community member he becomes more aware of the immediate implications for him of political decisions.

In addition, since political affairs become more familiar to a person as he matures, they seem less distant and unrealistic. The number of people who become politically active themselves, either as candidates or as party workers of one kind or another, is very small, but a much larger number of people acquire a certain familiarity with political goings on, and it seems likely that this fact is associated with an increasing identification of oneself with the party symbols.

Finally, for some people politics and parties may take on reality only as the result of some personal or national crisis. For example, many apparently inert people were stimulated to vote for the first time during the early years of the Great Depression. The Korean War appears to have activated several million people who had sat out the previous elections. On a more personal basis a business failure, a bad crop year, the loss of a job, or an encounter with the law may create a need for action and a sharpening of interest in what can be accomplished through political channels. Crises of large or small magnitude occur repeatedly during the lifetime of the ordinary citizen and serve to keep him alive to his role in the total political process.

Once a person has acquired some embryonic party attachment, it is easy for him to discover that most events in the ambiguous world of politics redound to the credit of his chosen party. As his perception of his party's virtue gains momentum in this manner, so his loyalty to it strengthens, and this fact in turn increases the probability that future events will be interpreted in a fashion that supports his partisan inclination. There are limits on the extent to which reality can be distorted to fit expectations and preferences, and exceptionally critical circumstances may induce a party identifier to cross party lines for a single election in the spirit of "time for a change." It is even possible that the flow of events may place his party in such an unfavorable position as to bring an actual change in his identification. But this is unusual; more typically party identification is not only sustained but strengthened by the passing show of political acts and actors.

It is matter of particular interest that party identification does not decline in significance in the later years of life; on the contrary, strong party attachment is more common among people of retirement age than it is at any other period. A close look at the comparatively few people who have changed their party identification during adulthood has given us reason to believe that intensity of party identification is directly related to the length of time a person has felt some degree of attachment to his party. As we move through the successive age cohorts we are consequently more and more likely to find people who have had a long unbroken experience of party identification. Older people have had more time to accumulate tenure in their party association, even those who in their earlier years moved from one party to the other. As they settle in their ultimate choice and their tenure with it grows, they become increasingly rigidly attached to it and less and less susceptible to cross-party pressures.

PARTISANSHIP OF IDENTIFICATION   It remains now to consider one further aspect of the relationship of age to political orientation. Republican identification increases progressively from the younger to the older age groups; 8 per cent of the 21–24 age group were strong Republican identifiers, compared with 24 per cent of those over 65 years old.

This peculiarity of the distribution of party identification presents an interesting question that we cannot fully answer. Is the Republican Party gradually aging and being replaced by a party that has captured the bulk of the young people coming into the electorate? If party identification is typically a life-long commitment, changed on the national scale only by major social cataclysms, it would be reasonable to conclude that the present age division in party identification is the consequence of the Depression and the New Deal and that the present Republican following must inevitably decrease as time replaces the older age groups with the younger groups in which people of Democratic commitment are more numerous.

To this explanation, however, one may oppose the hypothesis that the two parties have different appeals to people of different ages, and although the Democratic Party may have an advantage in its appeal to young people, this advantage may be gradually dissipated as these young Democrats grow older and respond differently to political stimuli. It would seem likely in a society in which the Republican Party was widely perceived as conservative and middle-class and the Democratic Party as liberal and working-class that the two parties would not be equally attractive to the older and younger members of the electorate.

If we examine in detail the reports of individual political history, we find that there was a substantial shift of party attachments during the New Deal period, most of it toward the Democratic Party. In each of the four-year periods during the last twenty years, however, there has been additional shifting, balancing out in each case to a relatively small advantage to the Republican Party. These findings lead us to doubt the proposition that either of the major parties is likely to expire as the result of old age. The great break toward the Democratic Party at the beginning of the Depression undoubtedly split the electorate along age lines. This split appears to have been maintained in the ensuing years by the heavy proportion of young people who declared themselves for the Democratic Party as they entered the electorate, but it has been offset by the Republican advantage in cross-party conversions among those in the older age brackets. During the 1950's these two components of the total following of the two parties appeared to balance each other very closely. Both the proportions of the electorate identifying themselves with each party and the age composition of each party's adherents remained constant throughout this period.

NOTES

[1] Herbert Hyman, *Political Socialization* (The Free Press, Glencoe, Ill., 1959).

[2] There are obvious weaknesses in this measure. Some of our respondents had undoubtedly carried an "inherited" party identification into early adulthood but had changed by the time we interviewed them.

[3] This formulation closely resembles a model for the explanation of attitude changes developed by George Katona. See his "Attitude Change: Instability of Response and Acquisition of Experience" (*Psychological Monographs*, Vol. 72, No. 10; Washington, D. C.: American Psychological Association, Inc., 1958).

[4] V. O. Key, *Politics, Parties and Pressure Groups* (4th ed., Thomas Y. Crowell Company, New York, 1958), p. 578.

[5] Lawrence H. Fuchs, *The Political Behavior of American Jews* (The Free Press, Glencoe, Ill., 1956), p. 56. See also Oscar Handlin, *The Uprooted* (Boston, Mass.: Little, Brown, 1951), p. 216.

14

NORMAN H. NIE, SIDNEY VERBA,
JOHN R. PETROCIK

THE RISE OF ISSUE VOTING

The role of party has declined as a guide to the vote. And, as party has declined in importance, the role of issues appears to have risen. These changes are not independent of each other. The following abstract analysis, into which we later place some data, helps us understand some of the dynamics of party- and issue-guided voting.

PARTY VOTING

The main rule of party voting is simple: when there is a choice between the candidate of the party with which you identify and the opposition party, vote for your party's candidate. Party voting therefore requires that:

1. A voter have a party identification. He or she must prefer one or the other of the two parties. This preference must be a relatively long-term preference; one that extends across elections. In some countries, party identification appears to be coterminus with voting intention; if a person is going to vote for or has just voted for the candidate of a party he will almost always say he identifies with that party.[1] But for there to be party voting, it must also be possible to vote in a way that deviates from the party; it must be meaningful to say "I am a Democrat, but I voted for a Republican."

2. The candidates must be from different parties, otherwise one cannot choose on the basis of party. There is no party vote in the Democratic primary.

3. The individual must use the party affiliation as the criterion (or at least as a major criterion) for choice. It is not always easy to tell whether this is the case. If someone who calls himself a Democrat votes for the Democratic candidate, that does not necessarily indicate that he voted that way for party reasons—he might have flipped a coin. But we can use the voting behavior of an aggregate of people who identify with the Democratic party to see if their behavior is consistent with the hypothesis that they vote on the basis of party. And we can go further and ask them why they voted as they did; or . . . ask them why they like a candidate and record whether they mention his party.

The notion of a party vote also implies that:

4. A voter with no party identification cannot vote on the basis of party. Thus

the growth in the number of Independents automatically reduces the number who can give a party vote.

5. A candidate not identified with one of the major parties cannot receive a party vote. This is an oversimplification, of course. Someone who has a long-term identification with the Socialist party and votes for the Socialist candidate gives a party vote. Furthermore, a candidate without the official nomination of one of the main parties may still be perceived by voters to be the candidate of that party. One can argue, as does Schneider, that Wallace in 1968 was perceived by many southern Democrats as the mainstream Democratic candidate, though this was not the case with northern democrats.[2] But for our purposes, a party vote will be considered to be a vote for one of the major party candidates.

ISSUE VOTING

Issue voting is analogous to party voting, but somewhat more complicated. The main rule of issue voting is similar to that for party voting: if there is an issue A and two positions on that issue (A_1 and A_2), the voter who prefers one of the two positions will vote for the candidate who holds that same position. Issue voting therefore requires:

1. That the individual have a preference for either A_1 or A_2 (just as he had to have a party identification for a party vote). Furthermore, just as party identification has to be more than a mere reflection of how one intends to vote or had just voted, so the issue preference of the individual must be more than a mere reflection of his preference for one candidate over the other. If the voter adopts an issue position because his preferred candidate adopts it, he will appear to cast an issue vote but it will not in fact be one.

2. The candidates must offer a choice on the issues. One candidate must support A_1, the other A_2; or one must support one of the positions and the other be neutral. If a candidate supports A_1 and the other takes no position, voters with issue positions can still vote on that basis: voters who prefer A_1 will vote for the candidate who also prefers it, and those who prefer position A_2 will vote for the neutral candidate. But if both candidates support the same position or are both neutral, issue voting is impossible.[3]

Issue voting, however, offers a number of complexities not found in party voting. For one thing, issues do not always offer clear dichotomous choices of A_1 versus A_2 as is the choice between the Republican and Democratic parties. There may be many possible positions on the issue. Sometimes the issue positions can be thought of as points along a continuum: the amount we ought to spend for defense can range from zero dollars to the total GNP, and we can imagine citizens with preferences somewhere along the continuum that runs from one point to the other. If there were such a continuum, we could change the general rule of issue voting to read: vote for the candidate whose position on the continuum is closest to your own. In figure 14-1, voter *a* votes for candidate 1; voter *c* for candidate 2. Voter *b* is close to an indifference point (he cannot make an issue vote if he is equidistant between the two candidates), but he is a touch

168   *Nie, Verba, and Petrocik*

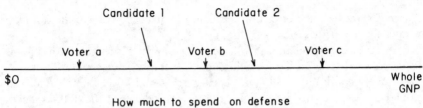

How much to spend on defense
FIGURE 14-1. HYPOTHETICAL ISSUE CONTINUUM

closer to candidate 1 and an issue vote would go to him. Note the important point: a voter has to be closer to one candidate than another to make an issue vote. The closer the two candidates are to each other, the more difficult is it to make such a vote. If the candidates do not differ, issue voting is impossible.

A second complexity is that issue positions may not always line up along a continuum. What should we do if there is an embargo on oil shipments by OPEC? Invade the Persian Gulf? Drastically reduce our energy consumption? Stop our support to Israel in the hope that OPEC will resume oil shipments? The three positions do not form a neat continuum, nor are they mutually exclusive. Casting an issue vote becomes more complicated under these circumstances, but it is still possible: vote for the candidate whose mix of positions is closest to your own.

Third, a more complicated situation arises when there is more than one relevant issue. Assume that there are two issues in an election, and each is equally salient to a voter. An issue voter would vote for the candidate who was closer to him on the two-dimensional plane defined by the two issues. Consider figure 14-2. Voter *a* should vote for candidate 1 if he casts an issue vote. Though he is closer to candidate 2 on issue A (candidate 1 is more liberal than voter *a* on that) he is further from candidate 2 on issue B than he is from candidate 1 on issue A. Voter *b*, on the other hand, is closer to candidate 2 on both issues and should vote for him if he casts an issue vote. The two-issue case can be extended to the three- or four-issue case. For our purposes what is important is the illustration this gives as to why issue consistency increases the potential for issue voting.

Issue consistency converts the two-dimensional space defined by the two-issue continuum into one dimension. This is illustrated in figure 14-3. If citizens take consistent positions across two issues, it means that they are found in the upper left (consistent liberal) and lower right (consistent conservative) positions. The greater the proportion of the citizenry with consistent positions, the more the issue space can be accurately simplified by the heavy line joining those two positions. As our analysis of issue consistency has shown, more citizens fall on that line after 1964 than before. . . .

Let us assume that candidates as well fall somewhere along the heavy line of issue consistency—that is, that they are likely to be consistent liberals, consistent middle of the roaders, or consistent conservatives. For the purpose of our argument, it is not necessary that they fall exactly on the line, but simply that

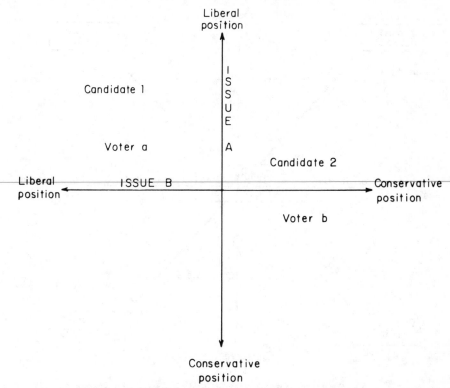

FIGURE 14-2. HYPOTHETICAL ISSUE CONTINUUM INVOLVING TWO ISSUES

they be closer to the line than is the average citizen (that is, that there is more "constraint" in their issue positions than there is on the part of the citizenry).

If candidates fall on that line, the proportion of citizens who give an issue vote (who are unambiguously closer to one candidate than another) will increase the more citizens there are on that line. For example, suppose candidate 1 is running against candidate 4 (a consistently liberal candidate versus a consistently conservative one—see figure 14-3). Citizens at either end of the liberal-conservative continuum have unambiguous issue choices. Consistent liberals will vote for candidate 1; consistent conservatives will vote for candidate 4. If there are some citizens who take a middle of the road position on both issues, they will not be able to choose between candidates 1 and 4 on the issues. They are equidistant between the two candidates. This is true as well for those citizens who have strong but "criss-cross" positions on the issues—that is, they are liberal on one issue and conservative on the other. Citizens in those positions (in the lower left and upper right of figure 14-3) are equidistant between the candidates 1 and 4 and cannot cast an issue vote.

As another example, suppose consistently liberal candidate 1 runs against candidate 3 who is a middle of the roader a touch to the right of center. Again the choice for the consistent liberals and consistent conservatives is fairly clear. In this case, the middle of the roaders have an issue choice as well—they are

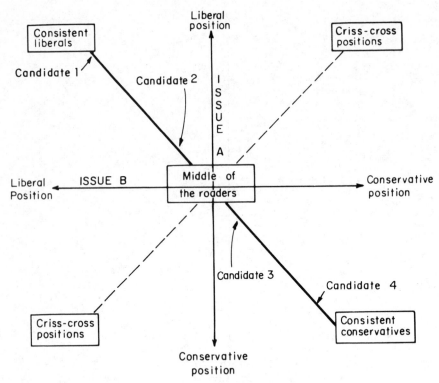

FIGURE 14-3.   VOTERS AND CANDIDATES ON A TWO-ISSUE SPACE

closer to candidate 3. The criss-crossed voter is also somewhat closer to candidate 3 but the distinction between candidate 3 and candidate 1 in terms of closeness is not as great as is the case for citizens on the liberal-conservative continuum. The citizen who is liberal on issue B but conservative on issue A likes candidate 1's position on the former, and dislikes his position on the latter. He is fairly indifferent to candidate 3's position on both issues. The situation is by no means as clear to him as it is to almost all citizens on the liberal-conservative continuum—especially to those at the ends of the continuum.

This is illustrated in figure 14-4. The consistent liberal is closer to candidate 1 by the full distance along the liberal-conservative continuum between candidates 1 and 3, the same is true for the consistent conservatives. But the criss-crossed voter is closer to candidate 3 than he is to candidate 1 by a smaller amount—the difference between lines x and y.

Lastly, consider a race between candidates 2 and 3 (on figure 14-3). Both are close to the middle of the road. Insofar as there is little issue distance between them, the opportunity for anyone to vote on an issue basis is reduced. But it should be clear from figure 14-4 that citizens at the consistent ends of the liberal-conservative continuum will be more sensitive to whatever difference exists between candidates 2 and 3 than will a citizen at one of the "criss-cross" positions.

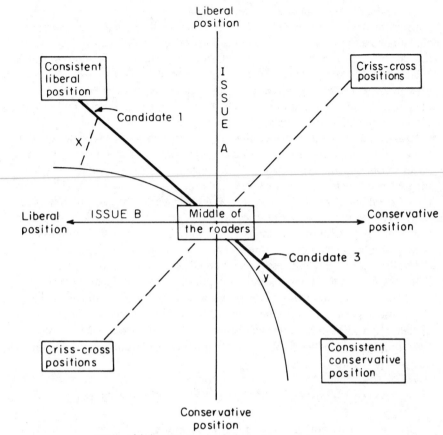

FIGURE 14-4.   ISSUE CONSISTENCY AND ISSUE DISTANCE

In sum, issue consistency has a potentially important impact on the voting decision. It simplifies the issue space for the voter and makes it easier for him to choose on the basis of his issue position. Voters with consistent issue positions will be more sensitive to the issue positions of candidates.

We have not paid much attention to issue salience. Another way in which a multiplicity of issues can be simplified is when one issue is overriding. In such a case, one has really returned to a single issue space for the voter who has an overriding issue.[4] There are, of course, many mixed circumstances—where one has multiple issues of varying salience and with varying degrees of consistency among them. These are important complexities, but ones we shall not explore.

One final complexity for issue voting: a good deal depends on the location of the candidates on the issues. Citizens with issue positions cannot vote those positions unless they are given a choice (consider the difficulty of issue voting when candidate 2 opposes candidate 3 as in figure 14-3). In this respect, issue voting differs from party voting.

The party affiliation of candidates is fairly clear and unambiguous. The major party candidates may fudge their party affiliation somewhat. They may make nonpartisan appeals or in other ways try to lower the salience of their party affiliation. However, in each of the elections since 1964 at least one candidate has taken a consistently liberal or conservative position: Goldwater in 1964; Wallace (as the third party candidate) in 1968; and McGovern in 1972. Thus, at least in these elections, the existence of a candidate with a position on the liberal-conservative continuum that is both unambiguous and fairly far from the center has facilitated issue voting.[5]

Lastly, there is some evidence that respondents consider candidates to have more consistent positions across a range of issues than the respondents themselves have. In the 1968 and 1972 election studies, respondents placed themselves on issue scales in connection with a number of issues. They also placed candidates on the same scales. We can measure the consistency of an individual's position across two issues by the "distance" between the positions he assigns himself on those two issues.[6] This can be compared with the distance between the positions he assigns to a candidate on the same pair of issues.

In all cases, respondents assign the candidates to more consistent positions than they choose for themselves. This applies to those candidates perceived as being at one or the other ends of the issue continuum—McGovern and Wallace. But it also applies to a candidate such as Nixon. He is placed a bit to the right of center by voters, on a number of issues. His position is thus that of a slightly right *consistent* middle of the roader. Thus he too would fall on the main diagonal on figure 14-3.

DATA ON ISSUE VOTING AND PARTY VOTING

Decline in party voting comes about in two ways: (1) the proportion of the electorate with no party affiliation has risen and, therefore, the proportion that can cast a party vote has fallen and (2) even among those who have a partisan identity, the proportion voting for the opposition party has grown. We have also seen . . . the rise in the number of citizens who can cast issue votes because they have consistent issue positions. As numerous analyses have demonstrated in recent years, there is a concomitant rise in the likelihood that they will vote in accord with their issue position.[7]

Figure 14-5 compares two correlations: the correlation between our summary index of attitudes and the direction of the presidential vote and the correlation between party identification and the vote.[8] Our concern is with changes in these correlations over time. The relationship between party identification and the vote is one with which we are familiar; from 1960, it falls precipitously. The square of the correlations reported in figure 14-5 tells us the proportion of variance in the vote that is explained by party identification. The variance explained was about 50 percent in 1956 and 1960; by 1972 it had fallen to 25 percent.

The contrast between the attitude/vote correlations and the party/vote correlations is dramatic. The relationship between issues and the voting decision rises

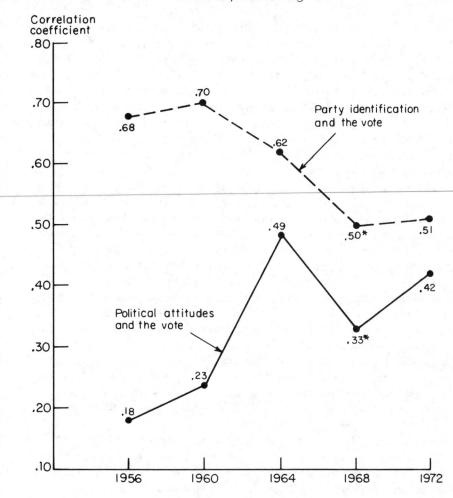

Correlation coefficient

* Weighted average of the correlation between attitudes and a Nixon/Humphrey choice, a Nixon/Wallace choice, and a Humphrey/Wallace choice.

FIGURE 14-5.   PEARSON CORRELATIONS BETWEEN PARTY IDENTIFICATION AND THE PRESIDENTIAL VOTE AND BETWEEN THE SUMMARY MEASURE OF POLITICAL BELIEFS AND THE PRESIDENTIAL VOTE, 1956–1972

sharply. In 1956, the correlation between issue position and the vote was .18. The correlation goes up dramatically in 1964 and remains substantially above the earlier years. In the pre-1964 period a citizen's position on the issues, as measured by our summary attitude scale, had little or no impact on the way in which he voted. Citizens on the left side of the scale were almost as likely to vote for a Republican as for a Democrat. Citizens on the right were almost as likely to vote Democratic as Republican. There was a small increase in the relationship between issue position and the vote in 1960, but the major shift seems to have come between 1960 and 1964. From 1964 on, there is a considerable association between left-right issue position and direction of the presidential vote.

We think it important that three major changes occur during the same time period, between the 1960 and 1964 elections. These are the increase in consistency among attitudes themselves, the increased relationship between attitudes and the vote, and the decreased relationship between party identification and the vote. The data suggest that the American public has been entering the electoral arena since 1964 with quite a different mental set than was the case in the late 1950s and early 1960s. They have become more concerned with issues and less tied to their parties.

There is substantial controversy in the political science literature as to what issue voting is and how one measures it. The increased correlation of position on our issue scale and the vote is consistent with the hypothesis that issues play a larger role in the voting decision after 1964 than before. But it is not direct evidence that the voting choice was made with issues as one of the criteria. We can present, however, some data on this. We have presented some of these data earlier, though in a slightly different form. In each presidential election study, citizens were asked to list the things they liked or disliked about the opposing candidates. We have already seen that the frequency of reference to political party as a reason for liking or disliking a candidate has declined, while the frequency of reference to issues or ideological position has risen. In figure 14-6 we summarize both changes. We compare the proportion of responses that clearly refer to the candidate in party terms (that is, where the candidate is liked or disliked because of his party ties) with those responses that refer to a specific issue or issue area and add a third category of responses that refer to the personal traits and characteristics of the candidate.[9]

The data from these questions are particularly appropriate for examining the way in which the citizens think about an election. The questions are completely open-ended and the respondent spontaneously lists the type of characteristics which lead him to like or dislike each of the candidates.[10]

The changing importance of party and issues in the voting decision is very clear from the data. There are sharp changes in the frequency of reference to the issue positions of candidates and to their party ties. References to the former climb; references to the latter fall. In the first three elections, references to the party ties of the candidates are slightly (about 10 percent) less frequent than references to their issue position. There is, however, a sharp change in 1964. In that year, references to the issue positions of the candidates are 43 percent more frequent than references to party ties. And the gap remains as large in 1972. Or, to look at the data somewhat differently, in 1952 almost half of the respondents mentioned party ties as a reason for liking or disliking a candidate. By 1972, only about one in five mention party. In contrast, before 1964, about half of the respondents mentioned issues. After 1964, the proportion rises to about three out of four. Again the most significant change appears to take place between 1960 and 1964.

In contrast to the data on issues and parties, the frequency of reference to the personal characteristics of the candidates remains high and relatively stable, till

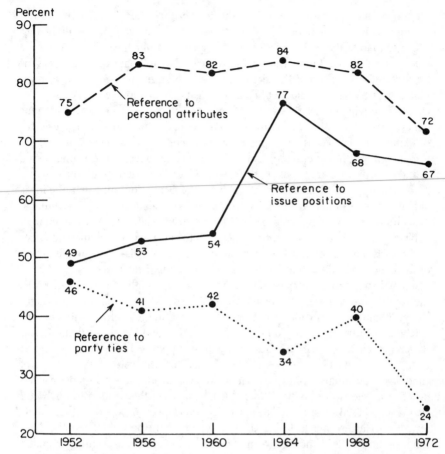

the 1972 election when there is some decline.[11] In short, there has been a significant change in the standards of evaluation invoked by citizens when they are asked about presidential candidates. In the pre-1964 elections, candidates were evaluated in terms of their personal characteristics and their party ties. After 1964, the party ties of the candidate receive less mention and evaluations depend more heavily on the issue position of the candidate, coupled with his personal characteristics. By 1972, more citizens mention the issue positions of the candidates when called on to evaluate them than mention either party ties or personal characteristics.

We can take these data one step further. Citizens use issues more frequently as a standard of candidate evaluation. But are those issue evaluations used as a basis of the vote? We test for the importance of issue evaluations as a basis of the voting decision in the following manner. For those respondents who mention the issue positions of one or both candidates when asked for evaluations of the candidates, we develop a score reflecting the extent to which the issue references are, on balance, favorable to one candidate over the other. (Those who do not mention issues are left out of the calculation.) Issues can be mentioned in response to four different questions: on the reasons for liking candidate A, on the reasons for disliking him, on the reasons for liking candidate B, on the reasons for disliking him. We use the fact that issues can be mentioned as a reason for liking or disliking a candidate to create our issue evaluation score. A couple of examples ought to make clear what we have done. Someone who mentions issues twice as a reason for liking candidate A and issues once as a reason for disliking candidate B has a net issue evaluation score of three in favor of A. If the respondent, on the other hand, had mentioned issues once as a reason for liking A and once as a reason for liking B, he would have a score of zero on our scale. The latter respondent uses issues as a standard of evaluation but when one looks at all the issue evaluations he gives, they do not on balance favor one candidate over the other. We developed parallel measures in relation to party references and personal references. The former measures the degree to which the references to the party affiliation of one or both candidates are on balance favorable to one of the candidates; the latter does the same for personal references.

These issue, party, and personal evaluation scores can then be correlated with the vote. In other words, we can ask whether the degree to which an individual's issue evaluations favor candidate A over B is related to the likelihood that he will vote for A rather than B. And we ask the same about party evaluation and personal evaluation. We plot these correlations in figure 14-7. Once again, the pattern in the data is quite clear. The impact on the vote of evaluations of candidates' personal attributes remains strong and relatively constant in each presidential election from 1952 to 1972. The data on the relationship between evaluations based on a candidate's party ties and the vote, on the other hand, reveal, once again, the declining salience of party in the post-1960 period. There is a drop in the correlation between 1964 and 1968 and an even more dramatic decline in 1972. Not only do citizens evaluate candidates less frequently in party terms in 1968 and 1972, but even among those who do make such party-based evaluations one cannot predict their vote on that basis as well as one could before 1964.

The pattern for issue-related references is in marked contrast. The correlations between issue evaluations and the vote remain relatively stable throughout the time period. Those who evaluated candidates in issue terms during the early years were as likely to vote in accord with those evaluations as are the issue evaluators in the later years. The difference, of course, is that there were many fewer issue evaluators in the earlier period.

The joint impact of the proportion of the electorate that uses the various evaluative criteria and the correlation between such evaluations and the vote is made apparent if we repeat the calculations reported on figure 14-7, but carry them out for all voters rather than for those who make the particular evaluation under question. In figure 14-7, for instance, we reported the correlation between the issue evaluation scores and the vote only for those who made some issue evaluation. In figure 14-8 we report the same correlation, but include those who make no issue evaluation in the calculation, scoring them as falling at the

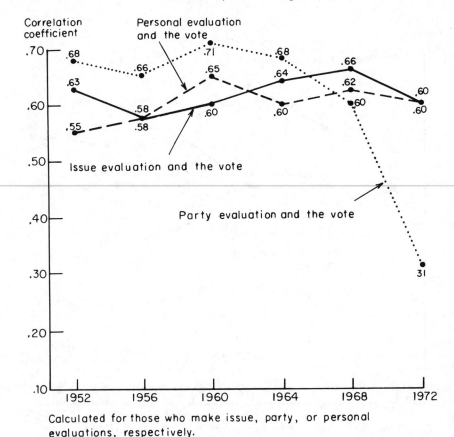

FIGURE 14-7.   PEARSON CORRELATIONS OF EVALUATIONS OF THE CANDIDATES IN TERMS OF PERSONAL TRAITS, PARTY TIES, AND ISSUE POSITIONS WITH THE PRESIDENTIAL VOTE, 1952–1972

neutral point of the scale. The effect of this is to increase the correlation when there are many who make issue evaluations and decrease it when few use issue criteria.

The comparison of the data on figure 14-8 with those on figure 14-7 is instructive. In both figures, the correlation of personal evaluations with the vote remains relatively steady throughout, reflecting the fact that both the proportion making such evaluations and the correlation of the evaluations with the vote are steady. The correlation of issue evaluations and the vote on figure 14-8, however, goes up between 1960 and 1964, reflecting the change in the proportion using issues as evaluative standards. This contrasts with the steady pattern on figure 14-7. Lastly, we observe an even more precipitous drop in the correlation of partisan evaluations and the vote, reflecting the declining proportion making such evaluations as well as the declining correlation of such evaluations with the vote.

The relationship between issue evaluations and the vote takes an interestingly

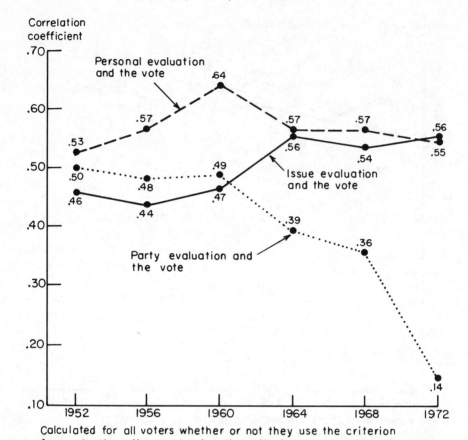

Calculated for all voters whether or not they use the criterion
for evaluation; those not using the criterion are considered neutral.

FIGURE 14-8.   PEARSON CORRELATIONS OF EVALUATIONS OF THE CANDIDATES IN TERMS OF
PERSONAL TRAITS, PARTY TIES, AND ISSUE POSITIONS WITH THE PRESIDENTIAL VOTE,
1952–1972

different shape from the relationship between party evaluations and the vote.
Over the two decade period, party evaluations have come to have less effect on
the vote for two reasons: fewer citizens make such evaluations and among those
who make them, the impact of the party evaluations on the vote goes down.
When it comes to issue evaluations, the increase in their impact on the vote
comes from the increased numbers who evaluate candidates in issue terms. If as
many people thought of candidates in issue terms during the earlier period, issue
evaluations would have been as potent a vote determining force in that period as
in the later period.

In this sense, the relationship of issue *evaluations* to the vote also differs from
the relationship of issue *position* (that is, the respondent's position on our
left-right attitude measure) to the vote. The impact of issue position on the vote
increases both because more citizens have coherent issue positions at one or the
other end of the issue spectrum and because the impact of those positions on

voting is greater. The data support an interesting speculation: that there has been less change in the way in which citizens use issues in relation to the vote than there is change in the kinds of issue positions that they have. Few citizens volunteered issues as reasons for liking or disliking candidates in the early years because the candidates did not present themselves in clear issue terms. However, for the voter who discerned some issue on the basis of which he could evaluate the candidates, the issue evaluation was as potent a force on the vote as were evaluations in later years. In contrast, the respondent's own issue position was not as potent a force in relation to the vote in the early years even among those who had coherent positions. The difference, we believe, has to do with the relationship between the voter's issue position and the positions presented by candidates.

Voters who use issues to evaluate candidates in response to the open-ended questions have selected issues important to them and on which they perceive the candidates to differ.[12] Fewer did this in early years, but those who did voted on that basis. Voters who have coherent issue positions on the left or the right, in contrast, cannot necessarily vote on the basis of those postions; they have to be given an issue choice by the candidate. In the earlier elections, this suggests, such choices were not offered to the public (or, at least, were not perceived by the public to be offered them). If voters in the later years vote in accord with issue position, it is because they are offered choices that allow them to do so.[13] In sum, the changes we observe appear to reflect an interaction between citizens and the choices they are offered. . . .

NOTES

[1] See David Butler and Donald E. Stokes, *Political Change in Britain* (New York: St. Martin's Press, 1969). This presumption that in most other countries voting and party preference is identical may be a result of an insensitivity to the different meaning assigned to similar phrases in different countries. It is at least possible that asking people if they are Conservative or Labour identifiers in Britain is not the equivalent of asking party identification in the United States. In the United States the party preference questions appear to inquire about whether the respondent prefers a party, while in England it may appear that the party identification questions are asking about formal membership in a party. The confusion between party identification and membership in a party can arise because dues paying membership in a party is as common to most party systems as it is infrequent in the United States.

[2] William Schneider, "Issues, Voting, and Cleavages," *American Behavioral Scientist*, 18 (September 1974), 111–146.

[3] This is the critical assumption of all studies of issue voting. See Anthony Downs, *An Economic Theory of Democracy* (New York: Harper & Row, 1957).

[4] On this see Sidney Verba and Norman H. Nie, *Participation in America* (New York: Harper & Row, 1972), chap. 7.

[5] Unambiguous issue positions among candidates and voters is the essential element for issue voting. In addition to Downs, *An Economic Theory of Democracy*, and Black, *The Theory of Committees and Elections*, a recent deductive model of voter choice is Otto Davis, Melvin H.

Hinch, and Peter C. Ordershook, "An Expository Development of a Mathematical Model of the Electoral Process," *American Political Science Review*, 64 (June 1970), 426–448. A more plausible empirical analysis is in M. J. Shapiro, "Rational Political Man, A Synthesis of Economic and Social Psychological Perspectives," *American Political Science Review*, 63 (December 1969), 1106–1119. The most sophisticated discussion of candidate positions in relation to voter choice is found in Benjamin I. Page, *Choices and Echoes in Presidential Elections* (Chicago: University of Chicago Press, 1978).

⁶ The scales have to be adjusted so that the liberal answer is always at the same end of the scale.

⁷ There is a considerable amount of research literature which attempts an estimate of issue voting. The bibliography in John Kessel, "Comment: The Issues in Issue Voting," *American Political Science Review*, 66 (June 1972), 459–465, is as complete a list as one will find, and Kessel offers some worthy observations on the topic. The assessment of issue voting versus party voting is cleverly done in Richard W. Boyd, "Popular Control of Public Policy: A Normal Vote Analysis of the 1968 Election," *American Political Science Review*, 66 (June 1972), 429–449. Although the published research is too voluminous to cite here, special attention might be paid to assessments of issue voting following the themes developed by David E. Repass, "Issue Salience and Party Choice," *American Political Science Review*, 65 (June 1971), 389–400, and David G. Lawrence, *Issue Voting and Demand Failure in American Presidential Elections: 1952–1968*, Ph.D. dissertation, University of Chicago, 1975. An excellent treatment is in Gerald Pomper, *The Voter's Choice* (New York: Dodd Mead, 1975), chap. 8.

⁸ We assume that the Democratic candidate is on the left, the Republican candidate on the right. Thus a positive correlation means that citizens on the liberal end of the issue scale are more likely to vote for the Democratic candidate, citizens at the conservative end more likely to vote Republican. The assumption of the position of the major party candidates since 1956 is, we believe, a realistic one, and is confirmed by all data we can find on the perception of citizens of the issue location of candidates.

In 1968, there is the complexity of the Wallace candidacy. In general, we have treated him as a candidate to the right of Nixon. The correlation between issue position and the vote for 1968, reported in figure 14-5, is an average of three correlations between issue position on the one hand and a Humphrey/Nixon, Humphrey/Wallace, and Nixon/Wallace choice, with the second-named candidate the concervative candidate in each pair.

⁹ Note in examining the data presented in this figure that respondents may give more than one of these three types of responses.

¹⁰ The merit of using the open-ended like-dislike questions to do this kind of analysis is argued in Repass, "Issue Salience and Party Choice," and in Lawrence, *Issue Voting and Demand Failure*. Other analyses using corresponding measures include: Angus Campbell and others, *The Voter Decides* (Evanston: Row-Peterson, 1954); Angus Cambell and others, *The American Voter* (New York: Wiley, 1960); Donald Stokes and Warren E. Miller, "Components of Electoral Decision," *American Political Science Review*, 52 (June 1958), 369–387; and Angus Campbell and Donald Stokes, "Partisan Attitudes and the Presidential Vote," in Eugene Burdick and Arthur J. Brodbeck, eds., *American Voting Behavior* (New York: Free Press, 1959), 353–371. Chapters 7, 8, and 9 use the same data differently in doing an analysis of attitudes and ideological conceptualization. For a longitudinal analysis of the vote choice using these particular data, see Donald E. Stokes, "Dynamic Elements of Contents for the Presidency," *American Political Science Review*, 60 (March 1966), 19–28.

¹¹ The decline in the proportion making personal references to candidates in 1972 does not mean that such personal evaluations were unimportant in that year. Quite the contrary. The decline in personal references involves largely a decline in positive references. Negative evaluations of the candidates—particularly of McGovern—were frequent and had an impact on the vote. See Arthur Miller and others, "A Majority Party in Disarray," paper presented at the Annual Meeting of the American Political Science Association, New Orleans, September 1974, pp. 53–54.

¹² Repass, "Issue Salience and Party Choice," shows how issue voting is greater if one uses as the measure of issue position the issue that the respondent chooses as most important.

¹³ We must add a note of caution. The data do not eliminate the alternative causal explanation: that people adopt issue positions to suit their already-selected voting choice—that is, if they prefer a

candidate (for whatever reason) they will accept his issue preferences. As Richard Brody and Benjamin Page point out, it is difficult if not impossible to choose between the two causal directions with the kinds of data available. The convergence of the data from the open-ended and closed questions leads us to believe that we are observing a real increase in the impact of issue position on the voting choice. But even if the causal direction were to run the other way, we could still conclude that issues had grown in importance. At minimum, it would mean that citizens after 1964 felt greater necessity to adopt issue positions consistent with their favored candidates or were more likely to rationalize their preference for a candidate in issue terms. We think we can say something stronger than that. But even if people are rationalizing, they are doing it on an issue basis much more than used to be the case. See Benjamin I. Page and Richard A. Brody, "Policy Voting and the Electoral Process: The Vietnam Issue," *American Political Science Review*, 66 (September 1972), pp. 979–995.

15

WALTER DEAN BURNHAM

THE CHANGING SHAPE OF THE AMERICAN POLITICAL UNIVERSE

. . . Even the crudest form of statistical analysis makes it abundantly clear that the changes which have occurred in the relative size and shape of the active electorate in this country have not only been quantitatively enormous but have followed a directional course which seems to be unique in the contemporary universe of democratic politics. In the United States these transformations over the past century have involved devolution, a dissociation from politics as such among a growing segment of the eligible electorate and an apparent deterioration of the bonds of party linkage between electorate and government. More precisely, these trends were overwhelmingly prominent between about 1900 and 1930, were only very moderately reversed following the political realignment of 1928–1936, and now seem to be increasing once again along several dimensions of analysis. Such a pattern of development is pronouncedly retrograde compared with those which have obtained almost everywhere else in the Western world during the past century.

Probably the best-known aspect of the changing American political universe has been the long-term trend in national voter turnout: a steep decline from 1900 to about 1930, followed by a moderate resurgence since that time.[1] As the figures in Table 15-1 indicate, nationwide turnout down through 1900 was quite high by contemporary standards—comparing favorably in presidential years with recent levels of participation in Western Europe—and was also marked by very low levels of drop-off. A good deal of the precipitate decline in turnout after 1896 can, of course, be attributed to the disfranchisement of Negroes in the South and the consolidation of its one-party regime. But as Table 15-2 and Fig. 15-1 both reveal, non-Southern states not only shared this decline but also have current turnout rates which remain substantially below 19th-century levels.[2]

The persistence of mediocre rates of American voting turnout into the present political era is scarcely news. It forms so obvious and continuing a problem of our democracy that a special presidential commission has recently given it intensive study.[3] Two additional aspects of the problem, however, emerge from a perusal of the foregoing data. In the first place, it is quite apparent that the political realignment of the 1930s, while it restored two-party competition to

TABLE 15-1. DECLINE AND PARTIAL RESURGENCE: MEAN LEVELS OF NATIONAL TURNOUT
AND DROP-OFF BY PERIODS, 1848–1962*

Period (Presidential Years)	Mean Estimated Turnout	Period (Off-Years)	Mean Estimated Turnout	Mean Drop-Off
	(%)		(%)	(%)
1848–1872	75.1	1850–1874	65.2	7.0
1876–1896	78.5	1878–1898	62.8	15.2
1900–1916	64.8	1902–1918	47.9	22.4
1920–1928	51.7	1922–1930	35.2	28.7
1932–1944	59.1	1934–1946	41.0	27.8
1948–1960	60.3	1950–1962	44.1	24.9

* Off-year turnout data based on total vote for congressional candidates in off years.

many states outside the South, did not stimulate turnout to return in most areas to 19th-century levels. Even if the mere existence of competitiveness precludes such low levels of turnout as are found in the South today, or as once prevailed in the northern industrial states, it falls far short of compelling a substantially full turnout under present-day conditions. Second, drop-off on the national level has shown markedly little tendency to recede in the face of increases in presidential-year turnout over the last thirty years. The component of peripheral voters in the active electorate has apparently undergone a permanent expansion from about one-sixth in the late 19th century to more than one-quarter in recent decades. If, as seems more than likely, the political regime established after 1896 was largely responsible for the marked relative decline in the active voting universe and the marked increase in peripherality among those who still occasionally voted, it is all the more remarkable that the dramatic political realignment of the 1930s has had such little effect in reversing these trends.

At least two major features of our contemporary polity, to be sure, are obviously related to the presently apparent ceiling on turnout. First, the American electoral system creates a major "double hurdle" for prospective voters which does not exist in Western Europe: the requirements associated with

TABLE 15-2. SECTIONALISM AND PARTICIPATION: MEAN TURNOUT IN SOUTHERN AND
NONSOUTHERN STATES IN PRESIDENTIAL ELECTIONS, 1868–1960

Period	Mean Turnout: 11 Southern States	Period	Mean Turnout: Non-Southern States
	(%)		(%)
1868–1880	69.4	1868–1880	82.6
1884–1896	61.1	1884–1896	85.4
1900 (transition)	43.4	1900	84.1
1904–1916	29.8	1904–1916	73.6
1920–1948	24.7	1920–1932	60.6
1952–1960	38.8	1936–1960	68.0

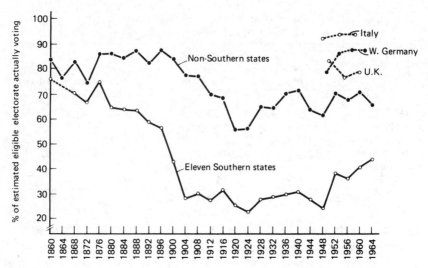

FIG. 15-1.   PATTERNS OF TURNOUT: UNITED STATES, 1860–1964, BY REGION, AND SELECTED WESTERN EUROPEAN NATIONS, 1948–1961

residence and registration, usually entailing periodic reregistration at frequent intervals, and the fact that elections are held on a normal working day in this employee society rather than on Sundays or holidays.[4] Second, it is very probably true that 19th-century elections were major sources of entertainment in an age unblessed by modern mass communications, so that it is more difficult for politicians to gain and keep public attention today than it was then.[5] Yet if American voters labor under the most cumbersome sets of procedural requirements in the Western world, this in itself is a datum which tends to support Schattschneider's thesis that the struggle for democracy is still being waged in the United States and that there are profound resistances within the political system itself to the adoption of needed procedural reforms.[6] Moreover, there are certain areas—such as all of Ohio outside the metropolitan counties and cities of at least 15,000 population—where no registration procedures have ever been established, but where no significant deviation from the patterns outlined here appears to exist. Finally, while it may well be true that the partial displacement by TV and other means of entertainment has inhibited expansion of the active voting universe during the past generation, it is equally true that the structure of the American voting universe—*i.e.*, the adult population—as it exists today was substantially formed in the period 1900–1920, *prior* to the development of such major media as the movies, radio and television.

As we move below the gross national level, the voting patterns discussed above stand out with far greater clarity and detail. Their divergences suggest something of the individual differences which distinguish each state subsystem from its fellows, as their uniformities indicate the universality of the broader secular trends. Five states have been selected for analysis here. During the latter part of the 19th century two of these, Michigan and Pennsylvania, were originally competitive states which tended to favor the Republican Party. They developed solidly one-party regimes after the realignment of 1896. These regimes were overthrown in their turn and vigorous party competition was restored in the wake of the New Deal realignment. In two other states, Ohio and New York, the 1896 alignment has no such dire consequences for two-party competition on the state level. These states have also shown a somewhat different pattern of development since the 1930s than Michigan and Pennsylvania. Our fifth state is Oklahoma, where a modified one-party system is structured heavily along sectional lines and operates in a socio-economic context unfavorable to the classic New Deal articulation of politics along ethnic-class lines of cleavage.

Michigan politics was marked from 1894 through 1930 by the virtual eclipse of a state Democratic Party which had formerly contested elections on nearly equal terms with the Republicans. The inverse relationships developing between this emergent one-partyism on the one hand, and both the relative size of the active voting universe and the strength of party linkage on the other, stand out in especially bold relief.

A decisive shift away from the stable and substantially fully mobilized voting patterns of the 19th century occurred in Michigan after the realignment of 1896, with a lag of about a decade between that election and the onset of disruption in those patterns. The first major breakthrough of characteristics associated with 20th-century American electorates occurred in the presidential year 1904, when the mean percentage Democratic for all statewide offices reached an unprecedented low of 35.6 and the rate of split-ticket voting jumped from almost zero to 17.1 per cent. A steady progression of decline in turnout and party competition, accompanied by heavy increases in the other criteria of peripherality, continued down through 1930.

The scope of this transformation was virtually revolutionary. During the civil-war era scarcely 15 per cent of Michigan's potential electorate appears to have been altogether outside the voting universe. About 7 per cent could be classified as peripheral voters by Campbell's definition, and the remainder—more than three-quarters of the total—were core voters. Moreover, as the extremely low 19th-century level of split-ticket voting indicates, these active voters overwhelmingly cast party-line ballots. By the 1920s, less than one-third of the potential electorate were still core voters, while nearly one-quarter were peripheral and nearly one-half remained outside the political system altogether. Drop-off and roll-off increased sixfold during this period, while the amplitude of partisan swing approximately doubled and the split-ticket-voting rate increased by a factor of approximately eight to twelve.

For the most part these trends underwent a sharp reversal as party competition in Michigan was abruptly restored during the 1930s and organized in its contemporary mode in 1948. As the mean Democratic percentage of the two-party vote increased and turnout—especially in off-year elections—showed a marked relative upswing, such characteristics of marginality as drop-off, roll-off, split-ticket voting and partisan swing declined in magnitude. Yet, as the means for the 1948–1962 period demonstrate, a large gap remains to be closed before anything like the *status quo ante* can be restored. Our criteria—except, of course, for the mean percentage Democratic of the two-party vote—have

TABLE 15-3. MICHIGAN, 1854–1962: DECAY AND RESURGENCE?

| Period | Mean Turnout | | Mean Drop-Off | Mean Roll-Off | Mean Split-Ticket Voting | Mean Partisan Swing | Mean % D of 2-Party Vote |
	PRES. YEARS	OFF-YEARS					
	(%)	(%)	(%)	(%)	(%)	(%)	
1854–1872	84.8	78.1	7.8	0.9	0.8	3.2	43.9
1878–1892	84.9	74.9	10.7	0.8	1.6	2.2	48.0
1894–1908	84.8	68.2	22.3	1.5	5.9	4.7	39.6
1910–1918	71.4	53.0	27.2	3.0	9.8	4.1	40.4*
1920–1930	55.0	31.5	42.9	6.0	10.0	7.3	29.8
1932–1946	63.6	47.3	25.9	6.7	6.0	7.4	47.9
1948–1962	66.9	53.6	19.1	4.1	5.8	4.9	51.0

* Democratic percentage of three-party vote in 1912 and 1914.

returned only to the levels of the transitional period 1900–1918. As is well known, exceptionally disciplined and issue-oriented party organizations have emerged in Michigan since 1948, and elections have been intensely competitive throughout this period.[7] In view of this, the failure of turnout in recent years to return to something approaching 19th-century levels is all the more impressive, as is the continuing persistence of fairly high levels of drop-off, roll-off, and split-ticket voting.[8]

The Michigan data have still more suggestive implications. Campbell's discussion of surge and decline in the modern context points to a cyclical process in which peripheral voters, drawn into the active voting universe only under unusual short-term stimuli, withdraw from it again when the stimuli are removed. It follows that declines in turnout are accompanied by a marked relative increase in the component of core voters in the electorate and by a closer approximation in off years to a "normal" partisan division of the vote.[9] This presumably includes a reduction in the level of split-ticket voting as well. But the precise opposite occurred as a secular process—not only in Michigan but, it would seem, universally—during the 1900–1930 era. Declines in turnout were accompanied by substantial, continuous increases in the indices of party and voter peripherality among those elements of the adult population which remained in the political universe at all. The lower the turnout during this period, the fewer of the voters still remaining who bothered to vote for the entire slate of officers in any given election. The lower the turnout in presidential years, the greater was the drop-off gap between the total vote cast in presidential and succeeding off-year elections. The lower the turnout, the greater were the incidence of split-ticket voting and the amplitude of partisan swing. Under the enormous impact of the forces which produced these declines in turnout and party competitiveness after 1896, the component of highly involved and party-oriented core voters in the active electorate fell off at a rate which more than kept pace with the progressive shrinking of that electorate's relative size. These developments necessarily imply a limitation upon the usefulness of the surge-decline model as it relates to secular movements prior to about 1934. They suggest, moreover, that the effects of the forces at work after 1896 to depress voter

TABLE 15-4. VOTING PATTERNS IN PENNSYLVANIA, 1876–1962:
DECLINE AND RESURGENCE?

Period	Mean Turnout		Mean Drop-Off	Mean Roll-Off	Mean Split-Ticket Voting	Mean Partisan Swing	Mean % D of 2-Party Vote
	PRES. YEARS	OFF-YEARS					
	(%)	(%)	(%)	(%)	(%)	(%)	
1876–1892	78.5	69.3	9.4	0.6	0.6	1.4	47.7
1894–1908	75.7	64.7	12.2	5.2	1.3	6.3	38.5
1910–1918	64.0	51.4	20.0	4.3	4.7	5.8	43.6*
1920–1930	50.4	39.5	28.0	5.2	8.9	7.1	32.8
1932–1948	61.5	51.9	14.9	2.2	1.4	6.1	49.0
1950–1962	67.5	56.3	12.2	1.8	3.1	3.3	49.3

* Combined major anti-Republican vote (Democrat, Keystone, Lincoln, Washington).

participation and to dislocate party linkage between voters and government were even more crushingly severe than a superficial perusal of the data would indicate.

Pennsylvania provides us with variations on the same theme. As in Michigan, the political realignment centering on 1896 eventually converted an industrializing state with a relatively slight but usually decisive Republican bias into a solidly one-party G.O.P. bastion. To a much greater extent than in Michigan, this disintegration of the state Democratic Party was accompanied by periodic outbursts of third-party ventures and plural party nominations of major candidates, down to the First World War. Thereafter, as in Michigan, the real contest between competing candidates and political tendencies passed into the Republican primary, where it usually remained until the advent of the New Deal. In both states relatively extreme declines in the rate of turnout were associated with the disappearance of effective two-party competition, and in both states these declines were closely paralleled by sharp increases in the indices of peripherality.

As Table 15-4 demonstrates, the parallel behavior of the Michigan and Pennsylvania electorates has also extended into the present; the now-familiar pattern of increasing turnout and party competition accompanied by marked declines in our other indices has been quite visible in the Keystone State since the advent of the New Deal. On the whole, indeed, a better approximation to the *status quo ante* has been reached in Pennsylvania than in Michigan or perhaps in most other states. But despite the intense competitiveness of its present party system, this restoration remains far from complete.

A more detailed examination of turnout and variability in turnout below the statewide level raises some questions about the direct role of immigration and woman suffrage in depressing voter participation. It also uncovers a significant transposition of relative voter involvement in rural areas and urban centers since about 1930.

It is frequently argued that declines in participation after the turn of the century were largely the product of massive immigration from Europe and of the advent of woman suffrage, both of which added very large and initially poorly

TABLE 15-5. DIFFERENTIALS IN AGGREGATE TURNOUT AND VARIATIONS OF TURNOUT IN
SELECTED PENNSYLVANIA COUNTIES: PRESIDENTIAL ELECTIONS, 1876–1960*

County and Type	N	% Foreign Stock, 1920	1876–1896		1900–1916		1920–1932		1936–1960	
			MEAN TURNOUT	COEF. VAR.	MEAN TURNOUT	COEF. VAR.	MEAN TURNOUT	COEF. VAR.	MEAN TURNOUT	COEF. VAR.
Urban:		(%)	(%)		(%)		(%)		(%)	
Allegheny	1	56.6	71.8	6.75	56.7	2.45	43.8	10.11	68.9	5.82
Philadelphia	1	54.3	85.2	4.61	72.9	6.42	50.5	12.57	68.8	4.40
Industrial-Mining:	4	49.9	88.1	4.48	72.8	4.41	54.2	11.63	64.7	10.88
Rural:	8	13.5	88.5	3.12	76.4	3.63	56.0	8.09	65.2	13.20

* The coefficient of variability is a standard statistical measure; see V. O. Key, Jr., A Primer of Statistics for Political Scientists (New York, 1954), pp. 44–52. Since secular trends, where present, had to be taken into account, this coefficient appears abnormally low in the period 1900–1916. During this period many counties registered a straight-line decline in turnout from one election to the next.

socialized elements to the potential electorate.[10] There is no question that these were influential factors. The data in Table 15-5 indicate, for example, that down until the Great Depression turnout was consistently higher and much less subject to variation in rural counties with relatively insignificant foreign-stock populations than in either the industrial-mining or metropolitan counties.

Yet two other aspects of these data should also be noted. First, the pattern of turnout decline from the 1876–1896 period to the 1900–1916 period was quite uniform among all categories of counties, though the rank order of their turnouts remained largely unchanged. It can be inferred from this that, while immigration probably played a major role in the evolution of Pennsylvania's political system as a whole, it had no visible direct effect upon the secular decline in rural voting participation. Broader systemic factors, including but transcending the factor of immigration, seem clearly to have been at work. Second, a very substantial fraction of the total decline in turnout from the 1870s to the 1920s—in some rural native-stock counties more than half—occurred *before* women were given the vote. Moreover, post-1950 turnout levels in Pennsylvania, and apparently in most other non-Southern states, have been at least as high as in the decade immediately preceding the general enfranchisement of women. If even today a higher percentage of American than European women fail to come to the polls, the same can also be said of such population groups as the poorly educated, farmers, the lower-income classes, Negroes and other deprived elements in the potential electorate.[11] In such a context woman suffrage, as important a variable as it certainly has been in our recent political history, seems to raise more analytical problems than it solves.

Particularly suggestive for our hypothesis of basic changes in the nature of American voting behavior over time is the quite recent transposition of aggregate turnout and variations in turnout as between our rural sample and the two metropolitan centers. In sharp contrast to the situation prevailing before 1900, turnout in these rural counties has tended during the past generation not only to

TABLE 15-6. URBAN-RURAL DIFFERENCES IN STABILITY OF POLITICAL INVOLVEMENT: 1936–1960 MEAN TURNOUT AND VARIABILITY OF TURNOUT AS PERCENTAGES OF 1876–96 MEAN TURNOUT AND VARIABILITY OF TURNOUT, PENNSYLVANIA

County and Type	N	1936–60 Turnout / 1876–96 Turnout	1936–60 Variability / 1876–96 Variability
		(%)	(%)
Urban:			
Allegheny	1	95.9	86.2
Philadelphia	1	80.8	95.4
Industrial-Mining:	4	73.4	249.6
Rural:	8	73.7	447.4

be slightly lower than in the large cities but also subject to far wider oscillations from election to election. In Bedford County, for example, turnout stood at 82.5 per cent in 1936, but sagged to an all-time low of 41.2 per cent in 1948. The comparable figures in Philadelphia were 74.3 and 64.8 per cent, and in Allegheny County 72.5 per cent (in 1940) and 60.6 per cent.

A major finding revealed by survey research is that the "farm vote" is currently one of the most unstable and poorly articulated elements in the American electorate.[12] It is said that since rural voters lack the solid network of group identifications and easy access to mass-communication media enjoyed by their city cousins, they tend to be both unusually apathetic and exceptionally volatile in their partisan commitments. As rural voting turnout was abnormally low in 1948, its rate of increase from 1948 to 1952 was exceptionally large and—fully consistent with Campbell's surge-decline model—was associated with a one-sided surge toward Eisenhower. A restatement of the data in Table 15-5 lends strong support to this evaluation of the relative position of the rural vote as a description of the *current* American voting universe.

But the data strongly imply that virtually the opposite of present conditions prevailed during the 19th century. Such variables as education level, communications and non-family-group interaction were probably much more poorly developed in rural areas before 1900 than they are today. Not only did this leave no visible mark on agrarian turnout; it seems extremely likely that the 19th-century farmer was at least as well integrated into the political system of that day as any other element in the American electorate. The awesome rates of turnout which can be found in states like Indiana, Iowa and Kentucky prior to 1900 indicate that this extremely high level of rural political involvement was not limited to Pennsylvania.[13] As a recent study of Indiana politics demonstrates, the primarily rural "traditional vote" in that state was marked prior to 1900 by an overwhelming partisan stability as well.[14]

Perhaps, following the arguments of C. Wright Mills and others, we can regard this extraordinary change in rural voting behavior as a function of the conversion of a cracker-barrel society into a subordinate element in a larger mass society.[15] In any event, this rural movement toward relatively low and widely fluctuating levels of turnout may well be indicative of an emergent political alienation in such areas. It is suggestive that these movements have been

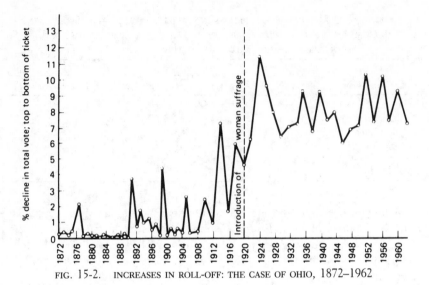

FIG. 15-2.   INCREASES IN ROLL-OFF: THE CASE OF OHIO, 1872–1962

accompanied generally in Pennsylvania as in states like West Virginia by a strongly positive Republican trend in these agrarian bailiwicks during the last thirty years.[16] The impression arises that the political realignment of the 1930s, which only imperfectly mobilized and integrated urban populations into the political system, had not even these limited positive effects in more isolated communities.

The behavior of the Ohio electorate down to about 1930 closely paralleled the patterns displayed in its neighbor states, Michigan and Pennsylvania. Since then a marked divergence has been manifest.

Two-party competition here was far less seriously affected by the sectional political alignment of 1896–1932 than in most other northern industrial states. Of the eighteen gubernatorial elections held in Ohio from 1895 to 1930, for example, Democrats won ten. But here as elsewhere are to be found the same patterns of decline in turnout and sharp increases in indices of voter peripherality after 1900. Indeed, while turnout bottomed out during the 1920s at a point considerably higher than in Michigan or Pennsylvania, it had also been considerably higher than in either of them during the 19th century. Here too such variables as woman suffrage seem to have played a smaller role as causal agents—at least so far as they affected the growing tendencies toward peripherality among active voters—than is commonly supposed. Drop-off from presidential to off-year elections began to assume its modern shape in Ohio between 1898 and 1910. As Figure 15-2 shows, roll-off—an especially prominent feature in contemporary Ohio voting behavior—emerged in modern form in the election of 1914.

Ohio, unlike either Michigan or Pennsylvania, has demonstrated only an extremely limited resurgence since the realignment of the 1930s. Presidential-year voting turnout in the period 1948–60 actually declined from the mean level of 1932–44, and was not appreciably higher than it had been in the trough of the

TABLE 15-7. PATTERNS OF VOTER PARTICIPATION IN OHIO, 1857–1962: DECLINE
WITHOUT RESURGENCE?

| Period | Mean Turnout | | Mean Drop-Off | Mean Roll-Off | Mean Split-Ticket Voting |
	PRES. YEARS	OFF-YEARS			
	(%)	(%)			
1857–1879	89.0	78.4	9.7	0.6	0.5
1880–1903	92.2	80.5	11.2	0.8	0.6
1904–1918	80.4	71.2	9.2	2.5	3.3
1920–1930	62.4	45.8	24.1	7.9	9.9
1932–1946	69.9	49.1	27.2	7.6	6.5
1948–1962	66.5	53.3	19.0	8.2	11.1

1920s. If mean drop-off has declined somewhat in recent years, it still stands at a level twice as high as in any period before 1920. Moreover, roll-off and the rate of split-ticket voting have actually increased to unprecedented highs since 1948. By 1962 the latter ratio touched an all-time high of 21.3% (except for the three-party election of 1924), suggesting that Ohio politics may be becoming an "every-man-for-himself" affair. This pattern of behavior stands in the sharpest possible contrast to 19th-century norms. In that period turnout had reached substantially full proportions, drop-off was minimal and well over 99 per cent of the voters cast both complete ballots and straight party tickets—an achievement that may have been partly an artifact of the party ballots then in use.[17] The political reintegration which the New Deal realignment brought in its wake elsewhere has scarcely become visible in Ohio.

Two recent discussions of Ohio politics may shed some light upon these characteristics. Thomas A. Flinn, examining changes over the past century in the partisan alignments of Ohio counties, concludes that until the first decade of

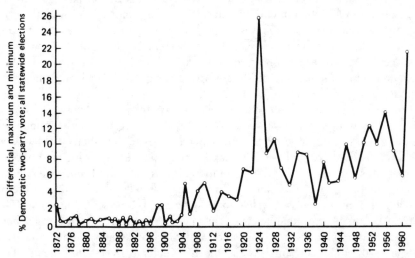

FIG. 15-3. INCREASES IN SPLIT-TICKET VOTING: THE CASE OF OHIO, 1872–1962.

the 20th century the state had a set of political alignments based largely on sectionalism within Ohio—a product of the diverse regional backgrounds of its settlers and their descendants. This older political system broke down under the impact of industrialization and a national class-ethnic partisan realignment, but no new political order of similar coherence or partisan stability has yet emerged to take its place.[18] Flinn's findings and the conclusions which Lee Benson has drawn from his study of New York voting behavior in the 1840s are remarkably similar.[19] In this earlier voting universe the durability of partisan commitment and the extremely high levels of turnout appear to have had their roots in a cohesive and persistent set of positive and negative group referents. These, as Flinn notes, provided "no clear-cut class basis for statewide party following from the time of Jackson to that of Wilson."[20]

John H. Fenton, discussing the 1962 gubernatorial campaign, carries the argument one step further.[21] Basic to Ohio's social structure, he argues, is an unusually wide diffusion of its working-class population among a large number of middle-sized cities and even smaller towns. The weakness of the labor unions and the chaotic disorganization of the state Democratic Party seem to rest upon this diffusion. Ohio also lacks agencies which report on the activities of politicians from a working-class point of view, such as have been set up by the United Automobile Workers in Detroit or the United Mine Workers in Pennsylvania or West Virginia. The result of this is that to a much greater extent than in other industrial states, potential recruits for a cohesive and reasonably well-organized Democratic Party in Ohio live in an isolated, atomized social milieu. Consequently they tend to vote in a heavily personalist, issueless way, as the middle and upper classes do not. Such a state of affairs may provide clues not only for the relative failure of voter turnout to increase during the past generation, but for the persistent and growing indications of voter peripherality in Ohio's active electorate as well.

The development of the voting universe in New York is more analogous to the situation in Ohio than in either Michigan or Pennsylvania. In New York, as in Ohio, two-party competition was not as dislocated by the 1896–1930 alignment as a hasty survey of the presidential-election percentages during that period might suggest. Democrats remained firmly in control of New York City, and this control helped them to capture the governorship eight out of eighteen times from 1896 through 1930. There were other parallels with Ohio as well, for here too this persistence of party competition did not prevent the normal post-1896 voting syndrome from appearing in New York. Nor has there been any pronounced resurgence in turnout levels or convincing declines in the other variables since the 1930s. Drop-off, roll-off, split-ticket voting and partisan swing are not only quite high in New York by 19th-century standards, but have been twice as great as in neighboring Pennsylvania during the past decade. This relative failure of political reintegration is revealed not only by the data presented in Table 15-8 but—in much more dramatic fashion—by the rise and persistence of labor-oriented third parties which are centered in New York City and have enjoyed a balance-of-power position between the two major party establishments. The existence of the American Labor and Liberal Parties, as well as the continuing

TABLE 15-8. NEW YORK VOTING PATTERNS, 1834–1962: DECLINE WITHOUT RESURGENCE?

Period	Mean Turnout (Pres. Years)	Mean Drop-Off	Mean Roll-Off	Mean Split-Ticket Voting	Mean Partisan Swing	Mean % D of 2-Party Vote
	(%)	(%)	(%)	(%)	(%)	
1834–1858	84.8	3.3	1.6	1.2	1.7	50.9*
1860–1879	89.3	7.9	0.4	0.6	2.6	50.1
1880–1898	87.9	10.4	1.2	1.6	5.0	50.5
1900–1908	82.5	8.3	1.1	2.2	3.7	47.2
1910–1918	71.9	10.9	5.1	3.3	3.8	46.2
1920–1930	60.4	17.3	5.5	9.5	8.3	49.6
1932–1946	71.3	22.5	4.9	3.4	3.2	53.2†
1948–1962	67.8	20.6	3.6	6.5	5.8	47.3†

* Elections from 1854 to 1858 excluded because of major third-party vote.

† The American Labor Party, 1936–46, and the Liberal Party, 1944–62, are included in Democratic vote when their candidates and Democratic candidates were the same.

vitality of anti-Tammany "reform" factions, are vocal testimony to the failure of the old-line New York Democratic Party to adapt itself successfully to the political style and goals of a substantial portion of the urban electorate.

Curiously enough, examination of the data thus far presented raises some doubt that the direct primary has contributed quite as much to the erosion of party linkages as has been often supposed.[22] There seems to be little doubt that it has indeed been a major eroding element in some of the states where it has taken root—especially in states with partially or fully one-party systems where the primary has sapped the minority party's monopoly of opposition. But comparison of New York with our other states suggests the need of further concentrated work on this problem. After a brief flirtation with the direct primary between 1912 and 1921, New York resumed its place as one of the very few states relying on party conventions to select nominees for statewide offices, as it does to this day. Despite this fact, the post-1896 pattern of shrinkage in turnout and increases in our other indices of political dissociation was virtually the same in New York as elsewhere. To take a more recent example, New York's split-ticket-voting ratio was 16.1 per cent in 1962, compared with 21.3 in Ohio, 7.1 in Michigan and 6.8 per cent in Pennsylvania. The overall pattern of the data suggests that since 1932 the latter two states may have developed a more cohesive party politics and a more integrated voting universe with the direct primary than New York has without it.

If the data thus far indicate some link between the relative magnitude of voter non-participation and marginality with the cohesiveness of the local party system, even greater secular trends of the same sort should occur where one of the parties has continued to enjoy a perennially dominant position in state politics. Oklahoma, a border state with a modified one-party regime, tends to support such an assumption.[23] The relatively recent admission of this state to the union naturally precludes analysis of its pre-1896 voting behavior. Even so, it is quite clear that the further back one goes toward the data of admission, the closer one comes to an approximation to a 19th-century voting universe. In Oklahoma,

TABLE 15-9. VOTER PERIPHERALITY AND PARTY DECAY? OKLAHOMA, 1907–1962

Period	Mean Turnout (Off-Years)	Mean Drop-Off	Mean Roll-Off*	Mean Split-Ticket Voting*	% of State and Congressional Elections Uncontested by Republicans	
					PER CENT	MEAN N†
	(%)	(%)	(%)	(%)		
1907–1918	52.9	12.1	6.1	3.6	2.1	32
1922–1930	40.1	13.0	13.9	9.7	2.1	31
1934–1946	37.1	32.2	16.4	8.1	14.8	32
1950–1962	44.5	26.3	14.0	10.5	41.3	29

* Roll-off and split-ticket voting are computed for contested elections only.
† Mean number of state and congressional races in each off-year election.

curiously enough, the secular decline in turnout and increases in the other indices continued into the New Deal era itself, measured by the off-year elections when—as in a growing number of states[24]—a full slate of statewide officers is elected. Since 1946 very little solid evidence of a substantial resurgence in turnout or of major declines in drop-off, roll-off or split-ticket voting has appeared, but there is some evidence that the minority Republican Party is atrophying.

The magnitude of drop-off and roll-off has become relatively enormous in Oklahoma since the 1920s, with a very slight reduction in both during the 1950–1962 period. While turnout has correspondingly increased somewhat since its trough in the 1934–1946 period, at no time since 1914 have as many as one-half of the state's potential voters come to the polls in these locally decisive off-year elections. Still more impressive is the almost vertical increase in the proportion of uncontested elections since the end of World War II. The 1958 and 1962 elections, moreover, indicate that the trend toward decomposition in the Republican party organization and its linkage with its mass base is continuing. In 1958 the party virtually collapsed, its gubernatorial candidate winning only 21.3 per cent of the two-party vote. Four years later the Republican candidate won 55.5 per cent of the two-party vote. The resultant partisan swings of 34.2 per cent for this office and 22.0 for all contested statewide offices was the largest in the state's history and one of the largest on record anywhere. But while 1962 marked the first Republican gubernatorial victory in the state's history, it was also the first election in which the Republican Party yielded more than half of the statewide and congressional offices to its opposition without any contest at all. Even among contested offices, the Oklahoma electorate followed a national trend in 1962 by splitting its tickets at the unprecedented rate of 17.3 per cent.

As Key has suggested, the direct primary has almost certainly had cumulatively destructive effects on the cohesion of both parties in such modified one-party states as Oklahoma.[25] The rapidly spreading device of "insulating" state politics from national trends by holding the major state elections in off years has also probably played a significant role. Yet it seems more than likely that these are variables which ultimately depend for their effectiveness upon the

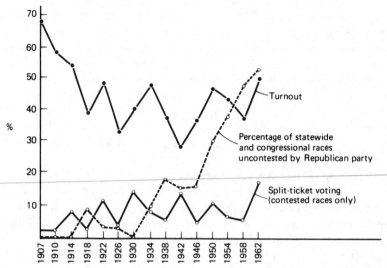

FIG. 15-4.   PATTERNS OF POLITICAL EVOLUTION: THE CASE OF OKLAHOMA, 1907–1962

nature of the local political culture and the socio-economic forces which underlie it. Pennsylvania, for example, also has a direct-primary. Since 1875, it has also insulated state from national politics by holding its major state elections in off years. Yet since the realignment of the 1930s, both parties have contested every statewide office in Pennsylvania as a matter of course. Indeed, only very infrequently have elections for seats in the state legislature gone by default to one of the parties, even in bailiwicks which it utterly dominates. [26]

These five statewide variations on our general theme suggest, as do the tentative explorations below the statewide level in Pennsylvania, that an extremely important factor in the recent evolution of the voting universe has been the extent to which the imperatives of the class-ethnic New Deal realignment have been relevant to the local social structure and political culture. In the absence of an effectively integrating set of state political organizations, issues and candidates around which a relatively intense polarization of voters can develop, politics is likely to have so little salience that very substantial portions of the potential electorate either exclude themselves altogether from the political system or enter it in an erratic and occasional way. As organized and articulated in political terms, the contest between "business" and "government" which has tended to be the linchpin of our national politics since the 1930s has obviously made no impression upon many in the lowest income strata of the urban population. It has also failed to demonstrate sustained organizing power in areas of rural poverty or among local political cultures which remain largely pre-industrial in outlook and social structure.

The conclusions which arise directly out of this survey of aggregate data and indices of participation seem clear enough. On both the national and state levels they point to the existence and eventual collapse of an earlier political universe in the United States—a universe in many ways so sharply different from the one we all take for granted today that many of our contemporary frames of analytical reference seem irrelevant or misleading in studying it. The late 19th-century voting universe was marked by a more complete and intensely party-oriented voting participation among the American electorate than ever before or since. Approximately two-thirds of the potential national electorate were then "core" voters, one-tenth fell into the peripheral category, and about one-quarter remained outside. In the four northern states examined in this survey the component of core elements in the potential electorate was even larger: about three-quarters core voters, one-tenth peripherals and about 15 per cent non-voters.

In other ways too this 19th-century system differed markedly from its successors. Class antagonisms as such appear to have had extremely low salience by comparison with today's voting behavior. Perhaps differentials in the level of formal education among various groups in the population contributed to differentials in 19th-century turnout as they clearly do now. But the unquestionably far lower *general* level of formal education in America during the last century did not preclude a much more intense and uniform mass political participation than any which has prevailed in recent decades. Though the evidence is still scanty, it strongly implies that the influence of rurality upon the intensity and uniformity of voting participation appears to have been precisely the opposite of what survey-research findings hold it to be today. This was essentially a pre-industrial democratic system, resting heavily upon a rural and small-town base. Apparently, it was quite adequate, both in partisan organization and dissemination of political information, to the task of mobilizing voters on a scale which compares favorably with recent European levels of participation.

There is little doubt that the model of surge and decline discussed above casts significant light upon the behavior of today's American electorate as it responds to the stimuli of successive elections. But the model depends for its validity upon the demonstrated existence of very large numbers both of peripheral voters and of core voters whose attachment to party is relatively feeble. Since these were not pronounced characteristics of the 19th-century voting universe, it might be expected that abnormal increases in the percentage of the vote won by either party would be associated with very different kinds of movements in the electorate, and that such increases would be relatively unusual by present-day standards.

Even a cursory inspection of the partisan dimensions of voting behavior in the 19th century tends to confirm this expectation. Not only did the amplitude of partisan swing generally tend to be much smaller then than now,[27] but nationwide landslides of the 20th-century type were almost non-existent.[28] Moreover, when one party did win an unusually heavy majority, this increase was usually associated with a pronounced and one-sided *decline* in turnout. Comparison of the 1848 and 1852 elections in Georgia and of the October gubernatorial and November presidential elections of 1872 in Pennsylvania, for example, makes it clear that the "landslides" won by one of the presidential contenders in 1852 and 1872 were the direct consequence of mass abstentions by voters who normally supported the other party.[29] Under 19th-century conditions, marked as they were by substantially full mobilization of the eligible electorate, the only play in the system which could provide extraordinary majorities had to come from a reversal of the modern pattern of surge and decline—a depression in turnout which was overwhelmingly confined to adherents of one of the parties.[30]

This earlier political order, as we have seen, was eroded away very rapidly after 1900. Turnout fell precipitately from 19th-century levels even before the advent of woman suffrage, and even in areas where immigrant elements in the electorates were almost nonexistent. As turnout declined, a larger and larger component of the still-active electorate moved from a core to a peripheral position, and the hold of the parties over their mass base appreciably deteriorated. This revolutionary contraction in the size and diffusion in the shape of the voting universe was almost certainly the fruit of the heavily sectional party realignment which was inaugurated in 1896. This "system of 1896," as Schattschneider calls it,[31] led to the destruction of party competition throughout much of the United States, and thus paved the way for the rise of the direct primary. It also gave immense impetus to the strains of anti-partisan and anti-majoritarian theory and practice which have always been significant elements in the American political tradition. By the decade of the 1920s this new regime and business control over public policy in this country were consolidated. During that decade hardly more than one-third of the eligible adults were still core voters. Another one-sixth were peripheral voters and fully one-half remained outside the active voting universe altogether. It is difficult to avoid the impression that while all the forms of political democracy were more or less scrupulously preserved, the functional result of the "system of 1896" was the conversion of a fairly democratic regime into a rather broadly based oligarchy.

The present shape and size of the American voting universe are, of course, largely the product of the 1928–1936 political realignment. Survey-research findings most closely approximate political reality as they relate to this next broad phase of American political evolution. But the characteristics of the present voting universe suggest rather forcefully that the New Deal realignment has been both incomplete and transitional. At present, about 44 per cent of the national electorate are core voters, another 16 or so are peripheral, and about 40 per cent are still outside the political system altogether. By 19th-century standards, indices of voter peripherality stand at very high levels. Party organizations remain at best only indifferently successful at mobilizing a stable, predictable mass base of support.

The data which have been presented here, though they constitute only a small fraction of the materials which must eventually be examined, tend by and large to support Schattschneider's functional thesis of American party politics.[32] We still need to know a great deal more than we do about the specific linkages between party and voter in the 19th century. Systematic research remains also to be done on the causes and effects of the great post-1896 transition in American political behavior. Even so, it seems useful to propose an hypothesis of transition in extension of Schattschneider's argument.

The 19th-century American political system, for its day, was incomparably the most thoroughly democratized of any in the world. The development of vigorous party competition extended from individual localities to the nation itself. It involved the invention of the first organizational machinery—the caucus, the convention and the widely disseminated party press—which was designed to deal with large numbers of citizens rather than with semi-aristocratic parliamentary cliques. Sooner than the British, and at a time when Prussia protected its elites through its three-class electoral system, when each new change of regime in France brought with it a change in the size of the electorate and the nature of *le pays légal*, and when the basis of representation in Sweden was still the estate, Americans had elaborated not only the machinery and media of mass politics but a franchise which remarkably closely approached universal suffrage. Like the larger political culture of which it was an integral part, this system rested upon both broad consensual acceptance of middle-class social norms as ground rules and majoritarian settlement (in "critical" elections from time to time), once and for all, of deeply divisive substantive issues on which neither consensus nor further postponement of a showdown was possible. Within the limits so imposed it was apparently capable of coherent and decisive action. It especially permitted the explicit formulation of sectional issues and—though admittedly at the price of civil war—arrived at a clear-cut decision as to which of two incompatible sectional modes of social and economic organization was henceforth to prevail.

But after several decades of intensive industrialization a new dilemma of power, in many respects as grave as that which had eventuated in civil war, moved toward the stage of overt crisis. Prior to the closing years of the century the middle-class character of the political culture and the party system, coupled with the afterglow of the civil-war trauma, had permitted the penetration and control of the cadres of both major parties by the heavily concentrated power of our industrializing elites. But this control was inherently unstable, for if and when the social dislocations produced by the industrial revolution should in turn produce a grass-roots counterrevolution, the party whose clienteles were more vulnerable to the appeals of the counterrevolutionaries might be captured by them.

The take-off phase of industrialization has been a brutal and exploitative process everywhere, whether managed by capitalists or commissars.[33] A vital functional political need during this phase is to provide adequate insulation of the industrializing elites from mass pressures, and to prevent their displacement by a coalition of those who are damaged by the processes of capital accumulation. This problem was effectively resolved in the Soviet Union under Lenin and Stalin by vesting a totalitarian monopoly of political power in the hands of Communist industrializing elites. In recent years developing nations have tended to rely upon less coercive devices such as non-totalitarian single-party systems or personalist dictatorship to meet that need, among others. The 19th-century European elites were provided a good deal of insulation by the persistence of feudal patterns of social deference and especially by the restriction of the right to vote to the middle and upper classes.

But in the United States the institutions of mass democratic politics and universal suffrage uniquely came into being *before* the onset of full-scale industrialization. The struggle for democracy in Europe was explicitly linked from the outset with the struggle for universal suffrage. The eventual success of this movement permitted the development in relatively sequential fashion of the forms of party organization which Duverger has described in detail.[34] In the United States—ostensibly at least—the struggle for democracy had already been won, and remarkably painlessly, by the mid-19th century. In consequence, the American industrializing elites were, and felt themselves to be, uniquely vulnerable to an anti-industrialist assault which could be carried out peacefully and in the absence of effective legal or customary sanctions by a citizenry possessing at least two generations' experience with political democracy.

This crisis of vulnerability reached its peak in the 1890s. Two major elements in the population bore the brunt of the exceptionally severe deprivations felt during this depression decade: the smaller cash-crop farmers of the Southern and Western "colonial" regions and the ethnically fragmented urban working class. The cash-crop farmers, typically overextended and undercapitalized, had undergone a thirty-years' decline in the prices for their commodities in the face of intense international competition. With the onset of depression in 1893, what had been acute discomfort for them became disaster. The workers, already cruelly exploited in many instances during this "take-off" phase of large-scale industrialization, were also devastated by the worst depression the country had thus far known. Characteristically, the farmers resorted to political organization while the workers sporadically resorted to often bloody strikes. The industrializers and their intellectual and legal spokesmen were acutely conscious that these two profoundly alienated groups might coalesce. Their alarm was apparently given quite tangible form when the agrarian insurgents captured control of the Democratic Party in 1896.

But the results of that great referendum revealed that the conservatives' fears and the anti-industrialists' hopes of putting together a winning coalition on a Jacksonian base were alike groundless. Not only did urban labor *not* flock to William Jennings Bryan, it repudiated the Democratic Party on an unprecedented scale throughout the industrialized Northeast. The intensity and permanence of this urban realignment was paralleled by the Democrats' failure to make significant inroads into Republican strength in the more diversified and depression-resistant farm areas east of the Missouri River, and by their nearly total collapse in rural New England. The Democratic-Populist effort to create a coalition of the dispossessed created instead the most enduringly sectional political alignment in American history—an alignment which eventually separated the Southern and Western agrarians and transformed the most industrially advanced region of the country into a bulwark of industrialist Republicanism.

This realignment brought victory beyond expectation to those who had sought to find some way of insulating American elites from mass pressures without formally disrupting the pre-existing democratic-pluralist political structure, without violence and without conspiracy. Of the factors involved in this victory three stand out as of particular importance. (1) The depression of 1893 began and deepened during a Democratic administration. Of course there is no way of ascertaining directly what part of the decisive minority which shifted its allegiance to the Republican Party reacted viscerally to the then incumbent party and failed to perceive that Cleveland and Bryan were diametrically opposed on the central policy issues of the day. But contemporary survey findings would tend to suggest that such a component in a realigning electorate might not be small. In this context it is especially worth noting that the process of profound break with traditional voting patterns began in the fall of 1893, not in 1896. In a number of major states like Ohio and Pennsylvania the voting pattern of 1896 bears far more resemblance to those of 1893–1895 than the latter did to pre-1893 voting patterns. Assuming that such visceral responses to the Democrats as the "party of depression" did play a major role in the realignment, it would follow that the strong economic upswing after 1897 would tend to strengthen this identification and its cognate, the identification of the Republicans as the "party of prosperity."

(2) The Democratic platform and campaign were heavily weighted toward the interests and needs of an essentially rural and semi-colonial clientele. Considerably narrowed in its programmatic base from the farmer-labor Populist platform of 1892, the Democratic Party focussed most of its campaign upon monetary inflation as a means of redressing the economic balance. Bryan's viewpoint was essentially that of the smallholder who wished to give the term "businessman" a broader definition than the Easterners meant by it, and of an agrarian whose remarks about the relative importance of farms and cities bespoke his profound misunderstanding of the revolution of his time. Silver mine owners and depressed cash-crop farmers could greet the prospect of inflation with enthusiasm, but it meant much less to adequately capitalized and diversified farmers in the Northeast, and less than nothing to the depression-ridden wage-earners in that region's shops, mines and factories. Bryan's appeal at base was essentially Jacksonian—a call for a return to the simpler and more virtuous economic and political arrangements which he identified with that bygone era. Such nostalgia could evoke a positive response among the native-stock rural elements whose political style and economic expectations had been shaped in the far-away past. But it could hardly seem a realistic political choice for the ethnically pluralist urban populations, large numbers of whom found such nostalgia meaningless since it related to nothing in their past or current experience. Programmatically, at least, these urbanites were presented with a two-way choice only one part of which seemed at all functionally related to the realities of an emergent industrial society. With the Democrats actually cast in the role of reactionaries despite the apparent radicalism of their platform and leader, and with no socialist alternative even thinkable in the context of the American political culture of the 1890s, the Republican Party alone retained some relevance to the urban setting. In this context, its massive triumph there was a foregone conclusion.

(3) An extremely important aspect of any political realignment is the unusually intense mobilization of negative-reference-group sentiments during the course of the campaign. 1896 was typical in this respect. Profound antagonisms in culture and political style between the cosmopolitan, immigrant, wet, largely non-

Protestant components of American urban populations and the parochial, dry, Anglo-Saxon Protestant inhabitants of rural areas can be traced back at least to the 1840s. Bryan was virtually the archetype of the latter culture, and it would have been surprising had he not been the target of intense ethnocultural hostility from those who identified with the former. He could hardly have appeared as other than an alien to those who heard him in New York in 1896, or to those who booed him off the stage at the Democratic Convention—also in New York—in 1924. Moreover, his remarks about the Northeast as "the enemy's country"—anticipating Senator Goldwater's views about that region in 1964— could only intensify a broadly sectional hostility to his candidacy and deepen the impression that he was attacking not only the Northeast's industrializing elites but the Northeast itself. Both in 1896 and 1964 this region gave every visible evidence of replying in kind.

As Schattschneider has perceptively observed, the "system of 1896" was admirably suited to its primary function. One of its major working parts was a judiciary which proceeded first to manufacture the needed constitutional restraints on democratic political action—a development presaged by such decisions as the Minnesota railroad rate case of 1890[35] and the income tax cases of 1894–1895[36]—and then to apply these restraints against certain sensitive categories of national and state economic legislation.[37] Another of the new system's basic components was the control which the sectional alignment itself gave to the Republican Party, and through it the corporate business community, over the scope and direction of national public policy. Democracy was not only placed in judicial leading-strings, it was effectively placed out of commission— at least so far as two-party competition was concerned—in more than half of the states. Yet it was one of the greatest, if unacknowledged, contributions of the "system of 1896" that democratic forms, procedures and traditions continued to survive.[38] Confronted with a narrowed scope of effective democratic options, an increasingly large proportion of the eligible adult population either left, failed to enter or—as was the case with Southern Negroes after the completion of the 1890–1904 disfranchisement movement in the Old Confederacy—was systematically excluded from the American voting universe. The results of this on the exercise of the franchise have already been examined here in some detail. It was during this 1896–1932 era that the basic characteristics associated with today's mass electorate were formed.

These characteristics, as we have seen, have already far outlived the 1896 alignment itself. There seems to be no convincing evidence that they are being progressively liquidated at the present time. If the re-emergence of a competitive party politics and its at least partial orientation toward the broader needs of an urban, industrialized society were welcome fruits of the New Deal revolution, that revolution has apparently exhausted most of its potential for stimulating turnout or party-oriented voting in America. The present state of affairs, to be sure, is not without its defenders. The civics-minded have tended to argue that the visible drift away from party-oriented voting among a growing minority of voters is a sign of increasing maturity in the electorate.[39] Others have argued that mediocre rates of turnout in the United States, paralleled by the normally low salience of issues in our political campaigns, are indicative of a "politics of happiness."[40] It is further contended that any sudden injection of large numbers of poorly socialized adults into the active voting universe could constitute a danger to the Republic.[41]

But there is another side to this coin. The ultimate democratic purpose of issue-formulation in a campaign is to give the people at large the power to choose their and their agents' options. Moreover, so far as is known, the blunt alternative to party government is the concentration of political power, locally or nationally, in the hands of those who already possess concentrated economic power.[42] If no adequate substitute for party as a means for mobilizing non-elite influence on the governing process has yet been discovered, the obvious growth of "image" and "personality" voting in recent decades should be a matter of some concern to those who would like to see a more complete restoration of the democratic process in the United States.

Moreover, recent studies—such as Murray Levin's examinations of the attitudes of the Boston and Massachusetts electorate—reveal that such phenomena as widespread ticket splitting may be associated quite readily with pervasive and remarkably intense feelings of political alienation.[43] Convinced that both party organizations are hopelessly corrupt and out of reach of popular control, a minority which is large enough to hold the balance of power between Republicans and Democrats tends rather consistently to vote for the lesser, or lesser-known, of two evils. It takes a mordant variety of humor to find a kind of emergent voter maturity in this alienation. For Levin's data are difficult to square with the facile optimism underlying the civics approach to independent voting. So, for that matter, are the conclusions of survey research about the behavior of many so-called "independent" voters.[44]

Findings such as these seem little more comforting to the proponents of the "politics of happiness" thesis. Granted the proposition that most people who have been immersed from birth in a given political system are apt to be unaware of alternatives whose explicit formulation that system inhibits, it is of course difficult to ascertain whether their issueless and apathetic political style is an outward sign of "real" happiness. We can surmise, however, that the kind of political alienation which Levin describes is incompatible with political happiness, whether real or fancied. A great many American voters, it would seem, are quite intelligent enough to perceive the deep contradiction which exists between the ideals of rhetorical democracy as preached in school and on the stump, and the actual day-to-day reality as that reality intrudes on his own *milieu*. Alienation arises from perception of that contradiction, and from the consequent feelings of individual political futility arising when the voter confronts an organization of politics which seems unable to produce minimally gratifying results. The concentration of socially deprived characteristics among the more than forty million adult Americans who today are altogether outside the voting universe suggests active alienation—or its passive equivalent, political apathy—on a scale quite unknown anywhere else in the Western world. Unless it is assumed as a kind of universal law that problems of existence which can be organized in political terms must fade out below a certain socio-economic level, this state of affairs is not inevitable. And if it is not inevitable, one may infer that the political system itself is responsible for its continued existence.

Yet such an assumption of fade-out is clearly untenable in view of what is known about patterns of voting participation in other democratic systems. Nor need it be assumed that substantial and rapid increases in American voting participation would necessarily, or even probably, involve the emergence of totalitarian mass movements. The possibility of such movements is a constant danger, to be sure, in any polity containing so high a proportion of apolitical elements in its potential electorate. But it would be unwise to respond to this possibility by merely expressing the comfortable hope that the apoliticals will remain apolitical, and by doing nothing to engage them in the system in a timely and orderly way. It is much more to the point to seek a way, if one can be found, to integrate the apolitical half of the American electorate into the political system before crisis arises.[45] Such integration need not be out of the question. The United States, after all, enjoyed intense mass political involvement without totalitarian movements during the last part of the 19th century, as do other Western democracies today.

No integration of the apoliticals can be carried out without a price to be paid. Underlying the failure of political organizations more advanced than the 19th-century middle-class cadre party to develop in this country has been the deeper failure of any except middle-class social and political values to achieve full legitimacy in the American political culture. It may not now be possible for our polity to make so great a leap as to admit non-middle-class values to political legitimacy and thus provide the preconditions for a more coherent and responsible mode of party organization. But such a leap may have to be made if full mobilization of the apolitical elements is to be achieved without the simultaneous emergence of manipulative radicalism of the left or the right. The heart of our contemporary political dilemma appears to lie in the conflict between this emergent need and the ideological individualism which continues so deeply to pervade our political culture. Yet the present situation perpetuates a standing danger that the half of the American electorate which is now more or less entirely outside the universe of active politics may someday be mobilized in substantial degree by totalitarian or quasi-totalitarian appeals. As the late President Kennedy seemed to intimate in his executive order establishing the Commission on Registration and Voting Participation, it also raises some questions about the legitimacy of the regime itself.[46]

NOTES

[1] See, *e.g.*, Robert E. Lane, *Political Life* (Glencoe, Ill., 1959), pp. 18–26.

[2] There are, of course, very wide divergences in turnout rates even among non-Southern states. Some of them, like Idaho, New Hampshire and Utah, have presidential-year turnouts which compare very favorably with European levels of participation. A detailed analysis of these differences

remains to be made. It should prove of the utmost importance in casting light upon the relevance of current forms of political organization and partisan alignments to differing kinds of electorates and political subsystems in the United States.

[3] *Report of the President's Commission on Registration and Voting Participation* (Washington, 1963), esp. pp. 5–9. Hereafter cited as *Report*.

[4] *Ibid.*, pp. 11–14, 31–42.

[5] See, *e.g.*, Stanley Kelley, "Elections and the Mass Media," *Law and Contemporary Problems*, Vol. 27, pp. 307–26 (1962).

[6] E. E. Schattschneider, *The Semi-Sovereign People* (New York, 1960), pp. 102–3.

[7] Joseph La Palombara, *Guide to Michigan Politics* (East Lansing, Mich., Michigan State University Press, 1960), pp. 22–35.

[8] This recalls Robinson and Standing's conclusion that voter participation in Indiana does not necessarily increase with increasing party competition. Of the eight Michigan gubernatorial elections from 1948 to 1962 only one was decided by a margin of 55% or more, while three were decided by margins of less than 51.5% of the two-party vote. Despite this intensely competitive situation, turnout—while of course much higher than in the 1920s—remains significantly below normal pre-1920 levels.

[9] Angus Campbell, "Surge and Decline: A Study of Electoral Change," *Public Opinion Quarterly*, Vol. 24, pp. 401–4 (1960).

[10] Herbert Tingsten, *Political Behavior* (Stockholm, Stockholm Economic Studies, No. 7, 1937), pp. 10–36. See also Charles E. Merriam and Harold F. Gosnell, *Non-Voting* (Chicago, University of Chicago Press, 1924), pp. 26, 109–22, for a useful discussion of the effect of woman suffrage on turnout in a metropolitan area immediately following the general enfranchisement of 1920.

[11] Survey-research estimates place current turnout among American women at 10% below male turnout. Angus Campbell *et al.*, *The American Voter* (New York, 1964), pp. 484–85. This sex-related difference in participation is apparently universal, but is significantly smaller in European countries which provide election data by sex, despite the far higher European level of participation by both sexes. The postwar differential has been 5.8% in Norway (1945–57 mean), 3.3% in Sweden (1948–60 mean), and 1.9% in Finland (1962 general election). While in 1956 only about 55% of American women went to the polls, the mean turnout among women in postwar elections was 76.1% in Norway and 79.4% in Sweden.

[12] *Ibid.*, pp. 402–40.

[13] The estimated rates of turnout in presidential elections from 1876 through 1896, mean turnout in the period 1936–60 and estimated turnout in 1964 were as follows in these states:

State	1876	1880	1884	1888	1892	1896	1936–60 (Mean)	1964 (Prelim.)
Indiana	94.6	94.4	92.2	93.3	89.0	95.1	75.0	73.3
Iowa	89.6	91.5	90.0	87.9	88.5	96.2	71.7	72.0
Kentucky	76.1	71.0	68.0	79.1	72.6	88.0	57.6	52.6

[14] V. O. Key, Jr., and Frank Munger, "Social Determinism and Electoral Decision," in Eugene Burdick and Arthur J. Brodbeck, eds., *American Voting Behavior* (Glencoe, Ill.: 1959), pp. 282–88.

[15] C. Wright Mills, *The Power Elite* (New York, Oxford University Press, 1956), pp. 298–324. See also Arthur J. Vidich and Joseph Bensman, *Small Town in Mass Society* (New York, 1960), pp. 5–15, 202–27, 297–320.

[16] John H. Fenton, *Politics in the Border States* (New Orleans, Hauser Press, 1957), pp. 117–20.

[17] However, Ohio's modern pattern of split-ticket voting, formed several decades ago, seems to have been little (if at all) affected by the 1950 change from party-column to office-block ballot forms. See Figure 15-3.

[18] Thomas A. Flinn, "Continuity and Change in Ohio Politics," *Journal of Politics*, Vol. 24, pp. 521–44 (1962).

[19] Lee Benson, *The Concept of Jacksonian Democracy* (Princeton, Princeton University Press, 1961), pp. 123–207, 288–328.

[20] Flinn, *op. cit.*, p. 542.

[21] John H. Fenton, "Ohio's Unpredictable Voters," *Harper's Magazine*, Vol. 225, pp. 61–65 (1962).

[22] This would seem to suggest a limitation on Key's findings, *American State Politics* (New York, 1956), pp. 169–96.

[23] This designation is given the state's political system in Oliver Benson, Harry Holloway, George Mauer, Joseph Pray and Wayne Young, *Oklahoma Votes: 1907–1962* (Norman, Okla., Bureau of Government Research, University of Oklahoma, 1964), pp. 44–52. For an extensive discussion of the sectional basis of Oklahoma politics, see *ibid.*, pp. 32–43, and V. O. Key, Jr., *American State Politics, op. cit.*, (New York: 1956), pp. 220–22.

[24] In 1936, 34 states (71%) elected governors for either two- or four-year terms in presidential years, and the three-year term in New Jersey caused major state elections to coincide with every fourth presidential election. By 1964, only 25 of 50 states (50%) still held some of their gubernatorial elections in presidential years. Two of these, Florida and Michigan, are scheduled to begin off-year gubernatorial elections for four-year terms in 1966.

[25] *American State Politics, op. cit.*, pp. 169–96.

[26] In the period 1956–62 there have been 840 general-election contests for the Pennsylvania House of Representatives. Of these all but six, or 0.7%, have been contested by both major political parties. No Pennsylvania state Senate seat has been uncontested during this period. Despite the 1962 Republican upsurge in Oklahoma, however, there were no contests between the parties in 11 of 22 Senate seats (50.0%) and in 73 of 120 House seats (60.9%). All the uncontested Senate seats and all but two of the uncontested House seats were won by Democrats.

[27] Mean national partisan swings in presidential elections since 1872 have been as follows: 1872–92, 2.3%; 1896–1916, 5.0%; 1920–32, 10.3%; 1936–64, 5.4%.

[28] If a presidential landslide is arbitrarily defined as a contest in which the winning candidate received 55% or more of the two-party vote, only the election of 1872 would qualify among the 16 presidential elections held from 1836 to 1896. Of 17 presidential elections held from 1900 through 1964, at least eight were landslide elections by this definition, and a ninth—the 1924 election, in which the Republican candidate received 54.3% and the Democratic candidate 29.0% of a three-party total—could plausibly be included.

[29] The total vote in Georgia declined from 92,203 in 1848 to 62,333 in 1852. Estimated turnout declined from about 88% to about 55% of the eligible electorate, while the Democratic share of the two-party vote increased from 48.5% in 1848 to 64.8% in 1852. The pattern of participation in the Pennsylvania gubernatorial and presidential elections of 1872 is also revealing:

Raw Vote	Governor, Oct. 1872	President, Nov. 1872	Absolute Decline
Total	671,147	562,276	−108,871
Democratic	317,760	213,027	−104,733
Republican	353,387	349,249	− 4,138

Estimated turnout in October was 82.0%, in November 68.6%. The Democratic percentage of the two-party vote was 47.3% in October and 37.9% in November.

[30] The only apparent exception to this generalization in the 19th century was the election of 1840. But this was the first election in which substantially full mobilization of the eligible electorate occurred. The rate of increase in the total vote from 1836 to 1860 was 60.0%, the largest in American history. Estimated turnout increased from about 58% in 1836 to about 80% in 1840. This election, with its relatively one-sided mobilization of hitherto apolitical elements in the potential electorate, not unnaturally bears some resemblance to the elections of the 1950s. But the increase in the Whig share of the two-party vote from 49.2% in 1836 to only 53.0% in 1840 suggests that the surge was considerably smaller than those of the 1950s.

[31] *The Semi-Sovereign People, op. cit.*, p. 81.

[32] *Ibid.*, esp. pp. 78–113. See also his "United States: The Functional Approach to Party Government," in Sigmund Neumann, ed., *Modern Political Parties* (Chicago, University of Chicago Press, 1956), pp. 194–215.

[33] Clark Kerr, John T. Dunlop, Frederick S. Harbison and Charles A. Myers, *Industrialism and Industrial Man* (Cambridge, Harvard University Press, 1960), pp. 47–76, 98–126, 193, 233. Walt

W. Rostow. *The Stages of Economic Growth* (Cambridge, Cambridge University Press, 1960), pp. 17–58.

[34] Maurice Duverger, *Political Parties* (New York, 2d. ed., 1959), pp. 1–60.

[35] Chicago, Milwaukee & St. Paul Railway Co. v. Minnesota, 134 U.S. 418 (1890).

[36] Pollock v. Farmers' Loan & Trust Co., 157 U.S. 429 (1895); (rehearing) 158 U.S. 601 (1895).

[37] The literature on this process of judicial concept-formulation from its roots in the 1870s through its formal penetration into the structure of constitutional law in the 1890s is extremely voluminous. Two especially enlightening accounts are: Benjamin Twiss, *Lawyers and the Constitution* (Princeton, Princeton University Press, 1942), and Arnold M. Paul, *Conservative Crises and the Rule of Law* (Ithaca, Cornell University Press, 1960).

[38] Paul, *ibid.*, pp. 131–58.

[39] See, among many other examples, *Congressional Quarterly Weekly Report*, Vol. 22 (May 1, 1964), p. 801.

[40] Heinz Eulau, "The Politics of Happiness," *Antioch Review*, Vol. 16, pp. 259–64 (1956); Seymour M. Lipset, *Political Man* (New York, 1960), pp. 179–219.

[41] *Ibid.*, pp. 216–19; Herbert Tingsten, *Political Behavior*, *op. cit.*, pp. 225–26.

[42] V. O. Key, Jr., *Southern Politics* (New York, 1949), pp. 526–28; E. E. Schattschneider, *The Semi-Sovereign People*, *op. cit.*, pp. 114–28.

[43] Murray B. Levin, *The Alienated Voter* (New York, 1960), pp. 58–75, and his *The Compleat Politician* (Indianapolis, 1962), esp. pp. 133–78. While one may hope that Boston and Massachusetts are extreme case studies in the pathology of democratic politics in the United States, it appears improbable that the pattern of conflict between the individual's expectations and reality is entirely unique to the Bay State.

[44] Angus Campbell *et al.*, *The American Voter*, *op. cit.*, pp. 143–45.

[45] The line of reasoning developed in this article—especially that part of it which deals with the possible development of political alienation in the United States—seems not entirely consistent with the findings of Gabriel A. Almond and Sidney Verba, *The Civic Culture* (Princeton, Princeton University Press, 1963), pp. 402–69, 472–505. Of course there is no question that relatively high levels of individual satisfaction with political institutions and acceptance of democratic norms may exist in a political system with abnormally low rates of actual voting participation, just as extremely high turnout may—as in Italy—be associated with intense and activist modes of political alienation. At the same time, the gap between American norms and the actual political activity of American individuals does exist, as Almond and Verba point out on pp. 479–87. This may represent the afterglow of a Lockean value consensus in an inappropriate socio-economic setting, but in a polity quite lacking in the disruptive discontinuities of historical development which have occurred during this century in Germany, Italy and Mexico. Or it may represent something much more positive.

[46] "Whereas less than sixty-five percent of the United States population of voting age cast ballots for Presidential electors in 1960; and

"Whereas popular participation in Government through elections is essential to a democratic form of Government; and

"Whereas the causes of nonvoting are not fully understood and more effective corrective action will be possible on the basis of a better understanding of the causes of the failure of many citizens to register and vote . . ." (emphasis supplied) The full text of the executive order is in *Report*, pp. 63–64. Compare with Schattschneider's comment in *The Semi-Sovereign People*, *op. cit.*, p. 112: "A greatly expanded popular base of political participation is the essential condition for public support of the government. This is the modern problem of democratic government. The price of support is participation. The choice is between participation and propaganda, between democratic and dictatorial ways of *changing consent into support, because consent is no longer enough.*" (Author's emphasis)

PART FIVE

INTEREST GROUPS

Private groups such as trade associations, labor unions, and farmers' organizations have long been recognized as an important feature of the American political community. Americans have a reputation for forming interest groups to promote their economic, political, or social objectives, and American government is thought to be responsive to, if not actually dependent upon, these associations. The classic literature on interest groups falls into three main categories. First, some authors have sought to explain why groups are formed and to delineate the different characteristics of associations according to such attributes as their size and purpose. It could be argued that this approach dates back to the 1830s when Alexis de Tocqueville observed that "Americans of all ages, all conditions, and all dispositions constantly form associations. They have not only commercial and manufacturing companies . . . but associations of a thousand other kinds, religious, moral, serious, futile, general or restricted, enormous or diminutive. . . . Wherever at the head of some new undertaking you see the government in France or a man of rank in England, in the United States you will be sure to find an association." Second, many have concentrated on the process by which groups advance their political interests. And, third, some have examined the impact of interest groups and their activities on the political system as a whole.

Mancur Olson's chapter on "The Logic" from *The Rise and Decline of Nations* (1982) is a preeminent example of the first approach, dealing with the dynamics of forming and maintaining private associations. Olson seeks to explain why individuals join and work for groups by addressing a fundamental paradox: "The individual in any large group with a common interest will reap only a minute share of the gains from whatever sacrifices the individual makes to achieve this common interest. Since any gain goes to everyone in the group, those who contribute nothing to the effort will get just as much as those who made a contribution. It pays to 'let George do it,' but George has little or no incentive to do anything in the group interest either. . . . The paradox, then, is that . . . large groups, at least if they are composed of rational individuals, will *not* act in their group interest." However, as Olson argues, this paradox can be resolved in practice through the use of selective incentives, both positive and negative, to prompt individuals to contribute to group activities. Olson also notes that since small organizations may not be able to function without contributions from each of their few members, the logic of individual participation indicates that "smaller groups will have a greater likelihood of engaging in collective action than larger ones."

The selection from Raymond A. Bauer, Ithiel de Sola Pool, and Lewis A. Dexter's *American Business and Public Policy* (1972) serves as a bridge between the first and second approaches. While concerned with the group dynamics of business organizations, Bauer and associates seek to relate these considerations to the processes through which business groups seek representation in the political system. They find, for instance, that, largely as a result of the groups' desire to retain members, "there is a pattern of avoidance of issues, suppression of controversy, and at least the pretense of unanimity." This drive for consensus therefore serves to limit business associations' political action. In addition, they conclude that interest groups are "far short of the omnipotent, well-oiled machines that are portrayed in political literature."[1] Moreover, they observe that pressure groups have worked best "when they could become auxiliaries to a legislator, not propagandists to him."[2] Thus, pressure politics, in their view, tends to be more of an informational and organizational process than one involving traditional notions of pressure, like that of bribery based on money or on the potential control of votes.

In some respects, the third approach to interest groups is of greatest concern. It analyzes the impact of the group process on the political system as a whole. In "The Scope and Bias of the Pressure System" (1960), E. E. Schattschneider concludes that "the notion that the pressure system is automatically representative of the whole community is a myth fostered by the universalizing tendency of modern group theories. Pressure politics is a selective process ill designed to serve diffuse interests. The system is skewed, loaded, and unbalanced in favor of a fraction of a minority."

Finally, Theodore J. Lowi's "Public Philosophy: Interest-Group Liberalism" (1967) considers the impact of the pressure group system on government itself. Lowi contends that the contemporary role of interest groups in government has three pronounced effects: "(1) the atrophy of institutions of popular control; (2) the maintenance of old and creation of new structures of privilege; and (3) conservatism, in several senses of the word."

NOTES

[1] Raymond A. Bauer, Ithiel de Sola Pool, and Lewis Anthony Dexter, *American Business and Public Policy* (Chicago: Aldine-Atherton, 1972), p. 349.
[2] Ibid., p. 357.

16

MANCUR OLSON, JR.

COLLECTIVE ACTION: THE LOGIC

I

. . . It has often been taken for granted that if everyone in a group of individuals or firms had some interest in common, then there would be a tendency for the group to seek to further this interest. Thus many students of politics in the United States for a long time supposed that citizens with a common political interest would organize and lobby to serve that interest. Each individual in the population would be in one or more groups and the vector of pressures of these competing groups explained the outcomes of the political process. Similarly, it was often supposed that if workers, farmers, or consumers faced monopolies harmful to their interests, they would eventually attain countervailing power through organizations such as labor unions or farm organizations that obtained market power and protective government action. On a larger scale, huge social classes are often expected to act in the interest of their members; the unalloyed form of this belief is, of course, the Marxian contention that in capitalist societies the bourgeois class runs the government to serve its own interests, and that once the exploitation of the proletariat goes far enough and "false consciousness" has disappeared, the working class will in its own interest revolt and establish a dictatorship of the proletariat. In general, if the individuals in some category or class had a sufficient degree of self-interest and if they all agreed on some common interest, then the group would to some extent also act in a self-interested or group-interested manner.

If we ponder the logic of the familiar assumption described in the preceding paragraph, we can see that it is fundamentally and indisputably faulty. Consider those consumers who agree that they pay higher prices for a product because of some objectionable monopoly or tariff, or those workers who agree that their skill deserves a higher wage. Let us now ask what would be the expedient course of action for an individual consumer who would like to see a boycott to combat a monopoly or a lobby to repeal the tariff, or for an individual worker who would like a strike threat or a minimum wage law that could bring higher wages. If the consumer or worker contributes a few days and a few dollars to organize a boycott or a union or to lobby for favorable legislation, he or she will have sacrificed time and money. What will this sacrifice obtain? The individual will at best succeed in advancing the cause to a small (often imperceptible) degree. In any case he will get only a minute share of the gain from his action. The very fact that the objective or interest is common to or shared by the group entails that the gain from any sacrifice an individual makes to serve this common purpose is shared with everyone in the group. The successful boycott or strike or lobbying action will bring the better price or wage for everyone in the relevant category, so the individual in any large group with a common interest will reap only a minute share of the gains from whatever sacrifices the individual makes to achieve this common interest. Since any gain goes to everyone in the group, those who contribute nothing to the effort will get just as much as those who made a contribution. It pays to "let George do it," but George has little or no incentive to do anything in the group interest either, so (in the absence of factors that are completely left out of the conceptions mentioned in the first paragraph) there will be little, if any, group action. The paradox, then, is that (in the absence of special arrangements or circumstances to which we shall turn later) large groups, at least if they are composed of rational individuals, will *not* act in their group interest.

This paradox is elaborated and set out in a way that lets the reader check every step of the logic in a book I wrote entitled *The Logic of Collective Action.* . . .[1]

II

One finding in *The Logic* is that the services of associations like labor unions, professional associations, farm organizations, cartels, lobbies (and even collusive group without formal organization) resemble the basic services of the state in one utterly fundamental respect. The services of such associations, like the elemental services or "public goods" provided by governments, if provided to anyone, go to everyone in some category or group. Just as the law and order, defense, or pollution abatement brought about by government accrue to everyone in some country or geographic area, so the tariff obtained by a farm organization's lobbying effort raises the price to all producers of the relevant commodity. Similarly, as I argued earlier, the higher wage won by a union applies to all employees in the pertinent category. More generally, every lobby obtaining a general change in legislation or regulation thereby obtains a public or collective good for everyone who benefits from that change, and every combination—that is, every "cartel"—using market or industrial action to get a higher price or wage must, when it restricts the quantity supplied, raise the price for every seller, thereby creating a collective good for all sellers.

If governments, on the one hand, and combinations exploiting their political or market power, on the other, produce public or collective goods that inevitably go to everyone in some group or category, then both are subject to the paradoxical logic set out above: that is, the individuals and firms they serve have in general no incentive voluntarily to contribute to their support.[2] It follows that if there is only voluntary and rational individual behavior,[3] then for the most part neither governments nor lobbies and cartels will exist, unless individuals support them for some reason *other* than the collective goods they provide. Of course, governments exist virtually everywhere and often there are lobbies and cartelistic organizations as well. If the argument so far is right, it follows that something *other* than the collective goods that governments and other organizations provide accounts for their existence.[4]

In the case of governments, the answer was explained before *The Logic of Collective Action* was written; governments are obviously supported by compulsory taxation. Sometimes there is little objection to this compulsion, presumably because many people intuitively understand that public goods cannot be sold in the marketplace or financed by any voluntary mechanism; as I have already argued, each individual would get only a minute share of any governmental services he or she paid for and would get whatever level of services was provided by others in any event.

In the case of organizations that provide collective goods to their client groups through political or market action, the answer has not been obvious, but it is no less clear-cut. Organizations of this kind, at least when they represent large groups, are again not supported because of the collective goods they provide, but rather because they have been fortunate enough to find what I have called *selective incentives*. A selective incentive is one that applies selectively to the individuals depending on whether they do or do not contribute to the provision of the collective good.

A selective incentive can be either negative or positive; it can, for example, be a loss or punishment imposed only on those who do *not* help provide the collective good. Tax payments are, of course, obtained with the help of negative selective incentives, since those who are found not to have paid their taxes must then suffer both taxes and penalties. The best-known type of organized interest group in modern democratic societies, the labor union, is also usually supported, in part, through negative selective incentives. Most of the dues in strong unions are obtained through union shop, closed shop, or agency shop arrangements which make dues paying more or less compulsory and automatic. There are often also informal arrangements with the same effect; David McDonald, former president of the United Steel Workers of America, describes one of these arrangements used in the early history of that union. It was, he writes, a technique

> which we called . . . visual education, which was a high-sounding label for a practice much more accurately described as dues picketing. It worked very simply. A group of dues-paying members, selected by the district director (usually more for their size than their tact) would stand at the plant gate with pick handles or baseball bats in hand and confront each worker as he arrived for his shift.[5]

As McDonald's "dues picketing" analogy suggests, picketing during strikes is another negative selective incentive that unions sometimes need; although picketing in industries with established and stable unions is usually peaceful, this is because the union's capacity to close down an enterprise against which it has called a strike is clear to all; the early phase of unionization often involves a great deal of violence on the part of both unions and anti-union employers and scabs.[6]

Some opponents of labor unions argue that, since many of the members of labor unions join only through the processes McDonald described or through legally enforced union-shop arrangements, most of the relevant workers do not want to be unionized. The Taft-Hartley Act provided that impartial governmentally administered elections should be held to determine whether workers did in fact want to belong to unions. As the collective-good logic set out here suggests, the same workers who had to be coerced to pay union dues voted for the unions with compulsory dues (and normally by overwhelming margins), so that this feature of the Taft-Hartley Act was soon abandoned as pointless.[7] The workers who as individuals tried to avoid paying union dues at the same time that they voted to force themselves all to pay dues are no different from taxpayers who vote, in effect, for high levels of taxation, yet try to arrange their private affairs in ways that avoid taxes. Because of the same logic, many professional associations also get members through covert or overt coercion (for example, lawyers in those states with a "closed bar"). So do lobbies and cartels of several other types; some of the contributions by corporate officials, for instance, to politicians useful to the corporation are also the result of subtle forms of coercion.[8]

Positive selective incentives, although easily overlooked, are also commonplace, as diverse examples in *The Logic* demonstrate.[9] American farm organizations offer prototypical examples. Many of the members of the stronger American farm organizations are members because their dues payments are automatically deducted from the "patronage dividends" of farm cooperatives or are included in the insurance premiums paid to mutual insurance companies associated with the farm organizations. Any number of organizations with urban clients also provide similar positive selective incentives in the form of insurance policies, publications, group air fares, and other private goods made available only to members. The grievance procedures of labor unions usually also offer selective incentives, since the grievances of active members often get most of the attention. The symbiosis between the political power of a lobbying organization and the business institutions associated with it often yields tax or other advantages for the business institution, and the publicity and other information flowing out of the political arm of a movement often generates patterns of preference or trust that make the business activities of the movement more remunerative. The surpluses obtained in such ways in turn provide positive selective incentives that recruit participants for the lobbying efforts.

III

Small groups, or occasionally large "federal" groups that are made up of many small groups of socially interactive members, have an additional source of both negative and positive selective incentives. Clearly most people value the companionship and respect of those with whom they interact. In modern societies solitary confinement is, apart from the rare death penalty, the harshest legal punishment. The censure or even ostracism of those who fail to bear a share of the burdens of collective action can sometimes be an important selective incentive. An extreme example of this occurs when British unionists refuse to speak to uncooperative colleagues, that is, "send them to Coventry." Similarly, those in a socially interactive group seeking a collective good can give special respect or honor to those who distinguish themselves by their sacrifices in the interest of the group and thereby offer them a positive selective incentive. Since most people apparently prefer relatively like-minded or agreeable and respectable company, and often prefer to associate with those whom they especially admire, they may find it costless to shun those who shirk the collective action and to favor those who oversubscribe.

Social selective incentives can be powerful and inexpensive, but they are available only in certain situations. As I have already indicated, they have little applicability to large groups, except in those cases in which the large groups can be federations of small groups that are capable of social interaction. It also is not possible to organize most large groups in need of a collective good into small, socially interactive subgroups, since most individuals do not have the time needed to maintain a huge number of friends and acquaintances.

The availability of social selective incentives is also limited by the social heterogeneity of some of the groups or categories that would benefit from a collective good. Everyday observation reveals that most socially interactive groups are fairly homogeneous and that many people resist extensive social interaction with those they deem to have lower status or greatly different tastes. Even Bohemian or other nonconformist groups often are made up of individuals who are similar to one another, however much they differ from the rest of society. Since some of the categories of individuals who would benefit from a collective good are socially heterogeneous, the social interaction needed for selective incentives sometimes cannot be arranged even when the number of individuals involved is small.

Another problem in organizing and maintaining socially heterogeneous groups is that they are less likely to agree on the exact nature of whatever collective good is at issue or on how much of it is worth buying. All the arguments showing the difficulty of collective action mentioned so far in this chapter hold even when there is perfect consensus about the collective good that is desired, the amount that is wanted, and the best way to obtain the good. But if anything, such as social heterogeneity, reduces consensus, collective action can become still less likely. And if there is nonetheless collective action, it incurs the extra cost (especially for the leaders of whatever organization or collusion is at issue) of accommodating and compromising the different views. The situation is slightly different in the very small groups to which we shall turn shortly. In such groups differences of opinion can sometimes provide a bit of an incentive to join an organization seeking a collective good, since joining might give the individual a significant influence over the organization's policy and the nature of any collective good it would obtain. But this consideration is not relevant to any group that is large enough so that a single individual cannot expect to affect the outcome.

Consensus is especially difficult where collective goods are concerned because the defining characteristic of collective goods—that they go to everyone in some group or category if they are provided at all—also entails that everyone in the relevant group gets more or less of the collective good together, and that they all have to accept whatever level and type of public good is provided. A country can have only one foreign and defense policy, however diverse the preferences and incomes of its citizenry, and (except in the rarely attainable case of a "Lindahl equilibrium")[10] there will not be agreement within a country on how much should be spent to carry out the foreign and defense policy. This is a clear implication of the arguments for "fiscal equivalence"[11] and of the rigorous models of "optimal segregation"[12] and "fiscal federalism."[13] Heterogeneous clients with diverse demands for collective goods can pose an even greater problem for private associations, which not only must deal with the disagreements but also must find selective incentives strong enough to hold dissatisfied clients.

In short, the political entrepreneurs who attempt to organize collective action will accordingly be more likely to succeed if they strive to organize relatively homogeneous groups. The political managers whose task it is to maintain organized or collusive action similarly will be motivated to use indoctrination and selective recruitment to increase the homogeneity of their client groups. This is true in part because social selective incentives are more likely to be available to the more nearly homogeneous groups, and in part because homogeneity will help achieve consensus.

IV

Information and calculation about a collective good is often itself a collective good. Consider a typical member of a large organization who is deciding how much time to devote to studying the policies or leadership of the organization. The more time the member devotes to this matter, the greater the likelihood that his or her voting and advocacy will favor effective policies and leadership for the organization. This typical member will, however, get only a small share of the gain from the more effective policies and leadership: in the aggregate, the other members will get almost all the gains, so that the individual member does not have an incentive to devote nearly as much time to fact-finding and thinking about the organization as would be in the group interest. Each of the members of the group would be better off if they all could be coerced into spending more time finding out how to vote to make the organization best further their interests. This is dramatically evident in the case of the typical voter in a national election in a large country. The gain to such a voter from studying issues and candidates until it is clear what vote is truly in his or her interest is given by the difference in the value to the individual of the "right" election outcome as compared with the "wrong" outcome, *multiplied by the probability a change in the individual's vote will alter the outcome of the election.* Since the probability that a typical voter will change the outcome of the election is vanishingly small, the typical citizen is usually "rationally ignorant" about public affairs.[14] Often, information about public affairs is so interesting or entertaining that it pays to acquire it for these reasons alone—this appears to be the single most important source of exceptions to the generalization that *typical* citizens are rationally ignorant about public affairs.

Individuals in a few special vocations can receive considerable rewards in private goods if they acquire exceptional knowledge of public goods. Politicians, lobbyists, journalists, and social scientists, for example, may earn more money, power, or prestige from knowledge of this or that public business. Occasionally, exceptional knowledge of public policy can generate exceptional profits in stock exchanges or other markets. Withal, the typical citizen will find that his or her income and life chances will not be improved by zealous study of public affairs, or even of any single collective good.

The limited knowledge of public affairs is in turn necessary to explain the effectiveness of lobbying. If all citizens had obtained and digested all pertinent information, they could not then be swayed by advertising or other persuasion. With perfectly informed citizens, elected officials would not be subject to the blandishments of lobbyists, since the constituents would then know if their interests were betrayed and defeat the unfaithful representative at the next election. Just as lobbies provide collective goods to special-interest groups, so their effectiveness is explained by the imperfect knowledge of citizens, and this in turn is due mainly to the fact that information and calculation about collective goods is also a collective good.

This fact—that the benefits of individual enlightenment about public goods are usually dispersed throughout a group or nation, rather than concentrated upon the individual who bears the costs of becoming enlightened—explains many other phenomena as well. It explains, for example, the "man bites dog" criterion of what is newsworthy. If the television newscasts were watched or newspapers were read solely to obtain the most important information about public affairs, aberrant events of little public importance would be ignored and typical patterns of quantitative significance would be emphasized; when the news is, by contrast, for most people largely an alternative to other forms of diversion or entertainment, intriguing oddities and human-interest items are in demand. Similarly, events that unfold in a suspenseful way or sex scandals among public figures are fully covered by the media, whereas the complexities of economic policy or quantitative analyses of public problems receive only minimal attention. Public officials, often able to thrive without giving the citizens good value for their tax monies, may fall over an exceptional mistake striking enough to be newsworthy. Extravagant statements, picturesque protests, and unruly demonstrations that offend much of the public they are designed to influence are also explicable in this way: they make diverting news and thus call attention to interests and arguments that might otherwise be ignored. Even some isolated acts of terrorism that are described as "senseless" can, from this perspective, be explained as effective means of obtaining the riveted attention of a public that otherwise would remain rationally ignorant.

This argument also helps us to understand certain apparent inconsistencies in the behavior of modern democracies. The arrangement of the income-tax brackets in all the major developed democracies is distinctly progressive, whereas the loopholes are more often tilted toward a minority of more prosperous taxpayers. Since both are the results of the same democratic institutions, why do they not have the same incidence? As I see it, the progression of the income tax is a matter of such salience and political controversy that much of the electorate knows about it, so populist and majoritarian considerations dictate a considerable degree of progression. The details of tax laws are far less widely known, and they often reflect the interests of small numbers of organized and usually more prosperous taxpayers. Several of the developed democracies similarly have adopted programs such as Medicare and Medicaid that are obviously inspired by the concerns about the cost of medical care to those with low or middle incomes, yet implemented or administered these programs in ways that resulted in large increases in income for prosperous physicians and other providers of medical care. Again, these diverse consequences seem to be explained by the fact that conspicuous and controversial choices of overall policies become known to the majorities who consume health care, whereas the many smaller choices needed to implement these programs are influenced primarily by a minority of organized providers of health care.

The fact that the typical individual does not have an incentive to spend much time studying many of his choices concerning collective goods also helps to explain some otherwise inexplicable individual contributions toward the provision of collective goods. The logic of collective action that has been described in this chapter is not immediately apparent to those who have never studied it; if it were, there would be nothing paradoxical in the argument with which this chapter opened, and students to whom the argument is explained would not react with initial skepticism.[15] No doubt the practical implications of this logic for the individual's own choices were often discerned before the logic was ever set out in print, but this does not mean that they were always understood even at the intuitive and practical level. In particular, when the costs of individual contributions to collective action are very small, the individual has little incentive to investigate whether or not to make a contribution or even to exercise intuition. If the individual knows the costs of a contribution to collective action in the interest of a group of which he is a part are trivially small, he may rationally not take the trouble to consider whether the gains are smaller still. This is particularly the case since the size of these gains and the policies that would maximize them are matters about which it is usually not rational for him to investigate.

This consideration of the costs and benefits of calculation about public goods leads to the testable prediction that voluntary contributions toward the provision of collective goods for large groups without selective incentives will often occur when the costs of the individual contributions are negligible, but that they will *not* often occur when the costs of the individual contributions are considerable. In other words, when the costs of individual action to help to obtain a desired collective good are small enough, the result is indeterminate and sometimes goes one way and sometimes the other, but when the costs get larger this indeterminacy disappears. We should accordingly find that more than a few people are willing to take the moment of time needed to sign petitions for causes they support, or to express their opinions in the course of discussion, or to vote for the candidate or party they prefer. Similarly, if the argument here is correct, we should not find many instances where individuals voluntarily contribute substantial sums of resources year after year for the purpose of obtaining some collective good for some large group of which they are a part. Before parting with a large amount of money or time, and particularly before doing so repeatedly, the rational individual will reflect on what this considerable sacrifice will accomplish. If the individual is a typical individual in a large group that would benefit from a collective good, his contribution will not make a perceptible difference in the amount that is provided. The theory here predicts that such contributions become less likely the larger the contribution at issue. [16]

V

Even when contributions are costly enough to elicit rational calculation, there is still one set of circumstances in which collective action can occur without selective incentives. This set of circumstances becomes evident the moment we think of situations in which there are only a few individuals or firms that would benefit from collective action. Suppose there are two firms of equal size in an industry and no other firms can enter the industry. It still will be the case that a higher price for the industry's product will benefit both firms and that legislation favorable to the industry will help both firms. The higher price and the favorable legislation are then collective goods to this "oligopolistic" industry, even though there are only two in the group that benefit from the collective goods. Obviously, each of the oligopolists is in a situation in which if it restricts output to raise the industry price, or lobbies for favorable legislation for the industry, it will tend to get half of the benefit. And the cost-benefit ratio of action in the common interest easily could be so favorable that, even though a firm bears the whole cost of its action and gets only half the benefit of this action, it could still profit from acting in the common interest. Thus if the group that would benefit from collective action is sufficiently small and the cost-benefit ratio of collective action for the group sufficiently favorable, there may well be calculated action in the collective interest even without selective incentives.

When there are only a few members in the group, there is also the possibility that they will bargain with one another and agree on collective action—then the action of each can have a perceptible effect on the interests and the expedient courses of action of others, so that each has an incentive to act strategically, that is, in ways that take into account the effect of the individual's choices on the choices of others. This interdependence of individual firms or persons in the group can give them an incentive to bargain with one another for their mutual advantage. Indeed, if bargaining costs were negligible, they would have an incentive to continue bargaining with one another until group gains were maximized, that is, until what we shall term a *group-optimal outcome* (or what economists sometimes call a "Pareto-optimal" outcome for the group) is achieved. One way the two firms mentioned in the previous paragraph could obtain such an outcome is by agreeing that each will bear half the costs of any collective action; each firm would then bear half the cost of its action in the common interest and receive half the benefits. It therefore would have an incentive to continue action in the collective interest until the aggregate gains of collective action were maximized. In any bargaining, however, each party has an incentive to seek the largest possible share of the group gain for itself, and usually also an incentive to threaten to block or undermine the collective action—that is, to be a "holdout"—if it does not get its preferred share of the group gains. Thus the bargaining may very well not succeed in achieving a group-optimal outcome and may also fail to achieve agreement on any collective action at all. The upshot of all this, as I explain elsewhere,[17] is that "small" groups can often engage in collective action without selective incentives. In certain small groups ("privileged groups") there is actually a presumption that some of the collective good will be provided. Nonetheless, even in the best of circumstances collective action is problematic and the outcomes in particular cases are indeterminate.

Although some aspects of the matter are complex and indeterminate, the essence of the relationship between the size of the group that would benefit from collective action and the extent of collective action is beautifully simple—yet somehow not widely understood. Consider again our two firms and suppose that they have *not* worked out any agreement to maximize their aggregate gains or to coordinate their actions in any way. Each firm will still get half the gains of any action it takes in the interest of the group, and thus it may have a substantial incentive to act in the group interest even when it is acting unilaterally. There is, of course, also a *group external economy*, or gain to the group for which the firm acting unilaterally is not compensated, of 50 percent, so unilateral behavior does not achieve a group-optimal outcome.[18] Now suppose there were a third firm of the same size—the group external economy would then be two thirds, and the individual firm would get only a third of the gain from any independent action it took in the group interest. Of course, if there were a hundred such firms, the group external economy would be 99 percent, and the individual firm would get only 1 percent of the gain from any action in the group interest. Obviously, when we get to large groups measured in millions or even thousands, the incentive for group-oriented behavior in the absence of selective incentives becomes insignificant and even imperceptible.

Untypical as my example of equal-sized firms may be, it makes the general point intuitively obvious: other things being equal, *the larger the number of individuals or firms that would benefit from a collective good, the smaller the share of the gains from action in the group interest that will accrue to the individual or firm that undertakes the action. Thus, in the absence of selective incentives, the incentive for group action diminishes as group size increases, so that large groups are less able to act in their common interest than small ones.* If an additional individual or firm that would value the collective good enters the scene, then the share of the gains from group-oriented action that anyone already in the group might take must diminish. This holds true whatever the relative sizes or valuations of the collective good in the group. . . .

The number of people who must bargain if a group-optimal amount of a collective good is to be obtained, and thus the costs of bargaining, must rise with the size of the group. This consideration reinforces the point just made. Indeed, both everyday observation and the logic of the matter suggest that for genuinely large groups, bargaining among all members to obtain agreement on the provision of a collective good is out of the question. The consideration mentioned earlier in this chapter, that social selective incentives are available only to small groups and (tenuously) to those larger groups that are federations of small groups, also suggests that small groups are more likely to organize than large ones.

The significance of the logic that has just been set out can best be seen by comparing groups that would have the same net gain from collective action, if they could engage in it, but that vary in size. Suppose there are a million individuals who would gain a thousand dollars each, or a billion in the aggregate, if they were to organize effectively and engage in collective action that had a total cost of a hundred million. If the logic set out above is right, they could not organize or engage in effective collective action without selective incentives. Now suppose that, although the total gain of a billion dollars from collective action and the aggregate cost of a hundred million remain the same, the group is composed instead of five big corporations or five organized municipalities, each of which would gain two hundred million. Collective action is not an absolute certainty even in this case, since each of the five could conceivably expect others to put up the hundred million and hope to gain the collective good worth two hundred million at no cost at all. Yet collective action, perhaps after some delays due to bargaining, seems very likely indeed. In this case any one of the five would gain a hundred million from providing the collective good even if it had to pay the whole cost itself; and the costs of bargaining among five would not be great, so they would sooner or later probably work out an agreement providing for the collective action. The numbers in this example are arbitrary, but roughly similar situations occur often in reality, and the contrast between "small" and "large" groups could be illustrated with an infinite number of diverse examples.

The significance of this argument shows up in a second way if one compares the operations of lobbies or cartels within jurisdictions of vastly different scale, such as a modest municipality on the one hand and a big country on the other. Within the town, the mayor or city council may be influenced by, say, a score of petitioners or a lobbying budget of a thousand dollars. A particular line of business may be in the hands of only a few firms, and if the town is distant enough from other markets only these few would need to agree to create a cartel. In a big country, the resources needed to influence the national government are likely to be much more substantial, and unless the firms are (as they sometimes are) gigantic, many of them would have to cooperate to create an effective cartel. Now suppose that the million individuals in our large group in the previous paragraph were spread out over a hundred thousand towns or jurisdictions, so that each jurisdiction had ten of them, along with the same proportion of citizens in other categories as before. Suppose also that the cost-benefit ratios remained the same, so that there was still a billion dollars to gain across all jurisdictions or ten thousand in each, and that it would still cost a hundred million dollars across all jurisdictions or a thousand in each. It no longer seems out of the question that in many jurisdictions the groups of ten, or subsets of them, would put up the thousand-dollar total needed to get the thousand for each individual. Thus we see that, if all else were equal, small jurisdictions would have more collective action per capita than large ones.

Differences in intensities of preference generate a third type of illustration of the logic at issue. A small number of zealots anxious for a particular collective good are more likely to act collectively to obtain that good than a larger number with the same aggregate willingness to pay. Suppose there are twenty-five individuals, each of whom finds a given collective good worth a thousand dollars in one case, whereas in another there are five thousand, each of whom finds the collective good worth five dollars. Obviously, the argument indicates that there would be a greater likelihood of collective action in the former case than in the latter, even though the aggregate demand for the collective good is the same in both. The great historical significance of small groups of fanatics no doubt owes something to this consideration.

VI

The argument in this chapter predicts that those groups that have access to selective incentives will be more likely to act collectively to obtain collective goods than those that do not, and that smaller groups will have a greater likelihood of engaging in collective action than larger ones. The empirical portions of *The Logic* show that this prediction has been correct for the United States. More study will be needed before we can be utterly certain that the argument also holds for other countries, but the more prominent features of the organizational landscape of other countries certainly do fit the theory. In no major country are large groups without access to selective incentives generally organized—the masses of consumers are not in consumers' organizations, the millions of taxpayers are not in taxpayers' organizations, the vast number of those with relatively low incomes are not in organizations for the poor, and the sometimes substantial numbers of unemployed have no organized voice. These groups are so dispersed that it is not feasible for any nongovernmental organization to coerce them; in this they differ dramatically from those, like workers in large factories or mines, who are susceptible to coercion through picketing. Neither does there appear to be any source of the positive selective incentives that might give individuals in these categories an incentive to cooperate with the many others with whom they share common interests.[19] By contrast, almost everywhere the social prestige of the learned professions and the limited numbers of practitioners of each profession in each community has helped them to organize. The professions have also been helped to organize by the distinctive susceptibility of the public to the assertion that a professional organization, with the backing of government, ought to be able to determine who is "qualified" to practice the profession, and thereby to control a decisive selective incentive. The small groups of (often large) firms in industry after industry, in country after country, are similarly often organized in trade associations or organizations or collusions of one kind or another. So, frequently, are the small groups of (usually smaller) businesses in particular towns or communities.

Even though the groups that the theory says cannot be organized do not appear to be organized anywhere, there are still substantial differences across societies and historical periods in the extent to which the groups that our logic says *could* be organized *are* organized. . . .

NOTES

[1] Cambridge: Harvard University Press, 1965, 1971. The 1971 version differs from the first 1965 printing only in the addition of an appendix. Some readers may have access to the first paperback edition published by Schocken Books (New York: 1968), which is identical to the 1965 Harvard version. Readers whose first language is not English may prefer *Die Logik des Kollektiven Handelns* (Tübingen: J. C. B. Mohr [Paul Siebeck], 1968), or *Logique de l'Action Collective* (Paris: Presses Universitaires de France, 1978). Translations in Japanese (from Minerva Shobo) and in Italian (from Feltrinelli) are forthcoming.

[2] There is a logically possible exception to this assertion, although not of wide practical importance, that is explained in footnote 68 of chapter 1 of *The Logic*, pp. 48–49.

[3] *Rational* need not imply *self-interested*. The argument in the text can hold even when there is altruistic behavior, although if particular types of altruistic behavior are strong enough it will not hold. Consider first altruistic attitudes about observable outcomes or results—suppose an individual would be willing to sacrifice some leisure or other personal consumption to obtain some amount of a collective good because of an altruistic concern that others should have this collective good. In other words, the individual's preference ordering takes account of the collective good obtained by others as well as personal consumption. This assumption of altruism does not imply irrationality, or a tendency to make choices that are inconsistent with the maximal satisfaction of the values or preferences the individual has. Altruism also does not call into question the normal diminishing marginal rates of substitution between any pair of goods or objectives; as more of any good or objective (selfish or altruistic) is attained, other things being equal, the extent to which other goods or objectives (selfish or altruistic) will be given up to attain more of that good or objective will diminish.

A typical altruistic and rational individual of the sort described will not make any substantial voluntary contributions to obtain a collective good for a large group. The reason is that in a sufficiently large group the individual's contribution will make only a small and perhaps imperceptible difference to the amount of collective good the group obtains, whereas at the same time every contribution reduces dollar-for-dollar the amount of personal consumption and private-good charity, and the diminishing marginal rates of substitution entail that these sacrifices become progressively more onerous. In equilibrium in large groups there is accordingly little or no voluntary contribution by the rational altruist to the provision of a collective good.

Jarring as it is to the common-sense notion of rationality, let us now make the special assumption that the altruist gets satisfaction not from observably better outcomes for others, but rather from his or her own sacrifices for them. On this assumption we can secure voluntary provision of collective goods even in the largest groups. Here each dollar of personal consumption that is sacrificed can bring a significant return in moral satisfaction, and the problem that substantial personal sacrifices bring little or no perceptible change in the level of public good provided is no longer relevant. Even though this latter participatory or "Kantian" altruism is presumably not the usual form of altruism, I think it does exist and helps to account for some observations of voluntary contributions to large groups. (Yet another possibility is that the altruist is result-oriented but neglects the observable levels of the public good, simply assuming that his or her sacrifices of personal consumption increase the utility of others enough to justify the personal sacrifice.) My own thinking on this issue has been clarified by reading Howard Margolis, *Selfishness, Altruism, and Rationality* (Cambridge: At the University Press, 1982).

⁴ This argument need not apply to small groups, which are discussed later in the chapter.

⁵ David J. McDonald, *Union Man* (New York: Dutton, 1969), p. 121, quoted in William A. Gamson, *The Strategy of Social Protest* (Homewood, Ill.: Dorsey Press, 1975), p. 68.

⁶ The references to the often violent interaction between employers and employees in the early stages of unionization should not obscure the consensual and informal "unionization" that also sometimes occurs because of employers' initiatives. This sort of labor organization or collusion arises because some types of production require that workers collaborate effectively. When this is the case, the employer may find it profitable to encourage team spirit and social interaction among employees. Staff conferences and work-group meetings, newsletters for employees, firm-sponsored employee athletic teams, employer-financed office parties, and the like are partly explained by this consideration. In firms that have the same employment pattern for some time, the networks for employee interaction that the employer created to encourage effective cooperation at work may evolve into informal collusions, or occasionally even unions, of workers, and tacitly or openly force the employer to deal with his employees as a cartelized group. This evolution is unlikely when employees are, for example, day laborers or consultants, but when stable patterns of active cooperation are important to production, the employer may gain more from the extra production that this cooperation brings about than he loses from the informal or formal cartelization that he helps to create. The evolution of this type of informal unionization implies that there is more organization of labor than the statistics imply, and that the differences between some ostensibly unorganized firms and unionized firms are not as great as might appear on the surface.

⁷ *The Logic*, p. 85.

⁸ This means in turn that sometimes individual corporations of substantial size can be political combinations with significant lobbying power. On less than voluntary corporate contributions, see J. Patrick Wright, *On a Clear Day You Can See General Motors* (Grosse Pointe, Mich.: Wright Enterprises, 1979), pp. 69–70.

⁹ *The Logic*, pp. 132–67.

¹⁰ Erik Lindahl, "Just Taxation—A Positive Solution," in Richard Musgrave and Alan T. Peacock, eds., *Classics in the Theory of Public Finance* (London: Macmillan, 1958), pp. 168–77 and 214–33. In a Lindahl equilibrium, the parties at issue are each charged a tax-price for marginal units of the public good that is equal to the value each places on a marginal unit of the good. When this condition holds, even parties that have vastly different evaluations of the collective good will want the same amount. It would take us far afield to discuss the huge literature on this matter now, but it may be helpful to nonspecialists to point out that in most circumstances in which the parties at issue expect Lindahl-type taxation, they would have an incentive to understate their true valuations of the collective good, since they would get whatever amount was provided however low their tax-price. There is an interesting literature on relatively subtle schemes that could give individuals an incentive to reveal their true valuations for public goods, thereby making Lindahl-equilibria attainable, but most of these schemes are a very long way indeed from practical application.

¹¹ See my primitive, early article, "The Principle of 'Fiscal Equivalence,'" *American Economic Review, Papers and Proceedings* 59 (May 1969):479–87.

¹² See, for a leading example, Martin C. McGuire, "Group Segregation and Optimal Jurisdictions," *Journal of Political Economy* 82 (1974):112–32.

¹³ See most notably Wallace Oates, *Fiscal Federalism* (New York: Harcourt Brace Jovanovich, Inc., 1972).

¹⁴ For very early work on the limited information voters may be expected to have, see Anthony Downs's classic *Economic Theory of Democracy* (New York: Harper, 1957).

¹⁵ I am indebted to Russell Hardin for calling this point to my attention. For a superb and rigorous analysis of the whole issue of collective action, see Hardin's *Collective Action* (Baltimore: The Johns Hopkins University Press, 1982).

¹⁶ There is another consideration that works in the same direction. Consider individuals who get pleasure from participating in efforts to obtain a collective good just as they would from ordinary consumption, and so are participation altruists (described in note 3). If the costs of collective action

to the individual are slight, the costs of consuming the participation pleasure or satisfying the moral impulse to be a participant are unlikely to prevent collective action. With the diminishing marginal rates of substitution that are described in note 3, however, the extent of collective action out of these motives will decrease as its price rises.

[17] *The Logic*, pp. 5–65.

[18] The assumption that there are two firms that place an equal value on the collective good is expositionally useful but will not often be descriptively realistic. In the much more common case, where the parties place different valuations on the public good, the party that places the larger absolute valuation on the public good is at an immense disadvantage. When it provides the amount of the collective good that would be optimal for it alone, then the others have an incentive to enjoy this amount and provide none at all. But the reverse is not true. So the larger party bears the whole burden of the collective good. (The party that places the larger value on the collective good has the option of trying to force the others to share the cost by withholding provision, but it is also at a disadvantage in the bargaining because it will lose more from this action than those with whom it is bargaining.) Thus a complete analysis of the likelihood of collective action must consider the relative sizes or valuations of the collective good of the parties involved as well as the size of the group; see the references in the next note [not printed here] on "the exploitation of the great by the small" and other consequences of intragroup variations in valuations of collective goods.

If the corner solution with the larger party bearing all the burden does not occur, and both firms provide some amount of the collective good under Cournot assumptions, then the two firms will tend to be of exactly the same size, as in the example chosen for expositional convenience in the text. Assume that each firm has to pay the same price for each unit of the collective good and that they have identical production functions for whatever private good they produce. Since they must, by the definition of a pure collective good, both receive the same amount of it, they can both be in equilibrium under Cournot assumptions only if their isoquants have the same slope at the relevant point. That is, the isoquants describing the output that results from each combination of the private good and public good inputs for each of the firms must have the same slope if the two firms enjoying the same amount of the collective good are each purchasing some of it at the same time. Under my identical production function and factor price assumptions, the two firms must then have exactly the same output or size.

Similarly remarkable results hold for consumers who share a collective good. Either the consumer that places the higher absolute valuation on the public good will bear the entire cost or else they will end up with equal incomes! When both consumers get the same amount of a collective good, they both can be continuing to purchase some under Cournot behavior only if they both have the same marginal rate of substitution between the public good and the private good, and thus (with identical utility functions and prices) identical incomes. Unless the two consumers have identical incomes *in the beginning*, there is inevitably exploitation of the great by the small. One possibility is that the richer consumer will bear the whole cost of the collective good. The only other possibility with independent adjustment is that the public good is so valuable that the richer consumer's initial purchases of it have such a large income effect on the poorer consumer that this poorer consumer ends up just as well off as the initially richer consumer, so both buy some amount of the collective good in equilibrium. I have profited from discussions of this point with my colleague Martin C. McGuire. For a stimulating and valuable, if partially incorrect, argument along related lines, see Ronald Jeremias and Asghar Zardkoohi, "Distributional Implications of Independent Adjustment in an Economy with Public Goods," *Economic Inquiry* 14 (June 1976):305–8.

[19] Even groups or causes that are so large or popular that they encompass almost everyone in the society cannot generate very substantial organizations. Consider those concerned about the quality of the environment. Although environmental extremists are a small minority, almost everyone is interested in a wholesome environment, and poll results suggest that in the United States, for example, there are tens of millions of citizens who think more ought to be done to protect the environment. In the late 1960s and early 1970s, certainly, environmentalism was faddish as well. Despite this, and despite subsidized postal rates for nonprofit organizations and reductions in the cost of direct mail solicitation due to computers, relatively few people pay dues each year to environmental organizations. The major environmental organizations in the United States have memberships measured in the tens or hundreds of thousands, with at least the larger (such as the

Audubon Society, with its products for bird-watchers) plainly owing much of their membership to selective incentives. There are surely more than 50 million Americans who value a wholesome environment, but in a typical year probably fewer than one in a hundred pays dues to any organization whose main activity is lobbying for a better environment. The proportion of physicians in the American Medical Association, or automobile workers in the United Automobile Workers union, or farmers in the Farm Bureau, or manufacturers in trade associations is incomparably greater.

17

RAYMOND A. BAUER, ITHIEL DE SOLA POOL, LEWIS
ANTHONY DEXTER

AMERICAN BUSINESS AND PUBLIC POLICY

QUASIUNANIMITY—PREMISE OF ACTION

. . . The usual pattern in American business and trade associations is one of unanimity, or, more accurately, quasiunanimity.[1]

Sometimes the minority preserves the façade of such unanimity if it does not feel that it has too much at stake. It then keeps its peace and does not obstruct. To quote one interview,

> His views are not the views of the association. . . . The association . . . has to be restrictive. . . . They have to look out for the interests of all the different parts of the industry. . . . While he wasn't much concerned with tariffs and trade and can be detached, the association has to try to protect anyone they can get protection for.

Thus, there can be dissent when the minority is relatively indifferent. The dissenters maintain the appearance of unanimity by self-restraint.

At other times, when the minority feels strongly on the issue, restraint is imposed on the majority. In this common situation, multipurpose organizations duck the controversial issues. Here is a description by one trade executive of conflicts of interests within his organization.

> It is necessary to distinguish different parts of the . . . industry. There are manufacturers of finished . . . products which are competitive with imports. There are manufacturers of finished . . . products which are noncompetitive with imports. There are manufacturers of unfinished parts which are competitive with imports, and there are manufacturers of unfinished parts which are noncompetitive with imports. The viewpoint of each would be different. . . .

That association took no stand at all on general tariff policy.

The problem becomes especially crucial in such catchall, multipurpose organizations as the Chamber of Commerce and the National Association of Manufacturers. Since such organizations are supposed to represent a wide range of interests in a wide range of businesses, special efforts are taken to avoid generating any avoidable internal conflict. Cautious procedures are employed for reaching a policy position, and spokesmen are confined to stating that position without elaboration, for fear that even the most cautious elaboration may produce dissension.

The pattern in the U.S. Chamber of Commerce is typical. The Chamber has over 3,000 affiliated local chambers with more than 1,500,000 individual members. In most cases, policy statements are recommended by one of the Chamber's specialized committees. They are reviewed by the board of directors and then sent to a vote, either by referendum or at the annual meeting. Each year the president of the Chamber for that year appoints such committees as the Foreign Commerce Department Committee or the Committee on International Political and Social Problems. He makes these appointments with the advice of the full-time managers of the various departments of the Chamber, who thus exert a degree of influence on the direction the committees may take. When a committee has formulated a policy statement, it is sent out for consideration at least six weeks before the annual meeting. If consensus is reached at that meeting, the policy statement is then published and ordinarily holds for three years, although it can be changed at any time. The procedure is majority vote, but there is a general understanding that no stand will be taken if opinion is sharply divided.

Once a policy has been adopted, any person testifying for the Chamber is limited to it. One respondent told us that he would never testify for the Chamber of Commerce again because, once he said his piece as expressed in the official resolution, there was no more he could say. If asked other questions, he must simply reply, "The Chamber has no position on that." This leaves Chamber witnesses relatively impotent, but maintains the possibility of unity for an organization purporting to represent all American business.

In this weak form, the Chamber supported the administration's trade program both in the 1950's and 1962. In 1962, however, the Chamber faced the problem of what to do about an embattled minority. In January, the Chamber's Foreign Commerce Committee endorsed the Kennedy program by a large majority. In February, the board of directors did the same, on the grounds that they were interpreting the still-binding general resolutions of past conventions. Chamber representatives testified accordingly at the House hearings. Dispute arose, however, over the bill's readjustment provisions. The board resolution attached minor strings to its endorsement of such aids, but, when the fiftieth annual convention met in May, protectionist groups led a bitter attack on such federal subsidies to business and "back-door" federal control of state unemployment benefit systems. Even though the protectionist attack was not directly on the trade issue, it would have left the Chamber leadership in the position of having its testimony repudiated. An unusual two-hour floor battle ensued, in which the official resolution was first rejected; much later, when, the protectionists alleged, half the delegates had left, a motion to reconsider was passed and the directors upheld. Such things happen, but only rarely, and the tension generated makes clear why an association that wants to represent all business cannot often afford such controversial stands.

The NAM procedure is similarly based on committee work and board action.

However, it seldom presents policy statements for a general vote by the members because it believes that only people with an active interest in a specific topic and who are informed on it should express an opinion. It, too, has an International Relations Committee. There are about 165 people on the committee, about half of them active, the rest joining to keep themselves informed on what is going on.

At the end of October, 1953, the NAM and its International Relations Committee went through a minor crisis. For some time, the NAM had been moving toward a more liberal trade policy. Strong influences were pushing it to adopt a statement supporting the President's program, as had the Chamber of Commerce and the Committee for Economic Development. NAM President Charles R. Sligh, Jr., had undergone a substantial conversion in views, attributed by his associates to his travels to Europe and contacts with European businessmen. During 1953, he had delivered speeches in which he had, for example, urged the United States to "work at a long-term tariff policy that will encourage the foreign producer to study his productivity problems, his merchandising and sales problems, and then compete intelligently in our markets over here." Some of the protectionist companies of the NAM had complained bitterly about these statements of personal views.

At the same time, the appropriate staff members of the NAM, almost to a man in favor of a liberal-trade policy, had been working hard with the members of the International Relations Committee, again overwhelmingly on the liberal-trade side, to draft a 400-page research report. This was the basis for a resolution drawn up by a steering group of the International Relations Committee and adopted by the committee in the middle of October. The board of directors was to decide on it on October 29. On the outside, the high powers of the Eisenhower administration were vigorously working on their business friends, for their strategy was in part to have all three major business associations—the Chamber, the CED, and the NAM—united behind the President's policy. A high administration source, for example, told us on October 20 to "watch for some surprising statements that will appear within the next month from some large business organizations." Arrangements were made to have Henning W. Prentiss, Jr., past president of the NAM and chairman of its International Relations Committee, testify before the Randall Commission on the afternoon of October 29, the very day of the board meeting, so that he could with full dramatic impact report the new policy. This was to be a major element in the strategy of winning a liberal report from the Randall Commission.

As the day of the board meeting approached, tension mounted and discussion increased. The NAM staff members who had guided this move could not predict the outcome. At the committee meeting, where they had expected a sharp fight, none developed. But in the board it was a different story. The majority was clearly for the resolution, but some individuals threatened to resign from the association if the resolution passed. The NAM remained without a policy.

Prentiss had to testify before the Randall Commission as follows:

The board of directors of the National Association of Manufacturers met today in New York to discuss the tariff and related issues.

For many years, the association has not endeavored to deal with the specific issue of the tariff.

It was our feeling that the membership was so evenly divided that no majority opinion could be established sufficiently strong to carry influence with those concerned with the development and implementation of national policy. Something over a year ago, however, following discussions in the board and in the International Relations Committee, the conclusion was reached that the topic should be put under study.

After several months of research and discussion and deliberation on the part of the International Relations Committee and the board of directors, the following resolution was adopted by the board early this afternoon:

. . . *Whereas, the National Association of Manufacturers has never adopted any position as to individual tariff rates and has no current policy as to other tariff matters, and*

Whereas, it is impracticable for the association to generalize in the national interest on a matter such as tariffs, which is so specific to the divergent points of view of its more than 20,000 members and their employees,

Therefore, be it resolved that:

The National Association of Manufacturers does not presume to speak in any way for its members as to tariff matters, and

Be it further resolved, that:

No existing positions or policies of the association on international economic matters shall be construed to be a position on tariffs.

The NAM and the Chamber of Commerce are constrained by the fact that they must try to speak for the full range of American business. They necessarily take positions only when business is relatively united.

But are specific industry associations more daring? Yes, but only to a degree. Here, too, we generally find the controlling principle to be quasiunanimity.

For example, the National Electrical Manufacturers Association had on the surface been one of the most active of the trade associations on the issue of protection; yet a close view reveals that it had taken no position. In July, 1953, the association decided to have a study of foreign-trade policies made. The occasion was the one-year extension of the Reciprocal Trade Act and creation of the Randall Commission. Accordingly, it had Donovan, Leisure, Newton, and Irvine make an analysis of legislation, treaties, and regulations affecting the ability of American manufacturers to compete with foreign producers, and it commissioned the National Industrial Conference Board to make a study called "United States and its Foreign Trade Position," which actually deals with electrical machinery. The more controversial phase of this, "The United States Electrical Manufacturing Industry in its Relation to the Security, Health, Safety and Welfare of the Country," was in turn subcontracted to Stone and Webster, an engineering corporation. To quote the NEMA,

All three organizations participating in the study were instructed to present factual conclusions only and to make no attempt at analysis, evaluation, or recommendation.

In view of this objective and factual approach, O. Glenn Saxon, Professor of Economics at Yale University, was asked to make an analysis and evaluation of the three documents and to prepare his own conclusions and recommendations as to foreign economic policy.

Note that nowhere had the association taken a stand. In April, 1954, however, a group of manufacturers in their own name issued some "Recommendations of Electrical Manufacturers on Foreign Trade Policy." The signatories included manufacturers representing $3⅓ billion of annual sales and more than 235,000 employees. They included Westinghouse and eight departments of General Electric, but not General Electric as such. Sensitivity to conflicting interests reached down even below the corporate level. The chairman of the board of G.E. testified before the House committee, supporting the Trade Agreements Act "in broad effect."

Many trade associations and also many major companies adopted this permissive pattern, evading an official position while permitting action which smacked of one. A vice-president of a very large company, himself a strong, able, and vocal protectionist, said of his company:

> They really had no general stand except a very broad "goody-goody" policy. He said this was because of conflicting interests in the company. . . . "I am having a rough time in trying to persuade the company to come around." . . . "You know, you will find very few companies, except possibly one which has just a single main product, that has a clear stand on policy. . . . The trade associations . . . have to take a stand except, of course, if they represent businesses with conflicting interests. . . . If you have equal and conflicting interests in an organization, you get no action. . . ." Each department at [his company] has its own export division, and "I have a hell of a time with the export managers."

Although the company has what this vice-president considers virtually no policy, in the public eye it is a leading protectionist company, and that primarily because of this man's dynamism and effective public action.

Executives of trade associations expressed concern over the danger of prejudicing their organizations' strength by attempting to take stands on issues on which unanimity was absent.

> An organization of this kind has a wide diversity of interests, and it should not get embroiled in tariff fights. You don't get anywhere; you split your organization; you decrease its effectiveness; you end up with a weak-kneed position which doesn't express anything. I am speaking frankly now; the businessmen who are interested have their own trade associations who can go to bat on it. . . . There is a definite feeling that it is better to have a strong association . . . rather than to weaken and debilitate the association by inside rows. The main position is to keep the organization strong.

A variant way of avoiding internal friction is for a parent body to have a policy but not to enforce it on its members. The best example of this was the labor movement. As noted in our chapter on Detroit, the national CIO leadership strongly favored a more liberal trade policy, but many member unions and even the United Auto Workers locals associated with bicycle manufacturing favored protection for their industries. National officials of the CIO and UAW were extremely anxious to avoid putting any appreciable pressure on their locals. The only difference between the stance of the CIO leaders and that of typical trade-association executives is that the CIO leadership did view itself as a policy-forming unit, whereas trade-association executives typically view themselves as arbitrators between forces in the organization and as the members' mouthpiece. National labor leaders have more freedom in setting policies than do trade-association executives because AFL-CIO affiliates and locals are unlikely to secede if in disagreement with a national policy. But the labor leadership, too, felt impotent to prevent dissenting members from expressing their points of view.

Thus, throughout, there is a pattern of avoidance of issues, suppression of controversy, and at least the pretense of unanimity.

Sometimes issues cannot be avoided. What happens when there are sharp differences of opinion in American trade associations? Here, the pattern is one of multiplication of associations. Most business firms belong to several associations, and large firms belong to scores. An industry is apt to have many associations covering the variety of interests represented within it. In the textile industry, for example, a quick count reveals fifty-one associations, and these do not include those concerned with either raw fibers and thread or garments and finished products. For some purposes, such as research, the widest unity of the industry is feasible. Thus, there is a Textile Research Institute, an American Association of Textile Technology, and a Textile Economics Bureau. There is also a Textile Salesmen's Association, a Textile Export Association, and a Webb-Pomerene Act Association. For other purposes, since the interests of different fabrics are competitive, there is a National Association of Wool Manufacturers; a Burlap Council; a Corduroy Council of America; an American Lace Manufacturers Association; a National Federation of Textiles, for rayons and other man-made fabrics; and many others. There was no nation-wide cotton association, for the Northern and Southern cotton textile industries were too sharply antagonistic to each other. There was, at the time of the study, the National Association of Cotton Manufacturers, which was the association of the Northern firms, and the American Cotton Manufacturers Institute, that of the Southern firms. Since then, under the impact of the merger movement, firms increasingly find themselves manufacturing more than one textile, so the Northern group has organized the Northern Textile Association to permit representation of firms whose interests extend beyond cotton.

Partial coalition and partial conflict of interests is the pattern throughout. Woolen manufacturers share with wool-growers an interest in research and in the promotion of the use of wool, but they are at odds on whether these be American or British woolens. The manufacturers' and growers' interests converge in wanting protection against woolen fabric imports, but they find themselves in conflict regarding imports of raw wool. Cheap raw-wool imports help the American manufacturer compete with his British rivals, but hurt the American grower. In conflict with both the manufacturers and the growers, importers want free trade in general. Thus, a multiplicity of associations is called into being to reflect these varied interests. Alongside the National Association of Woolen Manufacturers, the American Wool Council unites the producers and the dealers with the manufacturers. For purposes of wool promotion, the Wool Bureau unites the entire American industry. It is represented in the American Wool Council with the British International Wool Secretariat. Separated from these associations to represent special interests are the American Trade Association for British Woolens and, for the fabric wholesalers, the Woolen Jobbers Association.

This pattern of multiplication and division permits each association to follow the rule of quasiunanimity within its range of issues and to permit those of its own members who have a different viewpoint to express it through another and more appropriate association. Often, these divergent bodies actually operate from the same headquarters and share personnel. There are some business firms in the field of association management which provide staff and offices for a large number of very small associations. For the larger associations, which have their own staffs and offices, it is also convenient to have several faces for different purposes. Thus, the National Coal Association has in its large and well-staffed Washington office the Coal Exporters Association. The former has been the voice of protection for the coal industry and has played down the prospect of the coal export market; the latter has the duty to maximize that prospect, whatever it may be.

Situations constantly arise which call for discretion on the part of officers and staff members of trade associations. We think, for instance, of the president of a trade organization who was also president of a company which had taken a strong protectionist position. But, we were told, "They dissociate themselves from the association in such matters since they . . . recognize that their interests are different from the rest of the association."

To summarize, it is difficult to get multipurpose business associations to take stands on controversial issues. The broader and more heterogeneous the organization, the greater the probability that some subgroups will dissent on a given issue. In a sense this means that, the more an organization represents the business community as a whole, the more unlikely it is to become committed on such an issue as foreign-trade policy. For the man who is seeking organizational support, there are ways out of this dilemma. There is a good chance that, in the multiplicity of business and trade organizations, one of those to which his firm belongs may be substantially united on the particular issue. Another possibility is to form a new organization to work on the specific problem. Thus, in 1953–1962 we found in the special-purpose organizations—the Strackbein group, the Committee for a National Trade Policy, and the like—firms grouped together which had nothing in common except support for or opposition to the Reciprocal Trade Act.

FURTHER DIFFICULTIES
OF THE PRESSURE GROUPS

The efforts of business and trade associations to avoid disintegration over controversial issues lead to a proliferation of organizations and particularly to the formation of specialized pressure groups designed to deal with specific issues. Even such single-minded groups had difficulties we did not anticipate. They suffered from shortages of money, skilled personnel, information, and time.

"All That Money Being Thrown Around"

The image of lobbyists wallowing in ill-gotten and ill-spent lucre is one of the great myths of our time. There are few very-well-paid lobbyists even at the peak of the profession. However, there have been legislative issues on which a great deal of money has been spent. A dramatic example of an attempt to "buy" legislation was the Natural Gas Bill of 1956, though the exposure of paper bags full of cash defeated that bill. We think such instances to be atypical, but we are interested now in how much money the foreign-trade pressure groups had for their range of activities.

The reciprocal-trade controversy, like that over the Natural Gas Bill, was one on the outcome of which many people stood to gain or lose large sums of money. Despite that, the men we observed were not overfed lobbyists with lush bankrolls throwing swank cocktail parties, but rather hard-working organizers devoting an excessive portion of their time to raising enough money to keep their organizations going and constantly skimping on obvious things to do because the money was not available.

The lobbyists themselves are the source of part of the false public image of men with unbounded resources. Each side vastly overestimates the other. Each pictures the other as having an unlimited budget, an enormous staff, and all the operational possibilities which they themselves wish they had but feel frustrated because they have not. Each side sees itself as David against Goliath.

Let our respondents speak for themselves. Here are some comments by people on the low-tariff side describing the campaign of the protectionists:

> The coal people spent $1,000,000 in the first half of this year [1953] on the tariff fight.
>
> X said the interesting thing this year will be the . . . broad plastering of the Strackbein group. They have just hired a high-priced public-relations counsel to work for them who will spread the idea all over the country. I expect the Committee for a National Trade Policy, on the other hand, will spend most of its time at the telephone and do a hand-tooled job.

Here is what the protectionists say about those on the low-tariff side of the issue:

> "You know, we are just amateurs at this game." We replied, "Well, if you are

amateurs, who are the professionals?" He said, "People like the Ford people. We just have a typewriter and a mimeograph machine, and they have all sorts of money and resources."

Some independent oil producers to whom we spoke,

> . . . indicated . . . admiration and . . . even envy of Standard Oil of New Jersey. They said, for example, it is probably the only organization that has the facts and figures of what is going on in the coal industry. We asked them how Standard Oil was able to influence policy, and they said it was largely through their resources. When the government runs into a problem, it goes to them, and Standard gives them the data and sometimes even lends them personnel to work on problems for the government for a long period of time. We asked them what kept them from doing the same, and they shrugged their shoulders and said, "Simply money."

Another protectionist said:

> Ike has lines out to all the mass-production industries. You know, he has people like Wilson of General Motors, and all through the campaign you could see him around with people like this. He thinks that these people are the important people in the country. And the Coleman committee speaks for this group.

An interviewer reported of a protectionist lobbyist:

> I asked him if he thought they had been getting a fair break from the press. He laughed and said that [the press has] a stand and that therefore they gave fuller reporting to the other side. . . . Newsprint, pulp, and pulpwood are all on the free list. Together, the imports of them are $800,000,000 a year. He said that this means more to them than the second-class rate, and they are organizing a big fight on that.

Another reported:

> I then asked what he thought would likely be the outcome of the trade debate in the light of this political situation. He said, off the record, that Eisenhower will get what he wants. I asked if that doesn't discourage his [trade association] members from doing anything. He said that they feel desperate, they don't think they'll win. "They feel like Custer's last stand." [Our] industry is a $50,000,000-a-year industry. In Washington that doesn't mean a thing. It is chicken-feed.

The contestants on both sides would be shocked to discover how impotent their rivals feel. For example, one public-relations firm was described to us on several occasions as the leading one on the protectionist side. Here was what our interviewer found when he called on the firm in Washington:

> The offices of U, V, Y, and Z, though at a good address, were surprisingly modest. Four small rooms led into the reception room. There were one or two secretaries around and one man besides X. . . . X was fiddling inexpertly with a pile of papers. . . . I asked him when his firm had become involved in the trade issue. He

said that they had started on it last year when they represented A until July, when his money ran out. . . . In addition to representing A, they also worked for a group of big companies in the electrical and chemical fields . . . as more of an information service than public relations, since these companies were afraid to do anything. They lost that account, too. . . . X said that his firm will probably get out of this field. . . . Their present tariff accounts are the B industry and C industry. The big companies, in particular, won't stick their necks out. . . . He said that Strackbein got a little money from the big companies he had mentioned before, but not much.

On the low-tariff side, the story was much the same. The history of the Committee for a National Trade Policy can be written largely in terms of a struggle with finance. It started with a plan which called for the raising of $300,000. By the end of the first year, it had succeeded in raising about $200,000. The overhead amounted to $15,000 or $16,000 a month. Simple arithmetic shows how little money was left for campaign activities. None of the top staff people were particularly adept at or interested in fund-raising, so a professional fund-raiser was employed. He did not succeed and was dropped. Every mailing and advertisement had to be measured against the funds in the treasury.

A draft budget of October, 1953, though, like any other budget, not fully conforming to what actually happened, sheds some light on the operation. The budget was divided between operations and special activities. Operations included salaries, offices, and fund-raising. Salaries for fourteen employees, five or six of them clerical, were to come to about $11,000 a month. Rent and office costs were under $1,400 a month. Costs of fund-raising were estimated at $5,000 a month. Had these expenditures not been cut, and they are certainly not unreasonable for an organization intended to carry on a vigorous nation-wide campaign, the entire $200,000 would have disappeared there. The major budgeted special activity was preparing a mailing list of 100,000 names. That was expected to cost about $35,000. That would have been, for the most part, a one-time expense, but certainly an essential one for an effective organization. Lack of money prevented the completion of that job. After the first year, the financial position of the organization became even more stringent.

We have some less complete figures on other organizations. For example, the combined advertising and public-relations budget of the Swiss watch manufacturers in America reached $2,000,000 a year. Of this, most went for watch advertising which served both institutional and commercial purposes. (How can one distinguish the political effects of a Swiss watch advertisement from its sales purposes?) About $250,000 of the $2,000,000 went for public-relations activities in the campaign against tariff increases. Outside of that budget, there were some activities paid for by American assemblers using Swiss movements. There were also legal costs incurred in Tariff Commission hearings and activities of the Swiss Embassy which might well be chargeable in a complete accounting of what it cost to attempt to avoid a tariff increase.

One can argue that the sums expended on such a case are large or small, depending on the approach one takes. The total sums spent by all parties in a fight on a major national issue in which many millions of dollars are at stake may be very large indeed. In the instance of Swiss watches, the nonadvertising expenditures by one side may have substantially exceeded $500,000 a year. But that figure includes all the relevant activities of all the firms, all the trade associations, all the law cases, and also the relevant activities of the Swiss government. On the other hand, the sums available to any one lobbying or public-information organization or program are apt to be much too small to enable it to act in any decisive fashion or to acquire any megalomaniacal fantasies. The $120,000 to $150,000 a year that the major public-relations firm representing the watch assemblers received as its fee had first to cover its overhead and salaries. What was left for campaign purposes was hardly a stupendous figure.

We have no reason to believe that any one of the pressure groups on the trade issue wanted to buy votes. We know that Congressional votes were in general not available to be bought. But even if a group wished to turn from propaganda to corruption, no one of the organizations had the discretionary funds to undertake such an enterprise. Presumably, the funds of the natural-gas interests referred to above were more centrally channelled. However, as we have already indicated, the reciprocal-trade controversy was a more normal situation.

The failure to recognize the multiplicity and diversity of spending bodies, each with its individual goals, leads to a false image of pressure group processes. The total sums spent somehow leave the impression of plutocratic giants, able by their wealth to totally distort the public process. Clearly, if one takes the few instances concerning which we have reasonably reliable figures and projects those figures over the total number of organizations operating in this field and if one then adds to these organizational expenditures the amounts spent by business firms and individuals in their own contributed time and effort—for example, arranging meetings, making speeches, writing letters—one cannot escape the conclusion that the reciprocal-trade controversy cost the participants many millions of dollars a year. Yet, wherever one looked at the persons actually spending that money, one saw only harassed men with tight budgets and limited campaign funds, once their essential organizational overheads had been met.

Lack of Skilled Personnel

A profession needs an ideology to justify itself. Without a proud self-image, it will not attract its full potential in personnel. A man and his family are proud of the practice of law. Most mothers would say, "I didn't raise my boy to be a lobbyist." As long as that situation prevails, the best talent will not be found in pressure politics. One of our respondents described legislative work as a young man's game. A family man moves from it to more stable occupations. Many lobbyists were in fact older, but those were not generally the most gifted men. This is a difficult point to document. We have no evidence on intrinsic ability; yet it is our distinct impression that, except for a few highly capable men at the top of the heap, the best men leave the field.

Lack of Knowledge

The lack of money and personnel is compounded by such other problems as inadequate information. It takes able men and much money to do good research, and research is one thing every lobby needs. Facts are their stock in trade. Research is needed to write speeches, to put out pamphlets, to prepare testimony, to find the arguments which will convince doubters. It may not be research as the academician conceives it, but, such as it is, it takes much of the organizer's time.

At one level, if one asked what these association organizers did, we would answer in these terms: they produced publicity; they arranged meetings; they stimulated letters, articles, and speeches. In so doing, they raised the level of public discussion and awareness of public policy. We do not mean for a moment to suggest that they were educators in intent or that their products would meet the normal standards of scholarship. We suggest only that the net effect of all this discussion, counterdiscussion, statement, and correction is a certain degree of enlightenment.

The scholarly researcher may be both intrigued and disturbed as he observes the research activity conducted by interest groups and the standards of integrity in it. The prevailing attitude was least self-consciously expressed by one public-relations man from whose interview we quote:

> He said: "We did a survey recently which showed 300,000 unemployed as a result of foreign imports. That's probably about right, although no one can prove it one way or the other. . . ." I asked if some of the protectionists whom he dealt with who responded to particular injuries didn't have some trouble rationalizing their view in terms of the big picture. He said, "No, it doesn't bother them for long. They convince themselves that theirs is the national interest." He then cited himself as an example. He said: "Often I have doubts when I take a job, but after a while I find I am convinced. I like to tell myself that it is because I know more about the subject, but that is not really it. If that were it, why would I always find I am convinced of the side I am working on?" I suggested to him that there might be limits to this process. He said: "That's right. You don't get into a job in the first place if you don't like the looks of it. . . ." He said that he did a job on the oil cartel. "There are seven companies that divide up the world between them. We publicized that, and it is probably true."

In short, the job of an operator is to seek those facts which build his case. The operator here, as in psychological warfare, as in law cases, as in all fields except pure research, is balancing three standards. He wants the facts that will support his case, that will not kick back by exposing him as deceitful, and that are reliable because he himself objects in principle to lying. His assumption is that, since he is on the right side, there must be some facts that will help, not hurt. His job is to find them. He has no taboo against stating with great certitude something that is only probable or against stating broadly something that is only partially true; but he does not want to make his case out of whole cloth, nor does he believe that he can successfully do so. As one respondent put it:

He said that they tried to get informational bulletins out, and then he said half-apologetically, "We call them informational bulletins, but some people don't think they are just information. . . . You know, we may slant the data a little bit our way, but it has to be sound; we see to it that it is sound because we cannot get caught off base."

Thus, a large part of the activity of the organizers consists of research, and one of the reasons for their relative ineffectiveness is the lack of good research on both sides. Congressmen frequently said that they would talk to anybody who would bring them really fresh information. Bored to death by hearing the same old stories, they often expressed a real craving for some solid facts that they could believe. One may wonder whether this was not to some extent a search for a *deus ex machina*, a wistful feeling on the part of congressmen that there must be some objective answer that would get them out of difficult decisions. Yet, receptive to facts they were, whatever the reason.

Thus, information is often power. A complex example is provided by the petroleum industry. For good and sufficient reasons, major oil companies are afraid to be overtly politically aggressive. They collided with the antitrust laws once, and they have been a symbol of big business in the public mind. They hesitate to lobby, and they would probably never dream of organizing their employees in a letter-writing campaign. Their time-perspective is a long one, and they recognize that self-restraint on a momentary issue will in the end pay off in public acceptance of the industry. It is therefore somewhat of a mystery how these few large firms succeeded in holding off oil-import quotas as long as they did against the much more vigorous demands of the American independent producers for protection. The answer lies in part in the fund of expertise and knowledge which they have accumulated. As noted in a quotation above, when the government needs expert personnel for staffing policy jobs in the administration of petroleum, it is likely to find them among men who have worked for the major oil companies. When one needs facts about the world petroleum situation, he is likely to find them in the excellent library organized by Standard Oil of New Jersey. Indeed, in their fight against Standard and the other major producers, the independents turned to Standard Oil to get the basic data with which to fight them. The sensitivity of the big companies to public relations, their unwillingness to be aggressive, and the power that knowledge gives them are all illustrated by the fact that, when the independents went to Standard to get the data with which to fight Standard, the latter helped them and asked no questions. Standard thus won the respect and the frustrated awe which, we have noted, was felt by those who opposed it, but on the basis of imperfect knowledge.

Though information can be power, it is a power usually untapped by the pressure groups we studied. The amount of factual information most of them had assembled was limited indeed. Neither side budgeted much for research. The Coleman committee initially had some rather large research plans, but these were the first casualties of budgetary stress. One highly placed respondent noted that:

The figures which really substantiate a case of damage are never presented. Everyone claims damage, but when you ask them to prove it there just isn't any. The only statistics that are ever quoted are Picquet's.[2]

Another, who worked for a public-relations firm, also complained that Picquet's volume had become a bible for reciprocal-trade supporters and a target for protectionists, since it had almost a monopoly on the facts.

Lack of Time

The harassment we observed was not only financial. The life of a Washington pressure-group organizer is not a leisurely one. That is both its charm and its agony. In working for any legislative cause, whether as a lobbyist or as a congressman, there is just too much to do. An executive of a trade association has to concern himself, not only with national policies, but also with organization finances, membership, meetings, bulletins and magazines, correspondence, inquiries, staffing, and the like. He must follow legislative and administrative developments, not only on tariffs, but also on government contracts, taxes, and regulations of all sorts. He has to collect economic statistics, business news, and scientific and legislative reports. If he is in a single-issue organization, such as the CNTP or the Strackbein committee, he is concerned with changes in tariff rates and regulations for each of the products listed in the tariff rules. He is concerned, not only with the Reciprocal Trade Bill and all its ramifications, but also with customs simplification, GATT, OTC, Buy-American legislation, agricultural legislation, and such administrative proceedings as Tariff Commission escape-clause proceedings and State Department reciprocal-trade negotiations. In this day of big government, there is never enough time to do more than select from among its complexities what to cope with, or else to drift, pushed by events into a few of the many things one might do. Most pressure-group activity is emergency fire-fighting. There is seldom time to do much more. Long-range planning goes by default. . . .

PRESSURE GROUP OR SERVICE BUREAU?

Our survey of business leaders as well as our community studies showed that men tend to make and maintain contact with those who agree with them. This tendency also characterized the staffs of the pressure groups. An impediment to the effectiveness of these organizations was a deep resistance to approaching unfriendly people. Perhaps the kind of person who becomes a public-relations man or a lobbyist is more than usually other-directed and anxious to be approved and to please. Perhaps the lobbyist is simply the victim of a calculation that he is unlikely to convert any enemies; his most effective use of time is thus not to debate with his opponents but to stimulate his friends to act. That calculation is certainly part of the operational code of the American lobbyist, whether it is the result of bitter experience or whether it is a rationalization of a distaste for being rebuffed. We know that very few lobbyists spend any substantial amount of time working on those who do not already agree with them, and it became clear to us as outside observers that the result was frequently the missing of opportunities. The events of 1962 again require us to qualify our generalizations. The liberal traders had learned some lessons by then.[3] The strategy in 1962 was developed by men who already in 1953, in the Simpson bill controversy, had recognized the advantages of a direct approach to affected industries. In 1962, the liberal-trade high command successfully approached the textile industry and unsuccessfully approached the chemical industry. The basic 1962 strategy of splitting the protectionists by concessions to some of them necessitated negotiations with those foes. We shall have more to say about the textile case. The campaign by the administration on the chemical industry was carried as far as a private meeting between Howard C. Petersen, the President's special assistant on trade policy, and industry leaders in February at a session of the Manufacturing Chemists Association in New York. But, these exceptions notwithstanding, we observed no more common mistake than that of failing to push people who were movable because it was assumed that they were on the other side.

This became obvious to us as we watched the controversy from Capitol Hill. We note below how few were the congressmen who had heard anything from the major pressure groups and how many there were who were genuinely puzzled as to how they should vote and who would have appreciated clear indications of where their constituencies stood and what the issues were. They were the highly committed spokesmen of each side with whom in fact the pressure groups were in contact. There was a handful of protectionist spokesmen in Congress who were in constant communication with the major protectionist lobbies. There was also a handful of spokesmen for reciprocal trade who were in constant communication with the Coleman committee and with the Randall staff. For either set of lobbyists to have approached congressmen who were fully committed to the other side would have been indeed a foolish waste of effort and source of annoyance. It might in fact have been dangerous, for, as we have noted elsewhere, legitimate communications that do not annoy a congressman are not viewed as pressure, whereas those which threaten him are. A lobbyist approaching a real enemy is apt to invite a blast in *The Congressional Record* or elsewhere about selfish interests bringing pressures to bear.[4]

In short, it makes sense to avoid one's out-and-out opponents in Congress. But what of the moderates and mildly interested people in the middle? A lobbyist is a busy man. It is quite a chore to keep himself informed as to the views and desires of over 500 congressmen. Yet, to some extent each side tries to do just that. Late in 1953, Mrs. Rachel Bell, who had worked on the Hill on a series of international issues starting with the Committee to Defend America by Aiding the Allies, drafted for the Coleman committee a list of all the congressmen and where they might be expected to stand, based on past voting records modified by recent public statements. Our interviewer, familiar as he was with this issue, immediately spotted what he considered a number of wrong estimates. He asked, for example, about Congressman X, who was listed as undecided. After some discussion, it became clear that there was no knowledge at the CNTP that this congressman had issued a strongly protectionist statement approximately a year before. This is not a criticism, for, conversely, there were scores of congressmen on whom the committee had information where we would have pleaded ignorance. It is simply one more evidence of the enormity of the task. Eighteen months later, when a vote was taken, the list of the senators proved less than two-thirds correct, although thirteen had been listed as undecided. In the House, the prediction was three-quarters correct and one-quarter wrong, with a still larger proportion than in the Senate listed as undecided.

Thus, there was a great deal of uncertainty as to who stood where. In part, this was due to ignorance by the predictor; in part, it arose from the fact that many congressmen had not made up their minds.

This situation adds to the significance of the fact that lobbyists fear to enter where they may find a hostile reception. Since uncertainty is greatest precisely regarding those who are undecided, the lobbyist is apt to neglect contact with those very persons whom he might be able to influence. It is easy from an academic armchair to point this out and call it foolish, but if one puts oneself into the shoes or swivel chair of a harassed organizer, it is easy to see how it happens. The morning begins with a desk loaded with unfinished jobs and unanswered mail. There are hundreds of things which should be done, if only one could find the time for the effort required. Possibilities flash across the mind in the twinkle of an eye. One possibility may be to telephone a good friend, the assistant to a congressman, to ask that some article be read into *The Congressional Record*. Another may be to telephone the executive of another association with whom one works regularly to ask that it send a representative to a meeting. Another may be to line up a speaker in response to a request. Still another may be to arrange a luncheon with a possible source of funds. Finally, there may be the chronic awareness that he really ought to get in touch with any one of four or five congressmen about whose stand he is quite vague. Most of the first four possibilities simply involve picking up the telephone and having a pleasant conversation with a sympathetic and familiar colleague. Raising funds is painful, but the pressures to do it are never absent.

Approaching an unfamiliar congressman, however, immediately raises problems. To begin with, the fact that one views him as a question mark means that one's contact is limited. Our hypothetical organizer is puzzled. Perhaps he can write a letter to a businessman in the congressman's district and ask for information on likely reactions and on lines of approach. Until he gets an answer, he had better not walk brashly into what might prove a difficult situation and might do more harm than good. Some time later he gets an answer. Perhaps it doesn't tell him much, or perhaps it reinforces his notion that he ought to do something, but he may still need to find a way to make proper contact. Should he ask a mutual friend for an introduction? If so, he has put himself in debt to that friend, who may or may not be an advocate of his cause.

It is so much easier to carry on activities within the circle of those who agree and encourage you than it is to break out and find potential proselytes, that the day-to-day routine and pressure of business tend to shunt those more painful activities aside. The result is that *the lobbyist becomes in effect a service bureau for those congressmen already agreeing with him, rather than an agent of direct persuasion.*[5]

Breakfast at the Willard

This tendency to "work with our own people" was true on both sides of the controversy. One of the high points in the activities of the Strackbein committee was its cooperation with Congressman Simpson during the time that he served on the Randall Commission. The commission's deliberations were held entirely in executive session. Clarence Randall felt from the beginning that his only chance of getting a unanimous report was to avoid public controversy, for that would force members of the commission with special affiliations to make statements for the record which would be hard to reverse later. He himself adopted a policy of refusing to meet the press, and he urged his example on all commission members. Congressman Simpson, presumably in the minority on the commission, apparently felt that these rules of procedure were to his disadvantage. He maintained virtually daily contact with Oscar Strackbein in order to keep running pressure on the commission.

The commission, it will be recalled, permitted only two days of open hearings. Among those who testified was Strackbein. A few days later, his Nation-wide Committee of Industry, Agriculture, and Labor on Import-Export Policy held a meeting at the Willard Hotel, at which it adopted a resolution calling for the removal of Clarence Randall as commission chairman. The keynote speaker was Representative Simpson. Simpson himself avoided calling for Randall's removal, but his speech gave the meeting its newsworthiness. There seems little doubt that this meeting was arranged in response to Simpson's desire and to help him in his conflict with Randall. In this instance, the Strackbein committee was able to score because it could make itself an auxiliary of a person with power.

Helping Senator Gore

A similar high point of activity and effectiveness was reached by the Coleman committee in June, 1954, when it was able to put itself at the service of Sen. Albert Gore (D., Tenn.). To understand how a committee organized by Eisenhower supporters at the President's request ended up working for a Democratic senator, we need to know the background.

The administration had recognized the rising resistance to the Randall Commission proposals and had therefore agreed to a temporary, one-year extension of the Reciprocal Trade Act. To the ardent supporters of reciprocal trade, this was a defeat and in the eyes of some a sell-out. They anticipated continued uncertainty among foreign businessmen as to the prospects in the American market, and uncertainty is, as we have noted, at least as important as high tariffs in restricting trade development. They also foresaw the next renewal as coming in a less favorable juncture, although administration strategists believed, on the contrary, that time would work in their favor. In any case, the more ardent reciprocal-trade supporters saw themselves as betrayed. On the Senate floor, Senator Gore seized on this situation. He introduced an amendment giving the administration exactly the bill it had originally wished, with a three-year extension. This was obviously a political gesture designed to embarrass the President; the Democrats were offering him what he wanted after he had agreed to relinquish it. Randall and President Eisenhower resolved their dilemma by adhering to the agreement they had reached. They opposed the Gore amendment and urged their Republican supporters to vote against it.

The Committee for a National Trade Policy, however, made the opposite decision. It had long sought leadership from the White House which it did not feel it was getting. Now, for the first time, it suddenly found itself with strong leadership and a chance to be of service. True, nobody expected the Gore amendment to pass both houses of Congress. Still, rationally or irrationally, the staff of the CNTP saw in this unexpected event the chance to strike at least one blow for liberalized trade. It went into vigorous and forceful action. For that one and only time during the period of this study, it acted with some of the characteristics usually attributed to a pressure group.

Senator Gore recognized that one of his major problems was to persuade people, particularly Republicans, that his motion was not merely a slick political trick designed to embarrass the administration. To demonstrate that he was acting out of deep conviction and a sense of the importance of the issue, he decided to introduce the bill with a thoughtful four-hour speech. He instructed his assistants to prepare one.

For this they needed help, as they also did for the rounding-up of votes and support. First, they telephoned Clarence Randall and, quoting his own words to him, said they were getting him what he wanted and were sure that Randall would be glad to help. They wanted staff writers and a list of names of people whose supporting statements could be obtained. Randall was ambivalent but annoyed, feeling that the whole thing was political gunplay. As tactfully as he could, he declined and suggested that Gore's assistant approach the CNTP. When the CNTP picked up the Gore proposal, Randall was in fact perturbed, although of two minds. In retrospect, at least, he has said that it was perfectly proper for the CNTP as a bipartisan group committed on the issue to take the stand it did.

On Friday, June 18, one of Gore's assistants telephoned Meyer Rashish at the CNTP. That was the first time that they had had direct dealings. Between that Friday and the following Thursday, when the vote was taken, there were about four days available in which to prepare the speech. Working on it, besides Edward Robinson, William Allen, Senator Gore's assistants, and Rashish, was John Sharon, a general political aide of George Ball. Robinson also called upon Harold P. LaMarr, assistant to Howard Picquet in the Legislative Reference Service of the Library of Congress, whose job it was to prepare such material for congressmen.

One of the key decisions involved in writing the speech was to put the emphasis on lower American tariffs as a countermeasure to the Soviet trade offensive. We had been wondering for some time during 1954 why the liberal traders did not make use of this argument. The decision to use the approach was made by Senator Gore himself. It grew in part out of a clipping file which LaMarr and Picquet maintained. During the previous months, they had been struck by the rapid accumulation of material on the Soviet trade offensive and the fact that it was not being discussed in the context of American trade policy. From Gore's point of view, the anti-Soviet argument had the distinct advantage of putting stress on American exports of agricultural products, a topic to which he also wished to devote a considerable portion of the speech.

The next problem was that of lining up votes. Gore himself lined up the Democrats. Charles Taft was assigned the job of trying to obtain a half-dozen Republican votes to offset the few Democratic defections that were inevitable. Taft spoke to Senators Irving Ives (N.Y.), James Duff (Pa.), Margaret Chase Smith (Maine), George Aiken (Vt.), Prescott Bush (Conn.), and Frank Carlson (Kan.). Ives and Smith left the impression that they would vote for the bill. Duff telephoned the White House to ask how he should vote; he voted nay. Margaret Chase Smith did not show up for the vote.

On the Democratic side, the leadership, specifically Lyndon Johnson, had been won over and asked the whip to line up votes. In the end, the Gore amendment lost only six Democrats, but, with no Republicans supporting it, it could not pass. The key to the Democratic side was thought to be Senator George. A few Democrats—such as Matthew Neely of West Virginia, Pat McCarran of Nevada, Johnson of Colorado, and Pastore of Rhode Island—had been written off from the beginning because of needs for protection in their constituencies. Gore spoke to George three times in the hope that he might support the bill. On June 15, however, after some persuasion by Millikin, with whom he had a close working relationship in the Finance Committee, George withdrew his support from the movement for a three-year extension because "the President has backed up on his own proposal." At that moment, it looked as though the Gore proposal were dead. The odds were so strong against it that, in the opinion of Gore's associates, the protectionists fell down on the job. "They felt so safe they weren't even buttonholing anybody." Yet, as the political advantages for the Democrats became clearer, the rest of the Democrats in the Senate lined up ever more solidly. Adlai Stevenson, who had adopted a policy against becoming involved in legislative controversy, stepped out of his usual role, despite some Democratic National Committee opposition. He issued a statement supporting the move. This helped to remove the impression that it was a one-man effort on the part of a junior senator. Immediately after the reading of the Stevenson statement, however, George rose to oppose the Gore amendment. Still, only six Democrats opposed the bill.

The story illustrates many points, but the one with which we are concerned here is the activity of a pressure group when it is functioning at full steam. Its role became that of an auxiliary service bureau for a senator with whom it was in complete agreement. Its staff provided him with information, they helped him in writing, they arranged for statements of support (notably Stevenson's), and they even assumed the task of approaching a half-dozen amenable Republicans, something a Democratic senator could not well do.

Notes

[1] David Truman, *The Governmental Process* (New York: Alfred Knopf, 1955) has an interesting discussion of the problem of group cohesion, pp. 156–187. Although both his and our discussion cover much of the same ground, unless we read him incorrectly, he does not anticipate the second part of our argument, i.e., that unanimity (or cohesion) is maintained by the use of multiple group memberships for purposes which might produce conflict within a single given group. Truman sees multiple group memberships as a source of conflict, but does not emphasize that they may also reduce conflict.

[2] Howard S. Picquet, *Aid, Trade and the Tariff* (New York: Thomas Y. Crowell, 1953).

[3] We do not believe that one cause of the change was that a few of the proadministration organizers had read some chapters of this manuscript, but we owe it to the reader to note that this possible confounding of the evidence existed.

[4] An example of how "pressure" may backfire is the reaction in the fall of 1959 to the threatening letter that labor leader James Carey sent to congressmen who opposed his views on the labor reform bill.

[5] Other writers have made essentially the same point. Donald C. Blaisdell, *American Democracy Under Pressure* (New York: Ronald Press, 1957), p. 12, says: ". . . few lobbyists are crude enough today to attempt to persuade a legislator against his better judgment or against what he believes to be the majority sentiment of the people he represents." Bernard C. Cohen, *The Influence of Non-governmental Groups on Foreign Policy-Making* (Boston: World Peace Foundation, 1959), p. 14, comments: ". . . policy makers are not often persuaded to act (or not act) in favor of persons or groups with whom they are in basic ideological or political conflict. But more positively, there generally appears to be a close affinity between the policy makers and the individual or group whose position he is persuaded to support." Cohen goes on (p. 15) to cite an earlier study by John W. Masland ("Pressure Groups and American Foreign Policy preceding Pearl Harbor," *Public Opinion Quarterly*, Spring 1942, p. 121), in which Masland says: "The representatives of these various groups cultivated personal contact with members of Congress and of the Administration who were favorably inclined to their views. Fred Libby and Dorothy Detzer for many years worked closely with isolationists in Congress. General Wood moved into the office of Senator Wheeler for several days to assist in planning opposition strategy to revision of the Neutrality Act. Around the State Department, Clark Eichelberger found doors open at all times and consulted freely with officials, giving and receiving advice."

18

E. E. SCHATTSCHNEIDER

THE SCOPE AND BIAS OF THE PRESSURE SYSTEM

. . . As a matter of fact, the distinction between *public* and *private* interests is a thoroughly respectable one; it is one of the oldest known to political theory. In the literature of the subject, the public interest refers to general or common interests shared by all or by substantially all members of the community.[1] Presumably no community exists unless there is some kind of community of interests, just as there is no nation without some notion of national interests. If it is really impossible to distinguish between private and public interests, the group theorists have produced a revolution in political thought so great that it is impossible to foresee its consequences. For this reason the distinction ought to be explored with great care.

At a time when nationalism is described as one of the most dynamic forces in the world, it should not be difficult to understand that national interests actually do exist.[2] It is necessary only to consider the proportion of the American budget devoted to national defense to realize that the common interest in national survival is a great one. Measured in dollars this interest is one of the biggest things in the world. Moreover, it is difficult to describe this interest as special. The diet on which the American leviathan feeds is something more than a jungle of disparate special interests. In the literature of democratic theory the body of common agreement found in the community is known as the "consensus," without which it is believed that no democratic system can survive.

The reality of the common interest is suggested by demonstrated capacity of the community to survive. There must be something that holds people together.

In contrast with the common interests are the special interests. The implication of this term is that these are interests shared by only a few people or a fraction of the community; they *exclude* others and may be *adverse* to them. A special interest is exclusive in about the same way as private property is exclusive. In a complex society it is not surprising that there are some interests that are shared by all or substantially all members of the community and some interests that are not shared so widely. The distinction is useful precisely because conflicting claims are made by people about the nature of their interests in controversial matters.

Perfect agreement within the community is not always possible, but an interest may be said to have become public when it is shared so widely as to be substantially universal. Thus, the difference between 99 percent agreement and perfect agreement is not so great that it becomes necessary to argue that all interests are special, that the interests of the 99 percent are as special as the interests of the 1 percent. For example, the law is probably doing an adequate job of defining the public interest in domestic tranquility despite the fact that there is nearly always one dissenter at every hanging. That is, the law defines the public interest in spite of the fact that there may be some outlaws.

Since one function of theory is to explain reality, it is reasonable to add that it is a good deal easier to explain what is going on in politics by making a distinction between public and private interests than it is to attempt to explain *everything* in terms of special interests. The attempt to prove that all interests are special forces us into circumlocutions such as those involved in the argument that people have special interests in the common good. The argument can be made, but it seems a long way around to avoid a useful distinction.

What is to be said about the argument that the distinction between public and special interests is "subjective" and is therefore "unscientific"?

All discussion of interests, special as well as general, refers to the motives, desires, and intentions of people. In this sense the whole discussion of interests is subjective. We have made progress in the study of politics because people have observed some kind of relation between the political behavior of people and certain wholly impersonal data concerning their ownership of property, income, economic status, professions, and the like. All that we know about interests, private as well as public, is based on inferences of this sort. Whether the distinction in any given case is valid depends on the evidence and on the kinds of inferences drawn from the evidence.

The only meaningful way we can speak of the interests of an association like the National Association of Manufacturers is to draw inferences from the fact that the membership is a select group to which only manufacturers may belong and to try to relate that datum to what the association does. The implications, logic, and deductions are persuasive only if they furnish reasonable explanations of the facts. That is all that any theory about interests can do. It has seemed persuasive to students of politics to suppose that manufacturers do not join an association to which only manufacturers may belong merely to promote philanthropic or cultural or religious interests, for example. The basis of selection of the membership creates an inference about the organization's concerns. The conclusions drawn from this datum seem to fit what we know about the policies promoted by the association; i.e., the policies seem to reflect the exclusive interests of manufacturers. The method is not foolproof, but it works better than many other kinds of analysis and is useful precisely because special-interest groups often tend to rationalize their special interests as public interests.

Is it possible to distinguish between the "interests" of the members of the National Association of Manufacturers and the members of the American League to Abolish Capital Punishment? The facts in the two cases are not identical. First, *the members of the A.L.A.C.P. obviously do not expect to be hanged.* The membership of the A.L.A.C.P. is not restricted to persons under indictment for murder or in jeopardy of the extreme penalty. *Anybody* can join A.L.A.C.P. Its members oppose capital punishment, although they are not personally likely to benefit by the policy they advocate. The inference is therefore that the interest of the A.L.A.C.P. is not adverse, exclusive, or special. It is not like the interest of the Petroleum Institute in depletion allowances.

Take some other cases. The members of the National Child Labor Committee are not children in need of legislative protection against exploitation by employers. The members of the World Peace Foundation apparently want peace, but in the nature of things they must want peace for everyone because no group can be at peace while the rest of the community is at war. Similarly, even if the members of the National Defense League wanted defense only for themselves, they would necessarily have to work for defense for the whole country because national security is indivisible. Only a naive person is likely to imagine that the political involvements of the members of the American Bankers Association and members of the Foreign Policy Association are identical. In other words, we may draw inferences from the exclusive or the nonexclusive nature of benefits sought by organizations as well as we can from the composition of groups. The positions of these groups can be distinguished not on the basis of some subjective process, but by making reasonable inferences from verifiable facts.

On the other hand, because some special-interest groups attempt to identify themselves with the public interest it does not follow that the whole idea of the public interest is a fraud. Mr. Wilson's famous remark that what is good for General Motors is good for the country assumes that people generally do in fact desire the common good. Presumably, Mr. Wilson attempted to explain the special interest of General Motors in terms of the common interest because that was the only way he could talk to people who do not belong to the General Motors organization. *Within* the General Motors organization, discussions might be carried on in terms of naked self-interest, but a *public discussion must be carried on in public terms.*

All public discussion is addressed to the general community. To describe the conflict of special-interest groups as a form of politics means that the conflict has become generalized, has become a matter involving the broader public. In the nature of things *a political conflict among special interests is never restricted to the group most immediately interested.* Instead, it is an appeal (initiated by relatively small numbers of people) for the support of vast numbers of people who are sufficiently remote to have a somewhat different perspective on the controversy. It follows that Mr. Wilson's comment, far from demonstrating that the public interest is a fraud, proves that he thinks that the public interest is so important that even a great private corporation must make obeisance to it.

The distinction between public and special interests is an indispensable tool for the study of politics. To abolish the distinction is to make a shambles of political science by treating things that are different as if they were alike. The kind of distinction made here is a commonplace of all literature dealing with human society, but *if we accept it, we have established one of the outer limits of the subject;* we have split the world of interests in half and have taken one step toward defining the scope of this kind of political conflict.

We can now examine the second distinction, the distinction between organized and unorganized groups. The question here is not whether the distinction can be made but whether or not it is worth making. Organization has been described as "merely a stage or degree of interaction" in the development of a group.[3]

The proposition is a good one, but what conclusions do we draw from it? We do not dispose of the matter by calling the distinction between organized and unorganized groups a "mere" difference of degree because some of the greatest differences in the world are differences of degree. As far as special-interest politics is concerned the implication to be avoided is that a few workmen who habitually stop at a corner saloon for a glass of beer are essentially the same as the United States Army because the difference between them is merely one of degree. At this point we have distinction that makes a difference. The distinction between organized and unorganized groups is worth making because it ought to alert us against an analysis which begins as a general group theory of politics but ends with a defense of pressure politics as inherent, universal, permanent, and inevitable. This kind of confusion comes from the loosening of categories involved in the universalization of group concepts.

Since the beginning of intellectual history, scholars have sought to make progress in their work by distinguishing between things that are unlike and by dividing their subject matter into categories to examine them more intelligently. It is something of a novelty, therefore, when group theorists reverse this process by discussing their subject in terms so universal that they wipe out all categories, because this is the dimension in which it is least possible to understand anything.

If we are able, therefore, to distinguish between public and private interests and between organized and unorganized groups we have marked out the major boundaries of the subject; *we have given the subject shape and scope.* We are now in a position to attempt to define the area we want to explore. Having cut the pie into four pieces, we can now appropriate the piece we want and leave the rest to someone else. For a multitude of reasons *the most likely field of study is that of the organized, special-interest groups.* The advantage of concentrating on organized groups is that they are known, identifiable, and recognizable. The advantage of concentrating on special-interest groups is that they have one important characteristic in common; they are all exclusive. This piece of the pie (the organized special-interest groups) we shall call the *pressure system.* The pressure system has boundaries we can define; we can fix its scope and make an attempt to estimate its bias.

It may be assumed at the outset that all organized special-interest groups have some kind of impact on politics. A sample survey of organizations made by the Trade Associations Division of the United States Department of Commerce in 1942 concluded that "From 70 to 100 percent (of these associations) are planning activities in the field of government relations, trade promotion, trade practices, public relations, annual conventions, cooperation with other organizations, and information services."[4]

The subject of our analysis can be reduced to manageable proportions and brought under control if we restrict ourselves to the groups whose interests in politics are sufficient to have led them to unite in formal organizations having memberships, bylaws, and officers. A further advantage of this kind of definition is, we may assume, that the organized special-interest groups are the most self-conscious, best developed, most intense and active groups. Whatever claims can be made for a group theory of politics ought to be sustained by the evidence concerning these groups, if the claims have any validity at all.

The organized groups listed in the various directories (such as *National Associations of the United States*, published at intervals by the United States Department of Commerce) and specialty yearbooks, registers, etc. and the *Lobby Index*, published by the United States House of Representatives, probably include the bulk of the organizations in the pressure system. All compilations are incomplete, but these are extensive enough to provide us with some basis for estimating the scope of the system.

By the time a group has developed the kind of interest that leads it to organize, it may be assumed that it has also developed some kind of political bias because *organization is itself a mobilization of bias in preparation for action.* Since these groups can be identified and since they have memberships (i.e., they include and exclude people), it is possible to think of the *scope* of the system.

When lists of these organizations are examined, the fact that strikes the student most forcibly is that *the system is very small.* The range of organized, identifiable, known groups is amazingly narrow; there is nothing remotely universal about it. There is a tendency on the part of the publishers of directories of associations to place an undue emphasis on business organizations, an emphasis that is almost inevitable because the business community is by a wide margin the most highly organized segment of society. Publishers doubtless tend also to reflect public demand for information. Nevertheless, the dominance of business groups in the pressure system is so marked that it probably cannot be explained away as an accident of the publishing industry.

The business character of the pressure system is shown by almost every list available. *National Associations of the United States*[5] lists 1,860 business associations out of a total of 4,000 in the volume, though it refers without listing (p. VII) to 16,000 organizations of businessmen. One cannot be certain what the total content of the unknown associational universe may be, but, taken with the evidence found in other compilations, it is obvious that business is remarkably well represented. Some evidence of the over-all scope of the system is to be seen in the estimate that 15,000 national trade associations have a gross membership of about one million business firms.[6] The data are incomplete, but even if we do not have a detailed map this is the shore dimly seen.

Much more directly related to pressure politics is the *Lobby Index, 1946–1949* (an index of organizations and individuals registering or filing quarterly reports under the Federal Lobbying Act), published as a report of the House Select Committee on Lobbying Activities. In this compilation, 825 out of a total of 1,247 entries (exclusive of individuals and Indian tribes) represented business.[7] A selected list of the most important of the groups listed in the *Index* (the groups spending the largest sums of money on lobbying) published in the *Congressional Quarterly Log* shows 149 business organizations in a total of 265 listed.[8]

The business or upper-class bias of the pressure system shows up everywhere. Businessmen are four or five times as likely to write to their congressmen as manual laborers are. College graduates are far more apt to write to their congressmen than people in the lowest educational category are.[9]

The limited scope of the business pressure system is indicated by all available statistics. Among business organizations, the National Association of Manufacturers (with about 20,000 corporate members) and the Chamber of Commerce of the United States (about as large as the N.A.M.) are giants. Usually business associations are much smaller. Of 421 trade associations in the metal-products industry listed in *National Associations of the United States,* 153 have a membership of less than 20.[10] The median membership was somewhere between 24 and 50. Approximately the same scale of memberships is to be found in the lumber, furniture, and paper industries where 37.3 percent of the associations listed had a membership of less than 20 and the median membership was in the 25 to 50 range.[11]

The statistics in these cases are representative of nearly all other classifications of industry.

Data drawn from other sources support this thesis. Broadly, the pressure system has an upper-class bias. There is overwhelming evidence that participation in voluntary organizations is related to upper social and economic status; the rate of participation is much higher in the upper strata than it is elsewhere. The general proposition is well stated by Lazarsfeld:

> People on the lower SES levels are less likely to belong to any organizations than the people on high SES (Social and Economic Status) levels. (On an A and B level, we find 72 percent of these respondents who belong to one or more organizations. The proportion of respondents who are members of formal organizations decreases steadily as SES level descends until, on the D level only 35 percent of the respondents belong to any associations.)[12]

The bias of the system is shown by the fact that *even nonbusiness organizations reflect an upper-class tendency.*

Lazarsfeld's generalization seems to apply equally well to urban and rural populations. The obverse side of the coin is that large areas of the population appear to be wholly outside the system of private organization. A study made by Ira Reid of a Philadelphia area showed that in a sample of 963 persons, 85 percent belonged to no civic or charitable organization and 74 percent belonged to no occupational, business, or professional associations, while another Philadelphia study of 1,154 women showed that 55 percent belonged to no associations of any kind.[13]

A *Fortune* farm poll taken some years ago found that 70.5 percent of farmers belonged to no agricultural organizations. A similar conclusion was reached by two Gallup polls showing that perhaps no more than one third of the farmers of the country belonged to farm organizations,[14] while another *Fortune* poll showed that 86.8 percent of the low-income farmers belonged to no farm organizations.[15] All available data support the generalization that the farmers who do not participate in rural organizations are largely the poorer ones.

A substantial amount of research done by other rural sociologists points to the same conclusion. Mangus and Cottam say, on the basis of a study of 556 heads of Ohio farm families and their wives:

> The present study indicates that comparatively few of those who ranked low on the scale of living took any active part in community organizations as members, attendants, contributors, or leaders. On the other hand, those families that ranked high on the scale of living comprised the vast majority of the highly active participants in formal group activities. . . . Fully two-thirds of those in the lower class as defined in this study were non-participants as compared with only one-tenth of those in the upper class and one-fourth of those in the middle class. . . . When families were classified by the general level-of-living index, 16 times as large a proportion of those in the upper classes as of those in the lower class were active participants. . . .[16]

Along the same line Richardson and Bauder observe, "Socio-economic status was directly related to participation."[17] In still another study it was found that "a highly significant relationship existed between income and formal participation."[18] It was found that persons with more than four years of college education held twenty times as many memberships (per one hundred persons) as did those with less than a fourth-grade education and were forty times as likely to hold office in nonchurch organizations, while persons with an income over $5,000 hold ninety-four times as many offices as persons with incomes less than $250.[19]

D.E. Lindstrom found that 72 percent of farm laborers belonged to no organizations whatever.[20]

There is a great wealth of data supporting the proposition that participation in private associations exhibits a class bias.[21]

The class bias of associational activity gives meaning to the limited scope of the pressure system, because *scope and bias are aspects of the same tendency.* The data raise a serious question about the validity of the proposition that special-interest groups are a universal form of political organization reflecting *all* interests. As a matter of fact, to suppose that everyone participates in pressure-group activity and that all interests get themselves organized in the pressure system is to destroy the meaning of this form of politics. The pressure system makes sense only as the political instrument of a segment of the community. It gets results by being selective and biased; *if everybody got into the act, the unique advantages of this form of organization would be destroyed, for it is possible that if all interests could be mobilized the result would be a stalemate.*

Special-interest organizations are most easily formed when they deal with small numbers of individuals who are acutely aware of their exclusive interests. To describe the conditions of pressure-group organization in this way is, however, to say that it is primarily a business phenomenon. Aside from a few very large organizations (the churches, organized labor, farm organizations, and veterans' organizations) the residue is a small segment of the population. *Pressure politics is essentially the politics of small groups.*

The vice of the groupist theory is that it conceals the most significant aspects of the system. The flaw in the pluralist heaven is that the heavenly chorus sings with a strong upper-class accent. Probably about 90 percent of the people cannot get into the pressure system.

The notion that the pressure system is automatically representative of the whole community is a myth fostered by the universalizing tendency of modern group theories. *Pressure politics is a selective process* ill designed to serve diffuse interests. The system is skewed, loaded, and unbalanced in favor of a fraction of a minority.

On the other hand, pressure tactics are not remarkably successful in mobilizing general interests. When pressure-group organizations attempt to represent the interests of large numbers of people, they are usually able to reach only a small segment of their constituencies. Only a chemical trace of the fifteen million Negroes in the United States belong to the National Association for the Advancement of Colored People. Only one five hundredths of 1 percent of American women belong to the League of Women Voters, only one sixteen hundredths of 1 percent of the consumers belong to the National Consumers' League, and only 6 percent of American automobile drivers belong to the American Automobile Association, while about 15 percent of the veterans belong to the American Legion.

The competing claims of pressure groups and political parties for the loyalty of the American public revolve about the difference between the results likely to be achieved by small-scale and large-scale political organization. Inevitably, the outcome of pressure politics and party politics will be vastly different.

A CRITIQUE
OF GROUP THEORIES OF POLITICS

It is extremely unlikely that the vogue of group theories of politics would have attained its present status if its basic assumptions had not been first established by some concept of economic determinism. The economic interpretation of politics has always appealed to those political philosophers who have sought a single prime mover, a sort of philosopher's stone of political science around which to organize their ideas. The search for a single, ultimate cause has something to do with the attempt to explain *everything* about politics in terms of group concepts. The logic of economic determinism is to *identify the origins of conflict and to assume the conclusion.* This kind of thought has some of the earmarks of an illusion. The somnambulatory quality of thinking in this field appears also in the tendency of research to deal only with successful pressure campaigns or the willingness of scholars to be satisfied with having placed pressure groups on the scene of the crime without following through to see if the effect can really be attributed to the cause. What makes this kind of thinking remarkable is the fact that in political contests there are as many failures as there are successes. Where in the literature of pressure politics are the failures?

Students of special-interest politics need a more sophisticated set of intellectual tools than they have developed thus far. The theoretical problem involved in the search for a single cause is that all power relations in a democracy are reciprocal. Trying to find the original cause is like trying to find the first wave of the ocean.

Can we really assume that we know all that is to be known about a conflict if we understand its *origins*? Everything we know about politics suggests that a conflict is likely to change profoundly as it becomes political. It is a rare individual who can confront his antagonists without changing his opinions to some degree. Everything changes once a conflict gets into the political arena— *who* is involved, *what* the conflict is about, the resources available, etc. It is extremely difficult to predict the outcome of a fight by watching its beginning because we do not even know who else is going to get into the conflict. The logical consequence of the exclusive emphasis on the determinism of the private origins of conflict is to assign zero value to the political process.

The very expression "pressure politics" invites us to misconceive the role of special-interest groups in politics. The word "pressure" implies the use of some kind of force, a form of intimidation, something other than reason and information, to induce public authorities to act against their own best judgment. In Latham's famous statement . . . the legislature is described as a "referee" who "ratifies" and "records" the "balance of power" among the contending groups. [22]

It is hard to imagine a more effective way of saying that Congress has no mind or force of its own or that Congress is unable to invoke new forces that might alter the equation.

Actually the outcome of political conflict is not like the "resultant" of opposing forces in physics. To assume that the forces in a political situation could be diagramed as a physicist might diagram the resultant of opposing physical forces is to wipe the slate clean of all remote, general, and public considerations for the protection of which civil societies have been instituted.

Moreover, the notion of "pressure" distorts the image of the power relations involved. *Private conflicts are taken into the public arena precisely because someone wants to make certain that the power ratio among the private interests most immediately involved shall not prevail.* To treat a conflict as a mere test of the strength of the private interests is to leave out the most significant factors. This is so true that it might indeed be said that the only way to preserve private power ratios is to keep conflicts out of the public arena.

The assumption that it is only the "interested" who count ought to be re-examined in view of the foregoing discussion. The tendency of the literature of pressure politics has been to neglect the low-tension force of large numbers because it *assumes that the equation of forces is fixed at the outset.*

Given the assumptions made by the group theorists, the attack on the idea of the majority is completely logical. The assumption is that conflict is monopolized narrowly by the parties immediately concerned. There is no room for a majority when conflict is defined so narrowly. It is a great deficiency of the group

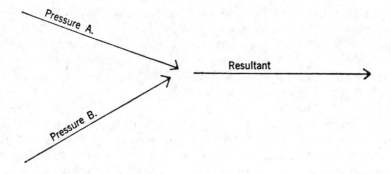

theory that it has found no place in the political system for the majority. The force of the majority is of an entirely different order of magnitude, something not to be measured by pressure-group standards.

Instead of attempting to exterminate all political forms, organizations, and alignments that do not qualify as pressure groups, would it not be better to attempt to make a synthesis, covering the whole political system and finding a place for all kinds of political life?

One possible synthesis of pressure politics and party politics might be produced by *describing politics as the socialization of conflict.* That is to say, the political process is a sequence: conflicts are initiated by highly motivated, high-tension groups so directly and immediately involved that it is difficult for them to see the justice of competing claims. As long as the conflicts of these groups remain *private* (carried on in terms of economic competition, reciprocal denial of goods and services, private negotiations and bargaining, struggles for corporate control or competition for membership), no political process is initiated. Conflicts become political only when an attempt is made to involve the wider public. Pressure politics might be described as a stage in the socialization of conflict. This analysis makes pressure politics an integral part of all politics, including party politics.

One of the characteristic points of origin of pressure politics is a breakdown of the discipline of the business community. The flight to government is perpetual. Something like this is likely to happen wherever there is a point of contact between competing power systems. It is the *losers in intrabusiness conflict who seek redress from public authority. The dominant business interests resist appeals to the government.* The role of the government as the patron of the defeated private interest sheds light on its function as the critic of private power relations.

Since the contestants in private conflicts are apt to be unequal in strength, it follows that *the most powerful special interests want private settlements* because they are able to dictate the outcome as long as the conflict remains private. If A is a hundred times as strong as B he does not welcome the intervention of a third party because he expects to impose his own terms on B; he wants to isolate B. He is especially opposed to the intervention of public authority, because public authority represents the most overwhelming form of outside intervention. Thus, if $A/B = 100/1$, it is obviously not to A's advantage to involve a third party a million times as strong as A and B combined. Therefore, it is the weak, not the strong, who appeal to public authority for relief. It is the weak who want to socialize conflict, i.e., to involve more and more people in the conflict until the balance of forces is changed. In the schoolyard it is not the bully but the defenseless smaller boys who "tell the teacher." When the teacher intervenes, the balance of power in the schoolyard is apt to change drastically. It is the function of public authority to *modify private power relations by enlarging the scope of conflict.* Nothing could be more mistaken than to suppose that public authority merely registers the dominance of the strong over the weak. The mere existence of public order has already ruled out a great variety of forms of private pressure. Nothing could be more confusing than to suppose that the refugees from the business community who come to Congress for relief and protection *force* Congress to do their bidding.

Evidence of the truth of this analysis may be seen in the fact that the big private interests do not necessarily win if they are involved in public conflicts with petty interests. The image of the lobbyists as primarily the agents of big business is not easy to support on the face of the record of congressional hearings, for example. The biggest corporations in the country tend to avoid the arena in which pressure groups and lobbyists fight it out before congressional committees. To describe this process exclusively in terms of an effort of business to intimidate congressmen is to misconceive what is actually going on.

It is probably a mistake to assume that pressure politics is the typical or even the most important relation between government and business. The pressure group is by no means the perfect instrument of the business community. What does big business want? The *winners* in intrabusiness strife want (1) to be let alone (they want autonomy) and (2) to preserve the solidarity of the business community. For these purposes pressure politics is not a wholly satisfactory device. The most elementary considerations of strategy call for the business community to develop some kind of common policy more broadly based than any special-interest group is likely to be.

The political influence of business depends on the kind of solidarity that, on the one hand, leads all business to rally to the support of *any* businessman in trouble with the government and, on the other hand, keeps internal business disputes out of the public arena. In this system businessmen resist the impulse to attack each other in public and discourage the efforts of individual members of the business community to take intrabusiness conflicts into politics.

The attempt to mobilize a united front of the whole business community does not resemble the classical concept of pressure politics. The logic of business politics is to keep peace within the business community by supporting as far as possible all claims that business groups make for themselves. The tendency is to support all businessmen who have conflicts with the government and support all businessmen in conflict with labor. In this way *special-interest politics can be converted into party policy.* The search is for a broad base of political mobilization grounded on the strategic need for political organization on a wider scale than is possible in the case of the historical pressure group. Once the business community begins to think in terms of a larger scale of political organization the Republican party looms large in business politics.

It is a great achievement of American democracy that business has been forced to form a political organization designed to win elections, i.e., has been forced to compete for power in the widest arena in the political system. On the other hand, *the power of the Republican party to make terms with business rests on the fact that business cannot afford to be isolated.*

The Republican party has played a major role in *the political organization of the business community*, a far greater role than many students of politics seem to have realized. The influence of business in the Republican party is great, but it is never absolute because business is remarkably dependent on the party. The business community is too small, it arouses too much antagonism, and its aims are too narrow to win the support of a popular majority. The political education of business is a function of the Republican party that can never be done so well by anyone else.

In the management of the political relations of the business community, the Republican party is much more important than any combination of pressure groups ever could be. The success of special interests in Congress is due less to the "pressure" exerted by these groups than it is due to the fact that Republican members of Congress are committed in advance to a general probusiness attitude. The notion that business groups coerce Republican congressmen into voting for their bills underestimates the whole Republican posture in American politics.[23]

It is not easy to manage the political interests of the business community because there is a perpetual stream of losers in intrabusiness conflicts who go to the government for relief and protection. It has not been possible therefore to maintain perfect solidarity, and when solidarity is breached the government is involved almost automatically. The fact that business has not become hopelessly divided and that it has retained great influence in American politics has been due chiefly to the over-all mediating role played by the Republican party. There has never been a pressure group or a combination of pressure groups capable of performing this function.

NOTES

[1] References to the public interest appear under a variety of headings in the literature of political theory.

See G. D. H. Cole's comment on "the will of all" and the "general will," pp. xxx and xxxi of his introduction to Everyman's edition of Rousseau's *Social Contract*, London, 1913.

See Ernst Cassirer, *The Myth of the State*, Garden City, 1955, pp. 88–93, for a discussion of Plato's concept of "justice" as the end of the state in his criticism of the sophists.

See S. D. Lindsay, *The Essentials of Democracy*, Philadelphia, 1929, p. 49, for a statement regarding consensus.

[2] It does not seem necessary to argue that nationalism and national interests are forces in the modern world. E. H. Carr writes about "the catastrophic growth of nationalism" in *Nationalism and After*, New York, 1945, p. 18. D. W. Brogan describes nations as "the only communities that now

exist," *The American Character*, New York, 1944, p. 169. "The outstanding and distinctive characteristic of the people of the Western States System is their devotion and allegiance to the 'nations' into which they have got themselves divided," Frederick L. Schumann, *International Politics*, 3d ed., New York, 1941, p. 300. A. D. Lindsay in *The Essentials of Democracy*, Philadelphia, 1929, p. 49, has stated the doctrine of the democratic consensus as follows: "Nationality, however produced, is a sense of belonging together, involving a readiness on the part of the members of a state to subordinate their differences to it. It involves something more. It has a connection with the notion of a distinctive culture—some sort of rough ideal of the kind of common life for which the community stands, which always exists in people's minds as a rough criticism by which political proposals are to be judged. This at least is clear, that where such common understanding and sense of belonging together either does not exist or is overshadowed by other differences, successful democracy is not really possible."

3 David Truman, *The Government Process*, New York, 1951, p. 51.

4 *National Associations of the United States*, p. xi.

5 Edited by Jay Judkins, Washington, 1949, p. viii.

6 *National Associations of the United States*, p. viii.

7 House Report No. 3197, 81st Congress, 2d Session, December 15, 1950, Washington.

8 *Congressional Quarterly Log*, week ending February 24, 1950, pp. 217 ff. Another compilation, the list of approximately one thousand associations and societies published in the *World Almanac* for 1953, reflects to a very great extent the economic, professional and leisure interests and activities of the upper economic strata of the community. Scarcely more than a dozen or so of the associations listed in the *World Almanac* can be described as proletarian in their outlook or membership.

9 *American Institute of Public Opinion*, May 29, 1946.

10 Four hundred fifty associations are listed, but figures for membership are given for only 421.

11 Membership statistics are given for only 177 of the 200 associations listed.

12 Lazarsfeld and Associates, *The People's Choice*, p. 145.

13 Reid and Ehle, "Leadership Selection in the Urban Locality Areas," *Public Opinion Quarterly* (1950), 14:262–284. See also Powell, *Anatomy of Public Opinion*, New York, 1951, pp. 180–181.

14 See Carey McWilliams, *Small Farm and Big Farm*, Public Affairs Pamphlet, No. 100.

15 *Fortune* poll, April, 1943.

16 A. R. Mangus and H. R. Cottam, *Level of Living, Social Participation, and Adjustment of Ohio Farm People*, Ohio Agricultural Experiment Station, Wooster, Ohio, Bull. 624, September, 1941, pp. 51, 53.

Another study (of New York farmers) shows that there is a direct relation between organizational activity and the economic status of farmers. The author concludes that "the operators of farms of less than 55 acres in size are represented in only very small proportions in membership in the farm bureau and in the Dairymen's League and other cooperatives." W. A. Anderson, *The Membership of Farmers in New York Organizations*, Cornell University Agricultural Experiment Station, Ithaca, N.Y., 1937, p. 20.

17 P. D. Richardson and Ward W. Bauder, *Participation in Organized Activities in a Kentucky Rural Community*. Kentucky Agricultural Experimental Station, University of Kentucky, Bulletin 598, 1953, Lexington, Kentucky, pp. 26, 28. "The number of memberships varied directly with the socio-economic score."

18 Harold F. Kaufman, *Participation in Organized Activities in Selected Kentucky Localities*, Bulletin 528, Kentucky Agricultural Experiment Station, University of Kentucky, Lexington, 1949, p. 19.

19 *Ibid.*, pp. 11, 12, 13, 21.

See also Mirra Komorovsky, "The Voluntary Association of Urban Dwellers," *American Sociological Review*, 11:686–698, 1946.

20 *Forces Affecting Participation of Farm People in Rural Organizations*, University of Illinois Agricultural Experiment Station, Bulletin 423, 1936, p. 103.

21 "Associational participation is greatest at the top of Jonesville society and decreases on the way down the class hierarchy. The upper class belongs to the greatest number of associations, the upper-middle class next, and so on down to the lower-lower class which belongs to the least." Warner, *Democracy in Jonesville*, New York, 1949, p. 117. See also pp. 138, 140, 141, 143.

"A higher proportion of the members of the upper class belong to more associations than the members of any other class." Warner, *Jonesville*, p. 131.

"The upper and upper-middle classes are highly organized, well integrated social groups. The lower-middle and lower classes are more loosely organized and have fewer devices for maintaining their own distinctiveness in the community." Warner, *Jonesville*, p. 148. See also p. 153.

"Many organized groups touch only a few people in a community. Studies in cities reveal that 40 to 60 per cent of adults are members of these organized groups if church membership is excluded. In rural communities the percentage is smaller. So when we bring in representatives from these organized groups, we should not pretend that we are getting a complete representation of the people of the community. The American practice of 'joining' is not as universal as popularly assumed." G. W. Blackwell, "Community Analysis," *Approaches to the Study of Politics*, Roland Young, ed., Northwestern University Press, 1958, p. 306.

"Aside from church participation, most urban individuals belong to one organization or none. Low socio-economic rank individuals and middle-rank individuals, usually belong to one organization at most, and it is usually work-connected for men, child-church connected for women. Only in the upper socio-economic levels is the 'joiner' to be found with any frequency. When attendance at organizations is studied, some twenty per cent of the memberships are usually 'paper' memberships." Scott Greer, "Individual Participation in Mass Society," *Approaches to the Study of Politics*, p. 332.

[22] Earl Latham, *The Group Basis of Politics*, Ithaca, N.Y., 1952, pp. 35–36.

[23] See *Reporter*, November 25, 1958, for story of Senator Bricker and the Ohio Right-to-Work referendum.

19

THEODORE J. LOWI

THE PUBLIC PHILOSOPHY: INTEREST-GROUP LIBERALISM

Until astonishingly recent times American national government played a marginal role in the life of the nation. Even as late as the eve of World War I, the State Department could support itself on consular fees. In most years revenues from tariffs supplied adequate financing, plus a surplus, from all other responsibilities. In 1800, there was less than one-half a federal bureaucrat per 1,000 citizens. On the eve of the Civil War there were only 1.5 federal bureaucrats per 1,000 citizens, and by 1900 that ratio had climbed to 2.7. This compares with 7 per 1,000 in 1940 and 13 per 1,000 in 1962—exclusive of military personnel.

The relatively small size of the public sphere was maintained in great part by the constitutional wall of separation between government and private life. The wall was occasionally scaled in both directions, but concern for the proper relation of private life and public order was always a serious and effective issue. Americans always talked pragmatism, in government as in all other things; but doctrine always deeply penetrated public dialogue. Power, even in the United States, needed justification.

Throughout the decades between the end of the Civil War and the Great Depression, almost every debate over a public policy became involved in the larger debate over the nature and consequences of larger and smaller spheres of government. This period was just as much a "constitutional period" as that of 1789–1820. Each period is distinguished by its effort to define (or redefine) and employ a "public philosophy."

Lippmann's term is taken here to mean any set of principles and criteria above and beyond the reach of government and statesmen by which the decisions of government are guided and justified. This is not far removed from Lippmann's usage, except that he had in mind the abstract but quite specific public

This article was made possible by a Social Science Research Council Fellowship. Thanks are also due Professors Richard Flathman, L. A. Froman, Jr., George LaNoue, and Grant McConnell for their many helpful criticisms and suggestions. For his considerable encouragement I am grateful to Max Ascoli of *The Reporter*, and to him, to Henry Kariel (in *The Decline of American Pluralism*) and to Grant McConnell I am doubly grateful for their early recognition of problems with pluralism.

philosophy of bills of rights and natural law.[1] A country either possesses it or does not, loses it or regains it. We may end up agreeing that what Lippmann had in mind is the only public philosophy worthy of the name. But by altering the definition as above, we can use it analytically and critically in the mainstream of modern political science: A public philosophy is something that every stable polity possesses. It is the "political formula"—the "legal and moral basis, or principle, on which the power of the political class rests."[2] It is something that can and does change over generations. Some types of public philosophy may be better, in various ways, than others. And it is possible to discover what the prevailing public philosophy is and to assess its significance by straightforward interpretation of the policies of government and their impact, real or threatened, on society.

In the constitutional epoch immediately preceding our own, ending in 1937, the perennial issue underlying all debate on public policy—and therefore the key to public philosophy in that period—was the question of the nature of government itself and whether expansion or contraction best produced public good. Liberal and conservative regimes derived their principles and rationalizations of governing and policy formulation from their positions on the question. Expansion of government was demanded by liberals as the only means of combating the injustices of a brutal physical and social world that would not change as long as it was taken as natural. Favoring government expansion became the mark of the contemporary liberal. His underlying assumption was that the instruments of government provided the means for conscious induction of social change; without capacity for such change no experimentation with any new institutional forms or means of expanding rights would be possible. Opposition to such means, but not necessarily those forms or those rights, became the mark of the contemporary conservative.

There was unanimity on the criteria underlying the distinction between the adversaries. All agreed that a man's position was determined by his attitude toward government and his attitude toward deliberate social change or "planning." All agreed (and many persist in agreeing) that these two attitudes are consistent and reinforcing both as a guide for leaders in their choices among policies and as a criterion for followers in their choices among leaders. For example:

> Conservatism is committed to a discriminating defense of the social order against change and reform (liberalism). . . . By the Right, I mean generally those parties and movements that are skeptical of popular government, oppose the bright plans of the reformers and dogooders, and draw particular support from men with a sizable stake in the established order. By the Left, I mean generally those parties and movements that demand wider popular participation in government, push actively for reform, and draw particular support from the disinherited, dislocated and disgruntled. As a general rule, to which there are historic exceptions, the Right is conservative or reactionary, the Left is liberal or radical.[3]

These two criteria arose out of a particular constitutional period, were appropriate to that period, and provided a mutually reinforcing basis for doctrine during the period. After 1937, the Constitution did not die from the Revolution, as many had predicted it would. But the basis for the doctrine of that period did die. Liberalism-conservatism as the source of the public philosophy no longer made any sense. Once the principle of positive government in a growing and indeterminable political sphere was established, criteria arising out of the very issue of *whether* such a principle should be established became extinguished. They were extinguished by the total victory of one side of the old dialogue over the other.

The old dialogue has passed into the graveyard of consensus. Yet it persists. Since it has no real, operable meaning any more, it is almost purely ritualistic. However, its persistence has had its real effects. The persistence of this state of affairs so far beyond its own day, has been responsible for two pathological conditions in the 1960's. The first is that the empty rhetoric has produced a crisis of public authority. Without a basis for meaningful adversary proceedings, there has been little, if any, conflict among political actors at the level where each is forced regularly into formulating general rules, applicable to individual acts of state and at one and the same time ethically plausible to the individual citizen. The tendency of individuals to accept governmental decisions because they are good has probably at no time in this century been less intense and less widely distributed in the United States. This is producing many problems of political cynicism and irresponsibility in everyday political processes; and these problems, in turn, have tended toward the second pathological condition, the emergence of an ersatz public philosophy that seeks to justify power and to end the crisis of public authority by parceling out public authority to private parties. That is, the emerging public philosophy seeks to solve the problem of public authority by defining it away. A most maladaptive "political formula," it will inevitably exacerbate rather than end the crisis, even though its short-run effect is one of consensus and stabilization.

THE OLD FORMULA VERSUS THE NEW TIMES

A brief look at a few hard cases will be sufficient to show how little can really be drawn from the old public philosophy to justify the key modern policies and practices in either the public or the private spheres. Table 19-1 helps to show at a glance just how irrelevant the old criteria are. Diagramming and analyzing policies as "techniques of control" was used to good effect by Dahl and Lindblom.[4] In Table 19-1 are arranged a few selected public policies and private policies or widely established practices. They are placed in two dimensions according to the two basic attributes of liberalism-conservatism. Above the line are public policies; below the line are private policies or examples of established business and group practices. This vertical dimension is a simple dichotomy.[5] Therefore, above the line is the "liberal" dimension, and below the line the "conservative" dimension. The horizontal dimension is a continuum. Each policy or practice is placed along the line from left to right roughly according to its real or probable impact upon the society. To the left is the liberal direction,

TABLE 19-1. SELECTED PUBLIC AND PRIVATE POLICIES ARRANGED ACCORDING TO THE PROBABLE EFFECT ON SOCIETY

Public policies (above the line)

Graduated income tax (potential)	Luxury taxes	Growth fiscal policies	Counter-cyclical fiscal policies	Social Security programs based on insurance principles (U.S.)	Existing farm programs	(Kennedy-Freeman farm proposals)
Social Security programs based on graduated income tax		Graduated Income Tax (United States)	Sales taxes			High tariffs
						Import quotas
Civil rights package	Real antitrust		Aids to small business	Direct regulation (e.g., FCC, ICC, CAB, etc.)	Restraint of competition (NRA, fair trade, anti-price discrim.)	Utilities
Low tariffs	"Yardstick" regulation (TVA)			Antitrust by consent decree	Tax on colored margarine	

Private policies (below the line)

Competition in agriculture	Competitive business	Oligopoly with research competition	Oligopoly without competition (steel, cigarettes)	Trade associations	Monopoly	Group representation on boards
New interest groups	Corporate philanthropy		Brand names	Pools	Old interest groups (NAM, AFL-CIO, TWU, etc.)	Strict gold standard with no bank money
	Merit hiring and promotion		Ethnic appeals of political campaigns	Basing points		
				Price leadership		
				Fair trade policies		
				Union unemployment and automation policies		

Note: *Above the line:* Public policies ("liberal")
Below the line: Private policies or practices ("conservative")
Toward the left side: Policies likely to produce change ("liberal")
Toward the right side: Policies likely to maintain existing practices ("conservative")

where policies are placed if they are likely to affect a direct change in things. To the right is the conservative direction, where policies and practices are placed if they tend directly to maintain one or another status quo.

If the two criteria—attitude toward government and attitude toward change— were consistent and if together they described and justified programs, then liberal policies would be concentrated in the upper left corner, and conservative policies would be concentrated below the line to the right. Little study of the Diagram is necessary to discover that the inconsistencies between the two criteria are extreme. And little reflection is necessary to see that policy makers are being guided by some other principles, if principles do guide at all. The fact that private and public policies range across the extremes of maintenance and change suggests the simple but significant proposition that no institution with the capacity and resources for affecting the society works always in the same direction.[6] Yet a public philosophy based upon public-private and change-maintenance criteria requires unidirectional institutions. Obviously, the liberal-conservative dialogue made sense only up until, but not after, the establishment of positive government.

Analysis of the real or potential impact of public policies shows how incomplete is the fit between the earlier public philosophy and the policies it is supposed to support and justify. It shows that those who espouse social change in the abstract, especially government-engineered social change, are seldom peddling policies that would clearly effect any such change. Conversely, it shows that those who harangue on principle against government and change are frequently in real life pushing for strong doses of each. If these criteria do not really guide the leaders, they offer almost no plausible justification for the intelligent follower. A few examples in detail follow.

(1) The income tax. All taxes discriminate. The political question arises over the kind of discrimination the society desires. The graduated or progressive income tax is capable of effecting drastic changes in the relations among classes and between man and his property. According to the two criteria in question, then, the steeply progressive income tax is "liberal" both because it is governmental and because it effects social change. Our own income tax structure can be called only mildly "liberal," if at all, because it is only mildly, if at all, progressive, allowing as it does full exemption on interest from public debt, fast write-offs, depletion allowances, a host of "Louis B. Mayer Amendments," privileges on real estate transactions, and so on *ad nauseum*. It is generally understood that the effective ceiling on taxes is not 91% or 75% but a good deal less than 50%. And considering all taxes together, it seems fairly clear that they comprise a bastion against rather than a weapon for fluidity among classes and channels of opportunity. This is not an argument in favor of the one tax structure or the other, but rather one in favor of the proposition that no trace of a sign can be found of liberal-conservative principles underlying taxation, not even as a guide to compromise. During the legislative action in 1963–64, there was much discussion and debate on the impact of the tax cut on the rate of aggregate economic growth. But there was almost no consideration of the tax structure or the tax cut for its significance to the society. In fact, plans for large-scale tax

reform were withdrawn altogether before the tax bill was ever formally proposed. As a consequence, taxation in the United States is a government policy to preserve the established economic relations among people and classes.

(2) The social security system. This is, of course, a bundle of policies, and accuracy would require classification of each. On balance, however, they are "liberal" only because they are governmental; they are conservative in their impact on social structure and opportunity. If they promote welfare, then, indeed, it is important to be able to say that a conservative policy *can* promote welfare. Above all else, old age insurance, unemployment compensation and the like are techniques of fiscal policy. They are, initially, important countercyclical devices, "automatic stabilizers," that work through the maintenance of demand throughout the business cycle and through the maintenance of existing economic relationships without dislocation. In this dimension, "liberals" are a good deal less willing to take chances than "conservatives."

At another dimension, social security in the United States is an even more interesting case of the gap between the old public philosophy and the real impact of established programs. For, social security programs are techniques of social as well as fiscal control, and as such they are clearly conservative. The American system of social security is based fairly strictly on an insurance principle, a principle of the spreading of risk through forced saving. Government's role is essentially paternalistic; speaking roughly, government raises the minimum wage by the amount of the employer's contribution, takes that plus about an equal amount from the employee's wages, and says, "This much of your income we'll not trust you to spend." This principle of contributory social security does not affect the class structure, the sum total of opportunity, or anything else; on the contrary, it tends to maintain existing patterns. It helps make people a little happier to be where they are doing what they are doing. The social security system is consistent with both criteria of liberalism only to the extent that it is based on a graduated income tax or to the extent that it supports those who did not contribute before entering the rolls. And that is a very small extent indeed.

The medicare program is significant as an addition to the scope and scale of social security, but in no important way does it change the social significance of social security. After President Kennedy proposed a medical care bill limited to the aged and based on "actuarial soundness," there was not even any need to debate the social significance of the bill. Actuarial soundness was a sufficient message that social security would remain altogether what it had been, except for the temporary addition of people who were already old and had made no contribution before entering the rolls. The only surprise in the medicare case was the difficulty of passage. But that was not due to a stalemate between liberalism and conservatism. It was due to a stalemate between the unorganized and apathetic elderly and the intensely felt and highly organized trade union interests of the American Medical Association. A program that originated with Bismarck was simply a while longer being needed in the United States.

(3) The farm programs provide an equally good case of the irrelevance of policy to the old public philosophy. High price supports with crop controls, the center of farm policy for a generation, are supported by "liberals"; but they are

"liberal" because and only because they are governmental. The entire establishment escaped death in 1949–50 only with urban-labor support, but that support proves nothing about liberalism.

What has been the purpose and what is the impact of such a program? Basically, the aim was to restore and to maintain a pre-1914 agriculture in face of extremely strong contrary financial, industrial and technological developments. The effect of the program has clearly been as intended, for far larger numbers of farmers and subsistence farms remain than are supportable in strictly economic terms. And the program perpetuates the established sizes of a farm and relationships among farmers by basing present quotas and controls upon past outputs, state by state, county by county, and farm by farm. The New Frontier and Great Society proposals must be ranked as even more "conservative," despite their governmental base, because they would have delegated to a few leading farmers or farm group leaders in each surplus commodity area the power to determine the quotas, thus allowing those most involved to decide *for themselves* just what there is about agriculture worth conserving. This is elevation of government-by-conflict-of-interest to a virtuous principle. Early in his presidency, Lyndon Johnson called the leaders of the major agriculture interest groups to formulate new policy solutions to agriculture. This was the beginning of the Johnson round. In music, a round is a form in which everything is repeated over and over again.

(4) Business practices. The "conservative" side of the argument comes out no better upon examination. Competitive business enterprise is a highly dynamic force that usually makes change normal, innovation necessary, and influence by ordinary individuals over economic decisions possible. For these reasons many forms of competitive enterprise should be thought of as supported by real liberals despite the fact that government is only in a marginal way responsible for it. But, except for martyrs from Thurmond Arnold to Walter S. Adams who have sought vainly to use government to decentralize industry, the net impact of attitudes toward business from conservatives as well as liberals has been to restrain the system. One might say that the only difference between old-school liberals and conservatives is that the former would destroy the market through public means and the latter through private means. This is very largely due to the fact that, lacking any independent standards, all politicians depend upon those organized interests that already have access to government and to the media of communication. According to the second criterion of liberalism-conservatism, *all established interest groups are conservative.*[7] Government policy is one of many strategies organized interests feel free to pursue. In this respect it is useless to distinguish between NAM and AFL-CIO. Trade associations, for example, exist to "stabilize the market," in other words, to maintain existing relations among members despite any fluctuations in their respective sectors of the economy. They, in turn, are the primary determiners of private as well as public policies toward business and business competition. Holding companies, pools, market sharing, information sharing, interlocking directorships, price leadership, competition through advertising and not prices, and collusion in bidding are typical non-governmental policies, which become inevitable if they are not illegal. On

the other hand, they are functionally in no way distinguishable from such governmental policies as basing points laws, fair trade laws, antiprice discrimination laws, NRA codes, and so on. To the extent that liberalism-conservatism is taken seriously as the source of public philosophy, liberals-conservatives become hemmed in by it, too rigid to withdraw their sentiments as new needs become old, vested interests. They are inevitably betrayed by the very groups that profited most by their support.

The enormous inconsistency between what public policy really is and what old doctrine supposes it to be may turn out to be merely true but still inconsequential. This might be the case if it could be shown that American public men were the original pragmatists and were never in need of any doctrine other than the loose social code that binds us all. This possibility must be rejected. Stable countries, with their highly rationalized political order, have great need of legitimizing rituals, perhaps more so than transitional societies where expectations are not so high. Moreover, the very persistence of the old criteria so far beyond their appropriate hour can be taken as an index to the need American elites have for doctrinal support.

The old public philosophy became outmoded because in our time it applies to the wrong class of objects. Statesmen simply no longer disagree about whether government should be involved; therefore they neither seek out the old criteria for guidance through their disagreements, nor do they really have need of the criteria to justify the mere governmental character of policies. But this does not mean that public men are not now being guided by some other, widely shared, criteria that do apply to the relevant class of objects. The good functionalist must insist upon being guided by the hypothesis that some political formula or public philosophy does exist. If it is obvious that public men are no longer governed by the older public philosophy, then the next logical proposition is this, that there is some other public philosophy with which public policy behaviors are consistent, but it may be one not clearly enough formulated to be well known yet beyond public men themselves.

I contend that such criteria have emerged in a new and already well-developed public philosophy through which public men are attempting to grapple with the pathologies created by the persistence of the old formula. I contend, further, that the new public philosophy is the source of important new political pathologies in America. I contend, finally, that the new public philosophy is pathological because it emerged not out of an evolution of the older but out of the total and complete silence of the older upon those objects with which any new public philosophy had to deal.

INTEREST-GROUP LIBERALISM

The weaknesses of the old liberalism-conservatism were not altogether clear before the 1960's. This tardiness is due simply to the intervention of two wars and then an eight-year period of relative quiescence in policy making and in the saliency of politics and government to the masses. Truman's Fair Deal agenda, already left over from the end of the New Deal, held fire for over a decade until it became a major part of the Democratic agenda of the 1960's and comprised a very large proportion of the successful record of the 89th Congress, the most actively legislating Congress since 1933. Even the historic *Brown* v. *Board of Education* decision failed to bring about noticeable expansion and intensification of political activity until the Little Rock debacle of 1957. With increasing pace thereafter, new pressures began to be placed upon political institutions, and another round of governmental activity was in the making. In many ways the period that began in 1957 with Little Rock and Sputnik was as much a constitutional revolution as that of the 1930's. In this decade—as measured by Federal budgets, personnel, the sheer proliferation of service and other agencies, or the expansion of public regulatory authority—there have clearly been a civil rights revolution, an educational revolution, and a scientific and technological revolution.

All of this activity proves that there is no end to government responsibility. It is not possible to automate all the stabilizers. The new activity in the 1960's also proves that the political apparatus of democracy can respond promptly once the constitutional barriers to democratic choice have been lowered. However, that is only the beginning of the story, because the almost total democratization of the Constitution and the contemporary expansion of the public sector has been accompanied by expansion, not by contraction, of a sense of illegitimacy about public objects. Here is a spectacular paradox. We witness governmental effort of gigantic proportion to solve problems forthwith and directly. Yet we witness expressions of personal alienation and disorientation increasing, certainly not subsiding, in frequency and intensity; and we witness further weakening of informal controls in the family, neighborhood and groups. We witness a vast expansion of effort to bring the ordinary citizen into closer rapport with the democratic process, including unprecedented efforts to confer upon the poor and ineducable the power to make official decisions involving their own fate. Yet at the very same time we witness crisis after crisis in the very institutions in which the new methods of decision-making seemed most appropriate.

It is as though each new program or program expansion were admission of prior governmental inadequacy or failure without necessarily being a contribution to order and well-being. The War on Poverty programs have become as often as not instruments of social protest. The Watts riots, the movements for police review boards in many cities, the sit-ins and marches even where no specifically evil laws are being enforced against a special race or group, the strikes and protests by civil servants, nurses, doctors, teachers, transport and defense workers, and others in vital occupations—all these and many others are evidence of increasing impatience with established ways of resolving social conflict and dividing up society's values. Verbal and organizational attacks on that vague being, the "power structure," even in cities with histories of strong reform movements and imaginative social programs, reflect increasing rejection of pluralistic patterns in favor of more direct prosecution of claims against society. Far from insignificant as a sign of the times is emergence of a third and a fourth national party movement, one on either extreme but alike in their opposition to centrist parties, electoral politics, and pre-election compromise. Many of these new patterns and problems may have been generated by racial issues, but it is clear that that was only a precipitant. The ironic fact is that the post-1937 political economy, either because of or in spite of government policies and two wars, had produced unprecedented prosperity, and as the national output increased arithmetically the rate of rising expectation must have gone up geometrically—in a modern expression of the Malthusian Law. Public authority was left to grapple with this alienating gap between expectation and reality.[8]

Prosperity might merely have produced a gigantic race among all to share in its benefits. The expansion of the public sector might have increased the legitimacy of government and other public objects through redistribution of opportunities to join the prosperity. Instead, the expansion of government that helped produce sustained prosperity also produced a crisis of public authority. Why? Because the old justification for that expansion had so little to say beyond the need for the expansion itself. The class of objects to which the new and appropriate public philosophy would have to apply should, it seems obvious, be the forms, structures and procedures of government control. There are vast technical, political and ethical questions involved in what are and what ought to be the consequences of the various ways in which power can be administered and employed. What constitutes "due process" in an age of positive government? What impact does one or another administrative process have upon society, upon the specific clientele whose compliance is sought, upon the sense of legitimacy among citizens, and upon the capacity of the next generation to respond, governmentally and otherwise, to the problems of its own time?

Out of the developing crisis in public authority has developed an ersatz political formula that does, for all its problems, offer the public man some guidance and some justification in his efforts to shape, form and provide for the administration of positive laws in the positive state. There are several possible names for this contemporary replacement of liberalism-conservatism. A strong possibility would be *corporatism*, but its history as a concept gives it several unwanted connotations, such as conservative Catholicism or Italian fascism, that keep it from being quite suitable. Another is *syndicalism*, but among many objections is the connotation of anarchy too far removed from American experience or intentions. However, the new American public philosophy is a variant of those two alien philosophies.

The most clinically accurate term to describe the American variant is *interest-group liberalism*. It may be called liberalism because it expects to use government in a positive and expansive role, it is motivated by the highest sentiments, and it possesses strong faith that what is good for government is good for the society. It is "interest-group liberalism" because it sees as both necessary and good that the policy agenda and the public interest be defined in terms of the organized interests in society. In brief sketch, the working model of the interest group liberal is a vulgarized version of the pluralist model of modern political science. It assumes: (1) Organized interests are homogeneous and easy to define, sometimes monolithic. Any "duly elected" spokesman for any interest is taken as speaking in close approximation for each and every member.[9] (2) Organized interests pretty much fill up and adequately represent most of the sectors of our lives, so that one organized group can be found effectively answering and checking some other organized group as it seeks to prosecute its claims against society.[10] And (3) the role of government is one of ensuring access particularly to the most effectively organized, and of ratifying the agreements and adjustments worked out among the competing leaders and their claims. This last assumption is supposed to be a statement of how our democracy works and how it ought to work. Taken together, these assumptions constitute the Adam Smith "hidden hand" model applied to groups. Ironically, it is embraced most strongly by the very people most likely to reject the Smith model applied in its original form to firms in the market.

These assumptions are the basis of the new public philosophy. The policy behaviors of old-school liberals and conservatives, of Republicans and Democrats, so inconsistent with liberalism-conservatism criteria, are fully consistent with the criteria drawn from interest-group liberalism: *The most important difference between liberals and conservatives, Republicans and Democrats—however they define themselves—is to be found in the interest groups they identify with. Congressmen are guided in their votes, Presidents in their programs, and administrators in their discretion, by whatever organized interests they have taken for themselves as the most legitimate; and that is the measure of the legitimacy of demands.*

The assumptions of the model and the concluding behavioral proposition constitute, for better or worse, an important part of the working methodology of modern, empirical political science. However, quite another story with quite different consequences is how all of this became elevated from an hypothesis about political behavior to an ideology about how the democratic system ought to work and then became ultimately elevated to that ideology most widely shared among contemporary public men.

Interest-Group Liberalism: An Intellectual History

The opening of the national government to positive action on a large scale was inevitably to have an impact upon political justification just as on political technique. However, the inventors of technique were less than inventive for justification of particular policies at particular times. Hansen, for instance, has observed that Keynes was no social reformer, nor had he any particular commitments to particular social ends.[11] Keynes helped discover the modern economic system and how to help it maintain itself, but his ideas and techniques could be used, and indeed have been used, to support many points of view. "Collective bargaining, trade unionism, minimum-wage laws, hours legislation, social security, a progressive tax system, slum clearance and housing, urban redevelopment and planning, education reform," Hansen observed of Keynes, "all these he accepted, but they were not among his preoccupations. In no sense could he be called the father of the welfare state."[12]

Nor was the doctrine of popular government and majority rule, which was so important in the victory of liberalism over conservatism, adequate guidance after the demise of liberalism-conservatism. If one reviews the New Deal period and thereafter he will see how little propensity Americans have had to use the majority rule justification. The reasons why are fairly apparent. Justification of positive government programs on the basis of popular rule required above all a proclamation of the supremacy of Congress. The abdication of Congress in the 1930's in the passage of the fundamental New Deal legislation could never have been justified in the name of popular government. With all due respect to Congressmen, little discernible effort was made to do so. Statutory and investigatory infringements on civil liberties during World War II and during the Cold War, plus the popular support of McCarthyism, produced further reluctance to fall back on Congress and majority rule as the fount of public policy wisdom. Many who wished to use this basis anyway sought support in the plebiscitary character of the Presidency. However, "presidential liberals" have had to blind themselves to many complications in the true basis of presidential authority and to the true—the bureaucratic—expression of presidental will.

The very practices that made convincing use of popular rule doctrine impossible—delegation of power to administrators, interest representation, outright delegation of power to trade associations, and so on—were what made interest-group liberalism so attractive an alternative. And because the larger interest groups did claim large memberships, they could be taken virtually as popular rule in modern dress. Interest-group liberalism simply corresponded impressively well with the realities of power. Thus, it possessed a little of science and some of the trappings of popular rule. Political scientists, after all, were pioneers in insisting upon recognition of the group, as well as in helping to elevate the pressure-group system from power to virtue. Political scientists had for a long time argued that the group is the necessary variable in political analysis for breaking through the formalisms of government.[13] However, there was inevitably an element of approval in their methodological argument, if only to counteract the kind of recognition of the group that Steffens and other progressives and Muckrakers were more than willing to accord. In 1929, Pendleton Herring concluded his inquiry with the argument that:

> [The national associations] represent a healthy democratic development. They rose in answer to certain needs. . . . They are part of our representative system. . . . These groups must be welcomed for what they are, and certain precautionary regulations worked out. The groups must be understood and their proper place in government allotted, if not by actual legislation, then by general public realization of their significance.[14]

Following World War II, one easily notes among political scientists the widespread acceptance of the methodology and, more importantly here, the normative position. Among political scientists the best expression of interest-group liberalism was probably that of Wilfred Binkley and Malcolm Moos. The fact that it was so prominent in their American government basic textbook suggests that it tended to reflect conventional wisdom among political scientists even in 1948. Binkley and Moos argued that the "basic concept for understanding the dynamics of government is the multi-group nature of modern society or the modern state."[15] Political reality could be grasped scientifically as a "parallelogram of forces" among groups, and the public interest is "determined and established" through the free competition of interest groups: "The necessary composing and compromising of their differences is the practical test of what constitutes the public interest."[16]

The fact that a doctrine has some support in the realities of power certainly helps to explain its appeal as a doctrine.[17] But there were also several strongly positive reasons for the emergence of this particular doctrine. The first, and once perhaps the only, is that it has helped flank the constitutional problems of federalism. Manifestations of the corporate state were once limited primarily to the Extension Service of the Department of Agriculture, with self-administration by the land grant colleges and the local farmers and commerce associations. Self-administration by organized groups was an attractive technique precisely because it could be justified as so decentralized and permissive as to be hardly federal at all.[18] Here began the ethical and conceptual mingling of the notion of organized private groups with the notions of "local government" and "self-government." Ultimately direct interest group participation in government became synonymous with self-government, first for reasons of strategy, then by belief that the two were indeed synonymous. As a propaganda strategy it eased acceptance in the courts, then among the locals who still believed the farmer was and should be independent. Success as strategy increased usage; usage helped elevate strategy to doctrine. The users began to believe in their own symbols.

A second positive appeal of interest-group liberalism is strongly related to the first. Interest-group liberalism helps solve a problem for the democratic politician in the modern state where the stakes are so high. This is the problem of enhanced conflict and how to avoid it. The politician's contribution to society is his skill in resolving conflict. However, direct confrontations are sought only by the zealous ideologues and "outsiders." The typical American politician displaces and defers and delegates conflict where possible; he squarely faces conflict only when he must. Interest-group liberalism offers a justification for keeping major combatants apart. It provides a theoretical basis for giving to each according to his claim, the price for which is a reduction of concern for what others are claiming. In other words, it transforms logrolling from necessary evil to greater good. This is the basis for the "consensus" so often claimed these days. It is also the basis for President Kennedy's faith that in our day ideology has given over to administration. It is inconceivable that so sophisticated a person as he could believe, for example, that his setting of guidelines for wage and price increases was a purely administrative act. Here, in fact, is a policy that will never be "administered" in the ordinary sense of the word. The guidelines provide a basis for direct and regular policy-making between the President (or his agent) and the spokesmen for industry and the spokesmen for labor. This is a new phase of government relations with management and labor, and it is another step consistent with the interest-group liberal criterion of direct access.

The third positive appeal of interest-group liberalism is that it is a direct, even if pathological, response to the crisis of public authority. The practice of dealing only with organized claims in formulating policy, and of dealing exclusively through organized claims in implementing programs helps create the sense that power need not be power at all, nor control control. If sovereignty is parceled out among the groups, then who's out anything? As Max Ways of *Fortune* put it, government power, group power and individual power may go up simultaneously. If the groups to be controlled control the controls, *then* "to administer does not always mean to rule."[19] The inequality of power, ultimately the involvement of coercion in government decisions, is always a gnawing problem in a democratic culture. Rousseau's General Will stopped at the boundary of a Swiss canton. The myth of the group and the group will is becoming the answer to Rousseau in the big democracy.

President Eisenhower talked regularly about the desirability of business-government "partnerships," despite the misgivings in his farewell address about the "military-industrial complex." However, explicit and systematic expression of interest-group liberalism is much more the contribution of the Democrats. There is little reason to believe that one party believes more ardently than the other; but the best evidence can be found among the more articulate Democrats, especially in the words of two of the leading Democratic intellectuals, Professors John Kenneth Galbraith and Arthur Schlesinger, Jr.[20] To Professor Galbraith: "Private economic power is held in check by the countervailing power of those who are subject to it. The first begets the second."[21] Concentrated economic power stimulates other business interests (in contrast to the Smithian consumer), which organize against it. This results in a natural tendency toward equilibrium. But Galbraith is not really writing a theoretical alternative to Adam Smith; he is writing a program of government action. For he admits to the limited existence of effective countervailing power and proposes that where it is absent or too weak, government policy should seek out and support or, where necessary, create the organizations capable of countervailing. Government thereby pursues the public interest and makes itself superfluous at the same time. This is a sure-fire, nearly scientific, guide to interest-group liberalism. Professor Schlesinger's views are summarized for us in the campaign tract he wrote in 1960. To Schlesinger, the essential difference between the Democratic and Republican parties is that the Democratic party is a truly multi-interest party in the grand tradition extending back to Federalist No. 10. In power, it offers multi-interest administration and therefore ought to be preferred over the Republican Party and:

> What is the essence of a multi-interest administration? It is surely that the leading interests in society are all represented in the interior processes of policy formation—which can be done only if members or advocates of these interests are included in key positions of government. . . .[22]

This theme Schlesinger repeated in his more serious and more recent work, *A Thousand Days*. Following his account of the 1962 confrontation of President Kennedy with the steel industry and the later decision to cut taxes and cast off for expansionary rather than stabilizing fiscal policy, Schlesinger concludes:

> The ideological debates of the past began to give way to a new agreement on the

practicalities of managing a modern economy. There thus developed in the Kennedy years a national accord on economic policy—a new consensus which gave hope of harnessing government, business and labor in rational partnership for a steadily expanding American economy.[23]

Interest-Group Liberalism and Public Policies in the 1960's

A significant point in the entire argument is that the Republicans would disagree with Schlesinger on the *facts* but not on the *basis* of his distinction. The Republican rejoinder would be, in effect, "Democratic Administrations are *not* more multi-interest than Republican." And, in my opinion, this would be almost the whole truth. This principle has been explicitly applied in the formulation of a large number of policies, especially since the return of the Democrats to power in 1961. That is, policy makers have in numerous new programs added elements of official group representation and have officially applied "participatory democracy" to the implementation as well as the formulation of law as part of the justification of their action. There are additional policies where evidence of the application of interest-group liberalism is clear even though not as consciously intended or as much a part of the record of self-praise.

President Kennedy provides an especially good starting point because his positions were clear and because justification was especially important to him. No attention need be paid to the elements of liberalism-conservatism in his program but only to the consistency of his requests with interest-group liberalism. John Kennedy was bred to a politics of well-organized and autonomous units of power. Locally they were more likely ethnic, religious and neighborhood organizations, but they had to be reckoned with as powerful interest groups. The national party he set out to win in 1956 was also a congeries of autonomous factions and blocs; and it has been said that he succeeded by recreating the "New Deal coalition." But there is a vast difference between pluralism inside political parties and legitimized pluralism built into government programs. The one does not necessarily follow from the other, unless leaders believe it is desirable. President Kennedy's proposals and rhetoric mark his belief in that desirability. Many of his most important proposals mark his very real contribution to the corporatizing of the government-group nexus in the United States.

The argriculture problem, high and early on the New Frontier agenda, was to be solved somewhat differently from all earlier attempts, and that difference is much to the point. At local levels, federal agriculture programs had always been corporative, with committees of local farm dignitaries applying the state and national standards to local conditions.[24] President Kennedy proposed simply to bring this pattern to the center and to have the farmers, represented by group leaders, *set* the standards as well as apply them. Essentially, this was NRA applied to agriculture.

There was no attempt to reinstitute an industrial NRA pattern, but there were, just the same, moves toward recognition of the organized side of industry in the "interior processes" of government. First, as earlier observed, by direct presidential act guidelines for profits and wages were set up. Notice was thereby served that henceforth "industrial policy" would be made by direct bargaining between President and each and every leader of an industrial sector. Quite separately, but along parallel industrial lines, this meant the same sort of bargaining between President and union leaders. It is beside the point to argue whether Kennedy or Johnson has been more lenient in applying the guidelines to the unions. It is even beside the point to argue whether this new technique of control means more government involvement and direction than alternative techniques. The point is that the pattern of control and the manner of its impact is basically corporativistic. "Partnership" is the measure of success.

Many other relations of government to industry have tended toward the same pattern in the 1960's, whether they come this way full-blown from President or emerge from Congress this way only at the end. COMSAT is a combination out of 1930's Italy and 1950's France. Like the Italian practice of "permanent receivership," COMSAT is a combine of kept private companies, sharing in stock and risk with the government. Like the many French public and mixed corporations, there is direct "interest representation" on the Board. The "public" stamp is placed on it by adding to the interest-laden Board three presidentially appointed members; but one of these is a representative of Big Labor and one a representative of Big Industry. By the end of 1966, there was already talk among the carriers (the communications industries) of forming a combine within the combine to regularize and stabilize losses suffered by any of them as a result of obsolescence and competition.

The Trade Expansion Act of 1962, for another example, was the first American tariff based upon broad categories of goods rather than single items. From the beginning, categorization of goods paralleled the lines of jurisdiction of the leading trade associations and organized farm commodities groups.[25] The semi-official role of trade associations was expected to increase and expand through those parts of the new law providing relief through subsidy for injuries proven to have been sustained by tariff cuts.

There were, of course, many Kennedy proposals that are economy-wide in intention, but even some of these have one peculiarity or another that distinguishes them less from the interest-group policies than first appearances suggest. The investment tax credit, for example, was industry-wide, but it involved a reduction rather than an enlargement of the governmental sphere. Appalachia involved a bold regional concept overwhelmingly broader than any organized groups; however, the strong veto power given the state governors allows for, and was expected to allow for, maximum return of group represen- tation through the back door. Appalachia is more clearly a case of interest-group liberalism if we include, as we should, state and local government agencies as groups to be directly represented in implementation of policies. This becomes an important characteristic of "creative federalism." In Appalachia the governors in the region commit Federal funds to development plans formulated by state agencies, local agencies, and private groups.

During the Johnson Administration the doctrines and policies of interest- group liberalism have been elevated to new highs of usage and rationalization.

It is coming of age by being provided with new and appropriate halo words. The most important is "creative federalism," about which President Johnson and his Great Society team have spoken frequently and enthusiastically. This and related terms—such as partnership, maximum feasible participation, and, above all, consensus—seem to be very sincerely felt by present government leaders. The sentiments are coming to be shared widely among non-government leaders and are at the bottom of the extraordinary business support Johnson received during his most active period of legislative creativity. Probably the most accurate and sympathetic analysis of creative federalism and the role it is playing in the Great Society has been provided by *Fortune* magazine. As *Fortune* and many other observers would agree, creative federalism is not federalism. Federalism divides sovereignty between duly constituted levels of government. "Creative federalism" is a parceling of powers between the central government and *all* structures of power, governments and non-governments. In fact, little distinction is made between what is government and what is not. It is, according to the enthusiastic definition of *Fortune* writer Max Ways, "a relation, cooperative and competitive, between a limited central power and other powers that are essentially independent of it." The difference between federalism and "creative federalism" is no mere academic distinction. Creative federalism involves a "new way of organizing federal programs . . . [in which simultaneously] the power of states and local governments will increase; the power of private organizations, including businesses, will increase; the power of individuals will increase."[26]

In line with the new rationale, President Johnson and his Administration have expanded the degree to which private organizations and local authorities become endowed with national sovereignty. Corporativistic programs inherited from the New Deal have been strengthened in the degree to which they can share in the new, explicit rationale. This has been particularly noticeable in the power and natural resources field, where policies are now quite explicitly left to the determination of those participants who know the "local situation" best. It is quite at the center of Great Society expansions of existing programs. When still Assistant Secretary for Education, Francis Keppel described federal education policy this way: "To speak of 'federal aid' [to education] simply confuses the issue. It is more appropriate to speak of federal support to special purposes . . . an investment made by a partner who has clearly in mind the investments of other partners—local, state and private."[27]

The most significant contribution of the Great Society to the growing ratio such corporativistic programs bear to the sum total of federal activity is the War on Poverty, particularly the community action program. To the old progressive the elimination of poverty was a passionate dream, to the socialist a philosophic and historic necessity. To the interest-group liberal, poverty is becoming just another status around which power centers ought to organize. If one hasn't organized, then organize it. In so organizing it, poverty is not eliminated, but inconsistency in the manner of government's relation to society is reduced. Organizing the poor, something that once was done only in the Threepenny Opera, helps legitimize the interest-group liberal's preference for dealing only with organized claims. The "Peachum factor" in public affairs is best personified in Sargent Shriver. In getting the War on Poverty under way Shriver was misunderstood in many matters, particularly on any insistence that the poor be represented in some mathematically exact way. But one aspect of the doctrine was clear all the time. This was (and is) that certain types of groups should always be involved some way. As he listed them they are: "governmental groups," philanthropic, religious, business, and labor groups, and "the poor."[28] The significance lies primarily in the equality of the listing. "Governmental groups" are simply one more type of participant.

Interest-group liberalism thus seems closer to being the established, operative ideology of the American elite than any other body of doctrine. The United States is far from 100 per cent a corporate state; but each administration, beginning with the New Deal revolution, has helped reduce the gap. And it is equally significant that few if any programs organized on the basis of direct interest representation or group self-administration have ever been eliminated. To the undoubted power of organized interests has now been added the belief in their virtue. There would always be delegation of sovereignty to interest groups in some proportion of the total body of governmental activities. The new context of justification simply means far more direct delegation than the realities of power, unsupported by legitimacy, would call for.

In sum, modern liberals are ambivalent about government. Government is obviously the most efficacious way of achieving good purposes in our age. But it is efficacious because it is involuntary; as one of the founders of modern social science put it, modern government possesses a monopoly of legal coercion in a society. To live with their ambivalence, modern policy makers have fallen into believing that public policy involves merely the identification of the problems toward which government ought to be aimed. It pretends, through "pluralism," "countervailing power," "creative federalism," "partnership," and "participatory democracy," that the unsentimental business of coercion is not involved and that the unsentimental decisions of how to employ coercion need not really be made at all. Stated in the extreme, the policies of interest-group liberalism are end-oriented. Few standards of implementation, if any, accompany delegations of power. The requirement of standards has been replaced by the requirement of participation. The requirement of law has been replaced by the requirement of contingency.

THE COSTS OF INTEREST-GROUP LIBERALISM

For all the political advantages interest-group liberals have in their ideology, there are high costs involved. Unfortunately, these costs are not strongly apparent at the time of the creation of a group-based program. As Wallace Sayre once observed, the gains of a change tend to be immediate, the costs tend to be cumulative. However, it takes no long-run patience or the spinning of fine webs to capture and assess the consequences of group-based policy solutions. Three major consequences are suggested and assessed here: (1) the atrophy of institutions of popular control; (2) the maintenance of old and creation of new structures of privilege; and (3) conservatism, in several senses of the word.

1. In his *The Public Philosophy*, Lippmann was rightfully concerned over the "derangement of power" whereby modern democracies tend first toward unchecked elective leadership and then toward drainage of public authority from elective leaders down into their constituencies. However, Lippmann erred if he thought of constituencies only as voting constituencies. Drainage has tended toward "support group constituencies," and with special consequence. Parceling out policy-making power to the most interested parties destroys political responsibility. A program split off with a special imperium to govern itself is not merely an administrative unit. It is a structure of power with impressive capacities to resist central political control.

Besides making conflict-of-interest a principle of government rather than a criminal act, participatory programs shut out the public. To be more precise, programs of this sort tend to cut out all that part of the mass that is not specifically organized around values strongly salient to the goals of the program. They shut out the public, first, at the most creative phase of policy making—the phase where the problem is first defined. Once problems are defined, alliances form accordingly and the outcome is both a policy and a reflection of superior power. If the definition is laid out by groups along lines of established group organization, there is always great difficulty for an amorphous public to be organized in any other terms. The public is shut out, secondly, at the phase of accountability. In programs in which group self-administration is legitimate, the administrators are accountable primarily to the groups, only secondarily to President or Congress as institutions. In brief, to the extent that organized interests legitimately control a program there is functional rather than substantive accountability. This means questions of equity, balance and equilibrium to the exclusion of questions of overall social policy and questions of whether or not the program should be maintained or discontinued. It also means accountability to experts first and amateurs last; and an expert is a man trained and skilled in the mysteries and technologies of the program. These propositions are best illustrated by at least ten separate, self-governing systems (representing over 10 billion dollars per year in spending and loaning) in agriculture alone.[29] There are many other, although perhaps less dramatic, illustrations.

Finally, the public is shut out by tendencies toward conspiracy to shut the public out. One of the assumptions underlying direct group representation is that on the boards and in the staff and among the recognized outside consultants there will be regular countervailing and checks and balances. In Schattschneider's terms, this would be expected to expand the "scope of conflict." But there is nothing inevitable about that, and the safer assumption might well be the converse. One meaningful illustration, precisely because it is an absurd extreme, is found in the French system of interest representation. Maurice Bye reports that as the communist-controlled union, the CGT, intensified its participation in post-war government it was able to influence representatives of interests other than the employees. In a desperate effort to insure the separation and countervailing of interests on the boards, the government issued the decree that "each member of the board must be *independent of the interests he is not representing*."[30] After a 1964 review of the politics of agriculture and of five major efforts of their post-war administrations to bring the ten separate self-governing agriculture systems under a minimum of central control, I was led to the following conclusion:

> These systems . . . have become practically insulated from the three central sources of democratic political responsibility. Thus, within the Executive branch, they are autonomous. Secretaries of Agriculture have tried and failed to consolidate or even to coordinate related programs. Within Congress, they are sufficiently powerful to be able to exercise an effective veto or create a stalemate. And they are almost totally removed from the view, not to mention the control, of the general public. (Throughout the 1950's, Victor Anfuso of Brooklyn was the only member of the House Agriculture Committee from a non-farm constituency.)[31]

This, I suggest, is a tendency in all similarly organized programs.

2. Programs following the principles of interest-group liberalism create privilege, and it is a type of privilege particularly hard to bear or combat because it is touched with the symbolism of the state. The large national interest groups that walk the terrains of national politics are already fairly tight structures of power. We need no more research to support Michels' iron tendency toward oligarchy in "private governments." Pluralists ease our problem of abiding the existence of organized interests by characterizing oligarchy as simply a negative name for organization: In combat people want and need to be organized and led. Another, somewhat less assuaging, assertion of pluralism is that the member approves the goals of the group or is free to leave it for another, or can turn his attention to one of his "overlapping memberships" in other groups. But however true these may be in pluralistic *politics*, everything changes when some of the groups are co-opted by the state in pluralistic *government*. The American Farm Bureau Federation is no "voluntary association" insofar as it is a legitimate functionary in Extension work. NAHB, NAREB, NAACP or NAM are no ordinary lobbies after they become part of the "interior processes of policy formation."

The more clear and legitimized the representation of a group or its leaders in policy formation, the less voluntary is membership in that group and the more necessary is loyalty to its leadership for people who share the interests in question. And, the more clear the official practice of recognizing only organized interests, the more hierarchy is introduced into the society. It is a well-recognized and widely appreciated function of formal groups in modern societies to provide much of the necessary every-day social control. However, when the very thought processes behind public policy are geared toward those groups they are bound to take on much of the involuntary character of *public* control. The classic example outside agriculture is probably the Rivers and Harbors Congress, a private agency whose decisions in the screening of public works projects have almost the effect of law. And, as David Truman observes, arrangements where "one homogeneous group is directly or indirectly charged with the administration of a function . . . [in a] kind of situation that characterizes the occupational licensing boards and similar 'independent' agencies . . . have become increasingly familiar in regulatory situations in all levels of government."[32]

Even when the purpose of the program is the uplifting of the underprivileged, the administrative arrangement favored by interest-group liberalism tends toward creation of new privilege instead. Urban redevelopment programs based upon federal support of private plans do not necessarily, but do all too easily, become means by which the building industry regularizes itself. An FHA run essentially by the standards of the NAREB became a major escape route for the middle class to leave the city for suburbia rather than a means of providing housing for all. Urban redevelopment, operating for nearly two decades on a principle of local government and local developer specification of federal policy, has been used in the South (and elsewhere) as an effective instrument for Negro removal. Organizing councils for the poverty program have become first and foremost means of elevating individual spokesmen for the poor and of determining which churches and neighborhood organizations shall be the duly recognized channels of legitimate demand. Encouragement of organization among Negroes and the White and non-White poor is important. Early recognition of a few among many emerging leaders and organizations as legitimate administrators or policy-makers takes a serious risk of destroying the process itself (more on this directly below).

3. Government by and through interest groups is in impact conservative in almost every sense of that term. Part of its conservatism can be seen in another look at the two foregoing objections: Weakening of popular government and support of privilege are, in other words, two aspects of conservatism. It is beside the point to argue that these consequences are not intended. A third dimension of conservatism, stressed here separately, is the simple conservatism of resistance to change. David Truman, who has not been a strong critic of self-government by interest groups, has, all the same, identified a general tendency of established agency-group relationships to be "highly resistant to disturbance." He continues:

> New and expanded functions are easily accommodated, provided they develop and operate through existing channels of influence and do not tend to alter the relative importance of those influences. Disturbing changes are those that modify either the content or the relative strength of the component forces operating through an administrative agency. In the face of such changes, or the threat of them, the "old line" agency is highly inflexible.[33]

If this is already a tendency in a pluralistic system, then agency-group relationships must be all the more inflexible to the extent that the relationship is official and legitimate.

The war-on-poverty pattern, even in its early stages, provides a rich testing ground. I observed above that early official cooption of poverty leaders creates privilege before, and perhaps instead of, alleviating poverty. Another side of this war is the war the established welfare groups are waging against the emergence of the newly organizing social forces. Many reports are already remarking upon the opposition established welfare and church groups are putting up against the new groups. Such opposition led to abandonment of Syracuse's organize-the-poor project and the retreat of Sargent Shriver's Office of Economic Opportunity to "umbrella groups" sponsored by City Hall. [34] Old and established groups doing good works might naturally look fearfully upon the emergence of competing, perhaps hostile, groups. That is well and good—until their difference is one of "who shall be the government?" Conservatism then becomes necessary as a matter of survival.

The tendency toward the extreme conservatism of sharing legitimate power with private organizations is possibly stronger in programs more strictly economic. Adams and Gray reviewed figures on assignment of FM radio broadcasting licenses and found that as of 1955, 90 per cent of the FM stations were merely "little auxiliaries" of large AM networks. They also note that the same pattern was beginning to repeat itself in FCC licensing of UHF television channels. [35] The mythology may explain this as a case of "interest group power," but that begs the question. Whatever power was held by the networks was based largely on the commitment the FCC implied in the original grants of licenses. Having granted exclusive privileges to private groups in the public domain (in this case the original assignment of frequencies) without laying down practical conditions for perpetual public retention of the domain itself, the FCC had actually given over sovereignty. The companies acquired property rights and legally vested interests in the grant that interfere enormously with later efforts to affect the grant. Thus, any FCC attempt to expand the communications business through FM would deeply affect the positions and "property" of the established AM companies and networks. Issuing FM licenses to new organizations would have required an open assault on property as well as the established market relations. Leaving aside all other judgements of the practice, it is clearly conservative. [36] Granting of licenses and other privileges unconditionally, and limiting sovereignty by allowing the marketing of properties to be influenced by the possession of the privilege, are practices also to be found in oil, in water power, in the newer sources of power, in transportation, in the "parity" programs of agriculture.

Wherever such practices are found there will also be found strong resistance to change. Already the pattern is repeating itself in form and consequences in the policies regarding our newest resource, outer space. As earlier observed, the private members of COMSAT very early in the life of the new corporation made arrangements to protect themselves against the impact of new developments on old facilities. In addition to that, and more significantly here, the constituents of COMSAT have moved to exclude all other possible entrants and alternative ways of organizing the economics of space communication. In response to Ford Foundation's proposal for a separate satellite system for educational television, COMSAT officially moved to cut off any chance of a rival by (1) opposing Ford vigorously, (2) interpreting the statute and charter to be a grant of trust for the entire public interest in the field, (3) seeking a ruling to that effect from the FCC, (4) showing that stockholders in COMSAT and in the carrier members of COMSAT, such as A.T.&T., would be dealt an unfair blow, and (5) producing an alternative plan whereby the Ford system would be created within COMSAT, being underwritten by all the major carriers and "users" (i.e., the telephone and telegraph companies and the commercial networks). [37]

There are social and psychological mechanisms as well as economic and vested interests working against change. As programs are split off and allowed to establish self-governing relations with clientele groups, professional norms usually spring up, governing the proper ways of doing things. These rules-of-the-game heavily weight access and power in favor of the established interests, just as American parliamentary rules-of-the-game have always tended to make Congress a haven for classes in retreat. For example, as public health moved from a regulatory to a welfare concept, local health agencies put up impressive resistance against efforts to reorganize city and county health departments accordingly. Herbert Kaufman chronicles the vain forty-year reorganization effort in New York City.[38] An important psychological mechanism working against change is one that can be found in criticisms of the electoral devices of proportional and occupational representation. PR tends to rigidify whatever social cleavages first provide the basis for PR, because PR encourages social interests to organize, then perpetuates them by allowing them to become "constituencies." This is all the more true as interests actually become not merely groups but parties represented by name and bloc in parliament.[39] Even in less formalized situations, legitimizing a group gives it the advantages of exposure and usage as well as direct power, access and privilege.

INTEREST-GROUP LIBERALISM AND HOW TO SURVIVE IT

Quite possibly all of these developments are part of some irresistible historical process. In that case policy-makers would never really have had any alternative when they created group-based programs. And in that case the ideology of interest-group liberalism simply reflects and rationalizes the realities of power. However, the best test of a deterministic hypothesis is whether real-world efforts to deny it fail. Thus, a consideration of remedies is worthwhile.

We might begin where Truman ended his extremely influential work on pluralistic America. After reviewing several possible "palliatives" Truman concludes essentially that the pluralistic political system is not doomed at all but, to the contrary, is self-corrective:

> To the extent that the kind of dynamic stability that permits gradual adaptation is a function of elements within the system itself, the key factors will not be new. The group process will proceed in the usual fashion. Whether it eventuates in disaster will depend in the future as in the past basically upon the effects of overlapping membership, particularly the vitality of membership in those potential groups based upon interests held widely throughout the society. The memberships are the means both of stability and of peaceful change. In the future as in the past, they will provide the answer to the ancient question: *quis custodiet ipsos custodes?* Guardianship will emerge out of the affiliations of the guardians.[40]

But it is self-corrective only if there is overlapping and confrontation among groups, and too many examples above suggest that (1) there is a strong tendency, supported by a great deal of conscious effort, to keep confrontation to a minimum and that (2) "membership in potential groups" is confined to values about the "rules-of-the-game" about which there is strong consensus in general but, due to their generality, extreme permissiveness in particular, short-run situations. Thus, it cannot be assumed that the conditions necessary for the self-corrective system necessarily exist. It is wrong to assume that social pluralism (which is an undeniable fact about America) produced *political* pluralism.

However, the important question is not whether Truman and others are wrong but whether the conditions necessary for their self-corrective system can be deliberately contrived. The effort here is to propose some such contrivances. Two introductory observations should be made about them. First, it is assumed that positive government is here to stay and expand. Thus, proposals for return to a principle of lesser government and for policies in the lower left-hand corner of the Diagram, while logical and perhaps desirable, are not acceptable. Second, it is assumed that *real* political pluralism is a desirable form of democracy and that it is a desirable democratic antidote to the "incorporated pluralism" which has been the object of criticism throughout this essay.

1. The first part of the remedy is attractive precisely because it is so obvious. This is to discredit interest-group liberalism as official ideology. Essentially, this is the effort of this paper. Unless we are locked in a predetermined secular trend, a change of ideology can affect the pattern of power just as the pattern of power can affect ideology. Certainly the egalitarian ideology has affected the distribution of power in every country where it has had any currency at all. A change of ideology could keep to a minimum the number of programs that merely incorporate the forces responsible for passage. Some other ideology would provide a basis for resisting many of the most outrageous claims for patronage and privilege made by organized interests.

2. The second part of the remedy is institutional and also suggests the direction a new ideology ought to take. This is to push direct group access back one giant step in the political process, somehow to insulate administrative agencies from full group participation. This means restoration of the Federalist No. 10 ideology in which "factions" are necessary evils that require regulation, not accommodation. Madison defined faction as "a number of citizens, whether amounting to a majority or minority of the whole, who are united and actuated by some common impulse of passion, or of interest, *adverse to the right of other citizens, or to the permanent and aggregate interests of the community*." As a manifestation of the ideology prevalent today, it is worth noting that Truman quotes Madison's definition but ends his quote just before the parts I emphasized above.[41] That part of Madison's definition should be returned to full faith and credit, and the only way to do that and to be sure that it and the true self-regulatory character of pluralism can be institutionalized is *to keep group interests in constant confrontation with one another in Congress*. Once an agency is "depoliticized" or "made independent" by handing it over to its organized clientele, the number of "factions" is reduced from a competitive to an oligopolistic situation; competition lasts only until the remaining few groups learn each other's goals and each adjusts to the others. Lippmann is concerned for a "derangement of power" in which *governing* has been drained away from

the executive to the assembly and to the electorate, and neither is qualified to govern. The American pattern would suggest another kind of derangement altogether, a derangement brought about by Congress's direct extension of its own principles of representation over into the executive.

Pushing group representation and "participatory democracy" back into Congress and away from the executive requires several relatively traditional steps. The first would be revival of a constitutional doctrine that is still valid but widely disregarded. This is the rule that the delegation of legislative power to administrative agencies must be accompanied by clear standards of implementation.[42] This involves revival of the rule of law to replace the rule of bargaining as a principle of administration. It does not involve reduction of the public sphere. It *is* likely to make more difficult the framing and passage of some programs; but one wonders why any program should be acceptable if its partisans cannot clearly state purpose and means. Revival of the rule of law would also tend to dispel much of the cynicism with which the most active citizen views public authority.

Another way to restore competition to groups and ultimately push them back to Congress is to foster a truly independent executive. Development of a real Senior Civil Service is vital to this in the way it would tend to develop a profession of public administration, as distinct from a profession of a particular technology and a career within a specific agency. The makings of a Senior Civil Service lie already within the grasp of the Civil Service Commission if it has the wit to perceive its opportunity in its Career Executive Roster and its Office of Career Development and its Executive Seminar Center. The independent Senior Civil Servant, who could be designed for weakness in agency loyalty, combined with the imposition of clearer standards and rules governing administrative discretion, together would almost necessarily centralize and formalize, without denying, group access to agencies. In turn this would almost necessarily throw more groups together, increase their competition, expand the scope of that competition, and ultimately require open, public settlement of their differences. This would throw groups back more frequently into Congress and would also increase presidential opportunity to control the bureaucracies. The legitimacy of these institutions would be further confirmed.

3. A third part of the remedy has to do with programs themselves, although the recommendation overlaps No. 2 in that it has much to do with institutional roles. This is to set a Jeffersonian absolute limit of from five to ten years on every enabling act. As the end approaches, established relations between agency and clientele are likely to be shaken by exposure and opposition. This is as important as the need for regular evaluation of the existence of the program itself and of whether it should be abolished, expanded or merged with some other program. There is a myth that programs are evaluated at least once a year through the normal appropriations process and that specialized appropriations and authorizations subcommittees review agency requests with a fine tooth comb. However, yearly evaluation, especially the appropriations process, gets at only the incremental and marginal aspects of most programs, rarely at the substance. Here is an example of the earlier distinction between functional and substantive

accountability. The very cost-consciousness and detail that makes yearly review functionally rational is the basis of its weakness as a substantively rational process.

This proposal, like the proposal for a return to a rule of law, injects an element of inefficiency into the system. But our affluence is hardly worth the trouble if we cannot spend some of it on maintaining due process, pluralism and other system values. It also injects instability, but it is the very sort of instability that is supposed to make the pluralistic system work. It is amazing and distressing how many 1930's left-wing liberals have become 1960's interest-group liberals out of a concern for instability.

4. The fourth and final part of a reform program bears some resemblance to an old-line constitutional argument. Restoration of the *Schechter* and *Panama* requirement would tend to do more than strengthen the rule of law, enhance real political competition, and dispel political cynicism. It might also provide a basis for establishing some practical and functional limitations on the scope of federal power. That is to say, if an applicable and understandable set of general rules must accompany every federal program, then, except in some clear emergency, federal power could not extend to those objects for which no general rules are either practicable or desirable. Where regional or local variation is to be encouraged, State Government is really the proper unit. Argument for restoration of State Government is not based on mere antiquarian admiration of federalism or fear of national domination. It is an immensely practical argument. State Governments have been systematically weakened by Home Rule, by federal absorption of tax base and by federal-local relations. Yet the cities, even with federal help, have proven unable to cope because the problems have outgrown their boundaries. The State possesses all the powers of its cities plus the territorial containment of most of the new metropolitan realities. The State may be the only governmental unit capable of coping with contemporary problems. Unconditional rebates of federal revenues to the States and obedience to a rule of law may leave the way open for expansion of federal activities in which there is reasonable chance of success without loss of federal control and without loss of legitimacy.

No individual interest group can be expected to take fullest account of the consequences of its own claims. This is what Presidents and Congresses are for, and this is what will continue to be delegated away as long as the ideology of interest-group liberalism allows. In effect this means that restoring pluralism as an effective principle of democratic politics requires destroying it as a principle of government. If this is to be accomplished, reform must begin with the replacement of interest-group liberalism with some contemporary version of the rule of law. The program of reform must include at least: debate that centers upon the actual consequences of public policies and of their forms of implementation; a legislative process that regularly treats enabling legislation rather than revision; political brokers that have to deal in substantive as well as functional issues; and adaptation of public controls to local needs through choice of appropriate level of government rather than through delegation of the choice to the most interested parties.

NOTES

[1] See especially Clinton Rossiter and James Lare (eds.), *The Essential Lippmann* (New York: Vintage, 1965), pp. 171ff.

[2] Gaetano Mosca, *The Ruling Class* (New York: McGraw-Hill, 1939), p. 70.

[3] Clinton Rossiter, *Conservatism in America* (New York: Knopf, 1955), pp. 12 and 15.

[4] Robert A. Dahl and Charles E. Lindblom, *Politics, Economics, and Welfare* (New York: Harper & Bros., 1953), Chapter 1.

[5] The distance above or below the line is not meant to convey additional information about the degree of public involvement. However, as Dahl and Lindblom's analysis suggests, that is a desirable and practicable consideration.

[6] Placement along the continuum is gross and informal. However, it is clear that no basis for placing these policies according to impact could reduce their spread. And, differences of opinion as to the placement of specific policies (should antitrust go in the middle or over on the left?) would lead to the very kind of policy analysis political scientists need to get involved in.

[7] They are so placed on Table 19-1. Interest groups are not policies strictly speaking. However, individuals and corporations belong to and support trade associations and other groups as a matter of policy; and each such group formulates relatively clear policies supported by the members. Placing "old interest groups" on Table 19-1 and to the right is meant to convey two hypotheses: (1) that the existence of the group is itself conservative, and (2) that it is highly probable that the policies formulated by such old groups will be conservative.

[8] The preceding two paragraphs were taken, with revision, from the Introductory Essay of my *Private Life and Public Order* (New York: W. W. Norton, 1967).

[9] For an excellent inquiry into this assumption and into the realities of the internal life of the interests, see: Grant McConnell, "The Spirit of Private Government," *American Political Science Review*, 52 (1963), 754–770; see also Clark Kerr, *Unions and Union Leaders of Their Own Choosing* (Santa Barbara: Fund for the Republic, 1957); and S. M. Lipset *et al.*, *Union Democracy* (New York: Anchor, 1962). See also Arthur S. Miller, *Private Governments and the Constitution* (Santa Barbara: Fund for the Republic, 1959).

[10] It is assumed that "countervailing power" usually crops up somehow. Where it does not, government ought to help create it. See John K. Galbraith, *American Capitalism* (Boston: Houghton Mifflin, 1952).

[11] Alvin H. Hansen, *The American Economy* (New York: McGraw-Hill, 1957), pp. 152ff.

[12] *Ibid.*, pp. 158–159. Keynes said ". . . the Class War will find me on the side of the educated bourgeoisie": quoted in *ibid.*, p. 158.

[13] For pioneer expressions, see Arthur F. Bentley, *The Process of Government* (Chicago: University of Chicago Press, 1908); and E. Pendleton Herring, *Group Representation Before Congress* (Baltimore: Johns Hopkins Press, 1929). More recent arguments of the same methodological sort are found in David Truman, *The Governmental Process* (New York: Knopf, 1951); and Earl Latham, *The Group Basis of Politics* (Ithaca: Cornell University Press, 1952).

[14] *Op. cit.*, p. 268.

[15] *A Grammar of American Politics* (New York: Knopf, 1950), p. 7.

[16] *Ibid.*, pp. 8–9. In order to preserve value-free science, many pluralists ("group theorists") denied public interest altogether, arguing instead that there is a "totally inclusive interest" and that it is served by letting groups interact without knowing what it is. Cf. Truman, *op. cit.*, pp. 50–51.

[17] For discussions of the extent to which group theory is a satisfactory statement of reality, see my "American Business, Public Policy, Case-Studies and Political Theory," *World Politics*, 16 (1964), pp. 677–715, and the excellent essays cited therein.

[18] For more on the expansion and justification of these practices in agriculture see my "How the Farmers Get What They Want," *Reporter*, May 21, 1964, pp. 35ff.

[19] " 'Creative Federalism' and the Great Society," *Fortune*, January, 1966, p. 122.

[20] A third major intellectual of the Kennedy Administration was Professor Richard E. Neustadt.

That he is a political scientist makes all the more interesting his stress upon the necessary independence of the Presidency rather than the desirability of presidential partnerships and countervailing power. See his *Presidential Power* (New York: Wiley, 1960).

[21] Galbraith, *op. cit.*, p. 118.

[22] Arthur Schlesinger, Jr., *Kennedy or Nixon—Does It Make Any Difference?* (New York: Macmillan, 1960), p. 43.

[23] Arthur M. Schlesinger, Jr., *A Thousand Days*, as reprinted in *Chicago Sun-Times*, January 23, 1966, Section 2, p. 3.

[24] See for example, "How the Farmers Get What They Want," *op. cit.*

[25] See Raymond Bauer *et al.*, *American Business and Public Policy* (New York: Atherton, 1963), pp. 73ff.

[26] *Op. cit.*, p. 122.

[27] Quoted in *Congressional Quarterly*, Weekly Report, April 22, 1966, p. 833.

[28] Jules Witcover and Erwin Knoll, "Politics and the Poor: Shriver's Second Thoughts," *Reporter*, December 30, 1965, p. 24.

[29] "How The Farmers Get What They Want," *op. cit.*

[30] Mario Einaudi *et al.*, *Nationalization in France and Italy* (Ithaca: Cornell University Press, 1955), pp. 100–101, emphasis added.

[31] "How The Farmers Get What They Want," *op. cit.*, p. 36.

[32] *Op. cit.*, p. 462. For a profound appreciation of the public power of private authorities in occupational licensing, see York Willbern, "Professionalization in State and Local Government: Too Little or Too Much?" *Public Administration Review*, Winter, 1954. See also Arthur S. Miller, *op. cit.*

[33] *Op. cit.*, pp. 467–468.

[34] Witcover and Knoll, *op. cit.*

[35] Walter S. Adams and Horace Gray, *Monopoly in America* (New York: Macmillan, 1955), pp. 48–50.

[36] Cf. *ibid.*, pp. 44–46, and their discussion, from a different point of view, of the "abridgement of sovereignty by grants of privilege." See also Merle Fainsod *et al.*, *Government and the American Economy* (New York: Norton, 1959), pp. 400–404. They observe the same thing happening in television and for the same reasons.

[37] See accounts in *New York Times*, August 2 and August 29, 1966, and *Time Magazine*, August 12, 1966, p. 38.

[38] Herbert Kaufman, "The New York City Health Centers," Inter-university Case Program. Wallace Sayre and Herbert Kaufman in *Governing New York City* (New York: Russell Sage, 1960), Chapter XIX, generalize on this pattern. They refer to "islands of functional power" as the formal power structure of the city. Each island enjoys considerable autonomy, each is a system of administrators and their "satellite groups," each resists interactions with other islands. The big city is possibly in an advanced stage of what in this paper is observed as an important tendency at the national level. Because of the tragic stalemate in the cities, these pronounced city patterns might serve as a better warning than my illustrations drawn from national practices. See also Herbert Kaufman, *Politics and Policies in State and Local Governments* (Englewood Cliffs: Prentice-Hall, 1963), Chapter V.

[39] Cf. Carl Friedrich, *Constitutional Government and Democracy* (Boston: Ginn and Co., 1950), pp. 291–294. See also a classic critique of occupational representation by Paul H. Douglas, "Occupational versus Proportional Representation," *American Journal of Sociology* (September, 1923); and David Truman, *op. cit.*, pp. 525–526.

[40] *Op. cit.*, p. 535.

[41] *Op. cit.*, p. 4.

[42] This rule is made more interesting for the argument here because it was given new currency in the *Schechter Poultry* and *Panama Refining* cases, both of which involved the most extreme instance of delegation of sovereignty to groups, the NRA. For a recent expression, see Judge Henry J. Friendly's *The Federal Administrative Agencies* (Cambridge: Harvard University Press, 1962), pp. 5ff.

PART SIX

THE CONGRESS

Woodrow Wilson once described the Congress as "the predominant and controlling force" in the American government. "The legislature," he concluded, "is the aggressive spirit." Writing some eighty-five years later, Samuel P. Huntington struck a different chord. Modern critics, he noted, frequently say that "Congress either does not legislate or legislates too little and too late." "Today's 'aggressive spirit,'" Huntington claimed, "is clearly the executive branch."

So disparate are Wilson's and Huntington's views that one wonders whether they were talking about the same subject. To be sure, the Congress has changed importantly since Wilson's day. Virtually all congressional scholars agree that the organizational structure of the Congress is now much more fragmented, and power within it much more dispersed. In his treatise *Congressional Government* (1885), excerpted here, Wilson observed too that "Authority [in Congress] is perplexingly subdivided and distributed, and responsibility has to be hunted down in out-of-the-way corners." Yet the unmistakable impression one gets from his account is that legislative leadership was far stronger in Wilson's day, and the role of party organs much greater, than today. In the nineteenth century as at the present time, committees ruled Congress, but in the House of Representatives the Speaker held absolute discretion over committee appointments. Individual legislators then were often unruly and freewheeling; still, party caucuses imposed more discipline than they do nowadays: "Any individual, or any minority of weak numbers or small influence, who has the temerity to neglect the decisions of the caucus is sure, if the offense be often repeated, or even once committed upon an important issue, to be read out of the party, almost without chance of reinstatement."

The real debate, however, is not *whether* the institution has become more fractionated and decentralized, but rather *what differences* such developments have made for the status and performance of the institution. According to Huntington, the dispersion of power—due to the increasingly specialized and elaborate committee system, loss of leadership control, and so forth—has weakened Congress in relation to the presidency. Abetting the trend, Huntington argues in his 1973 article, is the growing insulation of Congress as a political institution. New blood no longer flows easily into it; incumbents reign too long; committee chairmanships continue to be governed mostly by seniority; congressional leaders are older than were their predecessors; there is less lateral entry from other parts of the government, as congressional careers now typically follow a pattern of advancement within the institution itself. Additionally, Huntington finds, the strict territorial basis of congressional representation fails to reflect the increasingly national orientation of society's specialized economic and social interests.

Various facets of the issues raised in Huntington's article are explored in other essays that follow. The forces that in Huntington's opinion tend to insulate

Congress from present-day political and social realities are revealed by Nelson W. Polsby as characteristics of a broader phenomenon: "institutionalization." Polsby, in his 1970 article reprinted here, observes:

> One major consequence of this process of institutionalization has been to shift the balance in the careers and life-styles of legislators from amateur to professional, from the status of a temporary ambassador from home to that of member of the legislative group. Where Congress used to embody a popular will in some formal sense by its collective representativeness, it now does so *de facto* through the piecemeal pressures of case work for constituents, legislative committee hearings, and the appropriations process. Where representation, emphasizing the ambassadorial function, was once the characteristic, conscious activity of Congressmen and Senators, today it is deliberation, emphasizing the increasing centrality to Congressmen of their lives as members of a legislative work group and status system.

Polsby explores the implications of this change for the legislative process. He concludes by suggesting that three reforms could enhance Congress's performance: (1) a mandatory retirement system, (2) the improvement of technical knowledge available to Congress, and (3) the election of House committee chairmen at the start of each Congress.

Four years after Polsby published his article, Congress began to carry out a series of major internal reforms, including some related to Polsby's suggestions, with substantial implications for the relationship between the branches of government, as well as for the nature of Congress itself. Coming in the wake of the Vietnam War and the Watergate scandal, these developments marked a period of congressional resurgence and institutional change. Despite its reaffirmation of coequal status with the presidency since the mid-1970s, however, Congress's capacity to govern—that is, its ability to provide political leadership and policy integration—has remained problematical. No one has scrutinized this question more lucidly than James L. Sundquist in his study *The Decline and Resurgence of Congress* (1981). An important chapter of that book is reprinted here.

One feature of Congress that is central to almost all its functions is the standing committee system. Committees play a much more prominent role in the United States Congress than in most Western parliaments. Critics often stress this feature when lamenting the disaggregation of power in the American legislature. What the critics sometimes overlook, however, is that the roles of congressional committees differ widely. Some have much more power than others, and some, in fact, are such a potent force in the legislative process that, at least with respect to certain issues, they seem to steer the rest of the legislative body much as a group of party leaders might.

The definitive work on congressional committees remains Richard F. Fenno, Jr.'s *Congressmen in Committees*, published in 1973. Although Fenno's research predates the substantial changes in committee structure that took place in the ensuing years, most of his insights are still relevant. We have excerpted the key sections of three chapters providing a concise summary of his principal findings.

Briefly, Fenno studied six important committees in the House of Representatives: Appropriations, Ways and Means, Interior, Post Office, Education and Labor, and Foreign Affairs. He discovered that they behaved differently according to the goals pursued by their members, the external political constraints placed upon them by other interested parties, and the "decision rules" adopted to accommodate these pressures and to conduct committee business. In some cases, committees developed a high degree of consensus on goals and the rules of decision making; in others, much less. For some (for example, Education and Labor), external clientele groups were an especially salient constraint, whereas in others (for example, Appropriations and Ways and Means), the dominant imperative was to wield influence *inside* Congress—that is, within the full House itself. The Appropriations Committee, for instance, functioned in such a fashion as to ensure that the parent chamber would acquiesce to its recommendations almost routinely.

Finally, of particular interest to David R. Mayhew, in his 1974 article on congressional elections, is the fact that the proportion of "safe" seats in the House has been going up over the years. Mayhew discusses five possible explanations for the phenomenon: (1) that congressmen now value reelection more than formerly; (2) that incumbents are in a better position to "advertise" themselves to voters (via direct mailings, etc.); (3) that incumbents get credit for federal expenditures in their districts; (4) that improved voter survey methods have enabled incumbents to better adjust their policy stances to those of their constituents; and (5) that as voters respond less to party labels, the recognition value of incumbency provides an important cue. To some, of course, the growing advantage of incumbency in the House raises fundamental questions about the representativeness—indeed, about the democratic character—of the legislative branch. (Joseph Schumpeter defined modern democracy as "that institutional arrangement for arriving at political decisions in which individuals [i.e., representatives] acquire power to decide by means of a competitive struggle for the people's vote." With few House seats subject to genuinely "competitive struggles," one might wonder what is to ensure that our elected representatives remain accountable to us.) Yet, in some ways, the lengthening tenure of members of the House has strengthened Congress. Indeed, it could be argued that by making members more secure in office, and hence enhancing their autonomy, the legislature safeguards its independence from the executive. In Mayhew's words, "A Congress less affected by electoral tides is, on balance, one less susceptible to presidential wiles."

20

WOODROW WILSON

CONGRESSIONAL GOVERNMENT

> Political philosophy must analyze political history; it must distinguish
> what is due to the excellence of the people, and what to the excellence
> of the laws; it must carefully calculate the exact effect of each part of
> the constitution, though thus it may destroy many an idol of the
> multitude, and detect the secret of utility where but few imagined it
> to lie.
>
> BAGEHOT

Congress always makes what haste it can to legislate. It is the prime object of
its rules to expedite law-making. Its customs are fruits of its characteristic
diligence in enactment. Be the matters small or great, frivolous or grave, which
busy it, its aim is to have laws always a-making. Its temper is strenuously
legislative. That it cannot regulate all the questions to which its attention is
weekly invited is its misfortune, not its fault; is due to the human limitation of
its faculties, not to any narrow circumscription of its desires. If its committee
machinery is inadequate to the task of bringing to action more than one out of
every hundred of the bills introduced, it is not because the quick clearance of the
docket is not the motive of its organic life. If legislation, therfore, were the only
or the chief object for which it should live, it would not be possible to withhold
admiration from those clever hurrying rules and those inexorable customs which
seek to facilitate it. Nothing but a doubt as to whether or not Congress should
confine itself to law-making can challenge with a question the utility of its
organization as a facile statute-devising machine.

The political philosopher of these days of self-government has, however,
something more than a doubt with which to gainsay the usefulness of a sovereign
representative body which confines itself to legislation to the exclusion of all
other functions. Buckle declared, indeed, that the chief use and value of
legislation nowadays lay in its opportunity and power to remedy the mistakes of
the legislation of the past; that it was beneficent only when it carried healing in
its wings; that repeal was more blessed than enactment. And it is certainly true
that the greater part of the labor of legislation consists in carrying the loads
recklessly or bravely shouldered in times gone by, when the animal which is now
a bull was only a calf, and in completing, if they may be completed, the tasks

once undertaken in the shape of unambitious schemes which at the outset looked innocent enough. Having got his foot into it, the legislator finds it difficult, if not impossible, to get it out again. . . .

Legislation unquestionably generates legislation. Every statute may be said to have a long lineage of statutes behind it; and whether that lineage be honorable or of ill repute is as much a question as to each individual statute as it can be with regard to the ancestry of each individual legislator. Every statute in its turn has a numerous progeny, and only time and opportunity can decide whether its offspring will bring it honor or shame. Once begin the dance of legislation, and you must struggle through its mazes as best you can to its breathless end,—if any end there be.

It is not surprising, therefore, that the enacting, revising, tinkering, repealing of laws should engross the attention and engage the entire energy of such a body as Congress. It is, however, easy to see how it might be better employed; or, at least, how it might add others to this overshadowing function, to the infinite advantage of the government. Quite as important as legislation is vigilant oversight of administration; and even more important than legislation is the instruction and guidance in political affairs which the people might receive from a body which kept all national concerns suffused in a broad daylight of discussion. There is no similar legislature in existence which is so shut up to the one business of law-making as is our Congress. As I have said, it in a way superintends administration by the exercise of semi-judicial powers of investigation, whose limitations and insufficiency are manifest. But other national legislatures command administration and verify their name of "parliaments" by talking official acts into notoriety. Our extra-constitutional party conventions, short-lived and poor in power as they are, constitute our only machinery for that sort of control of the executive which consists in the award of personal rewards and punishments. This is the cardinal fact which differentiates Congress from the Chamber of Deputies and from Parliament, and which puts it beyond the reach of those eminently useful functions whose exercise would so raise it in usefulness and in dignity.

An effective representative body, gifted with the power to rule, ought, it would seem, not only to speak the will of the nation, which Congress does, but also to lead it to its conclusions, to utter the voice of its opinions, and to serve as its eyes in superintending all matters of government,—which Congress does not do. The discussions which take place in Congress are aimed at random. They now and again strike rather sharply the tender spots in this, that, or the other measure; but, as I have said, no two measures consciously join in purpose or agree in character, and so debate must wander as widely as the subjects of debate. Since there is little coherency about the legislation agreed upon, there can be little coherency about the debates. There is no one policy to be attacked or defended, but only a score or two of separate bills. To attend to such discussions is uninteresting; to be instructed by them is impossible. There is some scandal and discomfort, but infinite advantage, in having every affair of administration subjected to the test of constant examination on the part of the assembly which represents the nation. The chief use of such inquisition is, not the direction of those affairs in a way with which the country will be satisfied (though that itself is of course all-important), but the enlightenment of the people, which is always its sure consequence. Very few men are unequal to a danger which they see and understand; all men quail before a threatening which is dark and unintelligible, and suspect what is done behind a screen. If the people could have, through Congress, daily knowledge of all the more important transactions of the governmental offices, an insight into all that now seems withheld and private, their confidence in the executive, now so often shaken, would, I think, be very soon established. Because dishonesty *can* lurk under the privacies now vouchsafed our administrative agents, much that is upright and pure suffers unjust suspicion. Discoveries of guilt in a bureau cloud with doubts the trustworthiness of a department. As nothing is open enough for the quick and easy detection of peculation or fraud, so nothing is open enough for the due vindication and acknowledgment of honesty. The isolation and privacy which shield the one from discovery cheat the other of reward.

Inquisitiveness is never so forward, enterprising, and irrepressible as in a popular assembly which is given leave to ask questions and is afforded ready and abundant means of getting its questions answered. No cross-examination is more searching than that to which a minister of the Crown is subjected by the all-curious Commons. "Sir Robert Peel once asked to have a number of questions carefully written down which they asked him one day in succession in the House of Commons. They seemed a list of everything that could occur in the British empire or to the brain of a member of parliament." If one considered only the wear and tear upon ministers of state, which the plague of constant interrogation must inflict, he could wish that their lives, if useful, might be spared this blight of unending explanation; but no one can overestimate the immense advantage of a facility so unlimited for knowing all that is going on in the places where authority lives. The conscience of every member of the representative body is at the service of the nation. All that he feels bound to know he can find out; and what he finds out goes to the ears of the country. The question is his, the answer the nation's. And the inquisitiveness of such bodies as Congress is the best conceivable source of information. Congress is the only body which has the proper motive for inquiry, and it is the only body which has the power to act effectively upon the knowledge which its inquiries secure. The Press is merely curious or merely partisan. The people are scattered and unorganized. But Congress is, as it were, the corporate people, the mouthpiece of its will. It is a sovereign delegation which could ask questions with dignity, because with authority and with power to act.

Congress is fast becoming the governing body of the nation, and yet the only power which it possesses in perfection is the power which is but a part of government, the power of legislation. Legislation is but the oil of government. It is that which lubricates its channels and speeds its wheels; that which lessens the friction and so eases the movement. Or perhaps I shall be admitted to have hit upon a closer and apter analogy if I say that legislation is like a foreman set over the forces of government. It issues the orders which others obey. It directs, it admonishes, but it does not do the actual heavy work of governing. A good foreman does, it is true, himself take a hand in the work which he guides; and so I suppose our legislation must be likened to a poor foreman, because it stands altogether apart from that work which it is set to see well done. Members of Congress ought not to be censured too severely, however, when they fail to check evil courses on the part of the executive. They have been denied the means of doing so promptly and with effect. Whatever intention may have controlled the compromises of constitution-making in 1787, their result was to give us, not government by discussion, which is the only tolerable sort of government for a people which tries to do its own governing, but only *legislation* by discussion, which is no more than a small part of government by discussion. What is quite as indispensable as the debate of problems of legislation is the debate of all matters of administration. It is even more important to know how the house is being built than to know how the plans of the architect were conceived and how his specifications were calculated. It is better to have skillful work—stout walls, reliable arches, unbending rafters, and windows sure to "expel the winter's flaw"—than a drawing on paper which is the admiration of all the practical artists in the country. The discipline of an army depends quite as much upon the temper of the troops as upon the orders of the day.

It is the proper duty of a representative body to look diligently into every affair of government and to talk much about what it sees. It is meant to be the eyes and the voice, and to embody the wisdom and will of its constituents. Unless Congress have and use every means of acquainting itself with the acts and the disposition of the administrative agents of the government, the country must be helpless to learn how it is being served; and unless Congress both scrutinize these things and sift them by every form of discussion, the country must remain in embarrassing, crippling ignorance of the very affairs which it is most important that it should understand and direct. The informing function of Congress should be preferred even to its legislative function. The argument is not only that discussed and interrogated administration is the only pure and efficient administration, but, more than that, that the only really self-governing people is that people which discusses and interrogates its administration. The talk on the part of Congress which we sometimes justly condemn is the profitless squabble of words over frivolous bills or selfish party issues. It would be hard to conceive of there being too much talk about the practical concerns and processes of government. Such talk it is which, when earnestly and purposefully conducted, clears the public mind and shapes the demands of public opinion.

Congress could not be too diligent about such talking; whereas it may easily be too diligent in legislation. It often overdoes that business. It already sends to its Committees bills too many by the thousand to be given even a hasty thought; but its immense committee facilities and the absence of all other duties but that of legislation make it omnivorous in its appetite for new subjects for consideration. It is greedy to have a taste of every possible dish that may be put upon its table, as an "extra" to the constitutional bill of fare. This disposition on its part is the more notable because there is certainly less need for it to hurry and overwork itself at law-making than exists in the case of most other great national legislatures. It is not state and national legislature combined, as are the

Commons of England and the Chambers of France. Like the Reichstag of our cousin Germans, it is restricted to subjects of imperial scope. Its thoughts are meant to be kept for national interests. Its time is spared the waste of attention to local affairs. It is even forbidden the vast domain of the laws of property, of commercial dealing, and of ordinary crime. And even in the matter of caring for national interests the way has from the first been made plain and easy for it. There are no clogging feudal institutions to embarrass it. There is no long-continued practice of legal or of royal tyranny for it to cure,—no clearing away of old débris of any sort to delay it in its exercise of a common-sense dominion over a thoroughly modern and progressive nation. It is easy to believe that its legislative purposes might be most fortunately clarified and simplified, were it to square them by a conscientious attention to the paramount and controlling duty of understanding, discussing, and directing administration.

If the people's authorized representatives do not take upon themselves this duty, and by identifying themselves with the actual work of government stand between it and irresponsible, half-informed criticism, to what harassments is the executive not exposed? Led and checked by Congress, the prurient and fearless, because anonymous, animadversions of the Press, now so often premature and inconsiderate, might be disciplined into serviceable capacity to interpret and judge. Its energy and sagacity might be tempered by discretion, and strengthened by knowledge. One of our chief constitutional difficulties is that, in opportunities for informing and guiding public opinion, the freedom of the Press is greater than the freedom of Congress. It is as if newspapers, instead of the board of directors, were the sources of information for the stockholders of a corporation. We look into correspondents' letters instead of into the Congressional Record to find out what is a-doing and a-planning in the departments. Congress is altogether excluded from the arrangement by which the Press declares what the executive is, and conventions of the national parties decide what the executive shall be. Editors are self-constituted our guides, and caucus delegates our government directors. . . .

The plain tendency is towards a centralization of all the greater powers of government in the hands of the federal authorities, and towards the practical confirmation of those prerogatives of supreme overlordship which Congress has been gradually arrogating to itself. The central government is constantly becoming stronger and more active, and Congress is establishing itself as the one sovereign authority in that government. In constitutional theory and in the broader features of past practice, ours has been what Mr. Bagehot has called a "composite" government. Besides state and federal authorities to dispute as to sovereignty, there have been within the federal system itself rival and irreconcilable powers. But gradually the strong are overcoming the weak. If the signs of the times are to be credited, we are fast approaching an adjustment of sovereignty quite as "simple" as need be. Congress is not only to retain the authority it already possesses, but is to be brought again and again face to face with still greater demands upon its energy, its wisdom, and its conscience, is to have ever-widening duties and responsibilities thrust upon it without being granted a moment's opportunity to look back from the plough to which it has set its hands.

The sphere and influence of national administration and national legislation are widening rapidly. Our populations are growing at such a rate that one's reckoning staggers at counting the possible millions that may have a home and a work on this continent ere fifty more years shall have filled their short span. The East will not always be the centre of national life. The South is fast accumulating wealth, and will faster recover influence. The West has already achieved a greatness which no man can gainsay, and has in store a power of future growth which no man can estimate. Whether these sections are to be harmonious or dissentient depends almost entirely upon the methods and policy of the federal government. If that government be not careful to keep within its own proper sphere and prudent to square its policy by rules of national welfare, sectional lines must and will be known; citizens of one part of the country may look with jealousy and even with hatred upon their fellow-citizens of another part; and faction must tear and dissension distract a country which Providence would bless, but which man may curse. The government of a country so vast and various must be strong, prompt, wieldy, and efficient. Its strength must consist in the certainty and uniformity of its purposes, in its accord with national sentiment, in its unhesitating action, and in its honest aims. It must be steadied and approved by open administration diligently obedient to the more permanent judgments of public opinion; and its only active agency, its representative chambers, must be equipped with something besides abundant powers of legislation.

As at present constituted, the federal government lacks strength because its powers are divided, lacks promptness because its authorities are multiplied, lacks wieldiness because its processes are roundabout, lacks efficiency because its responsibility is indistinct and its action without competent direction. It is a government in which every officer may talk about every other officer's duty without having to render strict account for not doing his own, and in which the masters are held in check and offered contradiction by the servants. Mr. Lowell has called it "government by declamation." Talk is not sobered by any necessity imposed upon those who utter it to suit their actions to their words. There is no day of reckoning for words spoken. The speakers of a congressional majority may, without risk of incurring ridicule or discredit, condemn what their own Committees are doing; and the spokesmen of a minority may urge what contrary courses they please with a well-grounded assurance that what they say will be forgotten before they can be called upon to put it into practice. Nobody stands sponsor for the policy of the government. A dozen men originate it; a dozen compromises twist and alter it; a dozen offices whose names are scarcely known outside of Washington put it into execution.

This is the defect to which, it will be observed, I am constantly recurring; to which I recur again and again because every examination of the system, at whatsoever point begun, leads inevitably to it as to a central secret. It is the defect which interprets all the rest, because it is their common product. It is exemplified in the extraordinary fact that the utterances of the Press have greater weight and are accorded greater credit, though the Press speaks entirely without authority, than the utterances of Congress, though Congress possesses all authority. The gossip of the street is listened to rather than the words of the law-makers. The editor directs public opinion, the congressman obeys it. When a presidential election is at hand, indeed, the words of the political orator gain temporary heed. He is recognized as an authority in the arena, as a professional critic competent to discuss the good and bad points, and to forecast the fortunes of the contestants. There is something definite in hand, and he is known to have studied all its bearings. He is one of the managers, or is thought to be well acquainted with the management. He speaks "from the card." But let him talk, not about candidates, but about measures or about the policy of the government, and his observations sink at once to the level of a mere individual expression of opinion, to which his political occupations seem to add very little weight. It is universally recognized that he speaks without authority, about things which his vote may help to settle, but about which several hundred other men have votes quite as influential as his own. Legislation is not a thing to be known beforehand. It depends upon the conclusions of sundry Standing Committees. It is an aggregate, not a simple, production. It is impossible to tell how many persons' opinions and influences have entered into its composition. It is even impracticable to determine from this year's law-making what next year's will be like.

Speaking, therefore, without authority, the political orator speaks to little purpose when he speaks about legislation. The papers do not report him carefully; and their editorials seldom take any color from his arguments. The Press, being anonymous and representing a large force of inquisitive newshunters, is much more powerful than he chiefly because it *is* impersonal and seems to represent a wider and more thorough range of information. At the worst, it can easily compete with any ordinary individual. Its individual opinion is quite sure to be esteemed as worthy of attention as any other individual opinion. And, besides, it is almost everywhere strong enough to deny currency to the speeches of individuals whom it does not care to report. It goes to its audience; the orator must depend upon his audience coming to him. It can be heard at every fireside; the orator can be heard only on the platform or the hustings. There is no imperative demand on the part of the reading public in this country that the newspapers should report political speeches in full. On the contrary, most readers would be disgusted at finding their favorite columns so filled up. By giving even a notice of more than an item's length to such a speech, an editor runs the risk of being denounced as dull. And I believe that the position of the American Press is in this regard quite singular. . . . Since our politicians lack the credit of authority and responsibility, they must give place, except at election-time, to the Press, which is everywhere, generally well-informed, and always talking. It is necessarily "government by declamation" and editorial-writing.

It is probably also this lack of leadership which gives to our national parties their curious, conglomerate character. It would seem to be scarcely an exaggeration to say that they are homogeneous only in name. Neither of the two principal parties is of one mind with itself. Each tolerates all sorts of difference of creed and variety of aim within its own ranks. Each pretends to the same purposes and permits among its partisans the same contradictions to those purposes. They are grouped around no legislative leaders whose capacity has been tested and to whose opinions they loyally adhere. They are like armies without officers, engaged upon a campaign which has no great cause at its back. Their names and traditions, not their hopes and policy, keep them together.

It is to this fact, as well as to short terms which allow little time for differences to come to a head, that the easy agreement of congressional majorities should be attributed. In other like assemblies the harmony of majorities is constantly liable to disturbance. Ministers lose their following and find their friends falling away in the midst of a session. But not so in Congress. There, although the majority is frequently simply conglomerate, made up of factions not a few, and bearing in its elements every seed of discord, the harmony of party voting seldom, if ever, suffers an interruption. So far as outsiders can see, legislation generally flows placidly on, and the majority easily has its own way, acting with a sort of matter-of-course unanimity, with no suspicion of individual freedom of action. Whatever revolts may be threatened or accomplished in the ranks of the party outside the House at the polls, its power is never broken inside the House. This is doubtless due in part to the fact that there is no freedom of debate in the House; but there can be no question that it is principally due to the fact that debate is without aim, just because legislation is without consistency. Legislation is conglomerate. The absence of any concert of action amongst the Committees leaves legislation with scarcely any trace of determinate party courses. No two schemes pull together. If there is a coincidence of principle between several bills of the same session, it is generally accidental; and the confusion of policy which prevents intelligent cooperation also, of course, prevents intelligent differences and divisions. There is never a transfer of power from one party to the other during a session, because such a transfer would mean almost nothing. The majority remains of one mind so long as a Congress lives, because its mind is very vaguely ascertained, and its power of planning a split consequently very limited. It has no common mind, and if it had, has not the machinery for changing it. It is led by a score or two of Committees whose composition must remain the same to the end; and who are too numerous, as well as too disconnected, to fight against. It stays on one side because it hardly knows where the boundaries of that side are or how to cross them.

Moreover, there is a certain well-known piece of congressional machinery long ago invented and applied for the special purpose of keeping both majority and minority compact. The legislative caucus has almost as important a part in our system as have the Standing Committees, and deserves as close study as they. Its functions are much more easily understood in all their bearings than those of the Committees, however, because they are much simpler. The caucus is meant as an antidote to the Committees. It is designed to supply the cohesive principle which the multiplicity and mutual independence of the Committees so power-fully tend to destroy. Having no Prime Minister to confer with about the policy of the government, as they see members of parliament doing, our congressmen confer with each other in caucus. Rather than imprudently expose to the world the differences of opinion threatened or developed among its members, each party hastens to remove disrupting debate from the floor of Congress, where the speakers might too hastily commit themselves to insubordination, to quiet conferences behind closed doors, where frightened scruples may be reassured and every disagreement healed with a salve of compromise or subdued with the whip of political expediency. The caucus is the drilling-ground of the party. There its discipline is renewed and strengthened, its uniformity of step and gesture regained. The voting and speaking in the House are generally merely the movements of a sort of dress parade, for which the exercises of the caucus are designed to prepare. It is easy to see how difficult it would be for the party to keep its head amidst the confused cross-movements of the Committees without thus now and again pulling itself together in caucus, where it can ask itself its own mind and pledge itself anew to eternal agreement.

The credit of inventing this device is probably due to the Democrats. They appear to have used it so early as the second session of the eighth Congress. Speaking of that session, a reliable authority says: "During this session of Congress there was far less of free and independent discussion on the measures proposed by the friends of the administration than had been previously practiced in both branches of the national legislature. It appeared that on the most important subjects, the course adopted by the majority was the effect of caucus arrangement, or, in other words, had been previously agreed upon at meetings of the Democratic members held in private. Thus the legislation of Congress was constantly swayed by a party following feelings and pledges rather than according to sound reason or personal conviction." The censure implied in this last sentence may have seemed righteous at the time when such caucus pledges were in disfavor as new-fangled shackles, but it would hardly be accepted as just by the intensely practical politicians of to-day. They would probably prefer to put it thus: That the silvern speech spent in caucus secures the golden silence maintained on the floor of Congress, making each party rich in concord and happy in cooperation.

The fact that makes this defense of the caucus not altogether conclusive is that it is shielded from all responsibility by its sneaking privacy. It has great power without any balancing weight of accountability. Probably its debates would constitute interesting and instructive reading for the public, were they published; but they never get out except in rumors often rehearsed and as often amended. They are, one may take it for granted, much more candid and go much nearer the political heart of the questions discussed than anything that is ever said openly in Congress to the reporters' gallery. They approach matters without masks and handle them without gloves. It might hurt, but it would enlighten us to hear them. As it is, however, there is unhappily no ground for denying their power to override sound reason and personal conviction. The caucus cannot always silence or subdue a large and influential minority of dissentients, but its whip seldom fails to reduce individual malcontents and mutineers into submission. There is no place in congressional jousts for the free lance. The man who disobeys his party caucus is understood to disavow his party allegiance altogether, and to assume that dangerous neutrality which is so apt to degenerate into mere caprice, and which is almost sure to destroy his influence by bringing him under the suspicion of being unreliable,—a suspicion always conclusively damning in practical life. Any individual, or any minority of weak numbers or small influence, who has the temerity to neglect the decisions of the caucus is sure, if the offense be often repeated, or even once committed upon an important issue, to be read out of the party, almost without chance of reinstatement. And every one knows that nothing can be accomplished in politics by mere disagreement. The only privilege such recalcitrants gain is the privilege of disagreement; they are forever shut out from the privilege of confidential cooperation. They have chosen the helplessness of a faction.

It must be admitted, however, that, unfortunate as the necessity is for the existence of such powers as those of the caucus, that necessity actually exists and cannot be neglected. Against the fatal action of so many elements of disintegration it would seem to be imperatively needful that some energetic element of cohesion should be provided. It is doubtful whether in any other nation, with a shorter inheritance of political instinct, parties could long successfully resist the centrifugal forces of the committee system with only the varying attraction of the caucus to detain them. The wonder is that, despite the forcible and unnatural divorcement of legislation and administration and the consequent distraction of legislation from all attention to anything like an intelligent planning and superintendence of policy, we are not cursed with as many factions as now almost hopelessly confuse French politics. That we have had, and continue to have, only two national parties of national importance or real power is fortunate rather than natural. Their names stand for a fact, but scarcely for a reason.

An intelligent observer of our politics has declared that there is in the United States "a class, including thousands and tens of thousands of the best men in the country, who think it possible to enjoy the fruits of good government without working for them." Every one who has seen beyond the outside of our American life must recognize the truth of this; to explain it is to state the sum of all the most valid criticisms of congressional government. Public opinion has no easy vehicle for its judgments, no quick channels for its action. Nothing about the system is direct and simple. Authority is perplexingly subdivided and distributed, and responsibility has to be hunted down in out-of-the-way corners. So that the sum of the whole matter is that the means of working for the fruits of good government are not readily to be found. The average citizen may be excused for esteeming government at best but a haphazard affair, upon which his vote and all of his influence can have but little effect. How is his choice of a representative in Congress to affect the policy of the country as regards the questions in which he is most interested, if the man for whom he votes has no chance of getting on the Standing Committee which has virtual charge of those questions? How is it to make any difference who is chosen President? Has the President any very great authority in matters of vital policy? It seems almost a thing of despair to get any assurance that any vote he may cast will even in an infinitesimal degree affect the essential courses of administration. There are so many cooks mixing their ingredients in the national broth that it seems hopeless, this thing of changing one cook at a time.

The charm of our constitutional ideal has now been long enough wound up to enable sober men who do not believe in political witchcraft to judge what it has accomplished, and is likely still to accomplish, without further winding. The Constitution is not honored by blind worship. The more open-eyed we become, as a nation, to its defects, and the prompter we grow in applying with the unhesitating courage of conviction all thoroughly-tested or well-considered expedients necessary to make self-government among us a straightforward thing of simple method, single, unstinted power, and clear responsibility, the nearer will we approach to the sound sense and practical genius of the great and honorable statesmen of 1787. And the first step towards emancipation from the timidity and false pride which have led us to seek to thrive despite the defects of our national system rather than seem to deny its perfection is a fearless criticism of that system. When we shall have examined all its parts without sentiment, and gauged all its functions by the standards of practical common sense, we shall have established anew our right to the claim of political sagacity; and it will remain only to act intelligently upon what our opened eyes have seen in order to prove again the justice of our claim to political genius.

21

SAMUEL P. HUNTINGTON

CONGRESSIONAL RESPONSES TO THE TWENTIETH CENTURY

Congress is a perennial source of anguish to both its friends and its foes. The critics point to its legislative failure. The function of a legislature, they argue, is to legislate and Congress either does not legislate or legislates too little and too late. The intensity of their criticism varies inversely with the degree and dispatch with which Congress approves the President's legislative proposals. When in 1963 the Eighty-eighth Congress seemed to stymie the Kennedy legislative program, criticism rapidly mounted. "What kind of legislative body is it," asked Walter Lippmann, neatly summing up the prevailing exasperation, "that will not or cannot legislate?" When in 1964 the same Eighty-eighth Congress passed the civil rights, tax, and other bills, criticism of Congress correspondingly subsided. Reacting differently to this familiar pattern, the friends of Congress lamented its acquiescence to presidential dictate. Since 1933, they said, the authority of the executive branch—President, administration, and bureaucracy—has waxed, while that of Congress has waned. They warned of the constitutional perils stemming from the permanent subordination of one branch of government to another. In foreign and military policy, as well as domestic affairs, Congress is damned when it acquiesces in presidential leadership (Tonkin Gulf Resolution, 1964) and also when it attempts to seize the initiative (Mansfield Resolution, 1971). At the same time that it is an obstructive ogre to its enemies, Congress is also the declining despair of its friends. Can both images be true? In large part, they are. The dilemma of Congress, indeed, can be measured by the extent to which congressional assertion coincides with congressional obstruction.

This paradox has been at the root of the "problem" of Congress since the early days of the New Deal. Vis-à-vis the executive, Congress is an autonomous, legislative body. But apparently Congress can defend its autonomy only by refusing to legislate, and it can legislate only by surrendering its autonomy. In the past, there has been a familiar pattern: Congress balks, criticism rises, the clamoring voices of reformers fill the air with demands for the "modernization" of the "antiquated procedures" of an "eighteenth century" Congress so it can deal with "twentieth century realities." The demands for reform serve as counters in the legislative game to get the President's measures through Congress.

Independence thus provokes criticism; acquiescence brings approbation. If Congress legislates, it subordinates itself to the President; if it refuses to legislate, it alienates itself from public opinion. Congress can assert its power or it can pass laws; but it cannot do both.

LEGISLATIVE POWER AND INSTITUTIONAL CRISIS

The roots of this legislative dilemma lie in the changes in American society during the twentieth century. The twentieth century has seen: rapid urbanization and the beginnings of a postindustrial, technological society; the nationalization of social and economic problems and the concomitant growth of national organizations to deal with these problems; the increasing bureaucratization of social, economic, and governmental organizations; and the sustained high-level international involvement of the United States in world politics. These developments have generated new forces in American politics and initiated major changes in the distribution of power in American society. In particular, the twentieth century has witnessed the tremendous expansion of the responsibilities of the national government and the size of the national bureaucracy. In 1901, the national government had 351,798 employees or less than 1½ percent of the national labor force. In 1971 it had 5,637,000 employees, constituting almost 7 percent of the labor force. The expansion of the national government has been paralleled by the emergence of other large, national, bureaucratic organizations: manufacturing corporations, banks, insurance companies, labor unions, trade associations, farm organizations, newspaper chains, radio-TV networks. Each organization may have relatively specialized and concrete interests, but typically it functions on a national basis. Its headquarters are in New York or Washington; its operations are scattered across a dozen or more states. The emergence of these organizations truly constitutes, in Kenneth Boulding's expressive phrase, an "organizational revolution." The existence of this private "Establishment," more than anything else, distinguishes twentieth-century America from nineteenth-century America. The leaders of these organizations are the notables of American society: they are the prime wielders of social and economic power.

Adaptation Crises

These momentous social changes have confronted Congress with an institutional "adaptation crisis." Such a crisis occurs when changes in the environment of a governmental institution force the institution either to alter its functions, affiliation, and modes of behavior, or to face decline, decay, and isolation. Crises usually occur when an institution loses its previous sources of support or fails to adapt itself to the rise of new social forces. Such a crisis, for instance, affected the Presidency in the second and third decades of the nineteenth century. Under the leadership of Henry Clay the focal center of power in the national government was in the House of Representatives; the congressional caucus dictated presidential nominations; popular interest in and support for the Presidency were minimal. The "Executive," Justice Story remarked in 1818, "has no longer a commanding influence. The House of Representatives has absorbed all the popular feelings and all the effective power of the country." The Presidency was on the verge of becoming a weak, secondary instrumental organ of government. It was rescued from this fate by the Jacksonian movement, which democratized the Presidency, broadened its basis of popular support, and restored it as the center of vitality and leadership in the national government. The House of Commons was faced with a somewhat similar crisis during the agitation preceding the first Reform Bill of 1832. New social groups were developing in England which were demanding admission to the political arena and the opportunity to share in political leadership. Broadening the constituency of the House of Commons and reforming the system of election enabled the House to revitalize itself and to continue as the principal locus of power in the British government.

In both these cases a governmental institution got a new lease on life, new vigor, new power, by embodying within itself dynamic, new social forces. When an institution fails to make such an alignment, it must either restrict its own authority or submit to limitations upon its authority imposed from outside. In 1910, when the House of Lords refused to approve Lloyd George's budget, it was first compelled by governmental pressure, popular opinion, and the threat of the creation of new peers to acquiesce in the budget and then through a similar process to acquiesce in the curtailment of its own power to obstruct legislation approved by the Commons. In this case the effort to block legislation approved by the dominant forces in the political community resulted in a permanent diminution of the authority of the offending institution. A somewhat similar crisis developed with respect to the Supreme Court in the 1930s. Here again a less popular body attempted to veto the actions of more popular bodies. In three years the Court invalidated twelve acts of Congress. Inevitably this precipitated vigorous criticism and demands for reform, culminating in Roosevelt's court reorganization proposal in February of 1937. The alternatives confronting the Court were relatively clear-cut: it could "reform" or be "reformed." In "the switch in time that saved nine," it chose the former course, signaling its change by approving the National Labor Relations Act in April 1937 and the Social Security Act in May. With this switch, support for the reorganization of the Court drained away. The result was, in the words of Justice Jackson, "a failure of the reform forces and a victory of the reform."

Congress's Response

Each of these four institutional crises arose from the failure of a governmental institution to adjust to social change and the rise of new viewpoints, new needs, and new political forces. Congress's legislative dilemma and loss of power stem from the nature of its overall institutional response to the changes in American society. This response involves three major aspects of Congress as an institution: its affiliations, its structure, and its functions. During the twentieth century Congress gradually insulated itself from the new political forces which social change had generated and which were, in turn, generating more change. Hence the leadership of Congress lacked the incentive to take the legislative initiative in handling emerging national problems. Within Congress power became dispersed among many officials, committees, and subcommittees. Hence the central leadership of Congress lacked the ability to establish national legislative priorities. As a result, the legislative function of Congress declined in importance, while the growth of the federal bureaucracy made the administrative overseeing function of Congress more important. These three tendencies—toward insulation, dispersion, and oversight—have dominated the evolution of Congress during the twentieth century.

AFFILIATIONS: INSULATION FROM POWER

Congressional Evolution

Perhaps the single most important trend in congressional evolution for the bulk of this century was the growing insulation of Congress from other social groups and political institutions. In 1900 no gap existed between congressmen and the other leaders of American society and politics. Half a century later the changes in American society, on the one hand, and the institutional evolution of Congress, on the other, had produced a marked gap between congressional leaders and the bureaucratically oriented leadership of the executive branch and of the establishment. The growth of this gap can be seen in seven aspects of congressional evolution.

(1) *Increasing Tenure of Office*—In the nineteenth century few congressmen stayed in Congress very long. During the twentieth century the average tenure of congressmen has inexorably lengthened. In 1900 only 9 percent of the members of the House of Representatives had served five terms or more and less than 1 percent had served ten terms or more. In 1957, 45 percent of the House had served five terms or more and 14 percent ten terms or more. In 1897, for each representative who had served ten terms or more in the House, there were 34 representatives who had served two terms or less. In 1971 the ratio was down almost to equality, with 1.2 members who had served two terms or less for each ten-termer.[1] In the middle of the nineteenth century, only about half the representatives in any one Congress had served in a previous Congress, and only about one-third of the senators had been elected to the Senate more than once. By the second half of the twentieth century, close to 90 percent of the House were veterans, and almost two-thirds of the senators were beyond their first term. The biennial infusion of new blood had reached an all-time low.

(2) *The Increasingly Important Role of Seniority*—Increasing tenure of congressmen is closely linked to increasingly rigid adherence to the practices of seniority. The longer men stay in Congress, the more likely they are to see virtue in seniority. Conversely, the more important seniority is, the greater is the constituent appeal of men who have been long in office. The rigid system of seniority in *both* houses of Congress is a product of the twentieth century.

In the nineteenth century seniority was far more significant in the Senate than in the House. Since the middle of that century apparently only in five

TABLE 21-1. VETERAN CONGRESSMEN IN CONGRESS

Congress	Date	Representatives Elected to House More than Once	Senators Elected to Senate More than Once
42nd	1871	53%	32%
50th	1887	63	45
64th	1915	74	47
74th	1935	77	54
87th	1961	87	66
92nd	1971	88	65

Source: Figures for representatives for 1871–1915 are from Robert Luce, Legislative Assemblies (Boston: Houghton Mifflin Company, 1924), p. 365. Other figures were calculated independently. I am indebted to Emily Lieberman for assistance in updating these and other statistics in this essay.

instances—the last in 1925—has the chairmanship of a Senate committee been denied to the most senior member of the committee. In the House, on the other hand, the Speaker early received the power to appoint committees and to designate their chairmen. During the nineteenth century Speakers made much of this power. Committee appointment and the selection of chairmen were involved political processes, in which the Speaker carefully balanced factors of seniority, geography, expertise, and policy viewpoint in making his choices. Not infrequently prolonged bargaining would result as the Speaker traded committee positions for legislative commitments. Commenting on James G. Blaine's efforts at committee construction in the early 1870s, one member of his family wrote that Blaine "left for New York on Wednesday. He had cotton and wool manufacturers to meet in Boston, and, over and above all, pressure to resist or permit. As fast as he gets his committees arranged, just so fast some after-consideration comes up which overtopples the whole list like a row of bricks."[2] Only with the drastic curtailment of the powers of the Speaker in 1910 and 1911 did the seniority system in the House assume the inflexible pattern which it has today. Only twice in the years after the 1910 revolt—once in 1915 and once in 1921—was seniority neglected in the choice of committee chairmen.

In the 1960s seniority came under increasing criticism within Congress and some small steps away from it were taken. In 1965 the House Democratic caucus stripped two southern congressmen of their committee seniority for supporting Barry Goldwater in 1964. One of them, John Bell Williams of Mississippi, had been a member of the House since 1947 and was the second-ranking Democrat on the Committee on Interstate and Foreign Commerce. In 1967 a select House committee recommended punishing Representative Adam Clayton Powell by, among other things, taking away his seniority and hence his position as chairman of the Committee on Education and Labor. The House, however, instead voted to deny Mr. Powell a seat in the Ninetieth Congress. In 1971 the House Republican and Democratic caucuses decreed that the selection of committee chairmen should be subject to caucus approval; the Democratic caucus then approved as chairmen those who would have been chairmen by seniority. Nor was a serious effort made to change the seniority system in the Legislative Reorganization Act of 1970. These events suggest that the system will remain but that deviations from it (at least in the House) will occasionally occur and will be accepted as legitimate.

(3) *Extended Tenure: a Prerequisite for Leadership*—Before 1896 Speakers, at the time of their first election, averaged only 7 years' tenure in the House. Since 1896 Speakers have averaged 23 years of House service at their first election. In 1811 and in 1859 Henry Clay and William Pennington were elected Speaker when they first entered the House. In 1807 Thomas Jefferson arranged for the election of his friend, William C. Nicholas, to the House and then for his immediate selection by the party caucus as floor leader. Such an intrusion of leadership from the outside would now be unthinkable. Today the Speaker and other leaders of the House and, to a lesser degree, the leaders of the Senate are legislative veterans of long standing. In 1971 46 House leaders averaged over 23 years' service in the House while 40 leading senators averaged 17 years of senatorial service. The top House leaders (Speaker, floor leaders, chairmen and ranking minority members of Ways and Means, Appropriations, and Rules Committees) averaged 26 years in the House and 8 in leadership positions in 1971. Top Senate leaders (President *pro tem.*, floor leaders, chairmen, and ranking minority members of Finance, Foreign Relations, and Appropriations Committees) averaged 23 years of service in the Senate and 11 in leadership positions. Increasing tenure means increasing age. In the nineteenth century the leaders of Congress were often in their thirties. Clay was 34 when he became Speaker in 1811; Hunter, 30 when he became Speaker in 1839; White, 36 at his accession to the Speakership in 1841; and Ore, 35 when he became Speaker in 1857. In contrast, Rayburn was 58 when he became Speaker, Martin 63, McCormack 71, and Albert 62. In 1971 the top leaders of the House averaged 63 years, those of the Senate 69 years.

(4) *Leadership within Congress: a One-way Street*—Normally in American life becoming a leader in one institution opens up leadership possibilities in other institutions: corporation presidents head civic agencies or become cabinet officers; foundation and university executives move into government; leading lawyers and bankers take over industrial corporations. The greater one's prestige, authority, and accomplishments within one organization, the easier it is to move to other and better posts in other organizations. Such, however, is not the case with Congress. Leadership in the House of Representatives leads nowhere except to leadership in the House of Representatives. To a lesser degree, the same has been true of the Senate. The successful House or Senate leader has to identify himself completely with his institution, its mores, traditions, and ways of behavior. "The very ingredients which make you a powerful House leader," one representative has commented, "are the ones which keep you from being a public leader."[3] Representatives typically confront a "fourth-term crisis": if they wish to run for higher office—for governor or senator—they must usually do so by the beginning of their fourth term in the House. If they stay in the House for four or more terms, they in effect choose to make a career in the House and to forswear the other electoral possibilities of American politics. Leadership in the Senate is not as exclusive a commitment as it is in the House. But despite such notable exceptions as Taft and Johnson, the most influential men in the Senate

have typically been those who have looked with disdain upon the prospect of being anything but a United States Senator. Even someone with the high talent and broad ambition of Lyndon Johnson could not escape this exclusive embrace during his years as majority leader. In the words of Theodore H. White, the Senate, for Johnson, was "faith, calling, club, habit, relaxation, devotion, hobby, and love." Over the years it became "almost a monomania with him, his private life itself."[4] Such "monomania" is normally the prerequisite for Senate leadership. It is also normally an insurmountable barrier, psychologically and politically, to effective leadership outside the Senate.

(5) *The Decline of Personnel Interchange Between Congress and the Administration*—Movement of leaders in recent years between the great national institutions of the establishment and the top positions in the administration has been frequent, easy, and natural. This pattern of lateral entry distinguishes the American executive branch from the governments of most other modern societies. The circulation of individuals between leadership positions in governmental and private institutions eases the strains between political and private leadership and performs a unifying function comparable to that which common class origins perform in Great Britain or common membership in the Communist party does in the Soviet Union.

The frequent movement of individuals between administration and establishment contrasts sharply with the virtual absence of such movement between Congress and the administration or between Congress and the establishment. The gap between congressional leadership and administration leadership has increased sharply during this century. Seniority makes it virtually impossible for administration leaders to become leaders of Congress and makes it unlikely that leaders of Congress will want to become leaders of the administration. The separation of powers has become the insulation of leaders. Between 1861 and 1896, 37 percent of the people appointed to posts in the President's cabinet had served in the House or Senate. Between 1897 and 1940, 19 percent of the Cabinet positions were filled by former congressmen or senators. Between 1941 and 1963, only 15 percent of the cabinet posts were so filled. Former congressmen received only 4 percent of over 1,000 appointments of political executives made during the Roosevelt, Truman, Eisenhower, and Kennedy administrations.[5] In 1963, apart from the President and Vice-President, only one of the top 75 leaders of the Kennedy administration (Secretary of the Interior Udall) had served in Congress. The Nixon administration was somewhat more hospitable to legislators, but in 1971 only 4 of its 75 top leaders (apart from the President) had congressional experience.

Movement from the administration to leadership positions in Congress is almost equally rare. In 1971 only one of 84 congressional leaders (Senator Anderson) had previously served in the President's cabinet. Those members of the administration who do not move on to Congress are typically those who have come to the administration from state and local politics rather than from the great national institutions. Few congressmen and even fewer congressional leaders move from Congress to positions of leadership in national private organizations, and relatively few leaders of these organizations move on to

TABLE 21-2. GEOGRAPHICAL MOBILITY OF NATIONAL LEADERS

	Congressional Leaders		Administration Leaders		Political Executives	Business Leaders
	(1963) N-81	(1971) N-86	(1963) N-74	(1971) N-75	(1959) N-1865	(1952) N-8300
None	37%	43%	11%	13%	} 14%	} 40%
Intrastate	40	35	19	25		
Interstate, intraregion	5	8	9	3	10	15
Interregion	19	14	61	52	73	45
International	0	0	0	7	3	0

Sources: "Political Executives," Warner *et al.*, [see note 6], p. 332; business leaders, Warner and Abegglen, [see note 6], p. 82; congressional and administration leaders, independent calculation. Geographical mobility is measured by comparing birthplace with current residence. For administration leaders, current residence was considered to be last residence before assuming administration position. The nine regions employed in this analysis are defined in Warner *et al.*, [see note 6], pp. 42–43.

Congress. Successful men who have come to the top in business, law, or education naturally hesitate to shift to another world in which they would have to start all over again at the bottom. In some cases, establishment leaders also consider legislative office simply beneath them.

(6) *The Social Origins and Careers of Congressmen*—Congressmen are much more likely to come from rural and small-town backgrounds than are administration and establishment leaders. A majority of the senators holding office between 1947 and 1957 were born in rural areas. Of the 1959 senators 64 percent were raised in rural areas or in small towns, and only 19 percent in metropolitan centers. In contrast, 52 percent of the presidents of the largest industrial corporations grew up in metropolitan centers, as did a large proportion of the political executives appointed during the Roosevelt, Truman, Eisenhower, and Kennedy administrations. The contrast in origins is reflected in fathers' occupations. In the 1950s, the proportion of farmer fathers among senators (32 percent) was more than twice as high as it was among administration leaders (13 percent) and business leaders (9 to 15 percent).[6]

Of perhaps greater significance is the difference in geographical mobility between congressmen and private and public executives. Forty-one percent of the 1959 senators, but only 12 percent of the 1959 corporation presidents, were currently residing in their original hometowns. Seventy percent of the presidents had moved 100 miles or more from their hometowns but only 29 percent of the senators had done so.[7] In 1971 over two-fifths of the leaders of Congress but only 13 percent of administration leaders were still living in their places of birth. Seventy-five percent of the congressional leaders were living in their states of birth, while 62 percent of the administration leaders had moved out of their states of birth. Fifty-nine percent of administration leaders had moved from one region of the country to another, but only 16 percent of congressional leaders had similar mobility.

During the course of this century the career patterns of congressmen and of executive leaders have diverged. At an earlier period both leaderships had

TABLE 21-3. EXPERIENCE OF NATIONAL POLITICAL LEADERS IN STATE
AND LOCAL GOVERNMENT

Offices Held	Congressional Leaders			Administration Leaders		
	1903	1963	1971	1903	1963	1971
Any state or local office	75%	64%	71%	49%	17%	31%
Elective local office	55	46	37	22	5	4
State legislature	47	30	42	17	3	9
Appointive state office	12	10	16	20	7	12
Governor	16	9	5	5	4	7

extensive experience in local and state politics. In 1903 about one-half of executive leaders and three-quarters of congressional leaders had held office in state or local government. In 1971 the congressional pattern had not changed significantly, with 71 percent of the congressional leaders having held state or local office. The proportion of executive leaders with this experience, however, had dropped drastically. The proportion of administration leaders who had held state or local office was still less than half that of congressional leaders, although it had gone up to 31 percent from 17 percent in 1963. When coupled with the data presented earlier on the larger number of former congressmen in the Nixon administration than in the Kennedy administration, these figures suggest a slight shift in recruitment toward local politics and away from the national establishment for the former as compared to the latter.

In recent years, congressional leaders have also more often been professional politicians than they were earlier: in 1903 only 5 percent of the congressional leaders had no major occupation outside politics, while in 1963, 22 percent of the congressional leaders had spent almost all their lives in electoral politics. Roughly 90 percent of the members of Congress in recent years, it has been estimated, "have served apprenticeship in some segment of our political life." [8]

The typical congressman may have gone away to college, but he then returned to his home state to pursue an electoral career, working his way up through local office, the state legislature, and eventually to Congress. The typical political executive, on the other hand, like the typical corporation executive, went away to college and then did not return home but instead pursued a career in a metropolitan center or worked in one or more national organizations with frequent changes of residence. As a result, political executives have become divorced from state and local politics, just as the congressional leaders have become isolated from national organizations. Congressional leaders, in short, come up through a "local politics" line while executives move up through a "national organization" line.

The differences in geographical mobility and career patterns between congressional and administration leaders reflect two different styles of life which cut across the usual occupational groupings. Businessmen, lawyers, and bankers are found in both Congress and the administration. But those in Congress are more likely to be small businessmen, small-town lawyers, and small-town bankers. Among the 66 lawyers in the Senate in 1963, for instance, only 2—Joseph Clark and Clifford Case—had been "prominent corporation counsel[s]" before going into politics.[9] Administration leaders, in contrast, are far more likely to be affiliated with large national industrial corporations, with Wall Street or State Street law firms, and with New York banks.

(7) *The Provincialism of Congressmen*—The absence of mobility between Congress and the executive branch and the differing backgrounds of the leaders of the two branches of government stimulate different policy attitudes. Congressmen have tended to be oriented toward local needs and small-town ways of thought. The leaders of the administration and of the great private national institutions are more likely to think in national terms. Analyzing consensus-building on foreign aid, James N. Rosenau concluded that congressmen typically had "segmental" orientations while other national leaders had "continental" orientations. The segmentally oriented leaders "give highest priority to the subnational units which they head or represent" and are "not prepared to admit a discrepancy between" the national welfare and "their subnational concerns." The congressman is part of a local consensus of local politicians, local businessmen, local bankers, local trade union leaders, and local newspaper editors who constitute the opinion-making elite of their districts. As Senator Richard Neuberger noted: "If there is one maxim which seems to prevail among many members of our national legislature, it is that local matters must come first and global problems a poor second—that is, if the member of Congress is to survive politically." As a result, the members of Congress are "isolated" from other national leaders. At gatherings of national leaders, "members of Congress seem more conspicuous by their absence than by their presence." One piece of evidence is fairly conclusive: of 623 national opinion-makers who attended ten American Assembly sessions between 1956 and 1960, only 9 (1.4 percent) were members of Congress![10]

The differences in attitude between segmentally oriented congressmen and the other, continentally oriented national leaders are particularly marked in those areas of foreign policy (such as foreign aid) which involve the commitment of tangible resources for intangible ends. But they have also existed in domestic policy. The approaches of senators and corporation presidents to economic issues, Andrew Hacker found, were rooted in "disparate images of society." Senators were provincially oriented; corporation presidents "metropolitan" in their thinking. Senators might be sympathetic to business, but they thought of business in small-town, small-business terms. They might attempt to accommodate themselves to the needs of the national corporations, but basically they were "faced with a power they do not really understand and with demands about whose legitimacy they are uneasy." As a result, Hacker suggests, "serious tensions exist between our major political and economic institutions. . . . There is, at base, a real lack of understanding and a failure of communication between the two elites."[11]

"Segmental" or "provincial" attitudes are undoubtedly stronger in the House than they are in the Senate. But they have also existed in the Senate. Despite the increased unity of the country caused by mass communications and the growth of "national as distinguished from local or sectional industry," the Senate in the 1950s was, according to an admiring portraitist, "if anything progressively less national in its approach to most affairs" and "increasingly engaged upon the protection of what is primarily local or sectional in economic life."[12]

For both House and Senate these local patterns are being challenged and in some degree undermined by the nationalizing impact of the media and the geographical extension of party competition.[13] Yet within Congress old ideas, old values, and old beliefs linger on. The structure of Congress encourages their perpetuation. The newcomer to Congress is repeatedly warned that "to get along he must go along." To go along means to adjust to the prevailing mores and attitudes. The more the young congressman desires a career in the House or Senate, the more readily he makes these adjustments. The country at large has become urban, suburban, and metropolitan. Its economic, social, educational, and technological activities are increasingly performed by huge national bureaucratic organizations. In the 1960s these developments were only beginning to make themselves felt in Congress, as gradually younger and more adventurous congressmen took the initiative in challenging the old ways. On Capitol Hill the nineteenth-century ethos of the small town, the independent farmer, and the small businessman slowly wanes behind the institutional defenses which developed in this century to insulate Congress from the new America.

Defects in Representation

In the twentieth century the executive branch grew in power vis-à-vis Congress for precisely the same reason that the House of Representatives grew in power vis-à-vis the executive in the second and third decades of the nineteenth century. It became more powerful because it had become more representative. Congress lost power because it had two defects as a representative body. One, relatively minor and in part easily remedied, dealt with the representation of people as individuals; the other, more serious and perhaps beyond remedy, concerned the representation of organized groups and interests.

Congress was originally designed to represent individuals in the House and governmental units—the states—in the Senate. In the course of time the significance of the states as organized interests declined, and popular election of senators was introduced. In effect, both senators and representatives now represent relatively arbitrarily-defined territorial collections of individuals. This system of individual representation has suffered from two inequities. First, of course, is the constitutional equal representation of states in the Senate irrespective of population. Second, in the House, congressional districts have varied widely in size and may also be gerrymandered to benefit one party or group of voters. For much of this century the net effect of these practices was to place the urban and the suburban voter at a disadvantage vis-à-vis the rural and small-town voter. The correction of this imbalance moved rapidly ahead, however, following the Supreme Court decisions (*Baker* v. *Carr*, 1962; *Wesberry*

v. *Sanders*, 1964) mandating equal size for districts. As a result of the Court action, there was a net shift of between 10 and 19 districts from predominantly rural to predominantly urban during the 1960s.[14] The application of the new standards to the 1970 census population, it has been estimated, should result in 291 metropolitan districts in 1972 compared to 254 in 1962. Of these 129 would be suburban districts compared to 92 such districts in 1962. Central city representation, on the other hand, will drop to 100 congressmen from 106 in 1962 and a peak of 110 in 1966.[15] As Milton Cummings notes:

> In all this there is a very considerable irony. The battle for greater urban representation in the House in the 1950s and 1960s was often accompanied by rhetoric stressing the need to help the central cities, who, it was asserted, were penalized by rural overrepresentation. Now that the one-man/one-vote doctrine is being implemented, however, it is the suburbs, not the central cities, that stand to gain the most.[16]

The overall membership of the House will thus be increasingly metropolitan and suburban. Adherence to seniority, however, means that the leadership of the House will remain southern rural and northern urban for some years to come.

The second and more significant deficiency of Congress as a representative body concerns its insulation from the interests which have emerged in the twentieth century's "organizational revolution." How can national institutions be represented in a locally-elected legislature? In the absence of any easy answer to this question, the administration has tended to emerge as the natural point of access to the government for these national organizations and the place where their interests and viewpoints are brought into the policy-making process. In effect, the American system of government is moving toward a three-way system of representation. Particular territorial interests are represented in Congress; particular functional interests are represented in the administration; and the national interest is represented territorially and functionally in the Presidency.

Every four years the American people choose a President, but they elect an administration. In this century the administration has acquired many of the traditional characteristics of a representative body that Congress has tended to lose. The Jacksonian principle of "rotation in office" and the classic concept of the Cincinnatus-like statesman are far more relevant now to the administration than they are to Congress. Administration officials, unlike congressmen, are more frequently mobile amateurs in government than career professionals in politics. The patterns of power in Congress are rigid. The patterns of power in the administration are flexible. The administration is thus a far more sensitive register of changing currents of opinion than is Congress. A continuous adjustment of power and authority takes place within each administration; major changes in the distribution of power take place at every change of administration. The Eisenhower administration represented one combination of men, interests, and experience, the Kennedy-Johnson administration another, and the Nixon administration yet a third. Each time a new President takes office, the executive branch is invigorated in the same way that the House of Representatives was invigorated by Henry Clay and his western congressmen in 1811. A thousand new officials descend on Washington, coming fresh from the people, representing the diverse forces behind the new President, and bringing with them new demands, new ideas, and new power. Here truly is representative government along classic lines and of a sort which Congress has not known for decades. One key to the "decline" of Congress lies in the defects of Congress as a representative body.

STRUCTURE: THE DISPERSION OF POWER IN CONGRESS

The influence of Congress in our political system thus varies directly with its ties to the more dynamic and dominant groups in society. The power of Congress also varies directly, however, with the centralization of power in Congress. The corollary of these propositions is likewise true: centralization of authority within Congress usually goes with close connections between congressional leadership and major external forces and groups. The power of the House of Representatives was at a peak in the second decade of the nineteenth century, when power was centralized in the Speaker and when Henry Clay and his associates represented the dynamic new forces of trans-Appalachian nationalism. Another peak in the power of the House came during Reconstruction, when power was centralized in Speaker Colfax and the Joint Committee on Reconstruction as spokesmen for triumphant northern radicalism. A third peak in the power of the House came between 1890 and 1910, when the authority of the Speaker reached its height and Speakers Reed and Cannon reflected the newly established forces of nationalist conservatism. The peak in Senate power came during the post-Reconstruction period of the 1870s and 1880s. Within Congress, power was centralized in the senatorial leaders who represented the booming forces of the rising industrial capitalism and the new party machines. These were the years, as Wilfred Binkley put it, of "the Hegemony of the Senate."

Specialization Without Centralization

Since its first years, the twentieth century has seen no comparable centralization of power in Congress. Instead, the dominant tendency has been toward the dispersion of power. This leaves Congress only partially equipped to deal with the problems of modern society. In general, the complex modern environment requires in social and political institutions *both* a high degree of specialization and a high degree of centralized authority to coordinate and to integrate the activities of the specialized units. Specialization of function and centralization of authority have been the dominant trends of twentieth-century institutional development. Congress, however, has adjusted only half-way. Through its committees and subcommittees it has provided effectively for specialization, much more effectively, indeed, than the national legislature of any other country. But it has failed to combine increasing specialization of function with increasing centralization of authority. Instead the central leadership in Congress has been weakened, and as a result Congress lacks the central authority to integrate its specialized bodies. In a "rational" bureaucracy authority varies inversely with specialization. Within Congress authority usually varies directly with specialization.

The authority of the specialist is a distinctive feature of congressional behavior. "Specialization" is a key norm in both House and Senate. The man who makes a career in the House, one congressman has observed, "is primarily a worker, a specialist, and a craftsman—someone who will concentrate his energies in a particular field and gain prestige and influence in that." "The members who are most successful," another congressman concurred, "are those who pick a specialty or an area and become real experts in it."[17] The emphasis on specialization as a norm, of course, complements the importance of the committee as an institution. It also leads to a great stress on reciprocity. In a bureaucracy, specialized units compete with each other for the support of less specialized officials. In Congress, however, reciprocity among specialists replaces coordination by generalists. When a committee bill comes to the floor, the non-specialists in that subject acquiesce in its passage with the unspoken but complete understanding that they will receive similar treatment. "The traditional deference to the authority of one of its committees overwhelms the main body," one congressman has observed. "The whole fabric of Congress is based on committee expertise. . . ." Similarly, in the Senate "a large number of highly specialized experts generally accept each other's work without much criticism."[18] Reciprocity thus substitutes for centralization and confirms the diffusion of power among the committees.

History of Dispersion

The current phase of dispersed power in Congress dates from the second decade of this century. The turning point in the House came with the revolt against Speaker Cannon in 1910, the removal of the Speaker from the Rules Committee, and the loss by the Speaker of his power to appoint standing committees. For a brief period, from 1911 to 1915, much of the Speaker's former power was assumed by Oscar Underwood in his capacities as majority floor leader and chairman of the Ways and Means Committee. In 1915, however, Underwood was elected to the Senate, and the dispersion of power which had begun with the overthrow of the Speaker rapidly accelerated.

During the first years of the Wilson administration, authority in the Senate was concentrated in the floor leader, John Worth Kern, a junior senator first elected to the Senate in 1910. Under his leadership the seniority system was bypassed, and the Senate played an active and creative role in the remarkable legislative achievements of the Sixty-third Congress. Conceivably the long-entrenched position of seniority could have been broken at this point. "If the rule of 'seniority' was not destroyed in 1913," says Claude G. Bowers, "it was so badly shattered that it easily could have been given the finishing stroke."[19] Kern, however, was defeated for re-election in 1916, seniority was restored to its earlier position of eminence, and the power which Kern had temporarily centralized was again dispersed. Except for a brief reversal in the 1930s, this process of dispersion has intensified over the years. This is, it has been argued, the natural tendency of the Senate, with centralizing moves usually requiring some outside stimulus. In the late 1960s "important institutional positions" were "being dispersed ever more widely. . . ." As a result, "Virtually all senators acquire substantial legislative influence." The pattern is not even one of "decentralization"; it is one of "individualism."[20]

Thus since 1910 in the House and since 1915 in the Senate the overall tendency has been toward the weakening of central leadership and the strengthening of the committees. Most of the "reforms" which have been made in the procedures of Congress have contributed to this end. "Since 1910," observed the historian of the House in 1962, "the leadership of the House has been in commission. . . . The net effect of the various changes of the last 35 years in the power structure of the House of Representatives has been to diffuse the leadership, and to disperse its risks, among a numerous body of leaders."[21] The Budget and Accounting Act of 1921 strengthened the appropriations committees by giving them exclusive authority to report appropriations, but its primary effects were felt in the executive branch with the creation of the Bureau of the Budget. During the 1920s power was further dispersed among the Speaker, floor leaders, Rules, Appropriations, Ways and Means chairmen, and caucus chairman. In the following decade political development also contributed to the diffusion of influence when the conservative majority on the Rules Committee broke with the administration in 1937.

The dispersion of power to the committees of Congress was intensified by the Legislative Reorganization Act of 1946. In essence, this act was a "committee reorganization act" making the committees stronger and more effective. The reduction in the number of standing committees from 81 to 34 increased the importance of the committee chairmanships. Committee consolidation led to the proliferation of subcommittees, now estimated to number about 250. Thus the functions of integration and coordination which, if performed at all, would previously have been performed by the central leadership of the two houses, were now devolved on the leadership of the standing committees. Before the reorganization, for instance, committee jurisdictions frequently overlapped, and the presiding officers of the House and Senate could often influence the fate of a bill by exercising their discretion in referring it to committee. While jurisdictional uncertainties were not totally eliminated by the act, the discretion of the presiding officers was drastically curtailed. The committee chairman, on the other hand, could often influence the fate of legislation by manipulating the subcommittee structure of the committee and by exercising his discretion in referring bills to subcommittees. Similarly, the intention of the framers of the Reorganization Act to reduce, if not to eliminate, the use of special committees had the effect of restricting the freedom of action of the central leadership in the two houses at the same time that it confirmed the authority of the standing committees in their respective jurisdictions. The Reorganization Act also bolstered the committees by significantly expanding their staffs and by specifically authorizing them to exercise legislative overseeing functions with respect to the administrative agencies in their field of responsibility.

The act included few provisions strengthening the central leadership of Congress. Those which it did include in general did not operate successfully. A proposal for party policy committees in each house was defeated in the House of Representatives. The Senate subsequently authorized party policy committees in the Senate, but they did not become active or influential enough to affect the legislative process significantly. The act's provision for a Joint Committee on the Budget which would set an appropriation ceiling by February 15 of each year was implemented twice and then abandoned. In 1950 the appropriations committees reported a consolidated supply bill which cut the presidential estimates by $2 billion and was approved by Congress two months before the approval of the individual supply bills of 1949. Specialized interests within Congress, however, objected strenuously to this procedure, and it has not been attempted again. The net effect of the Reorganization Act was thus to further the dispersion of power, to strengthen and to institutionalize committee authority, and to circumscribe still more the influence of the central leadership. The Legislative Reorganization Act of 1970, a far more modest measure than that of 1946, reinforced these tendencies. It did not deal with seniority and none of its provisions was designed to strengthen central leadership. To the extent that it was implemented, its effects were, indeed, to disperse power still further within committees by reducing the prerogatives of the chairmen.

In the years after the 1946 reorganization, the issues which earlier had divided the central leadership and committee chairmen reappeared in each committee in struggles between committee chairmen and subcommittees. The chairmen attempted to maintain their own control and flexibility over the number, nature, staff, membership, and leadership of their subcommittees. Several of the most assertive chairmen either prevented the creation of subcommittees or created numbered subcommittees without distinct legislative jurisdictions, thereby reserving to themelves the assignment of legislation to the subcommittees. Those who wished to limit the power of the chairman, on the other hand, often invoked seniority as the rule to be followed in designating subcommittee chairmen. In 1961 31 of the 36 standing committees of the House and Senate had subcommittees and in 24 the subcommittees had fixed jurisdictions and significant autonomy, thus playing a major role in the legislative process. In many committees the subcommittees go their independent way, jealously guarding their autonomy and prerogatives against other subcommittees and their own committee chairman. "Given an active subcommittee chairman working in a specialized field with a staff of his own," one congressional staff member observes, "the parent committee can do no more than change the grammar of a subcommittee report."[22] In the Senate after World War II the predominant influence in legislation shifted from committee chairmen to subcommittee chairmen and individual senators. Specialization of function and dispersion of power, which once worked to the benefit of the committee chairmen, now work against them.

Position of Central Leaders

The Speaker and the majority floor leaders are the most powerful men in Congress, but their power is not markedly greater than that of many other congressional leaders. In 1959, for instance, thirteen of nineteen committee chairmen broke with the Speaker to support the Landrum-Griffin bill. "This graphically illustrated the locus of power in the House," one congressman commented. "The Speaker, unable to deliver votes, was revealed in outline against the chairmen. This fact was not lost on Democratic Members."[23] The power base of the central leaders has tended to atrophy, caught between the expansion of presidential authority and influence, on the one hand, and the institutionalization of committee authority, on the other.

At times individual central leaders have built up impressive networks of personal influence. These, however, have been individual, not institutional, phenomena. The ascendancy of Rayburn and Johnson during the 1950s, for instance, tended to obscure the difference between personal influence and institutional authority. With the departure of the Texas coalition their personal networks collapsed. "Rayburn's personal power and prestige," observed Representative Richard Bolling, "made the institution *appear* to work. When Rayburn died, the thing just fell apart."[24] Similarly, Johnson's effectiveness as Senate leader, in the words of one of his assistants, was "overwhelmingly a matter of personal influence. By all accounts, Johnson was the most personal among recent leaders in his approach. For years it was said that he talked to every Democratic senator every day. Persuasion ranged from the awesome pyrotechnics known as 'Treatment A' to the apparently casual but always purposeful exchange as he roamed the floor and the cloakroom."[25] When Johnson's successor was accused of failing to provide the necessary leadership to the Senate, he defended himself on the grounds that he was Mansfield and not Johnson. His definition of the leader's role was largely negative: "I am neither a circus ringmaster, the master of ceremonies of a Senate nightclub, a tamer of Senate lions, or a wheeler and dealer. . . ."[26] The majority leadership role was uninstitutionalized and the kindly, gentlemanly, easygoing qualities which Mansfield had had as Senator from Montana were not changed when he became majority leader. The power of the President has been institutionalized; the powers of the congressional committees and their chairmen have been institutionalized; but the power of the central leaders of Congress remains personal, *ad hoc*, and transitory.

In the House the dispersion of power has weakened the central leadership and strengthened committee and subcommittee chairmen. The latter, products of the seniority system, are normally legislative veterans of long standing. In the Senate, on the other hand, the more widespread dispersion of power within a smaller body has produced a more egalitarian situation in which freshmen senators are often able to take the initiative on important issues of particular concern to them or on which they have developed special expertise. The dispersion of power in the Senate, in short, has tended to open up that body to new and outside influences while in the House it has had the reverse effect.

In both houses, however, the dispersion of power makes obstruction easy and the development of a coherent legislative program difficult. Congress cannot play a positive role in the legislative process so long as it lacks a structure of power which makes positive leadership possible. During the last decades of the nineteenth century, for instance, the Speakers of the House centralized power, exercised personal leadership, and played an innovative role in policy. In subsequent years, in contrast, the Speakers "lost or gave away powers" and what initiative there was in policy came from the executive branch.[27] So long as the Speaker remains, in Bolling's words, "a weak King surrounded by strong Dukes," the House cannot organize itself to lead: "A strong Speaker is crucial to the House. He is the indispensable man for its legislative and political health, education, and welfare."[28] The same is true of the majority leader in the Senate. Perpetuation there of the dispersion of power, on the other hand, means that there is "no general plan for bringing bills to the floor in a given order or at a given time"; the legislative process as a whole becomes "highly segmented"; and the prospects for organized institutional reform are very low.[29]

FUNCTION: THE SHIFT TO OVERSIGHT

Loss of Initiative

The insulation of Congress from external social forces and the dispersion of power within Congress have stimulated significant changes in the functions of Congress. The congressional role in legislation has largely been reduced to delay and amendment; congressional activity in overseeing administration has expanded and diversified. During the nineteenth century Congress frequently took the legislative initiative in dealing with major national problems. Even when the original proposal came from the President, Congress usually played an active and positive role in reshaping the proposal into law. "The predominant and controlling force, the centre and source of all motive and of all regulative power," Woodrow Wilson observed in 1885, "is Congress. . . . The legislature is the aggressive spirit."[30] Since 1933, however, the initiative in formulating legislation, in assigning legislative priorities, in arousing support for legislation, and in determining the final content of the legislation enacted has clearly shifted to the executive branch. All three elements of the executive branch—President, administration, and bureaucracy—have gained legislative functions at the expense of Congress. Today's "aggressive spirit" is clearly the executive branch.

In 1908, it is reported, the Senate, in high dudgeon at the effrontery of the Secretary of the Interior, returned to him the draft of a bill which he had proposed, resolving to refuse any further communications from executive officers unless they were transmitted by the President himself.[31] Now, however, congressmen expect the executive departments to present them with bills. Eighty percent of the bills enacted into law, one congressman has estimated, originate in the executive branch. Indeed, in most instances congressmen do not admit a responsibility to take legislative action except in response to executive requests. Congress, as one senator has complained, "has surrendered its rightful place in the leadership in the lawmaking process to the White House. No longer is Congress the source of major legislation. It now merely filters legislative proposals from the President, straining out some and reluctantly letting others pass through. These days no one expects Congress to devise the important bills."[32] The President now determines the legislative agenda of Congress almost as thoroughly as the British cabinet sets the legislative agenda of Parliament. The institutionalization of this role was one of the more significant developments in presidential-congressional relations after World War II.[33]

Loss of Policy Control

Congress has conceded not only the initiative in originating legislation but—and perhaps inevitably as the result of losing the initiative—it has also lost the dominant influence it once had in shaping the final content of legislation. Between 1882 and 1909 Congress had a preponderant influence in shaping the content of 16 (55 percent) out of 29 major laws enacted during those years. It had a preponderant influence over 17 (46 percent) of 37 major laws passed between 1910 and 1932. During the constitutional revolution of the New Deal, however, its influence declined markedly: only 2 (8 percent) of 24 major laws passed between 1933 and 1940 were primarily the work of Congress.[34] Certainly its record after World War II was little better.

The loss of congressional control over the substance of policy was most marked, of course, in the area of national defense and foreign policy. At one time Congress did not hesitate to legislate the size and weapons of the armed forces. During the 1940s and 1950s this power—to raise and support armies, to provide and maintain a navy—came to rest firmly in the hands of the executive. Is Congress, one congressional committee asked plaintively in 1962, to play simply "the passive role of supine acquiescence" in executive programs or is it to be "an active participant in the determination of the direction of our defense policy?" The committee, however, already knew the answer:

> To any student of government, it is eminently clear that the role of the Congress in determining national policy, defense or otherwise, has deteriorated over the years. More and more the role of Congress has come to be that of a sometimes querulous but essentially kindly uncle who complains while furiously puffing on his pipe but who finally, as everyone expects, gives in and hands over the allowance, grants the permission, or raises his hand in blessing, and then returns to the rocking chair for another year of somnolence broken only by an occasional anxious glance down the avenue and a muttered doubt as to whether he had done the right thing.[35]

NOTES

[1] George B. Galloway, *History of the United States House of Representatives* (House Document 246, Eighty-seventh Congress, First Session, 1962), p. 31; T. Richard Witmer, "The Aging of the House," *Political Science Quarterly*, 79 (Dec. 1964), pp. 526–541. See Nelson Polsby, "The Institutionalization of the U.S. House of Representatives," *American Political Science Review*, 62 (March 1968), pp. 144–168, for documentation in historical detail for the House of Representatives of several of the trends posited here and analysis of them according to criteria of institutionalization (autonomy, coherence, complexity) which I elaborated in "Political Development and Political Decay," *World Politics*, 17 (April 1965), pp. 386–430.

[2] Gail Hamilton, *Life of James G. Blaine*, p. 263, quoted in DeAlva S. Alexander, *History and Procedure of the House of Representatives* (Boston: Houghton Mifflin, 1916), p. 69. On the development of the House seniority system, see Michael Abram and Joseph Cooper, "The Rise of Seniority in the House of Representatives," *Polity*, 1 (Fall 1968), pp. 52–85, and Nelson Polsby, Miriam Gallaher, and Barry Spencer Rundquist, "The Growth of the Seniority System in the U.S. House of Representatives," *American Political Science Review*, 63 (Sept. 1969), pp. 787–807. For the operation of the system, see, in general, Barbara Hinckley, *The Seniority System in Congress* (Bloomington: Ind. Univ. Press, 1971).

[3] Quoted in Charles L. Clapp, *The Congressman: His Work as He Sees It* (Washington: Brookings Institution, 1963), p. 21.

[4] Theodore H. White, *The Making of the President, 1960* (New York: Atheneum Press, 1961), p. 132.

[5] See Pendleton Herring, *Presidential Leadership* (New York: Farrar and Rinehart, 1940), pp. 164–165 for figures for 1861–1940; figures for 1940–1963 have been calculated on same basis as Herring's figures; see also Dean E. Mann, "The Selection of Federal Political Executives," *American Political Science Review*, 58 (March 1964), p. 97.

[6] See Andrew Hacker, "The Elected and the Anointed," *American Political Science Review*, 55 (Sept. 1961), pp. 540–541; Mann, *ibid.*, 58 (March 1964), pp. 92–93; Donald R. Matthews, *U.S. Senators and Their World* (Chapel Hill: Univ. of N.C. Press, 1960), pp. 14–17; W. Lloyd Warner *et al.*, *The American Federal Executive* (New Haven: Yale Univ. Press, 1963), pp. 11, 56–58, 333; W. Lloyd Warner and James C. Abegglen, *Occupational Mobility in American Business and Industry* (Minneapolis: Univ. of Minn. Press, 1955), p. 38; Suzanne Keller, "The Social Origins and Career Patterns of Three Generations of American Business Leaders" (Ph.D. dissertation, Columbia Univ., 1953), cited in Wendell Bell, Richard J. Hill, and Charles R. Wright, *Public Leadership* (San Francisco: Chandler Press, 1961), p. 106. Leroy N. Rieselbach has noted that congressmen in the 1950s and 1960s were not more rural or small-town in their birthplaces than the population of the country as a whole in 1900 and 1910. "Congressmen as 'Small Town Boys': A Research Note," *Midwest Journal of Political Science*, 14 (May 1970), pp. 321–330. His argument, however, involves a quite different question from that argued here which concerns not the representativeness of congressmen compared to the general population, but rather the similarity or difference in background of congressional and other elites.

[7] Hacker, *op. cit.*, p. 544. For further analysis of the limited geographical mobility of representatives, see Roger H. Davidson, *The Role of the Congressman* (New York: Pegasus, 1969), pp. 54–59.

[8] Davidson, *Role of the Congressman*, p. 54.

[9] Andrew Hacker, "Are There Too Many Lawyers in Congress?" *New York Times Magazine*, January 5, 1964, p. 74.

[10] James N. Rosenau, *National Leadership and Foreign Policy* (Princeton: Princeton Univ. Press, 1963), pp. 30–31, 347–350.

[11] Hacker, *op. cit.*, pp. 547–549.

[12] William S. White, *Citadel* (New York: Harper & Bros., 1956), p. 136.

[13] See John S. Saloma III, *Congress and the New Politics* (Boston: Little, Brown, 1969), pp. 68–69.

[14] Authorities vary on the exact impact of the Court decisions on the rural-urban balance in Congress, but they generally agree that it was less than had been anticipated. See Saloma, *Congress and the New Politics*, pp. 77–87; Andrew Hacker, *Congressional Districting: The Issue of Equal Representation* (Washington: Brookings Institution, rev. ed., 1964).

[15] Richard Lehne, "Shape of the Future," *National Civic Review*, 58 (Sept. 1969), pp. 351–355.

[16] Milton C. Cummings, Jr., "Reapportionment in the 1970's: Its Effects on Congress," in Nelson W. Polsby, ed., *Reapportionment in the 1970's* (Berkeley: Univ. of Cal. Press, 1971), p. 222.

[17] Clapp, *op. cit.*, pp. 23–24.

[18] Clem Miller, *Member of the House* (New York: Scribner's, 1962), p. 51; Randall B. Ripley, *Power in the Senate* (New York: St. Martin's Press, 1969), p. 172.

[19] Claude G. Bowers, *The Life of John Worth Kern* (Indianapolis: Hollenback Press, 1918), p. 840.

[20] Ripley, *Power in the Senate*, pp. 15–16, 53, 77, 185.

[21] Galloway, *op. cit.*, pp. 95, 98, 128.

[22] George Goodwin, Jr., "Subcommittees: The Miniature Legislatures of Congress," *American Political Science Review*, 56 (Sept. 1962), pp. 596–601.

[23] Miller, *op. cit.*, p. 110.

[24] Quoted in Stewart Alsop, "The Failure of Congress," *Saturday Evening Post*, 236 (December 7, 1963), p. 24.

[25] Ralph K. Huitt, "Democratic Party Leadership in the Senate," *American Political Science Review*, 55 (June 1961), p. 338.

[26] *Congressional Record* (Nov. 27, 1963), pp. 21, 758 (daily ed.).

[27] Randall B. Ripley, *Party Leaders in the House of Representatives* (Washington: Brookings Institution, 1967), pp. 16–17.

[28] Richard Bolling, *Power in the House: A History of the Leadership of the House of Representatives* (New York: E. P. Dutton, 1968), p. 29.

[29] Ripley, *Power in the Senate*, pp. 13–14.

[30] Woodrow Wilson, *Congressional Government* (Boston: Houghton Mifflin, 1885), pp. 11, 36.

[31] George B. Galloway, *The Legislative Process in Congress* (New York: Crowell, 1955), p. 9.

[32] Abraham Ribicoff, "Doesn't Congress Have Ideas of Its Own?" *Saturday Evening Post*, 237 (March 21, 1964), p. 6.

[33] Richard E. Neustadt, "Presidency and Legislation: Planning the President's Program," *American Political Science Review*, 49 (Dec. 1955), pp. 980–1021.

[34] Lawrence H. Chamberlain, *The President, Congress, and Legislation* (New York: Columbia Univ. Press, 1946), pp. 450–452.

[35] House Report 1406, Eighty-seventh Congress, Second Session (1962), p. 7.

22

NELSON W. POLSBY

STRENGTHENING CONGRESS IN NATIONAL POLICY-MAKING

The word is out that the Congress of the United States may have had something to do with the alteration over the past year and a half of American policy toward Southeast Asia. On the domestic scene, Congressmen can be observed taking the lead in tax reform and increasing federal appropriations for education. Consequently, it may briefly be fashionable to take Congress seriously, and perhaps those few of us who all along have been arguing this view *sotto voce* ought to say a word or two before Congress resumes its accustomed role of thwarting the domestic programs of liberal Presidents, and is once more relegated to the dustbin of historians if not of history.

To be sure it is easy enough to see why that popular guide to Washington politics, Casual Observer, finds Congress hard to understand. It is organized quite differently from the conventional bureaucracy, which Casual Observer professes to despise, but which he and his friends comprehend. Instead of having a single head, Congress looks like the hydra of Greek mythology. Instead of neatly delegating work downward and responsibility upward, Congress is a complex, redundant, not always predictable, and purposely unwieldy network of crisscrossing and overlapping lines of authority and information.

The mere contemplation of this organizational design customarily leads Casual Observer to assert overhastily that Congressional decision-making is inefficient, cumbersome, and in need of instant reform. Consider, for example, the frequently regretted fact that Cabinet officers are asked to justify certain aspects of their programs in much the same language before authorization and appropriation committees in both houses—four presentations in all. Clearly an inefficient use of a busy executive's time, according to the busy executive and his friends. Yet this same busy executive as a matter of course insists that programs coming up the line to his office be justified repeatedly to program review committees, bureau chiefs, department level staff, and departmental budget officers, and he would think nothing of justifying the program again to other interested executive branch departments, to the President and the Budget Bureau. Cabinet-level officers quite commonly make presentations, formal and informal, justifying their programs to the general public, to interest groups, to newspapermen. Why, then, does the need for Congress to hear justifications as well constitute such an intolerable inconvenience? Why should this alleged inconvenience lead to recommendations that Congress revamp its structure?

Casual Observer also finds Congress hard to fathom because the political theories that are currently available do not help him resolve some basic choices that he generally has to make in order to defend his preferences with respect to the distribution of power within the national government. Does he want a strong Congress? A strong Congress means precisely one capable of asserting its will, even though Presidents, interest groups, courts, and ephemeral majorities of public opinion may find it inconvenient. A weak Congress means less effective oversight of executive policy-making and of the bureaucracies, and such weakness diminishes the capacity of Congressmen and Senators to play the roles of critic, goad, and ombudsman. Further, he must decide whether to vest power in Congress or in the majority party within Congress. If the former, he must be prepared to tolerate coalitions which occasionally—and perhaps persistently— thwart the will of the majority of the majority party. Of such majorities are the conservative coalition—and the progressive one that unhorsed Joseph Cannon— made. If he opts for stricter party responsibility, he must accept the weakening of Congress vis-à-vis national parties, and whoever controls them—presumably quite often the President. For a long time, there were modish and unequivocal answers to these structural dilemmas, just as in the 'thirties Casual Observer's father knew what he thought of an innately reactionary institution like the Supreme Court. Now, however, while the idea of Congressional checks and balances and initiatives seems to make a little sense, it is possible to give these choices more evenhanded consideration.

The reasons why Congress and Presidents generally get along rather badly are too well known to require much reiteration. Differing constituencies arising from, on the one hand, the unit of rule of the electoral college and, on the other, from the differential effects of party competition, the residuum of malapportion- ment, and the seniority system account for part of the conflict. So do purely institutional factors, the most important of which is the differing time scale of Presidential and Congressional careers.

President Kennedy understood this problem quite well, as the following quotation from Theodore Sorensen's book suggests:

> "Wilbur Mills," he said one day, "knows that he was chairman of Ways and Means before I got here and that he'll still be chairman after I've gone—and he knows I know it. I don't have any hold on him."

More generally, the argument is that the career expectations of political actors influence the rates at which they are willing to expend resources. By the standards of the operational leaders of Congress—Congressional party leaders, committee and subcommittee chairmen, their minority counterparts, and leading up-and-coming members in both parties—the career of any President is short. In the 91st Congress considerably more than a majority of both houses had already served with at least three Presidents of the United States. More to the point, the vast majority in both houses could plausibly entertain the prospect of continuing to serve on into the indefinite future. Thus, while Presidents are under a constitutional injunction to seize the day, the men of Capitol Hill—even supposing they agree with the President and his programs—must calculate the consequences of their support against future demands upon their own resources. This leads to strategic dilemmas and to disagreements between Congress and the Presidency that are scarcely touched by proposals such as the four-year Congressional term of office, which seeks to coordinate the time of election but not the terminal points of Presidential and Congressional careers.

There is no definitive, universally acceptable answer to the question of how strong Congress should be. On the whole, gains in institutional strength are likely to be had at costs in institutional responsiveness. But there are many possible mixtures of these two qualities. A legislature that is merely an arena for the registering of the policy preferences of groups organized in the society at large is obviously not the only alternative to a legislature that is totally impervious to external sentiment. There is at present no very satisfactory description of Congress which assesses the developing balance between these somewhat incompatible goals. Thus Casual Observer is also handicapped in his attempts to understand Congress because Congress itself has been changing over the years, while our descriptions and justifications for it have not kept pace.

The accepted view of what a legislature contributes to government is that it represents the people, and it is as a representative body that Congress finds its ultimate justification in our political system. The difficulty that all modern legislatures face, of course, is the tremendous increase in the scale of modern government that makes it almost impossible for individual legislators genuinely to represent the people back home in any simple or straightforward fashion. And most legislatures collectively have pretty much stopped doing so. In most parliamentary systems, they are now mindless creatures of the political parties that run them.

But Congress is an exception. Principally because of historical accidents that destroyed the temporary unity of both the national parties earlier in this century, Congress built on some nineteenth-century precedents in ways that have maintained and in some cases enhanced its independence in the political system. One major consequence of this process of institutionalization has been to shift the balance in the careers and life-styles of legislators from amateur to professional, from the status of temporary ambassador from home to that of member of the legislative group. Where Congress used to embody a popular will in some formal sense by its collective representativeness, it now does so *de facto* through the piecemeal pressures of case work for constituents, legislative committee hearings, and the appropriations process. Where representation, emphasizing the ambassadorial function, was once the characteristic, conscious activity of Congressmen and Senators, today it is deliberation, emphasizing the increasing centrality to Congressmen of their lives as members of a legislative work group and status system.

Thus in a sense Congress has been modernizing itself, through processes which have shifted the loyalties and the attention of Congressmen and Senators toward Washington and away from the grass roots, differentiated its internal functions, and professionalized legislative service.

However, we have not yet developed a fully articulate rationale for a legislature that takes this developmental path; instead we are still relying both descriptively and evaluatively on notions of representation that made more sense when Congressmen spent most of their time at home and came from relatively knowable communities.

Thus a discussion of the strength of Congress in the political system might profitably consider the ways in which the House and the Senate organize to do business, as a means of gaining insight into how a legislature can cope with the complex demands of a large heterogeneous society, including the rest of a big government. This may serve to throw some light on how or whether an effective legislature can contribute to democratic government.

As institutions, the House and the Senate differ markedly in their contemporary characters. The House is a highly specialized instrument for processing legislation. Its great strength is its firmly structured division of labor. This provides the House with a toehold in the policy-making process by virtue of its capacity to specialize and hence, in some collective sense, to provide for the mastery of technical details. House members are frequently better prepared than Senators in legislative conferences, and usually have the better grasp of the peculiarities of the executive agencies they supervise. This is a consequence of the strong division of labor that the House maintains: members are generally assigned to one or two committees only. Floor debate is normally limited to participation by committee members. There is an expectation that members will concentrate their energies rather than range widely over the full spectrum of public policy.

Patterns of news coverage encourage specialization. General pronouncements by House members are normally not widely reported. Senators, because they are fewer, more socially prominent, and serve longer terms (hence are around long enough for newsmen to cultivate) and allegedly serve "larger" districts, can draw attention to themselves by well-timed press releases almost regardless of their content. One result of all this publicity (among other things) is that the Senate is increasingly the home of presidential hopefuls, and this of course tends to generate still more Senate publicity. Some years ago I inquired of the chief of an important Washington news bureau if there was an imbalance between House and Senate news coverage. His response (bowdlerized) was: "The House! Look at them! There's no presidential timber there at all."

The maintenance of a perennially timberless ecology like the House is difficult because it cannot entail excessive centralization of power. Decentralization of power is necessary for the House to sustain its capacity to cope with the outside world through its complex and specialized division of labor. The House's major career incentive is the opportunity accorded a tenth to a fifth of its members to possess the substance of power in the form of a committee or subcommittee chairmanship or membership on a key committee. At present seniority acts as a bulwark of this incentive system by guaranteeing a form of job security at least within the division of labor of the organization. Without decentralization of power there would quite likely be no incentive for able men to stay in the House; without able men (there are few enough of these at any rate) there would be no expertise. Without mastery of subject matter, initiatives taken and modifications made in public policy are capricious, responsive largely to prejudice, or ineffective, or failing that, detrimental.

The essence of the Senate is that it is a great forum, an echo chamber, a publicity machine. Thus "passing bills," which is central to the life of the House, is peripheral to the Senate. In the Senate the three central activities are cultivating national constituencies; formulating questions for debate and discussion on a national scale (especially in opposition to the President); and incubating new policy proposals that may at some future time find their way into legislation.

Where the House of Representatives is a large, impersonal, and highly specialized machine for processing bills and overseeing the executive branch, the Senate is, in a way, a theatre where dramas—comedies and tragedies, soap operas and horse operas—are staged to enhance the careers of its members and to influence public policy by means of debate and public investigation.

In both the House and Senate the first commandment to newcomers is "specialize." But this means different things in each house. "Specialize" to a Representative means "tend to your knitting": work hard on the committee to which you are assigned, pursue the interests of your state and region. Consider, however, the consequences of these well-known features of Senate organization: Every Senator has several committee assignments. Boundaries between committees are not strictly observed. On the floor, quite unlike the House, virtually any Senator may speak for any length of time about anything. Thus the institution itself gives few cues and no compulsions to new Senators wondering what they should specialize in. For the Senate, specialization seems to mean finding a subject matter and a nationwide constituency interested in the subject that has not already been preempted by some more senior Senator.

It is a cliché of academic political science that, in legislative matters, it is the President who initiates policy, and Congress which responds, amplifying and modifying and rearranging elements that are essentially originated in the executive branch. Not much work has been done, however, on following this river of bills-becoming-and-not-becoming-laws back to its sources. Where do innovations in policy come from *before* the President "initiates" them?

It appears that a great many newly enacted policies have "been around," "in the air" for quite a while. In the heat of a presidential campaign or later, when a President wants a "new" program, desk drawers fly open all over Washington. Pet schemes are constantly being fished out, dusted off, and tried out on political leaders. There is often a hiatus of years, sometimes decades, between the first proposal of a policy innovation and its appearance as a presidential "initiative"— much less a law.

It is certainly not generally true that policy innovation begins with a presidential message to Congress. For behind each presidential message lurk months of man-hours of work and sometimes years of advocacy and controversy. The two great fountainheads of new policy seem to be, first, generally acknowledged "problems" producing the demands upon government that spur bureaucrats to ad hoc problem solving. This often later has to be codified or rationalized as "policy." Second, a longer range buildup in the society of something that at first is not generally conceded to be a "problem." Those who see it that way may formulate demands upon the government in the guise of a "solution." This initiative may first be taken by a professor, or by staff professionals attached to an interest group, or by a government "expert." On rare occasions, experts attached to a Congressional committee will initiate a policy. More often, I think, Congress is in on the beginning of a policy innovation because it provides the first sympathy for an innovation concocted by outside experts.

Many of our most important policy innovations take years from initiation to enactment. Surely the idea of Medicare, to take an obvious example, was not "initiated" by the Johnson administration in the 89th Congress. Proposals incorporating its main features had been part of the Washington landscape since the early Truman administration. Medicare, like other great policy innovations, required *incubation*, a process in which men of Congress often play very significant roles. Incubation entails keeping a proposal alive while it picks up support, or waits for a better climate, or while a consensus begins to form that the problem to which it is addressed exists. Senators and (to a lesser extent) Representatives contribute to incubation by proposing bills that they know will not pass, making speeches, making demands for data and for support from interest groups favoring the proposal. Sometimes a sympathetic committee chairman can be persuaded to allow hearings on such a proposal. This focuses public attention, mobilizes interest groups for and against, and provides an occasion for the airing of a proposal's technical justifications. Policy incubation is, of course, not exclusively a Congressional activity; lobbyists may plant stories in the press, organizations may pass resolutions, professors may write books and articles. Most major policy innovations have been incubated by methods such as these.

The net effect of the Congressional process of incubation in any event is to develop a sense of community among far-flung interest groups that favor the innovation by giving them occasional opportunities to come in and testify. It provides an incentive for persons favoring the innovation to maintain up-to-date information on its prospective benefits and technical feasibility. And it accustoms the uncommitted to a new idea.

Thus the Senate is in some respects at a crucial nerve end of the polity. It articulates, formulates, shapes, and publicizes demands for significant policy innovation. Proposals to increase the structuredness of the Senate, to force germaneness in debates, to tighten committee assignment procedures, and reduce the number of assignments per Senator, misunderstand the nature of the Senate and the contribution it uniquely makes to the political system. What is needed in the Senate is as little structure as possible; its organizational flexibility enables it to incubate policy innovations, to advocate, to respond, to launch its great debates, in short, to pursue the continuous renovation of American public policy through the hidden self-promotion of its members.

I do not mean by this to suggest that Congress is entirely self-sufficient in the policy-making process, or that all demands on Congress are equally well treated. Far from it. In order finally to make new policy, Congress generally does need the power of the Presidency to set priorities and focus the energy sufficient to mobilize the successive majorities that law-making requires. A presidential priority is a tremendous advantage in clearing away obstacles, but the President's support is usually purchased at a price: the proposal becomes his. This is not merely a matter of credit, although who gets credit is no trivial matter. It also affects the substance of policy. The executive branch begins the process of bargaining by including some features of a proposal and dropping others, adding bait here and padding there. In some cases (e.g., foreign aid, civil rights) executive branch control over bargaining is tight and continues right through the legislative mill. In others (e.g., surtax, Medicare) influential members of Congress establish which provisions will survive and which will be sacrificed. Sometimes (e.g., the bill establishing a Department of Housing and Urban Development in the Kennedy administration) the most significant battle is precisely over who will control the bill.

But even with the President behind a bill, and despite years of Congressional incubation, the mortality rate for "new" proposals is high. Most Congressional policy-making takes place under adversary circumstances. Thus Congressional decision-makers ordinarily cannot enjoy the luxury of examining alternative means to stipulated ends. In an adversary process ends are not stipulated but contested. Agreement on means is often sought as a substitute for agreement on ends. Ends are often scaled down, pulled out of shape, or otherwise transformed. In short, from the standpoint of an outsider who cares about one or more pressing problems in society, the Congressional process of policy-making looks chaotic at best, perversely insensitive at worst.

If the perception of chaos is largely an optical illusion, the perception of insensitivity may not be. Insensitivity, slowness to register some kinds of new demands, exists in Congressional policy-making and is not altogether curable. It can come about because the strength of a demand in society as it is felt by an outsider has no counterpart equally strong within the Congressional process itself. Sometimes Congress does not reflect "needs" as defined in the society at large because Congress is malapportioned, or because the "wrong" sorts of people dominate the relevant committees. In this fashion a wave of short-run, intense demands might break futilely across the superstructure of any stable organization. Given the stately metabolism (fixed terms of office, staggered Senatorial elections) decreed for it by the founding fathers, Congress could hardly be expected to operate efficiently with respect to short-run demands in the best of circumstances.

A second source of Congressional insensitivity to innovation is of course the fact that many urgent demands are pressed upon Congress by groups with whom Congressmen—and quite often the bulk of their constituents—simply disagree. Not all righteous causes are popular. And, as a matter of fact, not all momentarily popular causes are necessarily righteous. Congressmen often have a keen appreciation of this.

It may be said that Congressmen are more concerned than they should be with popularity. But this constraint on their judgment is the result of the fact that they are popularly elected. They must ask who will get the credit or the blame for public policies. They must know who is for what and how strongly, because these matters affect not only their own future efficacy but also the present chances that a majority can be assembled.

Is there a practical alternative to a process of legislative policy-making in which alternative policies are put to stringent tests of internal political accept-ability? If the internal politics of the institution did not matter, the legislature would be a mere arena, a place for forces as they exist in the outside society to contend. The group that captures such an organization may find it marginally useful in pressing claims upon leaders situated elsewhere since victory in some arenas can give legitimacy to a cause. But as an organization develops independent power and internal structure at the same time that it begins to devote a portion of its resources to self-maintenance, it also develops a measure of insensitivity. To require total responsiveness of a legislature is to require it to be powerless.

Although Congress has developed institutional strength within its political system to a degree unrivaled by most contemporary legislatures, it does not follow that nothing can be done to increase its sensitivity to social problems, or increase its effectiveness within the logic of its own developing character. To me the reason most reform proposals are uninteresting is not because reforms are necessarily less appealing than the status quo, but because they are usually addressed rather arbitrarily to "needs," and typically neither needs nor solutions are discussed within the context that includes the relevant features of the ongoing system.

A number of meritorious reforms have been suggested that do not bear on the operations of the Congressional collectivity except insofar as the general reputations of all members are affected by the transgressions of a few. Reforms bearing on conflict of interest, disclosure of income, and other such matters do not materially affect the strength of the institution except as the institution's strength is mirrored in its general reputation.

Problems of Congressional morality cannot really be addressed responsibly without considering comparable problems in the private sector. Even under the new tax law American taxpayers will be giving rather substantial subsidies, far exceeding in their magnitude salaries and perquisites furnished Congress, to certain privileged persons and industries—most conspicuously oil companies and banks. How relevant is it to condemn Congressmen for allegedly taking "junkets" at taxpayer expense while in the private sector all manner of extravagance is routinely charged off to "business expenses" as a tax dodge? When Congress recently voted to raise Congressional salaries the news media were generally outraged. The fact is, considering the weight of their responsi-bilities, even at the new rates, Congressmen are far from overcompensated. It is necessary for them to maintain out of pocket two bases of operation. Their campaign expenses are not deductible as business expenses. Consider, also, the compensation of men in positions of comparable responsibility in the private sector. I doubt that the top 535 men in the automotive industry, or on Wall Street, or in television make do with the equivalent of salaries of $42,500 plus small change in the way of stationery allowances, inexpensive haircuts, a few overseas junkets, and occasional trips home on military aircraft.

All this provides no excuse for Congressmen not to bring themselves within the scope of the conflict-of-interest laws as they presently apply to political executives. This may be more technically difficult than it sounds, since like the everyday activities of the Secretary of the Treasury, their votes touch everything, so no investment of capital is immune to a conflict-of-interest problem. There are, however, enough violations of propriety to make the problem worth thinking about.

Important as these matters are for public morality, they do not touch the institutional life of Congress. I want to list three suggestions that are pertinent to the functioning of the collectivity. They embody changes in present arrangements, but do not disturb most existing institutional values except in ways I shall describe.

First, a scheme for mandatory retirement. Mortality is a melancholy fact, which comes upon us in different ways, and at different rates of speed. Most modern organizations protect themselves against its creeping effects by requiring the retirement of members after a certain age is reached. Congress now has a generous pension plan that works no economic hardship upon most members forced into retirement by electoral defeat. Instead of relying wholly upon local party systems to replace ailing, failing, and senile members, Congress should protect the efficiency and integrity of its functioning by providing for mandatory retirement at a stated age. If on college campuses these days thirty years of age seems about right for this purpose, perhaps for Congress the age seventy is suitable.

It will be argued in opposition to this proposal that many valuable persons make Congress their second career, and Congress would be depriving itself of much-needed maturity and good judgment in legislative affairs; that no similar impositions are contemplated for other political officers, and thus that the proposal is inequitable; and that the proposal places an unnecessary requirement upon electors in states and districts.

All three objections lack weight. The first ignores the extent to which Congress is presently a young man's game though, to be sure, a young man's waiting game. Men who arrive in Congress past the age of fifty-five rarely have a chance to accumulate sufficient seniority to acquire institutionally-based influence. This proposal would over the short run, in fact, give some older new arrivals more of a chance to shine, since it would clear the most senior men out of the way at a predictable rate. But it would not materially affect the incentive system as it currently applies differentially to men of different ages.

The second objection, that the proposal is inequitable, has no merit with respect to the executive branch, since the President's term of office is strictly limited by other means, and other political officials serve at his pleasure. As for the judicial branch, I have no desire to reopen the issue of court packing, but neither have I any objection in principle to the imposition of mandatory retirement upon all federal judges.

Finally, there is the matter of the protection of the interests of voters. Presumably, if they want to send elderly Representatives and Senators to Congress, they should be allowed to do so. I merely assert a competing interest, one that has grown in importance over the years, namely the interest that Congress has as an institution in maintaining a membership sufficiently vigorous to conduct its increasingly demanding business successfully. Surely each Congressional district and each state contains more than one potential Congressman or Senator, so the disability the requirement of mandatory retirement places on the voters of each district must be regarded as minimal. A more impressive objection is that the proposal is unconstitutional. This was not fully apparent until the Supreme Court decided Powell v. McCormack last year, holding that Congressmen could be excluded from sitting only if they failed to meet qualifications specified in the Constitution. It now appears that it will take remarkable agility at textual construction by future courts or two-thirds votes by each House of Congress respectively to expel in individual cases, or a Constitutional amendment, in order to give effect to a general retirement scheme.

The second suggestion has to do with the improvement of technical knowledge available to Congress. Congress gets technical knowledge principally from committee staff personnel who make themselves knowledgeable in the subject matter coming before them. But while the executive branch has systematically been engaged in professionalizing its means of technical understanding over the past decade or more, Congress on the whole has not done so. It is romantic for Congressmen to think of themselves as not in need of expert and detailed explicit analysis because they are "generalists." Generalism is too often a genteel name for ignorance. The professionalization of economic forecasting and defense procurement in the executive branch led to tremendous increases in the power of political decision-makers to identify options and choose among them. This is precisely the capacity many Congressmen feel they are losing. And, if they choose to do so, they can professionalize their own committee staffs, thereby increasing the efficiency of their explicit analytical activities and enhancing their own knowledge and power.

To "professionalize" entails continuous contact with a community outside the world of Capitol Hill. Professional men—economists, operations researchers, psychologists, and so on—maintain standards of performance by knowing and participating in their professional communities. Typically, nowadays, the top economists of the executive branch—the men who formulate fiscal policy, antitrust policy, international trade policy, and so forth—are first and foremost professional economists. Their loyalty to professional standards means (in general) that the options presented to political executives will be feasible and technically sound.

Typically, Congressional committees are staffed by means of an older, less effective process of patronage. This produces loyal service and, by the standards of an earlier day, highly competent service. But unswerving loyalty to the chairman is seldom enough to produce technically informed criticism of executive proposals, sophisticated insight into alternatives, or sensitive awareness of emerging problems in the world. Yet these are what Congress needs. Hence, two corrective proposals. Committees should be encouraged to constitute outside advisory groups to advise the chairman on the technical competence of the work the committee is receiving from its staff. Secondly, more extensive exchanges for one- or two-year hitches of service should be instituted between Congressional committee staffs and comparable staff in the executive branch, private business, labor unions, social service organizations, and universities.

The purpose of these proposals is to bring to bear upon explicit policy analysis on Capitol Hill the standards—and the considerations—that are commonly employed in policy analysis within the executive branch and elsewhere in society. Steps such as these will not necessarily bring Congress into harmony with the executive branch in areas where they now disagree, since there is no reason to suppose that a large number of disagreements over national policy are based on ignorance—though some may be. These disagreements should be resolved. Other disagreements may occur if Congress chooses to equip itself with more professional analytic personnel, since not all executive branch proposals are free from controversy even when they are grounded in thorough professional knowledge. Thus more professionalism in explicit analysis can assist Congress in finding disagreements and weak spots in executive branch recommendations and can increase the probability that Congress itself can initiate policy. These proposals, therefore, genuinely attempt to strengthen Congress rather than to weaken it.

My third suggestion is a simple endorsement of Representative Morris Udall's proposal to elect House committee chairmen at the start of each Congress. Udall's plan is not a return to king caucus. Rather, it provides for the selection of committee chairmen from a slate of the three most senior members of the majority party to be elected by secret ballot by all majority caucus members, with the ranking member on the minority side to be picked by a similar process in his caucus. This provides an institutional hedge against a too-arbitrary chairman, or one who is incapacitated or hopelessly out of step with his colleagues, without wholly vitiating the advantages of seniority or placing chairmanships in the hands of some centralized authority.

I have mentioned that the great advantage of the seniority system is that it decentralizes power in the House of Representatives by creating multiple centers of policy influence and increasing the number of good Congressional jobs. This adds to the incentives of the Congressional career. Proposals to centralize power must always be weighed against the damage they may do to this incentive system. Effective legislatures in world history have been fragile and rare. In most places and at most times legislatures have been little more than arenas for the registering of organized group interests or electoral colleges for cabinets. The Udall plan has the advantage of even further decentralizing power—to Congressional party rank and file—rather than placing it in the hands of party leaders, and thus this plan increases the general level of incentives for House members to make careers in the House.

These proposals recognize that institutions must provide means by which they can respond to outside demands, yet at the same time retain the capacity to exercise independent choice. They recognize the peculiar contributions the House and the Senate make, individually and together, to American politics, and seek to enhance the participation of these institutions in the processes of policy-making by improving their capabilities rather than destroying their power.

23

JAMES L. SUNDQUIST

MISSING CAPABILITIES: POLITICAL LEADERSHIP AND POLICY INTEGRATION

"The thing that is missing in the Senate today is that we get caught up so often in these day-to-day debates without a national or a broad perspective, without an overview, or foresight capacity." So complained Senator Bill Brock, Republican of Tennessee, cochairman of a committee established to reform the Senate's committee system, in 1976.[1] And the Democratic cochairman, Adlai E. Stevenson of Illinois, agreed:

> We are compartmentalists; we have sliced our daily routines into superficial fragments, and we have divided and subdivided large problems into a host of committee cubbyholes. It is no wonder that there is little consistency or coherence to what we do here. Do we have anything that could fairly be called a "policy" in such fields as energy conservation, environmental protection, or health care? If we do, it would be hard to find evidence of it in our fragmented committee system.[2]

That was in the fourth year of the congressional resurgence, but these were time-worn criticisms, by members of both houses. And they had led to the time-tested remedy: where "a broad perspective" and "consistency" and "coherence" were needed, the Congress had become accustomed to turn to an executive branch that at the top, in the person of a single individual and in the staff agencies that with him make up the presidency, has the capacity to blend and unify disparate views. So the Congress prescribed an annual executive budget as long ago as 1921, and subsequently, as it recognized the need for broad and integrated policies in other areas—economic growth and stability, national security, urban growth, and so on—it directed the president in successive acts to assemble and present those policies.

But these specific acts reflected, as well as abetted, the rise of the presidency to the preeminent position in American government and society that in the twentieth century it has come to occupy. The president has become the prime center of legislative initiation not merely because he heads the vast apparatus of the executive branch but, perhaps primarily, because he is given a mandate by the people as the political leader of the country. After his inauguration, he is expected by his opponents and supporters alike to restate authoritatively the philosophy and the programs that he presented in his victorious campaign—to pronounce the goals that he will seek, to define the programs and propose the allocation of resources to attain those goals, and to use his unmatched, and unmatchable, access to the media to mobilize public support. The short word for all this is to *lead*. By mid-century, what may be called the presidential leadership model was firmly in place. The president was accepted even as the legislature's own leader, expected to set the goals for its legislative sessions, to assemble the agenda, to plan the strategy for the passage of individual bills, to negotiate the necessary compromises, and then even to round up the votes for their enactment.

Within the presidential leadership model, the Congress had developed for itself a complementary role, which was more than one of simple followership. If the president in his program provided the broad perspective, the Congress contributed the narrow one; it examined the presidential program from the viewpoint of nearly half a thousand separate constituencies. The American congressman, deeply rooted in his state and district, constantly in touch with his constituents, individualistic, and not tightly bound to support any party line, specialized as *representative*, in the literal meaning of the word. The president proposed, from the national perspective, and the Congress disposed, from the perspectives of an aggregate of separate constituencies.

That was the implicit principle of executive-legislative relations that evolved in the age of congressional decline. The president would be the nation's policy planner and initiator. He would also be the decisive doer; when quick decision and action were required, he would be empowered to decide and to act. The Congress would not seek to alter the structural characteristics—cure the endemic weaknesses—that prevented it from fulfilling those roles. It would, instead, concentrate on doing what it does best, assigning to the executive branch those functions the latter could perform better.

When the system worked, the president set the general direction of national policy, and the Congress modified the specific policies and programs, to soften or enhance their impact on particular constituencies. The system did not always work, of course, for the president might not always lay out clear goals and programs, or the Congress might choose not to accept them if he did. At such times, the country entered one of the periods of "deadlock and drift" that James MacGregor Burns has characterized as the normal state of American democracy.[3] For there could be no alternative to presidential leadership, as long as the Congress had not organized within itself the capacity to proclaim an alternative set of national objectives and devise comprehensive and consistent programs to achieve them.

TURNING AWAY
FROM PRESIDENTIAL LEADERSHIP

The significance of the congressional resurgence of the 1970s is that it has challenged the fundamental concepts of the presidential leadership model. A resurgent Congress, by definition, is one that has turned away from its old dependence on the executive. But what, in the American system, is to take the place of presidential leadership? In its day of introspection and resolve, in 1973, the Congress did not confront that question in any abstract form. As always, its members were responding to a condition, not a theory. They knew the relationship they wished to overturn, concretely, but they were less clear as to the relationship they sought. While they denounced unilateral presidential government, only in their more extreme bursts of rhetoric did they talk of substituting anything like congressional government. When Senate Majority Leader Mike Mansfield declared, "The people have not chosen to be governed by one branch of government alone," he referred, presumably, to the legislative as well as the executive. The most common expression of a goal was "coequal" status for the Congress. What the advocates of change seemed to be groping for was a relationship of equality within which the two branches, harnessed somehow in tandem, would lead the government together. "The essential point," said one of the leaders of the debate, Representative Lee Hamilton, Democrat of Indiana, "is that the decisions of government, both domestic and foreign, be shared decisions."[4]

But when it came to defining that relationship in specific bills, over the ensuing years, the Congress had to confront the inherent fallacy in the conception. For the two branches can lead the government in tandem only when they agree on the direction it should go. When they agree, however, there is no problem with the old presidential leadership model. It is when they disagree that institutional relationships become crucial, because they determine the means by which deadlocks are broken, compromises forced, and when compromise is impossible which branch prevails. Who prevails on what matters defines the balance of power between the branches.

That balance of power was what the constitutional crisis of the Nixon years was all about. The policy differences between the president and the Congress were real, and they were sharpened by the struggle for partisan advantage. On some matters where the branches disagreed—welfare reform, for example—the usual deadlock ensued and could be accepted, for there was no compulsion for immediate action. But other issues simply had to be resolved. At any given time, the government had to have a budget and a fiscal policy. In its international affairs, it had to act, one way or another. When compromise could not be achieved, Nixon felt impelled to act to assure that the executive branch prevailed and, in so doing, shifted the balance of power decisively in favor of the executive. The Congress cried "usurpation" and moved to set the balance right, by its standards. That meant undoing not merely the specific shifts that Nixon had wrought but, to the degree it could, the whole of what it saw as forty years of continuous decline.

The congressional actions did not result in any tandem arrangements. As they grappled with specific problem areas, the advocates of change could set up institutional arrangements that encouraged consultation and a free flow of information, but in the end they had to assign responsibility clearly to one branch or the other in order to avert deadlock and permit the government to function. In fiscal policy, they claimed the last word for the Congress, by ending the practice of impoundment. In war powers, they conceded the first word to the president but instituted a procedure to require the Congress to affirm or reverse his course. Wherever the legislative veto was applied, they reserved the final decision for the Congress.

To assert its right to make the ultimate decisions, the Congress did not need to alter the role of the president as policy initiator. While Republican presidents were in office, the Democratic congressional leaders did encourage initiatives independent of the White House, but for reasons more of partisan than of institutional rivalry. "The Constitution does not require us to await proposals from the Executive Branch," Majority Leader Mansfield reminded the Senate at the opening of the heady Ninety-third Congress, in 1973, as he recited a list of pending issues, including measures vetoed by President Nixon the preceding year.[5] To an extent, in the next four years, the Congress did strike out on its own, most notably in developing and enacting its series of economic stimulus measures in 1973. But once the Democrats recaptured the White House, the democratic majorities lapsed back to their old habits. In a not untypical instance, when Senator Daniel P. Moynihan of New York learned in April 1977 that the new Carter administration would not be sending its welfare reform proposals to the Congress until autumn, he reportedly declared angrily that someone "with a first-rate mind and three months experience could draft legislation in a morning."[6] Moynihan had the experience and surely the mind—he was one of the principal authors of the Nixon family assistance plan of 1969—and presumably he could spare a morning. Yet neither he nor anyone else suggested that in a resurgent Congress the subcommittee on public assistance that he headed should draft its own bill. Moynihan himself would only promise to begin action immediately when the president's program arrived.[7]

The idea for a "summit" conference of business, labor, and other groups on the state of the economy early in President Ford's term originated on Capitol Hill, but the legislators prevailed on the chief executive to call it and preside over it. In this same period, Majority Leader Mansfield, appearing on national television, described graphically the congressional dependence on the executive on economic matters—even when that executive is the political opponent of the congressional majority. "We tried to do something about the inflation and the recession through advocating wage, price, rent and profit controls . . . and other matters, but we just can't seem to get the votes. That's why it is necessary, in my opinion, for one man, the President, to take the lead, and for the Congress to cooperate as much as it can." The lead has to come from the "chief of state," said Mansfield, because "535 men and women in the Congress cannot do so."[8]

None of the legislation that over the years had imposed on the president responsibilities to plan and to initiate was changed during the congressional resurgence. Even in setting up the congressional budget process, the Congress left intact the executive budget process it had established in 1921. The president still presents the budget as he always has, in the same form, and the new budget committees, like the appropriations committees, use it as a starting point. Moreover, the stream of directives to the president to prepare comprehensive plans, and the authorization of new units in the Executive Office of the President for the purpose, flowed unstemmed. In 1976 the legislators established in the Executive Office an Office of Science and Technology Policy, to assist the president in, among other things, preparing an annual report to the Congress and a legislative program dealing with "critical and emerging national prob- lems."[9] Senators who sought a national policy on "balanced growth" initiated legislation for a White House conference on the subject, to be convened by the president (and held in early 1978). In establishing the Department of Energy, the Congress directed the president to prepare and submit, by April 1 of each odd-numbered year, a National Energy Policy Plan. The Full Employment and Balanced Growth Act of 1978[10] specified that the president, in his annual Economic Report, should include numerical goals for levels of employment, unemployment, production, real income, productivity, and prices, and a program for achieving those goals. And the requirement for an annual report by the president on housing production objectives and a program of legislative and administrative action to achieve them, established in 1968 for a ten-year period, was made permanent.

Only in the Congressional Budget and Impoundment Control Act, among all these measures, did the Congress impose on itself the same requirement for comprehensive thinking and action. The case of the National Energy Policy Plan is particularly instructive, because sponsors of the idea—Senators Jacob K. Javits, Republican of New York, and John Glenn, Democrat of Ohio— originally proposed that the Congress do just that. As passed by the Senate, the president's plan would be referred to the "appropriate committees" in each house, which would modify the plan as they found necessary and desirable and report a joint resolution embodying the plan as modified. The Congress would then, by October 1 of the odd-numbered year, adopt a final plan, which would assure, said Javits, that the Congress would not revert to the "random and short-term energy policies that have been so characteristic of our actions in the past."[11] The weakness in the bill, however, was that, unlike the budget act, it did not create a centralized congressional machinery. Indeed, it did not even specify which of the existing committees would have responsibility for writing the joint resolution. So the Congress went on responding to crises, on a "random and short-term" basis.[12]

But while the Congress still looks to the president for comprehensive planning and for legislative initiative, it is in the response to that initiative that the relationship has changed. On decisions where the Congress once normally deferred to the president, in the 1970s it asserted its own views more aggressively and felt less compunction in substituting its judgment for the president's. A habit of deference, in other words, had given way to a habit of self-assertion.

Yet when the Congress deliberately turned away from the presidential leadership model that it had in large measure itself designed, it raised grave questions as to what might take its place. If the president was diminished as a leader, could the Congress fill the resulting vacuum? Could a legislative branch so long conditioned and organized to follow now step out in front and point the way? Two elements of the president's leadership responsibility are crucial: first, his position as the political leader of the nation; second, his function as integrator of the government's policies and programs. Neither of these roles, at the end of the resurgent 1970s, was the Congress prepared to play.

THE CONGRESS AS POLITICAL LEADER

"One of the most universal cravings of our time is a hunger for compelling and creative leadership," are the opening words of James MacGregor Burns's treatise on that subject. Leadership, he goes on, "is exercised when persons with certain motives and purposes mobilize, in competition or conflict with others, institutional, political, psychological, and other resources so as to arouse, engage, and satisfy the motives of followers."[13] In the presidential leadership model, it is the president who mobilizes the resources. Leadership in the presidency, Burns tells us, means identifying and enunciating the national values of liberty and equality, confronting "the overriding moral and social issues facing the country"—making that high office, in Franklin Roosevelt's oft-cited words, "preeminently a place of moral leadership."[14] As Burns acknowledges, some disagree that presidents ought to talk in moral terms about the national purpose and national values. But presidential leadership surely does consist, at a less exalted level, of defining national objectives, goals, and policies that "arouse, engage, and satisfy" the majority of the country. The Monroe Doctrine and the Truman Doctrine, the Emancipation Proclamation and the Atlantic Charter, the Fourteen Points and the Four Freedoms, the economic bill of rights and the war on poverty were all presidentially proclaimed goals that aroused, engaged, and satisfied the preponderance of national opinion—for a time, at least.

On a whole range of more prosaic matters, the country wants to be satisfied that it is heading, if not toward clearly defined goals, at least in the right general direction. It wants to be assured, at any time, that fiscal policy is sound, that the government is steering the economy wisely, that the United States is meeting its international challenges successfully, that tax and welfare policies are equitable, that the environment is protected, that the urban condition is being improved, that opportunities for human development are being extended. At this particular time, the country would like to think that its interminable energy problem is on its way to being resolved. All these are quite apart from leadership in crises like Iran or Afghanistan or Watts, when the people instinctively turn to the single individual in the White House as the only person who can unify the country and point the way.

In the presidential leadership model, it is the president who sets the direction of the country, who proclaims the policies and programs he contends will move the nation toward its goals. He does not do this arbitrarily, of course. He gets advice from a huge executive establishment and from a circle of close associates. He is sensitive to public opinion, he has the benefit of sophisticated polling data, and he tries to give the public what it wants. He listens to members of the Congress and to his own particular constituency. Sometimes he is more follower than leader. But, in any case, it is the president who in the end must announce where he means to take the country, and how he means to get it there. If he does not, the cry goes up, sooner or later, for "leadership," for "vision." Lack of leadership becomes a campaign issue and a president's challengers seek to displace or succeed him by promising a greater measure of the leadership the people want.

In the great quadrennial political competition, presidential leadership is legitimized—at times unmistakably mandated. In every presidential campaign, the candidates present their philosophies and their programs, and the people, in choosing one from among those candidates, decide the general direction of governmental policy. Sometimes they register their views incontestably, in favor of change or in favor of continuity, in a landslide election—as in 1932, 1936, 1952, and 1964—that endorses both the candidate for president and the congressional candidates of his party who share his policy commitments. After such elections, the presidential leadership model has every chance to work. The mandate is to a party as well as to a person, but the mandate to lead is clearly fixed—in the president. He was chosen for that purpose by the party itself, at its convention. He was the chief and only authoritative spokesman for the party, in the campaign. And he and his vice president were the only persons for whom the entire nation had the opportunity to vote.

In every less decisive election, however, the model is put on trial. In a split decision—and four of the seven elections from 1956 through 1980 chose the president and the majorities of one or both houses of Congress from opposing parties—who has the people's mandate? Even when the presidency and the Congress are of the same party, the presidential leadership model may be vitiated, if the president's victory is a narrow one. President Kennedy, in his brief term, found himself thwarted repeatedly by the conservative coalition. And President Carter, who ran weaker than the Democratic congressional candidates in virtually every state and district—and who, moreover, ran as an outsider to the party establishment—never won full acceptance as leader of his party in the resurgent and individualistic Congress of that time.

At all such times, when the presidential leadership model has been rejected—whether on principle during periods of divided government or as the consequence of defections from party discipline when majorities are small—there has been no alternative model of congressional leadership. The institutional structure of the Congress and its patterns of behavior have evolved to enable it to follow and to respond, but not to lead.

And that creates profound consequences for the democratic system. Even when the voters give the president an uncooperative Congress, he remains the only source of effective leadership, and the people understand that as a fact of life and expect him to be the leader. He is still the one person who presented a philosophy and a program to all the voters, asked for a mandate to lead the country in a more or less defined direction, and received it. The people sent him to Washington to take charge, and one of his jobs is to lead the legislature, to stop the incessant bickering and get things done. Even when they elect a president of one philosophy and congressmen of another, it is surely doubtful that the people are mandating deadlock and inaction. They may be expressing ambivalence and uncertainty, but they are more likely to be simply paying respect to incumbency or personal acquaintanceship in voting for Congress—particularly for members of the House. The superior mandate is still the president's.

If elections are to have meaning, then—which is to say, if democracy is to have meaning—the country must be able to make some progress in the direction the president told the people he would lead it, at least for the first two years until the voters can again express themselves. If it does not so move, the whole democratic electoral system has failed in its fundamental purpose: the people have not been able, by their votes, to set the course of government. The election, it turns out, did not make the difference that was promised; the voters might as well have stayed at home. Confidence is shattered, disillusionment sets in. One of the common complaints against Jimmy Carter throughout his term was that of "broken promises"—which in most cases reflected not a reversal of his own position but the rejection of his leadership by the Congress. So the normal rise of optimism that marks each quadrennial election and inauguration season was reversed more quickly than usual as President Carter failed to deliver on his pledges. And when Carter came down from Camp David in July 1979 and made his extraordinary televised speech deploring the national "malaise," his political opponents, at least, were quick to make the connection between the country's mood and the weakness of presidential leadership. As Senator Edward Kennedy opened his campaign against Carter, he made "leadership" the issue and found the "malaise" to reside "not in our people but in our leadership."[15]

Unless the presidential leadership model can somehow be restored, simply changing the occupant of the White House will not satisfy the "universal craving . . . for compelling and creative leadership." The Congress cannot make up the loss, short of radical changes in the constitutional and party systems. Alternative congressional structures tried out in the past are likely to be as faulty for the future as they proved to be when they were in effect. Stronger congressional leadership is not the answer: even if the trend of seven decades could somehow be reversed and the centralized power stripped from Czar Cannon and from Nelson Aldrich and his allies be restored to their successors, the new leaders still could not speak for all the people. The link that binds followers to leader was never forged through the process of a national election. So it was that when Cannon tried to govern the country from his post as speaker, Cannonism became an issue and Cannon inevitably lost. A modern speaker or Senate leader who sought to arrive at his policies through a truly democratic process—acting as spokesman for the party caucus and a representative party policy committee—would have a stronger claim to speak for the nation. Conceivably, leaders who renewed their mandates continuously through those instruments could compete with the president for public respect, particularly in a period of divided government. But for them to be effective in announcing, and then executing, a set of policies and programs would require radical change back to institutions and practices long since discarded in most of the United States: binding caucuses and party discipline. In other words, a new political party system would have to take form on Capitol Hill, and it could not emerge unless a new party system evolved in the states and districts that send their representatives to Washington.

In the meantime, the present party system moves toward an ever more rampant individualism. No one can speak with authority for the Congress as a whole, or even for either house. Probably more than ever before in its history, unless the Congress follows the president it emits a cacophony of sounds. In crisis, it does not act with sureness, with decision, unless the president sets its course. Between crises, it does not have a program, or goals, or a sense of direction, of its own, for it deliberately has looked to the president for those. In sum, to the extent that presidential leadership is rejected, there is no substitute.

THE CONGRESS AS POLICY INTEGRATOR

To give the country a sense of progress toward any of its accepted goals, leadership must mobilize institutional, political, and psychological resources, as Burns points out. The activities of the government must be concerted in support of the objectives, and where objectives conflict—energy development and environmental protection, for example—the opposing considerations must be balanced through open processes and with apparent equity. The government's programs must support its goals, functional or sectoral policies must be brought into consistency with broad objectives, decisions that affect one another must be related so that the totality makes sense. All this calls for policy integration, or planning. The lack of capacity of a fragmented Congress to perform this function is one of the endemic weaknesses of the legislative branch that led it to erect the edifice of the modern presidency, brick by brick.

In the presidential leadership model of American government, then, policy integration was made the responsibility of the presidency. Whether or not it has always performed that function well, the executive branch is at least well designed for the purpose. With its hierarchical structure, it can represent diverse views in the many departments and agencies but reconcile them in the Executive Office of the President, with a point of decision in the chief executive himself.

In its policymaking processes, of course, the executive branch may appear more rational and orderly than it really is. And in its rivalry with the Congress, every public relations advantage is with the executive. Its strengths are exaggerated in the communications process, its weaknesses can be largely hidden. If on a given policy situation it flounders in indecision for months on end, if it is stalemated by internal policy conflicts, if it finally yields to the demands of narrow special interests, if its ultimate product is badly compromised and sloppy, all those weaknesses are likely to remain partially or wholly concealed. Dissenters within the executive branch do not take their case to the public, unless they resign. Investigative reporters can report and columnists can gossip, but their findings rarely make the seven o'clock news. The first the public at large hears of a policy decision is normally when the president announces it. Then he speaks with decision and authority, and his presentation is so well organized and well documented that his policies appear to flow from a systematic, balanced, and orderly consideration of the public interest—and only that.

The Congress, in contrast, does its floundering in public. Every conflict, delay, stalemate, and hastily-arrived-at compromise is in the open. So is every concession to the lobbyists. And the Congress, unlike the executive branch, is bipartisan, which means that on the inside of its deliberations at every stage is a minority whose political mission is to discredit the majority—to expose its weaknesses, disputes, and indecision. And the president, who may have temporized a year or more before making up his own mind, always presses the Congress for instant action, once he announces his program, and appeals for help to the people directly and through the media. The contrast in the public view is between a president who knows what he wants and where he is going and a Congress that cannot seem to come to grips with the agenda he has given it. The Congress is bound to look worse, and the executive branch better, than each really is.

But after that is said, the fact remains that the executive branch does have the capability of being more decisive than the legislative branch when it has to be, and of bringing its policies into a more consistent whole, simply because it is a hierarchy. At the top is an authoritative Executive Office of the President where policies can be looked at in relation to one another and their conflicts reconciled. In charge of it all is a single individual—the president—with the power to say "This is it" and command his subordinates to fall in line with his decision.

Each autumn the executive branch goes through an elaborate process of policy integration, out of which emerges "the program of the president."[16] That program—and it is significant that it is viewed as a single program—is embodied at the beginning of each year in a series of state papers that are supposed to be, and in fact are in their major aspects, mutually reinforcing, with any serious contradictions usually discovered and ironed out. Beginning with the State of the Union Message, they include the Economic Report of the President and the Budget, followed by supplementary special messages spelling out specific legislative proposals. If the Congress rejects the program of the president, the question is whether it can substitute a corresponding, equally well-integrated, program of its own. Can it establish the necessary centralized institutions that it has lacked, and endow them with authority? If it cannot, if its own decisions lack national perspective and consistency and coherence, the resurgence of Congress must lead to an inferior policy product.

The problem of policy integration in the Congress appears at three levels: first, in each committee; second, in each house as a whole; third, between the houses.

The last of these is a territory almost wholly unexplored. To find a bicameral policymaking mechanism with broad responsibility one must go back more than a century, to the Joint Committee of Fifteen on Reconstruction. Recent years have seen only an occasional experiment, such as the Joint Committee on Atomic Energy, now abolished, and the Joint Economic Committee, which has never had legislative jurisdiction. In an era of fragmentation and individualism, the trend has been away from centralization of power even within individual houses, let alone in the Congress as a whole. Anyway, acceptance of presidential leadership of the legislative process by both houses made joint devices appear dispensable. Coordination of legislative policies and program was to be attained in meetings of the leaders of the two bodies at the White House with the president. Coordination of the details was to be left to committee chairmen and their staffs, with cabinet members and other administration officials acting as intermediaries if necessary.[17]

During the six Eisenhower and eight Nixon-Ford years of divided government, presidential meetings with the congressional majority leaders—when they were held—were limited in scope and inevitably took on the character of negotiating and communicating, rather than policy planning, sessions. Presidents discussed legislative strategy on controversial questions at separate meetings with the minority Republican leadership, and the Democratic majorities were left to their own devices to coordinate House and Senate legislative policies and programs. Nevertheless, even in these periods the Congress did not develop any new joint mechanisms for integrating policy. In designing its new congressional budget process, it did create a central research and advisory organization—the Congressional Budget Office—but the legislative responsibilities were assigned to separate committees in the two houses in the usual fashion. So in this as in all other fields of legislation (except atomic energy, when the joint committee was still in existence), policy differences between the two houses were negotiated piecemeal, by conference committees appointed separately for every piece of legislation. From 1977 through 1980, the executive branch resumed its former coordinating role.

At the committee levels and in the separate houses the Congress has periodically grappled with the problem of policy integration, through internal redistribution of power. The degree to which these experiments succeeded is an indicator of the potential of structural reform.

The Limits of Committee Restructuring

At the committee level, improvement of the capacity for policy integration has been sought through reduction in the number of committees and elimination of jurisdictional overlap. The reform temper of the 1970s invited new attempts to simplify committee structure on the pattern of the highly successful effort of 1946 and the less productive undertaking in the mid-1960s. The Bolling committee was established by the House in 1973 and the Stevenson-Brock committee by the Senate in 1976. The former presented a plan to rationalize committee jurisdictions that was, for the most part, rejected by the Democratic caucus,[18] but the Senate group was more successful. It managed to eliminate three standing committees, reducing the number from eighteen to fifteen. And through its recommendation to limit the number of subcommittee chairmanships each senator could hold—a proposal made more stringent through amendment on the Senate floor—the number of subcommittees was cut from 135 in 1976 to 100 in 1978 (compared to 121 in 1972). This helped.[19] But reducing the number of committees and subcommittees cannot begin to solve the problem of policy integration. Policy still has to be sliced into segments—if not 150, then at least 100 or so—and even if that number could conceivably be cut in half, virtually every major problem would still be bound to overlap the defined jurisdictions. Yet, except in the field of budget policy, there is no continuing institutional machinery for reassembling the segments of an issue for consideration whole.

One of the aims of the Stevenson-Brock enterprise, for example, was to bring into a single committee responsibility for as many aspects as possible of the newly emergent problem of energy. The old Interior Committee was therefore converted into a Committee on Energy and Natural Resources; the Joint Committee on Atomic Energy was abolished, and its nonmilitary jurisdiction, along with some of the functions of half a dozen other committees, were transferred to the new committee. Yet when President Carter sent his National Energy Plan to the Congress in 1977, a large element of the legislative action concerned taxation, which remained the responsibility of Finance, and the conflict between two blocs of senators led by two aggressive chairmen—Henry M. Jackson (Democrat of Washington) of Energy and Natural Resources and Russell B. Long (Democrat of Louisiana) of Finance—deadlocked the Senate members of the House-Senate conference committee for over a year. The result, in the end, was anything but a comprehensive and coherent program. To transfer jurisdiction over energy taxation to the Energy and Natural Resources Committee would not solve the overlap problem, of course, for then consideration of revenue policy would be divided.

The Bolling committee in the House, struggling with the same problem, had earlier proposed a similar solution—a new committee on energy and environment, to be built on the existing Interior and Insular Affairs Committee, with areas of jurisdiction transferred from several other committees, including Commerce. But environmental and consumer groups, fearing capture of the new committee by producer interests, rallied to defeat it.[20] A new House Select Committee on Committees, appointed in 1979 as a successor to the Bolling group and headed by Jerry M. Patterson, Democrat of California, conceived a more limited approach, proposing to promote Commerce's Subcommittee on Energy and Power to full committee status with only minor disturbance to the jurisdictions of other committees. Rejecting this approach, the House renamed the Interstate and Foreign Commerce Committee the Energy and Commerce Committee but left important aspects of energy legislation outside its scope. The locus of policy integration therefore remained largely as before, in the whole House as the mediator among committees.

Even where jurisdiction over particular problems can be nicely concentrated in single major committees, moreover, the committees have lost much of their power as integrating forces. The autocratic chairmen of the past, however one may view their other attributes, could coordinate and direct the work of their committees and control the product if they chose to do so and possessed the necessary skill and determination. But in the new democracy, most of the jurisdiction, and the accompanying staff resources, have been assigned to the subcommittees, and full committee chairmen have been reduced in many cases to a first-among-equals—some say to a figurehead—status. What comes to the floors of the House and Senate now is usually less a committee than a subcommittee product. It may be routinely approved by the full committee, through a logrolling process among subcommittee leaders. It is managed by the subcommittee, rather than the full committee, chairman on the floor. Committee members are less inclined to support the committee product as a matter of principle. Floor amendments are more freely offered, and more freely accepted. In sum, what begins as piecemeal consideration of problems in subcommittees of limited jurisdiction continues as piecemeal action all the way through the legislative process.

An occasional committee chairman with the right combination of knowledge, skill, charm, and untiring effort can still dominate his committee. Russell Long of Senate Finance was perhaps the chairman most often cited as a surviving embodiment of the baronial tradition, but even he was not always able to carry his control of events from the committee to the Senate floor. No matter what his personal qualities, Al Ullman could never have become the force as chairman of House Ways and Means that his predecessor, Wilbur Mills, was for so many years; too much of the institutional power of the Ways and Means chairman was deliberately stripped away when the committee was enlarged and directed to establish subcommittees, and when it ceased to function also as the Democratic committee on committees. To some degree, the power of every chairman has been similarly diffused.

The Use of Ad Hoc Committees

At the level of the whole house, the most promising innovation in policy-integration machinery—apart from the budget process—has been the use by the House of Representatives of ad hoc committees which cut across the jurisdictional lines of the standing committees to deal with broad problems. Both the Bolling and Stevenson-Brock committees were aware that the problem of overlap, and the need for policy integration, could not be met by a reshuffling of committee jurisdictions, no matter how designed. The solution devised by the Bolling committee, which was adopted by the House, gave the speaker additional control over the flow of legislation by authorizing him to refer bills to more than one committee simultaneously or sequentially, to create ad hoc select committees with the approval of the House, and to make "such other provisions as may be considered appropriate" to expedite the consideration of important bills.[21]

Ad hoc committees showed some early promise of evolving as a mechanism for policy integration. Such committees had been created on occasion in both houses in the past to make studies and prepare reports, but until the Bolling committee recommendation was adopted in 1975 they had not, in modern times, had *legislative* jurisdiction;[22] the combined power of the standing committee chairmen was sufficient to forestall any invasion of their domain. But, with the barons gone from the scene, Speaker Albert used the new authority once in 1975, and Speaker O'Neill twice two years later. All three proposals, carefully negotiated by the leadership with the leaders of the affected committees, were approved by the House without opposition. All are worth attention as promising designs for the development of a capacity for policy integration in both houses.

In the first action, Speaker Albert had the House create a Select Committee on the Outer Continental Shelf, with members drawn from three standing committees, to review and bring up to date the 1953 law that governed the development of oil and gas in the seabed. Headed by Representative John M. Murphy, New York Democrat, it produced a bill that set new rules for oil and gas leasing, which was rejected by the House late in 1976 but enacted in modified form in 1978. The committee's life was then extended into 1980 for purposes of oversight.

Speaker O'Neill's first experimental body, the Ad Hoc Committee on Energy, was not, in contrast, assigned original jurisdiction over energy legislation but instead sat in a review capacity over the bills reported by the regular committees. Most of the measures called for in President Carter's 1977 National Energy Plan were referred to two committees—Commerce and Ways and Means—but minor elements went to three others. All five, as well as two more that had some interest in the broad subject, were represented on the forty-member ad hoc body, which was chaired by Thomas L. Ashley of Ohio, a twenty-three-year veteran who was not identified with either the producer or the consumer side of the highly controversial energy issue and who could be counted on to work closely with the leadership. The other twenty-six Democratic members were "hand-picked" so as to make sure the committee would be "friendly" to the Carter program; "packed" was the Republican term for it.[23] In referring the measure's elements to the regular committees, O'Neill gave them a ten-week deadline—which all of them met. The president's program survived that stage almost intact, the main casualty being his proposal for an increase of five cents in the gasoline tax in any year during which consumption rose. The principal contributions of the ad hoc committee—which made its decisions through a caucus of its Democratic members—were to restore the proposed increase in the gasoline tax and to somewhat liberalize price controls on natural gas to stave off a move for deregulation on the floor. The strategy was half successful; the compromise on control of gas prices was accepted, while the gasoline tax lost. But all the other major elements of the Carter program survived the House. O'Neill, who had master-minded the entire exercise, was credited with an extraordinary feat of generalship in steering the whole complex package through the chamber in a bare three months. "A lot of people have been crying for leadership," commented Representative Toby Moffett, a second-term Connecticut Democrat. "And now they've got it."[24]

In the third experiment, O'Neill negotiated an arrangement with three committees for a combined "super-subcommittee" (as distinct from an ad hoc select committee) to consider the president's welfare reform program, transmitted to the Congress in August 1977. Headed by James C. Corman, Democrat of California, a Ways and Means committee member and supporter of the president's approach, the ad hoc subcommittee consisted of fifteen members of Ways and Means and seven each from Agriculture and from Education and Labor. In this case, however, the speaker set no deadlines. While the subcommittee served its purpose in holding a single set of hearings on the entire plan and in approving it nearly as submitted, the legislation subsequently bogged down in the three committees to which the Corman panel reported—particularly in Ways and Means, whose chairman, Al Ullman, had an alternate proposal.

The ad hoc structure served to facilitate negotiations with the White House, however, and in June 1978 a compromise was reportedly agreed on. But that turned out to be too late; O'Neill concluded that even if the scaled-down compromise measure could be put through the House, the Senate would not have time to act on it in that election year. So he pronounced the issue dead for the Ninety-fifth Congress. Despite the ultimate collapse of the effort, however, the structural device that was employed establishes a third useful precedent for the handling of complex problems where a comprehensive approach is required. The device did permit all of the facets of the welfare problem and the administration's proposed solution to be considered in an integrated way, and at the initial stage an integrated policy did emerge from the subcommittee. That the policy lacked sufficient support to pass the Congress does not reflect on the procedure.

With the Bolling committee recommendation as its model, the Stevenson-Brock committee recommended in 1976 that the Senate place in the majority and minority leaders, acting jointly, the same authority that the House had given to its speaker. But some members of the Senate Rules Committee, to which the Stevenson-Brock report was referred, contended that the leaders already had the authority to propose ad hoc arrangements at any time, and Majority Leader Byrd did not press the issue. If the power exists, however, it has not been used, and issues that overlap committee jurisdictions continue to be handled in a piecemeal fashion.[25] As a case in point, the Carter energy program that was put through the House with only minor modifications under the auspices of the Ashley committee was parceled out among Senate committees and nothing that could be called a national energy plan was ever put together. No significant energy legislation at all emerged in 1977, and after a deadlock that lasted throughout most of the next year the Carter plan was decimated, with no substitute congressional plan in its place. Thus ended an essay at national energy planning in the manner that the Senate itself had called for in the Javits-Glenn amendment to the Department of Energy Act of 1977.[26] In the House, Speaker O'Neill did not continue in the Ninety-sixth Congress of 1979–80 his experiments with ad hoc committees.

In sum, the period of congressional resurgence has brought about no fundamental improvement in the integrative capacity of the Congress, with the single, though major, exception of the budget process. The House and Senate Budget committees provide the perspective and the overview capacity that is missing elsewhere, and their budget resolutions are expressions of integrated policy, of general fiscal goals with which all program decisions are to be made consistent. What, then, is the potential for creating similar integrating mechanisms in other fields?

The Congressional Budget Process as a Model

When the Congress and the executive branch agree on their general fiscal policy—as during the Carter years—relations in this field resemble a modified version of the presidential leadership model. As party leader and chief legislator, President Carter was actually in a stronger position than were his predecessors, for the congressional budget committees exist to mobilize support for the party's consensus program and safeguard it from piecemeal damage. They provide a channel for orderly communication between the branches. Antagonisms are reduced and party cohesion improved, yet with the full participation of the assertive Congress.

But when the president and the congressional majorities are of opposite parties, or the branches disagree for other reasons, the budget process approaches what may be termed a congressional leadership model. In those times, when the president's fiscal policy is going to be overturned in any case, the new budget process enables the Congress to supersede the administration's integrated program with one of its own that is coherent also, assembled through a process not markedly less rational and orderly than the one the president used. That is what happened in the first two years of the act's operation, when Gerald Ford was in the White House.

True, the budget committees have no power of decision; they are on a par with other committees advocating other policy positions, and contested issues are ultimately resolved in trials of strength on the floors of the two houses between the broad and the particularist perspectives. But budget-makers do not necessarily have the last word in the executive branch either. There it is the president who balances the goals of fiscal policy against other policy objectives and makes the choices. This is as it should be. Fiscal policy is an element of national policy that has to be reconciled with other elements; it is not always, as those who seek to write the country's fiscal policy into the Constitution would have it be, the overriding element.

When the Congress each year completes the reconciliation process, and thus brings the fiscal consequences of every action into harmony with a general fiscal policy, it solves much of the total problem of policy integration. Once the fiscal reconciliation is achieved, the formation of tax policy, social security policy, agricultural policy, welfare policy, resource development policy, and so on can perhaps proceed well enough on a piecemeal basis, as they always have. If this means philosophical contradictions—government regulation being extended in some areas while being contracted in others, for example, or some programs being devolved to state and local governments while others are being centralized—that may be untidy but probably harmless enough.[27] Nevertheless, there are areas in addition to fiscal policy where the need for policy integration seems to be generally acknowledged. These include economic policy, urban or urban growth policy, environmental policy, and energy policy. Most crucial of all, perhaps, is the need for coordination of foreign and military policies—a need conceded when the Congress created the National Security Council in 1946. Then, in some aspects at least, foreign policy has to be linked to domestic policy, and energy policy and growth policy and fiscal policy all tied together. It is difficult to escape the conclusion that additional mechanisms are needed to enable the Congress to at least *consider* whether critical linkages exist among the policy decisions that it takes and, where it finds that the policies are interrelated, to make the decisions consistent. All of the arguments that have been accepted by the Congress for integrating all of the elements of fiscal policy can be put forward with equal force on behalf of integration in other policy areas—indeed, on behalf of integration of all policy into a "program of the Congress" that corresponds to the "program of the president."

There are severe limits, however, to the extent to which a model of congressional leadership could be applied. That model appears to be working in the field of fiscal policy; and in theory it could work in some other areas of domestic policy—such as urban growth policy, or energy policy, or economic policy. But it is not suited to national security and foreign affairs, or for linking foreign and domestic policy, for the reasons set out [previously]. And in domestic areas each new integrating committee inserted into the policymaking process compounds the total problem of integration at the same time that it may solve a segment of it. It is one thing to require that all policies have to be harmonized with a fiscal policy, but quite another to demand that they be harmonized with an energy policy, an urban policy, an economic policy, and perhaps an environmental policy, as well, and then that all of these be reconciled with one another. With each new integrating device that might be conceived for any one segment of the total policymaking process, the complexity advances by geometrical progression.[28]

Then what of a supercommittee to integrate them all and produce the *single* congressional program that would correspond with—and supersede if necessary—the program of the president? That, in one form, was what the Legislative Reorganization Act of 1946 contemplated, with its provision for a majority and minority policy committee in each house. But the idea failed then, and it would be rash to believe it would work better now. To produce an integrated program, the supercommittee would have to do more than react to policy proposals or individual bills after they came from the regular committees, which is about all the committees created since 1946 have ever done. It would have to do its work in advance, much as the budget committees now do, laying out the general policy and program to which—after adoption by the bodies—the regular committees would be obliged to conform. But such an undertaking would be all but impossible to fit into the already bulging annual congressional schedule. Moreover, it would require an extraordinarily able staff, which would have to be granted a large measure of power and influence, and that would hardly be acceptable to elected members of Congress who found their views overruled by mere employees. Even if the staff could be kept submerged, to place an effective power of program integration in an elite group of members in each house would run counter to all the forces that have produced the new individualism of the Congress. The other members, singly or in committees, would not be likely for long to submit peacefully to a supercommittee, even if they could be lured into creating it in the first place. The idea of a central policymaking apparatus for the Senate or the House has an engineer's simplicity of form, but the last time either house was organized on hierarchical lines was in 1910, and it turned out then that neither the members nor the public would stand for it. Since then, the centrifugal forces of individualism have gained strength with every passing year.

The capacity to produce a comprehensive and integrated program, then, remains missing in Congress. "The effort of the Congress to assert itself should not be misunderstood to mean that the Congress can truly become an equal branch of the government," Representative Hamilton said in 1974, in the early days of the resurgence. "It is simply too difficult for strong-minded, aggressive persons 'to get it all together' on all the issues on the nation's agenda. The Congress cannot control inflation, solve the energy shortage, or negotiate trade agreements. Congress may win some battles, restrain the President here and there, but it will remain essentially a body which confirms or rejects Presidential proposals, and reviews them after the fact."[29] That was an accurate forecast. Three Congresses later, Senator Gary Hart, Democrat of Colorado, was complaining: "In the Senate . . . we almost never debate what this country's long-term strategy is." "The United States has no trade strategy," declared Senator Stevenson shortly afterward. "It has no industrial policy. It has no food policy."[30] His criticism was directed at the government as a whole, not just at the Congress, but insofar as either branch felt a responsibility for developing long-term strategies on such matters, it was the executive. Except in the fiscal field, policy coordination remained, no less than before the congressional revolt against the Nixon leadership, a function delegated to the executive. The Congress remained compartmentalized, organized as the executive branch would be if the latter had only departments and no Executive Office of the President—indeed, no president. The independent work of individual committees and subcommittees cannot be integrated without instrumentalities for that purpose, and the conceptual and practical obstacles to creating such instrumentalities appear insuperable. Moreover, the motivation to take any decisive steps in that direction is lacking.

NOTES

[1] *First Report, with Recommendations of the Temporary Select Committee to Study the Senate Committee System*, S. Rept. 94-1395, 94 Cong. 2 sess. (U.S. Government Printing Office, 1976), p. 5.

[2] *Congressional Record*, September 30, 1976, p. 34018.

[3] *The Deadlock of Democracy* (Prentice-Hall, 1963), p. 2.

[4] *Congressional Record*, June 24, 1974, p. 4176.

[5] Ibid., January 4, 1973, p. 325.

[6] United Press International dispatch, April 26, 1977.

[7] *Congressional Record*, April 25, 1977, p. 11965.

[8] "Face the Nation," CBS television program, October 27, 1974.

[9] Public Law 94-282. This revived an office that President Kennedy had established by reorganization plan but President Nixon had abolished in a subsequent plan.

[10] Better known as the Humphrey-Hawkins Act, for its principal sponsors, Senators Hubert H. Humphrey and, after his death, Muriel Humphrey, both Democrats of Minnesota, and Representative Augustus F. Hawkins, Democrat of California.

[11] *Congressional Record*, May 18, 1977, pp. 15280–81.

[12] Anticipating the statutory requirement, President Carter had already come forward, in April 1977, with a document bravely—and misleadingly—entitled "The National Energy Plan." It was not

a *national plan*, at all, let alone *the* plan; it was only a proposal for a plan. And, in the absence of a congressional mechanism and process analogous to those created in the budget act, it never became a plan.

[13] *Leadership* (Harper and Row, 1978), pp. 1, 18.

[14] Ibid., pp. 389–90, xi.

[15] David S. Broder, *Washington Post*, November 19, 1979.

[16] In a year of presidential transition, the program is that of the outgoing president, but it is presented to the Congress with the same formality as though the incumbent president were continuing in office. And much of it survives the change of incumbents, for the presidency—as distinct from the president—has its own continuity.

[17] The *Washington Post*, April 22, 1978, relates an incident of shuttle diplomacy that is not atypical: "The separation of powers doctrine was fairly blurred Thursday night as congressional conferees on natural gas pricing . . . invited in the administration, in the person of Energy Secretary James Schlesinger, to help solve their differences. For much of the session, which lasted until 3 a.m., House and Senate members caucused in separate rooms . . . and Schlesinger in his shirtsleeves padded from one closed meeting to another trying to mediate differences and persuade one side or the other not to break off talks and go home."

[18] The work of the House Select Committee on Committees, chaired by Representative Richard Bolling, Democrat of Missouri, is analyzed by two former members of its staff, Roger H. Davidson and Walter J. Oleszek, in *Congress Against Itself* (Indiana University Press, 1977).

[19] The number remained at the new level in 1979–80. Meanwhile . . . the number of House subcommittees continued to rise, from 119 in 1972 to 144 in 1976 and 148 in 1979.

[20] Davidson and Oleszek, *Congress Against Itself*, pp. 176–78, 196–97, 212–13, 250.

[21] "Committee Reform Amendments of 1974," H. Res. 988, p. 35.

[22] The only exception in the preceding thirty years, apart from groups (such as the Bolling committee itself) set up to deal with internal House matters, was a select committee on survivor benefits for deceased members or former members of the armed services. David J. Vogler, "The Rise of Ad Hoc Committees in the House of Representatives," paper prepared for the 1978 annual meeting of the American Political Science Association.

[23] *Congressional Quarterly Almanac, 1977*, pp. 721–22. Richard Corrigan, "Carter's Energy Crusade Becomes Tip's Party Caucus," *National Journal*, vol. 9 (July 30, 1977), p. 1196.

[24] Corrigan, "Carter's Energy Crusade," p. 1197.

[25] The Senate had, of course, utilized devices for coordination directly between existing committees, as distinct from creating new committees. G. Calvin Mackenzie, "Committee Coordination and Policy Integration in the Senate," in *Committees and Senate Procedures*, papers prepared for the Commission on the Operation of the Senate, 94 Cong. 2 sess. (GPO, 1977), pp. 74–93, reports that 7 percent of all Senate public bills in 1975 were referred to more than one committee (but this device, he notes, does not ensure agreement, and if it is not reached, some other mode of coordination must be employed), that committees held 107 joint hearings, and that assignment of members of one committee to be ex officio members of another sometimes helped to bridge the gap between committees. He also reviews the use of temporary study committees, which he finds are usually "regarded as weak stepsisters in the legislative process" that rarely seek "to provide balanced and integrated responses to complex policy questions" (p. 87). Mackenzie recommends invigorating the majority Policy Committee as the arbiter of committee jurisdiction and the coordination of legislative action.

[26] In a letter to Majority Leader Mansfield in 1975, Senator Frank E. Moss, Democrat of Utah, pointed out that "twenty-six subcommittees held hearings or mark-up sessions on energy legislation in the first session of the 93rd Congress (1973) alone. This dispersal of responsibility prevented the Senate from developing a national energy policy." *Congressional Record*, February 18, 1975, p. 3344.

[27] The classic argument for achieving coordination of policy *without* benefit of an authoritative central mechanism—through "partisan mutual adjustment"—is Charles E. Lindblom's *The Intelligence of Democracy* (Free Press, 1965). But Lindblom acknowledges that neither mechanism is a complete substitute for the other, and that coordination of policy through central decisionmaking is the superior process in some circumstances (pp. 293–94).

[28] This is especially true if the integrating body is simply imposed on the existing structure without a rationalization of the whole—as was the case when the budget committees were established. If the Congress were being organized anew, it may be doubted that a three-tier structure would be designed, with budget, authorizing, and appropriations committees all involved in the major decisions on every program every year.

[29] *Congressional Record*, June 24, 1974, p. 4174.

[30] Ibid., daily edition, October 5, 1979, p. S14173; December 20, 1979, p. S19286.

24

RICHARD F. FENNO, JR.

CONGRESSMEN IN COMMITTEES

. . . We have begun our committee analysis by trying to find out what the individual members of each committee want for themselves from their present committee service. And we have found three quite different patterns, each of which gives special prominence to one of the three basic goals of House members. Furthermore, we found a remarkable consensus on goals among each committee's membership, a discovery that has persuaded us to ground our analysis here. Moreover, each of the three goals (and this was more fortuitous than planned) is the consensual one for two of our six committees. Appropriations and Ways and Means are populated mostly by influence-oriented members; Interior and Post Office are populated mostly by re-election-oriented members; Education and Labor and Foreign Affairs are populated mostly by policy-oriented members. Such modal characterizations are admittedly oversimplifications. But they do have sufficient validity to serve as a basis for predicting gross similarities and differences in committee behavior. Assuming that members will work in committee to achieve their stated goals, committees with similar goal patterns should display important similarities in behavior, and committees with different goal patterns should display important differences in behavior. More specifically, these similarities and differences should appear with respect to decision-making processes and decisions. But even such rudimentary predictions as these will hold only when "all other things are equal." And we know enough about committees to know that such a condition does not obtain. Most important, perhaps, we know that each committee works in a somewhat different environment. We need, therefore, to add this key variable to the analysis.

. . . The question now arises: how far do committee patterns that are based on members' goals correspond to committee patterns based on environmental constraints? That is, do committees whose members have similar goals operate in similar environments? The answer to both questions, we would now have to conclude is: "a little, but not much."

The two committees with distinctively influence-oriented members are also the two committees with the parent chamber as the most prominent environmental element. Similarly, the two committees whose members are re-election-oriented are also the two committees for which clientele groups are the most prominent environmental element. This is what we mean by "a little." On the other hand, for each of these two pairs of committees, there are some marked dissimilarities in environment. The policy coalitions facing Ways and Means are more complex and more partisan than those facing Appropriations. And the policy coalitions facing Interior are more complex and more pluralistic than those facing Post Office. In terms of their environments, the influence-oriented and re-election-oriented committees are as much unlike as they are like one another.

The environments of the two policy-oriented committees have almost nothing in common. The policy coalitions facing Education and Labor are more complex than those confronting Foreign Affairs. The environment of Foreign Affairs most closely resembles that of Post Office in its monolithic character. And the environment of Education and Labor most nearly resembles that of Ways and Means in its partisan character. Overall, within each pair of committees, one committee seems to confront a distinctly more complex, more pluralistic policy coalition than the other. The policy environment of the Ways and Means is more complex than that of Appropriations, that of Interior more complex than Post Office, and that of Education and Labor more complex than Foreign Affairs. As we move to describe committee behavior, we might expect it to be more difficult to predict the behavior of a committee operating in a complex environment than that of a committee, composed of members with the same goals, subject to a relatively simple set of constraints.

What seems most striking, in answering our earlier question, is the degree to which the environments of our pairs differ from one another. None of our three pairs, alike in member goals, is wholly alike with regard to the environment. We conclude, therefore, that the environmental variable is a largely *independent* one. It is not possible to predict the characteristics of a committee's environment by knowing only its members' goals. Nor is it possible to predict the goals simply by knowing the environment. Each variable can be expected to make an independent contribution in explaining a committee's behavior. And each must be investigated carefully. We do not mean there is no relationship between member goals and environmental constraints. The small degree of interconnection we have noted indicates that there are some linkages. And we would certainly expect that for any given committee, a change in one variable might produce a change in the other. But, clearly, each must be given independent weight throughout the analysis which follows.

. . . We have viewed the committee environment in terms of the influence outsiders have on committee members. But if one is searching for the antecedents of these external constraints, one finds that the subject of the policy and its associated characteristics must be given a central place. We have compared the relative prominence of four categories of interested outsiders. But we have found, again and again, that similarities and, more often, differences in their interest and prominence are related to the policy area itself. Our idea of "policy coalition" is intended to acknowledge the importance of policy subjects, without, at the same time, making them an independent variable of the analysis. Some readers will probably wish we had done just that—developed a classification of policy subjects and/or policy characteristics to serve as major independent variables. Those who feel this way should be encouraged to try. There is nothing in this study to challenge and much to confirm Capitol Hill wisdom that committee differences are related to policy differences. From the foregoing analysis, one might suggest that such policy characteristics as their importance to the parent institution, their salience, and their fragmentation would be useful categories. But we have chosen to compare committees at one level removed from their policy subjects because to do so helps us to advance the argument we have been making. We have given special emphasis to the goals of committee members; it is more in keeping with that emphasis to consider the environment in terms of people actively applying constraints to the members. From this perspective, policy subjects become important primarily because of the outsiders that take an interest in them and, hence, in the committee. It is obviously necessary to know about policy characteristics in order to locate the crucially important outsiders. But it is the outsiders that interest us most in this analysis. . . .

On every committee the members try to accommodate their personal goals to important environmental expectations and to embody this accommodation in broad, underlying guidelines for decision making. No two committees, it appears, will produce the same set of guiding premises. One explanation is, of course, that no two committees share the same set of member goals and the same set of environmental constraints. Another explanation might be that no two committees deal with the same area of policy. For, once again, we find differences among our variables related to differences in policy subject. In this chapter as in the previous one, however, we have conducted our analysis at one level removed from policy subjects. We have been interested, here, in the *perceptions* that each committee's members have of their policy area—on the assumption that members' behavior is based on members' perceptions of policy subjects and not on the objective characteristics of the policies themselves. At least we would argue this way until such time as a satisfactory categorization of policy subjects could be made from which one could deduce members' perceptions. For now, we might simply underscore the value of knowing: that Appropriations members perceive their subject matter to be nonideological, while Education and Labor members perceive their subject matter to be ideological; that Ways and Means members think of their business as freighted with consequences, while Post Office members think of their business as inconsequential; that Interior members view their policy area as specific and detailed, while Foreign Affairs members see theirs as general and vague. These differences in perceptions of subject matter help to account for differences in the decision-making processes of the committees. For example, the perceptions of subject matter held by Appropriations, Ways and Means, and Interior are more conducive to developing and sustaining expertise as a basis for decision making than are the perceptions held by the other three committees.

Despite the uniqueness of each committee's decision rules, two interesting patterns did emerge—interesting because both of them distinguish Appropriations, Ways and Means, and Interior on the one hand from Education and Labor, Foreign Affairs, and Post Office on the other. Each of the first three committees has achieved a consensus on its decision rules; each of the latter three committees has not. Furthermore, the decision rules of the first three committees are all, in one way or another, oriented toward insuring success on the House floor; the decision rules of the latter three are not. By *floor success*, we mean to include *both* House members' reactions to the content of a committee's decisions and House members' reactions to the committee as a decision-making collectivity. Obviously, the explanation for the two patterns—in terms of members' goals, environmental constraints, and strategic problems—differs within and across the two clusters of committees. We have tried to supply committee-by-committee explanations as we went along.

It may be that the two patterns are related. The more a committee concerns itself about floor success, the more likely it is, perhaps, to come to agreement on an operative set of decision rules. Or, perhaps, the greater its agreement on decision rules, the more likely will a committee enjoy success on the floor. Or it may be that the two patterns are not connected at all. Starting with the observation, however, we can ask whether the three high-consensus, House-oriented committees will display different decision-making processes from those of the three low-consensus, non-House-oriented committees. . . .

We have tried to demonstrate . . . that each committee's internal decision-making processes are shaped by its members' goals, by the constraints placed upon the members by interested outside groups, and by the strategic premises that members adopt in order to accommodate their personal goals to environmental constraints. One overall comparative dimension suggested by the independent variables of the analysis involves the relative impact of the members themselves and of external groups on decision-making processes. We might think of the dimension as *decision-making autonomy*. The greater the relative influence of the members, the more autonomous the committee; the greater the relative influence of outside groups, the less autonomous the committee. Making only the grossest kinds of distinctions, it appears that Ways and Means, Appropriations, and Interior are more autonomous decision makers than Foreign Affairs, Education and Labor, and Post Office. That is, members of the first three committees have a more independent influence on their own decision-making processes than do the members of the second three. For Ways and Means, we might mention the restraints on partisanship and the leadership of Wilbur Mills; for Appropriations, there are the specialization and internal influence of its subcommittees; for Interior, there are its participatory democracy and the leadership of Wayne Aspinall. The sources of committee autonomy are not always the same, but the result—a marked degree of internal, member control of decision making—is the same. With the other three committees, it is the environmental impact on decision making that seems most noteworthy. For Foreign Affairs, it is executive domination; for Education and Labor, it is the permeation of partisan policy coalitions; for Post Office, it is clientele domination. The three more autonomous committees emphasize expertise in decision making more than the three less autonomous ones, suggesting that perception of subject matter is related to decision-making processes.

The clustering of committees with regard to decision-making autonomy parallels the clustering noted in the last chapter, based on some similarities and differences in the committees' decision rules. Appropriations, Ways and Means, and Interior have, in common, a consensus on decision rules, a House-oriented set of decision rules, and decision-making autonomy. The three characteristics are probably closely interrelated. But the main thrust of our argument would be that the first two contribute to the third. When a committee's members agree on what they should do, they are more likely to be able to control their own decision making than when they cannot agree on what to do. When a committee's decision rules are oriented toward success (i.e., winning plus respect and confidence) on the House floor, the committee will have a greater desire to establish its operating independence than when its strategies are not especially concerned with floor success. House members, we recall, *want* their committees to be relatively autonomous, relatively expert decision makers. They are more likely, therefore, to follow and to respect committees that can demonstrate some political and intellectual independence of outside, non-House groups. Whether or not distinguishing the two clusters of committees will, in turn, help us to differentiate and explain committee decisions is a question we will keep in mind as we turn to a discussion of that subject. . . .

We have presented evidence to demonstrate that committee decisions do, indeed, follow those decision rules that each committee's members have devised to accommodate their personal goals to the constraints of their environment. That is, a committee's decisions are explainable in terms of its members' goals, the constraints of its environment, its decision strategies, and—to a lesser, refining degree, perhaps—by its decision-making processes. Enough evidence has been mustered, we hope, to lend strength to the line of argument we have pursued. We have not, of course, *proven* anything, for we have not tried very determinedly to muster a contrary body of evidence. Those who find themselves resisting our selective use of evidence are invited to provide counterexamples and to fashion another line of argument. We hope that what we have presented will seem worth that kind of further development and testing.

To the degree that a committee's decisions follow its decision rules, committee members and the most interested outside groups should be reasonably satisfied with committee performance. For those rules are, after all, an effort to accommodate the views of each. We have not found a measure of satisfaction that would allow us to describe and compare amounts of internal and/or external satisfaction. But we have detected varying degrees of it. For member satisfaction, a necessary condition would seem to be committee *activity*. No member goal can be achieved without some minimal level of activity. Post Office members' dissatisfaction arose because that Committee slipped below an acceptable level of activity; it "wasn't doing anything." Foreign Affairs has simmered with dissatisfaction because its members have felt they "weren't doing enough." Both would have been satisfied with increased activity. The other committees have been active. For Education and Labor members, indeed, their increased activity was the basis for their newly found satisfaction in the Powell years.

Members of our other three committees require an additional condition for their satisfaction. They feel the need to make an *independent* contribution to decision making. Especially, they want to feel a measure of independence relative to the executive branch—in both an institutional and a policy sense. They want to preserve autonomous decision-making processes and they want to develop substantive expertise. When they do achieve such independence, they develop a psychological feeling of group identity, which further strengthens their independence. Ways and Means, Appropriations, and Interior members' satisfaction, then, seems to be based on both their *activity* and their *independence*. During the period studied, these three committees maintained a higher and steadier level of satisfaction with their own performance than did the three other committees.

It is hard to generalize about the conditions of satisfaction for the groups comprising the environment. Perhaps it is enough to remind ourselves, again, that individual committees face quite varied sets of environmental constraints. For two of our committees, the institutional constraints of the parent chamber are most important. House expectations call for a balance between autonomous and responsive decision making. And, so far, Ways and Means and Appropriations seem to have maintained a balance satisfactory to House leaders and House majorities. For the other four, the policy coalitions of their environments are more important. But dominance in those policy coalitions varies, so that the expectations confronting the four committees also vary. The executive-led coalition confronting Foreign Affairs wants legitimation plus assessments of political feasibility. The clientele-led coalitions facing Interior and Post Office want access to members plus sympathetic committee member spokesmen. The party-led coalitions facing Education and Labor want all these things plus a partisanship that will abet victory at the polls. How can we compare levels of satisfaction across such diverse expectations? Is the executive branch more satisfied with the legitimation it gets than clientele groups are with the spokesmanship they get? All we can say is that the leaders of each coalition do seem pretty well satisfied with the committees that interest them—the executive with Foreign Affairs, the postal employees with Post Office, all but the preservationist groups with Interior, the Democrats and Republicans with Education and Labor.

Looking across the six committees, some of the gross similarities and differences noted earlier do appear to carry through to their decisions. That is, Ways and Means, Appropriations, and Interior remain strikingly similar to one another and strikingly different from Education and Labor, Foreign Affairs, and Post Office. The three committees with a consensus on House-oriented decision rules do seem to be more successful on the House floor than the three committees whose decision rules are not House-oriented. Members of the same three, more autonomous committees express a greater overall satisfaction with their committee's decision processes and decisions than do the members of the three less autonomous committees with theirs. And from the autonomy and satisfaction of the first three flows a sense of corporate identity and corporate pride that is missing in the three less autonomous, less satisfied committees. On the other hand, the decisions of our three less autonomous committees seem to bring relatively greater satisfaction to interested and influential environmental groups than do the decisions of our three more autonomous committees. Education and Labor, Foreign Affairs, and Post Office are more permeable and, hence, relatively more responsive to the wishes of people outside the Congress than are Ways and Means, Appropriations, and Interior.

Utilizing these *relative* distinctions, we find two types of House committees. One type is identified by the House orientation of its decision rules, the autonomy of its decision-making processes, its emphasis on committee expertise, its success on the House floor, its members' sense of group identity, and the relatively higher ratio of member to nonmember satisfaction with its performance. The other type is identified by its extra-House-oriented decision rules, the permeability of its decision-making processes, the de-emphasis on committee expertise, its lack of success on the House floor, the absence of any feeling of group identification, and the relatively higher ratio of nonmember to member satisfaction with its performance.

Since no committee falls completely into one category or the other, we probably should think of these as "ideal types" toward which committees tend—a *corporate* type, on the one hand, and a *permeable* type, on the other. Committees of the corporate type tend to be more influential but less responsive than permeable committees. Permeable committees tend to be more responsive but less influential than corporate committees. Ways and Means, Appropriations and Interior come closest to the corporate type of committee. Education and Labor, Foreign Affairs, and Post Office come closest to the permeable type of committee. And, we might add, all Senate committees tend toward the permeable category. There are no corporate committees in the Senate.

25

DAVID R. MAYHEW

CONGRESSIONAL ELECTIONS: THE CASE OF THE VANISHING MARGINALS

Of the electoral instruments voters have used to influence American national government few have been more important than the biennial "net partisan swing" in United States House membership. Since Jacksonian times ups and downs in party seat holdings in the House have supplied an important form of party linkage.

The seat swing is, in practice, a two-step phenomenon. For a party to register a net gain in House seats there must occur (*a*) a gain (over the last election) in the national proportion of popular votes cast for House candidates of the party in question. That is, the party must be the beneficiary of a national trend in popular voting for the House.[1] But there must also occur (*b*) a translation of popular vote gains into seat gains.[2] Having the former without the latter might be interesting but it would not be very important.

The causes of popular vote swings have only recently been traced with any precision. There is voter behavior that produces the familiar mid-term sag for parties in control of the presidency.[3] There is the long-run close relation between changes in economic indices and changes in the House popular vote.[4] There are doubtless other matters that can give a national cast to House voting, including wars.[5]

The consequences of partisan seat swings (built on popular vote swings) have been more elusive but no less arresting. As in the case of the Great Society Congress (1965–1966), House newcomers can supply the votes to pass bills that could not have been passed without them. Presidents with ambitious domestic programs (Woodrow Wilson, Franklin Roosevelt, Lyndon Johnson) have relied heavily on the votes of temporarily augmented Democratic House majorities. No clear argument can be made, of course, that a bill-passing binge like that of 1965–1966 offers a direct conversion of popular wishes into laws. The evidence is more ambiguous. At the least a House election like the one of 1964 produces a rotation of government elites that has policy consequences; at the most there is some detectable relation between what such temporarily empowered elites do and what popular wishes are. Over time the working of the seat swing has sometimes given a dialectical cast to national policy-making, with successive elites making successive policy approximations. A case in point is the enactment of the Wagner Act in the Democratic Seventy-fourth Congress followed by its Taft-Hartley revision in the Republican Eightieth. Because of all the translation uncertainties the House seat swing has been a decidedly blunt voter instrument, but it has been a noteworthy instrument nonetheless.

The foregoing is a preface to a discussion of some recent election data. The data, for the years 1956–1972, suggest strongly that the House seat swing is a phenomenon of fast declining amplitude and therefore of fast declining signif-icance. The first task here will be to lay out the data—in nearly raw form—in order to give a sense of their shape and flow. The second task will be to speculate about causes of the pattern in the data, the third to ponder the implications of this pattern.

I

The data are presented in Figure 25-1, an array of 22 bar graphs that runs on for five pages. If the pages are turned sideways and read as if they were one long multi-page display, the graphs appear in three columns of nine, nine, and four. It will be useful to begin with an examination of the four graphs in the right-hand column.

Each of the four right-hand graphs is a frequency distribution in which congressional districts are sorted according to percentages of the major-party presidential vote cast in them in one of the four presidential elections of the years 1956–1968.[6] The districts are cumulated vertically in percentages of the total district set of 435 rather than in absolute numbers. The horizontal axis has column intervals of five percent, ranging from a far-left interval for districts where the Democratic presidential percentage was 0–4.9 to a far-right interval where the percentage was 95–100. Thus the 1956 graph shows that the Stevenson-Kefauver ticket won 50 to 54.9 percent of the major-party vote in about 7 percent of the districts (actual district N = 30) and a modal 40 to 44.9 percent of the vote in about 20 percent of the districts (actual N = 87).

In themselves these presidential graphs hold no surprises; they are presented for the purpose of visual comparison with the other data. The presidential mode travels well to the left of the 50 percent mark in 1956 and well to the right in 1964, but the four distributions are fundamentally alike in shape—highly peaked, unimodal, not far from normal.

The center and left columns give frequency distributions, organized on the same principles as the four presidential graphs, in which House districts are sorted according to percentages of the major-party House vote cast in them in each of the nine congressional elections in the years 1956–1972. But for each House election there are two graphs side by side. For each year the graph in the left column gives a distribution of returns for all districts in which an incumbent congressman was running, the center column a set of returns for districts with no incumbents running.[7]

The center graphs, the "open seat" distributions, are erratically shaped because the N's are small. The number of House districts without incumbents

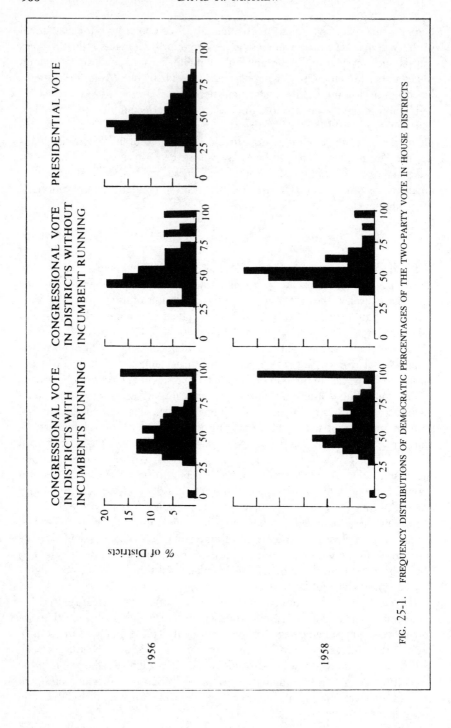

FIG. 25-1.   FREQUENCY DISTRIBUTIONS OF DEMOCRATIC PERCENTAGES OF THE TWO-PARTY VOTE IN HOUSE DISTRICTS

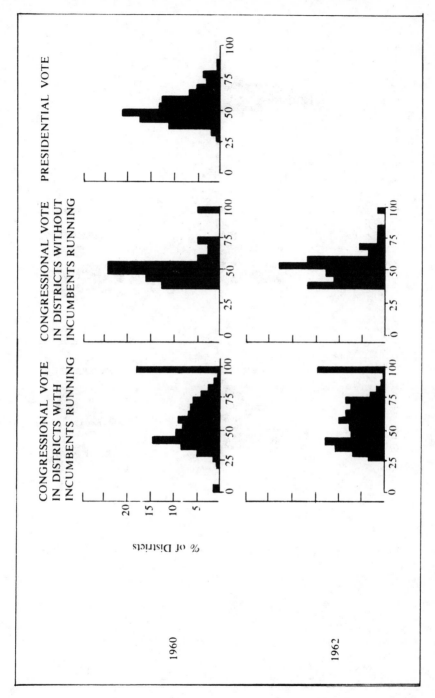

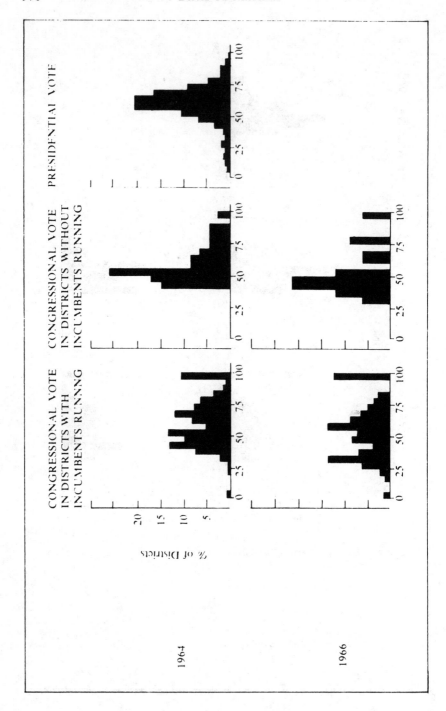

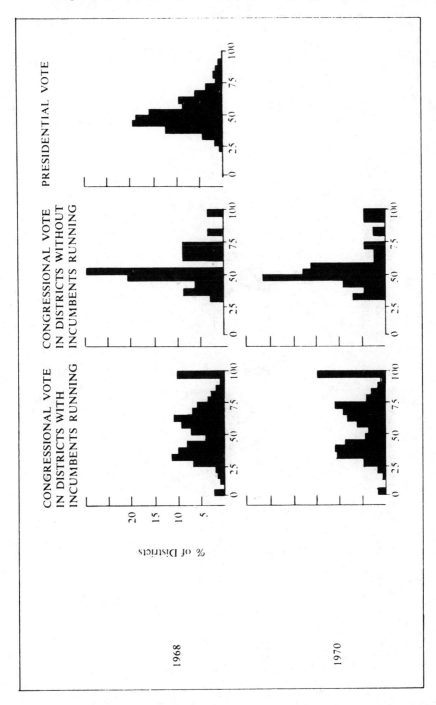

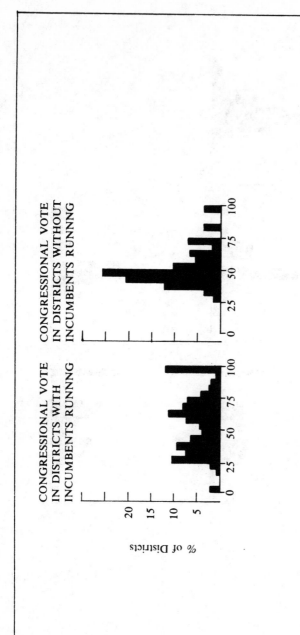

running averages 43 (about a tenth of the membership) and ranges from 31 (in 1956) to 59 (in 1972); there is no discernible upward or downward trend in the series. With allowances made for erratic shape these nine "open seat" distributions are much alike. All are highly peaked and centrally clustered. In 1958 and 1968 nearly 30 percent of the readings appear in the modal interval (in both cases the 50–54.9 percent Democratic interval). Over the set of nine elections the proportion of "open seat" outcomes falling in the 40–59.9 percent area ranges from 54.8 percent to 70.2 percent, the proportion in the 45–54.9 percent area from 29.0 percent to 50.1 percent. All of which imparts the simple and obvious message that House elections without incumbents running tend to be closely contested.

The nine graphs in the left-hand column give distributions for districts with incumbents running.[8] Thus in 1956 about 9 percent of districts with incumbents running yielded returns in the 45–49.9 percent Democratic interval. In some of these cases the incumbents were Democrats who thereby lost their seats; in any of these nine graphs the election reading for a losing incumbent will appear on what was, from his standpoint, the unfortunate side of the 50 percent line. In an Appendix the nine data sets are disaggregated to show where in fact incumbents lost.

Immediately visible on each of these incumbency graphs is the isolated mode in the 95–100 percent interval, recording the familiar phenomenon of uncontested Democratic victories—mostly in the South. But, if these right-flush modes can be ignored for a moment, what has recently been happening in the contested range is far more interesting. In 1956 and 1960 the distributions in the contested range are skewed a little to the right, but still not far from normal in shape. In the 1958 and 1962 midterm years the distributions are somewhat flatter and more jagged.[9] In 1964 and 1966 they appear only tenuously normal. In 1968, 1970, and 1972 they have become emphatically bimodal in shape. Or, to ring in the uncontested Democratic seats again, the shape of incumbency distributions has now become strikingly trimodal. Thus in the 1972 election there was a range of reasonably safe Republican seats (with the 25–29.9 percent and 35–39.5 percent intervals most heavily populated), a range of reasonably safe Democratic seats (peaked in the 60–64.9 percent interval), and a set of 44 uncontested Democratic seats.

The title of this paper includes the phrase, "The Case of the Vanishing Marginals." The "vanishing marginals" are all those congressmen whose election percentages could, but now do not, earn them places in the central range of these incumbency distributions. In the graphs for the most recent elections the trough between the "reasonably safe" Republican and Democratic modes appears in the percentage range that we are accustomed to calling "marginal." Figure 25-2 captures the point, with time series showing how many incumbent congressmen have recorded percentages in the "marginal" range in each election from 1956 through 1972.[10] The lower series on the two Figure 25-2 graphs show, for comparative purposes, the number of "open seat" outcomes in the marginal range. In one graph marginality is defined narrowly (45–54.9 Democratic percentage of the major-party vote), in the other broadly

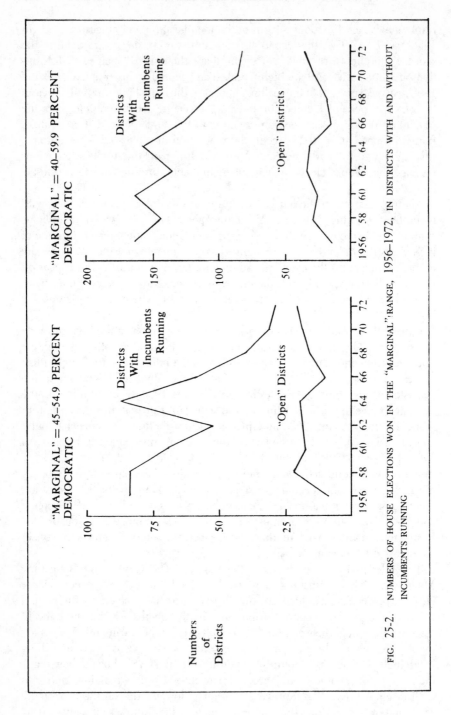

FIG. 25-2.   NUMBERS OF HOUSE ELECTIONS WON IN THE "MARGINAL" RANGE, 1956–1972, IN DISTRICTS WITH AND WITHOUT INCUMBENTS RUNNING

(40–59.9 percent). By either definition the number of incumbents running in the marginal zone has roughly halved over the sixteen-year period.[11] For some reason, or reasons, it seems to be a lot easier now than it used to be for a sitting congressman to win three-fifths of the November vote.

II

Why the decline in incumbent marginality? No clear answer is available.[12] Adding complexity to the problem is the fact that the proportion of House seats won in the marginal range has been slowly declining for over a century.[13] Whatever mix of causes underlies the long-run change could account for much of the rapid current change as well. On the assumption that the contemporary decline is not ephemeral, perhaps the most useful thing to do here is to set out some hypotheses which may singly or in combination account for it. Five hypotheses are offered below. Some have a more persuasive ring than others; none is wholly implausible. The first has to do with district line-drawing, the next three with congressmen's actions designed to attract votes, the last with voter behavior not inspired by congressmen's actions.

(1) The line-drawing explanation is easy to reach for. In the last decade of chronic redistricting the possibility of building districts to profit incumbents has not been lost on House members or others acting in their interest. With county lines less sacred than they once were, ingenious districts can be and have been drawn. And there are good examples of cross-party districting deals among congressmen of large state delegations.[14] But the problem with the line-drawing hypothesis is that it seems not to explain very much. Manipulation of the aggregate national data does not yield an impressive relation between redistricting and electoral benefit.[15] Moreover, if voters are being partitioned into safe House districts it can be argued that bimodal patterns ought to appear sooner or later in presidential and "open seat" distributions of the sort displayed in Figure 25-1. Of bimodalism the relevant Figure 25-1 graphs give no trace, although it must be said that the evidence is inconclusive. The evidence on redistricting generally is incomplete and inconclusive. But the odds are that it will not explain very much. If all 435 congressmen were suddenly to retire in 1974, and if elections to replace them were conducted in the 1972 district set, the odds are that a distribution of new member percentages would look like a presidential or an evened out "open seat" distribution—unimodal and roughly normal, though perhaps still with a modest isolated mode for uncontested Southerners.

The next four hypotheses hinge on the assumption that House incumbency now carries with it greater electoral advantages than it has in the past. There is evidence that it does.[16] One way to try to find out is to look at what happens to party fortunes in districts where congressmen die, retire, or lose primaries—to compare the last November percentages of veteran incumbents with the percentages of their successor nominees. Table 25-1 does this for the six elections in the years 1962–1972. Figures are given for transitions in which the retirees were at least two-term veterans and where the bracketing elections were both contested by both parties. It is hard to tease conclusions out of these data; the

TABLE 25-1. CHANGE IN PARTY PERCENTAGE IN HOUSE DISTRICTS WHERE INCUMBENTS HAVE RETIRED, DIED, OR LOST PRIMARIES

| | Transitions in Districts without Line Changes | | | | | | Transitions in Districts with Line Changes | |
| | DEMOCRATIC DISTRICTS | | REPUBLICAN DISTRICTS | | ALL DISTRICTS | | ALL DISTRICTS | |
	N	MEAN	N	MEAN	N	MEAN	N	MEAN
1962	(4)	−5.2	(4)	−0.2	(8)	−2.7	(9)	+1.3
1964	(12)	+5.5	(13)	−8.2	(25)	−1.6	*	
1966	(3)	−6.2	(3)	−2.5	(6)	−4.3	(7)	−7.7
1968	(4)	+1.1	(3)	−14.9	(7)	−5.8	(12)	−8.6
1970	(15)	−4.9	(17)	−7.9	(32)	−6.5	(4)	−5.7
1972	(2)	−26.7	*		(2)	−26.7	(25)	−9.5

Transitions in Districts with and without Line Changes

| | DEMOCRATIC DISTRICTS | | REPUBLICAN DISTRICTS | | ALL DISTRICTS | | ALL DISTRICTS | | ALL DISTRICTS | |
| | | | | | | | | WGHT'D | | |
	N	MEAN	N	MEAN	N	MEAN	N	MEAN	N	MEDIAN
1962	(5)	−6.0	(12)	+1.8	(17)	−0.5	(17)	−2.1	(17)	−3.1
1964	(12)	+5.5	(13)	−8.2	(25)	−1.6	(25)	−1.3	(25)	−3.1
1966	(8)	−8.9	(5)	−1.8	(13)	−6.2	(13)	−5.4	(13)	−8.2
1968	(10)	−1.4	(9)	−14.5	(19)	−7.6	(19)	−8.0	(19)	−4.7
1970	(19)	−5.1	(17)	−7.9	(36)	−6.4	(36)	−6.0	(36)	−5.6
1972	(12)	−13.1	(15)	−9.0	(27)	−10.8	(27)	−11.1	(27)	−10.2

universes for the six elections are small, the districts in each inter-election set vary widely in their change percentages, national trends affect Democrats and Republicans differently, and there is the redistricting problem throughout. But these are all of the data there are on the point. Most of the columns in the table include figures on districts with line changes. Including these raises the obvious problem that redistricting itself can affect party percentages. But there is some justification for the inclusion. For one thing, no systematic difference appears here between what happens electorally in redrawn and untouched districts. For another, it is impossible to get any reading at all on the 1972 election without inspecting the redrawn districts; 25 of the 27 "succession nominations" occurred in 1972 in districts with line changes. If handled carefully the altered districts can yield information. Redrawn districts are covered here if they were treated in the press as being more or less "the same" as districts preceding them; thus, for example, Paul Cronin is commonly regarded as Bradford Morse's successor in the fifth Massachusetts district although Cronin's 1972 boundaries are somewhat different from Morse's old ones.

What to look for in Table 25-1 is whether switches in party nominees bring about drops in party percentages. The bigger the drop the higher the putative value of incumbency. Inter-election changes in party percentage are calculated here by comparing party shares of the total congressional district vote in the bracketing elections.[17] The first three columns in the table give data only on districts without line changes. Thus in 1962 there were four Democratic retirements (or deaths, etc.) in districts with 1960 lines intact; the Democratic share of the total vote fell an average of 5.2 percent in these four districts between 1960 and 1962. In the four Republican retirement districts in 1962 the Republican share of the total vote fell an average of 0.2 percent. In 1964 there was an understandable party gain in the Democratic retirement districts, and an especially heavy mean loss in the Republican set. Fortuitously the numbers of retirement districts for the two parties are almost identical in each of the five elections in 1962 through 1970, so it makes sense to calculate mean change values for all retirement districts regardless of party in each year in order to try to cancel out the effects of election-specific national trends. This is done in the third column, a list of cross-party percentage change means for the six elections. (Thus in 1964 the average change in the 25 retirement seats was a negative 1.6 percent even though the average party values were far apart; Republicans generally lost more in their transitions than Democrats gained in theirs.) Here there emerges some fairly solid evidence. Mean drops in percentage were higher in 1966, 1968, and 1970 than in 1962 and 1964. (1972, with its N of 2, can be ignored.) The best evidence is for 1964 and 1970, with their large N's. Loss of incumbents cost the parties a mean of 1.6 percent in 1964, a mean of 6.5 percent in 1970.

In the fourth column figures on transitions in redrawn districts are introduced. The values are mean changes for redrawn retirement districts by year regardless of party. It will be seen that these values differ in no systematic way from the values for undisturbed districts in the third column. There is the same general trend toward bigger drops in percentage. Especially striking is the 1972 value of minus 9.5 percent, lower than any other reading in the list of values for redrawn districts. The fifth, sixth, and seventh columns of the table give mean values by year, respectively, for Democratic, Republican, and all retirement districts, with no distinctions being made between altered and unaltered districts. The eighth column gives a weighted mean for each year, a simple average of the party averages. Finally the ninth column gives a median value for the set of all readings in each year.

These readings, tenuous as they are, all point in the same direction. Incumbency does seem to have increased in electoral value, and it is reasonable to suppose that one effect of this increase has been to boost House members of both parties out of the marginal electoral range. If incumbency has risen in value, what accounts for the rise? The second, third, and fourth hypotheses below focus on electorally useful activities that House members may now be engaging in more effectively than their predecessors did ten or twenty years ago.

(2) House members may now be advertising themselves better. Simple name recognition counts for a lot in House elections, as the Survey Research Center data show.[18] A name perceived with a halo of good will around it probably counts for more. If House members have not profited from accelerated advertising in the last decade, it is not from want of trying. The time series in Figure 25-3 shows, in millions of pieces, how much mail was sent out from the

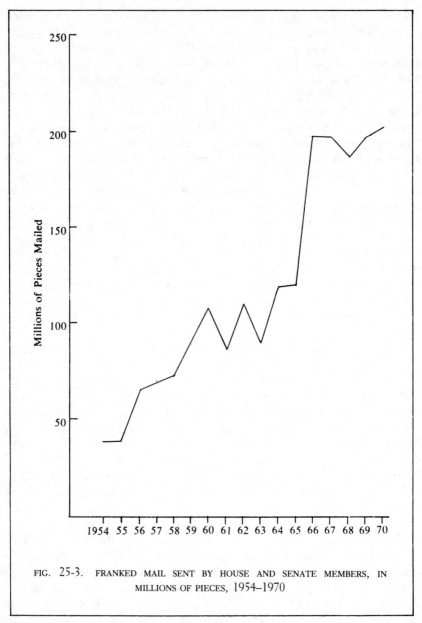

FIG. 25-3.   FRANKED MAIL SENT BY HOUSE AND SENATE MEMBERS, IN MILLIONS OF PIECES, 1954–1970

SOURCE: U.S. Congress, House, Committee on Appropriations, *Hearings Before a Subcommittee of the Committee on Appropriations, Legislative Branch Appropriations for 1970*, 91st Cong., 1st sess., 1969, ·p. 501 has 1954–1968 data. Subsequent annual hearings update estimated franking use.

Capitol (by both House and Senate members) in each year from 1954 through 1970.[19] The mail includes letters, newsletters, questionnaires, child-care pamphlets, etc., some of them mailed to all district box-holders. Peak mailing months are the Octobers of even-numbered years. Mail flow more than sextupled over the sixteen-year period, with an especially steep increase between 1965 and 1966. In fact the mail-flow curve matches well any incumbency-advantage curve derivable from the data in Table 25-1. There is no let-up in sight; one recent estimate has it that House members will send out about 900,000 pieces of mail per member in 1974, at a total public cost of $38.1 million.[20] So the answer to the incumbency advantage question could be a remarkably simple one: the more hundreds of thousands of messages congressmen rain down on constituents the more votes they get. Whether all this activity has significantly raised the proportion of citizens who know their congressmen's names is uncertain. There are some Gallup readings showing that the share of adults who could name their congressmen rose from 46 to 53 percent between 1966 and 1970.[21]

(3) Another possibility is that House members may be getting more political mileage out of federal programs. The number of grant-in-aid programs has risen in the last decade at something like the rate of Capitol mail flow. The more programs there are, the more chances House members have to claim credit ostentatiously for the local manifestations of them—housing grants, education grants, anti-pollution grants, etc.

(4) Yet another possibility is that House members have become more skilled at public position-taking on "issues." The point is a technological one. If more congressmen are commissioning and using scientific opinion polls to plumb district sentiment, then House members may have become, on balance, more practiced at attuning themselves to district opinion.[22] There is a possibility here, however hard it is to try to measure. There may be a greater general sophistication today about polling and its uses. In 1964, forty-nine Republican House members running for re-election signed a pre-convention statement endorsing Senator Goldwater. It was claimed that Goldwater's nomination would help the party ticket. The forty-nine suffered disproportionately in November.[23] In 1972 there was no comparable rush among House Democrats to identify themselves with Senator McGovern.

(5) The fifth and last hypothesis has to do with changes in voter behavior not inspired by changes in incumbent activities. It is possible that incumbents have been profiting not from any exertions of their own but from changes in voter attitudes. A logic suggests itself. Voters dissatisfied with party cues could be reaching for any other cues that are available in deciding how to vote. The incumbency cue is readily at hand. This hypothesis assumes a current rise in discontent with parties; it assumes nothing about changes in the cues voters have been receiving from congressmen.

There is no point in speculating further here about causes. But it is important that the subject be given further treatment, if for no other reason than that some of the variables can be legally manipulated. The congressional franking privilege comes first to mind.

TABLE 25-2. HOUSE VOTE SWINGS AND SEAT SWINGS, 1956–1972

	Change in National Popular Vote over Last Election	Net Partisan Seat Swing over Last Election	Incumbent Losses to Opposite Party Challengers		
			D	R	TOTAL
1956	1.5% D	2 D	8	7	15
1958	5.1% D	49 D	1	34	35
1960	1.1% R	20 R	22	3	25
1962	2.2% R	2 R	9	5	14
1964	4.7% D	36 D	5	39	44
1966	6.2% R	47 R	39	1	40
1968	0.4% R	5 R	5	0	5
1970	3.3% D	12 D	2	9	11
1972	1.4% R	12 R	6	3	9

III

If fewer House members are winning elections narrowly, and if the proportion of "open seats" per election is not rising, it ought to follow that congressional seat swings are declining in amplitude. The argument requires no assumption that national swings in the House popular vote are changing in amplitude—and indeed there is no evidence in the contemporary data that they are. It does require the assumption that a congressman's percentage showing in one election supplies information on his strength as he goes into the next. That is, a House member running at the 60 percent level is less likely to be unseated by an adverse 5 percent party trend next time around than one running at the 54 percent level. It is easy to predict that a popular voting trend will cut less of a swath through a set of congressmen whose last-election percentages are arrayed like those in the 1968, 1970, and 1972 incumbency graphs of Figure 25-1 than through a set whose percentages are centrally and normally distributed.

There is evidence suggesting that the flight from marginality is having its posited effect. Edward Tufte has found that a "swing ratio"—a rate of translation of votes into seats—built on data from the 1966, 1968, and 1970 elections yields an exceptionally low value when compared with ratios for other election triplets over the last century.[24] The figures in Table 25-2 point in the same direction. Supplied here are data on popular vote swings, net partisan seat swings, and incumbency defeats for each and both parties in the election years from 1956 through 1972.[25] It is worth noting that the large seat swings of 1958, 1964, and 1966 were heavily dependent upon defeats of incumbents. Very few incumbents have lost since 1966. (Almost all the 1972 losers were victims of line changes.) Especially interesting are the figures for 1970, a year in which the popular vote swing was a fairly sizable 3.3 percent. Yet only nine incumbents of the disfavored party lost and the net swing over 1968 was only twelve—of which three changed over in 1969 by-elections. Part of the explanation here is doubtless that the disfavored party had relatively few incumbents in the vulnerable range to protect. Only 47 Republicans running in 1970 had won under the 60 percent mark in

1968, whereas there had been 82 comparably exposed Republicans running in 1958, 76 Republicans in 1964, and 79 Democrats in 1966.

What general conclusions can be drawn? If the trends hold we are witnesses to the blunting of a blunt instrument. It may be too soon to say that seat swings of the 1958 or 1964 variety can be consigned to the history books, but it is hard to see how they could be equaled in the newer electoral circumstances. There is probably another manifestation here of what Walter Dean Burnham calls "electoral disaggregation"—a weakening of the peculiar links that party has supplied between electorate and government.[26] There is a concomitant triumph for the Madisonian vision; a Congress less affected by electoral tides is, on balance, one less susceptible to presidential wiles. But there is a long-run danger that a Congress that cannot supply quick electoral change is no match for a presidency that can.

APPENDIX

The columns of figures below are frequency distributions of Democratic percentages of the November two-party House vote recorded in districts with incumbents of either (but not both) of the parties running, in biennial elections from 1956 through 1972, with separate columns for each year for districts harboring Democratic and Republican incumbents. Thus in 1956 there were twenty-eight districts with Republican incumbents running in which Democratic percentages were in the 45–49.9 percent range. There were also eight districts with Democratic incumbents running in which Democratic percentages were in the 45–49.9 percent range; these eight Democrats thereby lost their seats. Squares or rectangles are drawn around cells below which contain values for incumbents who lost seats to opposite-party challengers.

Numbers of Districts, by Year and by Party of Incumbent

Democratic % of the Two-Party Vote	1956 D	1956 R	1958 D	1958 R	1960 D	1960 R	1962 D	1962 R	1964 D	1964 R	1966 D	1966 R	1968 D	1968 R	1970 D	1970 R	1972 D	1972 R
0– 4.9		3		1		3		1		1		4		9		5		7
5– 9.9																		
10–14.9														1				
15–19.9						1						3		3		2		2
20–24.9				1		1				1		8		6		5		7
25–29.9		13		11		3		11		1		24		25		15		38
30–34.9		28		27		16		24		7		53		47		40		27
35–39.9		54		44		33		39	2	25	1	26		39		41		36
40–44.9		54		50	3	56	2	45	2	47	8	6		31		34	2	22
45–49.9	8	28	1		19	19	7	19	1	38	30	3	5	10	2	15	4	10

	1956		1958		1960		1962		1964		1966		1968		1970		1972	
	D	R	D	R	D	R	D	R	D	R	D	R	D	R	D	R	D	R
50– 54.9	40	6	4	27	28	3	23	4	14	35	28	1	26		8	7	15	2
55– 59.9	28	1	11	7	36		36	1	18	4	53		38		20	1	27	1
60– 64.9	28		33		27		32		35		34		43		28	1	40	
65– 69.9	21		19		26		27		45		26		24		35		30	
70– 74.9	10		26		21		31		29		20		22		42		26	
75– 79.9	7		17		16		11		24		13		12		15		16	
80– 84.9	2		10		11		4		13		9		10		12		9	
85– 89.9	4		1		4		2		4				4		4		7	
90– 94.9	1		5		3		1		2				1		1		1	
95–100.0	68		95		72		56		40		51		41		56		44	

NOTES

[1] To put it yet another way, voting for House candidates must have a "national component" to it. See Donald E. Stokes, "Parties and the Nationalization of Electoral Forces," ch. 7 in William N. Chambers and Walter D. Burnham, *The American Party Systems* (New York: Oxford University Press, 1967).

[2] The best analysis of translation formulas is in Edward R. Tufte, "The Relation Between Seats and Votes in Two Party Systems," *American Political Science Review*, 67 (June, 1973), 540–554.

[3] Angus Campbell, "Surge and Decline: A Study in Electoral Change," ch. 3 in Campbell et al., *Elections and the Political Order* (New York: Wiley, 1966).

[4] Gerald H. Kramer, "Short-Term Fluctuations in U.S. Voting Behavior, 1896–1964," *American Political Science Review*, 65 (1971), 131–143.

[5] Ibid., p. 140.

[6] At the time of writing no comparable figures were yet available for the 1972 election. Dealing with the 1968 returns by calculating percentages of the major-party vote poses obvious problems—especially in the South—but so does any alternative way of dealing with them. Congressional district data used in Figure 25-1 and following tables and figures were taken from *Congressional Quarterly* compilations.

[7] An incumbent is defined here as a congressman who held a seat at the time he was running in a November election, even if he had first taken the seat in a recent by-election.

[8] The center graphs cover districts with no incumbents, the left-hand graphs districts with one incumbent. This leaves no place in the diagram for districts with two opposite-party incumbents running against each other. There were 16 of these throw-in cases over the period: 7 in 1962, 1 in 1966, 4 in 1968, 1 in 1970, 3 in 1972. Republicans won in 10 of them.

[9] On balance it can be expected that distributions will be more centrally clustered in presidential than in midterm years, for the reason that presidential elections enroll expanded electorates in which disproportionate numbers of voters violate district partisan habits in their congressional voting. See Harvey Kabaker, "Estimating the Normal Vote in Congressional Elections," *Midwest Journal of Political Science*, 13 (1969), 58–83.

[10] Again, the 16 throw-in cases are not included. It should be recalled here that some of these incumbents in the marginal range moved across the 50 percent mark and lost their seats. (See the Appendix.) Of the 198 incumbents who lost elections to opposite-party challengers in the 1956–1972 period, only 4 plummeted far enough to fall outside the broadly defined (40–59.9 percent) marginal range.

[11] The decline has come in spite of Republican inroads in Southern House districts. One reason here is that, once they have gotten their seats, Southern Republican incumbents tend to win elections handily; 16 of 22 of them won with over 60 percent of the major-party vote in 1970, 18 of 22 in 1972.

[12] Albert D. Cover [conducted] research at Yale on incumbency and marginality in the 1960's.

[13] I owe this point to Walter D. Burnham. On long-run decline in House turnover see Charles O. Jones, "Inter-Party Competition for Congressional Seats," *Western Political Quarterly*, 17 (1964), 461–476.

[14] Some strategies and examples are discussed in David R. Mayhew, "Congressional Representation: Theory and Practice in Drawing the Districts," ch. 7 in Nelson W. Polsby, ed., *Reapportionment in the 1970's* (Berkeley: University of California Press, 1971), pp. 274–284.

[15] On the 1966 election see Robert J. Erikson, "Malapportionment, Gerrymandering, and Party Fortunes in Congressional Elections," *American Political Science Review*, 66 (1972), 1238.

[16] Robert Erikson estimates that incumbency status was worth about 2 percent of the vote in the 1950's and early 1960's, but about 5 percent in 1966 and thereafter. Erikson, "The Advantage of Incumbency in Congressional Elections," *Polity*, 3 (1971), 395–405. Erikson, "Malapportionment, Gerrymandering, and Party Fortunes in Congressional Elections," op. cit., 1240.

17 Figures 25-1 and 25-2 are built on candidate percentage of the major-party vote, Table 25-1 on percentages of the total vote.

18 Donald E. Stokes and Warren E. Miller, "Party Government and the Saliency of Congress," ch. 11 in Angus Campbell, et al., *Elections and the Political Order* (New York: Wiley, 1966), pp. 204–209.

19 Data supplied by Albert D. Cover.

20 Norman C. Miller, "Yes, You Are Getting More Politico Mail; And It Will Get Worse," *Wall Street Journal*, March 6, 1973.

21 Gallup survey in *Washington Post*, September 20, 1970.

22 There is a discussion of roll-call position-taking and its electoral effects in Robert Erikson, "The Electoral Impact of Congressional Roll Call Voting," *American Political Science Review*, 65 (1971), 1018–1032.

23 Robert A. Schoenberger, "Campaign Strategy and Party Loyalty: the Electoral Relevance of Candidate Decision-Making in the 1964 Congressional Elections," *American Political Science Review*, 63 (1969), 515–520.

24 Op. cit., pp. 549–550.

25 The incumbency defeat figures cover only losses to opposite-party challengers. Thus once again the 16 throw-in cases are disregarded. Also ignored are the November losses of two highly visible Democrats—Brooks Hays (1958) and Louise Day Hicks (1972)—to independents who thereupon enrolled as Democrats themselves in Washington. It might be added here that some incumbents do after all lose their primaries. The figures for losses to primary challengers are: 6 in 1956, 4 in 1958, 5 in 1960, 8 in 1962, 5 in 1964, 5 in 1966, 3 in 1968, 9 in 1970, 8 in 1972. The figures for losses where redistricting has thrown incumbents into the same primary: 5 in 1962, 3 in 1964, 3 in 1966, 1 in 1968, 1 in 1970, 6 in 1972. Whatever their qualitative effects, primaries have not rivaled the larger November swings in turnover leverage.

26 "The End of American Party Politics," *Trans-Action*, 7 (December, 1969), 18–20.

PART SEVEN

THE PRESIDENCY

With the advent of President Franklin D. Roosevelt's New Deal in the 1930s, the presidency emerged as the focal point of American government. Whereas in the nineteenth century it was possible to think in terms of "Congressional Government," today it is far more common to come across books with titles such as *A Presidential Nation*[1] and *The Imperial Presidency*.[2] Not only has the president taken on greater and more complex roles and the executive office expanded dramatically in conjunction with this development, but popular expectations of the president have also risen disproportionately to the president's ability to fulfill them. Indeed, as Thomas Cronin laments, the president is now considered almost synonymous with American government itself: "The President's values, his qualities of character and intellect, his capacity for leadership, his political skills, his definition of his own role, and the way he performs it—*these* are fundamental determinants of the working of the American government and of American politics."[3] However, as popular attention focused on the presidential office, the paradoxical nature of the presidency became more evident. According to several contemporary political scientists the office is currently at once too powerful and too weak, too large and yet inadequately staffed, too political and not political enough. In part these paradoxes are due to the Founders' inability to develop a clear theory of the presidency. Indeed, they voted twelve times on how to choose a president and five on the term of office. To the extent that the Founders had a general approach to the office, it was to create a presidency that was independent and strong enough to resist the legislature, but also too limited to take far-reaching independent action. Obviously, this would be a precarious balance; indeed, it is one that some would argue needs to be reestablished today.

Perhaps the best place to begin considering the American presidency is with the question of popular expectations, because it is these demands upon the chief executive that have made the president the focal point of the political community and laid bare the various limitations and problems inherent in the office. James D. Barber's "The Presidency: What Americans Want" (1971) is a clear and enduring statement of the issue. Barber believes that the American people look to the president to satisfy at least three sets of needs: reassurance, progress and action, and legitimacy. He also observes that "the strong focus on getting elected has somehow increasingly divorced that problem from the problem of governing." This situation is dangerous, as Barber observes: "People are hungry for a hero, one who fits the new age. Soon they will find one. A good deal is riding on the question of whether they will find a demagogue or a democrat as they search out a way to link their passions to their government."

James Bryce's "Why Great Men Are Not Chosen Presidents" sheds the light

[1] Joseph Califano, Jr., *A Presidential Nation* (New York: W. W. Norton, 1975).
[2] Arthur Schlesinger, Jr., *The Imperial Presidency* (Boston: Houghton Mifflin, 1973).
[3] Quoted by Thomas E. Cronin, *The State of the Presidency* (Boston: Little, Brown, 1975), p. 30.

of historical perspective on Barber's question. Although the piece was originally published in the 1880s, the reader may agree that some of the problems Bryce addresses have been quite persistent. For instance, he notes that only a limited proportion of "first-rate ability" is drawn to politics, that the electoral system tends to reward geographically and politically balanced tickets, and that many individuals of great personal merit, who might be good presidents, would be very poor campaigners.

Richard Neustadt's "Power to Persuade" from *Presidential Power* (1960, 1976) considers the problem of limited presidential capacity from a different perspective. Neustadt argues that formal presidential powers are inadequate for effective presidential performance and that the essence of presidential power is the power to persuade. As he states it, "Presidential 'powers' may be inconclusive when a president commands, but always remain relevant as he persuades."

Thomas Cronin's essay on "The Swelling of the Presidency" (1973) suggests that the quest for persuasive power and the other demands placed upon the presidency have encouraged the development of a large and unwieldy Executive Office of the President (EOP). Almost all observers, including presidents themselves, agree that this makes it *more* difficult for the president to coordinate his roles. It also places considerable political power in the hands of unelected presidential staffers. Despite the growth of presidential offices and staff, Cronin observes, "The presidency remains sorely overburdened—with both functions and functionaries—and needs very much to be cut back in both."

26

JAMES D. BARBER

THE PRESIDENCY:
WHAT AMERICANS WANT

Every leader with any understanding of what he is about knows that he has two jobs: to move the enterprise forward and to keep his people happy. Often these tasks interfere with one another. The press for action disrupts the harmony of the team, or the price of a happy organization may be lassitude. The trick is to make of these two problems two resources, to reinforce the thrust for action with high morale and to make achievement a source of satisfaction. But that is hard to bring off; most leaders fail at it.

In our peculiar presidency one way of working this out is precluded: the division of labor. Studies of small decision-making groups have frequently discovered two leaders, one who emphasizes the objective tasks, another who handles the group's emotional life, the pair of them Mutt-and-Jeffing their way to success. To a degree the assignment of the Vice-President to "politics" is a try in this direction. But in the main we lean on the President for leadership in making the government work and in making us happy about our country. We elect a politician and insist that he also be a king. The British solution probably never was available to us; in any case President Washington, by his superb performance as monarch, quashed for all time the idea of the President as a mere clerk to execute the will of the Congress. One man, in full sight of us all, must if he is to succeed bless us with inspiration as he goads us to action.

A second solution is alternation: the President is king for a while and then shifts to being politician for a while, and back again. President Nixon has this propensity, I think, and it has contributed to all the uncertainties observers have felt in characterizing a man who is now the very image of calm self-restraint, now the independent fighter. His emphasis on time and timing reinforces this adaptive technique as does, in a much more fundamental way, his memory of the contrasting styles of his forebears. But it is a dangerous game; once it is understood—once the public perceives it—its effectiveness wanes and what sticks is an impression of shiftiness.

I think we need a larger time frame to get at the basic relation between the man in the White House and the mood of the country. I think we have seen, in Kennedy, Johnson, and in Nixon so far, a series of failures, traceable to interesting causes, in meeting the emotional demands Americans place on the presidency. And I believe we may be able to use some simple psychological concepts to project the more likely implications for 1972 and 1976. To get at the topic requires first a closer look at the nature of the emotions surrounding the presidency and at the psychological implications of the passage of time.

Americans look to their President to satisfy at least three sets of needs. First is the need for reassurance. It is clear in studies of reactions to the death of Presidents (McKinley, Garfield, Harding, Roosevelt, as well as Kennedy) and in the propensity of children to want to believe the President is a good man, that people turn to the President for a sense that things will be all right, that in the midst of trouble is a core of serenity. Harding had this appeal down pat with his normalcy, his ability to "bloviate" the common clichés so reassuringly to an emotionally exhausted citizenry. People want to be taken care of; they place ultimate responsibility for that on the President.

Beyond reassurance, people want a sense of progress and action. The contradiction may be only a trivially logical one—part of what was reassuring about Franklin Roosevelt was the feeling that he was taking effective action, moving forward with some kind of program, at least at first. At times the people react strongly against "do-nothing" government, more specifically against a President who seems to be holding the office but not playing the role. There was some of that feeling against Eisenhower, a questioning of his political competence and drive amidst a general aura of respect and affection. The President is supposed to be a take-charge man, a doer, a turner of the wheels, a producer of progress even if that means some sacrifice of serenity.

Then people want a sense of legitimacy from and in the presidency. Again there is an apparent contradiction: he should be a master politician who is above politics. He should have a right to his place and a rightful way of acting in it. The responsibility—even religiosity—of the office has to be protected by a man who presents himself as defender of the faith. There is more to this than dignity, though, more than an air of propriety. The President is expected to personify our betterness in an inspiring way, to express in what he does and is (not just in what he says) a moral idealism which, in much of the public mind, is the very opposite of "politics."

I think close study would show that Franklin Roosevelt, Truman, and Eisenhower, in somewhat different ways, exemplified these themes. For all his deviousness, Roosevelt was a master reassurer (no slouch as a mover and shaker, either, or as king-hero to most). His humor, his air of patrician calm, his simplicity of expression, and his masterful use of intimacy over the radio calmed a trembling nation even when his policies were faltering badly. People who were politically aware then, have that memory with them now, that model to hold up against the current reassurers. Indeed we grew up with Roosevelt from 1933 to 1945; over all those years the office and the man seemed to grow together into one thing, one oaken trunk of stability in the midst of national and world chaos.

Truman put great store in maintaining the dignity of the office, but of course his strength was his fighting courage in the face of adversity. To the "average man" (for or against him) Truman was a quite satisfactory battler—direct, open, definite, aggressive, persistent, unswerved in his pursuits—or so he seemed. Even his intense personal loyalties, which eventually sullied his image as a legitimator, fit the picture of a man who stuck to his guns. And he decided; he seemed to know where he was going and how to get there without a lot of delicate hesitation. He left behind a memory of the President as a man moving strong and straight toward a goal. That was not just the way Harry acted. That was Harry himself.

Eisenhower's very bumbling seemed to confirm his legitimacy. The 1950s' word for him was "sincere" and if his idealism took expression in mimickable form its content struck home to a people ready for spiritual uplift. What other politician could have said what Ike said—about the duty he felt to serve his country, about his second crusade—and be believed? Truman angrily dismissed Ike's promise to go to Korea as a publicity gimmick; what politician today could get that seen as a straightforward attempt to end a war? Ike was believed, and believed in, as a President-king-archbishop of an American brand. Much of his moral indignation went into justifying *not* taking action in various circumstances, in retreating from the rolling political tides. But that was all right with the public. By 1956, all other reasons for preferring him paled in comparison to the simple statement of preference itself—"I like Ike"—and he left the office barely touched by the Adams scandal. He left a legacy, a memory trace that reminds us that whatever else a President should be, he should be a damn good man.

Reassurance, action, legitimacy—at least a sense of those—encompass most of what Americans want to feel about their President. The people want those feelings so much that they will get projected onto a new President until he proves himself otherwise. Americans want and need to believe that the ordinary men they elevate to the presidency (or might elevate) are "Lincolnesque," bearers of the torch, benevolent leaders. All this they try to confirm in the allegiance they pay the man as he takes office. From that high point he tends to descend in a remarkably regular curve, broken by upward leaps in popular esteem when crisis comes to remind us of the uniqueness of his charge. (Possibly there is some deep and wide current in the public mind that wants to experience vicariously the tragic drama of kings falling, which requires setting him up high in the first place.) In any case, the criteria of emotional evaluation, as distinguished from evaluation of his policies and practices considered objectively, do not seem to change much. He ought to keep us safely in his care. He ought to get the country moving. And he ought to inspire our higher selves with an example of principled goodness.

If we consider these needs as motives, what happens when they are frustrated? If the need is superficial, frustration will eventually eliminate or at least trivialize it—people will stop worrying about it and turn to other things. But although most American political motives are shallow, as shown by general lack of interest in or emotional attachment to political activity and information, those centered in the President are different—much more intense, much more persistent. If the need is intense and persistent, frustration will not easily dispel it. Up to a point, the longer gratification is delayed, the more drive accumulates, the less sufficient minor gratifications become in satisfying the need. There is a building up, a heightening of expectation, an increase in demand for satisfaction. Typically the person probes around for substitutes, for example in aggressive behavior. But the broad and simple pattern is probably the right one: frustrate an important need now and you only intensify the demand for its satisfaction later.

I think the public has experienced in the last three presidencies a good deal of disappointment in their desires for presidential reassurance, activism, and legitimacy. They have also been disappointed in some dimensions of public policy objectively considered, but I do not see any very unambiguous connection between the actual achievements of an administration in policy terms and its success or failure along this emotional dimension. Whatever their "real" accomplishments, Kennedy, Johnson, and Nixon have in different ways let us down, frustrated our fundamental needs for kingliness in the White House.

The modal response to Kennedy once elected was, I think, centered in his activist image. He was the young prince elevated to the throne, insisting that his predecessor's standards were not good enough for a new generation, promising forward motion with a new vitality. People were ready to give him a chance. But from the start there was something vaguely unsatisfying about Kennedy as fighter for progress. He had that edge of restrained rage that comes through so effectively on television. But he was, or seemed, iron and ice, not fire and brimstone. Many appreciated him who could not quite identify with him. One could get angry beside Harry Truman; one could only get indignant beside John Kennedy—or so it seemed at a distance.

Then came the practical restraints. Empowered in a narrow victory, he [Kennedy] had to move cautiously in Washington, waiting out the congressional elders, learning that they could not be pushed as easily as the campaign politicians. Results came slowly. For high adventure the public had to make do with the Peace Corps and the space program, both of them probes away from the tangle of home politics. The Kennedy administration seemed to shape itself not so much around a team of fighting partisans as around a technology, a rational, statistical approach to mechanized decision making. It is hard for people to find excitement in a new accounting system. In many of these ways, President Kennedy, though he remained a vessel of hope and good intentions, came across as too cool, too slick, too stylish (stylized?) to rile up America between the Appalachians and Lake Tahoe. The people rushed, figuratively, to his side in crisis, but that seemed more a dutiful rally than a heartfelt leap into the fray.

Then the sharp horror of the assassinations, for which disappointment is too pale a word. But clearly one aspect of that was dashed hopes, the sudden curtaining of the drama of President Kennedy as leader of the nation's progressive, activist forces. This was the ultimate disappointment.

Lyndon Johnson came on as the dedicated, determined continuer. A good deal of early speculation concerned his background as a wheeler and dealer and his adequacy to fill John Kennedy's shoes. But I think there was another feeling: something desperately immoral had happened, a gigantic disruption of tradition. People were perhaps less interested in what Johnson would continue than that he would continue, would uphold and sustain the government's legitimate succession. Johnson quickly picked up these themes. For all his colorful private conversation, he presented himself to the public as Old Reliable, as Preacher Lyndon, interestingly, more in the Eisenhower than in the Roosevelt mode. His war on poverty and his championing of civil rights were advanced as highly moralized stands on principle.

At a deeper level, Lyndon Johnson may have suffered the strains of intense personal ambition and power hunger, may have experienced some desperate need to confirm himself as a real person with his own preferences rather than a mere compromiser. But his public rhetoric reached out for the people's need to believe that their President embodied American values. Possibly part of the interpretation of his incredible victory over Goldwater was that Johnson, in contrast, seemed to be upholding the traditional principles against some bizarre and uncertain threat from the right. Johnson would be the national President, the voice from the White House calling on the people to do the right thing.

I think he saw the Vietnam War that way. At least to the public, he passed quickly over the details of possible compromises with the enemy to get to the main points: honor, coming to the aid of victims of aggression, standing up for what you believe in.

But in the end, much like that other President Johnson of a century earlier, Lyndon Johnson frustrated the popular need for legitimacy. The credibility gap cracked open under his feet and no amount of preaching could close it. People moved from suspicion to despair, with much help from the press and television. His popularity plummeted and the forces of youthful idealism took out after him. In the end he gave the impression of a leader at bay, grasping at resignation on principle as a way to reassert his personal legitimacy, only to have that dismissed as a calculated ploy. For all his ponderous moralizing, Johnson came to stand in the mind of much of the public as a moral pariah. The point is not the justice or injustice of that characterization, but that it represented a failure, despite immense effort, to satisfy the people's need for sincerity and simple idealism in the presidency.

It is too early yet to be very sure about Richard Nixon's resonance with the emotional tides around the presidency, but he began with "lowered voices," a plea for peace and quiet echoing Harding's normalcy. I think he sensed the national desire for a surcease of anxiety—the need for reassurance—and wanted to meet that by conveying an impression of calm, professional, un-ideological rulership. He seemed to shy away from dramatics, even as he was announcing various historic firsts. His Cabinet had no famous heroes or villains; he had to describe their "extra dimensions" to the nation. He meant to get on with the task and be judged by results to be achieved with quiet efficiency.

But even now it is obvious Nixon has not succeeded in reassuring the nation. Not only is there harsh division among the people, but a good deal of worry about the fact of that division—polarization is a scare word now. The year 1970 was far from a comfortable one in terms of political emotions, and there is not yet much sign that 1971 will bring domestic or foreign peace. Much as many people want to believe Nixon—almost want to foist some sort of greatness upon him—they have not yet, I think, felt they could drop their emotional guard and leave the troubles up to him. Uncertainty about just who Nixon is and where he is going adds to the national anxiety, and not only in the nervous northeast. Here again, then, the people have been disappointed in their hope and expectation that the President could help still palpitations of a scared country.

Disappointment with the President is not, to say the least, the root cause of our current national turmoil. Nor does the fault of it necessarily lie in some personal moral flaw in the President himself. It is one factor, one more on top of all the others, reinforcing politically unhealthy tendencies, and it can happen to the best of men. Its larger implication is that stored-up needs for reassurance, activism, and legitimacy—for emotional sustenance from the White House—can emerge to distort political choices and divert energies from productive action. These bottled-up, frustrated needs make it harder to find presidential candidates who could satisfy them and at the same time produce genuine social progress. On the other hand, a candidate who combined this kind of charisma with extraordinary competence in policy making would be an immense national resource.

Insofar as the man's character and style are factors in the equation, the lack of fit between President and public mood is not hard to fathom. President Nixon's character was formed in another era, modeled after old-fashioned heroes of the past. His style was, in many cases, an invention of his early political emergence, suited to the time he found himself politically, but almost inevitably out of kilter with the present. I think it is possible to find out the main thrust of a political character once we discern his rate of political activity and his affective stance toward that activity—basically whether he works hard or takes it easy, and whether he generally seems to like what he does or not. His style is a later accretion. The clearest clue to style—the way the man manages his political rhetoric, interpersonal relations, and decision making—is to be found in his first independent political success, that time when he found a special way to make words, other people, and work pay off in personal success, usually in late adolescence or early adulthood.

People are trained for leadership long before they assume it, and therefore are always, to a degree, regressive in their attempts to adapt to the present. In a fast-moving political culture, that can be a source of important strain, of disparity between the man's and the nation's ways of life.

Perhaps another set of factors contributing to the President's troubles in meeting the public's emotional needs is the increasing rationalization of politics. The process of electing a President has become a high-powered business enterprise, a technical, organized, systematic production. The strong focus on getting elected has somehow increasingly divorced that problem from the problem of governing. For all the manipulation of sentiment, the election process has acquired a technocratic tone which seems to work against emotional expression. The resonance between candidate and people is shallow, temporary, calculated—and known to be calculated. The steam has gone out of the drama. What is left is the image of the clean machine, the blinking computer. Undoubtedly television has helped this along with its emphasis on cool wit rather than belly laughs, mild disdain rather than free anger.

Similarly in government itself there is the elevation of technique over value. Despite a good deal of emotive language, the picture of government run by a combination of technocrats and clever political manipulators comes through. Perhaps this is best symbolized in the physical White House: no longer a pleasant shrine, but a plantation facade hiding a political factory.

These and other culture developments make it ever harder to articulate convincingly the religious-emotional themes which have for so long been a part of our politics. The result is a symbolic thrashing around—with the flag, for example—in search of some heartfelt connection between government and people. Given the centrality of the presidency to our political emotions, the chances that these feelings will fasten themselves to the President and presidential candidates are great. They are even greater after a period of emotional disappointment, of accumulating frustration.

For these reasons, I think we will see, perhaps in 1972, a search for candidates who can elicit strong emotional responses from the public. A cool image on television will not be enough; nor will piling up delegates' votes through local-issue primaries or chicken-dinnering suffice. The connection will not be made by a candidate who supposes that the more social turmoil there is, the calmer he should come across.

People are hungry for a hero, one who fits the new age. Soon they will find one. A good deal is riding on the question whether they will find a demagogue or a democrat as they search out a way to link their passions to their government.

27

JAMES BRYCE

WHY GREAT MEN
ARE NOT CHOSEN PRESIDENTS

Europeans often ask, and Americans do not always explain, how it happens that this great office, the greatest in the world, unless we except the papacy, to which any man can rise by his own merits, is not more frequently filled by great and striking men? In America, which is beyond all other countries the country of a "career open to talents," a country, moreover, in which political life is unusually keen and political ambition widely diffused, it might be expected that the highest place would always be won by a man of brilliant gifts. But since the heroes of the Revolution died out with Jefferson and Adams and Madison some sixty years ago, no person except General Grant has reached the chair whose name would have been remembered had he not been president, and no president except Abraham Lincoln has displayed rare or striking qualities in the chair. Who now knows or cares to know anything about the personality of James K. Polk or Franklin Pierce? The only thing remarkable about them is that being so commonplace they should have climbed so high.

Several reasons may be suggested for the fact, which Americans are themselves the first to admit.

One is that the proportion of first-rate ability drawn into politics is smaller in America than in most European countries. This is a phenomenon whose causes must be elucidated later: in the meantime it is enough to say that in France and Italy, where half-revolutionary conditions have made public life exciting and accessible; in Germany, where an admirably-organized civil service cultivates and develops statecraft with unusual success; in England, where many persons of wealth and leisure seek to enter the political arena, while burning questions touch the interests of all classes and make men eager observers of the combatants, the total quantity of talent devoted to parliamentary or administrative work is far larger, relatively to the population, than in America, where much of the best ability, both for thought and for action, for planning and for executing rushes into a field which is comparatively narrow in Europe, the business of developing the material resources of the country.

Another is that the methods and habits of Congress, and indeed of political life generally, seem to give fewer opportunities for personal distinction, fewer modes in which a man may commend himself to his countrymen by eminent capacity in thought, in speech, or in administration, than is the case in the free countries of Europe.

A third reason is that eminent men make more enemies, and give those enemies more assailable points, than obscure men do. They are therefore in so far less desirable candidates. It is true that the eminent man has also made more friends, that his name is more widely known, and may be greeted with louder cheers. Other things being equal, the famous man is preferable. But other things never are equal. The famous man has probably attacked some leaders in his own party, has supplanted others, has expressed his dislike to the crotchet of some active section, has perhaps committed errors which are capable of being magnified into offences. No man stands long before the public and bears a part in great affairs without giving openings to censorious criticism. Fiercer far than the light which beats upon a throne is the light which beats upon a presidential candidate, searching out all the reasons of his past life. Hence, when the choice lies between a brilliant man and a safe man, the safe man is preferred. Party feeling, strong enough to carry in on its back a man without conspicuous positive merits, is not always strong enough to procure forgiveness for a man with positive faults.

A European finds that this phenomenon needs in its turn to be explained, for in the free countries of Europe brilliancy, be it eloquence in speech, or some striking achievement in war or administration, or the power through whatever means of somehow impressing the popular imagination, is what makes a leader triumphant. Why should it be otherwise in America? Because in America party loyalty and party organization have been hitherto so perfect that any one put forward by the party will get the full party vote if his character is good and his "record," as they call it, unstained. The safe candidate may not draw in quite so many votes from the moderate men of the other side as the brilliant one would, but he will not lose nearly so many from his own ranks. Even those who admit his mediocrity will vote straight when the moment for voting comes. Besides, the ordinary American voter does not object to mediocrity. He has a lower conception of the qualities requisite to make a statesman than those who direct public opinion in Europe have. He likes his candidate to be sensible, vigorous, and, above all, what he calls "magnetic," and does not value, because he sees no need for, originality or profundity, a fine culture or a wide knowledge. Candidates are selected to be run for nomination by knots of persons who, however expert as party tacticians, are usually commonplace men; and the choice between those selected for nomination is made by a very large body, an assembly of over eight hundred delegates from the local party organizations over the country, who are certainly no better than ordinary citizens. How this process works will be seen more fully when I come to speak of those nominating conventions which are so notable a feature in American politics.

It must also be remembered that the merits of a President are one thing and those of a candidate another thing. An eminent American is reported to have said to friends who wished to put him forward, "Gentlemen, let there be no mistake. I should make a good president, but a very bad candidate." Now to a party it is more important that its nominee should be a good candidate than that he should turn out a good president. A nearer danger is a greater danger. As Saladin says in *The Talisman*, "A wild cat in a chamber is more dangerous than a lion in a distant desert." It will be a misfortune to the party, as well as to the country, if the candidate elected should prove a bad president. But it is a greater misfortune to the party that it should be beaten in the impending election, for the evil of losing national patronage will have come four years sooner. "B" (so reason the leaders), "who is one of our possible candidates, may be an abler man than A, who is the other. But we have a better chance of winning with A than with B, while X, the candidate of our opponents, is anyhow no better than A. We must therefore run A." This reasoning is all the more forcible because the previous career of the possible candidates has generally made it easier to say who will succeed as a candidate than who will succeed as a president; and because the wire-pullers with whom the choice rests are better judges of the former question than of the latter.

After all, too, and this is a point much less obvious to Europeans than to Americans, a president need not be a man of brilliant intellectual gifts. Englishmen, imagining him as something like their prime minister, assume that he ought to be a dazzling orator, able to sway legislatures or multitudes, possessed also of the constructive powers that can devise a great policy or frame a comprehensive piece of legislation. They forget that the president does not sit in Congress, that he ought not to address meetings, except on ornamental and (usually) nonpolitical occasions, that he cannot submit bills nor otherwise influence the action of the legislature. His main duties are to be prompt and firm in securing the due execution of the laws and maintaining the public peace, careful and upright in the choice of the executive officials of the country. Eloquence, whose value is apt to be overrated in all free countries, imagination, profundity of thought or extent of knowledge, are all in so far a gain to him that they make him a bigger man, and help him to gain a greater influence over the nation, an influence which, if he be a true patriot he may use for its good. But they are not necessary for the due discharge in ordinary times of the duties of his post. A man may lack them and yet make an excellent president. Four-fifths of his work is the same in kind as that which devolves on the chairman of a commercial company or the manager of a railway, the work of choosing good subordinates, seeing that they attend to their business, and taking a sound practical view of such administrative questions as require his decision. Firmness, common sense, and most of all, honesty, an honesty above all suspicion of personal interest, are the qualities which the country chiefly needs in its chief magistrate.

So far we have been considering personal merits. But in the selection of a candidate many considerations have to be regarded besides personal merits, whether they be the merits of a candidate, or of a possible president. The chief of these considerations is the amount of support which can be secured from different states or from different regions, or, as the Americans say, "sections," of the Union. State feeling and sectional feeling are powerful factors in a presidential election. The Northwest, including the states from Ohio to Dakota, is now the most populous region of the Union, and therefore counts for most in an election. It naturally conceives that its interests will be best protected by one who knows them from birth and residence. Hence *prima facie* a Northwestern man makes the best candidate. A large state casts a heavier vote in the election; and every state is of course more likely to be carried by one of its own children than by a stranger, because his fellow-citizens, while they feel honoured by the choice, gain also a substantial advantage, having a better prospect of such favours as the administration can bestow. Hence, *coeteris paribus*, a man from a large state is preferable as a candidate. New York casts thirty-six votes in the presidential election, Pennsylvania thirty, Ohio twenty-three, Illinois twenty-two, while Vermont and Rhode Island have but four, Delaware, Nevada, and Oregon only three votes each. It is therefore, parties being usually very evenly balanced, better worth while to have an inferior candidate from one of the larger states, who may carry the whole weight of his state with him, than a somewhat superior candidate from one of the smaller states, who will carry only three or four votes. The problem is further complicated by the fact that some states are already safe for one or other party, while others are doubtful. The Northwestern and New England states are most of them certain to go Republican: the Southern States are (at present) all of them certain to go Democratic. It is more important to gratify a doubtful state than one you have got already; and hence *coeteris paribus*, a candidate from a doubtful state, such as New York or Indiana, is to be preferred.

Other minor disqualifying circumstances require less explanation. A Roman Catholic, or an avowed disbeliever in Christianity, would be an undesirable candidate. Since the close of the Civil War, any one who fought, especially if he fought with distinction, in the Northern army, has enjoyed great advantages, for the soldiers of that army, still numerous, rally to his name. The two elections of General Grant, who knew nothing of politics, and the fact that his influence survived the faults of his long administration, are evidence of the weight of this consideration. It influenced the selection both of Garfield and of his opponent Hancock. Similarly a person who fought in the Southern army would be a bad candidate, for he might alienate the North.

On a railway journey in the Far West in 1883 I fell in with two newspaper men from the state of Indiana, who were taking their holiday. The conversation turned on the next presidential election. They spoke hopefully of the chances for nomination by their party of an Indiana man, a comparatively obscure person, whose name I had never heard. I expressed some surprise that he should be thought of. They observed that he had done well in state politics, that there was nothing against him, that Indiana would work for him. "But," I rejoined, "ought you not to have a man of more commanding character? There is Senator A. Everybody tells me that he is the shrewdest and most experienced man in your party, and that he has a perfectly clean record. Why not run him?" "Why, yes," they answered, "that is all true. But you see he comes from a small state, and we have got that state already. Besides, he wasn't in the war. Our man was. Indiana's vote is worth having, and if our man is run, we can carry Indiana."

"Surely the race is not to the swift, nor the battle to the strong, neither yet bread to the wise, nor yet riches to men of understanding, nor yet favour to men of skill, but time and chance happeneth to them all."

These secondary considerations do not always prevail. Intellectual ability and force of character must influence the choice of a candidate, and their influence is sometimes decisive. They count for more when times are so critical that the need for a strong man is felt. Reformers declare that their weight will go on increasing as the disgust of good citizens with the methods of professional politicians increases. But for many generations past it is not the greatest men in the Roman Church that have been chosen popes, nor the most brilliant men in the Anglican Church that have been appointed archbishops of Canterbury.

Although several presidents have survived their departure from office by many years, only one, John Quincy Adams, has played a part in politics after quitting the White House. It may be that the ex-president has not been a great leader before his accession to office; it may be that he does not care to exert himself after he has held and dropped the great prize, and found (one may safely add) how little of a prize it is. Something however, must also be ascribed to other features of the political system of the country. It is often hard to find a vacancy in the representation of a given state through which to re-enter Congress; it is disagreeable to recur to the arts by which seats are secured. Past greatness is rather an encumbrance than a help to resuming a political career. Exalted power, on which the unsleeping eye of hostile critics was fixed, has probably disclosed all a president's weaknesses, and has either forced him to make enemies by disobliging adherents, or exposed him to censure for subservience to party interests. He is regarded as having had his day; he belongs already to the past, and unless, like Grant, he is endeared to the people by the memory of some splendid service, he soon sinks into the crowd or avoids neglect by retirement. Possibly he may deserve to be forgotten; but more frequently he is a man of sufficient ability and character to make the experience he has gained valuable to the country, could it be retained in a place where he might turn it to account. They managed things better at Rome in the days of the republic, gathering into their Senate all the fame and experience, all the wisdom and skill, of those who had ruled and fought as consuls and praetors at home and abroad.

"What shall we do with our ex-presidents?" is a question often put in America, but never yet answered. The position of a past chief magistrate is not a happy one. He has been a species of sovereign at home. He is received—General Grant was—with almost royal honours abroad. His private income may be unsufficient to enable him to live in ease, yet he cannot without loss of dignity, the country's dignity as well as his own, go back to practice at the bar or become partner in a mercantile firm. If he tries to enter the Senate, it may happen that there is no seat vacant for his own state, or that the majority in the state legislature is against him. It has been suggested that he might be given a seat in that chamber as an extra member; but to this plan there is the objection that it would give to the state from which he comes a third senator, and thus put other states at a disadvantage. In any case, however, it would seem only right to bestow such a pension as would relieve him from the necessity of re-entering business or a profession.

We may now answer the question from which we started. Great men are not chosen presidents, firstly, because great men are rare in politics; secondly, because the method of choice does not bring them to the top; thirdly, because they are not, in quiet times, absolutely needed. I may observe that the presidents, regarded historically, fall into three periods, the second inferior to the first, the third rather better than the second.

Down till the election of Andrew Jackson in 1828, all the presidents had been statesmen in the European sense of the word, men of education, of administrative experience, of a certain largeness of view and dignity of character. All except the first two had served in the great office of secretary of state; all were well known to the nation from the part they had played. In the second period, from Jackson till the outbreak of the Civil War in 1861, the presidents were either mere politicians, such as Van Buren, Polk, or Buchanan, or else successful soldiers, such as Harrison or Taylor, whom their party found useful as figureheads. They were intellectual pigmies beside the real leaders of that generation—Clay, Calhoun, and Webster. A new series begins with Lincoln in 1861. He and General Grant his successor, who cover sixteen years between them, belong to the history of the world. The other less distinguished presidents of this period contrast favourably with the Polks and Pierces of the days before the war, but they are not, like the early presidents, the first men of the country. If we compare the eighteen presidents who have been elected to office since 1789 with the nineteen English prime ministers of the same hundred years, there are but six of the latter, and at least eight of the former whom history calls personally insignificant, while only Washington, Jefferson, Lincoln, and Grant can claim to belong to a front rank represented in the English list by seven or possibly eight names. It would seem that the natural selections of the English parliamentary system, even as modified by the aristocratic habits of that country, has more tendency to bring the highest gifts to the highest place than the more artificial selection of America.

28

RICHARD E. NEUSTADT

THE POWER TO PERSUADE

The limits on command suggest the structure of our government. The constitutional convention of 1787 is supposed to have created a government of "separated powers." It did nothing of the sort. Rather, it created a government of separated institutions *sharing* powers.[1] "I am part of the legislative process," Eisenhower often said in 1959 as a reminder of his veto.[2] Congress, the dispenser of authority and funds, is no less part of the administrative process. Federalism adds another set of separated institutions. The Bill of Rights adds others. Many public purposes can only be achieved by voluntary acts of private institutions; the press, for one, in Douglass Cater's phrase, is a "fourth branch of government."[3] And with the coming of alliances abroad, the separate institutions of a London, or a Bonn, share in the making of American policy.

What the Constitution separates our political parties do not combine. The parties are themselves composed of separated organizations sharing public authority. The authority consists of nominating powers. Our national parties are confederations of state and local party institutions, with a headquarters that represents the White House, more or less, if the party has a president in office. These confederacies manage presidential nominations. All other public offices depend upon electorates confined within the states.[4] All other nominations are controlled within the states. The president and congressmen who bear one party's label are divided by dependence upon different sets of voters. The differences are sharpest at the stage of nomination. The White House has too small a share in nominating congressmen, and Congress has too little weight in nominating presidents for party to erase their constitutional separation. Party links are stronger than is frequently supposed, but nominating processes assure the separation.[5]

The separateness of institutions and the sharing of authority prescribe the terms on which a president persuades. When one man shares authority with another, but does not gain or lose his job upon the other's whim, his willingness to act upon the urging of the other turns on whether he conceives the action right for him. The essence of a president's persuasive task is to convince such men that what the White House wants of them is what they ought to do for their sake and on their authority.

Persuasive power, thus defined, amounts to more than charm or reasoned argument. These have their uses for a president, but these are not the whole of his resources. For the men he would induce to do what he wants done on their own responsibility will need or fear some acts by him on his responsibility. If they share his authority, he has some share in theirs. Presidential "powers" may be inconclusive when a president commands, but always remain relevant as he persuades. The status and authority inherent in his office reinforce his logic and his charm.

Status adds something to persuasiveness; authority adds still more. When Truman urged wage changes on his secretary of commerce while the latter was administering the steel mills, he and Secretary Sawyer were not just two men reasoning with one another. Had they been so, Sawyer probably would never have agreed to act. Truman's status gave him special claims to Sawyer's loyalty, or at least attention. In Walter Bagehot's charming phrase "no man can *argue* on his knees." Although there is no kneeling in this country, few men—and exceedingly few cabinet officers—are immune to the impulse to say "yes" to the president of the United States. It grows harder to say "no" when they are seated in his oval office at the White House, or in his study on the second floor, where almost tangibly he partakes of the aura of his physical surroundings. In Sawyer's case, moreover, the president possessed formal authority to intervene in many matters of concern to the secretary of commerce. These matters ranged from jurisdictional disputes among the defense agencies to legislation pending before Congress and, ultimately, to the tenure of the secretary, himself. There is nothing in the record to suggest that Truman voiced specific threats when they negotiated over wage increases. But given his *formal* powers and their relevance to Sawyer's other interests, it is safe to assume that Truman's very advocacy of wage action conveyed an implicit threat.

A president's authority and status give him great advantages in dealing with the men he would persuade. Each "power" is a vantage point for him in the degree that other men have use for his authority. From the veto to appointments, from publicity to budgeting, and so down a long list, the White House now controls the most encompassing array of vantage points in the American political system. With hardly an exception, the men who share in governing this country are aware that at some time, in some degree, the doing of *their* jobs, the furthering of *their* ambitions, may depend upon the president of the United States. Their need for presidential action, or their fear of it, is bound to be recurrent if not actually continuous. Their need or fear is his advantage.

A president's advantages are greater than mere listing of his "powers" might suggest. The men with whom he deals must deal with him until the last day of his term. Because they have continuing relationships with him, his future, while it lasts, supports his present influence. Even though there is no need or fear of him today, what he could do tomorrow may supply today's advantage. Continuing relationships may convert any "power," any aspect of his status, into vantage points in almost any case. When he induces other men to do what he wants done, a president can trade on their dependence now *and* later.

The president's advantages are checked by the advantages of others. Continuing relationships will pull in both directions. These are relationships of mutual dependence. A president depends upon the men he would persuade; he has to reckon with his need or fear of them. They too will possess status, or authority, or both, else they would be of little use to him. Their vantage points confront his own; their power tempers his.

Persuasion is a two-way street. Sawyer, it will be recalled, did not respond at once to Truman's plan for wage increases at the steel mills. On the contrary, the secretary hesitated and delayed and only acquiesced when he was satisfied that publicly he would not bear the onus of decision. Sawyer had some points of vantage all his own from which to resist presidential pressure. If he had to reckon with coercive implications in the president's "situations of strength," so had Truman to be mindful of the implications underlying Sawyer's place as a department head, as steel administrator, and as a cabinet spokesman for business. Loyalty is reciprocal. Having taken on a dirty job in the steel crisis, Sawyer had strong claims to loyal support. Besides, he had authority to do some things that the White House could ill afford. Emulating Wilson, he might have resigned in a huff (the removal power also works two ways). Or emulating Ellis Arnall, he might have declined to sign necessary orders. Or, he might have let it be known publicly that he deplored what he was told to do and protested its doing. By following any of these courses Sawyer almost surely would have strengthened the position of management, weakened the position of the White House, and embittered the union. But the whole purpose of a wage increase was to enhance White House persuasiveness in urging settlement upon union and companies alike. Although Sawyer's status and authority did not give him the power to prevent an increase outright, they gave him capability to undermine its purpose. If his authority over wage rates had been vested by a statute, not by revocable presidential order, his power of prevention might have been complete. So Harold Ickes demonstrated in the famous case of helium sales to Germany before the Second World War.[6]

The power to persuade is the power to bargain. Status and authority yield bargaining advantages. But in a government of "separated institutions sharing powers," they yield them to all sides. With the array of vantage points at his disposal, a president may be far more persuasive than his logic or his charm could make him. But outcomes are not guaranteed by his advantages. There remain the counter pressures those whom he would influence can bring to bear on him from vantage points at their disposal. Command has limited utility; persuasion becomes give-and-take. It is well that the White House holds the vantage points it does. In such a business any president may need them all—and more.

This view of power as akin to bargaining is one we commonly accept in the sphere of congressional relations. Every textbook states and every legislative session demonstrates that save in times like the extraordinary Hundred Days of 1933—times virtually ruled out by definition at mid-century—a president will often be unable to obtain congressional action on his terms or even to halt action he opposes. The reverse is equally accepted: Congress often is frustrated by the president. Their formal powers are so intertwined that neither will accomplish very much, for very long, without the acquiescence of the other. By the same token, though, what one demands, the other can resist. The stage is set for that great game, much like collective bargaining, in which each seeks to profit from the other's needs and fears. It is a game played catch-as-catch-can, case by case. And everybody knows the game, observers and participants alike.

The concept of real power as a give-and-take is equally familiar when applied to presidential influence outside the formal structure of the federal government. The Little Rock affair may be extreme, but Eisenhower's dealings with the governor—and with the citizens—become a case in point. Less extreme but no less pertinent is the steel seizure case with respect to union leaders, and to workers, and to company executives as well. When he deals with such people a president draws bargaining advantage from his status or authority. By virtue of their public places or their private rights they have some capability to reply in kind.

In spheres of party politics the same thing follows, necessarily, from the confederal nature of our party organizations. Even in the case of national nominations a president's advantages are checked by those of others. In 1944 it is by no means clear that Roosevelt got his first choice as his running mate. In 1948 Truman, then the president, faced serious revolts against his nomination. In 1952 his intervention from the White House helped assure the choice of Adlai Stevenson, but it is far from clear that Truman could have done as much for any other candidate acceptable to him.[7] In 1956 when Eisenhower was president, the record leaves obscure just who backed Harold Stassen's effort to block Richard Nixon's renomination as vice-president. But evidently everything did not go quite as Eisenhower wanted, whatever his intentions may have been.[8] The outcomes in these instances bear all the marks of limits on command and of power checked by power that characterize congressional relations. Both in and out of politics these checks and limits seem to be quite widely understood.

Influence becomes still more a matter of give-and-take when presidents attempt to deal with allied governments. A classic illustration is the long unhappy wrangle over Suez policy in 1956. In dealing with the British and the French before their military intervention, Eisenhower had his share of bargaining advantages but no effective power of command. His allies had their share of counter pressures, and they finally tried the most extreme of all: action despite him. His pressure then was instrumental in reversing them. But had the British government been on safe ground *at home*, Eisenhower's wishes might have made as little difference after intervention as before. Behind the decorum of diplomacy—which was not very decorous in the Suez affair—relationships among allies are not unlike relationships among state delegations at a national convention. Power is persuasion and persuasion becomes bargaining. The concept is familiar to everyone who watches foreign policy.

In only one sphere is the concept unfamiliar: the sphere of executive relations. Perhaps because of civics textbooks and teaching in our schools, Americans instinctively resist the view that power in this sphere resembles power in all others. Even Washington reporters, White House aides, and congressmen are not immune to the illusion that administrative agencies comprise a single structure, "the" executive branch, where presidential word is law, or ought to be.

Yet we have seen . . . that when a president seeks something from executive officials his persuasiveness is subject to the same sorts of limitations as in the case of congressmen, or governors, or national committeemen, or private citizens, or foreign governments. There are no generic differences, no differences in kind and only sometimes in degree. The incidents preceding the dismissal of MacArthur and the incidents surrounding seizure of the steel mills make it plain that here as elsewhere influence derives from bargaining advantages; power is a give-and-take.

Like our governmental structure as a whole, the executive establishment consists of separated institutions sharing powers. The president heads one of these; cabinet officers, agency administrators, and military commanders head others. Below the departmental level, virtually independent bureau chiefs head many more. Under mid-century conditions, federal operations spill across dividing lines on organization charts; almost every policy entangles many agencies; almost every program calls for interagency collaboration. Everything somehow involves the president. But operating agencies owe their existence least of all to one another—and only in some part to him. Each has a separate statutory base; each has its statutes to administer; each deals with a different set of subcommittees at the Capitol. Each has its own peculiar set of clients, friends, and enemies outside the formal government. Each has a different set of specialized careerists inside its own bailiwick. Our Constitution gives the president the "take-care" clause and the appointive power. Our statutes give him central budgeting and a degree of personnel control. All agency administrators are responsible to him. But they *also* are responsible to Congress, to their clients, to their staffs, and to themselves. In short, they have five masters. Only after all of those do they owe any loyalty to each other.

"The members of the cabinet," Charles G. Dawes used to remark, "are a president's natural enemies." Dawes had been Harding's budget director, Coolidge's vice-president, and Hoover's ambassador to London; he also had been General Pershing's chief assistant for supply in the First World War. The words are highly colored, but Dawes knew whereof he spoke. The men who have to serve so many masters cannot help but be somewhat the "enemy" of any one of them. By the same token, any master wanting service is in some degree the "enemy" of such a servant. A president is likely to want loyal support but not to relish trouble on his doorstep. Yet the more his cabinet members cleave to him, the more they may need help from him in fending off the wrath of rival masters. Help, though, is synonymous with trouble. Many a cabinet officer with loyalty ill-rewarded by his lights and help withheld, has come to view the White House as innately hostile to department heads. Dawes' dictum can be turned around.

A senior presidential aide remarked to me in Eisenhower's time: "If some of these cabinet members would just take time out to stop and ask themselves 'What would I want if I were president?', they wouldn't give him all the trouble he's been having." But even if they asked themselves the question, such officials often could not act upon the answer. Their personal attachment to the president is all too often overwhelmed by duty to their other masters.

Executive officials are not equally advantaged in their dealings with a president. Nor are the same officials equally advantaged all the time. Not every officeholder can resist like a MacArthur, or like Arnall, Sawyer, Wilson, in a rough descending order of effective counter pressure. The vantage points conferred upon officials by their own authority and status vary enormously. The variance is heightened by particulars of time and circumstance. In mid-October 1950, Truman, at a press conference, remarked of the man he had considered firing in August and would fire the next April for intolerable insubordination:

> Let me tell you something that will be good for your souls. It's a pity that you . . . can't understand the ideas of two intellectually honest men when they meet. General MacArthur . . . is a member of the Government of the United States. He is loyal to that Government. He is loyal to the President. He is loyal to the President in his foreign policy. . . . There is no disagreement between General MacArthur and myself. . . .[9]

MacArthur's status in and out of government was never higher than when Truman spoke those words. The words, once spoken, added to the general's credibility thereafter when he sought to use the press in his campaign against the president. And what had happened between August and October? Near-victory had happened, together with that premature conference on *post*-war plans, the meeting at Wake Island.

If the bargaining advantages of a MacArthur fluctuate with changing circumstances, this is bound to be so with subordinates who have at their disposal fewer "powers," lesser status, to fall back on. And when officials have no "powers" in their own right, or depend upon the president for status, their counter pressure may be limited indeed. White House aides, who fit both categories, are among the most responsive men of all, and for good reason. As a director of the budget once remarked to me,

> Thank God I'm here and not across the street. If the President doesn't call me, I've got plenty I can do right here and plenty coming up to me, by rights, to justify my calling him. But those poor fellows over there, if the boss doesn't call them, doesn't ask them to do something, what *can* they do but sit?

Authority and status so conditional are frail reliances in resisting a president's own wants. Within the White House precincts, lifted eyebrows may suffice to set an aide in motion; command, coercion, even charm aside. But even in the White House a president does not monopolize effective power. Even there persuasion is akin to bargaining. A former Roosevelt aide once wrote of cabinet officers:

> Half of a President's suggestions, which theoretically carry the weight of orders, can be safely forgotten by a Cabinet member. And if the President asks about a suggestion a second time, he can be told that it is being investigated. If he asks a third time, a wise Cabinet officer will give him at least part of what he suggests. But only occasionally, except about the most important matters, do Presidents ever get around to asking three times.[10]

The rule applies to staff as well as to the cabinet, and certainly has been applied *by* staff in Truman's time and Eisenhower's.

Some aides will have more vantage points than a selective memory. Sherman Adams, for example, as the assistant to the president under Eisenhower, scarcely deserved the appellation "White House aide" in the meaning of the term before his time or as applied to other members of the Eisenhower entourage. Although Adams was by no means "chief of staff" in any sense so sweeping—or so simple—as press commentaries often took for granted, he apparently became no more dependent on the president than Eisenhower on him. "I need him," said the president when Adams turned out to have been remarkably imprudent in the Goldfine case, and delegated to him even the decision on his own departure.[11] This instance is extreme, but the tendency it illustrates is common enough. Any aide who demonstrates to others that he has the president's consistent confidence and a consistent part in presidential business will acquire so much business on his own account that he becomes in some sense independent of his chief. Nothing in the Constitution keeps a well-placed aide from converting status into power of his own, usable in some degree even against the president—an outcome not unknown in Truman's regime or, by all accounts, in Eisenhower's.

The more an officeholder's status and his "powers" stem from sources independent of the president, the stronger will be his potential pressure *on* the president. Department heads in general have more bargaining power than do most members of the White House staff; but bureau chiefs may have still more, and specialists at upper levels of established career services may have almost unlimited reserves of the enormous power which consists of sitting still. As Franklin Roosevelt once remarked:

> The Treasury is so large and far-flung and ingrained in its practices that I find it is almost impossible to get the action and results I want—even with Henry [Morgenthau] there. But the Treasury is not to be compared with the State Department. You should go through the experience of trying to get any changes in the thinking, policy, and action of the career diplomats and then you'd know what a real problem was. But the Treasury and the State Department put together are nothing compared with the Na-a-vy. The admirals are really something to cope with—and I should know. To change anything in the Na-a-vy is like punching a feather bed. You punch it with your right and you punch it with your left until you are finally exhausted, and then you find the damn bed just as it was before you started punching.[12]

[Three pages of original text omitted at this point.]

The essence of a president's persuasive task with congressmen and everybody else, *is to induce them to believe that what he wants of them is what their own appraisal of their own responsibilities requires them to do in their interest, not his.* Because men may differ in their views on public policy, because differences in outlook stem from differences in duty—duty to one's office, one's constituents, oneself—that task is bound to be more like collective bargaining than like a reasoned argument among philosopher kings. Overtly or implicitly, hard bargaining has characterized all illustrations offered up to now. This is the reason why: persuasion deals in the coin of self-interest with men who have some freedom to reject what they find counterfeit.

NOTES

[1] The reader will want to keep in mind the distinction between two senses in which the word *power* is employed. When I have used the word (or its plural) to refer to formal constitutional, statutory, or customary authority, it is either qualified by the adjective "formal" or placed in quotation marks as "power(s)." Where I have used it in the sense of effective influence upon the conduct of others, it appears without quotation marks (and always in the singular). Where clarity and convenience permit, *authority* is substituted for "power" in the first sense and *influence* for power in the second sense.

[2] See, for example, his press conference of July 22, 1959, as reported in the *New York Times* for July 23, 1959.

[3] See Douglass Cater, *The Fourth Branch of Government* (Boston: Houghton Mifflin, 1959).

[4] With the exception of the vice-presidency, of course.

[5] See David B. Truman's illuminating study of party relationships in the 81st Congress, *The Congressional Party* (New York: Wiley, 1959), especially chaps. 4, 6, and 8.

[6] As secretary of the interior in 1939, Harold Ickes refused to approve the sale of helium to Germany despite the insistence of the State Department and the urging of President Roosevelt. Without the secretary's approval, such sales were forbidden by statute. See *The Secret Diaries of Harold L. Ickes*, vol. 2 (New York: Simon and Schuster, 1954), especially pp. 391–393, 396–399. See also Michael J. Reagan, "The Helium Controversy" in the forthcoming case book on civil-military relations prepared for the Twentieth Century Fund under the editorial direction of Harold Stein.

In this instance the statutory authority ran to the secretary as a matter of *his* discretion. A president is unlikely to fire cabinet officers for the conscientious exercise of such authority. If the president did so, their successors might well be embarrassed both publicly and at the Capitol were they to reverse decisions previously taken. As for a president's authority to set aside discretionary determinations of this sort, it rests, if it exists at all, on shaky legal ground not likely to be trod save in the gravest of situations.

[7] Truman's *Memoirs* indicate that having tried and failed to make Stevenson an avowed candidate in the spring of 1952, the president decided to support the candidacy of Vice President Barkley. But Barkley withdrew early in the convention for lack of key northern support. Though Truman is silent on the matter, Barkley's active candidacy nearly was revived during the balloting, but the forces then aligning to revive it were led by opponents of Truman's Fair Deal, principally southerners. As a practical matter, the president could not have lent his weight to *their* endeavors and could back no one but Stevenson to counter them. The latter's strength could not be shifted, then, to Harriman or Kefauver. Instead the other northerners had to be withdrawn. Truman helped withdraw them. But he had no other option. See Memoirs by Harry S. Truman, vol. 2, *Years of Trial and Hope* (Garden City: Doubleday, 1956, copr. 1956 Time Inc.), pp. 495–496.

[8] The reference is to Stassen's public statement of July 23, 1956, calling for Nixon's replacement on the Republican ticket by Governor Herter of Massachusetts, the later secretary of state. Stassen's statement was issued after a conference with the president. Eisenhower's public statements on the vice-presidential nomination, both before and after Stassen's call, permit of alternative inferences: either that the president would have preferred another candidate, provided this could be arranged without a showing of White House dictation, or that he wanted Nixon on condition that the latter could show popular appeal. In the event, neither result was achieved. Eisenhower's own remarks lent strength to rapid party moves which smothered Stassen's effort. Nixon's nomination thus was

guaranteed too quickly to appear the consequence of popular demand. For the public record on this matter see reported statements by Eisenhower, Nixon, Stassen, Herter, and Leonard Hall (the Republican National Chairman) in the *New York Times* for March 1, 8, 15, 16; April 27; July 15, 16, 25–31; August 3, 4, 17, 23, 1956. See also the account from private sources by Earl Mazo in *Richard Nixon: A Personal and Politial Portrait* (New York: Harper, 1959), pp. 158–187.

[9] Stenographic transcript of presidential press conference, October 19, 1950, on file in the Truman Library at Independence, Missouri.

[10] Jonathan Daniels, *Frontier on the Potomac* (New York: Macmillan, 1946), pp. 31–32.

[11] Transcript of presidential press conference, June 18, 1958, in *Public Papers of the Presidents: Dwight D. Eisenhower*, 1958 (Washington: The National Archives, 1959), p. 479. In the summer of 1958, a congressional investigation into the affairs of a New England textile manufacturer, Bernard Goldfine, revealed that Sherman Adams had accepted various gifts and favors from him (the most notoriety attached to a vicuña coat). Adams also had made inquiries about the status of a Federal Communications Commission proceeding in which Goldfine was involved. In September 1958, Adams was allowed to resign. The episode was highly publicized and much discussed in that year's congressional campaigns.

[12] As reported in Marriner S. Eccles, *Beckoning Frontiers* (New York: Knopf, 1951), p. 336.

29

THOMAS E. CRONIN

THE SWELLING OF THE PRESIDENCY

The advent of Richard Nixon's second term in the White House is marked by an uncommon amount of concern, in Congress and elsewhere, about the expansion of presidential power and manpower. Even the president himself is ostensibly among those who are troubled. Soon after his reelection, Mr. Nixon announced that he was planning to pare back the presidential staff. And in recent days, the president has said he is taking action to cut the presidential workforce in half and to "substantially" reduce the number of organizations that now come under the White House. Mr. Nixon's announcements have no doubt been prompted in part by a desire to add drama and an aura of change to the commencement of his second term. But he also seems genuinely worried that the presidency may have grown so large and top-heavy that it now weakens rather than strengthens his ability to manage the federal government. His fears are justified.

The presidency has, in fact, grown a full 20 percent in the last four years alone in terms of the number of people who are employed directly under the president. It has swelled to the point where it is now only a little short of the State Department's sprawling domestic bureaucracy in size.

This burgeoning growth of the presidency has, in the process, made the traditional civics textbook picture of the executive branch of our government nearly obsolete. According to this view, the executive branch is more or less neatly divided into cabinet departments and their secretaries, agencies and their heads, and the president. A more contemporary view takes note of a few prominent presidential aides and refers to them as the "White House staff." But neither view adequately recognizes the large and growing coterie that surrounds the president and is made up of dozens of assistants, hundreds of presidential advisers, and thousands of members of an institutional amalgam called the Executive Office of the President. While the men and women in these categories all fall directly under the president in the organizational charts, there is no generally used term for their common terrain. But it has swelled so much in size and scope in recent years, and has become such an important part of the federal government, that it deserves its own designation. Most apt perhaps is the Presidential Establishment.

The Presidential Establishment today embraces more than twenty support staffs (the White House Office, National Security Council, and Office of Management and Budget, etc.) and advisory offices (Council of Economic Advisers, Office of Science and Technology, and Office of Telecommunications Policy, etc.). It has spawned a vast proliferation of ranks and titles to go with its proliferation of functions (Counsel to the President, Assistant to the President, Special Counselor, Special Assistant, Special Consultant, Director, Staff Director, etc.). "The White House now has enough people with fancy titles to populate a Gilbert and Sullivan comic opera," Congressman Morris Udall has reasonably enough observed.

There are no official figures on the size of the Presidential Establishment, and standard body counts vary widely depending on who is and who is not included in the count, but by one frequently used reckoning, between five and six thousand people work for the president of the United States. Payroll and maintenance costs for this staff run between $100 million and $150 million a year. (These figures include the Office of Economic Opportunity (OEO), which is an Executive Office agency and employs two thousand people, but not the roughly fifteen-thousand-man Central Intelligence Agency, although that, too, is directly responsible to the chief executive.) These "White House" workers have long since outgrown the White House itself and now occupy not only two wings of the executive mansion but three nearby high-rise office buildings as well.

The expansion of the Presidential Establishment, it should be emphasized, is by no means only a phenomenon of the Nixon years. The number of employees under the president has been growing steadily since the early 1900s when only a few dozen people served in the White House entourage, at a cost of less than a few hundred thousand dollars annually. Congress's research arm, the Congressional Research Service, has compiled a count that underlines in particular the accelerated increase in the last two decades. This compilation shows that between 1954 and 1971 the number of presidential advisers has grown from 25 to 45, the White House staff from 266 to 600, and the Executive Office staff from 1,175 to 5,395.

But if the growth of the Presidential Establishment antedates the current administration, it is curious at least that one of the largest expansions ever, in both relative and absolute terms, has taken place during the first term of a conservative, management-minded president who has often voiced his objection to any expansion of the federal government and its bureaucracy.

Under President Nixon, in fact, there has been an almost systematic bureaucratization of the Presidential Establishment, in which more new councils and offices have been established, more specialization and division of labor and layers of staffing have been added, than at any time except during World War II. Among the major Nixonian additions are the Council on Environmental Quality, Council on International Economic Policy, Domestic Council, and Office of Consumer Affairs.

The numbers in the White House entourage may have decreased somewhat since November when the president announced his intention to make certain staff cuts. They may shrink still more if, as expected, the OEO is shifted from

White House supervision to cabinet control, mainly under the Department of Health, Education, and Welfare. Also, in the months ahead, the president will probably offer specific legislative proposals, as he has done before, to reprogram or repackage the upper reaches of the executive.

Even so, any diminution of the Presidential Establishment has so far been more apparent than real, or more incidental than substantial. Some aides, such as former presidential counselor Robert Finch, who have wanted to leave anyway, have done so. Others, serving as scapegoats on the altar of Watergate, are also departing.

In addition, the president has officially removed a number of trusted domestic-policy staff assistants from the White House rolls and dispersed them to key sub-cabinet posts across the span of government. But this dispersal can be viewed as not so much reducing as creating yet another expansion—a virtual setting up of White House outposts (or little White Houses?) throughout the cabinet departments. The aides that are being sent forth are notable for their intimacy with the president, and they will surely maintain direct links to the White House, even though these links do not appear on the official organizational charts.

Then, too, one of the most important of the president's recent shifts of executive branch members involves an unequivocal addition to the Presidential Establishment. This is the formal setting up of a second office—with space and a staff in the White House—for Treasury Secretary George Shultz as chairman of yet another new presidential body, the Council on Economic Policy. This move makes Shultz a member of a White House inner cabinet. He will now be over-secretary of economic affairs alongside Henry Kissinger, over-secretary for national security affairs, and John Ehrlichman, over-secretary for domestic affairs.

In other words, however the names and numbers have changed recently or may be shifted about in the near future, the Presidential Establishment does not seem to be declining in terms of function, power, or prerogative; in fact, it may be continuing to grow as rapidly as ever.

Does it matter? A number of political analysts have argued recently that it does, and I agree with them. Perhaps the most disturbing aspect of the expansion of the Presidential Establishment is that it has become a powerful inner sanctum of government, isolated from traditional, constitutional checks and balances. It is common practice today for anonymous, unelected, and unratified aides to negotiate sensitive international commitments by means of executive agreements that are free from congressional oversight. Other aides in the Presidential Establishment wield fiscal authority over billions of dollars in funds that Congress has appropriated, yet the president refuses to spend, or that Congress has assigned to one purpose and the administration routinely redirects to another—all with no semblance of public scrutiny. Such exercises of power pose an important, perhaps vital, question of governmental philosophy: Should a political system that has made a virtue of periodic electoral accountability accord an ever-increasing policy-making role to White House counselors who neither are confirmed by the U.S. Senate nor, because of the doctrine of "executive privilege," are subject to questioning by Congress?

Another disquieting aspect of the growth of the Presidential Establishment is that the increase of its powers has been largely at the expense of the traditional sources of executive power and policy-making—the cabinet members and their departments. When I asked a former Kennedy-Johnson cabinet member a while ago what he would like to do if he ever returned to government, he said he would rather be a presidential assistant than a cabinet member. And this is an increasingly familiar assessment of the relative influence of the two levels of the executive branch. The Presidential Establishment has become, in effect, a whole layer of government between the president and the cabinet, and it often stands above the cabinet in terms of influence with the president. In spite of the exalted position that cabinet members hold in textbooks and protocol, a number of cabinet members in recent administrations have complained that they could not even get the president's ear except through an assistant. In his book *Who Owns America?*, former Secretary of the Interior Walter Hickel recounts his combat with a dozen different presidential functionaries and tells how he needed clearance from them before he could get to talk to the president, or how he frequently had to deal with the assistants themselves because the president was "too busy." During an earlier administration, President Eisenhower's chief assistant, Sherman Adams, was said to have told two cabinet members who could not resolve a matter of mutual concern: "Either make up your mind or else tell me and I will do it. We must not bother the president with this. He is trying to keep the world from war." Several of President Kennedy's cabinet members regularly battled with White House aides who blocked them from seeing the president. And McGeorge Bundy, as Kennedy's chief assistant for national security affairs, simply sidestepped the State Department in one major area of department communications. He had all important incoming State Department cables transmitted simultaneously to his office in the White House, part of an absorption of traditional State Department functions that visibly continues to this day with presidential assistant Henry Kissinger. Indeed, we recently witnessed the bizarre and telling spectacle of Secretary of State William Rogers insisting that he *did* have a role in making foreign policy.

In a speech in 1971, Senator Ernest Hollings of South Carolina plaintively noted the lowering of cabinet status. "It used to be," he said,

> that if I had a problem with food stamps, I went to see the secretary of agriculture, whose department had jurisdiction over that problem. Not anymore. Now, if I want to learn the policy, I must go to the White House to consult John Price [a special assistant]. If I want the latest on textiles, I won't get it from the secretary of commerce, who has the authority and responsibility. No, I am forced to go to the White House and see Mr. Peter Flanigan. I shouldn't feel too badly. Secretary Stans [Maurice Stans, then secretary of commerce] has to do the same thing.

If cabinet members individually have been downgraded in influence, the cabinet itself as a council of government has become somewhat of a relic, replaced by more specialized comminglings that as often as not are presided over by White House staffers. The cabinet's decline has taken place over several administrations. John Kennedy started out his term declaring his intentions of using the cabinet as a major policy-making body, but his change of mind was swift, as his postmaster general, J. Edward Day, has noted. "After the first two or three meetings," Day has written,

> one had the distinct impression that the President felt that decisions on major matters were not made—or even influenced—at Cabinet sessions, and that discussion there was a waste of time. . . . When members spoke up to suggest or to discuss major administration policy, the President would listen with thinly disguised impatience and then postpone or otherwise bypass the question.

Lyndon Johnson was equally disenchanted with the cabinet as a body and characteristically held cabinet sessions only when articles appeared in the press talking about how the cabinet was withering away. Under Nixon, the cabinet is almost never convened at all.

Not only has the Presidential Establishment taken over many policy-making functions from the cabinet and its members, it has also absorbed some of the operational functions. White House aides often feel they should handle any matters that they regard as ineptly administered, and they tend to intervene in internal departmental operations at lower and lower levels. They often feel underemployed, too, and so are inclined to reach out into the departments to find work and exercise authority for themselves.

The result is a continuous undercutting of cabinet departments—and the cost is heavy. These intrusions can cripple the capacity of cabinet officials to present policy alternatives, and they diminish self-confidence, morale, and initiative within the departments. George Ball, a former undersecretary of state, noted the effects on the State Department:

> Able men, with proper pride in their professional skills, will not long tolerate such votes of no-confidence, so it should be no surprise that they are leaving the career service, and making way for mediocrity with the result that, as time goes on, it may be hopelessly difficult to restore the Department.

The irony of this accretion of numbers and functions to the Presidential Establishment is that the presidency is finding itself increasingly afflicted with the very ills of the traditional departments that the expansions were often intended to remedy. The presidency has become a large, complex bureaucracy itself, rapidly acquiring many dubious characteristics of large bureaucracies in the process: layering, overspecialization, communication gaps, interoffice rivalries, inadequate coordination, and an impulse to become consumed with short-term, urgent operational concerns at the expense of thinking systematically about the consequences of varying sets of policies and priorities and about important long-range problems. It takes so much of the president's time to deal with the members of his own bureaucracy that it is little wonder he has little time to hear counsel from cabinet officials.

Another toll of the burgeoning Presidential Establishment is that White House aides, in assuming more and more responsibility for the management of government programs, inevitably lose the detachment and objectivity that is so essential for evaluating new ideas. Can a lieutenant vigorously engaged in implementing the presidential will admit the possibility that what the president wants is wrong or not working? Yet a president is increasingly dependent on the judgment of these same staff members, since he seldom sees his cabinet members.

Why has the presidency grown bigger and bigger? There is no single villain or systematically organized conspiracy promoting this expansion. A variety of factors is at work. The most significant is the expansion of the role of the presidency itself—an expansion that for the most part has taken place during national emergencies. The reason for this is that the public and Congress in recent decades have both tended to look to the president for the decisive responses that were needed in those emergencies. The Great Depression and World War II in particular brought sizable increases in presidential staffs. And once in place, many stayed on, even after the emergencies that brought them had faded. Smaller national crises have occasioned expansion in the White House entourage, too. After the Russians successfully orbited *Sputnik* in 1957, President Eisenhower added several science advisers. After the Bay of Pigs, President Kennedy enlarged his national security staff.

Considerable growth in the Presidential Establishment, especially in the post-World War II years, stems directly from the belief that critical societal problems require that wise men be assigned to the White House to alert the President to appropriate solutions and to serve as the agents for implementing these solutions. Congress has frequently acted on the basis of this belief, legislating the creation of the National Security Council, the Council of Economic Advisers, and the Council on Environmental Quality, among others. Congress has also increased the chores of the presidency by making it a statutory responsibility for the president to prepare more and more reports associated with what are regarded as critical social areas—annual economic and manpower reports, a biennial report on national growth, etc.

Most recently, President Nixon responded to a number of troublesome problems that defy easy relegation to any one department—problems like international trade and drug abuse—by setting up special offices in the Executive Office with sweeping authority and sizable staffs. Once established, these units rarely get dislodged. And an era of permanent crisis ensures a continuing accumulation of such bodies.

Another reason for the growth of the Presidential Establishment is that occupants of the White House frequently distrust members of the permanent government. Nixon aides, for example, have viewed most civil servants not only as Democratic but as wholly unsympathetic to such objectives of the Nixon administration as decentralization, revenue sharing, and the curtailment of several Great Society programs. Departmental bureaucracies are viewed from the White House as independent, unresponsive, unfamiliar, and inaccessible. They are suspected again and again of placing their own, congressional, or special-interest priorities ahead of those communicated to them from the White House. Even the president's own cabinet members soon become viewed in the same light; one of the strengths of cabinet members, namely their capacity to make a compelling case for their programs, has proved to be their chief liability with presidents.

Presidents may want this type of advocacy initially, but they soon grow weary and wary of it. Not long ago, one White House aide accused a former labor secretary of trying to "out-Meany Meany." Efforts by former Interior Secretary Hickel to advance certain environmental programs and by departing Housing and Urban Development Secretary George Romney to promote innovative housing construction methods not only were unwelcome but after a while were viewed with considerable displeasure and suspicion at the White House.

Hickel writes poignantly of coming to this recognition during his final meeting with President Nixon, in the course of which the president frequently referred to him as an "adversary." "Initially," writes Hickel,

> I considered that a compliment because, to me, an adversary is a valuable asset. It was only after the President had used the term many times and with a disapproving inflection that I realized he considered an adversary an enemy. I could not understand why he would consider me an enemy.

Not only have recent presidents been suspicious about the depth of the loyalty of those in their cabinets, but they also invariably become concerned about the possibility that sensitive administration secrets may leak out through the departmental bureaucracies, and this is another reason why presidents have come to rely more on their own personal groups, such as task forces and advisory commissions.

Still another reason that more and more portfolios have been given to the presidency is that new federal programs frequently concern more than one federal agency, and it seems reasonable that someone at a higher level is required to fashion a consistent policy and to reconcile conflicts. Attempts by cabinet members themselves to solve sensitive jurisdictional questions frequently result in bitter squabbling. At times, too, cabinet members themselves have recommended that these multidepartmental issues be settled at the White House. Sometimes new presidential appointees insist that new offices for program coordination be assigned directly under the president. Ironically, such was the plea of George McGovern, for example, when President Kennedy offered him the post of director of the Food-for-Peace program in 1961. McGovern attacked the buildup of the Presidential Establishment in his campaign against Nixon, but back in 1961 he wanted visibility (and no doubt celebrity status) and he successfully argued against his being located outside the White House—either in the State or Agriculture departments. President Kennedy and his then campaign manager Robert Kennedy felt indebted to McGovern because of his efforts in assisting the Kennedy presidential campaign in South Dakota. Accordingly, McGovern was granted not only a berth in the Executive Office of the President but also the much-coveted title of special assistant to the president.

The Presidential Establishment has also been enlarged by the representation of interest groups within its fold. Even a partial listing of staff specializations that have been grafted onto the White House in recent years reveals how interest-group brokerage has become added to the more traditional staff activities of counseling and administration. These specializations form a veritable index of American society:

> Budget and management, national security, economics, congressional matters, science and technology, drug abuse prevention, telecommunications, consumers, national goals, intergovernmental relations, environment, domestic policy, international economics, military affairs, civil rights, disarmament, labor relations, District of Columbia, cultural affairs, education, foreign trade and tariffs, past Presidents, the aged, health and nutrition, physical fitness, volunteerism, intellectuals, blacks, youth, women, "the Jewish community," Wall Street, governors, mayors, "ethnics," regulatory agencies and related industry, state party chairmen, Mexican-Americans.

It is as if interest groups and professions no longer settle for lobbying Congress, or having one of their number appointed to departmental advisory boards or sub-cabinet positions. It now appears essential to "have your own man right there in the White House." Once this foothold is established, of course, interest groups can play upon the potential political backlash that could arise should their representation be discontinued.

One of the more disturbing elements in the growth of the Presidential Establishment is the development, particularly under the current administration, of a huge public-relations apparatus. More than 100 presidential aides are now engaged in various forms of press-agentry or public relations, busily selling and reselling the president. This activity is devoted to the particular occupant of the White House, but inevitably it affects the presidency itself, by projecting or reinforcing images of the presidency that are almost imperial in their suggestions of omnipotence and omniscience. Thus the public-relations apparatus not only has directly enlarged the presidential workforce but has expanded public expectations about the presidency at the same time.

Last, but by no means least, Congress, which has grown increasingly critical of the burgeoning power of the presidency, must take some blame itself for the expansion of the White House. Divided within itself and ill-equipped, or simply disinclined to make some of the nation's toughest political decisions in recent decades, Congress has abdicated more and more authority to the presidency. The fact that the recent massive bombing of North Vietnam was ordered by the president without even a pretense of consultation with Congress buried what little was left of the semblance of that body's war-making power. Another recent instance of Congress's tendency to surrender authority to the presidency, an extraordinary instance, was the passage by the House (though not the Senate) of a grant to the president that would give him the right to determine which programs are to be cut whenever the budget goes beyond a $250 billion ceiling limit—a bill which, in effect, would hand over to the president some of Congress's long-cherished "power of the purse."

What can be done to bring the Presidential Establishment back down to size? What can be done to bring it to a size that both lightens the heavy accumulation of functions that it has absorbed and allows the Presidential Establishment to perform its most important functions more effectively and wisely?

First, Congress should curb its own impulse to establish new presidential agencies and to ask for yet additional reports and studies from the president. In the past Congress has been a too willing partner in the enlargement of the presidency. If Congress genuinely wants a leaner presidency, it should ask more of itself. For instance, it could well make better use of its own General Accounting Office and Congressional Research Service for chores that are now often assigned to the president.

Congress should also establish in each of its houses special committees on Executive Office operations. Most congressional committees are organized to deal with areas such as labor, agriculture, armed services, or education, paralleling the organization of the cabinet. What we need now are committees designed explicitly to oversee the White House. No longer can the task of overseeing presidential operations be dispersed among dozens of committees and subcommittees, each of which can look at only small segments of the Presidential Establishment.

Some will complain that adding yet another committee to the already overburdened congressional system is just like adding another council to the overstuffed Presidential Establishment. But the central importance of what the presidency does (and does not do) must rank among the most critical tasks of the contemporary Congress. As things are organized now, the presidency escapes with grievously inadequate scrutiny. Equally important, Congress needs these committees to help protect itself from its own tendency to relinquish to the presidency its diminishing resources and prerogatives. Since Truman, presidents have had staffs to oversee Congress; it is time Congress reciprocated.

Similar efforts to let the salutary light of public attention shine more brightly on the presidency should be inaugurated by the serious journals and newspapers of the nation. For too long, publishers and editors have believed that covering the presidency means assigning a reporter to the White House press corps. Unfortunately, however, those who follow the president around on his travels are rarely in a position to do investigative reporting on what is going on inside the Presidential Establishment. Covering the Executive Office of the President requires more than a president watcher; it needs a specialist who understands the arcane language and highly complex practices that have grown up in the Presidential Establishment.

Finally, it is time to reverse the downgrading of the cabinet. President Nixon ostensibly moved in this direction with his designation several days ago of three cabinet heads—HEW's Caspar W. Weinberger, Agriculture's Earl L. Butz, and HUD's James T. Lynn—as, in effect, super-secretaries of "human resources," "natural resources," and "community development" respectively. The move was expressly made in the name of cabinet consolidation, plans for which Mr. Nixon put forward in 1971 but which Congress has so far spurned.

The three men will hold onto their cabinet posts, but they have been given

White House offices as well—as presidential counselors—and so it may be that the most direct effect of the appointments is a further expansion of the Presidential Establishment, rather than a counter-bolstering of the cabinet. But if the move does, in fact, lead to cabinet consolidation under broader divisions, it will be a step in the right direction.

Reducing the present number of departments would strengthen the hand of cabinet members vis-à-vis special interests, and might enable them to serve as advisers, as well as advocates, to the president. Cabinet consolidation would also have another very desirable effect: it would be a move toward reducing the accumulation of power within the Presidential Establishment. For much of the power of budget directors and other senior White House aides comes from their roles as penultimate referees of interdepartmental jurisdictional disputes. Under consolidated departments, a small number of strengthened cabinet officers with closer ties to the president would resolve these conflicts instead. With fewer but broader cabinet departments, there would be less need for many of the interest-group brokers and special councils that now constitute so much of the excessive baggage in the overburdened presidency.

Meantime, the presidency remains sorely overburdened—with both functions and functionaries—and needs very much to be cut back in both. Certainly, the number of presidential workers can and should be reduced. Harry Truman put it best, perhaps, when he said with characteristic succinctness: "I do not like this present trend toward a huge White House staff . . . . Mostly these aides get in each other's way." But while the number of functionaries is the most tangible and dramatic measure of the White House's expansion, its increasing absorption of governmental functions is more profoundly disturbing. The current White House occupant may regard cutting down (or transferring) a number of his staff members as a way of mollifying critics who charge that the American presidency has grown too big and bloated, but it is yet another thing to reduce the president's authority or his accumulated prerogatives. As the nation's number-one critic of the swelling of government, President Nixon will, it is hoped, move—or will continue to move if he has truly already started—to substantially deflate this swelling in one of the areas where it most needs to be deflated—at home, in the White House.

PART EIGHT

THE BUREAUCRACY

PART EIGHT

THE BUREAUCRACY

American government has become bureaucratized. Today there are close to 3 million federal civil servants and about 12 million state and local public employees. These individuals are engaged in the making and implementing of public policy. They have discretionary authority over large sums of money and over the ways in which public policies will be formulated and applied. American public service is characterized by hierarchy, specialization, formalization, impersonality, and the selection and promotion of employees on the basis of some conception of merit and seniority. The extent of bureaucratization was unanticipated by the Founders; nor was it envisioned in the Constitution. Not surprisingly, therefore, dealing effectively with the phenomenon has been difficult.

As James Q. Wilson points out in "The Rise of the Bureaucratic State" (1975), the development of a large-scale federal bureaucracy has created several political problems. Foremost among these is the basic incompatibility of bureaucratic government and democratic government. In order to function, democracy requires pluralism, equality, liberty, rotation in office, equal access to participation in politics, and elections. Bureaucracy, by contrast, relies upon unity, hierarchy, command, long duration in office, differentiated access to participation in policy-making, and appointment. Though many scholars and public officials have sought ways in which to reduce this incompatibility, the fact remains that a great deal of political power and influence is currently concentrated in the hands of unelected, largely irremovable, and somewhat uncontrollable public bureaucrats. Each essay in this section addresses this problem from a different perspective.

Wilson traces the development of the federal bureaucracy and discusses several of the issues raised by the bureaucratization of American government. Ultimately, he concludes that bureaucratization is not damaging in itself, but rather that "the crucial test of [agencies'] value is their behavior, and that can be judged only by applying economic and welfare criteria to the policies they produce. But if such judgments should prove damning, as increasingly has been the case, then the problem of finding the authority with which to alter or abolish such organizations becomes acute. In this regard the theory of the separation of powers has proved unhelpful." Wilson, like many others, believes that although Congress has the constitutional power and organizational ability to control the federal bureaucracy, it lacks the will to do so.

Norton E. Long's essay, "Power and Administration," (1949) was one of the first works to confront the politicality of the federal bureaucracy directly. Long believes that "the lifeblood of administration is power" and as a result of the fragmentation found in the American political system, public bureaucrats "must supplement the resources available through the hierarchy with those they can muster on their own." Unlike Wilson, however, Long argues that bureaucratic power can be harmonized with democratic government if administrative decisions are responsive to organized interest groups. "The bureaucracy is recognized by all interested groups as a major channel of representation to such an extent that Congress rightly feels the competition of a rival."

Hugh Heclo's essay on "Political Executives" (1977) addresses the same issues from the perspective of the executive branch. Political executives are political appointees to the top levels of bureaucratic agencies. Heclo finds that as a result of their limited experience and short tenure, and the nature of executive branch politics and organization, it is fruitless to expect political executives, including cabinet members, to bridge the gap between democracy and bureaucracy: "Despite all the resources devoted to more topside staff, new management initiatives, more elaborate analytic techniques, and so on, there remain few—probably fewer than ever—places where political executives can look for reliable political support in any efforts at leadership in the bureaucracy. Political appointees in Washington are substantially on their own and vulnerable to bureaucratic power."

Graham T. Allison's article, "Conceptual Models and the Cuban Missile Crisis" (1969), explores the role of bureaucracy in American foreign policy-making. This selection is essentially an abbreviated version of his seminal book on the subject, *Essence of Decision*. Although Allison uses three alternative theoretical perspectives (or "conceptual lenses") to explain the dramatic events in the fall of 1962, his most enduring insights center on the influence of bureaucratic standard operating procedures, "bureaucratic politics," and organizational behavior in the decision-making process.

30

JAMES Q. WILSON

THE RISE
OF THE BUREAUCRATIC STATE

During its first 150 years, the American republic was not thought to have "bureaucracy," and thus it would have been meaningless to refer to the "problems" of a "bureaucratic state." There were, of course, appointed civilian officials: Though only about 3,000 at the end of the Federalist period, there were about 95,000 by the time Grover Cleveland assumed office in 1881, and nearly half a million by 1925. Some aspects of these numerous officials were regarded as problems—notably, the standards by which they were appointed and the political loyalties to which they were held—but these were thought to be matters of proper character and good management. The great political and constitutional struggles were not over the power of the administrative apparatus, but over the power of the President, of Congress, and of the states.

The Founding Fathers had little to say about the nature or function of the executive branch of the new government. The Constitution is virtually silent on the subject and the debates in the Constitutional Convention are almost devoid of reference to an administrative apparatus. This reflected no lack of concern about the matter, however. Indeed, it was in part because of the Founders' depressing experience with chaotic and inefficient management under the Continental Congress and the Articles of Confederation that they had assembled in Philadelphia. Management by committees composed of part-time amateurs had cost the colonies dearly in the War of Independence and few, if any, of the Founders wished to return to that system. The argument was only over how the heads of the necessary departments of government were to be selected, and whether these heads should be wholly subordinate to the President or whether instead they should form some sort of council that would advise the President and perhaps share in his authority. In the end, the Founders left if up to Congress to decide the matter.

There was no dispute in Congress that there should be executive departments, headed by single appointed officials, and, of course, the Constitution specified that these would be appointed by the President with the advice and consent of the Senate. The only issue was how such officials might be removed. After prolonged debate and by the narrowest of majorities, Congress agreed that the

President should have the sole right of removal, thus confirming that the infant administrative system would be wholly subordinate—in law at least—to the President. Had not Vice-President John Adams, presiding over a Senate equally divided on the issue, cast the deciding vote in favor of presidential removal, the administrative departments might conceivably have become legal dependencies of the legislature, with incalculable consequences for the development of the embryonic government.

THE "BUREAUCRACY PROBLEM"

The original departments were small and had limited duties. The State Department, the first to be created, had but nine employees in addition to the Secretary. The War Department did not reach 80 civilian employees until 1801; it commanded only a few thousand soldiers. Only the Treasury Department had substantial powers—it collected taxes, managed the public debt, ran the national bank, conducted land surveys, and purchased military supplies. Because of this, Congress gave the closest scrutiny to its structure and its activities.

The number of administrative agencies and employees grew slowly but steadily during the 19th and early 20th centuries and then increased explosively on the occasion of World War I, the Depression, and World War II. It is difficult to say at what point in this process the administrative system became a distinct locus of power or an independent source of political initiatives and problems. What is clear is that the emphasis on the sheer *size* of the administrative establishment—conventional in many treatments of the subject—is misleading.

The government can spend vast sums of money—wisely or unwisely—without creating that set of conditions we ordinarily associate with the bureaucratic state. For example, there could be massive transfer payments made under government auspices from person to person or from state to state, all managed by a comparatively small staff of officials and a few large computers. In 1971, the federal government paid out $54 billion under various social insurance programs, yet the Social Security Administration employs only 73,000 persons, many of whom perform purely routine jobs.

And though it may be harder to believe, the government could in principle employ an army of civilian personnel without giving rise to those organizational patterns that we call bureaucratic. Suppose, for instance, that we as a nation should decide to have in the public schools at least one teacher for every two students. This would require a vast increase in the number of teachers and schoolrooms, but almost all of the persons added would be performing more or less identical tasks, and they could be organized into very small units (e.g., neighborhood schools). Though there would be significant overhead costs, most citizens would not be aware of any increase in the "bureaucratic" aspects of education—indeed, owing to the much greater time each teacher would have to devote to each pupil and his or her parents, the citizenry might well conclude that there actually had been a substantial reduction in the amount of "bureaucracy."

To the reader predisposed to believe that we have a "bureaucracy problem," these hypothetical cases may seem farfetched. Max Weber, after all, warned us that in capitalist and socialist societies alike, bureaucracy was likely to acquire an "overtowering" power position. Conservatives have always feared bureaucracy, save perhaps the police. Humane socialists have frequently been embarrassed by their inability to reconcile a desire for public control of the economy with the suspicion that a public bureaucracy may be as immune to democratic control as a private one. Liberals have equivocated, either dismissing any concern for bureaucracy as reactionary quibbling about social progress or embracing that concern when obviously nonreactionary persons (welfare recipients, for example) express a view toward the Department of Health and Human Services indistinguishable from the view businessmen take of the Internal Revenue Service.

POLITICAL AUTHORITY

There are at least three ways in which political power may be gathered undesirably into bureaucratic hands: by the growth of an administrative apparatus so large as to be immune from popular control, by placing power over a governmental bureaucracy of any size in private rather than public hands, or by vesting discretionary authority in the hands of a public agency so that the exercise of that power is not responsive to the public good. These are not the only problems that arise because of bureaucratic organization. From the point of view of their members, bureaucracies are sometimes uncaring, ponderous, or unfair; from the point of view of their political superiors, they are sometimes unimaginative or inefficient; from the point of view of their clients, they are sometimes slow or unjust. No single account can possibly treat of all that is problematic in bureaucracy; even the part I discuss here—the extent to which political authority has been transferred undesirably to an unaccountable administrative realm—is itself too large for a single essay. But it is, if not the most important problem, then surely the one that would most have troubled our Revolutionary leaders, especially those that went on to produce the Constitution. It was, after all, the question of power that chiefly concerned them, both in redefining our relationship with England and in finding a new basis for political authority in the Colonies.

To some, following in the tradition of Weber, bureaucracy is the inevitable consequence and perhaps necessary concomitant of modernity. A money economy, the division of labor, and the evolution of legal-rational norms to justify organizational authority require the efficient adaptation of means to ends and a high degree of predictability in the behavior of rulers. To this, Georg Simmel added the view that organizations tend to acquire the characteristics of those institutions with which they are in conflict, so that as government becomes more bureaucratic, private organizations—political parties, trade unions, voluntary associations—will have an additional reason to become bureaucratic as well.

By viewing bureaucracy as an inevitable (or, as some would put it, "functional") aspect of society, we find ourselves attracted to theories that explain the growth of bureaucracy in terms of some inner dynamic to which all agencies respond and which makes all barely governable and scarcely tolerable. Bureaucracies grow, we are told, because of Parkinson's Law: Work and personnel expand to consume the available resources. Bureaucracies behave, we believe, in accord with various other maxims, such as the Peter Principle: In hierarchial organizations, personnel are promoted up to that point at which their incompetence becomes manifest—hence, all important positions are held by incompetents. More elegant, if not essentially different, theories have been propounded by scholars. The tendency of all bureaus to expand is explained by William A. Niskanen by the assumption, derived from the theory of the firm, that "bureaucrats maximize the total budget of their bureau during their tenure"—hence, "all bureaus are too large." What keeps them from being not merely too large but all-consuming is that fact that a bureau must deliver to some degree on its promised output, and if it consistently underdelivers, its budget will be cut by unhappy legislators. But since measuring the output of a bureau is often difficult—indeed, even *conceptualizing* the output of the State Department is mind-boggling—the bureau has a great deal of freedom within which to seek the largest possible budget.

Such theories, both the popular and the scholarly, assign little importance to the nature of the tasks an agency performs, the constitutional framework in which it is embedded, or the preferences and attitudes of citizens and legislators. Our approach will be quite different: Different agencies will be examined in historical perspective to discover the kinds of problems—if any, to which their operation give rise, and how those problems were affected—perhaps determined—by the tasks which they were assigned, the political system in which they operated, and the preferences they were required to consult. What follows will be far from a systematic treatment of such matters, and even farther from a rigorous testing of any theory of bureaucratization. Our knowledge of agency history and behavior is too sketchy to permit that.

BUREAUCRACY AND SIZE

During the first half of the 19th century, the growth in the size of the federal bureaucracy can be explained, not by the assumption of new tasks by the government or by the imperialistic designs of the managers of existing tasks, but by the addition to existing bureaus of personnel performing essentially routine, repetitive tasks for which the public demand was great and unavoidable. The principal problem facing a bureaucracy thus enlarged was how best to coordinate its activities toward given and noncontroversial ends.

The increase in the size of the executive branch of the federal government at this time was almost entirely the result of the increase in the size of the Post Office. From 1816 to 1861, federal civilian employment in the executive branch increased nearly eightfold (from 4,837 to 36,672), but 86 percent of this growth was the result of additions to the postal service. The Post Office Department was expanding as population and commerce expanded. By 1869 there were 27,000 post offices scattered around the nation; by 1901, nearly 77,000. In New York alone, by 1894 there were nearly 3,000 postal employees, the same number required to run the entire federal government at the beginning of that century.

The organizational shape of the Post Office was more or less fixed in the administration of Andrew Jackson. The Postmaster General, almost always appointed because of his partisan position, was aided by three (later four) assistant postmaster generals dealing with appointments, mail-carrying contracts, operations, and finance. There is no reason in theory why such an organization could not deliver the mails efficiently and honestly: The task is routine, its performance is measurable, and its value is monitored by millions of customers. Yet the Post Office, from the earliest years of the 19th century, was an organization marred by inefficiency and corruption. The reason is often thought to be found in the making of political appointments to the Post Office. "Political hacks," so the theory goes, would inevitably combine dishonesty and incompetence to the disservice of the nation; thus, by cleansing the department of such persons these difficulties could be avoided. Indeed, some have argued that it was the advent of the "spoils system" under Jackson that contributed to the later inefficiencies of the public bureaucracy.

The opposite is more nearly the case. The Jacksonians did not seek to make the administrative apparatus a mere tool of the Democratic party advantage, but to purify that apparatus not only of what they took to be Federalist subversion but also of personal decadence. The government was becoming not just large, but lax. Integrity and diligence were absent, not merely from government, but from social institutions generally. The Jacksonians were in many cases concerned about the decline in what the Founders had called "republican virtue," but what their successors were more likely to call simplicity and decency. As Matthew Crenson has recently observed in his book *The Federal Machine*, Jacksonian administrators wanted to "guarantee the good behavior of civil servants" as well as to cope with bigness, and to do this they sought both to place their own followers in office and—what is more important—to create a system of depersonalized, specialized bureaucratic rule. Far from being the enemies of bureaucracy, the Jacksonians were among its principal architects.

Impersonal administrative systems, like the spoils system, were "devices for strengthening the government's authority over its own civil servants"; these bureaucratic methods were, in turn, intended to "compensate for a decline in the disciplinary power of social institutions" such as the community, the professions, and business. If public servants, like men generally in a rapidly growing and diversifying society, could no longer be relied upon "to have a delicate regard for their reputations," accurate bookkeeping, close inspections, and regularized procedures would accomplish what character could not.

Amos Kendall, Postmaster General under President Jackson, set about to achieve this goal with a remarkable series of administrative innovations. To prevent corruption, Kendall embarked on two contradictory courses of action: He sought to bring every detail of the department's affairs under his personal scrutiny and he began to reduce and divide the authority on which that scrutiny depended. Virtually every important document and many unimportant ones had to be signed by Kendall himself. At the same time, he gave to the Treasury Department the power to audit his accounts and obtained from Congress a law requiring that the revenues of the department be paid into the Treasury rather than retained by the Post Office. The duties of his subordinates were carefully defined and arranged so that the authority of one assistant would tend to check that of another. What was installed was not simply a specialized management system, but a concept of the administrative separation of powers.

Few subsequent postmasters were of Kendall's ability. The result was predictable. Endless details flowed to Washington for decision, but no one in Washington other than the Postmaster General had the authority to decide. Meanwhile, the size of the postal establishment grew by leaps and bounds. Quickly the department began to operate on the basis of habit and local custom: Since everybody reported to Washington, in effect no one did. As Leonard D. White was later to remark, "the system could work only because it was a vast, repetitive, fixed, and generally routine operation." John Wanamaker, an able businessman who became Postmaster General under President Cleveland, proposed decentralizing the department under 26 regional supervisors. But Wanamaker's own assistants in Washington were unenthusiastic about such a diminution in their authority and, in any event, Congress steadfastly refused to endorse decentralization.

Civil service reform was not strongly resisted in the Post Office; from 1883 on, the number of its employees covered by the merit system expanded. Big-city postmasters were often delighted to be relieved of the burden of dealing with hundreds of place-seekers. Employees welcomed the job protection that civil service provided. In time, the merit system came to govern Post Office personnel almost completely, yet the problems of the department became, if anything, worse. By the mid-20th century, slow and inadequate service, an inability technologically to cope with the mounting flood of mail, and the inequities of its pricing system became all too evident. The problem with the Post Office, however, was not omnipotence but impotence. It was a government monopoly. Being a monopoly, it had little incentive to find the most efficient means to manage its services; being a government monopoly, it was not free to adopt such means even when found—communities, Congressmen, and special-interest groups saw to that.

THE MILITARY ESTABLISHMENT

Not all large bureaucracies grow in response to demands for service. The Department of Defense, since 1941 the largest employer of federal civilian officials, has become, as the governmental keystone of the "military-industrial complex," the very archetype of an administrative entity that is thought to be so vast and so well-entrenched that it can virtually ignore the political branches of government, growing and even acting on the basis of its own inner imperatives. In fact, until recently the military services were a major economic and political force only during wartime. In the late 18th and early 19th centuries, America was a neutral nation with only a tiny standing army. During the Civil War, over two million men served on the Union side alone and the War Department expanded enormously, but demobilization after the war was virtually complete, except for a small Indian-fighting force. Its peacetime authorized strength was only 25,000 enlisted men and 2,161 officers, and its actual strength for the rest of the century was often less. Congress authorized the purchase and installation of over 2,000 coastal defense guns, but barely 6 percent of these were put in place.

When war with Spain broke out, the army was almost totally unprepared. Over 300,000 men eventually served in that brief conflict, and though almost all were again demobilized, the War Department under Elihu Root was reorganized and put on a more professional basis with a greater capacity for unified central control. Since the United States had become an imperial power with important possessions in the Caribbean and the Far East, the need for a larger military establishment was clear; even so, the average size of the army until World War I was only about 250,000.

The First World War again witnessed a vast mobilization—nearly five million men in all—and again an almost complete demobilization after the war. The Second World War involved over 16 million military personnel. The demobilization that followed was less complete than after previous engagements owing to the development of the Cold War, but it was substantial nonetheless—the Army fell in size from over eight million men to only half a million. Military spending declined from $91 billion in the first quarter of 1945 to only slightly more than $10 billion in the second quarter of 1947. For the next three years it remained relatively flat. It began to rise rapidly in 1950, partly to finance our involvement in the Korean conflict and partly to begin the construction of a military force that could counterbalance the Soviet Union, especially in Europe.

In sum, from the Revolutionary War to 1950, a period of over 170 years, the size and deployment of the military establishment in this country was governed entirely by decisions made by political leaders on political grounds. The military did not expand autonomously, a large standing army did not find wars to fight, and its officers did not play a significant role except in wartime and occasionally as presidential candidates. No bureaucracy proved easier to control, at least insofar as its size and purposes were concerned.

A "MILITARY-INDUSTRIAL COMPLEX"?

The argument for the existence of an autonomous, bureaucratically led military-industrial complex is supported primarily by events since 1950. Not only has the United States assumed during this period worldwide commitments that necessitate a larger military establishment, but the advent of new, high-technology weapons has created a vast industrial machine with an interest in sustaining a high level of military expenditures, especially on weapons research, development, and acquisition. This machine, so the argument goes, is allied with the Pentagon in ways that dominate the political officials nominally in charge of the armed forces. There is some truth in all this. We have become a world military force, though that decision was made by elected officials in 1949–1950 and not dictated by a (then nonexistent) military-industrial complex. High-cost, high-technology weapons have become important and a number of industrial concerns will prosper or perish depending on how contracts for those weapons are let. The development and purchase of weapons is sometimes made in a wasteful, even irrational, manner. And the allocation of funds among the several armed services is often dictated as much by inter-service rivalry as by strategic or political decisions.

But despite all this, the military has not been able to sustain itself at its preferred size, to keep its strength constant or growing, or to retain for its use a fixed or growing portion of the Gross National Product. Even during the last two decades, the period of greatest military prominence, the size of the Army has varied enormously—from over 200 maneuver battalions in 1955, to 174 in 1965, rising to 217 at the peak of the Vietnam action in 1969, and then declining rapidly to 138 in 1972. Even military hardware, presumably of greater interest to the industrial side of the military-industrial complex, has often declined in quantity, even though per unit price has risen. The Navy had over 1,000 ships in 1955; it has only 700 today. The Air Force had nearly 24,000 aircraft in 1955; it has fewer than 14,000 today. This is not to say the combat strength of the military is substantially less than it once was, and there is greater firepower now at the disposal of each military unit, and there are various missile systems now in place, for which no earlier counterparts existed. But the total budget, and thus the total force level, of the military has been decided primarily by the President and not in any serious sense forced upon him by subordinates. (For example, President Truman decided to allocate one third of the federal budget to defense, President Eisenhower chose to spend no more than 10 percent of the Gross National Product on it, and President Kennedy strongly supported Robert McNamara's radical and controversial budget revisions.) Even a matter of as great significance as the size of the total military budget for research and development has proved remarkably resistant to inflationary trends: In constant dollars, since 1964 that appropriation has been relatively steady (in 1972 dollars, about $30 billion a year).

The principal source of growth in the military budget in recent years has arisen from Congressionally determined pay provisions. The legislature has voted for more or less automatic pay increases for military personnel with the result that the military budget has gone up even when the number of personnel in the military establishment has gone down.

The bureaucratic problems associated with the military establishment arise mostly from its internal management and are functions of its complexity, the uncertainty surrounding its future deployment, conflicts among its constituent services over mission and role, and the need to purchase expensive equipment without the benefit of a market economy that can control costs. Complexity, uncertainty, rivalry, and monopsony are inherent (and frustrating) aspects of the military as a bureaucracy, but they are very different problems from those typically associated with the phrase "the military-industrial complex." The size and budget of the military are matters wholly within the power of civilian authorities to decide—indeed, the military budget contains the largest discretionary items in the entire federal budget.

If the Founding Fathers were to return to review their handiwork, they would no doubt be staggered by the size of both the Post Office and the Defense Department, and in the case of the latter, be worried about the implications of our commitments to various foreign powers. They surely would be amazed at the technological accomplishments but depressed by the cost and inefficiency of both departments; but they would not, I suspect, think that our Constitutional arrangements for managing these enterprises have proved defective or that there had occurred, as a result of the creation of these vast bureaus, an important shift in the locus of political authority.

They would observe that there have continued to operate strong localistic pressures in both systems—offices are operated, often uneconomically, in some small communities because small communities have influential Congressmen; military bases are maintained in many states because states have powerful Senators. But a national government with localistic biases is precisely the system they believed they had designed in 1787, and though they surely could not have then imagined the costs of it, they just as surely would have said (Hamilton possibly excepted) that these costs were the defects of the system's virtues.

BUREAUCRACY AND CLIENTELISM

After 1861, the growth in the federal administrative system could no longer be explained primarily by an expansion of the postal service and other traditional bureaus. Though these continued to expand, new departments were added that reflected a new (or at least greater) emphasis on the enlargement of the scope of government. Between 1861 and 1901, over 200,000 civilian employees were added to the federal service, only 52 percent of whom were postal workers. Some of these, of course, staffed a larger military and naval establishment stimulated by the Civil War and the Spanish-American War. By 1901 there were over 44,000 civilian defense employees, mostly workers in government-owned arsenals and shipyards. But even those could account for less than one fourth of the increase in employment during the preceding 40 years.

What was striking about the period after 1861 was that the government began to give formal, bureaucratic recognition to the emergence of distinctive interest in a diversifying economy. As Richard L. Schott has written, "whereas earlier federal department had been formed around specialized governmental functions (foreign affairs, war, finance, and the like), the new departments of this period— Agriculture, Labor, and Commerce—were devoted to the interests and aspirations of particular economic groups."

The original purpose behind these clientele-oriented departments was neither to subsidize nor to regulate, but to promote, chiefly by gathering and publishing statistics and (especially in the case of agriculture) by research. The formation of the Department of Agriculture in 1862 was to become a model, for better or worse, for later political campaigns for government recognition. A private association representing an interest—in this case the United States Agricultural Society—was formed. It made every President from Fillmore to Lincoln an honorary member, it enrolled key Congressmen, and it began to lobby for a new department. The precedent was followed by labor groups, especially the Knights of Labor, to secure creation in 1888 of a Department of Labor. It was broadened in 1903 to be a Department of Commerce and Labor, the parts were separated and the two departments we now know were formed.

There was an early 19th-century precedent for the creation of these client-serving departments: the Pension Office, then in the Department of the Interior. Begun in 1833 and regularized in 1849, the Office became one of the largest bureaus of the government in the aftermath of the Civil War, as hundreds of thousands of Union Army veterans were made eligible for pensions if they had incurred a permanent disability or injury while on military duty; dependent widows were also eligible if their husbands had died in service or of service-connected injuries. The Grand Army of the Republic (GAR), the leading veterans' organization, was quick to exert pressure for more generous pension laws and for more liberal administration of such laws as already existed. In 1879 Congressmen, noting the number of ex-servicemen living (and voting) in their states, made veterans eligible for pensions retroactively to the date of their discharge from the service, thus enabling thousands who had been late in filing applications to be rewarded for their dilatoriness. In 1890 the law was changed again to make it unnecessary to have been injured in the service—all that was necessary was to have served and then to have acquired a permanent disability by any means other than through "their own vicious habits." And whenever cases not qualifying under existing law came to the attention of Congress, it promptly passed a special act making those persons eligible by name.

So far as is known, the Pension Office was remarkably free of corruption in the administration of this windfall—and why not, since anything an administrator might deny, a legislator was only too pleased to grant. By 1891 the Commissioner of Pensions observed that this was "the largest executive bureau in the world." There were over 6,000 officials supplemented by thousands of local physicians paid on a fee basis. In 1900 alone, the Office had to process 477,000 cases. Fraud was rampant as thousands of persons brought false or exaggerated claims; as Leonard D. White was later to write, "pensioners and their attorneys seemed to have been engaged in a gigantic conspiracy to defraud their own government." Though the Office struggled to be honest, Congress was indifferent—or more accurately, complaisant: The GAR was a powerful electoral force and it was ably and lucratively assisted by thousands of private pension attorneys. The pattern of bureaucratic clientelism was set in a way later to become a familiar feature of the governmental landscape—a subsidy was initially provided, because it was either popular or unnoticed, to a group that was powerfully benefited and had few or disorganized opponents; the beneficiaries were organized to supervise the administration and ensure the funding of the program; the law authorizing the program, first passed because it seemed the right thing to do, was left intact or even expanded because politically it became the only thing to do. A benefit once bestowed cannot easily be withdrawn.

PUBLIC POWER AND PRIVATE INTERESTS

It was at the state level, however, that client-oriented bureaucracies proliferated in the 19th century. Chief among these were the occupational licensing agencies. At the time of Independence, professions and occupations either could be freely entered (in which case the consumer had to judge the quality of service for himself) or entry was informally controlled by the existing members of the profession or occupation by personal tutelage and the management of reputations. The later part of the 19th century, however, witnessed the increased use of law and bureaucracy to control entry into a line of work. The state courts generally allowed this on the grounds that it was a proper exercise of the "police power" of the state, but as Morton Keller has observed, "when state courts approved the licensing of barbers and blacksmiths, but not of horseshoers, it was evident that the principles governing certification were—to put it charitably— elusive ones." By 1952, there were more than 75 different occupations in the United States for which one needed a license to practice, and the awarding of these licenses was typically in the hands of persons already in the occupation, who could act under color of law. These licensing boards—for plumbers, dry cleaners, beauticians, attorneys, undertakers, and the like—frequently have been criticized as particularly flagrant examples of the excesses of a bureaucratic state. But the problems they create—of restricted entry, higher prices, and lengthy and complex initiation procedures—are not primarily the result of some bureaucratic pathology but of the possession of public power by persons who use it for private purposes. Or more accurately, they are the result of using public power in ways that benefited those in the profession in the sincere but unsubstantiated conviction that doing so would benefit the public generally.

The New Deal was perhaps the high water mark of at least the theory of bureaucratic clientelism. Not only did various sectors of society, notably agriculture, begin receiving massive subsidies, but the government proposed, through the National Industrial Recovery Act (NRA), to cloak with public power a vast number of industrial groupings and trade associations so that they might control production and prices in ways that would end the depression. The NRA's Blue Eagle fell before the Supreme Court—the wholesale delegation of public power to private interests was declared unconstitutional. But the piecemeal delegation was not, as the continued growth of specialized promotional agencies attests. The Civil Aeronautics Board, for example, erroneously thought to be exclusively a regulatory agency, was formed in 1938 "to promote" as well as regulate civil aviation and it has done so by restricting entry and maintaining above-market rate fares.

Agriculture, of course, provides the leading case of clientelism. Theodore J. Lowi finds "at least 10 separate, autonomous, local self-governing systems" located in or closely associated with the Department of Agriculture that control to some significant degree the flow of billions of dollars in expenditures and loans. Local committees of farmers, private farm organizations, agency heads, and committee chairmen in Congress dominate policy-making in this area— not, perhaps, to the exclusion of the concerns of other publics, but certainly in ways not powerfully constrained by them.

"COOPERATIVE FEDERALISM"

The growing edge of client-oriented bureaucracy can be found, however, not in government relations with private groups, but in the relations among governmental units. In dollar volume, the chief clients of federal domestic expenditures are state and local government agencies. To some degree, federal involvement in local affairs by the cooperative funding or management of local enterprises has always existed. The Northwest Ordinance of 1784 made public land available to finance local schools and the Morrill Act of 1862 gave land to support state colleges, but what Morton Grodzins and Daniel Elazar have called "cooperative federalism," though it always existed, did not begin in earnest until the passage in 1913 of the 16th Amendment to the Constitution allowed the federal government to levy an income tax on citizens and thereby to acquire access to vast sources of revenue. Between 1914 and 1917, federal aid to states and localities increased a thousandfold. By 1948 it amounted to over one tenth of all state and local spending; by 1970, to over one sixth.

The degree to which such grants, and the federal agencies that administer them, constrain or even direct state and local bureaucracies is a matter of dispute. No general answer can be given—federal support of welfare programs has left considerable discretion in the hands of the states over the size of benefits and some discretion over eligibility rules, whereas federal support of highway construction carries with it specific requirements as to design, safety, and (since 1968) environmental and social impact.

A few generalizations are possible, however. The first is that the states and not the cities have been from the first, and remain today, the principal client group for grants-in-aid. It was not until the Housing Act of 1937 that money was given in any substantial amount directly to local governments and though many additional programs of this kind were later added, as late as 1970 less than 12 percent of all federal aid went directly to cities and towns. The second general observation is that the 1960s mark a major watershed in the way in which the purposes of federal aid are determined. Before that time, most grants were for purposes initially defined by the states—to build highways and airports, to fund unemployment insurance programs, and the like. Beginning in the 1960s, the federal government, at the initiative of the President and his advisors, increasingly came to define the purposes of these grants—not necessarily over the objection of the states, but often without any initiative from them. Federal money was to be spent on poverty, ecology, planning, and other "national" goals for which, until the laws were passed, there were few, if any, well-organized and influential constituencies. Whereas federal money was once spent in response to the claims of distinct and organized clients, public or private, in the contemporary period federal money has increasingly been spent in ways that have *created* such clients.

And once rewarded or created, they are rarely penalized or abolished. What David Stockman has called the "social pork barrel" grows more or less steadily. Between 1950 and 1970, the number of farms declined from about 5.6 million to fewer than three million, but government payments to farmers rose about $283 million to $3.2 billion. In the public sector, even controversial programs have grown. Urban renewal programs have been sharply criticized, but federal support for the program rose from $281 million in 1965 to about $1 billion in 1972. Public housing has been enmeshed in controversy, but federal support for it rose from $206 million in 1965 to $845 million in 1972. Federal financial support for local poverty programs under the Office of Economic Opportunity has actually declined in recent years, but this cut is almost unique and it required the steadfast and deliberate attention of a determined President who was bitterly assailed both in the Congress and in the courts.

SELF-PERPETUATING AGENCIES

If the Founding Fathers were to return to examine bureaucratic clientelism, they would, I suspect, be deeply discouraged. James Madison clearly foresaw that American society would be "broken into many parts, interests and classes of citizens" and that this "multiplicity of interests" would help ensure against "the tyranny of the majority," especially in a federal regime with separate branches of government. Positive action would require a "coalition of a majority"; in the process of forming this coalition, the rights of all would be protected, not merely by self-interested bargains, but because in a free society such a coalition "could seldom take place on any other principles than those of justice and the general good." To those who wrongly believed that Madison thought of men as acting only out of base motives, the phrase is instructive: Persuading men who disagree to compromise their differences can rarely be achieved solely by the parceling out of relative advantage; the belief is also required that what is being agreed to is right, proper, and defensible before public opinion.

Most of the major new social programs of the United States, whether for the good of the few or the many, were initially adopted by broad coalitions appealing to general standards of justice or to conceptions of the public weal. This is certainly the case with most of the New Deal legislation—notably such programs as Social Security—and with most Great Society legislation—notably Medicare and aid to education; it was also conspicuously the case with respect to post-Great Society legislation pertaining to consumer and environmental concerns. State occupational licensing laws were supported by majorities instead in, among other things, the contribution of these statutes to public safety and health.

But when a program supplies particular benefits to an existing or newly created interest, public or private, it creates a set of political relationships that make exceptionally difficult further alteration of that program by coalitions of the majority. What was created in the name of the common good is sustained in the name of the particular interest. Bureaucratic clientelism becomes self-perpetuating, in the absence of some crisis or scandal, because a single interest group to which the program matters greatly is highly motivated and well-situated to ward off the criticisms of other groups that have a broad but weak interest in the policy.

In short, a regime of separated powers makes it difficult to overcome objections and contrary interests sufficiently to permit the enactment of a new program or the creation of a new agency. Unless the legislation can be made to pass either with little notice or at a time of crisis or extraordinary majorities—and sometimes even then—the initiation of new programs requires public interest arguments. But the same regime works to protect agencies, once created, from unwelcome change because a major change is, in effect, new legislation that must overcome the same hurdles as the original law, but this time with one of the hurdles—the wishes of the agency and its client—raised much higher. As a result, the Madisonian system makes it relatively easy for the delegation of public power to private groups to go unchallenged and, therefore, for factional interests that have acquired a supportive public bureaucracy to rule without submitting their interests to the effective scrutiny and modification of other interests.

BUREAUCRACY AND DISCRETION

For many decades, the Supreme Court denied to the federal government any general "police power" over occupations and businesses, and thus most such regulation occurred at the state level and even there under the constraint that it must not violate the notion of "substantive due process"—that is, the view that there were sharp limits to the power of any government to take (and therefore to regulate) property. What clearly was within the regulatory province of the federal government was interstate commerce, and thus it is not surprising that the first major federal regulatory body should be the Interstate Commerce Commission (ICC), created in 1887.

What does cause, if not surprise, then at least dispute, is the view that the Commerce Act actually was intended to regulate railroads in the public interest. It has become fashionable of late to see this law as a device sought by the railroads to protect themselves from competition. The argument has been given its best-known formulation by Gabriel Kolko. Long-haul railroads, facing ruinous price wars and powerless to resist the demands of big shippers for rebates, tried to create voluntary cartels or "pools" that would keep rates high. These pools always collapsed, however, when one railroad or another would cut rates in order to get more business. To prevent this, the railroads turned to the federal government seeking a law to compel what persuasion could not induce. But the genesis of the act was in fact more complex: Shippers wanted protection from high prices charged by railroads that operated monopolistic services in certain communities; many other shippers served by competing lines wanted no legal barriers to prevent competition from driving prices down as far as possible; some railroads wanted regulation to ease competition, while others feared regulation. And the law as finally passed in fact made "pooling" (or cartels to keep prices up) illegal.

The true significance of the Commerce Act is not that it allowed public power to be used to make secure private wealth but that it created a federal commission with broadly delegated powers that would have to reconcile conflicting goals (the desire for higher or lower prices) in a political environment characterized by a struggle among organized interests and rapidly changing technology. In short, the Commerce Act brought forth a new dimension to the problem of bureaucracy: not those problems, as with the Post Office, that resulted from size and political constraints, but those that were caused by the need to make binding choices without any clear standards for choice.

The ICC was not, of course, the first federal agency with substantial discretionary powers over important matters. The Office of Indian Affairs, for a while in the War Department but after 1849 in the Interior Department, coped for the better part of a century with the Indian problem equipped with no clear policy, beset on all sides by passionate and opposing arguments, and infected with a level of fraud and corruption that seemed impossible to eliminate. There were many causes of the problem, but at root was the fact that the government was determined to control the Indians but could not decide toward what end that control should be exercised (extermination, relocation, and assimilation all had their advocates) and, to the extent the goal was assimilation, could find no method by which to achieve it. By the end of the century, a policy of relocation had been adopted *de facto* and the worse abuses of the Indian service had been eliminated—if not by administrative skill, then by the exhaustion of things in Indian possession worth stealing. By the turn of the century, the management of the Indian question had become more or less routine administration of Indian schools and the allocation of reservation land among Indian claimants.

REGULATION VERSUS PROMOTION

It was the ICC and agencies and commissions for which it was the precedent that became the principal example of federal discretionary authority. It is important, however, to be clear about just what this precedent was. Not everything we now call a regulatory agency was in fact intended to be one. The ICC, the Antitrust Division of the Justice Department, the Federal Trade Commission (FTC), the Food and Drug Administration (FDA), the National Labor Relations Board (NRLB)—all these *were* intended to be genuinely regulatory bodies created to handle under public auspices matters once left to private arrangements. The techniques they were to employ varied: approving rates (ICC), issuing cease-and-desist orders (FTC), bringing civil or criminal actions in the courts (the Antitrust Division), defining after a hearing an appropriate standard of conduct (NLRB), or testing a product for safety (FDA). In each case, however, Congress clearly intended that the agency either define its own standards (a safe drug, a conspiracy in restraint of trade, a fair labor practice) or choose among competing claims (a higher or lower rate for shipping grain).

Other agencies often grouped with these regulatory bodies—the Civil Aeronautics Board, the Federal Communications Commission, the Maritime Commission—were designed, however, not primarily to regulate, but to *promote* the development of various infant or threatened industries. However, unlike fostering agriculture or commerce, fostering civil aviation or radio broadcasting was thought to require limiting entry (to prevent "unsafe" aviation or broadcast interference); but at the time these laws were passed few believed that the restrictions on entry would be many or that the choices would be made on any but technical or otherwise noncontroversial criteria. We smile now at their naïveté, but we continue to share it—today we sometimes suppose that choosing an approved exhaust emission control system or a water pollution control system can be done on the basis of technical criteria and without affecting production and employment.

MAJORITARIAN POLITICS

The creation of regulatory bureaucracies has occurred, as is often remarked, in waves. The first was the period between 1887 and 1890 (the Commerce Act and the Antitrust Act), the second between 1906 and 1915 (the Pure Food and Drug Act, the Meat Inspection Act, the Federal Trade Commission Act, the Clayton Act), the third during the 1930s (the Food, Drug, and Cosmetic Act, the Public Utility Holding Company Act, the Securities Exchange Act, the Natural Gas Act, the National Labor Relations Act), and the fourth during the latter part of the 1960s (the Water Quality Act, the Truth in Lending Act, the National Traffic and Motor Vehicle Safety Act, various amendments to the drug laws, the Motor Vehicle Pollution Control Act, and many others).

Each of these periods was characterized by progressive or liberal Presidents in office (Cleveland, T. R. Roosevelt, Wilson, F. D. Roosevelt, Johnson); one was a period of national crisis (the 1930s); three were periods when the President enjoyed extraordinary majorities of his own party in both house of Congress (1914–1916, 1932–1940, and 1964–1968); and only the first period preceded the emergence of the national mass media of communication. These facts are important because of the special difficulty of passing any genuinely regulatory legislation: A single interest, the regulated party, sees itself seriously threatened by a law proposed by a policy entrepreneur who must appeal to an unorganized majority, the members of which may not expect to be substantially or directly benefited by the law. Without special political circumstances—a crisis, a scandal, extraordinary majorities, an especially vigorous President, the support of media—the normal barriers to legislative innovation (i.e., to the formation of a "coalition of the majority") may prove insuperable.

Stated another way, the initiation of regulatory programs tends to take the form of majoritarian rather than coalition politics. The Madisonian system is placed in temporary suspense: Exceptional majorities propelled by a public mood and led by a skillful policy entrepreneur take action that might not be possible under ordinary circumstances (closely divided parties, legislative-executive checks and balances, popular indifference). The consequence of majoritarian politics for the administration of regulatory bureaucracies is great. To initiate and sustain the necessary legislative mood, strong, moralistic, and sometimes ideological appeals are necessary—leading, in turn, to the granting of broad mandates of power to the new agency (a modest delegation of authority would obviously be inadequate if the problem to be resolved is of crisis proportions) or to the specifying of exacting standards to be enforced (e.g., *no* carcinogenic products may be sold; 95 percent of the pollutants must be eliminated), or to both.

Either in applying a vague but broad rule ("the public interest, convenience, and necessity") or in enforcing a clear and strict standard, the regulatory agency will tend to broaden the range and domain of its authority, to lag behind technological and economic change, to resist deregulation, to stimulate corruption, and to contribute to the bureaucratization of private institutions.

It will broaden its regulatory reach out of a variety of motives: to satisfy the demand of the regulated enterprise that it be protected from competition, to make effective the initial regulatory action by attending to the unanticipated side effects of that action, to discover or stretch the meaning of vague statutory language, or to respond to new constituencies induced by the existence of the agency to convert what were once private demands into public pressures. For example, the Civil Aeronautics Board, out of a desire both to promote aviation and to protect the regulated price structure of the industry, will resist the entry into the industry of new carriers. If a Public Utilities Commission sets rates too low for a certain class of customers, the utility will allow service to those customers to decline in quality, leading in turn to a demand that the Commission also regulate the quality of service. If the Federal Communications Commission cannot decide who should receive a broadcast license by applying the "public interest" standard, it will be powerfully tempted to invest that phrase with whatever preferences the majority of the Commission then entertains, leading in turn to the exercise of control over many more aspects of broadcasting than merely signal interference—all in the name of deciding what the standard for entry shall be. If the Antitrust Division can prosecute conspiracies in restraint of trade, it will attract to itself the complaints of various firms about business practices that are neither conspiratorial not restraining but merely competitive, and a "vigorous" antitrust lawyer may conclude that these practices warrant prosecution.

BUREAUCRATIC INERTIA

Regulatory agencies are slow to respond to change for the same reason all organizations with an assured existence are slow: There is no incentive to respond. Furthermore, the requirements of due process and of political conciliation will make any response time-consuming. For example, owing to the complexity of the matter and the money at stake, any comprehensive review of the long-distance rates of the telephone company will take years, and possibly may take decades.

Deregulation, when warranted by changed economic circumstances or undesired regulatory results, will be resisted. Any organization, and *a fortiori* any public organization, develops a genuine belief in the rightness of its mission that is expressed as a commitment to regulation as a process. This happened to the ICC in the early decades of this century as it steadily sought both enlarged powers (setting minimum as well as maximum rates) and a broader jurisdiction (over trucks, barges, and pipelines as well as railroads). It even urged incorporation into the Transportation Act of 1920 language directing it to prepare a comprehensive transportation plan for the nation. Furthermore, any regulatory agency will confer benefits on some group or interest, whether intended or not; those beneficiaries will stoutly resist deregulation. (But in happy proof of the fact that there are no iron laws, even about bureaucracies, we note the recent proposals emanating from the Federal Power Commission that the price of natural gas be substantially deregulated.)

The operation of regulatory bureaus may tend to bureaucratize the private sector. The costs of conforming to many regulations can be met most easily— often, *only*—by large firms and institutions with specialized bureaucracies of their own. Smaller firms and groups often must choose between unacceptably high overhead costs, violating the law, or going out of business. A small bakery producing limited runs of a high-quality product literally may not be able to meet the safety and health standards for equipment or to keep track of and administer fairly its obligations to its two employees; but unless the bakery is willing to break the law, it must sell out to a big bakery and can afford to do these things, but may not be inclined to make and sell good bread. I am not aware of any data that measure private bureaucratization or industrial concentration as a function of the economies of scale produced by the need to cope with the regulatory environment, but I see no reason why such data could not be found.

Finally, regulatory agencies that control entry, fix prices, or substantially affect the profitability of an industry create a powerful stimulus for direct or indirect forms of corruption. The revelations about campaign finance in the 1972 presidential election show dramatically that there will be a response to that stimulus. Many corporations, disproportionately those in regulated industries (airlines, milk producers, oil companies), made illegal or hard to justify campaign contributions involving very large sums.

THE ERA OF CONTRACT

It is far from clear what the Founding Fathers would have thought of all this. They were not doctrinaire exponents of laissez-faire, nor were 18th-century governments timid about asserting their powers over the economy. Every imaginable device of fiscal policy was employed by the states after the Revolutionary War. Mother England had, during the mercantilist era, fixed prices and wages, licensed merchants, and granted monopolies and subsidies. (What were the royal grants of American land to immigrant settlers but the greatest of subsidies, sometimes—as in Pennsylvania—almost monopolistically given?) European nations regularly operated state enterprises, controlled trade, and protected industry. But as William D. Grampp has noted, at the Constitutional Convention the Founders considered authorizing only four kinds of economic controls, and they rejected two of them. They agreed to allow the Congress to regulate international and interstate commerce and to give monopoly protection in the form of copyrights and patents. Even Madison's proposal to allow the federal government to charter corporations was rejected. Not one of the 85 *Federalist* papers dealt with economic regulation; indeed, the only reference to commerce was the value to it of a unified nation and a strong navy.

G. Warren Nutter has speculated as to why our Founders were so restrained in equipping the new government with explicit regulatory powers. One reason may have been the impact of Adam Smith's *Wealth of Nations*, published the same year as the Declaration of Independence, and certainly soon familiar to many rebel leaders, notably Hamilton. Smith himself sought to explain the American prosperity before the Revolution by the fact that Britain, through "salutary neglect," had not imposed mercantilist rules on the colonial economy. "Plenty of good land, and liberty to manage their own affairs in their own way" were the "two great causes" of colonial prosperity. As Nutter observes, there was a spirit of individualistic venture among the colonies that found economic expression in the belief that voluntary contracts were the proper organization principle of enterprise.

One consequence of this view was that the courts in many states were heavily burdened with cases testing the provisions of contracts and settling debts under them. In one rural county in Massachusetts the judges heard over 800 civil cases during 1785. As James Willard Hurst has written, the years before 1875 were "above all else, the years of contract in our law."

The era of contract came to an end with the rise of economic organizations so large or with consequences so great that contracts were no longer adequate, in the public's view, to adjust corporate behavior to the legitimate expectations of other parties. The courts were slower to accede to this change than were many legislatures, but in time they acceded completely, and the era of administrative regulation was upon us. The Founders, were they to return, would understand the change in the scale and social significance of enterprise, would approve of many of the purposes of regulation, perhaps would approve of the behavior of some of the regulatory bureaus seeking to realize those purposes, but surely would be dismayed at the political cost resulting from having vested vast discretionary authority in the hands of officials whose very existence—to say nothing of whose function—was not anticipated by the Constitutional Convention and whose effective control is beyond the capacity of the governing institutions which that Convention had designed.

THE BUREAUCRATIC STATE AND THE REVOLUTION

The American Revolution was not only a struggle for independence but a fundamental rethinking of the nature of political authority. Indeed, until that reformulation was completed the Revolution was not finished. What made political authority problematic for the colonists was the extent to which they believed Mother England had subverted their liberties despite the protection of the British constitution, until then widely regarded in America as the most perfect set of governing arrangements yet devised. The evidence of usurpation is now familiar: unjust taxation, the weakening of the independence of the judiciary, the stationing of standing armies, and the extensive use of royal patronage to reward office-seekers at colonial expense. Except for the issue of taxation, which raised for the colonists major questions of representation, almost all of their complaints involved the abuse of *administrative* powers.

The first solution proposed by Americans to remedy this abuse was the vesting of most (or, in the case of Pennsylvania and a few other states, virtually all) powers in the legislature. But the events after 1776 in many colonies, notably Pennsylvania, convinced the most thoughtful citizens that legislative abuses were as likely as administrative ones: In the extreme case, citizens would suffer from the "tyranny of the majority." Their solution to this problem was, of course, the theory of the separation of powers by which, as brilliantly argued in *The Federalist* papers, each branch of government would check the likely usurpations of the other.

This formulation went essentially unchallenged in theory and unmodified by practice for over a century. Though a sizable administrative apparatus had come into being by the end of the 19th century, it constituted no serious threat to the existing distribution of political power because it either performed routine tasks (the Post Office) or dealt with temporary crises (the military). Some agencies wielding discretionary authority existed, but they either dealt with groups whose liberties were not of much concern (the Indian Office) or their exercise of discretion was minutely scrutinized by Congress (the Land Office, the Pension Office, the Customs Office). The major discretionary agencies of the 19th century flourished at the very period of greatest Congressional domination of the political process—the decades after the Civil War—and thus, though their supervision was typically inefficient and sometimes corrupt, these agencies were for most practical purposes direct dependencies of Congress. In short, their existence did not call into question the theory of the separation of powers.

But with the growth of client-serving and regulatory agencies, grave questions began to be raised—usually implicitly—about that theory. A client-serving bureau, because of its relations with some source of private power, could become partially independent of both the executive and legislative branches—or in the case of the latter, dependent upon certain committees and independent of others and of the views of the Congress as a whole. A regulatory agency (that is to say, a truly regulatory one and not a clientelist or promotional agency hiding behind a regulatory fig leaf) was, in the typical case, placed formally outside the existing branches of government. Indeed, they were called "independent" or "quasi-judicial" agencies (they might as well have been called "quasi-executive" or "quasi-legislative") and thus the special status that clientelist bureaus achieved *de facto*, the regulatory ones achieved *de jure*.

It is, of course, inadequate and misleading to criticize these agencies, as has often been done, merely because they raise questions about the problem of sovereignty. The crucial test of their value is their behavior, and that can be judged only by applying economic and welfare criteria to the policies they produce. But if such judgments should prove damning, as increasingly has been the case, then the problem of finding the authority with which to alter or abolish such organizations becomes acute. In this regard the theory of the separation of powers has proved unhelpful.

The separation of powers makes difficult, in ordinary times, the extension of public power over private conduct—as a nation, we came more slowly to the welfare state than almost any European nation, and we still engage in less central planning and operate fewer nationalized industries than other democratic regimes. But we have extended the regulatory sway of our national government as far as or farther than that of most other liberal regimes (our environmental and safety codes are now models for much of Europe), and the bureaus wielding these discretionary powers are, once created, harder to change or redirect than would be the case if authority were more centralized.

The shift of power toward the bureaucracy was not inevitable. It did not result simply from increased specialization, the growth of industry, or the imperialistic designs of the bureaus themselves. Before the second decade of this century, there was no federal bureaucracy wielding substantial discretionary powers. That we have one now is the result of political decisions made by elected representatives. Fifty years ago, the people often wanted more of government than it was willing to provide—it was, in that sense, a republican government in which representatives moderated popular demands. Today, not only does political action follow quickly upon the stimulus of public interest, but government itself creates that stimulus and sometimes acts in advance of it.

All democratic regimes tend to shift resources from the private to the public sector and to enlarge the size of the administrative component of government. The particularistic and localistic nature of American democracy has created a particularistic and client-serving administration. If our bureaucracy often serves special interests and is subject to no central direction, it is because our legislature often serves special interests and is subject to no central leadership. For Congress to complain of what it has created and it maintains is, to be charitable, misleading. Congress could change what it has devised, but there is little reason to suppose it will.

31

NORTON E. LONG

POWER AND ADMINISTRATION

I

There is no more forlorn spectacle in the administrative world than an agency and a program possessed of statutory life, armed with executive orders, sustained in the courts, yet stricken with paralysis and deprived of power. An object of contempt to its enemies and of despair to its friends.

The lifeblood of administration is power. Its attainment, maintenance, increase, dissipation, and loss are subjects the practitioner and student can ill afford to neglect. Loss of realism and failure are almost certain consequences. This is not to deny that important parts of public administration are so deeply entrenched in the habits of the community, so firmly supported by the public, or so clearly necessary as to be able to take their power base for granted and concentrate on the purely professional side of their problems. But even these islands of the blessed are not immune from the plague of politics, as witness the fate of the hapless Bureau of Labor Statistics and the perennial menace of the blind 5 per cent across-the-board budget cut. Perhaps Carlyle's aphorism holds here, "The healthy know not of their health but only the sick." To stay healthy one needs to recognize that health is a fruit, not a birthright. Power is only one of the considerations that must be weighed in administration, but of all it is the most overlooked in theory and the most dangerous to overlook in practice.

The power resources of an administrator or an agency are not disclosed by a legal search of titles and court decisions or by examining appropriations or budgetary allotments. Legal authority and a treasury balance are necessary but politically insufficient bases of administration. Administrative rationality requires a critical evaluation of the whole range of complex and shifting forces on whose support, acquiescence, or temporary impotence the power to act depends.

Analysis of the sources from which power is derived and the limitations they impose is as much a dictate of prudent administration as sound budgetary procedure. The bankruptcy that comes from an unbalanced power budget has consequences far more disastrous than the necessity of seeking a deficiency appropriation. The budgeting of power is a basic subject matter of a realistic science of administration.

It may be urged that for all but the top hierarchy of the administrative structure

448

the question of power is irrelevant. Legislative authority and administrative orders suffice. Power adequate to the function to be performed flows down the chain of command. Neither statute nor executive order, however, confers more than legal authority to act. Whether Congress or President can impart the substance of power as well as the form depends upon the line-up of forces in the particular case. A price control law wrung from a reluctant Congress by an amorphous and unstable combination of consumer and labor groups is formally the same as a law enacting a support price program for agriculture backed by the disciplined organizations of farmers and their congressmen. The differences for the scope and effectiveness of administration are obvious. The Presidency, like Congress, responds to and translates the pressures that play upon it. The real mandate contained in an Executive order varies with the political strength of the group demand embodied in it, and in the context of other group demands.

Both Congress and President do focus the general political energies of the community and so are considerably more than mere means for transmitting organized pressures. Yet power is not concentrated by the structure of government or politics into the hands of a leadership with a capacity to budget it among a diverse set of administrative activities. A picture of the Presidency as a reservoir of authority from which the lower echelons of administration draw life and vigor is an idealized distortion of reality.

A similar criticism applies to any like claim for an agency head in his agency. Only in varying degrees can the powers of subordinate officials be explained as resulting from the chain of command. Rarely is such an explanation a satisfactory account of the sources of power.

To deny that power is derived exclusively from superiors in the hierarchy is to assert that subordinates stand in a feudal relation in which to a degree they fend for themselves and acquire support peculiarly their own. A structure of interests friendly or hostile, vague and general or compact and well-defined, encloses each significant center of administrative discretion. This structure is an important determinant of the scope of possible action. As a source of power and authority it is a competitor of the formal hierarchy.

Not only does political power flow in from the sides of an organization, as it were; it also flows up the organization to the center from the constituent parts. When the staff of the Office of War Mobilization and Reconversion advised a hard-pressed agency to go out and get itself some popular support so that the President could afford to support it, their action reflected the realities of power rather than political cynicism.

It is clear that the American system of politics does not generate enough power at any focal point of leadership to provide the conditions for an even partially successful divorce of politics from administration. Subordinates cannot depend on the formal chain of command to deliver enough political power to permit them to do their jobs. Accordingly they must supplement the resources available through the hierarchy with those they can muster on their own, or accept the consequences in frustration—a course itself not without danger. Administrative rationality demands that objectives be determined and sights set in conformity with a realistic appraisal of power position and potential.

II

The theory of administration has neglected the problem of the sources and adequacy of power, in all probability because of a distaste for the disorderliness of American political life and a belief that this disorderliness is transitory. An idealized picture of the British parliamentary system as a Platonic form to be realized or approximated has exerted a baneful fascination in the field. The majority party with a mandate at the polls and a firmly seated leadership in the Cabinet seems to solve adequately the problem of the supply of power necessary to permit administration to concentrate on the fulfillment of accepted objectives. It is a commonplace that the American party system provides neither a mandate for a platform nor a mandate for a leadership.

Accordingly, the election over, its political meaning must be explored by the diverse leaders in the executive and legislative branches. Since the parties have failed to discuss issues, mobilize majorities in their terms, and create a working political consensus on measures to be carried out, the task is left for others—most prominently the agencies concerned. Legislation passed and powers granted are frequently politically premature. Thus the Council of Economic Advisers was given legislative birth before political acceptance of its functions existed. The agencies to which tasks are assigned must devote themselves to the creation of an adequate consensus to permit administration. The mandate that the parties do not supply must be attained through public relations and the mobilization of group support. Pendleton Herring and others have shown just how vital this support is for agency action.

The theory that agencies should confine themselves to communicating policy suggestions to executive and legislature, and refrain from appealing to their clientele and the public, neglects the failure of the parties to provide either a clear-cut decision as to what they should do or an adequately mobilized political support for a course of action. The bureaucracy under the American political system has a large share of responsibility for the public promotion of policy and even more in organizing the political basis for its survival and growth. It is generally recognized that the agencies have a special competence in the technical aspects of their fields which of necessity gives them a rightful policy initiative. In addition, they have or develop a shrewd understanding of the politically feasible in the group structure within which they work. Above all, in the eyes of their supporters and their enemies they represent the institutionalized embodiment of policy, an enduring organization actually or potentially capable of mobilizing power behind policy. The survival interests and creative drives of administrative organizations combine with clientele pressures to compel such mobilization. The party system provides no enduring institutional representation for group interest at all comparable to that of the bureaus of the Department of Agriculture. Even the subject matter committees of Congress function in the shadow of agency permanency.

The bureaucracy is recognized by all interested groups as a major channel of representation to such an extent that Congress rightly feels the competition of a rival. The weakness in party structure both permits and makes necessary the present dimensions of the political activities of the administrative branch— permits because it fails to protect administration from pressures and fails to provide adequate direction and support, makes necessary because it fails to develop a consensus on a leadership and a program that makes possible administration on the basis of accepted decisional premises.

Agencies and bureaus more or less perforce are in the business of building, maintaining, and increasing their political support. They lead and in large part are led by the diverse groups whose influence sustains them. Frequently they lead and are themselves led in conflicting directions. This is not due to a dull-witted incapacity to see the contradictions in their behavior but is an almost inevitable result of the contradictory nature of their support.

Herbert Simon has shown that administrative rationality depends on the establishment of uniform value premises in the decisional centers of organization. Unfortunately, the value premises of those forming vital elements of political support are often far from uniform. These elements are in Barnard's and Simon's sense "customers" of the organization and therefore parts of the organization whose wishes are clothed with a very real authority. A major and most time-consuming aspect of administration consists of the wide range of activities designed to secure enough "customer" acceptance to survive and, if fortunate, develop a consensus adequate to program formulation and execution.

To varying degrees, dependent on the breadth of acceptance of their programs, officials at every level of significant discretion must make their estimates of the situation, take stock of their resources, and plan accordingly. A keen appreciation of the real components of their organization is the beginning of wisdom. These components will be found to stretch far beyond the government payroll. Within the government they will encompass Congress, congressmen, committees, courts, other agencies, presidential advisers, and the President. The Aristotelian analysis of constitutions is equally applicable and equally necessary to an understanding of administrative organization.

The broad alliance of conflicting groups that makes up presidential majorities scarcely coheres about any definite pattern of objectives, nor has it by the alchemy of the party system had its collective power concentrated in an accepted leadership with a personal mandate. The conciliation and maintenance of this support is a necessary condition of the attainment and retention of office involving, as Madison so well saw, "the spirit of party and faction in the necessary and ordinary operations of government." The President must in large part be, if not all things to all men, at least many things to many men. As a consequence, the contradictions in his power base invade administration. The often criticized apparent cross-purposes of the Roosevelt regime cannot be put down to inept administration until the political facts are weighed. Were these apparently self-defeating measures reasonably related to the general maintenance of the composite majority of the Administration? The first objective—ultimate patriotism apart—of the administrator is the attainment and retention of the power on which his tenure of office depends. This is the necessary pre-condition for the accomplishment of all other objectives.

The same ambiguities that arouse the scorn of the naive in the electoral campaigns of the parties are equally inevitable in administration and for the same reasons. Victory at the polls does not yield either a clear-cut grant of power or a unified majority support for a coherent program. The task of the Presidency lies in feeling out the alternatives of policy which are consistent with the retention and increase of the group support on which the Administration rests. The lack of a budgetary theory (so frequently deplored) is not due to any incapacity to apply rational analysis to the comparative contribution of the various activities of government to a determinate hierarchy of purposes. It more probably stems from a fastidious distaste for the frank recognition of the budget as a politically expedient allocation of resources. Appraisal in terms of their political contribution to the Administration provides almost a sole common denominator between the Forest Service and the Bureau of Engraving.

Integration of the administrative structure through an over-all purpose in terms of which tasks and priorities can be established is an emergency phenomenon. Its realization, only partial at best, has been limited to war and the extremity of depression. Even in wartime the Farm Bureau Federation, the American Federation of Labor, the Congress of Industrial Organizations, the National Association of Manufacturers, the Chamber of Commerce, and a host of lesser interests resisted coordination of themselves and the agencies concerned with their interests. A Presidency temporarily empowered by intense mass popular support acting in behalf of a generally accepted and simplified purpose can, with great difficulty, bribe, cajole, and coerce a real measure of joint action. The long-drawn-out battle for conversion and the debacle of orderly reconversion underline the difficulty of attaining, and the transitory nature of, popularly based emergency power. Only in crises are the powers of the Executive nearly adequate to impose a common plan of action on the executive branch, let alone the economy.

In ordinary times the manifold pressures of our pluralistic society work themselves out in accordance with the balance of forces prevailing in Congress and the agencies. Only to a limited degree is the process subject to responsible direction or review by President or party leadership.

The program of the President cannot be a Gosplan for the government precisely because the nature of his institutional and group support gives him insufficient power. The personal unity of the Presidency cannot perform the function of Hobbes' sovereign since his office lacks the authority of Hobbes' contract. Single headedness in the executive gives no assurance of singleness of purpose. It only insures that the significant pressures in a society will be brought to bear on one office. Monarchy solves the problem of giving one plan to a multitude only when the plenitude of its authority approaches dictatorship. Impatient social theorists in all ages have turned to the philosopher king as a substitute for consensus. Whatever else he may become, it is difficult to conceive of the American president ruling as a philosopher king, even with the advice of the Executive Office. The monarchical solution to the administrative problems posed by the lack of a disciplined party system capable of giving firm leadership and a program to the legislature is a modern variant of the dreams of the eighteenth century savants and well nigh equally divorced from a realistic appraisal of social realities.

Much of administrative thought, when it does not assume the value of coordination for coordination's sake, operates on the assumption that there must be something akin to Rousseau's *volonté générale* in administration to which the errant *volonté de tous* of the bureaus can and should be made to conform. This will-o'-the-wisp was made the object of an illuminating search by Pendleton Herring in his *Public Administration and the Public Interest.* The answer for Rousseau was enlightened dictatorship or counting the votes. The administrative equivalent to the latter is the resultant of the relevant pressures, as Herring shows. The first alternative seems to require at least the potency of the British Labour party and elsewhere has needed the disciplined organization of a fascist, nazi, or communist party to provide the power and consensus necessary to coordinate the manifold activities of government to a common plan.

Dictatorship, as Sigmund Neumann has observed, is a substitute for institutions which is required to fill the vacuum when traditional institutions break down. Force supplies the compulsion and guide to action in place of the normal routines of unconscious habit. Administrative organizations, however much they may appear the creations of art, are institutions produced in history and woven in the web of social relationships that gives them life and being. They present the same refractory material to the hand of the political artist as the rest of society of which they form a part.

Just as the economists have attempted to escape the complexities of institutional reality by taking refuge in the frictionless realm of theory, so some students of administration, following their lead, have seen in the application of the doctrine of opportunity costs a clue to a science of administration. Valuable as this may be in a restricted way, Marx has more light to throw on the study of institutions. It is in the dynamics and interrelations of institutions that we have most hope of describing and therefore learning to control administrative behavior.

III

The difficulty of coordinating government agencies lies not only in the fact that bureaucratic organizations are institutions having survival interests which may conflict with their rational adaptation to over-all purpose, but even more in their having roots in society. Coordination of the varied activities of a modern government almost of necessity involves a substantial degree of coordination of the economy. Coordination of government agencies involves far more than changing the behavior and offices of officials in Washington and the field. It involves the publics that are implicated in their normal functioning. To coordinate fiscal policy, agricultural policy, labor policy, foreign policy, and military policy, to name a few major areas, moves beyond the range of government charts and the habitat of the bureaucrats to the market place and to where the people live and work. This suggests that the reason why government reorganization is so difficult is that far more than government in the formal sense is involved in reorganization. One could overlook this in the limited government of the nineteenth century but the multi-billion dollar government of the mid-twentieth permits no facile dichotomy between government and economy. Economy and efficiency are the two objectives a laissez faire society can prescribe in peacetime as over-all government objectives. Their inadequacy either as motivation or standards has long been obvious. A planned economy clearly requires a planned government. But, if one can afford an unplanned economy, apart from gross extravagance, there seems no compelling and therefore, perhaps, no sufficiently powerful reason for a planned government.

Basic to the problem of administrative rationality is that of organizational identification and point of view. To whom is one loyal—unit, section, branch, division, bureau, department, administration, government, country, people, world history, or what? Administrative analysis frequently assumes that organizational identification should occur in such a way as to merge primary organization loyalty in a larger synthesis. The good of the part is to give way to the reasoned good of the whole. This is most frequently illustrated in the rationalizations used to counter self-centered demands of primary groups for funds and personnel. Actually the competition between governmental power centers, rather than the rationalizations, is the effective instrument of coordination.

Where there is a clear common product on whose successful production the sub-groups depend for the attainment of their own satisfaction, it is possible to demonstrate to almost all participants the desirability of cooperation. The shoe factory produces shoes, or else, for all concerned. But the government as a whole and many of its component parts have no such identifiable common product on which all depend. Like the proverbial Heinz, there are fifty-seven or more varieties unified, if at all, by a common political profit and loss account.

Administration is faced by somewhat the same dilemma as economics. There are propositions about the behavior patterns conducive to full employment— welfare economics. On the other hand, there are propositions about the economics of the individual firm—the counsel of the business schools. It is possible to show with considerable persuasiveness that sound considerations for the individual firm may lead to a depression if generally adopted, a result desired by none of the participants. However, no single firm can afford by itself to adopt the course of collective wisdom; in the absence of a common power capable of enforcing decisions premised on the supremacy of the collective interest, *sauve qui peut* is common sense.

The position of administrative organizations is not unlike the position of particular firms. Just as the decisions of the firms could be coordinated by the imposition of a planned economy so could those of the component parts of the government. But just as it is possible to operate a formally unplanned economy by the loose coordination of the market, in the same fashion it is possible to operate a government by the loose coordination of the play of political forces through its institutions.

The unseen hand of Adam Smith may be little in evidence in either case. One need not believe in a doctrine of social or administrative harmony to believe that formal centralized planning—while perhaps desirable and in some cases necessary—is not a must. The complicated logistics of supplying the city of New York runs smoothly down the grooves of millions of well adapted habits projected from a distant past. It seems naive on the one hand to believe in the possibility of a vast, intricate, and delicate economy operating with a minimum of formal over-all direction, and on the other to doubt that a relatively simple mechanism such as the government can be controlled largely by the same play of forces.

Doubtless the real reasons for seeking coordination in the government are the same that prompt a desire for economic planning. In fact, apart from waging war with its demand for rapid change, economic planning would seem to be the only objective sufficiently compelling and extensive to require a drastic change in our system of political laissez faire. Harold Smith, testifying before the Senate Banking and Currency Committee on the Employment Act of 1946, showed how extensive a range of hitherto unrelated activities could be brought to bear on a common purpose—the maintenance of maximum employment and purchasing power. In the flush of the war experience and with prophecies of reconversion unemployment, a reluctant Congress passed a pious declaration of policy. Senator Flanders has recorded the meager showing to date.

Nevertheless, war and depression apart, the Employment Act of 1946 for the first time provides an inclusive common purpose in terms of which administrative activities can be evaluated and integrated. While still deficient in depth and content, it provides at least a partial basis for the rational budgeting of government activities. The older concept of economy and efficiency as autonomous standards still lingers in Congress, but elsewhere their validity as ends in themselves is treated with skepticism.

If the advent of Keynesian economics and the erosion of laissez faire have created the intellectual conditions requisite for the formulation of over-all government policy, they do not by any means guarantee the political conditions necessary for its implementation. We can see quite clearly that the development of an integrated administration requires an integrating purpose. The ideals of Locke, Smith, Spencer, and their American disciples deny the need for such a purpose save for economy and efficiency's sake. Marx, Keynes, and their followers by denying the validity of the self-regulating economy have endowed the state with an over-arching responsibility in terms of which broad coordination of activities is not only intellectually possible but theoretically, at least, necessary. Intellectual perception of the need for this coordination, however, has run well ahead of the public's perception of it and of the development of a political channeling of power adequate to its administrative implementation.

Most students of administration are planners of some sort. Most congressmen would fly the label like the plague. Most bureaucrats, whatever their private faith, live under two jealous gods, their particular clientele and the loyalty check. Such a condition might, if it exists as described, cast doubt on whether even the intellectual conditions for rational administrative coordination exist. Be that as it may, the transition from a government organized in clientele departments and bureaus, each responding to the massive feudal power of organized business, organized agriculture, and organized labor, to a government integrated about a paramount national purpose will require a political power at least as great as that which tamed the earlier feudalism. It takes a sharp eye or a tinted glass to see such an organized power on the American scene. Without it, administrative organization for over-all coordination has the academic air of South American constitution making. One is reminded of the remark attributed to the Austrian economist Mises; on being told that the facts did not agree with his theory, he replied *"desto schlechter für die Tatsache."*

IV

It is highly appropriate to consider how administrators should behave to meet the test of efficiency in a planned polity; but in the absence of such a polity and while, if we like, struggling to get it, a realistic science of administration will teach administrative behavior appropriate to the existing political system.

A close examination of the presidential system may well bring one to conclude that administrative rationality in it is a different matter from that applicable to the British ideal. The American Presidency is an office that has significant monarchical characteristics despite its limited term and elective nature. The literature on court and palace has many an insight applicable to the White House. Access to the President, reigning favorites, even the court jester, are topics that show the continuity of institutions. The maxims of LaRochefoucauld and the memoirs of the Duc de Saint Simon have a refreshing realism for the operator on the Potomac.

The problem of rival factions in the President's family is as old as the famous struggle between Jefferson and Hamilton, as fresh and modern as the latest cabal against John Snyder. Experience seems to show that this personal and factional struggle for the President's favor is a vital part of the process of representation. The vanity, personal ambition, or patriotism of the contestants soon clothes itself in the generalities of principle and the clique aligns itself with groups beyond the capital. Subordinate rivalry is tolerated if not encouraged by so many able executives that it can scarcely be attributed to administrative ineptitude. The wrangling tests opinion, uncovers information that would otherwise never rise to the top, and provides effective opportunity for decision rather than mere ratification of prearranged plans. Like most judges, the Executive needs to hear argument for his own instruction. The alternatives presented by subordinates in large part determine the freedom and the creative opportunity of their superiors. The danger of becoming a Merovingian is a powerful incentive to the maintenance of fluidity in the structure of power.

The fixed character of presidential tenure makes it necessary that subordinates be politically expendable. The President's men must be willing to accept the blame for failures not their own. Machiavelli's teaching on how princes must keep the faith bears re-reading. Collective responsibility is incompatible with a fixed term of office. As it tests the currents of public opinion, the situation on the Hill, and the varying strength of the organized pressures, the White House alters and adapts the complexion of the Administration. Loyalties to programs or to groups and personal pride and interest frequently conflict with whole-souled devotion to the Presidency. In fact, since such devotion is not made mandatory by custom, institutions, or the facts of power, the problem is perpetually perplexing to those who must choose.

The balance of power between executive and legislature is constantly subject to the shifts of public and group support. The latent tendency of the American Congress is to follow the age-old parliamentary precedents and to try to reduce the President to the role of constitutional monarch. Against this threat and to secure his own initiative, the President's resources are primarily demagogic, with the weaknesses and strengths that dependence on mass popular appeal implies. The unanswered question of American government—"who is boss?"—constantly plagues administration. The disruption of unity of command is not just the problem of Taylor's functional foreman, but goes to the stability and uniformity of basic decisional premises essential to consequent administration.

It is interesting to speculate on the consequences for administration of the full development of congressional or presidential government. A leadership in Congress that could control the timetable of the House and Senate would scarcely content itself short of reducing the President's Cabinet to what in all probability it was first intended to be, a modified version of the present Swiss executive. Such leadership could scarcely arise without centrally organized, disciplined, national parties far different from our present shambling alliances of state and local machines.

A Presidency backed by a disciplined party controlling a majority in Congress would probably assimilate itself to a premiership by association of legislative leadership in the formulation of policy and administration. In either line of development the crucial matter is party organization. For the spirit of the party system determines the character of the government.

That the American party system will develop toward the British ideal is by no means a foregone conclusion. The present oscillation between a strong demagogic Presidency and a defensively powerful congressional oligarchy may well prove a continuing pattern of American politics, as it was of Roman. In the absence of a party system providing an institutionalized centripetal force in our affairs, it is natural to look to the Presidency as Goldsmith's weary traveler looked to the throne.

The Presidency of the United States, however, is no such throne as the pre-World War I *Kaiserreich* that provided the moral and political basis for the Prussian bureaucracy. Lacking neutrality and mystique, it does not even perform the function of the British monarchy in providing a psychological foundation for the permanent civil service. A leaderless and irresponsible Congress frequently makes it appear the strong point of the republic. The Bonapartist experience in France, the Weimar Republic, and South American examples nearer home, despite important social differences, are relevant to any thoughtful consideration of building a solution to legislative anarchy on the unity of the executive.

The present course of American party development gives little ground for optimism that a responsible two party system capable of uniting Congress and Executive in a coherent program will emerge. The increasingly critical importance of the federal budget for the national economy and the inevitable impact of world power status on the conduct of foreign affairs make inescapable the problem of stable leadership in the American system. Unfortunately they by no means insure a happy or indeed any solution.

Attempts to solve administrative problems in isolation from the structure of power and purpose in the polity are bound to prove illusory. The reorganization of Congress to create responsibility in advance of the development of party responsibility was an act of piety to principle, of educational value; but as a practical matter it raised a structure without foundation. In the same way, reorganization of the executive branch to centralize administrative power in the Presidency while political power remains dispersed and divided may effect improvement, but in a large sense it must fail. The basic prerequisite to the administration of the textbooks is a responsible two party system. The means to its attainment are a number one problem for students of administration. What Schattschneider calls the struggle for party government may sometime yield us the responsible parliamentary two party system needed to underpin our present administrative theory. Until that happy time, exploration of the needs and necessities of our present system is a high priority task of responsible scholarship.

32

HUGH HECLO

POLITICAL EXECUTIVES:
A GOVERNMENT OF STRANGERS

To speak of political appointees in Washington is obviously to embrace a wide variety of people and situations. Political appointments cover everything from the temporary file clerk recouping a campaign obligation to the cabinet secretary heading a department organization larger than many state governments or the national administrations of some foreign countries. [Table 32-1] shows the number and types of what are considered to be the most clearly political appointments in the executive branch.

My focus in this [essay] is on the political executives at or near the top of government agencies. Volumes could be devoted to describing the maze of special circumstances in which these roughly 700 men and women find themselves. Here, however, attention will be given to some important points of common reference—the political executives' recruitment problems, inexperience, transience, disunity, and—not least—their strategically vulnerable position. Despite the large variety of government agencies and types of appointment, the most interesting thing is how much U.S. political executives actually have in common.

THE POLITICAL EXECUTIVE SYSTEM

From the outset political executives share one broad feature: all hold an ambivalent leadership position in what might loosely be termed the American "system" of public executives. To appreciate the peculiarity of their political situation, one must return to the basic rationale for having a number of nonelected political appointees in the executive branch in the first place. According to the Founding Fathers' design, power for the legislative functions of government was spread among the various representatives from states and congressional districts; for the executive function, power was deliberately unified in one elected chief executive. A single president to nominate and supervise the principal officers of the executive branch would promote the unity and vigor of executive operations, while requiring the Senate's consent to make appointments final would safeguard against any presidential abuse of the appointment power

TABLE 32-1. FULL-TIME POLITICAL APPOINTMENTS IN THE EXECUTIVE BRANCH, JUNE 1976

	Political Officials				
SCHEDULE	PRESIDENTIAL APPOINTMENTS WITH SENATE CONFIRMATION	PRESIDENTIAL APPOINTMENTS WITHOUT SENATE CONFIRMATION	SCHEDULE C APPOINTMENTS	NONCAREER EXECUTIVE ASSIGN- MENTS	MISCELLANEOUS[a]
Executive schedule					
I	12	—	—	—	—
II	61	10	—	—	—
III	109	4	1	—	1
IV	311	12	27	—	3
V	113	3	66	—	12
General schedule supergrades					
18	30	13	6	178	20
17	36	1	6	184	19
16	49	4	14	171	38
(16–18)[b]	—	18	—	—	24
General schedule lower grades					
15	10	2	282	—	15
14	36	—	98	—	16
13	54	—	63	—	20
12	1	—	75	—	14
11 and below	1	—	500	—	126
Total[c]	823	67	1,138	533	308

Source: Compiled from official estimates and sources.

[a] Includes certificated White House staff, some Veterans Administration personnel, and others.

[b] The grade level is administratively determined within this range and in a few cases can include executive schedule V.

[c] Excludes a number of positions that are exempted from civil service examinations (although insiders argue about whether they are or are not "political" jobs). Thus the table does not include schedules A and B mentioned [previously] or 162 noncareer positions that fall under the Foreign Assistance Act.

and would stabilize administration.[1] Theorists of party government later elaborated on what some of the founders only hinted at—that competition in the electoral marketplace would result in choices between alternative political teams and policies.[2]

The idea of a single chief executive entering office to promote his measures through a band of loyal political supporters in the executive branch is an easily understood model. It fits well with the media's desire to focus on the central presidential personality, and the notion of undertaking public service at the call of the president attracts many new political appointees to Washington. Astute scholars have pointed out that in reality the president's formal power as the single chief executive is often illusory, that even within his own executive branch he must persuade others and calculate his power stakes rather than cudgel his minions. This revisionist view, however, has not altered the customary concentration on the president and, like the standard constitutional or party government models, it relegates the bulk of political executives to a secondary, derivative role in the executive branch.

As noted earlier, the problem with relying on such president-centered models of executive politics is that they all depend on a tenuous political chain of events. The links of this chain are unlikely to hold from a preelection formulation of intentions, through an election contest giving a clear mandate to a particular president and his measures, to the installation of his team of executives in positions of control over government actions, to faithful administrative implementation of the promised policies. Nevertheless, there is an underlying psychological validity to the president-centered models. In good times and bad the president *is* the focus of national political attention. His popular following and public stature give him resources for bargaining and leadership that no political executive in the departments can hope to match.

Hence, even if one disregarded all the policy challenges and personnel trends . . . , U.S. federal executives would still find themselves in an extraordinarily difficult political situation. In theory political executives are supposed to provide departmental leadership and to work together under the president. But there are no "natural" political forces bolstering such expectations. Where, after all, does the political strength of these executives lie?

In elections? Departmental appointees are supposed to be helping the president make and carry out public policies affecting millions of lives, but no one has elected them. Typically, in fact, they will have played little part in the election responsible for their presence in Washington. Can ties to the president supply political strength? The president's closest companions are those who have followed him—not necessarily the party—and they will often have done so throughout the long march to the White House. Knowing the source of their power, they usually prefer proximity as White House aides rather than isolation as executive appointees somewhere "out" in the departments. And in any event a president who calculates his own power stakes is unlikely to let department executives borrow heavily on his political resources. Might political executives look for strength in their managerial authority? Hardly. Their second-hand mandate from the president competes with the mandates of elected congressmen who call the hearings, pass the enabling legislation, and appropriate the money. What about interest groups and clienteles? Obviously they have power, and many new political appointees do arrive in office closely tied to one or another such group.[3] But if this is the executive's exclusive source of political backing, any leadership role will be severely constrained. A public executive's responsibility is supposed to entail something more than advocacy for private groups.

Since these are "political" appointees, can strength perhaps be derived from political parties? As this [essay] will show, new political executives may be outsiders, but they are not outsiders who have been linked together politically during periods of opposition. Whatever central campaign machinery there is belongs largely to the individual president rather than to a set of national party leaders. At the vital state and local party level, those ambitious for their own elective careers know they must prepare their true political bases back home rather than in the Washington bureaucracy. Political parties are in no position to reward appointed executives for their successes or punish them for their failures.

On all of these counts, Washington's political executives have as few incentives to pull together as they have resources to stand alone as political leaders. Like the president, they must persuade rather than command others, but they lack the president's preeminent position to improve their bargaining power. The glare of White House attention may occasionally sweep across their agencies' activity, but for most political executives the president's traditional handshake and photograph will be his way of saying both hello and goodbye. In the constitutional structure and in the public eye, they are distinctly secondary figures to the single chief executive, yet the president's limited time, interests, and fighting power will make him utterly dependent on them for most of what is done by the executive branch. That they exist in such a twilight zone of political leadership is the first and primary fact of life shared by political appointees. . . .

CHARACTERISTICS OF POLITICAL EXECUTIVES

Although reliable information about political executives' behavior is lacking, a surfeit of data exists concerning their biographical characteristics. These data add up to a description of a statistical elite—statistical because there is little evidence of a self-conscious group seeking agreed upon goals and screening out other entrants; elite because political appointees in the federal government are consistently drawn from the most socially and economically advantaged portions of the population. With a degree of certainty rare in social science, political executives can be predicted to be disproportionately white, male, urban, affluent, middle-aged, well educated at prestige schools, and pursuers of high-status white-collar careers. They are unlikely to be female, nonwhite, wage-earning, from a small town, or possessors of average educational and social credentials.[4]

Work Experience

These socioeconomic data, however, reveal little about the kind of experience political executives gain on the job. For this type of information, researchers have examined job tenure and mobility in hopes of describing the government executives' opportunities to learn about their working environments. Such information does not entirely support several commonly held assumptions about the characteristics of political appointees. One is that the top political layers are filled with newcomers to government—politically imported outsiders credited by defenders with introducing a fresh view of government operations and labeled by detractors as ignorant intruders. Another common view (and one of the chief justifications for the extensive use of political appointments in government) is that those in the top strata resemble the Founding Fathers, in that they are "in-and-outers," that is, people who periodically interrupt their private careers to move in and out of the public service. Qualifying, if not entirely dispelling, each of these assumptions leaves behind a more realistic picture of the public careers of political executives.

TABLE 32-2. POLITICAL EXECUTIVES' YEARS OF EXPERIENCE IN THE FEDERAL
GOVERNMENT, 1970[a] (PERCENT)

Years of Government Experience	Presidential Appointees	Noncareer Supergrades	Career Supergrades
Less than 2	69	40	3
2–5	19	7	11
6–10	6	14	9
Over 10	6	39	77
Total	100	100	100

Source: Reproduced with the permission of Joel D. Aberbach and the Comparative Elite Project at the University of Michigan. The project is a comparative study of the attitudes of high-level administrators and elected officials in Western Europe and the United States. More information on the American portion of the study can be found in Joel D. Aberbach, James D. Chesney, and Bert A. Rockman, "Exploring Elite Political Attitudes," *Political Methodology* 2 (1975): 1-28.

[a] Figures refer to years of continuous or noncontinuous experience at the time of the survey (1970) and therefore overstate the amount of experience in government enjoyed by these officials (17 presidential appointees, 43 noncareer supergrades, and 64 career supergrades) at the time of their appointment to executive positions.

Compared with the government experience of civil servants, that of the men and women coming to top political positions naturally seems meager. [Table 32-2] shows that in 1970 the highest political executives (presidential appointees) had the least experience in the federal government, the next echelon of political appointees (noncareerists in the supergrade range of GS 16–18) had somewhat more, and higher civil servants had the longest experience of all.[5]

It is worth emphasizing the general point evident in such data: unlike the situation in most private organizations, in the U.S. executive branch those in the top positions of formal authority are likely to be substantially less familiar with their working environment than both their civil service and political subordinates.

But . . . this relative inexperience at the top does not mean that political executives are complete novices to government. One bureaucratic-type feature of the layers of political executives is the tendency (particularly after the early days of a new administration) for recruitment to occur from subordinate to superordinate political positions. Studies of top political executives from the Roosevelt to Johnson administrations have shown that the large majority had some previous experience in the federal government. During those years 29 percent of the senior appointees (cabinet secretaries, undersecretaries, assistant secretaries, general counsels, administrators, deputy administrators, and commissioners) had previously held high political positions in the same agency and 11 percent in other agencies; 24 percent had held lower-echelon political appointments (special assistants, personal aides, etc.) in the same agency and 37 percent in other agencies. All together about two-thirds of the top political executives had federal administrative service before their appointment by the President.[6] Lower-level political appointees, *i.e.*, noncareer executives in the supergrades, also are often recruited from among people with narrow experience inside government. During 1974, for example, over three-quarters of noncareer vacancies were filled from within the same agency, 11 percent from other agencies, and only 13 percent from outside government.[7]

These statistics, however, should not summon up images of a top government layer peopled with men of public affairs who, like modern counterparts of Cincinnatus or George Washington, repeatedly exchange private lives for public offices. While prominent examples of such men do exist (Nelson Rockefeller, Clark Clifford, Averell Harriman, etc.), true in-and-out careers are much less common than usually thought. Such careers would presumably show a periodic interchange of public service and private employment, possibly with several appointments in different administrations. In fact, these characteristics are uncommon. Between 1933 and 1965 nine out of ten top political executives had no more than two government appointments. Four-fifths served only one president and while most appointees reported their principal occupations to be in the private sector, seven out of ten held government rather than private positions immediately before their presidential appointment. Since nine out of ten of these top political executives served in only one agency, it is also difficult to see how the in-and-outers can be thought to supply anything like a general, government-wide capability for political leadership in the bureaucracy. Similar tendencies are evident in the lower-level political appointments, i.e., the noncareer executive assignments in the supergrade range. Very few of these noncareer executives have repeated spells of government service and rarely have they worked in more than one agency. In 1975, noncareer supergrades actually had somewhat less experience outside their agency than did the relatively immobile career bureaucrats at the same grade level.[8]

In sum, political appointees are generally people who will move in and sometimes up. They will cope as best they can and move out without returning. The few top executives with continual government experience may be extraordinarily valuable, but as a former civil servant said, "What most people don't realize is that an in-and-outer usually ends up staying an outer." The conventional image of Washington in-and-outers erroneously suggests a political team of utility players, when what actually exists is a one-time sequence of pinch hitters.

Birds of Passage

The single most obvious characteristic of Washington's political appointees is their transience. While most take up their appointments with somewhat more government experience and have a more terminal government career than is usually assumed, political executives are not likely to be in any one position for very long. The standard figure quoted is that the average undersecretary or assistant secretary remains in his job for about twenty-two months. More detailed breakdowns show this average to contain a large number of very short tenures; about half the top political executives can expect to stay in their jobs less than two years. (See Table 32-3.) The Nixon administration provided an extreme example of the general tendency when its personnel office in 1970 (*before* large-scale

TABLE 32-3. TENURE OF POLITICAL EXECUTIVES, 1960–1972 (PERCENT)

	Months on the Job		
TYPE OF EXECUTIVE	LESS THAN 12	12–24	OVER 24
Cabinet secretaries	16	25	59
Undersecretaries	16	35	49
Assistant secretaries	22	32	46

Source: Arch Patton, "Government's Revolving Door," *Business Week* (September 22, 1973): 12.

purges by the White House) found there was already an annual turnover rate of 27–30 percent in presidential and executive-level appointments to the departments and agencies. The tenure of cabinet secretaries declined from a previous average of forty months to eighteen months during the Nixon administration.

Again, those in the lower rather than in the higher political echelons have a better chance to acquire job experience. Unlike the high political executives just mentioned, noncareer supergrade appointees have an average tenure of fifteen years in the federal service. But . . . up to one-half of these "political appointees" are in effect former career officials. One year after the Johnson–Nixon transition about 90 percent of these civil-servant-type appointees were still in their jobs, and the turnover rate was in line with what could be expected of comparable civil servants. As for the other half (the 300 or so younger outsiders), two-thirds were no longer in their jobs a year after the Johnson–Nixon transition.[9]

Much more important than the experience or inexperience of political appointees as individuals is their transience as a group. Cabinet secretaries may bring with them a cadre of personal acquaintances to fill some of their subordinate political positions, but in general public executives will be strangers with only a fleeting chance to learn how to work together. This characteristic is worth examining in a little more detail.

One of the most persistent themes in comments from political executives of all recent administrations is the absence of teamwork characterizing the layers of appointees. This absence of unifying ties is foreordained, given the fractionalized, changing, and job-specific sets of forces that make up the selection process. But it is not only methods of selection that put mutually reinforcing loyalties at a premium. Rapid turnover intensifies all the other problems of political teamwork.

In many ways what matters most is not so much an individual's job tenure as the duration of his executive relationships. Those in superior positions need to assess the capacities of their subordinates; subordinates need to learn what is expected of them. Political appointees at the same hierarchial level need to learn each other's strengths, weaknesses, priorities, and ways of communicating. Normally the opportunity to develop these working relationships is even shorter than the time span for learning a particular job. As the following percentages show, during the Kennedy, Johnson, and Nixon administrations, almost two-thirds of the undersecretaries and four-fifths of the assistant secretaries worked two years or less for the same immediate political superiors:[10]

TABLE 32-4.

	Under 12 Months (Percent)	12–24 Months (Percent)	Over 2 Years (Percent)
Same undersecretary— cabinet secretary relationship	29	34	37
Same assistant secretary— undersecretary relationship	39	38	23

The effects of this group instability are reflected in countless ways, all expressive of the fundamental point that a political executive in Washington must operate amid kaleidoscopic sets of interpersonal relations. These situations are predictable only in the sense that they are likely to arise in unexpected ways to affect the chances for political leadership in the bureaucracy. For example, with one set of personalities and circumstances, a cabinet officer dealing with an assistant secretary may bypass an undersecretary but create little difficulty. An undersecretary who found himself in this position said, "It was something I knew [the cabinet secretary] was interested in. I was made to feel welcome if I wanted to get into it, so why should I be upset?" Later, with other people and in other circumstances: "There was [the undersecretary] from the California crowd. [The cabinet secretary] had no trouble with that because he simply outflanked him by bringing in his own man as assistant secretary. So there was poor old [the undersecretary] between the hammer and the anvil." But within another two years turnover in the assistant secretary's slot brought a new constellation of forces. "[The new man] made it clear he wasn't going to perform the same sort of hatchet job on the undersecretary. He was going to be strictly nonpartisan, and you could see things becoming more politically sanitized." One political appointee found that the cabinet secretary regularly used meetings to alert him that he "was being torpedoed by [a political colleague] who was always cutting deals on his own." Another man formally in the same position found himself "going to meetings, and people would want to know why I was there."

The Larger Picture

The unstable teams within departments are positively collegial when compared with the attenuated relations of political appointees across departments. At least within departments there may be the shared need to protect and promote a common set of agency programs. Weighed against this territorial imperative, political appointees elsewhere can seem like alien tribes.

Few political appointees are likely to be united by bonds of party loyalty, the academics' favorite prescription for overcoming political incoherence in Washington. Though they may be in broad agreement with the president's general approach, political executives usually will not have been active members of his party and only a small minority will have struggled together against common opponents in electoral campaigns. Civil servants are identifying a fundamental characteristic of executive leadership in Washington when they report that they have worked for many political appointees but rarely for a politician.[11] Most would probably agree with the assistant secretary who said, "As far as I can tell, in this town a political appointee is simply someone whose career isn't in this department."

None of this inexperience necessarily means a lack of partisanship in "nonpolitical" political appointees. Quite the opposite. Many of those eventually known as the most partisan of Nixon's appointees came from backgrounds with a minimum of party-political experience. "I came to Washington with absolutely no party or political background," one of them said. "I had a naive idea of managing as in private enterprise but quickly learned political factors are all pervasive."

The record of the Nixon White House demonstrated in a number of cases how those least politically experienced can be susceptible to developing more extreme personal partisanship than those accustomed to regular political interaction and its inevitable compromises. Often the zealousness of the new convert to Washington politics can make effective political teamwork that much more difficult. One official summed up his experience in four administrations by observing: "Inexperienced people tend to lack the political instinct. . . . Sometimes the political instinct means the best politics is no politics. And it knows where that's true, it's not pure partisanship."

Lacking any larger political forces to help unify political executives, the lines of mutual interdependence normally run vertically down the departments and their loosely related programs—not horizontally across the layers of political leadership in various departments. Insofar as top political executives need each other (as opposed to needing the president's support or endorsement) the needs are temporary and issue-specific, not enduring. Even at the height of public criticism concerning the placement of Nixon loyalists in the departments, many of those placed recognized the lack of any workable horizontal contacts. As one appointee said:

> For all the talk about teams, I have no contact that amounts to anything with other appointees outside the department. The few lunches we have aren't of much use for getting business done. There is no strong mechanism for getting political appointees together. As a group there's no trust.

It would be a mistake, however, to conclude that political executives are averse to creating alliances. At any given moment, informal communications and networks do exist throughout the political levels and across the departments in Washington. But as participants and issues change frequently, so do the nature and location of these relationships. Some political appointees will have enough common objectives and mutual knowledge to create fairly close informal groups. "There are me and six other assistant secretaries from other departments," said one such man. "We've got some management techniques we want to move on." A year later two of these executives were left in government. Another appointee was trying to draw his counterparts into monthly meetings but recognized "the problem is how to get continuity and institutionalize this sort of thing to keep it going." A year later, he too was gone and his group largely dismantled.

Equally revealing of the flux confronting any outsider is the fact that the last man quoted was like many resigning political appointees. He did not depart for reasons bearing any relation to the substance of what he was doing in government but because his own political patrons were leaving. While resignation for reasons of conscience or policy are relatively rare,[12] the chancy circumstances that create political executives in the first place can just as easily lead to their departure. Political executives and their particular sets of relationships with each other not only fade, but fade fortuitously. Even a close observer of these political comings and goings is likely to pick up confusing signals about whether an executive personnel change is a case of tactics, accident, or grand political strategy.

In recent years greater efforts have been made to formalize cross-departmental ties, with the hope of institutionalizing more permanent and general-purpose relationships than those that usually prevail. The Undersecretaries' Group, begun informally toward the end of the Johnson administration, is a good example. Formal organization occurred in 1968–69 at the urging of Bureau of the Budget officials and mainly, as one of the founders described it, "to get more political weight behind some procedural reforms we were pushing."[13] Nixon's advisers attempted later to broaden the scope of the Undersecretaries' Group and to establish regular meetings of a governmentwide team identified with the administration as a whole. According to one of the plan's promoters:

> It was something we should have done a lot earlier in the administration. We started monthly meetings, even had an executive order. We had a weekend session at Camp David with the wives along. The undersecretaries got to know each other. We talked about where we should be going and had some very thought-provoking sessions. . . . I think these people at this level are interested in things bigger than the department. I think they realize their success is measured by the success of the president.

Unfortunately, sociability and big thinking could not provide a foundation for serious working relationships. After one year, another presidential aide more closely connected with the activities of the group concluded:

> I didn't get the feeling they were acting like prima donnas, [but] it's just generally hard to get their attention, even concerning the federal regional councils, if they don't feel it's important to their departmental operations. . . . They just weren't interested in talking about these broader issues. Where they'd had a problem, they'd already met to settle it informally.

Undoubtedly every administration could help itself by doing more to exchange information and create understanding across political levels. But government-wide teamwork is another question. One undersecretary, generally recognized as a leading member of the group, went to the heart of the matter:

> You can't build a government-wide executive team through artificial structures like the

Undersecretaries' Group. It's a group in search of a mission. You can't build an executive team by pressing issues that aren't particularly relevant to people just for the sake of having everybody in on them. You can't do it by bypassing people to get to another layer. [Insofar as there is going to be a team] it has to begin at the top and use the cabinet secretaries.

Yet if there were to be such a serious effort at decisionmaking by enduring teams of political leaders across the top of departments, the U.S. presidency would look far different than it does today or ever has. In such a system cabinet secretaries would need each other as a group more than they would need their departmental identifications and more than they would need any individual member, including the president. Presidents may be advised that they need more collegial help and reactivated cabinets, and they may with good reason even take such advice, at least for a while. But barring any profound institutional and structural changes, no modern president can be expected to be like a foreign prime minister, merely the first among equals. He needs the particular colleagues in his cabinet too little; his colleagues need him too much and each other too little for that to happen. No public executive short of the president has a vested interest in coordinating political leadership in the executive branch as a whole. Political appointees out in the departments and agencies can expect to remain in their twilight zone.

Because the executive branch has a single head, its political leadership is inherently noncollegial—except for a sharing of some executive powers with Congress. That is the way the founders designed it. That is the way it functions. But "single" does not mean unitary. The political executives' very lack of coequality—no one is the president's peer—means that their successes are likely to be expropriated by the president, their failures left behind in the departments with little effect on the appointees' real vocations outside government. Since there is only one chief executive but many sources of political support and inspiration, top political appointees do not necessarily hang separately if they fail to hang together. *E unibus plurum.*

A SUMMARY AND LOOK FORWARD

Any commitment to democratic values necessarily means accepting a measure of instability in the top governing levels. Democratic elections are, after all, "a political invention to assure uncertainty of leadership, in what are deemed to be optimum amounts and periods of time."[14] But to the inherent electoral changes, the American executive political system adds a considerably greater range of nonelectoral uncertainty to political leadership. This system produces top executives who are both expendable over time and in a relatively weak, uncertain position at any one time.

The number of political executives is small vis-à-vis the bureaucracy but large and fragmented in relation to any notion of a trim top-management structure. To the normal confusions of pluralistic institutions and powers in Washington, the selection process contributes its own complexities. White House personnel efforts have rarely been effectively organized. Political forces intervene from many quarters, and their interests in political appointments often bear little relation to presidential needs or to qualifications required for effective perform-ance by public executives. White House efforts at political recruitment can be effective, but the organizational requirements are difficult to master. A White House operation that veers too far in the direction of centralized control can easily become self-defeating by overlooking the need for political executives to balance their responsiveness to the president with their usefulness to the departments.

While political appointees are more experienced in government than might be assumed, their government service does not usually provide continuity of experience, either through periodic spells of officeholding or long tenure in particular jobs. This is especially true at the higher political levels. Hence without a very steep learning curve, political appointees are likely to find that their capacities for effective action have matured at just about the time they are leaving office. As one assistant secretary said, "You're given this particular situation for one moment in time . . . you've got to get on your feet quickly." The entire process does not produce long-suffering policymakers who realize their major changes will come gradually through persistence. Most political appointees are more impatient. Any civil servant who offers the standard and often sensible bureaucratic advice to watch, wait, and be careful can expect to arouse more than a little suspicion.

All these tendencies are vastly intensified by the instability and uncertainty of working relationships among political appointees as a group. Over time, changes in the Washington community, particularly the declining role of parties, have provided even fewer points of political reference to help orient leadership in the executive branch. Despite the conventional models, political interaction is less like regularly scheduled matches between competing teams of partisans (presi-dent versus Congress, Republicans versus Democrats) and more like a sandlot pick-up game, with a variety of strangers, strategies, and misunderstandings. Such working relationships as exist are created and recreated sporadically as the political players come and go. Each largely picks up his lore anew—how to make his way, look for support, and deal with officialdom. It is circumstances such as these that lead many civil servants and experienced political executives to echo the words of one presidential appointee (in fact a Nixon placement in the supposedly enemy territory of the Department of Health, Education, and Welfare): "In my time I've come to the conclusion you can't say it's the damn bureaucrats. With some exceptions, that's not the problem. What's lacking is the political leadership." Political executives have no common culture for dealing with the problems of governing, and it is seldom that they are around long enough or trust one another enough to acquire one.

Weaknesses among political executives lead inevitably to White House complaints about their "going native" in the bureaucracy. The image is apt. To a large extent the particular agencies and bureaus *are* the native villages of executive politics. Even the most presidentially minded political executive will discover that his own agency provides the one relatively secure reference point amid all the other uncertainties of Washington. In their own agencies, appointees usually have at least some knowledge of each other and a common identity with particular programs. Outside the agency it is more like life in the big city among large numbers of anonymous people who have unknown lineages. Any common kinship in the political party or a shared political vocation is improbable, and in the background are always the suspicions of the president's "true" family of supporters in the White House. Political appointees in the larger Washington environment may deal frequently with each other, but these are likely to be the kind of ad hoc, instrumental relations of the city, where people interact without truly knowing each other.

Yet the political appointee's situation is not so simple that he can act as if he is surrounded by a random collection of strangers outside the confines of his agency village. Everywhere extensive networks of village folk in the bureaucracy, Congress, and lobby organizations share experiences, problems, and readings on people and events. An appointee may or may not be in touch with people in these networks, but they are certain to be in touch with each other independently of him. In sociological terms his networks are thin, transient, and single-stranded; theirs are dense, multiple, and enduring. Among public executives themselves there is little need to worry about any joint action to enforce community norms, because there is no community. In dealing with outside villagers who know each other, however, appointees can find that reprisals for any misdeeds are extraordinarily oblique and powerful. The political executive system may be a government of strangers, but its members cannot act as if everyone else is.

Now one can begin to see the real challenge to the political executives' statecraft in Washington. They must be able to move in two worlds—the tight, ingrown village life of the bureaucratic community and the open, disjointed world of political strangers. A public executive in Washington needs the social sensitivity of a villager and the political toughness of a city streetfighter. It is an increasingly unlikely combination. Despite all the resources devoted to more topside staff, new management initiatives, more elaborate analytic techniques, and so on, there remain few—probably fewer than ever—places where political executives can look for reliable political support in any efforts at leadership in the bureaucracy. Political appointees in Washington are substantially on their own and vulnerable to bureaucratic power.

NOTES

[1] For the political appointment process and the decision against a plural executive, see Arthur Taylor Prescott, *Drafting the Federal Constitution* (Louisiana State University Press, 1941), pp. 544–646; and Alexander Hamilton, James Madison, and John Jay, *The Federalist*, ed. Max Beloff (Oxford: Basil Blackwell, 1948), nos. 70, 72, and 76. There is some question about how far the founders actually intended the president to function alone or with the cabinet and Senate as a semicollegial group.

² Alexander Hamilton contended that after an election,

the person substituted is warranted in supposing that the dismission of his predecessor has proceeded from a dislike to his measures, and that the less he resembles him, the more he will recommend himself to the favor of his constituents. These considerations, and the influence of personal confidences and attachments, would be likely to induce every new president to promote a change of men to fill the subordinate stations. . . . (*Ibid.*, no. 72, p. 370)

³ See for example, U.S., Congress, Senate, Committee on Commerce, *Appointments to the Regulatory Agencies*, 94th Cong. 2nd sess. (Washington, D.C.: U.S. Government Printing Office, 1976); and Common Cause, *Serving Two Masters: A Common Cause Study of Conflicts of Interest in the Executive Branch* (Washington: Common Cause, 1976; processed).

⁴ See David T. Stanley, Dean E. Mann, and Jameson W. Doig, *Men Who Govern* (Brookings Institution, 1967), pp. 9–36; and Thomas R. Dye and John W. Pickering, "Governmental and Corporate Elites," *Journal of Politics* 37 (1974): 913–15.

⁵ Nixon political executives in 1970, however, had somewhat less government experience than those in previous administrations, including Eisenhower's.

⁶ Stanley, Mann, and Doig, *op. cit.*, table 3-5, p. 45, and table E-5, p. 137.

⁷ U.S. Civil Service Commission, *Executive Manpower in the Federal Service* (Washington, D.C.: U.S. Government Printing Office, 1975), table 15, p. 19.

⁸ Information on presidential appointees between 1933 and 1965 is from Stanley, Mann, and Doig, *op. cit.*, pp. 6, 8, 34, 50. Data on noncareer supergrades in 1975 is in unpublished tables prepared by the U.S. Civil Service Commission, Bureau of Executive Manpower.

⁹ U.S. Civil Service Commission, Bureau of Executive Manpower, "Non-Career Executive Assignments" (July 1975; processed).

¹⁰ See Arch Patton, "Government's Revolving Door," *Business Week* (September 22, 1973): 13.

¹¹ Although data are not entirely comparable, certainly less than half the political executives in all recent administrations had any record of political party activity, if by that is meant experience as campaign or party officials, conventional delegates, elected officials, or political candidates or their staff members. See Stanley, Mann, and Doig, *op. cit.*, table E-1, p. 132; and Dean E. Mann, *The Assistant Secretaries* (Brookings Institution, 1965), table A-9, p. 295.

¹² See Edward Weisband and Thomas Franck, *Resignation and Protest* (Penguin, 1976), especially pp. 121–63 and fig. 1, app. B, p. 201.

¹³ These procedural reforms are described in Joint Administrative Task Force, *Reducing Federal Grant-in-Aid Processing Time: Final Report*, An Interagency Report to the President (Washington, D.C.: U.S. Government Printing Office, March 1968).

¹⁴ Dwight Waldo, *Perspectives on Administration* (University of Alabama Press, 1956), p. 14.

33

GRAHAM T. ALLISON

CONCEPTUAL MODELS AND THE CUBAN MISSILE CRISIS

The Cuban missile crisis is a seminal event. For thirteen days of October 1962, there was a higher probability that more human lives would end suddenly than ever before in history. Had the worst occurred, the death of 100 million Americans, over 100 million Russians, and millions of Europeans as well would make previous natural calamities and inhumanities appear insignificant. Given the probability of disaster—which President Kennedy estimated as "between 1 out of 3 and even"—our escape seems awesome.[1] This event symbolizes a central, if only partially thinkable, fact about our existence. That such consequences could follow from the choices and actions of national governments obliges students of government as well as participants in governance to think hard about these problems.

Improved understanding of this crisis depends in part on more information and more probing analyses of available evidence. To contribute to these efforts is part of the purpose of this study. But here the missile crisis serves primarily as grist for a more general investigation.

This study proceeds from the premise that marked improvement in our understanding of such events depends critically on more self-consciousness about what observers bring to the analysis. What each analyst sees and judges to be important is a function not only of the evidence about what happened but also of the "conceptual lenses" through which he looks at the evidence. The principal purpose of this essay is to explore some of the fundamental assumptions and categories employed by analysts in thinking about problems of governmental behavior, especially in foreign and military affairs.

The general argument can be summarized in three propositions:

A longer version of this paper was presented at the Annual Meeting of the American Political Science Association, September, 1968 (reproduced by the Rand Corporation, P-3919). The paper is part of a larger study [*Essence of Decision: Explaining the Cuban Missile Crisis* (Boston, 1971).] For support in various stages of this work I am indebted to the Institute of Politics in the John F. Kennedy School of Government and the Center for International Affairs, both at Harvard University, the Rand Corporation, and the Council on Foreign Relations. For critical stimulation and advice I am especially grateful to Richard E. Neustadt, Thomas C. Schelling, Andrew W. Marshall, and Elisabeth K. Allison.

1. Analysts think about problems of foreign and military policy in terms of largely implicit conceptual models that have significant consequences for the content of their thought.[2]

Though the present product of foreign policy analysis is neither systematic nor powerful, if one carefully examines explanations produced by analysts, a number of fundamental similarities emerge. Explanations produced by particular analysts display quite regular, predictable features. This predictability suggests a substructure. These regularities reflect an analyst's assumptions about the character of puzzles, the categories in which problems should be considered, the types of evidence that are relevant, and the determinants of occurrences. The first proposition is that clusters of such related assumptions constitute basic frames of reference or conceptual models in terms of which analysts both ask and answer the questions: What happened? Why did the event happen? What will happen?[3] Such assumptions are central to the activities of explanation and prediction, for in attempting to explain a particular event, the analyst cannot simply describe the full state of the world leading up to that event. The logic of explanation requires that he single out the relevant, important determinants of the occurrence.[4] Moreover, as the logic of prediction underscores, the analyst must summarize the various determinants as they bear on the event in question. Conceptual models both fix the mesh of the nets that the analyst drags through the material in order to explain a particular action or decision and direct him to cast his net in select ponds, at certain depths, in order to catch the fish he is after.

2. Most analysts explain (and predict) the behavior of national governments in terms of various forms of one basic conceptual model, here entitled the Rational Policy Model (Model I).[5]

In terms of this conceptual model, analysts attempt to understand happenings as the more or less purposive acts of unified national governments. For these analysts, the point of an explanation is to show how the nation or government could have chosen the action in question, given the strategic problem that it faced. For example, in confronting the problem posed by the Soviet installation of missiles in Cuba, rational policy model analysts attempt to show how this was a reasonable act from the point of view of the Soviet Union, given Soviet strategic objectives.

3. Two "alternative" conceptual models, here labeled an Organizational Process Model (Model II) and a Bureaucratic Politics Model (Model III) provide a base for improved explanation and prediction.

Although the standard frame of reference has proved useful for many purposes, there is powerful evidence that it must be supplemented, if not supplanted, by frames of reference which focus upon the large organizations and political actors involved in the policy process. Model I's implication that important events have important causes, i.e., that monoliths perform large actions for big reasons, must be balanced by an appreciation of the facts (a) that monoliths are black boxes covering various gears and levers in a highly differentiated decision-making structure, and (b) that large acts are the consequences of innumerable and often conflicting smaller actions by individuals at various levels of bureaucratic organizations in the service of a variety of only partially compatible conceptions of national goals, organizational goals, and political objectives. Recent developments in the field of organization theory provide the foundation for the second model. According to this organizational process model, what Model I categorizes as "acts" and "choices" are instead *outputs* of large organizations functioning according to certain regular patterns of behavior. Faced with the problem of Soviet missiles in Cuba, a Model II analyst identifies the relevant organizations and displays the patterns of organizational behavior from which this action emerged. The third model focuses on the internal politics of a government. Happenings in foreign affairs are understood, according to the bureaucratic politics model, neither as choices nor as outputs. Instead, what happens is categorized as *outcomes* of various overlapping bargaining games among players arranged hierarchically in the national government. In confronting the problem posed by Soviet missiles in Cuba, a Model III analyst displays the perceptions, motivations, positions, power, and maneuvers of principal players from which the outcome emerged.[6]

A central metaphor illuminates differences among these models. Foreign policy has often been compared to moves, sequences of moves, and games of chess. If one were limited to observations on a screen upon which moves in the chess game were projected without information as to how the pieces came to be moved, he would assume—as Model I does—that an individual chess player was moving the pieces with reference to plans and maneuvers toward the goal of winning the game. But a pattern of moves can be imagined that would lead the serious observer, after watching several games, to consider the hypothesis that the chess player was not a single individual but rather a loose alliance of semi-independent organizations, each of which moved its set of pieces according to standard operating procedures. For example, movement of separate sets of pieces might proceed in turn, each according to a routine, the king's rook, bishop, and their pawns repeatedly attacking the opponent according to a fixed plan. Furthermore, it is conceivable that the pattern of play would suggest to an observer that a number of distinct players, with distinct objectives but shared power over the pieces, were determining the moves as the resultant of collegial bargaining. For example, the black rook's move might contribute to the loss of a black knight with no comparable gain for the black team, but with the black rook becoming the principal guardian of the "palace" on that side of the board.

The space available does not permit full development and support of such a general argument.[7] Rather, the sections that follow simply sketch each conceptual model, articulate it as an analytic paradigm, and apply it to produce an explanation. But each model is applied to the same event: the U.S. blockade of Cuba during the missile crisis. These "alternative explanations" of the same happening illustrate differences among the models—*at work.*[8] A crisis decision, by a small group of men in the context of ultimate threat, this is a case of the rational policy model *par excellence*. The dimensions and factors that Models II and III uncover in this case are therefore particularly suggestive. The concluding section of this paper suggests how the three models may be related and how they can be extended to generate predictions.

MODEL I: RATIONAL POLICY

Rational Policy Model Illustrated

Where is the pinch of the puzzle raised by the *New York Times* over Soviet deployment of an antiballistic missile system?[9] The question, as the *Times* states it, concerns the Soviet Union's objective in allocating such large sums of money for this weapon system while at the same time seeming to pursue a policy of increasing détente. In former President Johnson's words, "the paradox is that this [Soviet deployment of an antiballistic missile system] should be happening at a time when there is abundant evidence that our mutual antagonism is beginning to ease."[10] This question troubles people primarily because Soviet antiballistic missile deployment, and evidence of Soviet actions towards détente, when juxtaposed in our implicit model, produce a question. With reference to what objective could the Soviet government have rationally chosen the simultaneous pursuit of these two courses of actions? This question arises only when the analyst attempts to structure events as purposive choices of consistent actors.

How do analysts attempt to explain the Soviet emplacement of missiles in Cuba? The most widely cited explanation of this occurrence has been produced by two RAND Sovietologists, Arnold Horelick and Myron Rush.[11] They conclude that "the introduction of strategic missiles into Cuba was motivated chiefly by the Soviet leaders' desire to overcome . . . the existing large margin of U.S. strategic superiority."[12] How do they reach this conclusion? In Sherlock Holmes style, they seize several salient characteristics of this action and use these features as criteria against which to test alternative hypotheses about Soviet objectives. For example, the size of the Soviet deployment, and the simultaneous emplacement of more expensive, more visible intermediate range missiles as well as medium range missiles, it is argued, exclude an explanation of the action in terms of Cuban defense—since that objective could have been secured with a much smaller number of medium range missiles alone. Their explanation presents an argument for one objective that permits interpretation of the details of Soviet behavior as a value-maximizing choice.

How do analysts account for the coming of the First World War? According to Hans Morgenthau, "the first World War had its origin exclusively in the fear of a disturbance of the European balance of power.[13] In the period preceding World War I, the Triple Alliance precariously balanced the Triple Entente. If either power combination could gain a decisive advantage in the Balkans, it would achieve a decisive advantage in the balance of power. "It was this fear," Morgenthau asserts, "that motivated Austria in July 1914 to settle its accounts with Serbia once and for all, and that induced Germany to support Austria unconditionally. It was the same fear that brought Russia to the support of Serbia, and France to the support of Russia."[14] How is Morgenthau able to resolve this problem so confidently? By imposing on the data a "rational outline."[15] The value of this method, according to Morgenthau, is that "it provides for rational discipline in action and creates astounding continuity in foreign policy which makes American, British, or Russian foreign policy appear as an intelligent, rational continuum . . . regardless of the different motives, preferences, and intellectual and moral qualities of successive statesmen."[16]

Stanley Hoffmann's essay "Restraints and Choices in American Foreign Policy" concentrates, characteristically, on "deep forces": the international system, ideology, and national character—which constitute restraints, limits, and blinders.[17] Only secondarily does he consider decisions. But when explaining particular occurrences, though emphasizing relevant constraints, he focuses on the choices of nations. American behavior in Southeast Asia is explained as a reasonable choice of "downgrading this particular alliance (SEATO) in favor of direct U.S. involvement," given the constraint: "one is bound by one's commitments; one is committed by one's mistakes."[18] More frequently, Hoffmann uncovers confusion or contradiction in the nation's choice. For example, U.S. policy towards underdeveloped countries is explained as "schizophrenic."[19] The method employed by Hoffmann in producing these explanations as rational (or irrational) decisions, he terms "imaginative reconstruction."[20]

Deterrence is the cardinal problem of the contemporary strategic literature. Thomas Schelling's *Strategy of Conflict* formulates a number of propositions focused upon the dynamics of deterrence in the nuclear age. One of the major propositions concerns the stability of the balance of terror: in a situation of mutual deterrence, the probability of nuclear war is reduced not by the "balance" (the sheer equality of the situation) but rather by the *stability* of the balance, i.e., the fact that neither opponent in striking first can destroy the other's ability to strike back.[21] How does Schelling support this proposition? Confidence in the contention stems not from an inductive canvass of a large number of previous cases, but rather from two calculations. In a situation of "balance" but vulnerability, there are values for which a rational opponent could choose to strike first, e.g., to destroy enemy capabilities to retaliate. In a "stable balance" where no matter who strikes first, each has an assured capability to retaliate with unacceptable damage, no rational agent could choose such a course of action (since that choice is effectively equivalent to choosing mutual homicide). Whereas most contemporary strategic thinking is driven *implicitly* by the motor upon which this calculation depends, Schelling explicitly recognizes that strategic theory does assume a model. The foundation of a theory of strategy is, he asserts: "the assumption of rational behavior—not just of intelligent behavior, but of behavior motivated by conscious calculation of advantages, calculation that in turn is based on an explicit and internally consistent value system."[22]

What is striking about these examples from the literature of foreign policy and international relations are the similarities among analysts of various styles when they are called upon to produce explanations. Each assumes that what must be explained is an action, i.e., the realization of some purpose or intention. Each assumes that the actor is the national government. Each assumes that the action is chosen as a calculated response to a strategic problem. For each, explanation consists of showing what goal the government was pursuing in committing the act and how this action was a reasonable choice, given the nation's objectives. This set of assumptions characterizes the rational policy model. The assertion that Model I is the standard frame of reference implies no denial of highly visible differences among the interests of Sovietologists, diplomatic historians, international relations theorists, and strategists. Indeed, in most respects, differences among the work of Hans Morgenthau, Stanley Hoffmann, and Thomas Schelling could not be more pointed. Appreciation of the extent to which each relies predominantly on Model I, however, reveals basic similarities among Morgenthau's method of "rational reenactment," Hoffmann's "imaginative reconstruction," and Schelling's "vicarious problem solving"; family resemblances among Morgenthau's "rational statesman," Hoffmann's "roulette player," and Schelling's "game theorist."[23]

Most contemporary analysts (as well as laymen) proceed predominantly—albeit most often implicitly—in terms of this model when attempting to explain happenings in foreign affairs. Indeed, that occurrences in foreign affairs are the *acts* of *nations* seems so fundamental to thinking about such problems that this underlying model has rarely been recognized: to explain an occurrence in foreign policy simply means to show how the government could have rationally chosen that action.[24] These brief examples illustrate five uses of the model. To prove that most analysts think largely in terms of the rational policy model is not possible. In this limited space it is not even possible to illustrate the range of employment of the framework. Rather, my purpose is to convey to the reader a grasp of the model and a challenge; let the reader examine the literature with which he is most familiar and make his judgment.

The general characterization can be sharpened by articulating the rational policy model as an "analytic paradigm" in the technical sense developed by Robert K. Merton for sociological analyses.[25] Systematic statement of basic assumptions, concepts, and propositions employed by Model I analysts highlights the distinctive thrust of this style of analysis. To articulate a largely implicit framework is of necessity to caricature. But caricature can be instructive. . . .

The U.S. Blockade of Cuba: A First Cut[26]

The U.S. response to the Soviet Union's emplacement of missiles in Cuba must be understood in strategic terms as simple value-maximizing escalation. American nuclear superiority could be counted on to paralyze Soviet nuclear power; Soviet transgression of the nuclear threshold in response to an American use of lower levels of violence would be wildly irrational since it would mean virtual destruction of the Soviet Communist system and Russian nation. American local superiority was overwhelming: it could be initiated at a low level while threatening with high credibility an ascending sequence of steps short of the nuclear threshold. All that was required was for the United States to bring to bear its strategic and local superiority in such a way that American determination to see the missiles removed would be demonstrated, while at the same time allowing Moscow time and room to retreat without humiliation. The naval blockade—euphemistically named a "quarantine" in order to circumvent the niceties of international law—did just that.

The U.S. government's selection of the blockade followed this logic. Apprised of the presence of Soviet missiles in Cuba, the President assembled an Executive Committee (ExCom) of the National Security Council and directed them to "set aside all other tasks to make a prompt and intense survey of the dangers and all possible courses of action."[27] This group functioned as "fifteen individuals on our own, representing the President and not different departments."[28] As one of the participants recalls, "The remarkable aspect of those meetings was a sense of complete equality."[29] Most of the time during the week that followed was spent canvassing all the possible tracks and weighing the arguments for and against each. Six major categories of action were considered.

1. Do nothing. U.S. vulnerability to Soviet missiles was no new thing. Since the U.S. already lived under the gun of missiles based in Russia, a Soviet capability to strike from Cuba too made little real difference. The real danger stemmed from the possibility of U.S. over-reaction. The U.S. should announce the Soviet action in a calm, casual manner thereby deflating whatever political capital Khrushchev hoped to make of the missiles.

This argument fails on two counts. First, it grossly underestimates the military importance of the Soviet move. Not only would the Soviet Union's missile capability be doubled and the U.S. early warning system outflanked. The Soviet Union would have an opportunity to reverse the strategic balance by further installations, and indeed, in the longer run, to invest in cheaper, shorter-range rather than more expensive longer-range missiles. Second, the political importance of this move was undeniable. The Soviet Union's act challenged the American President's most solemn warning. If the U.S. failed to respond, no American commitment would be credible.

2. Diplomatic pressures. Several forms were considered: an appeal to the U.N. or O.A.S. for an inspection team, a secret approach to Khrushchev, and a direct approach to Khrushchev, perhaps at a summit meeting. The United States would demand that the missiles be removed, but the final settlement might include neutralization of Cuba, U.S. withdrawal from the Guantanamo base, and withdrawal of U.S. Jupiter missiles from Turkey or Italy.

Each form of the diplomatic approach had its own drawbacks. To arraign the Soviet Union before the U.N. Security Council held little promise since the Russians could veto any proposed action. While the diplomats argued, the missiles would become operational. To send a secret emissary to Khrushchev demanding that the missiles be withdrawn would be to pose untenable alternatives. On the one hand, this would invite Khrushchev to seize the diplomatic initiative, perhaps committing himself to strategic retaliation in response to an attack on Cuba. On the other hand, this would tender an ultimatum that no great power could accept. To confront Khrushchev at a summit would guarantee demands for U.S. concessions, and the analogy between U.S. missiles in Turkey and Russian missiles in Cuba could not be erased.

But why not trade U.S. Jupiters in Turkey and Italy, which the President had previously ordered withdrawn, for the missiles in Cuba? The U.S. had chosen to withdraw these missiles in order to replace them with superior, less vulnerable Mediterranean Polaris submarines. But the middle of the crisis was no time for concessions. The offer of such a deal might suggest to the Soviets that the West would yield and thus tempt them to demand more. It would certainly confirm European suspicions about American willingness to sacrifice European interests when the chips were down. Finally, the basic issue should be kept clear. As the President stated in reply to Bertrand Russell, "I think your attention might well be directed to the burglars rather than to those who have caught the burglars."[30]

3. A secret approach to Castro. The crisis provided an opportunity to separate Cuba and Soviet Communism by offering Castro the alternatives, "split or fall." But Soviet troops transported, constructed, guarded, and controlled the missiles. Their removal would thus depend on a Soviet decision.

4. Invasion. The United States could take this occasion not only to remove the missiles but also to rid itself of Castro. A Navy exercise had long been scheduled in which Marines, ferried from Florida in naval vessels, would liberate the imaginary island of Vieques.[31] Why not simply shift the point of disembarkment? (The Pentagon's foresight in planning this operation would be an appropriate antidote to the CIA's Bay of Pigs!)

Preparations were made for an invasion, but as a last resort. American troops would be forced to confront 20,000 Soviets in the first Cold War case of direct contact between the troops of the super powers. Such brinksmanship courted nuclear disaster, practically guaranteeing an equivalent Soviet move against Berlin.

5. Surgical air strike. The missile sites should be removed by a clean, swift conventional attack. This was the effective counter-action which the attempted deception deserved. A surgical strike would remove the missiles and thus eliminate both the danger that the missiles might become operational and the fear that the Soviets would discover the American discovery and act first.

The initial attractiveness of this alternative was dulled by several difficulties. First, could the strike really be "surgical"? The Air Force could not guarantee destruction of all the missiles.[32] Some might be fired during the attack; some might not have been identified. In order to assure destruction of Soviet and Cuban means of retaliating, what was required was not a surgical but rather a massive attack—of at least 500 sorties. Second, a surprise air attack would of course kill Russians at the missile sites. Pressures on the Soviet Union to retaliate would be so strong that an attack on Berlin or Turkey was highly probable. Third, the key problem with this program was that of advance warning. Could the President of the United States, with his memory of Pearl Harbor and his vision of future U.S. responsibility, order a "Pearl Harbor in reverse"? For 175 years, unannounced Sunday morning attacks had been an anathema to our tradition.[33]

6. Blockade. Indirect military action in the form of a blockade became more attractive as the ExCom dissected the other alternatives. An embargo on military shipments to Cuba enforced by a naval blockade was not without flaws, however. Could the U.S. blockade Cuba without inviting Soviet reprisal in Berlin? The likely solution to joint blockades would be the lifting of both blockades, restoring

the new *status quo,* and allowing the Soviets additional time to complete the missiles. Second, the possible consequences of the blockade resembled the drawbacks which disqualified the air strike. If Soviet ships did not stop, the United States would be forced to fire the first shot, inviting retaliation. Third, a blockade would deny the traditional freedom of the seas demanded by several of our close allies and might be held illegal, in violation of the U.N. Charter and international law, unless the United States could obtain a two-thirds vote in the O.A.S. Finally, how could a blockade be related to the problem, namely, some 75 missiles on the island of Cuba, approaching operational readiness daily? A blockade offered the Soviets a spectrum of delaying tactics with which to buy time to complete the missile installations. Was a *fait accompli* not required?

In spite of these enormous difficulties the blockade had comparative advantages: (1) It was a middle course between inaction and attack, aggressive enough to communicate firmness of intention, but nevertheless not so precipitous as a strike. (2) It placed on Khrushchev the burden of choice concerning the next step. He could avoid a direct military clash by keeping his ships away. His was the last clear chance. (3) No possible military confrontation could be more acceptable to the U.S. than a naval engagement in the Caribbean. (4) This move permitted the U.S., by flexing its conventional muscle, to exploit the threat of subsequent non-nuclear steps in each of which the U.S. would have significant superiority.

Particular arguments about advantages and disadvantages were powerful. The explanation of the American choice of the blockade lies in a more general principle, however. As President Kennedy stated in drawing the moral of the crisis:

> Above all, while defending our own vital interests, nuclear powers must avert those confrontations which bring an adversary to a choice of either a humiliating retreat or a nuclear war. To adopt that kind of course in the nuclear age would be evidence only of the bankruptcy of our policy—of a collective death wish for the world.[34]

The blockade was the United States' only real option.

MODEL II: ORGANIZATIONAL PROCESS

For some purposes, governmental behavior can be usefully summarized as action chosen by a unitary, rational decisionmaker: centrally controlled, completely informed, and value maximizing. But this simplification must not be allowed to conceal the fact that a "government" consists of a conglomerate of semi-feudal, loosely allied organizations, each with a substantial life of its own. Government leaders do sit formally, and to some extent in fact, on top of this conglomerate. But governments perceive problems through organizational sensors. Governments define alternatives and estimate consequences as organizations process information. Governments act as these organizations enact routines. Government behavior can therefore be understood according to a second conceptual model, less as deliberate choices of leaders and more as *outputs* of large organizations functioning according to standard patterns of behavior.

To be responsive to a broad spectrum of problems, governments consist of large organizations among which primary responsibility for particular areas is divided. Each organization attends to a special set of problems and acts in quasi-independence on these problems. But few important problems fall exclusively within the domain of a single organization. Thus government behavior relevant to any important problem reflects the independent output of several organizations, partially coordinated by government leaders. Government leaders can substantially disturb, but not substantially control, the behavior of these organizations.

To perform complex routines, the behavior of large numbers of individuals must be coordinated. Coordination requires standard operating procedures: rules according to which things are done. Assured capability for reliable performance of action that depends upon the behavior of hundreds of persons requires established "programs." Indeed, if the eleven members of a football team are to perform adequately on any particular down, each player must not "do what he thinks needs to be done" or "do what the quarterback tells him to do." Rather, each player must perform the maneuvers specified by a previously established play which the quarterback has simply called in this situation.

At any given time, a government consists of *existing* organizations, each with a *fixed* set of standard operating procedures and programs. The behavior of these organizations—and consequently of the government—relevant to an issue in any particular instance is, therefore, determined primarily by routines established in these organizations prior to that instance. But organizations do change. Learning occurs gradually, over time. Dramatic organizational change occurs in response to major crises. Both learning and change are influenced by existing organizational capabilities.

Borrowed from studies of organizations, these loosely formulated propositions amount simply to *tendencies*. Each must be hedged by modifiers like "other things being equal" and "under certain conditions." In particular instances, tendencies hold—more or less. In specific situations, the relevant question is: more or less? But this is as it should be. For, on the one hand, "organizations" are no more homogeneous a class than "solids." When scientists tried to generalize about "solids," they achieved similar results. Solids tend to expand when heated, but some do and some don't. More adequate categorization of the various elements now lumped under the rubric "organizations" is thus required. On the other hand, the behavior of particular organizations seems considerably more complex than the behavior of solids. Additional information about a particular organization is required for further specification of the tendency statements. In spite of these two caveats, the characterization of government action as organizational output differs distinctly from Model I. Attempts to understand problems of foreign affairs in terms of this frame of reference should produce quite different explanations.[35] . . .

The U.S. Blockade of Cuba: A Second Cut

ORGANIZATIONAL INTELLIGENCE   At 7:00 P.M. on October 22, 1962, President Kennedy disclosed the American discovery of the presence of Soviet strategic missiles in Cuba, declared a "strict quarantine on all offensive military equipment under shipment to Cuba," and demanded that "Chairman Khrushchev halt and eliminate this clandestine, reckless, and provocative threat to world peace."[36] This decision was reached at the pinnacle of the U.S. Government after a critical week of deliberation. What initiated that precious week were photographs of Soviet missile sites in Cuba taken on October 14. These pictures might not have been taken until a week later. In that case, the President speculated, "I don't think probably we would have chosen as prudently as we finally did."[37] U.S. leaders might have received this information three weeks earlier—if a U-2 had flown over San Cristobal in the last week of September.[38] What determined the context in which American leaders came to choose the blockade was the discovery of missiles on October 14.

There has been considerable debate over alleged American "intelligence failures" in the Cuban missile crisis.[39] But what both critics and defenders have neglected is the fact that the discovery took place on October 14, rather than three weeks earlier or a week later, as a consequence of the established routines and procedures of the organizations which constitute the U.S. intelligence community. These organizations were neither more nor less successful than they had been the previous month or were to be in the months to follow.[40]

The notorious "September estimate," approved by the United States Intelligence Board (USIB) on September 19, concluded that the Soviet Union would not introduce offensive missiles into Cuba.[41] No U-2 flight was directed over the western end of Cuba (after September 5) before October 4.[42] No U-2 flew over the western end of Cuba until the flight that discovered the Soviet missiles on October 14.[43] Can these "failures" be accounted for in organizational terms?

On September 19 when USIB met to consider the question of Cuba, the "system" contained the following information: (1) shipping intelligence had noted the arrival in Cuba of two large-hatch Soviet lumber ships, which were riding high in the water; (2) refugee reports of countless sightings of missiles, but also a report that Castro's private pilot, after a night of drinking in Havana, had boasted: "We will fight to the death and perhaps we can win because we have everything, including atomic weapons"; (3) a sighting by a CIA agent of the rear profile of a strategic missile; (4) U-2 photos produced by flights of August 29, September 5 and 17 showing the construction of a number of SAM sites and other defensive missiles.[44] Not all of this information was on the desk of the estimators, however. Shipping intelligence experts noted the fact that large-hatch ships were riding high in the water and spelled out the inference: the ships must be carrying "space consuming" cargo.[45] These facts were carefully included in the catalogue of intelligence concerning shipping. For experts sensitive to the Soviets' shortage of ships, however, these facts carried no special signal. The refugee report of Castro's private pilot's remark had been received at Opa Locka,

Florida, along with vast reams of inaccurate reports generated by the refugee community. This report and a thousand others had to be checked and compared before being sent to Washington. The two weeks required for initial processing could have been shortened by a large increase in resources, but the yield of this source was already quite marginal. The CIA agent's sighting of the rear profile of a strategic missile had occurred on September 12; transmission time from agent sighting to arrival in Washington typically took 9 to 12 days. Shortening this transmission time would impose severe cost in terms of danger to sub-agents, agents, and communication networks.

On the information available, the intelligence chiefs who predicted that the Soviet Union would not introduce offensive missiles into Cuba made a reasonable and defensible judgment.[46] Moreover, in the light of the fact that these organizations were gathering intelligence not only about Cuba but about potential occurrences in all parts of the world, the informational base available to the estimators involved nothing out of the ordinary. Nor, from an organizational perspective, is there anything startling about the gradual accumulation of evidence that led to the formulation of the hypothesis that the Soviets were installing missiles in Cuba and the decision on October 4 to direct a special flight over western Cuba.

The ten-day delay between the decision and the flight is another organizational story.[47] At the October 4 meeting, the Defense Department took the opportunity to raise an issue important to its concerns. Given the increased danger that a U-2 would be downed, it would be better if the pilot were an officer in uniform rather than a CIA agent. Thus the Air Force should assume responsibility for U-2 flights over Cuba. To the contrary, the CIA argued that this was an intelligence operation and thus within the CIA's jurisdiction. Moreover, CIA U-2's had been modified in certain ways which gave them advantages over Air Force U-2's in averting Soviet SAM's. Five days passed while the State Department pressed for less risky alternatives such as drones and the Air Force (in Department of Defense guise) and CIA engaged in territorial disputes. On October 9 a flight plan over San Cristobal was approved by COMOR, but to the CIA's dismay, Air Force pilots rather than CIA agents would take charge of the mission. At this point details become sketchy, but several members of the intelligence community have speculated that an Air Force pilot in an Air Force U-2 attempted a high altitude overflight on October 9 that "flamed out", i.e., lost power, and thus had to descend in order to restart its engine. A second round between Air Force and CIA followed, as a result of which Air Force pilots were trained to fly CIA U-2's. A successful overflight took place on October 14.

This ten-day delay constitutes some form of "failure." In the face of well-founded suspicions concerning offensive Soviet missiles in Cuba that posed a critical threat to the United States' most vital interest, squabbling between organizations whose job it is to produce this information seems entirely inappropriate. But for each of these organizations, the question involved the issue: "*Whose* job was it to be?" Moreover, the issue was not simply, which organization would control U-2 flights over Cuba, but rather the broader issue of ownership of U-2 intelligence activities—a very long standing territorial dispute. Thus though this delay was in one sense a "failure," it was also a nearly inevitable consequence of two facts: many jobs do not fall neatly into precisely defined organizational jurisdictions; and vigorous organizations are imperialistic.

ORGANIZATIONAL OPTIONS Deliberations of leaders in ExCom meetings produced broad outlines of alternatives. Details of these alternatives and blueprints for their implementation had to be specified by the organizations that would perform these tasks. These organizational outputs answered the question: What, specifically, *could* be done?

Discussion in the ExCom quickly narrowed the live options to two: an air strike and a blockade. The choice of the blockade instead of the air strike turned on two points: (1) the argument from morality and tradition that the United States could not perpetrate a "Pearl Harbor in reverse"; (2) the belief that a "surgical" air strike was impossible.[48] Whether the United States *might* strike first was a question not of capability but of morality. Whether the United States *could* perform the surgical strike was a factual question concerning capabilities. The majority of the members of the ExCom, including the President, initially preferred the air strike.[49] What effectively foreclosed this option, however, was the fact that the air strike they wanted could not be chosen with high confidence of success.[50] After having tentatively chosen the course of prudence—given that the surgical air strike was not an option—Kennedy reconsidered. On Sunday morning, October 21, he called the Air Force experts to a special meeting in his living quarters where he probed once more for the option of a *"surgical"* air strike.[51] General Walter C. Sweeny, Commander of Tactical Air Forces, asserted again that the Air Force could guarantee no higher than ninety percent effectiveness in a surgical air strike.[52] That "fact" was false.

The air strike alternative provides a classic case of military estimates. One of the alternatives outlined by the ExCom was named "air strike." Specification of the details of this alternative was delegated to the Air Force. Starting from an existing plan for massive U.S. military action against Cuba (prepared for contingencies like a response to a Soviet Berlin grab), Air Force estimators produced an attack to guarantee success.[53] This plan called for extensive bombardment of all missile sites, storage depots, airports, and, in deference to the Navy, the artillery batteries opposite the naval base at Guantanamo.[54] Members of the ExCom repeatedly expressed bewilderment at military estimates of the number of sorties required, likely casualties, and collateral damage. But the "surgical" air strike that the political leaders had in mind was never carefully examined during the first week of the crisis. Rather, this option was simply excluded on the grounds that since the Soviet MRBM's in Cuba were classified "mobile" in U.S. manuals, extensive bombing was required. During the second week of the crisis, careful examination revealed that the missiles were mobile, in the sense that small houses are mobile: that is, they could be moved and reassembled in 6 days. After the missiles were reclassified "movable" and detailed plans for surgical air strikes specified, this action was added to the list of live options for the end of the second week.

ORGANIZATIONAL IMPLEMENTATION Ex Com members separated several types of blockade: offensive weapons only, all armaments, and all strategic goods including POL (petroleum, oil, and lubricants). But the *"details"* of the operation were left to the Navy. Before the President announced the blockade on Monday evening, the first stage of the Navy's blueprint was in motion, and a problem loomed on the horizon.[55] The Navy had a detailed plan for the blockade. The President had several less precise but equally determined notions concerning what should be done, when, and how. For the Navy the issue was one of effective implementation of the Navy's blockade—without the meddling and interference of political leaders. For the President, the problem was to pace and manage events in such a way that the Soviet leaders would have time to see, think, and blink.

A careful reading of available sources uncovers an instructive incident. On Tuesday the British Ambassador, Ormsby-Gore, after having attended a briefing on the details of the blockade, suggested to the President that the plan for intercepting Soviet ships far out of reach of Cuban jets did not facilitate Khrushchev's hard decision.[56] Why not make the interception much closer to Cuba and thus give the Russian leader more time? According to the public account and the recollection of a number of individuals involved, Kennedy "agreed immediately, called McNamara, and over emotional Navy protest, issued the appropriate instructions."[57] As Sorensen records, "in a sharp clash with the Navy, he made certain his will prevailed."[58] The Navy's plan for the blockade was thus changed by drawing the blockade much closer to Cuba.

A serious organizational orientation makes one suspicious of this account. More careful examination of the available evidence confirms these suspicions, though alternative accounts must be somewhat speculative. According to the public chronology, a quarantine drawn close to Cuba became effective on Wednesday morning, the first Soviet ship was contacted on Thursday morning, and the first boarding of a ship occurred on Friday. According to the statement by the Department of Defense, boarding of the *Marcula* by a party from the *John R. Pierce* "took place at 7:50 A.M., E.D.T., 180 miles northeast of Nassau."[59] The *Marcula* had been trailed since about 10:30 the previous evening.[60] Simple calculations suggest that the *Pierce* must have been stationed along the Navy's original arc which extended 500 miles out to sea from Cape Magsi, Cuba's easternmost tip.[61] The blockade line was *not* moved as the President ordered, and the accounts report.

What happened is not entirely clear. One can be certain, however, that Soviet ships passed through the line along which American destroyers had posted themselves before the official "first contact" with the Soviet ship. On October 26 a Soviet tanker arrived in Havana and was honored by a dockside rally for "running the blockade." Photographs of this vessel show the name *Vinnitsa* on the side of the vessel in Cyrillic letters.[62] But according to the official U.S. position, the first tanker to pass through the blockade was the *Bucharest*, which was hailed by the Navy on the morning of October 25. Again simple mathematical calculation excludes the possibility that the *Bucharest* and the

Vinnitsa were the same ship. It seems probable that the Navy's resistance to the President's order that the blockade be drawn in closer to Cuba forced him to allow one or several Soviet ships to pass through the blockade after it was officially operative.[63]

This attempt to leash the Navy's blockade had a price. On Wednesday morning, October 24, what the President had been awaiting occurred. The 18 dry cargo ships heading towards the quarantine stopped dead in the water. This was the occasion of Dean Rusk's remark, "We are eyeball to eyeball and I think the other fellow just blinked."[64] But the Navy had another interpretation. The ships had simply stopped to pick up Soviet submarine escorts. The President became quite concerned lest the Navy—already riled because of Presidential meddling in its affairs—blunder into an incident. Sensing the President's fears, McNamara became suspicious of the Navy's procedures and routines for making the first interception. Calling on the Chief of Naval Operations in the Navy's inner sanctum, the Navy Flag Plot, McNamara put his questions harshly.[65] Who would make the first interception? Were Russian-speaking officers on board? How would submarines be dealt with? At one point McNamara asked Anderson what he would do if a Soviet ship's captain refused to answer questions about his cargo. Picking up the Manual of Navy Regulations the Navy man waved it in McNamara's face and shouted, "It's all in there." To which McNamara replied, "I don't give a damn what John Paul Jones would have done; I want to know what you are going to do, now."[66] The encounter ended on Anderson's remark: "Now, Mr. Secretary, if you and your Deputy will go back to your office the Navy will run the blockade."[67]

MODEL III: BUREAUCRATIC POLITICS

The leaders who sit on top of organizations are not a monolithic group. Rather, each is, in his own right, a player in a central, competitive game. The name of the game is bureaucratic politics: bargaining along regularized channels among players positioned hierarchically within the government. Government behavior can thus be understood according to a third conceptual model not as organizational outputs, but as outcomes of bargaining games. In contrast with Model I, the bureaucratic politics model sees no unitary actor but rather many actors as players, who focus not on a single strategic issue but on many diverse intra-national problems as well, in terms of no consistent set of strategic objectives but rather according to various conceptions of national, organizational, and personal goals, making government decisions not by rational choice but by the pulling and hauling that is politics.

The apparatus of each national government constitutes a complex arena for the intra-national game. Political leaders at the top of this apparatus plus the men who occupy positions on top of the critical organizations form the circle of central players. Ascendancy to this circle assures some independent standing. The necessary decentralization of decisions required for action on the broad range of foreign policy problems guarantees that each player has considerable discretion. Thus power is shared.

The nature of problems of foreign policy permits fundamental disagreement among reasonable men concerning what ought to be done. Analyses yield conflicting recommendations. Separate responsibilities laid on the shoulders of individual personalities encourage differences in perceptions and priorities. But the issues are of first order importance. What the nation does really matters. A wrong choice could mean irreparable damage. Thus responsible men are obliged to fight for what they are convinced is right.

Men share power. Men differ concerning what must be done. The differences matter. This milieu necessitates that policy be resolved by politics. What the nation does is sometimes the result of the triumph of one group over others. More often, however, different groups pulling in different directions yield a resultant distinct from what anyone intended. What moves the chess pieces is not simply the reasons which support a course of action, nor the routines of organizations which enact an alternative, but the power and skill of proponents and opponents of the action in question.

This characterization captures the thrust of the bureaucratic politics orientation. If problems of foreign policy arose as discreet issues, and decisions were determined one game at a time, this account would suffice. But most "issues," e.g., Vietnam or the proliferation of nuclear weapons, emerge piecemeal, over time, one lump in one context, a second in another. Hundreds of issues compete for players' attention every day. Each player is forced to fix upon his issues for that day, fight them on their own terms, and rush on to the next. Thus the character of emerging issues and the pace at which the game is played converge to yield government "decisions" and "actions" as collages. Choices by one player, outcomes of minor games, outcomes of central games, and "foul-ups"— these pieces, when stuck to the same canvas, constitute government behavior relevant to an issue.

The concept of national security policy as political outcome contradicts both public imagery and academic orthodoxy. Issues vital to national security, it is said, are too important to be settled by political games. They must be "above" politics. To accuse someone of "playing politics with national security" is a most serious charge. What public conviction demands, the academic penchant for intellectual elegance reinforces. Internal politics is messy; moreover, according to prevailing doctrine, politicking lacks intellectual content. As such, it constitutes gossip for journalists rather than a subject for serious investigation. Occasional memoirs, anecdotes in historical accounts, and several detailed case studies to the contrary, most of the literature of foreign policy avoids bureaucratic politics. The gap between academic literature and the experience of participants in government is nowhere wider than at this point. . . .

The U.S. Blockade of Cuba: A Third Cut

THE POLITICS OF DISCOVERY   A series of overlapping bargaining games determined both the *date* of the discovery of the Soviet missiles and the *impact* of this discovery on the Administration. An explanation of the politics of the discovery is consequently a considerable piece of the explanation of the U.S. blockade.

Cuba was the Kennedy Administration's "political Achilles' heel."[68] The months preceding the crisis were also months before the Congressional elections, and the Republican Senatorial and Congressional Campaign Committee had announced that Cuba would be "the dominant issue of the 1962 campaign."[69] What the administration billed as a "more positive and indirect approach of isolating Castro from developing, democratic Latin America," Senators Keating, Goldwater, Capehart, Thurmond, and others attacked as a "do-nothing" policy.[70] In statements on the floor of the House and Senate, campaign speeches across the country, and interviews and articles carried by national news media, Cuba—particularly the Soviet program of increased arms aid—served as a stick for stirring the domestic political scene.[71]

These attacks drew blood. Prudence demanded a vigorous reaction. The President decided to meet the issue head-on. The Administration mounted a forceful campaign of denial designed to discredit critics' claims. The President himself manned the front line of this offensive, though almost all Administration officials participated. In his news conference on August 19, President Kennedy attacked as "irresponsible" calls for an invasion of Cuba, stressing rather "the totality of our obligations" and promising to "watch what happens in Cuba with the closest attention."[72] On September 4, he issued a strong statement denying any provocative Soviet action in Cuba.[73] On September 13 he lashed out at "loose talk" calling for an invasion of Cuba.[74] The day before the flight of the U-2 which discovered the missiles, he campaigned in Capehart's Indiana against those "self-appointed generals and admirals who want to send someone else's sons to war."[75]

On Sunday, October 14, just as a U-2 was taking the first pictures of Soviet missiles, McGeorge Bundy was asserting:

> I *know* that there is no present evidence, and I think that there is no present likelihood that the Cuban government and the Soviet government would, in combination, attempt to install a major offensive capability.[76]

In this campaign to puncture the critics' charges, the Administration discovered that the public needed positive slogans. Thus, Kennedy fell into a tenuous semantic distinction between "offensive" and "defensive" weapons. This distinction originated in his September 4 statement that there was no evidence of "offensive ground to ground missiles" and warned "were it to be otherwise, the gravest issues would arise."[77] His September 13 statement turned on this distinction between "defensive" and "offensive" weapons and announced a firm commitment to action if the Soviet Union attempted to introduce the latter into Cuba.[78] Congressional committees elicited from administration officials testimony which read this distinction and the President's commitment into the *Congressional Record*.[79]

What the President least wanted to hear, the CIA was most hesitant to say plainly. On August 22 John McCone met privately with the President and voiced suspicions that the Soviets were preparing to introduce offensive missiles into Cuba.[80] Kennedy heard this as what it was: the suspicion of a hawk. McCone left Washington for a month's honeymoon on the Riviera. Fretting at Cap Ferrat, he bombarded his deputy, General Marshall Carter, with telegrams, but Carter, knowing that McCone had informed the President of his suspicions and received a cold reception, was reluctant to distribute these telegrams outside the CIA.[81] On September 9 a U-2 "on loan" to the Chinese Nationalists was downed over mainland China.[82] The Committee on Overhead Reconnaissance (COMOR) convened on September 10 with a sense of urgency.[83] Loss of another U-2 might incite world opinion to demand cancellation of U-2 flights. The President's campaign against those who asserted that the Soviets were acting provocatively in Cuba had begun. To risk downing a U-2 over Cuba was to risk chopping off the limb on which the President was sitting. That meeting decided to shy away from the western end of Cuba (where SAMs were becoming operational) and modify the flight pattern of the U-2s in order to reduce the probability that a U-2 would be lost.[84] USIB's unanimous approval of the September estimate reflects similar sensitivities. On September 13 the President had asserted that there were no Soviet offensive missiles in Cuba and committed his Administration to act if offensive missiles were discovered. Before Congressional committees, Administration officials were denying that there was any evidence whatever of offensive missiles in Cuba. The implications of a National intelligence estimate which concluded that the Soviets were introducing offensive missiles into Cuba were not lost on the men who constituted America's highest intelligence assembly.

The October 4 COMOR decision to direct a flight over the western end of Cuba in effect "overturned" the September estimate, but without officially raising that issue. The decision represented McCone's victory for which he had lobbied with the President before the September 10 decision, in telegrams before the September 19 estimate, and in person after his return to Washington. Though the politics of the intelligence community is closely guarded, several pieces of the story can be told.[85] By September 27, Colonel Wright and others in DIA believed that the Soviet Union was placing missiles in the San Cristobal area.[86] This area was marked suspicious by the CIA on September 29 and certified top priority on October 3. By October 4 McCone had the evidence required to raise the issue officially. The members of COMOR heard McCone's argument, but were reluctant to make the hard decision he demanded. The significant probability that a U-2 would be downed made overflight of western Cuba a matter of real concern.[87]

THE POLITICS OF ISSUES   The U-2 photographs presented incontrovertible evidence of Soviet offensive missiles in Cuba. This revelation fell upon politicized players in a complex context. As one high official recalled, Khrushchev had caught us "with our pants down." What each of the central participants saw, and what each did to cover both his own and the Administration's nakedness, created the spectrum of issues and answers.

At approximately 9:00 A.M., Tuesday morning, October 16, McGeorge Bundy went to the President's living quarters with the message: "Mr. President, there is now hard photographic evidence that the Russians have offensive missiles in Cuba."[88] Much has been made of Kennedy's "expression of surprise,"[89] but "surprise" fails to capture the character of his initial reaction. Rather, it was one of startled anger, most adequately conveyed by the exclamation: "He can't do that to *me!*"[90] In terms of the President's attention and priorities at that moment, Khrushchev had chosen the most unhelpful act of all. Kennedy had staked his full Presidential authority on the assertion that the Soviets would not place offensive weapons in Cuba. Moreover, Khrushchev had assured the President through the most direct and personal channels that he was aware of the President's domestic political problem and that nothing would be done to exacerbate this problem. The Chairman had *lied* to the President. Kennedy's initial reaction entailed action. The missiles must be removed.[91] The alternatives of "doing nothing" or "taking a diplomatic approach" could not have been less relevant to *his* problem.

These two tracks—doing nothing and taking a diplomatic approach—were the solutions advocated by two of his principal advisors. For Secretary of Defense McNamara, the missiles raised the spectre of nuclear war. He first framed the issue as a straightforward strategic problem. To understand the issue, one had to grasp two obvious but difficult points. First, the missiles represented an inevitable occurrence: narrowing of the missile gap. It simply happened sooner rather than later. Second, the United States could accept this occurrence since its conse-quences were minor: "seven-to-one missile 'superiority,' one-to-one missile 'equality,' one-to-seven missile 'inferiority'—the three postures are identical." McNamara's statement of this argument at the first meeting of the ExCom was summed up in the phrase, "a missile is a missile."[92] "It makes no great difference," he maintained, "whether you are killed by a missile from the Soviet Union or Cuba."[93] The implication was clear. The United States should not initiate a crisis with the Soviet Union, risking a significant probability of nuclear war over an occurrence which had such small strategic implications.

The perceptions of McGeorge Bundy, the President's Assistant for National Security Affairs, are the most difficult of all to reconstruct. There is no question that he initially argued for a diplomatic track.[94] But was Bundy laboring under his acknowledged burden of responsibility in Cuba I? Or was he playing the role of devil's advocate in order to make the President probe his own initial reaction and consider other options?

The President's brother, Robert Kennedy, saw most clearly the political wall against which Khrushchev had backed the President. But he, like McNamara, saw the prospect of nuclear doom. Was Khrushchev going to force the President to an insane act? At the first meeting of the ExCom, he scribbled a note, "Now I know how Tojo felt when he was planning Pearl Harbor."[95] From the outset he searched for an alternative that would prevent the air strike.

The initial reaction of Theodore Sorensen, the President's Special Counsel and "alter ego," fell somewhere between that of the President and his brother. Like the President, Sorensen felt the poignancy of betrayal. If the President had been the architect of the policy which the missiles punctured, Sorensen was the draftsman. Khrushchev's deceitful move demanded a strong counter-move. But like Robert Kennedy, Sorensen feared lest the shock and disgrace lead to disaster.

To the Joint Chiefs of Staff the issue was clear. *Now* was the time to do the job for which they had prepared contingency plans. Cuba I had been badly done; Cuba II would not be. The missiles provided the *occasion* to deal with the issue: cleansing the Western Hemisphere of Castro's Communism. As the President recalled on the day the crisis ended, "An invasion would have been a mistake— a wrong use of our power. But the military are mad. They wanted to do this. It's lucky for us that we have McNamara over there."[96]

McCone's perceptions flowed from his confirmed prediction. As the Cassandra of the incident, he argued forcefully that the Soviets had installed the missiles in a daring political probe which the United States must meet with force. The time for an air strike was now.[97]

THE POLITICS OF CHOICE   The process by which the blockade emerged is a story of the most subtle and intricate probing, pulling, and hauling; leading, guiding, and spurring. Reconstruction of this process can only be tentative. Initially the President and most of his advisers wanted the clean, surgical air strike. On the first day of the crisis, when informing Stevenson of the missiles, the President mentioned only two alternatives: "I suppose the alternatives are to go in by air and wipe them out, or to take other steps to render them inoperable."[98] At the end of the week a sizeable minority still favored an air strike. As Robert Kennedy recalled: "The fourteen people involved were very significant. . . . If six of them had been President of the U.S., I think that the world might have been blown up."[99] What prevented the air strike was a fortuitous coincidence of a number of factors—the absence of any one of which might have permitted that option to prevail.

First, McNamara's vision of holocaust set him firmly against the air strike. His initial attempt to frame the issue in strategic terms struck Kennedy as particularly inappropriate. Once McNamara realized that the name of the game was a strong response, however, he and his deputy Gilpatric chose the blockade as a fallback. When the Secretary of Defense—whose department had the action, whose reputation in the Cabinet was unequaled, in whom the President demonstrated full confidence—marshalled the arguments for the blockade and refused to be moved, the blockade became a formidable alternative.

Second, Robert Kennedy—the President's closest confidant—was unwilling to see his brother become a "Tojo." His arguments against the air strike on moral grounds struck a chord in the President. Moreover, once his brother had stated these arguments so forcefully, the President could not have chosen his initially preferred course without, in effect, agreeing to become what RFK had condemned.

The President learned of the missiles on Tuesday morning. On Wednesday morning, in order to mask our discovery from the Russians, the President flew to Connecticut to keep a campaign commitment, leaving RFK as the unofficial chairman of the group. By the time the President returned on Wednesday evening, a critical third piece had been added to the picture. McNamara had presented his argument for the blockade. Robert Kennedy and Sorensen had joined McNamara. A powerful coalition of the advisers in whom the President had the greatest confidence, and with whom his style was most compatible, had emerged.

Fourth, the coalition that had formed behind the President's initial preference gave him reason to pause. *Who* supported the air strike—the Chiefs, McCone, Rusk, Nitze, and Acheson—as much as *how* they supported it, counted. Fifth, a piece of inaccurate information, which no one probed, permitted the blockade advocates to fuel (potential) uncertainties in the President's mind. When the President returned to Washington Wednesday evening, RFK and Sorensen met him at the airport. Sorensen gave the President a four-page memorandum outlining the areas of agreement and disagreement. The strongest argument was that the air strike simply could not be surgical.[100] After a day of prodding and questioning, the Air Force had asserted that it could not guarantee the success of a surgical air strike limited to the missiles alone.

Thursday evening, the President convened the ExCom at the White House. He declared his tentative choice of the blockade and directed that preparations be made to put it into effect by Monday morning.[101] Though he raised a question about the possibility of a surgical air strike subsequently, he seems to have accepted the experts' opinion that this was no live option.[102] (Acceptance of this estimate suggests that he may have learned the lesson of the Bay of Pigs—"Never rely on experts"—less well than he supposed.)[103] But this information was incorrect. That no one probed this estimate during the first week of the crisis poses an interesting question for further investigation.

A coalition, including the President, thus emerged from the President's initial decision that something had to be done; McNamara, Robert Kennedy, and Sorensen's resistance to the air strike; incompatibility between the President and the air strike advocates; and an inaccurate piece of information.[104]

CONCLUSION

This essay has obviously bitten off more than it has chewed. For further developments and synthesis of these arguments the reader is referred to the larger study.[105] In spite of the limits of space, however, it would be inappropriate to stop without spelling out several implications of the argument and addressing the question of relations among the models and extensions of them to activity beyond explanation.

At a minimum, the intended implications of the argument presented here are four. First, formulation of alternative frames of reference and demonstration that different analysts, relying predominantly on different models, produce quite different explanations should encourage the analyst's self-consciousness about the nets he employs. The effect of these "spectacles" in sensitizing him to particular aspects of what is going on—framing the puzzle in one way rather than another, encouraging him to examine the problem in terms of certain categories rather than others, directing him to particular kinds of evidence, and relieving puzzlement by one procedure rather than another—must be recognized and explored.

Second, the argument implies a position on the problem of "the state of the art." While accepting the commonplace characterization of the present condition of foreign policy analysis—personalistic, non-cumulative, and sometimes insightful—this essay rejects both the counsel of despair's justification of this condition as a consequence of the character of the enterprise, and the "new frontiersmen's" demand for *a priori* theorizing on the frontiers and *ad hoc* appropriation of "new techniques."[106] What is required as a first step is non-casual examination of the present product: inspection of existing explanations, articulation of the conceptual models employed in producing them, formulation of the propositions relied upon, specification of the logic of the various intellectual enterprises, and reflection on the questions being asked. Though it is difficult to overemphasize the need for more systematic processing of more data, these preliminary matters of formulating questions with clarity and sensitivity to categories and assumptions so that fruitful acquisition of large quantities of data is possible are still a major hurdle in considering most important problems.

Third, the preliminary, partial paradigms presented here provide a basis for serious reexamination of many problems of foreign and military policy. Model II and Model III cuts at problems typically treated in Model I terms can permit significant improvements in explanation and prediction.[107] Full Model II and III analyses require large amounts of information. But even in cases where the information base is severely limited, improvements are possible. Consider the problem of predicting Soviet strategic forces. In the mid-1950s, Model I style calculations led to predictions that the Soviets would rapidly deploy large numbers of long-range bombers. From a Model II perspective, both the frailty of the Air Force within the Soviet military establishment and the budgetary implications of such a buildup, would have led analysts to hedge this prediction. Moreover, Model II would have pointed to a sure, visible indicator of such a buildup: noisy struggles among the Services over major budgetary shifts. In the late 1950s and early 1960s, Model I calculations led to the prediction of immediate, massive Soviet deployment of ICBMs. Again, a Model II cut would have reduced this number because, in the earlier period, strategic rockets were controlled by the Soviet Ground Forces rather than an independent Service, and in the later period, this would have necessitated massive shifts in budgetary splits. Today, Model I considerations lead many analysts both to recommend that an agreement not to deploy ABMs be a major American objective in upcoming strategic negotiations with the USSR, and to predict success. From a Model II vantage point, the existence of an ongoing Soviet ABM program, the strength of the organization (National Air Defense) that controls ABMs, and the fact that an agreement to stop ABM deployment would force the virtual dismantling of this organization, make a viable agreement of this sort much less likely. A Model III cut suggests that (a) there must be significant differences among perceptions and priorities of Soviet leaders over strategic negotiations, (b) any agreement will affect some players' power bases, and (c) agreements that do not require extensive cuts in the sources of some major players' power will prove easier to negotiate and more viable.

Fourth, the present formulation of paradigms is simply an initial step. As such it leaves a long list of critical questions unanswered. Given any action, an imaginative analyst should always be able to construct some rationale for the government's choice. By imposing, and relaxing, constraints on the parameters of rational choice (as in variants of Model I) analysts can construct a large number of accounts of any act as a rational choice. But does a statement of reasons why a rational actor would choose an action constitute an explanation of the *occurrence* of that action? How can Model I analysis be forced to make more systematic contributions to the question of the determinants of occurrences? Model II's explanation of t in terms of $t - 1$ is explanation. The world is contiguous. But governments sometimes make sharp departures. Can an organizational process model be modified to suggest where change is likely? Attention to organizational change should afford greater understanding of why particular programs and SOPs are maintained by identifiable types of organizations and also how a manager can improve organizational performance. Model III tells a fascinating "story." But its complexity is enormous, the information requirements are often overwhelming, and many of the details of the bargaining may be superfluous. How can such a model be made parsimonious? The three models are obviously not exclusive alternatives. Indeed, the paradigms highlight the partial emphasis of the framework—what each emphasizes and what it leaves out. Each concentrates on one class of variables, in effect, relegating other important factors to a *ceteris paribus* clause. Model I concentrates on "market factors": pressures and incentives created by the "international strategic marketplace." Models II and III focus on the internal mechanism of the government that chooses in this environment. But can these relations be more fully specified? Adequate synthesis would require a typology of decisions and actions, some of which are more amenable to treatment in terms of one model and some to another. Government behavior is but one cluster of factors relevant to occurrences in foreign affairs. Most students of foreign policy adopt this focus (at least when explaining and predicting). Nevertheless, the dimensions of the chess board, the character of the pieces, and the rules of the game—factors considered by international systems theorists—constitute the context in which the pieces are moved. Can the major variables in the full function of determinants of foreign policy outcomes be identified?

Both the outline of a partial, *ad hoc* working synthesis of the models, and a sketch of their uses in activities other than explanation can be suggested by generating predictions in terms of each. Strategic surrender is an important problem of international relations and diplomatic history. War termination is a new, developing area of the strategic literature. Both of these interests lead scholars to address a central question: *Why* do nations surrender *when*? Whether implicit in explanations or more explicit in analysis, diplomatic historians and strategists rely upon propositions which can be turned forward to produce predictions. Thus at the risk of being timely—and in error—the present situation

(August, 1968) offers an interesting test case: Why will North Vietnam surrender when?[108]

In a nutshell, analysis according to Model I asserts: nations quit when costs outweigh the benefits. North Vietnam will surrender when she realizes "that continued fighting can only generate additional costs without hope of compensating gains, this expectation being largely the consequence of the previous application of force by the dominant side."[109] U.S. actions can increase or decrease Hanoi's strategic costs. Bombing North Vietnam increases the pain and thus increases the probability of surrender. This proposition and prediction are not without meaning. That—"other things being equal"—nations are more likely to surrender when the strategic cost-benefit balance is negative, is true. Nations rarely surrender when they are winning. The proposition specifies a range within which nations surrender. But over this broad range, the relevant question is: why do nations surrender?

Models II and III focus upon the government machine through which this fact about the international strategic marketplace must be filtered to produce a surrender. These analysts are considerably less sanguine about the possibility of surrender *at the point* that the cost-benefit calculus turns negative. Never in history (i.e., in none of the five cases I have examined) have nations surrendered at that point. Surrender occurs sometime thereafter. *When* depends on process of organizations and politics of players within these governments—as they are affected by the opposing government. Moreover, the effects of the victorious power's action upon the surrendering nation cannot be adequately summarized as increasing or decreasing strategic costs. Imposing additional costs by bombing a nation may increase the probability of surrender. But it also may reduce it. An appreciation of the impact of the acts of one nation upon another thus requires some understanding of the machine which is being influenced. For more precise prediction, Models II and III require considerably more information about the organizations and politics of North Vietnam than is publicly available. On the basis of the limited public information, however, these models can be suggestive.

Model II examines two sub-problems. First, to have lost is not sufficient. The government must know that the strategic cost-benefit calculus is negative. But neither the categories, nor the indicators, of strategic costs and benefits are clear. And the sources of information about both are organizations whose parochial priorities and perceptions do not facilitate accurate information or estimation. Military evaluation of military performance, military estimates of factors like "enemy morale," and military predictions concerning when "the tide will turn" or "the corner will have been turned" are typically distorted. In cases of highly decentralized guerrilla operations, like Vietnam, these problems are exacerbated. Thus strategic costs will be underestimated. Only highly *visible* costs can have direct impact on leaders without being filtered through organizational channels. Second, since organizations define the details of options and execute actions, surrender (and negotiation) is likely to entail considerable bungling in the early stages. No organization can define options or prepare programs for this treasonous act. Thus, early overtures will be uncoordinated with the acts of other organizations, e.g., the fighting forces, creating contradictory "signals" to the victor.

Model III suggests that surrender will not come at the point that strategic costs outweigh benefits, but that it will not wait until the leadership group concludes that the war is lost. Rather the problem is better understood in terms of four additional propositions. First, strong advocates of the war effort, whose careers are closely identified with the war, rarely come to the conclusion that costs outweigh benefits. Second, quite often from the outset of a war, a number of members of the government (particularly those whose responsibilities sensitize them to problems other than war, e.g., economic planners or intelligence experts) are convinced that the war effort is futile. Third, surrender is likely to come as the result of a political shift that enhances the effective power of the latter group (and adds swing members to it). Further, the course of the war, particularly actions of the victor, can influence the advantages and disadvantages of players in the loser's government. Thus, North Vietnam will surrender not when its leaders have a change of heart, but when Hanoi has a change of leaders (or a change of effective power within the central circle). How U.S. bombing (or pause), threats, promises, or action in the South affect the game in Hanoi is subtle but nonetheless crucial.

That these three models could be applied to the surrender of governments other than North Vietnam should be obvious. But that exercise is left for the reader.

NOTES

[1] Theodore Sorensen, *Kennedy* (New York, 1965), p. 705.

[2] In attempting to understand problems of foreign affairs, analysts engage in a number of related, but logically separable enterprises: (a) description, (b) explanation, (c) prediction, (d) evaluation, and (e) recommendation. This essay focuses primarily on explanation (and by implication, prediction).

[3] In arguing that explanations proceed in terms of implicit conceptual models, this essay makes no claim that foreign policy analysts have developed any satisfactory, empirically tested theory. In this essay, the use of the term "model" without qualifiers should be read "conceptual scheme."

[4] For the purpose of this argument we shall accept Carl G. Hempel's characterization of the logic of explanation: an explanation "answers the question, 'Why did the explanandum-phenomenon occur?' by showing that the phenomenon resulted from particular circumstances, specified in C_1, $C_2, \ldots C_k$, in accordance with laws $L_1, L_2, \ldots L_r$. By pointing this out, the argument shows that, given the particular circumstances and the laws in question, the occurrence of the phenomenon was to be *expected*; and it is in this sense that the explanation enables us to understand why the phenomenon occurred." *Aspects of Scientific Explanation* (New York, 1965), p. 337. While various patterns of explanation can be distinguished, *viz.*, Ernest Nagel, *The Structure of Science: Problems in the Logic of Scientific Explanation* (New York, 1961), satisfactory scientific explanations exhibit this basic logic. Consequently prediction is the converse of explanation.

[5] Earlier drafts of this argument have aroused heated arguments concerning proper names for these models. To choose names from ordinary language is to court confusion, as well as familiarity. Perhaps it is best to think of these models as I, II, and III.

6 In strict terms, the "outcomes" which these three models attempt to explain are essentially actions of national governments, i.e., the sum of activities of all individuals employed by a government relevant to an issue. These models focus not on a state of affairs, i.e., a full description of the world, but upon national decision and implementation. This distinction is stated clearly by Harold and Margaret Sprout, "Environmental Factors on the Study of International Politics," in James Rosenau (ed.), *International Politics and Foreign Policy* (Glencoe, Illinois, 1961), p. 116. This restriction excludes explanations offered principally in terms of international systems theories. Nevertheless, this restriction is not severe, since few interesting explanations of occurrences in foreign policy have been produced at that level of analysis. According to David Singer, "The nation state—our primary actor in international relations . . . is clearly the traditional focus among Western students and is the one which dominates all of the texts employed in English-speaking colleges and universities." David Singer, "The Level-of-Analysis Problem in International Relations," Klaus Knorr and Sidney Verba (eds.), *The International System* (Princeton, 1961). Similarly, Richard Brody's review of contemporary trends in the study of international relations finds that "scholars have come increasingly to focus on acts of nations. That is, they all focus on the behavior of nations in some respect. Having an interest in accounting for the behavior of nations in common, the prospects for a common frame of reference are enhanced."

7 For further development and support of these arguments see the author's larger study [*Essence of Decision: Explaining the Cuban Missile Crisis* (Boston, 1971)]. In its abbreviated form, the argument must, at some points, appear overly stark. The limits of space have forced the omission of many reservations and refinements.

8 Each of the three "case snapshots" displays the work of a conceptual model as it is applied to explain the U.S. blockade of Cuba. But these three cuts are primarily exercises in hypothesis generation rather than hypothesis testing. Especially when separated from the larger study, these accounts may be misleading. The sources for these accounts include the full public record plus a large number of interviews with participants in the crisis.

9 *New York Times*, February 18, 1967.

10 *Ibid.*

11 Arnold Horelick and Myron Rush, *Strategic Power and Soviet Foreign Policy* (Chicago, 1965). Based on A. Horelick, "The Cuban Missile Crisis: An Analysis of Soviet Calculations and Behavior," *World Politics* (April, 1964).

12 Horelick and Rush, *Strategic Power and Soviet Foreign Policy*, p. 154.

13 Hans Morgenthau, *Politics Among Nations* (3rd ed.; New York, 1960), p. 191.

14 *Ibid.*, p. 192.

15 *Ibid.*, p. 5.

16 *Ibid.*, pp. 5–6.

17 Stanley Hoffmann, *Daedalus* (Fall, 1962); reprinted in *The State of War* (New York, 1965).

18 *Ibid.*, p. 171.

19 *Ibid.*, p. 189.

20 Following Robert MacIver; see Stanley Hoffmann, *Contemporary Theory in International Relations* (Englewood Cliffs, 1960), pp. 178–179.

21 Thomas Schelling, *The Strategy of Conflict* (New York, 1960), p. 232. This proposition was formulated earlier by A. Wohlstetter, "The Delicate Balance of Terror," *Foreign Affairs* (January, 1959).

22 Schelling, *op. cit.*, p. 4.

23 See Morgenthau, *op. cit.*, p. 5; Hoffmann, *Contemporary Theory*, pp. 178–179; Hoffmann, "Roulette in the Cellar," *The State of War*; Schelling, *op. cit.*

24 The larger study examines several exceptions to this generalization. Sidney Verba's excellent essay "Assumptions of Rationality and Non-Rationality in Models of the International System" is less an exception than it is an approach to a somewhat different problem. Verba focuses upon models of rationality and irrationality of *individual* statesmen: in Knorr and Verba, *The International System*.

25 Robert K. Merton, *Social Theory and Social Structures* (Revised and Enlarged Edition; New York, 1957), pp. 12–16. Considerably weaker than a satisfactory theoretical model, paradigms nevertheless represent a short step in that direction from looser, implicit conceptual models. Neither the concepts nor the relations among the variables are sufficiently specified to yield propositions

deductively. "Paradigmatic Analysis" nevertheless has considerable promise for clarifying and codifying styles of analysis in political science. Each of the paradigms stated here can be represented rigorously in mathematical terms. For example, Model I lends itself to mathematical formulation along the lines of Herbert Simon's "Behaviorial Theory of Rationality," *Models of Man* (New York, 1957). But this does not solve the most difficult problem of "measurement and estimation."

[26] As stated in the introduction, this "case snapshot" presents, without editorial commentary, a Model I analyst's explanation of the U.S. blockade. The purpose is to illustrate a strong, characteristic rational policy model account. This account is (roughly) consistent with prevailing explanations of these events.

[27] Theodore Sorensen, *op. cit.*, p. 675.

[28] *Ibid.*, p. 679.

[29] *Ibid.*, p. 679.

[30] Elie Abel, *The Missile Crisis* (New York, 1966), p. 144.

[31] *Ibid.*, p. 102.

[32] Sorensen, *op. cit.*, p. 684.

[33] *Ibid.*, p. 685. Though this was the formulation of the argument, the facts are not strictly accurate. Our tradition against surprise attack was rather younger than 175 years. For example President Theodore Roosevelt applauded Japan's attack on Russia in 1904.

[34] *New York Times*, June, 1963.

[35] The influence of organizational studies upon the present literature of foreign affairs is minimal. Specialists in international politics are not students of organization theory. Organization theory has only recently begun to study organizations as decisionmakers and has not yet produced behavioral studies of national security organizations from a decision-making perspective. It seems unlikely, however, that these gaps will remain unfilled much longer. Considerable progress has been made in the study of the business firm as an organization. Scholars have begun applying these insights to government organizations, and interest in an organizational perspective is spreading among institutions and individuals concerned with actual government operations. The "decisionmaking" approach represented by Richard Snyder, R. Bruck, and B. Sapin, *Foreign Policy Decision-Making* (Glencoe, Illinois, 1962), incorporates a number of insights from organization theory.

[36] U.S. Department of State, *Bulletin*, XLVII, pp. 715–720.

[37] Schlesinger, *op. cit.*, p. 803.

[38] Theodore Sorensen, *Kennedy*, p. 675.

[39] See U.S. Congress, Senate, Committee on Armed Services, Preparedness Investigation Subcommittee, *Interim Report on Cuban Military Build-up*, 88th Congress, 1st Session, 1963, p. 2; Hanson Baldwin, "Growing Risks of Bureaucratic Intelligence," *The Reporter* (August 15, 1963), 48–50; Roberta Wohlstetter, "Cuba and Pearl Harbor," *Foreign Affairs* (July, 1965), 706.

[40] U.S. Congress, House of Representatives, Committee on Appropriations, Subcommittee on Department of Defense Appropriations, *Hearings*, 88th Congress, 1st Session, 1963, 25 ff.

[41] R. Hilsman, *To Move a Nation* (New York, 1967), pp. 172–173.

[42] Department of Defense Appropriations, *Hearings*, p. 67.

[43] *Ibid.*, pp. 66–67.

[44] For (1) Hilsman, *op. cit.*, p. 186; (2) Abel, *op. cit.*, p. 24; (3) Department of Defense Appropriations, *Hearings*, p. 64; Abel, *op. cit.*, p. 24; (4) Department of Defense Appropriations, *Hearings*, pp. 1–30.

[45] The facts here are not entirely clear. This assertion is based on information from (1) "Department of Defense Briefing by the Honorable R. S. McNamara, Secretary of Defense, State Department Auditorium, 5:00 p.m., February 6, 1963." A verbatim transcript of a presentation actually made by General Carroll's assistant, John Hughes; and (2) Hilsman's statement, *op. cit.*, p. 186. But see R. Wohlstetter's interpretation, "Cuba and Pearl Harbor," 700.

[46] See Hilsman, *op. cit.*, pp. 172–174.

[47] Abel, *op. cit.*, pp. 26 ff; Weintal and Bartlett, *Facing the Brink* (New York, 1967), pp. 62 ff; *Cuban Military Build-up*; J. Daniel and J. Hubbell, *Strike in the West* (New York, 1963), pp. 15 ff.

[48] Schlesinger, *op. cit.*, p. 804.

[49] Sorensen, *Kennedy*, p. 684.

[50] *Ibid.*, pp. 684 ff.

[51] *Ibid.*, pp. 694–697.

[52] *Ibid.*, p. 697; Abel, *op. cit.*, pp. 100–101.

[53] Sorensen, *Kennedy*, p. 669.

[54] Hilsman, *op. cit.*, p. 204.

[55] See Abel, *op. cit.*, pp. 97 ff.

[56] Schlesinger, *op. cit.*, p. 818.

[57] *Ibid.*

[58] Sorensen, *Kennedy*, p. 710.

[59] *New York Times*, October 27, 1962.

[60] Abel, *op. cit.*, p. 171.

[61] For the location of the original arc see Abel, *op. cit.*, p. 141.

[62] *Facts on File*, Vol. XXII, 1962, p. 376, published by Facts on File, Inc., New York, yearly.

[63] This hypothesis would account for the mystery surrounding Kennedy's explosion at the leak of the stopping of the *Bucharest*. See Hilsman, *op. cit.*, p. 45.

[64] Abel, *op. cit.*, p. 153.

[65] See *ibid.*, pp. 154 ff.

[66] *Ibid.*, p. 156.

[67] *Ibid.*

[68] Sorensen, *Kennedy*, p. 670.

[69] *Ibid.*

[70] *Ibid.*, pp. 670 ff.

[71] *New York Times*, August, September, 1962.

[72] *New York Times*, August 20, 1962.

[73] *New York Times*, September 5, 1962.

[74] *New York Times*, September 14, 1962.

[75] *New York Times*, October 14, 1962.

[76] Cited by Abel, *op. cit.*, p. 13.

[77] *New York Times*, September 5, 1962.

[78] *New York Times*, September 14, 1962.

[79] Senate Foreign Relations Committee; Senate Armed Services Committee; House Committee on Appropriation; House Select Committee on Export Control.

[80] Abel, *op. cit.*, pp. 17–18. According to McCone, he told Kennedy, "The only construction I can put on the material going into Cuba is that the Russians are preparing to introduce offensive missiles." See also Weintal and Bartlett, *op. cit.*, pp. 60–61.

[81] Abel, *op. cit.*, p. 23.

[82] *New York Times*, September 10, 1962.

[83] See Abel, *op. cit.*, pp. 25–26; and Hilsman, *op. cit.*, p. 174.

[84] Department of Defense Appropriations, *Hearings*, 69.

[85] A basic, but somewhat contradictory, account of parts of this story emerges in the Department of Defense Appropriations, *Hearings*, 1–70.

[86] Department of Defense Appropriations, *Hearings*, 71.

[87] The details of the 10 days between the October 4 decision and the October 14 flight must be held in abeyance.

[88] Abel, *op. cit.*, p. 44.

[89] *Ibid.*, pp. 44 ff.

[90] See Richard Neustadt, "Afterword," *Presidential Power* (New York, 1964).

[91] Sorensen, *Kennedy*, p. 676; Schlesinger, *op. cit.*, p. 801.

[92] Hilsman, *op. cit.*, p. 195.

[93] *Ibid.*

[94] Weintal and Bartlett, *op. cit.*, p. 67; Abel, *op. cit.*, p. 53.

[95] Schlesinger, *op. cit.*, p. 803.

[96] *Ibid.*, p. 831.

[97] Abel, *op. cit.*, p. 186.

[98] *Ibid.*, p. 49.

[99] Interview, quoted by Ronald Steel, *New York Review of Books*, March 13, 1969, p. 22.

[100] Sorensen, *Kennedy*, p. 686.

[101] *Ibid.*, p. 691.

[102] *Ibid.*, pp. 691–692.

[103] Schlesinger, *op. cit.*, p. 296.

[104] Space will not permit an account of the path from this coalition to the formal government decision on Saturday and action on Monday.

[105] [*Essence of Decision* (Boston, 1971)].

[106] Thus my position is quite distinct from both poles in the recent "great debate" about international relations. While many "traditionalists" of the sort Kaplan attacks adopt the first posture and many "scientists" of the sort attacked by Bull adopt the second, this third posture is relatively neutral with respect to whatever is in substantive dispute. See Hedly Bull, "International Theory: The Case for a Classical Approach," *World Politics* (April, 1966); and Morton Kaplan, "The New Great Debate: Traditionalism vs. Science in International Relations," *World Politics* (October, 1966).

[107] A number of problems are now being examined in these terms both in the Bureaucracy Study Group on Bureaucracy and Policy of the Institute of Politics at Harvard University and at the Rand Corporation.

[108] In response to several readers' recommendations, what follows is reproduced *verbatim* from the paper delivered at the September, 1968 Association meetings (Rand P-3919). The discussion is heavily indebted to Ernest R. May.

[109] Richard Snyder, *Deterrence and Defense* (Princeton, 1961), p. 11. For a more general presentation of this position see Paul Kecskemeti, *Strategic Surrender* (New York, 1964).

PART NINE

THE JUDICIARY

When we addressed the uniqueness of the American political culture in the first section, we pointed out that some classic interpretations attribute much of American political development to "constitutionalism." The place of the Constitution in American life is clearly unique among the world's democratic political systems. The document is used not only as a guide in public policymaking, but also as a restraint upon the exercise of political power. It even provides moral and ethical guidance in the implementation of policy. Ever since Tocqueville's time, political observers have noted the American tendency to discuss policy issues in terms of their constitutionality. Today, issues such as abortion, affirmative action, and religious displays on public property are examples.

A major consequence of American constitutionalism is that it bestows great power on the judiciary, especially on the Supreme Court. The Court has long since established the power of judicial review—that is, the power to declare the acts of other units of government, both federal and state, unconstitutional. There is no true equivalent to this judicial power in other nations. As "keeper" of the Constitution, the Supreme Court is, as Alexander Bickel points out, "the most extraordinarily powerful court of law the world has ever known." Paradoxically, though, even the world's most powerful court is weak in comparison to the presidency and to Congress. Its size, budget, and much of its jurisdiction are established by legislation, not by the Constitution itself. The judiciary also must rely on the executive branch to carry out its decisions. In Alexander Hamilton's words in the seventy-eighth *Federalist Paper*, "The judiciary . . . has no influence over either the sword or the purse; no direction either of the strength or of the wealth of the society, and can take no active resolution whatever. It may truly be said to have neither FORCE nor WILL but merely judgment." Thus, the judiciary's overriding political task is to secure its power through its judgment; to do so it must maintain and constantly strive to strengthen its legitimacy. It is around these themes that all the classic works on the American judiciary revolve.

Edward S. Corwin's " 'Higher Law' Background of American Constitutional Law" (1928, 1955) reaches back into the history of Western development to explain American constitutionalism. Corwin concludes that the supremacy of the Constitution in American politics cannot be attributed solely to that document's origins and ratification. Rather, he suggests, the Constitution's place in American political life is due to its content, its "embodiment of an essential and unchanging justice"; it is to these elemental principles that American public officials must be faithful.

Federalist Paper Number 78 is a remarkable essay. It foresaw the use of judicial review well before there was a consensus among the population or its leaders as to the appropriateness of such a power. It also anticipated the fundamental problems inherent in providing this power to unelected officials holding what are essentially lifetime terms of office. Hamilton rationalized this antidemocratic situation in the following words: "Whoever attentively considers the different departments of power must perceive that, in a government in which they are separated from each other, the judiciary, from the nature of its functions, will always be the least dangerous to the political rights of the Constitution; because it will be least in a capacity to annoy or injure them."

Alexander M. Bickel's discussion of the "Establishment and General Justification of Judicial Review" (1962) is far more complex and subtle. Unlike Hamilton, Bickel comes to grips with "the essential reality that judicial review is a deviant institution in the American democracy." Yet he also considers judicial review to be a crucial aspect of the American political system and its culture. The institution is deviant because it does not rest on popular election; it is crucial because it enables the Constitution to be adapted to changing conditions. In roughly the same vein as Corwin, he addresses the symbolic, or even "mystic," functions of the Supreme Court: "But the Supreme Court as a legitimating force in society also casts a less palpable yet larger spell. With us the symbol of nationhood, of continuity, of unity and common purpose, is, of course, the Constitution, without particular reference to what exactly it means in this or that application. . . . [A]nd . . . it has in large part been left to the Supreme Court to concretize the symbol of the Constitution."

But what *does* the Constitution mean exactly "in this or that application"? It is the task of the judges to decide, but upon what grounds must they reach their decisions? Perhaps the essence of judicial decision making was conveyed most succinctly by Chief Justice Earl Warren when he remarked, "We serve only the public interest as we see it, guided only by the Constitution and our own consciences."[1] These bases of decision making—the Constitution and individual conscience—are addressed in the essay by C. Herman Pritchett.

Pritchett compares the judiciary, particularly the Supreme Court, to a legislature that votes on issues of public policy. He rejects the view that judges simply "look up the law" in order to decide cases. Rather, they exercise their own preferences, but within the institutional and procedural framework that places checks upon them. Pritchett develops a "box score" of the Supreme Court justices' records on libertarian issues during the 1946–1951 terms. His analysis shows substantial variation among the justices. Subsequently, better statistical techniques were developed to scale justices' values and to enable the researcher to understand judicial behavior. Conceptually, however, more recent approaches continue to reflect Pritchett's view that judges are public policymakers whose preferences and values can be understood best through analysis of their decisions.

To complete this section we have included, in abridged form, three Supreme Court decisions of fundamental importance.[2] Two were delivered by Chief

---

[1] Quoted in James F. Simon, *In His Own Image: The Supreme Court in Richard Nixon's America* (New York: David McKay, 1973), p. 2.

[2] In the text of these cases, abbreviations and capitalization have been modernized, citations have been omitted, and second references to cases mentioned by the Supreme Court have been shortened to include the name of the first party only.

Justice John Marshall, a major architect of American constitutionalism: *Marbury v. Madison* (1803), in which judicial review was established, and *McCulloch v. Maryland* (1819), in which a broad view of national power was asserted with the words "Let the end be legitimate, let it be within the scope of the Constitution, and all means which are appropriate, which are plainly adapted to that end, which are not prohibited, but consistent with the letter and spirit of the Constitution," are constitutional. The third case, *Brown v. Board of Education* (1954), declared that laws requiring racial segregation in public schools are unconstitutional. It is the most important statement in American history of the idea that the Constitution forbids governmental actions intended to promote racial segregation or racial inequality.

34

EDWARD S. CORWIN

THE "HIGHER LAW" BACKGROUND OF AMERICAN CONSTITUTIONAL LAW

> Theory is the most important part of the dogma of the law, as the
> architect is the most important man who takes part in the building of
> a house.
>
> *Collected Legal Papers,* HOLMES

The Reformation superseded an infallible Pope with an infallible Bible; the
American Revolution replaced the sway of a king with that of a document. That
such would be the outcome was not unforeseen from the first. In the same
number of *Common Sense* which contained his electrifying proposal that
America should declare her independence from Great Britain, [Thomas] Paine
urged also a "Continental Conference," whose task he described as follows:

> The conferring members being met, let their business be to frame a Continental
> Charter, or Charter of the United Colonies; (answering to what is called the Magna
> Charta of England) fixing the number and manner of choosing members of congress
> and members of assembly . . . and drawing the line of business and jurisdiction
> between them: (always remembering, that our strength is continental, not provincial)
> securing freedom and property to all men . . . with such other matter as it is necessary
> for a charter to contain. . . . But where, say some, is the King of America? Yet that
> we may not appear to be defective even in earthly honors, let a day be solemnly set
> apart for proclaiming the charter; let it be brought forth placed in the divine law, the
> word of God; let a crown be placed thereon, by which the world may know, that so far
> as we approve of monarchy, that in America the law is King.[1]

This suggestion, which was to eventuate more than a decade later in the
Philadelphia Convention, is not less interesting for its retrospection than it is for
its prophecy.

In the words of the younger Adams, "the Constitution itself had been extorted
from the grinding necessity of a reluctant nation";[2] yet hardly had it gone into
operation than hostile criticism of its provisions not merely ceased but gave place
to "an undiscriminating and almost blind worship of its principles"[3]—a worship
which continued essentially unchallenged till the other day. Other creeds have

waxed and waned, but "worship of the Constitution" has proceeded unabated.[4] It is true that the Abolitionists were accustomed to stigmatize the Constitution as "an agreement with Hell," but their shrill heresy only stirred the mass of Americans to renewed assertion of the national faith. Even Secession posed as loyalty to the *principles* of the Constitution and a protest against their violation, and in form at least the constitution of the Southern Confederacy was, with a few minor departures, a studied reproduction of the instrument of 1787. For by far the greater reach of its history, Bagehot's appraisal of the British monarchy is directly applicable to the Constitution: "The English Monarchy strengthens our government with the strength of religion."[5]

The fact that its adoption was followed by a wave of prosperity no doubt accounts for the initial launching of the Constitution upon the affections of the American people. Travelling through various parts of the United States at this time, Richard Bland Lee found "fields a few years ago waste and uncultivated filled with inhabitants and covered with harvests, new habitations reared, contentment in every face, plenty on every board. . . ." "To produce this effect," he continued, "was the intention of the Constitution, and it has succeeded." Indeed it is possible that rather too much praise was lavished upon the Constitution on this score. "It has been usual with declamatory gentlemen," complained the astringent Maclay, "in their praises of the present government, by way of contrast, to paint the state of the country under the old (Continental) congress, as if neither wood grew nor water ran in America before the happy adoption of the new Constitution"; and a few years later, when the European turmoil at once assisted, and by contrast advertised, our own blissful state, Josiah Quincy voiced a fear that "we have grown giddy with good fortune, attributing the greatness of our prosperity to our own wisdom, rather than to a course of events, and a guidance over which we had no influence."[6]

But while the belief that it drew prosperity in its wake may explain the beginning of the worship of the Constitution, it leaves a deeper question unanswered. It affords no explanation why this worship came to ascribe to the Constitution the precise virtues it did as an efficient cause of prosperity. To answer this question we must first of all project the Constitution against a background of doctrinal tradition which, widespread as European culture, was at the time of the founding of the English colonies especially strong in the mother country, though by the irony of history it had become a century and a half later the chief source of division between mother country and colonies.

It is customary nowadays to ascribe the *legality* as well as the *supremacy* of the Constitution—the one is, in truth, but the obverse of the other—exclusively to the fact that, in its own phraseology, it was "ordained" by "the people of the United States." Two ideas are thus brought into play. One is the so-called "positive" conception of law as a general expression merely for the particular commands of a human lawgiver, as a series of acts of human will;[7] the other is that the highest possible source of such commands, because the highest possible embodiment of human will, is "the people." The same two ideas occur in conjunction in the oft-quoted text of Justinian's *Institutes*: "Whatever has pleased the prince has the force of law, since the Roman people by the *lex regia* enacted concerning his *imperium*, have yielded up to him all their power and authority."⁸ The sole difference between the Constitution of the United States and the imperial legislation justified in this famous text is that the former is assumed to have proceeded immediately from the people, while the latter proceeded from a like source only mediately.

The attribution of supremacy to the Constitution on the ground solely of its rootage in popular will represents, however, a comparatively late outgrowth of American constitutional theory. Earlier the supremacy accorded to constitutions was ascribed less to their putative source than to their supposed content, to their embodiment of an essential and unchanging justice. The theory of law thus invoked stands in direct contrast to the one just reviewed. *There are*, it is predicated, *certain principles of right and justice which are entitled to prevail of their own intrinsic excellence, altogether regardless of the attitude of those who wield the physical resources of the community. Such principles were made by no human hands; indeed, if they did not antedate deity itself, they still so express its nature as to bind and control it. They are external to all Will as such and interpenetrate all Reason as such. They are eternal and immutable. In relation to such principles, human laws are, when entitled to obedience save as to matters indifferent, merely a record or transcript, and their enactment and act not of will or power but one of discovery and declaration.*⁹ The Ninth Amendment of the Constitution of the United States, in stipulating that "the enumeration of certain rights in this Constitution shall not prejudice other rights not so enumerated," illustrates this theory perfectly except that the principles of transcendental justice have been here translated into terms of personal and private rights. The relation of such rights, nevertheless, to governmental power is the same as that of the principles from which they spring and which they reflect. They owe nothing to their recognition in the Constitution—such recognition was necessary if the Constitution was to be regarded as complete.

Thus the *legality* of the Constitution, its *supremacy*, and its claim to be worshipped, alike find common standing ground on the belief in a law superior to the will of human governors. Certain questions arise: Whence came this idea of a "higher law"? How has it been enabled to survive, and in what transformations? What special forms of it are of particular interest for the history of American constitutional law and theory? By what agencies and as a result of what causes was it brought to America and wrought into the American system of government? . . .

NOTES

¹ Paine, *Political Writings* (1837) 45–46.
² Adams, *Jubilee Discourse on the Constitution* (1839) 55.
³ Woodrow Wilson, *Congressional Government* (13th ed. 1898) 4.

4 On the whole subject, see 1 Von Holst, *Constitutional History* (1877) c. 2; Schechter, *Early History of the Tradition of the Constitution* (1915) 9 Am. Pol. Sci. Rev. 707 *et seq.*

5 Bagehot, *English Constitution* (2d ed. 1925) 39. "The monarchy by its religious sanction now confirms all our political order. . . . It gives . . . a vast strength to the entire constitution, by enlisting on its behalf the credulous obedience of enormous masses." *Ibid.* 43–44.

6 Schechter, *supra* note 4, at 720–21.

7 Bentham, as quoted in Holland, *Elements of Jurisprudence* (12th ed. 1916) 14. For further definitions of "positive law," see *ibid.* 22–23; Willoughby, *Fundamental Concepts of Public Law* (1924) c. 10.

8 *Inst.* I, 2, 6: "Quod principi placuit, legis habet vigorem, cum lege regia quae de ejus imperio lata est, populus ei et in eum, omne imperium suum et potestatem concessit." The source is Ulpian, *Dig.* I, 4, 1. The Romans always regarded the people as the source of the legislative power. "Lex est, quod populus Romanus senatorie magistratu interrogante, veluti Consule, constituebat." *Inst.* I, 2, 4. During the Middle Ages the question was much debated whether the *lex regia* effected an absolute alienation (*translatio*) of the legislative power to the Emperor, or was a revocable delegation (*cessio*). The champions of popular sovereignty at the end of this period, like Marsiglio of Padua in his *Defensor Pacis*, took the latter view. See Gierke, *Political Theories of the Middle Ages* (Maitland's tr. 1922) 150, notes 158, 159.

9 For definitions of law incorporating this point of view, see Holland, *op. cit. supra* note 7, at 19–20, 32–36. *Cf.* 1 Blackstone, *Commentaries*, Intro.

35

"PUBLIUS" (ALEXANDER HAMILTON)

FEDERALIST PAPER NUMBER 78

We proceed now to an examination of the judiciary department of the proposed government.

In unfolding the defects of the existing Confederation, the utility and necessity of a federal judicature have been clearly pointed out. It is the less necessary to recapitulate the considerations there urged as the propriety of the institution in the abstract is not disputed; the only questions which have been raised being relative to the manner of constituting it, and to its extent. To these points, therefore, our observations shall be confined.

The manner of constituting it seems to embrace these several objects: 1st. The mode of appointing the judges. 2nd. The tenure by which they are to hold their places. 3rd. The partition of the judiciary authority between different courts and their relations to each other.

First. As to the mode of appointing the judges: this is the same with that of appointing the officers of the Union in general and has been so fully discussed in the two last numbers that nothing can be said here which would not be useless repetition.

Second. As to the tenure by which the judges are to hold their places: this chiefly concerns their duration in office, the provisions for their support, the precautions for their responsibility.

According to the plan of the convention, all judges who may be appointed by the United States are to hold their offices *during good behavior*; which is conformable to the most approved of the State constitutions, and among the rest, to that of this State. Its propriety having been drawn into question by the adversaries of that plan is no light symptom of the rage for objection which disorders their imaginations and judgments. The standard of good behavior for the continuance in office of the judicial magistracy is certainly one of the most valuable of the modern improvements in the practice of government. In a monarchy it is an excellent barrier to the despotism of the prince; in a republic it is a no less excellent barrier to the encroachments and oppressions of the representative body. And it is the best expedient which can be devised in any government to secure a steady, upright, and impartial administration of the laws.

Whoever attentively considers the different departments of power must perceive that, in a government in which they are separated from each other, the judiciary, from the nature of its functions, will always be the least dangerous to the political rights of the Constitution; because it will be least in a capacity to annoy or injure them. The executive not only dispenses the honors but holds the sword of the community. The legislature not only commands the purse but prescribes the rules by which the duties and rights of every citizen are to be regulated. The judiciary, on the contrary, has no influence over either the sword or the purse; no direction either of the strength or of the wealth of the society, and can take no active resolution whatever. It may truly be said to have neither FORCE nor WILL but merely judgment; and must ultimately depend upon the aid of the executive arm even for the efficacy of its judgments.

This simple view of the matter suggests several important consequences. It proves incontestably that the judiciary is beyond comparison the weakest of the three departments of power;[1] that it can never attack with success either of the other two; and that all possible care is requisite to enable it to defend itself against their attacks. It equally proves that though individual oppression may now and then proceed from the courts of justice, the general liberty of the people can never be endangered from that quarter; I mean so long as the judiciary remains truly distinct from both the legislature and the executive. For I agree that "there is no liberty if the power of judging be not separated from the legislative and executive powers."[2] And it proves, in the last place, that as liberty can have nothing to fear from the judiciary alone, but would have everything to fear from its union with either of the other departments; that as all the effects of such a union must ensue from a dependence of the former on the latter, notwithstanding a nominal and apparent separation; that as, from the natural feebleness of the judiciary, it is in continual jeopardy of being overpowered, awed, or influenced by its co-ordinate branches; and that as nothing can contribute so much to its firmness and independence as permanency in office, this quality may therefore be justly regarded as an indispensable ingredient in its constitution, and, in a great measure, as the citadel of the public justice and the public security.

The complete independence of the courts of justice is peculiarly essential in a limited Constitution. By a limited Constitution, I understand one which contains certain specified exceptions to the legislative authority; such, for instance, as that it shall pass no bills of attainder, no *ex post facto* laws, and the like. Limitations of this kind can be preserved in practice no other way than through the medium of courts of justice, whose duty it must be to declare all acts contrary to the manifest tenor of the Constitution void. Without this, all the reservations of particular rights or privileges would amount to nothing.

Some perplexity respecting the rights of the courts to pronounce legislative acts void, because contrary to the Constitution, has arisen from an imagination that the doctrine would imply a superiority of the judiciary to the legislative power. It is urged that the authority which can declare the acts of another void must necessarily be superior to the one whose acts may be declared void. As this doctrine is of great importance in all the American constitutions, a brief discussion of the grounds on which it rests cannot be unacceptable.

There is no position which depends on clearer principles than that every act of a delegated authority, contrary to the tenor of the commission under which it is exercised, is void. No legislative act, therefore, contrary to the Constitution, can be valid. To deny this would be to affirm that the deputy is greater than his principal; that the servant is above his master; that the representatives of the people are superior to the people themselves; that men acting by virtue of powers may do not only what their powers do not authorize, but what they forbid.

If it be said that the legislative body are themselves the constitutional judges of their own powers and that the construction they put upon them is conclusive upon the other departments it may be answered that this cannot be the natural presumption where it is not to be collected from any particular provisions in the Constitution. It is not otherwise to be supposed that the Constitution could intend to enable the representatives of the people to substitute their *will* to that of their constituents. It is far more rational to suppose that the courts were designed to be an intermediate body between the people and the legislature in order, among other things, to keep the latter within the limits assigned to their authority. The interpretation of the laws is the proper and peculiar province of the courts. A constitution is, in fact, and must be regarded by the judges as, a fundamental law. It therefore belongs to them to ascertain its meaning as well as the meaning of any particular act proceeding from the legislative body. If there should happen to be an irreconcilable variance between the two, that which has the superior obligation and validity ought, of course, to be preferred; or, in other words, the Constitution ought to be preferred to the statute, the intention of the people to the intention of their agents.

Nor does this conclusion by any means suppose a superiority of the judicial to the legislative power. It only supposes that the power of the people is superior to both, and that where the will of the legislature, declared in its statutes, stands in opposition to that of the people, declared in the Constitution, the judges ought to be governed by the latter rather than the former. They ought to regulate their decisions by the fundamental laws rather than by those which are not fundamental.

This exercise of judicial discretion in determining between two contradictory laws is exemplified in a familiar instance. It not uncommonly happens that there are two statutes existing at one time, clashing in whole or in part with each other and neither of them containing any repealing clause or expression. In such a case, it is the province of the courts to liquidate and fix their meaning and operation. So far as they can, by any fair construction, be reconciled to each other, reason and law conspire to dictate that this should be done; where this is impracticable, it becomes a matter of necessity to give effect to one in exclusion of the other. The rule which has obtained in the courts for determining their relative validity is that the last in order of time shall be preferred to the first. But this is a mere rule of construction, not derived from any positive law but from the nature and reason of the thing. It is a rule not enjoined upon the courts by legislative provision but adopted by themselves, as consonant to truth and propriety, for the direction of their conduct as interpreters of the law. They thought it reasonable that between the interfering acts of an *equal* authority that which was the last indication of its will should have the preference.

But in regard to the interfering acts of a superior and subordinate authority of an original and derivative power, the nature and reason of the thing indicate the converse of that rule as proper to be followed. They teach us that the prior act of a superior ought to be preferred to the subsequent act of an inferior and subordinate authority; and that accordingly, whenever a particular statute contravenes the Constitution, it will be the duty of the judicial tribunals to adhere to the latter and disregard the former.

It can be of no weight to say that the courts, on the pretense of a repugnancy, may substitute their own pleasure to the constitutional intentions of the legislature. This might as well happen in the case of two contradictory statutes; or it might as well happen in every adjudication upon any single statute. The courts must declare the sense of the law; and if they should be disposed to exercise WILL instead of JUDGMENT, the consequence would equally be the substitution of their pleasure to that of the legislative body. The observation, if it proved anything, would prove that there ought to be no judges distinct from that body.

If, then, the courts of justice are to be considered as the bulwarks of a limited Constitution against legislative encroachments, this consideration will afford a strong argument for the permanent tenure of judicial offices, since nothing will contribute so much as this to that independent spirit in the judges which must be essential to the faithful performance of so arduous a duty.

This independence of the judges is equally requisite to guard the Constitution and the rights of individuals from the effects of those ill humors which the arts of designing men, or the influence of particular conjunctures, sometimes disseminate among the people themselves, and which, though they speedily give place to better information, and more deliberate reflection, have a tendency, in the meantime, to occasion dangerous innovations in the government, and serious oppressions of the minor party in the community. Though I trust the friends of the proposed Constitution will never concur with its enemies[3] in questioning that fundamental principle of republican government which admits the right of the people to alter or abolish the established Constitution whenever they find it inconsistent with their happiness; yet it is not to be inferred from this principle that the representatives of the people, whenever a momentary inclination happens to lay hold of a majority of their constituents incompatible with the provisions in the existing Constitution would, on that account, be justifiable in a violation of those provisions; or that the courts would be under a greater obligation to connive at infractions in this shape than when they had proceeded wholly from the cabals of the representative body. Until the people have, by some solemn and authoritative act, annulled or changed the established form, it is binding upon themselves collectively, as well as individually; and no presumption, or even knowledge of their sentiments, can warrant their representatives in a departure from it prior to such an act. But it is easy to see that it would require an uncommon portion of fortitude in the judges to do their duty as faithful guardians of the Constitution, where legislative invasions of it had been instigated by the major voice of the community.

But it is not with a view to infractions of the Constitution only that the independence of the judges may be an essential safeguard against the effects of occasional ill humors in the society. These sometimes extend no farther than to the injury of the private rights of particular classes of citizens, by unjust and partial laws. Here also the firmness of the judicial magistracy is of vast importance in mitigating the severity and confining the operation of such laws. It not only serves to moderate the immediate mischiefs of those which may have been passed but it operates as a check upon the legislative body in passing them; who, perceiving that obstacles to the success of an iniquitous intention are to be expected from the scruples of the courts, are in a manner compelled, by the very motives of the injustice they meditate, to qualify their attempts. This is a circumstance calculated to have more influence upon the character of our governments than but few may be aware of. The benefits of the integrity and moderation of the judiciary have already been felt in more States than one; and though they may have displeased those whose sinister expectations they may have disappointed, they must have commanded the esteem and applause of all the virtuous and disinterested. Considerate men of every description ought to prize whatever will tend to beget or fortify that temper in the courts; as no man can be sure that he may not be tomorrow the victim of a spirit of injustice, by which he may be a gainer today. And every man must now feel that the inevitable tendency of such a spirit is to sap the foundations of public and private confidence and to introduce in its stead universal distrust and distress.

That inflexible and uniform adherence to the rights of the Constitution, and of individuals, which we perceive to be indispensable in the courts of justice, can certainly not be expected from judges who hold their offices by a temporary commission. Periodical appointments, however regulated, or by whomsoever made, would, in some way or other, be fatal to their necessary independence. If the power of making them was committed either to the executive or legislature there would be danger of an improper complaisance to the branch which possessed it; if to both, there would be an unwillingness to hazard the displeasure of either; if to the people, or to persons chosen by them for the special purpose, there would be too great a disposition to consult popularity to justify a reliance that nothing would be consulted but the Constitution and the laws.

There is yet a further and a weighty reason for the permanency of the judicial offices which is deducible from the nature of the qualifications they require. It has been frequently remarked with great propriety that a voluminous code of laws is one of the inconveniences necessarily connected with the advantages of a free government. To avoid an arbitrary discretion in the courts, it is indispensable that they should be bound down by strict rules and precedents which serve to define and point out their duty in every particular case that comes before them; and it will readily be conceived from the variety of controversies which grow out of the folly and wickedness of mankind that the records of those precedents must unavoidably swell to a very considerable bulk and must demand long and laborious study to acquire a competent knowledge of them. Hence it is that there can be but few men in the society who will have sufficient skill in the laws to qualify them for the stations of judges. And making the proper deductions for the ordinary depravity of human nature, the number must be still smaller of those who unite the requisite integrity with the requisite knowledge. These considerations apprise us that the government can have no great option between fit characters; and that a temporary duration in office which would naturally discourage such characters from quitting a lucrative line of practice to accept a seat on the bench would have a tendency to throw the administration of justice into hands less able and less well qualified to conduct it with utility and dignity. In the present circumstances of this country and in those in which it is likely to be for a long time to come, the disadvantages on this score would be greater than they may at first sight appear; but it must be confessed that they are far inferior to those which present themselves under the other aspects of the subject.

Upon the whole, there can be no room to doubt that the convention acted wisely in copying from the models of those constitutions which have established *good behavior* as the tenure of their judicial offices, in point of duration; and that so far from being blamable on this account, their plan would have been inexcusably defective if it had wanted this important feature of good government. The experience of Great Britain affords an illustrious comment on the excellence of the institution.

Publius
(Alexander Hamilton)

NOTES

[1] The celebrated Montesquieu, speaking of them, says: "Of the three powers above mentioned, the JUDICIARY is next to nothing."—*Spirit of Laws*, Vol. I, page 186.

[2] *Idem*, page 181.

[3] *Vide Protest of the Minority of the Convention of Pennsylvania*, Martin's speech, etc.

36

ALEXANDER M. BICKEL

ESTABLISHMENT AND GENERAL JUSTIFICATION OF JUDICIAL REVIEW

The least dangerous branch of the American government is the most extraordinarily powerful court of law the world has ever known. The power which distinguishes the Supreme Court of the United States is that of constitutional review of actions of the other branches of government, federal and state. Curiously enough, this power of judicial review, as it is called, does not derive from any explicit constitutional command. The authority to determine the meaning and application of a written constitution is nowhere defined or even mentioned in the document itself. This is not to say that the power of judicial review cannot be placed in the Constitution; merely that it cannot be found there. . . .

THE MORAL APPROVAL OF THE LINES: HISTORY

[W]e come to examine foundations for the doctrine of judicial review other than textual exegesis. *Marbury* v. *Madison*, relating to the power to hold federal statutes unconstitutional, and *Martin* v. *Hunter's Lessee* and *Cohens* v. *Virginia*, which assumed the power of judicial review of state actions, were decided, respectively, in 1803, 1816, and 1821. They met with controversy, to be sure, which has also recurred sporadically since. But their doctrines have held sway for roughly a century and a half. So long have they been among the realities of our national existence. Settled expectations have formed around them. The life of a nation that now encompasses 185 million people spread over a continent and more depends upon them in a hundred different aspects of its organization and coherence. It is late for radical changes. Perhaps *Marbury* v. *Madison* is a historical accident attributable to the political configuration of the earliest years, to Marshall's political antecedents, and to the force and statesmanlike deviousness of his personality. It was a half century before the power to strike down an act of Congress was again exercised, and at that time, in the *Dred Scott Case* of exceedingly bad odor, it was asserted in a fashion that would have assured its evanescence rather than permanence. But *Marbury* v. *Madison* did occur, and if it was an accident, it was not the first to play an important role in the permanent shaping of a government. One of the reasons that the "accident" has endured is that Marshall's own view of the scope of legislative power had grandeur. He undertook to expound the Constitution with finality, but it was Marshall himself who enjoined his posterity never to forget "that it is a *constitution* we are expounding," a living charter, embodying implied as well as expressed powers, "adapted to the various *crises* of human affairs," open to change, capable of growth. This was the Marshall of *McCulloch* v. *Maryland*, decided in 1819. If assumption of the power was accident, the vision and wisdom with which it was exercised in the early years cannot have been. And if it was accident, it had nevertheless been somewhat arranged; if *Marbury* v. *Madison* was *ex tempore*, it had nonetheless been well prepared. For, although the Framers of the Constitution had failed to be explicit about the function of judicial review, the evidence of their deliberations demonstrates that they foresaw—indeed, invited—it.

This has frequently been denied, whenever the impulse to radical change has come upon people. And *Marbury* v. *Madison* has been attacked, not merely for its apparent frailties, but as an act of "usurpation." Yet, as Professor Felix Frankfurter wrote in 1924: "Lack of historical scholarship, combined with fierce prepossessions, can alone account for the persistence of this talk. One would suppose that, at least, after the publication of Beard, *The Supreme Court and the Constitution*, there would be an end to this empty controversy." Beard wrote in 1912; Farrand published *The Records of the Federal Convention* in 1911 and *The Framing of the Constitution* in 1913. There have been some further accessions to our knowledge since, to be sure, and the books of history are never closed. Nor are historical hypotheses provable with mathematical precision. But it is as clear as such matters can be that the Framers of the Constitution specifically, if tacitly, expected that the federal courts would assume a power—of whatever exact dimensions—to pass on the constitutionality of actions of the Congress and the President, as well as of the several states. Moreover, not even a colorable showing of decisive historical evidence to the contrary can be made. Nor can it be maintained that the language of the Constitution is compellingly the other way. At worst it may be said that the intentions of the Framers cannot be ascertained with finality; that there were some who thought this and some that, and that it will never be entirely clear just exactly where the collective judgment—which alone is decisive—came to rest. In any debate over the force of the tradition, such is the most that can be said against the claims of judicial review.

Continuity with the past, said Holmes, is not a duty; it is merely a necessity. But Holmes also told us that it is "revolting to have no better reason for a rule of law than that so it was laid down in the time of Henry IV. It is still more revolting if the grounds upon which it was laid down have vanished long since, and the rule simply persists from blind imitation of the past." Judicial review is a present instrument of government. It represents a choice that men have made, and ultimately we must justify it as a choice in our own time. What are the elements of choice?

THE COUNTER-MAJORITARIAN DIFFICULTY

The root difficulty is that judicial review is a counter-majoritarian force in our system. There are various ways of sliding over this ineluctable reality. Marshall did so when he spoke of enforcing, in behalf of "the people," the limits that they have ordained for the institutions of a limited government. And it has been done ever since in much the same fashion by all too many commentators. Marshall himself followed Hamilton, who in the 78th *Federalist* denied that judicial review implied a superiority of the judicial over the legislative power—denied, in other words, that judicial review constituted control by an unrepresentative minority of an elected majority. "It only supposes," Hamilton went on, "that the power of the people is superior to both; and that where the will of the legislature, declared in its statutes, stands in opposition to that of the people, declared in the Constitution, the judges ought to be governed by the latter rather than the former." But the word "people" so used is an abstraction. Not necessarily a meaningless or a pernicious one by any means; always charged with emotion, but nonrepresentational—an abstraction obscuring the reality that when the Supreme Court declares unconstitutional a legislative act or the action of an elected executive, it thwarts the will of representatives of the actual people of the here and now; it exercises control, not in behalf of the prevailing majority, but against it. That, without mystic overtones, is what actually happens. It is an altogether different kettle of fish, and it is the reason the charge can be made that judicial review is undemocratic.

Most assuredly, no democracy operates by taking continuous nose counts on the broad range of daily governmental activities. Representative democracies— that is to say, all working democracies—function by electing certain men for certain periods of time, then passing judgment periodically on their conduct of public office. It is a matter of a laying on of hands, followed in time by a process of holding to account—all through the exercise of the franchise. The elected officials, however, are expected to delegate some of their tasks to men of their own appointment, who are not directly accountable at the polls. The whole operates under public scrutiny and criticism—but not at all times or in all parts. What we mean by democracy, therefore, is much more sophisticated and complex than the making of decisions in town meeting by a show of hands. It is true also that even decisions that have been submitted to the electoral process in some fashion are not continually resubmitted, and they are certainly not continually unmade. Once run through the process, once rendered by "the people" (using the term now in its mystic sense, because the reference is to the people in the past), myriad decisions remain to govern the present and the future despite what may well be fluctuating majorities against them at any given time. A high value is put on stability, and that is also a counter-majoritarian factor. Nevertheless, although democracy does not mean constant reconsideration of decisions once made, it does mean that a representative majority has the power to accomplish a reversal. This power is of the essence, and no less so because it is often merely held in reserve.

I am aware that this timid assault on the complexities of the American democratic system has yet left us with a highly simplistic statement, and I shall briefly rehearse some of the reasons. But nothing in the further complexities and perplexities of the system, which modern political science has explored with admirable and ingenious industry, and some of which it has tended to multiply with a fertility that passes the mere zeal of the discoverer—nothing in these complexities can alter the essential reality that judicial review is a deviant institution in the American democracy.

It is true, of course, that the process of reflecting the will of a popular majority in the legislature is deflected by various inequalities of representation and by all sorts of institutional habits and characteristics, which perhaps tend most often in favor of inertia. Yet it must be remembered that statutes are the product of the legislature and the executive acting in concert, and that the executive represents a very different constituency and thus tends to cure inequities of over- and underrepresentation. Reflecting a balance of forces in society for purposes of stable and effective government is more intricate and less certain than merely assuring each citizen his equal vote. Moreover, impurities and imperfections, if such they be, in one part of the system are no argument for total departure from the desired norm in another part. A much more important complicating factor—first adumbrated by Madison in the 10th *Federalist* and lately emphasized by Professor David B. Truman and others—is the proliferation and power of what Madison foresaw as "faction," what Mr. Truman calls "groups," and what in popular parlance has always been deprecated as the "interests" or the "pressure groups."

No doubt groups operate forcefully on the electoral process, and no doubt they seek and gain access to and an effective share in the legislative and executive decisional process. Perhaps they constitute also, in some measure, an impurity or imperfection. But no one has claimed that they have been able to capture the governmental process except by combining in some fashion, and thus capturing or constituting (are not the two verbs synonymous?) a majority. They often tend themselves to be majoritarian in composition and to be subject to broader majoritarian influences. And the price of what they sell or buy in the legislature is determined in the biennial or quadrennial electoral marketplace. It may be, as Professor Robert A. Dahl has written, that elections themselves, and the political competition that renders them meaningful, "do not make for government by majorities in any very significant way," for they do not establish a great many policy preferences. However, "they are a crucial device for controlling leaders." And if the control is exercised by "groups of various types and sizes, all seeking in various ways to advance their goals," so that we have "minorities rule" rather than majority rule, it remains true nevertheless that only those minorities rule which can command the votes of a majority of individuals in the electorate. In one fashion or another, both in the legislative process and at elections, the minorities must coalesce into a majority. Although, as Mr. Dahl says, "it is fashionable in some quarters to suggest that everything believed about democratic politics prior to World War I, and perhaps World War II, was nonsense," he makes no bones about his own belief that "the radical democrats who, unlike

Madison, insist upon the decisive importance of the election process in the whole grand strategy of democracy are essentially correct."

The insights of Professor Truman and other writers into the role that groups play in our society and our politics have a bearing on judicial review. They indicate that there are other means than the electoral process, though subordinate and subsidiary ones, of making institutions of government responsive to the needs and wishes of the governed. Hence one may infer that judicial review, although not responsible, may have ways of being responsive. But nothing can finally depreciate the central function that is assigned in democratic theory and practice to the electoral process; nor can it be denied that the policy-making power of representative institutions, born of the electoral process, is the distinguishing characteristic of the system. Judicial review works counter to this characteristic.

It therefore does not follow from the complex nature of a democratic system that, because admirals and generals and the members, say, of the Federal Reserve Board or of this or that administrative agency are not electorally responsible, judges who exercise the power of judicial review need not be responsible either, and in neither case is there a serious conflict with democratic theory. For admirals and generals and the like are most often responsible to officials who are themselves elected and through whom the line runs directly to a majority. What is more significant, the policies they make are or should be interstitial or technical only and are reversible by legislative majorities. Thus, so long as there has been a meaningful delegation by the legislature to administrators, which is kept within proper bounds, the essential majority power is there, and it is felt to be there—a fact of great consequence. Nor will it do to liken judicial review to the general lawmaking function of judges. In the latter aspect, judges are indeed something like administrative officials, for their decisions are also reversible by any legislative majority—and not infrequently they are reversed. Judicial review, however, is the power to apply and construe the Constitution, in matters of the greatest moment, against the wishes of a legislative majority, which is, in turn, powerless to affect the judicial decision.

"For myself," said the late Judge Learned Hand,

> it would be most irksome to be ruled by a bevy of Platonic Guardians, even if I knew how to choose them, which I assuredly do not. If they were in charge, I should miss the stimulus of living in a society where I have, at least theoretically, some part in the direction of public affairs. Of course I know how illusory would be the belief that my vote determined anything; but nevertheless when I go to the polls I have a satisfaction in the sense that we are all engaged in a common venture. If you retort that a sheep in the flock may feel something like it; I reply, following Saint Francis, "My brother, the Sheep."

This suggests not only the democratic value that inheres in obtaining the broad judgment of a majority of the people in the community and thus tending to produce better decisions. Judge Hand, if anything, rather deprecated the notion that the decisions will be better, or are affected at all. Some might think that he deprecated it beyond what is either just or realistic when he said that the belief that his vote determined anything was illusory. Hardly altogether. But the strong emphasis is on the related idea that coherent, stable—and *morally supportable*—government is possible only on the basis of consent, and that the secret of consent is the sense of common venture fostered by institutions that reflect and represent us and that we can call to account.

It has been suggested that the Congress, the President, the states, and the people (in the sense of current majorities) have from the beginning and in each generation acquiesced in, and thus consented to, the exercise of judicial review by the Supreme Court. In the first place, it is said that the Amending Clause of the Constitution has been employed to reverse the work of the Court only twice, perhaps three times; and it has never been used to take away or diminish the Court's power. But the Amending Clause itself incorporates an extreme minority veto. The argument then proceeds to draw on the first Judiciary Act, whose provisions regarding the jurisdiction of the federal courts have been continued in effect to this day. Yet we have seen that the Judiciary Act can be read as a grant of the power to declare federal statutes unconstitutional only on the basis of a previously and independently reached conclusion that such a power must exist. And even if the Judiciary Act did grant this power, as it surely granted the power to declare state actions unconstitutional, it amounted to an expression of the opinion of the first Congress that the Constitution implies judicial review. It is, in fact, extremely likely that the first Congress thought so. That is important; but it merely adds to the historical evidence on the point, which, as we have seen, is in any event quite strong. Future Congresses and future generations can only be said to have acquiesced in the belief of the first Congress that the Constitution implies this power. And they can be said to have become resigned to what follows, which is that the power can be taken away only by constitutional amendment. That is a very far cry from consent to the power on its merits, as a power freely continued by the decision or acquiescence of a majority in each generation. The argument advances not a step toward justification of the power on other than historical grounds.

A further, crucial difficulty must also be faced. Besides being a counter-majoritarian check on the legislature and the executive, judicial review may, in a larger sense, have a tendency over time seriously to weaken the democratic process. Judicial review expresses, of course, a form of distrust of the legislature. "The legislatures," wrote James Bradley Thayer at the turn of the century,

> are growing accustomed to this distrust and more and more readily inclined to justify it, and to shed the considerations of constitutional restraints,—certainly as concerning the exact extent of these restrictions,—turning that subject over to the courts; and what is worse, they insensibly fall into a habit of assuming that whatever they could constitutionally do they may do,—as if honor and fair dealing and common honesty were not relevant to their inquiries. The people, all this while, become careless as to whom they send to the legislature; too often they cheerfully vote for men whom they would not trust with an important private affair, and when these unfit persons are found to pass foolish and bad laws, and the courts step in and disregard them, the

people are glad that these few wiser gentlemen on the bench are so ready to protect them against their more immediate representatives. . . . [I]t should be remembered that the exercise of it [the power of judicial review], even when unavoidable, is always attended with a serious evil, namely, that the correction of legislative mistakes comes from the outside, and the people thus lose the political experience, and the moral education and stimulus that comes from fighting the question out in the ordinary way, and correcting their own errors. The tendency of a common and easy resort to this great function, now lamentably too common, is to dwarf the political capacity of the people, and to deaden its sense of moral responsibility. It is no light thing to do that.

To this day, in how many hundreds of occasions does Congress enact a measure that it deems expedient, having essayed consideration of its constitutionality (that is to say, of its acceptability on principle), only to abandon the attempt in the declared confidence that the Court will correct errors of principle, if any? It may well be, as has been suggested, that any lowering of the level of legislative performance is attributable to many factors other than judicial review. Yet there is no doubt that what Thayer observed remains observable. It seemed rather a puzzle, for example, to a scholar who recently compared British and American practices of legislative investigation. Professor Herman Finer wrote, with what might have seemed to Thayer charming ingenuousness:

> Is it not a truly extraordinary phenomenon that in the United States, where Congress is not a sovereign body, but subordinate to a constitution, there appear to be less restraints upon the arbitrary behavior of members in their . . . rough handling of the civil rights of the citizen during investigations . . . ? Though Parliament is sovereign and can legally do anything it likes, its practices are kinder, more restrained, and less invasive of the rights of those who come under its investigative attention. The student is forced to pause and reflect upon this remarkable reversal of demeanor and status.

Finally, another, though related, contention has been put forward. It is that judicial review runs so fundamentally counter to democratic theory that in a society which in all other respects rests on that theory, judicial review cannot ultimately be effective. We pay the price of a grave inner contradiction in the basic principle of our government, which is an inconvenience and a dangerous one; and in the end to no good purpose, for when the great test comes, judicial review will be unequal to it. The most arresting expression of this thought is in a famous passage from a speech of Judge Learned Hand, a passage, Dean Eugene V. Rostow has written, "of Browningesque passion and obscurity," voicing a "gloomy and apocalyptic view." Absent the institution of judicial review, Judge Hand said:

> I do not think that anyone can say what will be left of those [fundamental principles of equity and fair play which our constitutions enshrine]; I do not know whether they will serve only as counsels; but this much I think I do know—that a society so riven that the spirit of moderation is gone, no court *can* save; that a society where that spirit flourishes, no court *need* save; that in a society which evades its responsibility by thrusting upon the courts the nurture of that spirit, that spirit in the end will perish.

Over a century before Judge Hand spoke, Judge Gibson of Pennsylvania, in his day perhaps the ablest opponent of the establishment of judicial review, wrote: "Once let public opinion be so corrupt as to sanction every misconstruction of the Constitution and abuse of power which the temptation of the moment may dictate, and the party which may happen to be predominant will laugh at the puny efforts of a dependent power to arrest it in its course." And Thayer also believed that "under no system can the power of courts go far to save a people from ruin; our chief protection lies elsewhere."

THE MORAL APPROVAL
OF THE LINES: PRINCIPLE

Such, in outline, are the chief doubts that must be met if the doctrine of judicial review is to be justified on principle. Of course, these doubts will apply with lesser or greater force to various forms of the exercise of the power. For the moment the discussion is at wholesale, and we are seeking a justification on principle, quite aside from supports in history and the continuity of practice. The search must be for a function which might (indeed, must) involve the making of policy, yet which differs from the legislative and executive functions; which is peculiarly suited to the capabilities of the courts; which will not likely be performed elsewhere if the courts do not assume it; which can be so exercised as to be acceptable in a society that generally shares Judge Hand's satisfaction in a "sense of common venture"; which will be effective when needed; and whose discharge by the courts will not lower the quality of the other departments' performance by denuding them of the dignity and burden of their own responsibility. It will not be possible fully to meet all that is said against judicial review. Such is not the way with questions of government. We can only fill the other side of the scales with countervailing judgments on the real needs and the actual workings of our society and, of course, with our own portions of faith and hope. Then we may estimate how far the needle has moved.

The point of departure is a truism; perhaps it even rises to the unassailability of a platitude. It is that many actions of government have two aspects: their immediate, necessarily intended, practical effects, and their perhaps unintended or unappreciated bearing on values we hold to have more general and permanent interest. It is a premise we deduce not merely from the fact of a written constitution but from the history of the race, and ultimately as a moral judgment of the good society, that government should serve not only what we conceive from time to time to be our immediate material needs but also certain enduring values. This in part is what is meant by government under law. But such values do not present themselves ready-made. They have a past always, to be sure, but they must be continually derived, enunciated, and seen in relevant application. And it remains to ask which institution of our government—if any single one in particular—should be the pronouncer and guardian of such values.

Men in all walks of public life are able occasionally to perceive this second aspect of public questions. Sometimes they are also able to base their decisions on it; that is one of the things we like to call acting on principle. Often they do not do so, however, particularly when they sit in legislative assemblies. There, when the pressure for immediate results is strong enough and emotions ride high enough, men will ordinarily prefer to act on expediency rather than take the long view. Possibly legislators—everything else being equal—are as capable as other men of following the path of principle, where the path is clear or at any rate discernible. Our system, however, like all secular systems, calls for the evolution of principle in novel circumstances, rather than only for its mechanical application. Not merely respect for the rule of established principles but the creative establishment and renewal of a coherent body of principled rules—that is what our legislatures have proven themselves ill equipped to give us.

Initially, great reliance for principled decision was placed in the Senators and the President, who have more extended terms of office and were meant to be elected only indirectly. Yet the Senate and the President were conceived of as less closely tied to, not as divorced from, electoral responsibility and the political marketplace. And so even then the need might have been felt for an institution which stands altogether aside from the current clash of interests, and which, insofar as is humanly possible, is concerned only with principle. We cannot know whether, as Thayer believed, our legislatures are what they are because we have judicial review, or whether we have judicial review and consider it necessary because legislatures are what they are. Yet it is arguable also that the partial separation of the legislative and judicial functions—and it is not meant to be absolute—is beneficial in any event, because it makes it possible for the desires of various groups and interests concerning immediate results to be heard clearly and unrestrainedly in one place. It may be thought fitting that somewhere in government, at some stage in the process of law-making, such felt needs should find unambiguous expression. Moreover, and more importantly, courts have certain capacities for dealing with matters of principle that legislatures and executives do not possess. Judges have, or should have, the leisure, the training, and the insulation to follow the ways of the scholar in pursuing the ends of government. This is crucial in sorting out the enduring values of a society, and it is not something that institutions can do well occasionally, while operating for the most part with a different set of gears. It calls for a habit of mind, and for undeviating institutional customs. Another advantage that courts have is that questions of principle never carry the same aspect for them as they did for the legislature or the executive. Statutes, after all, deal typically with abstract or dimly foreseen problems. The courts are concerned with the flesh and blood of an actual case. This tends to modify, perhaps to lengthen, everyone's view. It also provides an extremely salutary proving ground for all abstractions; it is conducive, in a phrase of Holmes, to thinking things, not words, and thus to the evolution of principle by a process that tests as it creates.

Their insulation and the marvelous mystery of time give courts the capacity to appeal to men's better natures, to call forth their aspirations, which may have been forgotten in the moment's hue and cry. This is what Justice Stone called the opportunity for "the sober second thought." Hence it is that the courts, although they may somewhat dampen the people's and the legislatures' efforts to educate themselves, are also a great and highly effective educational institution. Judge Gibson, . . . highly critical as he was, took account of this. "In the business of government," he wrote, "a recurrence to first principles answers the end of an observation at sea with a view to correct the dead reckoning; and, for this purpose, a written constitution is an instrument of inestimable value. It is of inestimable value also, in rendering its principles familiar to the mass of the people. . . ." The educational institution that both takes the observation to correct the dead reckoning and makes it known is the voice of the Constitution: the Supreme Court exercising judicial review. The Justices, in Dean Rostow's phrase, "are inevitably teachers in a vital national seminar." No other branch of the American government is nearly so well equipped to conduct one. And such a seminar can do a great deal to keep our society from becoming so riven that no court will be able to save it. Of course, we have never quite been that society in which the spirit of moderation is so richly in flower that no court need save it.

Thus, as Professor Henry M. Hart, Jr., has written, and as surely most of the profession and of informed laity believe; for if not this, what and why?—thus the Court appears "predestined in the long run, not only by the thrilling tradition of Anglo-American law but also by the hard facts of its position in the structure of American institutions, to be a voice of reason, charged with the creative function of discerning afresh and of articulating and developing impersonal and durable principles. . . ." This line of thought may perhaps blunt, if it does not meet, the force of all the arguments on the other side. No doubt full consistency with democratic theory has not been established. The heart of the democratic faith is government by the consent of the governed. The further premise is not incompatible that the good society not only will want to satisfy the immediate needs of the greatest number but also will strive to support and maintain enduring general values. I have followed the view that the elected institutions are ill fitted, or not so well fitted as the courts, to perform the latter task. This rests on the assumption that the people themselves, by direct action at the ballot box, are surely incapable of sustaining a working system of general values specifically applied. But that much we assume throughout, being a representative, deliberative democracy. Matters of expediency are not generally submitted to direct referendum. Nor should matters of principle, which require even more intensive deliberation, be so submitted. Reference of specific policies to the people for initial decision is, with few exceptions, the fallacy of the misplaced mystics, or the way of those who would use the forms of democracy to undemocratic ends. It is not the way in which working democracies live. But democracies do live by the idea, central to the process of gaining the consent of the governed, that the majority has the ultimate power to displace the decision-makers and to reject any part of their policy. With that idea, judicial review must achieve some measure of consonance.

Democratic government under law—the slogan pulls in two opposed directions, but that does not keep it from being applicable to an operative polity. If it carries the elements of explosion, it doesn't contain a critical mass of them. Yet if the critical mass is not to be reached, there must be an accommodation, a degree of concord between the diverging elements. Having been checked, should the people persist; having been educated, should the people insist, must they not win over ever fundamental principle save one—which is the principle that they must win? Are we sufficiently certain of the permanent validity of any other principle to be ready to impose it against a consistent and determined majority, and could we do so for long? Have not the people the right of peaceable revolution, as assuredly, over time, they possess the capacity for a bloody one?

The premise of democracy is egalitarian, and, as Professor Herbert J. Muller has written, every bright sophomore knows how to punch holes in it. Yet, as Mr. Muller goes on to say, there is "no universal standard of superiority," there are no sure scales in which to weigh all the relevant virtues and capacities of men, and many a little man may rightly claim to be a better citizen than the expert or the genius. Moreover, and most significantly, "all men are in fact equal in respect of their common structure and their common destiny." Hence, to repeat the insight of Judge Hand, government must be their common venture. Who will think it moral ultimately to direct the lives of men against the will of the greater number of them? Or wise? "Man's historical experience should sober the revolutionaries who know the certain solution to our problems, and sober as well the traditionalists whose solution is a return to the ancient faiths, which have always failed in the past."

To bring judicial review into concord with such presuppositions requires a closer analysis of the actual operation of the process in various circumstances. The preliminary suggestions may be advanced that the rule of principle imposed by the Court is seldom rigid, that the Court has ways of persuading before it attempts to coerce, and that, over time, sustained opinion running counter to the Court's constitutional law can achieve its nullification, directly or by desuetude. It may further be that if the process is properly carried out, an aspect of the current—not only the timeless, mystic—popular will finds expression in constitutional adjudication. The result may be a tolerable accommodation with the theory and practice of democracy.

THE MYSTIC FUNCTION

This inquiry into a general justification of judicial review cannot end without taking account of a most suggestive and perceptive argument recently advanced by Professor Charles L. Black, Jr. It begins by emphasizing that the Court performs not only a checking function but also a legitimating one, as Mr. Black well calls it. Judicial review means not only that the Court may strike down a legislative action as unconstitutional but also that it may validate it as within constitutionally granted powers and as not violating constitutional limitations. Mr. Black contends, further, that the legitimating function would be impossible of performance if the checking function did not exist as well: what is the good of a declaration of validity from an institution which is by hypothesis required to validate everything that is brought before it? This is plainly so, though it is oddly stated. The picture is accurate, but it is stood on its head. The truth is that the legitimating function is an inescapable, even if unintended, by-product of the checking power. But what follows? What is the nature of this legitimating function, and what the need for it?

With a relish one can readily share, Mr. Black cites the story of the French intellectual who, upon arrival in New York harbor, exclaims: "It is wonderful to breathe the sweet air of legitimacy!" He contends essentially that what filled the Frenchman's lungs, what smelled to him so different from the succession of short-lived empires and republics endemic to his homeland, was the sweet odor of the Supreme Court of the United States. But I think it much simpler and nearer the reality of both the American and the French experience to begin with the proposition that legitimacy comes to a regime that is felt to be good and to have proven itself as such to generations past as well as in the present. Such a government must be principled as well as responsible; but it must be felt to be the one without having ceased to be the other, and unless it is responsible it cannot in fact be stable, and is not in my view morally supportable. Quite possibly, there have been governments that were electorally responsible and yet failed to attain stability. But that is not to say that they would have attained it by rendering themselves less responsible—that is, by divorcing the keepers of their principles from the electoral process. Legitimacy, being the stability of a good government over time, is the fruit of consent to specific actions or to the authority to act; the consent to the exercise of authority, whether or not approved in each instance, of as unified a population as possible, but most importantly, of a present majority.

Very probably, the stability of the American Republic is due in large part, as Professor Louis Hartz has eloquently argued, to the remarkable Lockeian consensus of a society that has never known a feudal regime; to a "moral unity" that was seriously broken only once, over the extension of slavery. This unity makes possible a society that accepts its principles from on high, without fighting about them. But the Lockeian consensus is also a limitation on the sort of principles that will be accepted. It is putting the cart before the horse to attribute the American sense of legitimacy to the institution of judicial review. The latter is more nearly the fruit of the former, although the "moral unity" must be made manifest, it must be renewed and sharpened and brought to bear—and this is an office that judicial review can discharge.

No doubt it is in the interest of the majority to obtain the acquiescence of the minority as often and in as great a degree as possible. And no doubt the Court can help bring about acquiescence by assuring those who have lost a political fight that merely momentary interest, not fundamental principle, was in play. Yet is it reasonable to assume that the majority would wish to see itself checked from time to time just to have an institution which, when it chooses to go along with the majority's will, is capable of helping to assuage the defeated minority? That is too much of an indirection. The checking power must find its own justification, particularly in a system which, in a number of important ways (e.g., the Senate's reflection of the federal structure, practices of legislative apportionment), offers prodigious political safeguards to the minority.

Thus the legitimating function of judicial review cannot be accepted as an independent justification for it. Yet it exists. Not only is the Supreme Court capable of generating consent for hotly controverted legislative or executive measures; it has the subtler power of adding a certain impetus to measures that the majority enacts rather tentatively. There are times when the majority might, because of strong minority feelings, be inclined in the end to deny itself, but when it comes to embrace a measure more firmly, and the minority comes to accept it, because the Court—intending perhaps no such consequence—has declared it consistent with constitutional principle. This tendency touches on Thayer's anxiety that judicial review will "dwarf the political capacity of the people" and "deaden its sense of moral responsibility." We shall return to it as a consideration that should cause the Court to stay its hand from time to time.

But the Supreme Court as a legitimating force in society also casts a less palpable yet larger spell. With us the symbol of nationhood, of continuity, of unity and common purpose, is, of course, the Constitution, without particular reference to what exactly it means in this or that application. The utility of such a symbol is a commonplace. Britain—the United Kingdom, and perhaps even the Commonwealth—is the most potent historical demonstration of the efficaciousness of a symbol, made concrete in the person of the Crown. The President in our system serves the function somewhat, but only very marginally, because the personification of unity must be above the political battle, and no President can fulfill his office while remaining above the battle. The effective Presidents have of necessity been men of power, and so it has in large part been left to the Supreme Court to concretize the symbol of the Constitution. Keeping in mind that this is offered as an observation, not as justification, it is surely true that the Court has been able to play the role partly—but only partly—by virtue of its power of judicial review.

The Court is seen as a continuum. It is never, like other institutions, renewed at a single stroke. No one or two changes on the Court, not even if they include the advent of a new Chief Justice, are apt to be as immediately momentous as a turnover in the presidency. To the extent that they are instruments of decisive change, Justices are time bombs, not warheads that explode on impact. There are exceptions, to be sure. In 1870, President Grant made two appointments that promptly resulted in the reversal of a quite crucial recent decision concerning the monetary powers of the federal government. And it may seem that strong new doctrine became ascendant soon after the first of President Roosevelt's appointees, Mr. Justice Black, came on the Bench in 1937. But on the whole, the movements of the Court are not sudden and not suddenly affected by new appointments. Continuity is a chief concern of the Court, as it is the main reason for the Court's place in the hearts of its countrymen.

No doubt, the Court's symbolic—or, if you will, mystic—function would not have been possible, would not have reached the stage at which we now see it, if the Court did not exercise the power of judicial review. It could scarcely personify the Constitution unless it had the authority finally to speak of it. But as the symbol manifests itself today, it seems not always to depend on judicial review. It seems at times to have as much to do with the life tenure of the Court's members and with the fact of the long government service of some of them, not only on the Court; in short, with the total impression of continuity personified.

Here the human chain goes back unbroken in a small, intimate group to the earliest beginnings. Take two recent retirements. Mr. Justice Minton, who left in October 1956, was a fire-eating New Deal Senator, and when he retired from the Court men no doubt remembered his stance in the 'thirties and thought, perhaps a little self-deprecatingly, of the emotions it had aroused. Mr. Justice Reed, who retired early in 1957, had, some twenty years earlier, when he was Solicitor General, argued a number of celebrated New Deal cases. His was the second of President Franklin Roosevelt's appointments, and he sat with Hughes and Brandeis and McReynolds. When McReynolds went, in 1941, a remembrance of the Wilson era and of trust-busting in the early 1900's went with him. Justice Van Devanter, a contemporary of McReynolds who retired in 1937, had been appointed by Taft, had held office under McKinley, and had sat with appointees of Cleveland and of Hayes. And so on back.

Senior members of the Court are witnesses to the reality and validity of our present—distracted, improbable, illegitimate as it often appears—because in their persons they assure us of its link to the past which they also witnessed and in which they were themselves once the harbingers of something outrageously new. This is true not only of those who are constructive and creative; it is true of Justices who oppose all that is not as they knew it. Say what they will, their very existence among us reassures us. When the great Holmes, who was wounded at Ball's Bluff and at Antietam, retired in 1932, being past ninety, the emotional public response was not due wholly to his undoubted greatness. It was also that his years, his years alone, fulfilled one of the functions of the Supreme Court.

37

C. HERMAN PRITCHETT

LIBERTARIAN MOTIVATIONS ON THE VINSON COURT

Justice Frankfurter is fond of quoting an old English saying that "the devil himself knoweth not the mind of men." The mind of a man who happens to be a judge is the center of many contending impulses when he is making it up, and an external reconstruction of the process is quite impossible. However, the rules of the game require that judges supply clues to their thought processes in the form of written opinions. In every major case decided by the Supreme Court, one or more of its members provided a written justification for the decision announced. The individualistic tradition of Anglo-Saxon jurisprudence, moreover, permits justices who do not agree with the views of their brethren to say so, and to give their reasons for dissenting. Thus the Supreme Court on decision day takes on the aspect of a small legislature in which votes are cast pro and con on significant issues of public policy, with accompanying explanations much more coherent and systematic and better-reasoned than are customarily available in explanation of votes cast, say, in the United States Senate.

While it has not been usual to do so, these judicial votes can be subjected to the same kinds of analysis as have been traditionally employed for the study of legislative voting behavior. Thus Table 37-1 undertakes to throw light on the attitudes of members of the recent Court toward civil liberties claims by recording their votes as favoring or opposing the claimed liberties in some 84 nonunanimous cases decided during the six terms from October, 1946 to June, 1952.

Such a table is useful, however, only if the analyst has some tenable hypothesis about the nature of the relations between a justice's decisions and his personal convictions. It would be naive to assume that justices in deciding cases are completely free to vote their own preferences, or that a voting record necessarily mirrors a justice's inner convictions. On the other hand, it would be even more naive to assume that a Supreme Court justice merely "looks up the law" on a subject and applies it to the case in hand.

A workable hypothesis on Supreme Court decision-making must be formulated with an appreciation of the operating conditions under which the judge makes his choices. In many respects his situation is quite comparable with that

TABLE 37-1. VOTING RECORDS OF JUSTICES IN NONUNANIMOUS CIVIL LIBERTIES
DECISIONS, 1946–51 TERMS

	No. Cases	For Free Speech Claims	For Alien Claims	For Criminal Defendants' Claims		Total
				FEDERAL	STATE	
NO. CASES		23	18	17	26	84
Murphy	42	100%	100%	100%	100%	100%
Rutledge	43	100	100	85	100	95
Douglas	72	100	64	87	96	89
Black	83	96	100	53	88	86
Frankfurter	82	50	76	82	42	60
Majority	84	26	33	53	37	37
Jackson	82	23	44	59	13	32
Clark	23	13	0	33	38	22
Burton	84	17	28	18	15	19
Minton	36	19	18	0	17	17
Vinson	84	13	33	0	12	14
Reed	84	22	6	12	12	13

of any individual who must make decisions on important matters within an institutional framework which brings to him questions for decision and provides mechanisms for making those decisions effective. Appellate courts share with legislatures the problem of decision-making in a collectivity of equals, in contrast to the conditions of decision-making in a hierarchy. We may tend to think of legislators as having greater freedom than judges in arriving at policy choices, but upon reflection it becomes obvious that legislators no more than judges are able to vote as free agents. They must think about what is good for their party. They must give some account of the probable effect of their vote on the prospects for reelection. They may decide to vote for something they do not want in order to get support for something they want very much. They may decide to vote for less than they want because their practical judgment tells them that is all they can get.

A Supreme Court justice finds himself in much the same situation, though operating within a judicial rather than a legislative context does make for some differences. He does not have a constituency of electors or a party position to consider. But the rules and traditions of the Court supply institutional preferences with which his own preferences must compete. One of these institutional preferences, for example, is *stare decisis*, the rule of precedent. The individual judge may think that the precedents are wrong, or outmoded. If so, he may follow his personal preference and state his reasons for voting to change the law. He is free to do that. He is not free to ignore the precedents, to act as though they did not exist. He has free choice, but among limited alternatives and only after he has satisfied himself that he has met the obligations of consistency and respect for settled principles which his responsibility to the Court imposes upon him.

His private views as an individual help to form and may be incorporated into his public views as a justice, but they are not the same thing.

What this means, in more concrete terms, is that when a civil liberties case comes to the Supreme Court, the justices are not asked whether they are more or less in favor of civil liberties. They are asked how the Court, consistently with its role as the highest judicial body in a federal system, should dispose of a proceeding, the basic facts in which have been found and the form of which has been given by lower judicial bodies. Under these circumstances some justices may not even choose to think of the civil liberties issue in the case. They may see the controlling problem as adherence or non-adherence to the precedents. They may think of the issue as judicial respect for legislative action. As participants in the judicial process they have a perfect right to choose from among the alternatives presented the ones which determine their view of the case.

Thus it is that a statistical table or "box score" such as Table 37-1 cannot be accepted as an index of personal attachment to libertarian values on the part of the justices. These votes were cast, not in their personal but in their judicial capacity, and represented their resolution of situations where many legitimate values may have been competing for attention. What the table does establish is the degree to which each member of the Court found it possible or desirable as a judge to prefer libertarian values over others present in the proceedings. These are what Mark DeWolfe Howe calls "relational statistics," and while Howe is a bitter critic of the statistical method as applied to judicial decisions, he is willing to admit that if interpreted on this basis box scores may be acceptable. But he adds the warning that relational statistics "have significance only when discriminating account is taken of all the values which are brought into relationship."

Obviously it is impossible to identify all the values which each justice may have related to the decision of a case. But our working hypothesis is that a decision involving civil liberties questions will be primarily influenced by the interaction of two factors. One is the direction and intensity of a justice's libertarian sympathies, which will vary according to his weighting of the relative claims of liberty and order in our society. Theoretically, positions on a liberty-order attitude scale could range from an individualist anarchism at one extreme to rigid authoritarianism on the other. The orthodoxy required for a Supreme Court appointment ensures, however, that the spread of opinion among members of that body will be much narrower.

The second factor is the conception which the justice holds of his judicial role and the obligations imposed on him by his judicial function. Every justice in deciding a case must give some thought to what is appropriate for him as a judge to do. The pressures which bear upon him are many, and they are mostly toward a pattern of conformity—conformity with precedents, conformity with the traditions of the law, conformity with public expectations as to how a judge should act, conformity toward established divisions of authority in a federal system based on the principle of separation of powers. While no justice can be oblivious to these pressures, they are not self-enforcing, and he is free to make his own interpretations of their requirements in guiding his own judicial conduct. The attitude scale involved may be thought of as ranging from an expansionist to a contractionist judicial philosophy, from broad to narrow judicial review, from judicial activism to judicial restraint.

Any attempt to rank justices on these two scales in an absolute fashion would be hopeless, but it should not be as difficult to locate them relatively to each other, and particularly by reference to their deviation from the Court's majority position at any one time. Table 37-1 shows that five members of the Vinson Court—Murphy, Rutledge, Douglas, Black, and Frankfurter—voted for libertarian claims substantially more often than the Court majority. In the terms of our hypothesis, the extremely high rate of support for libertarian claims registered by the first four of these justices suggests that they are strongly positive on both scales; their personal preferences must be strongly libertarian, and they must have a conception of their judicial function which permits or even requires them to give judicial effect to their libertarian preferences. Without assuming any absolute identity of views on their part, the motivation of these four justices can be characterized as libertarian activism.

38

MARBURY V. MADISON (1803)

Mr. Chief Justice Marshall delivered the opinion of the Court:

At the last term on the affidavits then read and filed with the clerk, a rule was granted in this case, requiring the secretary of state to show cause why a *mandamus* should not issue, directing him to deliver to William Marbury his commission as a justice of the peace for the county of Washington, in the District of Columbia.

No cause has been shown, and the present motion is for a *mandamus*. The peculiar delicacy of this case, the novelty of some of its circumstances, and the real difficulty attending the points which occur in it, require a complete exposition of the principles on which the opinion to be given by the Court is founded.

These principles have been, on the side of the applicant, very ably argued at the bar. In rendering the opinion of the Court, there will be some departure in form, though not in substance, from the points stated in that argument.

In the order in which the Court has viewed this subject, the following questions have been considered and decided.

1st. Has the applicant a right to the commission he demands?

2d. If he has a right, and that right has been violated, do the laws of his country afford him a remedy?

3d. If they do afford him a remedy, is it a *mandamus* issuing from this Court?

The first object of inquiry is,

Has the applicant a right to the commission he demands? . . .

It is . . . decidedly the opinion of the Court, that when a commission has been signed by the president, the appointment is made; and that the commission is complete when the seal of the United States has been affixed to it by the secretary of state.

Just before leaving office, President John Adams appointed William Marbury to the post of justice of the peace in Washington, D.C. However, in the presidential transition, Marbury failed to receive his commission—a legal document enabling him to exercise the authority of that position. After taking office, the new secretary of state, James Madison, refused to deliver the commission and was sued by Marbury. The technical issue before the Supreme Court involved section 13 of the Judiciary Act of 1789. The act gave the Supreme Court original jurisdiction and authority to issue writs of mandamus in such cases. The latter are binding legal directives issued to members of the executive branch. The political problem facing the Court was the very real prospect that for partisan reasons Madison would ignore such a writ, if issued. The Court's decision was to declare section 13 unconstitutional because it expanded the Court's original jurisdiction, which was established by the Constitution. Thus, the Court asserted the power of judicial review and avoided confrontation with the executive branch, but left Marbury without his commission.—Eds.

Where an officer is removable at the will of the executive, the circumstance which completes his appointment is of no concern; because the act is at any time revocable; and the commission may be arrested, if still in the office. But when the officer is not removable at the will of the executive, the appointment is not revocable, and cannot be annulled. It has conferred legal rights which cannot be resumed.

The discretion of the executive is to be exercised, until the appointment has been made. But having once made the appointment, his power over the office is terminated, in all cases where, by law, the officer is not removable by him. The right to the office is then in the person appointed, and he has the absolute unconditional power of accepting or rejecting it.

Mr. Marbury, then, since his commission was signed by the president, and sealed by the secretary of state, was appointed; and as the law creating the office, gave the officer a right to hold for five years, independent of the executive, the appointment was not revocable, but vested in the officer legal rights, which are protected by the laws of his country.

To withhold his commission, therefore, is an act deemed by the Court not warranted by law, but violative of a vested legal right.

This brings us to the second inquiry; which is,

If he has a right, and that right has been violated, do the laws of this country afford him a remedy?

The very essence of civil liberty certainly consists in the right of every individual to claim the protection of the laws, whenever he receives an injury. One of the first duties of government is to afford that protection. . . .

The government of the United States has been emphatically termed a government of laws, and not of men. It will certainly cease to deserve this high appellation, if the laws furnish no remedy for the violation of a vested legal right.

If this obloquy is to be cast on the jurisprudence of our country, it must arise from the peculiar character of the case.

It behooves us, then, to inquire whether there be in its composition any ingredient which shall exempt it from legal investigation, or exclude the injured party from legal redress. . . .

Is it in the nature of the transaction? Is the act of delivering or withholding a commission to be considered as a mere political act, belonging to the executive department alone, for the performance of which entire confidence is placed by our Constitution in the supreme executive; and for any misconduct respecting which, the injured individual has no remedy? That there may be such cases is not to be questioned; but that every act of duty, to be performed in any of the great departments of government, constitutes such a case, is not to be admitted. . . .

It follows, then, that the question, whether the legality of an act of the head of a department be examinable in a court of justice or not, must always depend on the nature of that act.

If some acts be examinable, and others not, there must be some rule of law to guide the court in the exercise of its jurisdiction.

In some instances, there may be difficulty in applying the rule to particular cases; but there cannot, it is believed, be much difficulty in laying down the rule.

By the Constitution of the United States, the president is invested with certain important political powers, in the exercise of which he is to use his own discretion, and is accountable only to his country in his political character and to his own conscience. To aid him in the performance of these duties, he is authorized to appoint certain officers, who act by his authority, and in conformity with his orders.

In such cases, their acts are his acts; and whatever opinion may be entertained of the manner in which executive discretion may be used, still there exists, and can exist, no power to control that discretion. The subjects are political. They respect the nation, not individual rights, and being intrusted to the executive, the decision of the executive is conclusive. The application of this remark will be perceived by adverting to the act of Congress for establishing the department of foreign affairs. This officer, as his duties were prescribed by that act, is to conform precisely to the will of the president. He is the mere organ by whom that will is communicated. The acts of such an officer, as an officer, can never be examinable by the courts.

But when the legislature proceeds to impose on that officer other duties; when he is directed peremptorily to perform certain acts; when the rights of individuals are dependent on the performance of those acts; he is so far the officer of the law; is amenable to the laws for his conduct; and cannot at his discretion sport away the vested rights of others.

The conclusion from this reasoning is, that where the heads of departments are the political or confidential agents of the executive, merely to execute the will of the president, or rather to act in cases in which the executive possesses a constitutional or legal discretion, nothing can be more perfectly clear than that their acts are only politically examinable. But where a specific duty is assigned by law, and individual rights depend upon the performance of that duty, it seems equally clear that the individual who considers himself injured, has a right to resort to the laws of his country for a remedy. . . .

It is, then, the opinion of the Court,

1st. That by signing the commission of Mr. Marbury, the president of the United States appointed him a justice of peace for the county of Washington, in the District of Columbia; and that the seal of the United States, affixed thereto by the secretary of state, is conclusive testimony of the verity of the signature, and of the completion of the appointment, and that the appointment conferred on him a legal right to the office for the space of five years.

2dly. That, having this legal title to the office, he has a consequent right to the commission; a refusal to deliver which is a plain violation of that right, for which the laws of his country afford him a remedy.

It remains to be inquired whether,

3dly. Is he entitled to the remedy for which he applies?

This depends on—1st. The nature of the writ applied for; and 2dly. The power of this court.

The nature of the writ. . . .

This writ, if awarded, would be directed to an officer of government, and its mandate to him would be, to use the words of Blackstone, "to do a particular thing therein specified, which appertains to his office and duty, and which the court has previously determined, or at least supposes, to be consonant to right and justice." Or, in the words of Lord Mansfield, the applicant, in this case, has a right to execute an office of public concern, and is kept out of possession of that right.

These circumstances certainly concur in this case.

Still, to render the *mandamus* a proper remedy, the officer to whom it is to be directed, must be one to whom, on legal principles, such writ may be directed; and the person applying for it must be without any other specific and legal remedy.

With respect to the officer to whom it would be directed.

The intimate political relation subsisting between the president of the United States and the heads of departments, necessarily renders any legal investigation of the acts of one of those high officers peculiarly irksome, as well as delicate; and excites some hesitation with respect to the propriety of entering into such investigation. Impressions are often received without much reflection or examination, and it is not wonderful that in such a case as this the assertion, by an individual, of his legal claims in a court of justice, to which claims it is the duty of that court to attend, should at first view be considered by some, as an attempt to intrude into the cabinet, and to intermeddle with the prerogatives of the executive.

It is scarcely necessary for the court to disclaim all pretentions to such jurisdiction. An extravagance, so absurd and excessive, could not have been entertained for a moment. The province of the court is, solely, to decide on the rights of individuals, not to inquire how the executive, or executive officers, perform duties in which they have a discretion. Questions in their nature political, or which are, by the Constitution and laws, submitted to the executive, can never be made in this Court.

But, if this be not such a question; if, so far from being an intrusion into the secrets of the cabinet, it respects a paper which, according to law, is upon record, and to a copy of which the law gives a right, on the payment of ten cents; if it be no intermeddling with a subject over which the executive can be considered as having exercised any control; what is there in the exalted station of the officer, which shall bar a citizen from asserting, in a court of justice, his legal rights, or shall forbid a court to listen to the claim, or to issue a *mandamus* directing the performance of a duty, not depending on executive discretion, but on particular acts of Congress, and the general principles of law?

. . . [W]here [the head of a department] is directed by law to do a certain act affecting the absolute rights of individuals, in the performance of which he is not placed under the particular direction of the president, and the performance of which the president cannot lawfully forbid, and therefore is never presumed to have forbidden; as for example to record a commission, or a patent for land, which has received all the legal solemnities; or to give a copy of such record; in such cases, it is not perceived on what ground the courts of the country are further excused from the duty of giving judgment that right be done to an injured individual, than if the same services were to be performed by a person not the head of a department. . . .

This, then, is a plain case for a *mandamus*, either to deliver the commission, or a copy of it from the record; and it only remains to be inquired,

Whether it can issue from this Court.

The act to establish the judicial courts of the United States authorizes the Supreme Court "to issue writs of *mandamus* in cases warranted by the principles and usages of law, to any courts appointed, or persons holding office, under the authority of the United States."

The secretary of state, being a person holding an office under the authority of the United States, is precisely within the letter of the description, and if this court is not authorized to issue a writ of *mandamus* to such an officer, it must be because the law is unconstitutional, and therefore absolutely incapable of conferring the authority, and assigning the duties which its words purport to confer and assign.

The Constitution vests the whole judicial power of the United States in one Supreme Court, and such inferior courts as Congress shall, from time to time, ordain and establish. This power is expressly extended to all cases arising under the laws of the United States; and, consequently, in some form, may be exercised over the present case; because the right claimed is given by a law of the United States.

In the distribution of this power it is declared that "the Supreme Court shall have original jurisdiction in all cases affecting ambassadors, other public ministers and consuls, and those in which a state shall be a party. In all other cases, the Supreme Court shall have appellate jurisdiction."

It has been insisted, at the bar, that as the original grant of jurisdiction, to the Supreme and inferior courts, is general, and the clause, assigning original jurisdiction to the Supreme Court, contains no negative or restrictive words, the power remains to the legislature, to assign original jurisdiction to that Court in other cases than those specified in the article which has been recited; provided those cases belong to the judicial power of the United States.

If it had been intended to leave it in the discretion of the legislature to apportion the judicial power between the supreme and inferior courts according to the will of that body, it would certainly have been useless to have proceeded further than to have defined the judicial power, and the tribunals in which it should be vested. The subsequent part of the section is mere surplusage, is entirely without meaning, if such is to be the construction. If Congress remains at liberty to give this Court appellate jurisdiction, where the Constitution has declared their jurisdiction shall be original; and original jurisdiction where the Constitution has declared it shall be appellate; the distribution of jurisdiction, made in the Constitution, is form without substance.

Affirmative words are often, in their operation, negative of other objects than those affirmed; and in this case, a negative or exclusive sense must be given to them, or they have no operation at all.

It cannot be presumed that any clause in the Constitution is intended to be without effect; and, therefore, such a construction is inadmissible, unless the words require it.

If the solicitude of the convention, respecting our peace with foreign powers, induced a provision that the Supreme Court should take original jurisdiction in cases which might be supposed to affect them; yet the clause would have proceeded no further than to provide for such cases, if no further restriction on the powers of Congress had been intended. That they should have appellate jurisdiction in all other cases, with such exceptions as Congress might make, is no restriction; unless the words be deemed exclusive of original jurisdiction. . . .

To enable this court, then, to issue a *mandamus*, it must be shown to be an exercise of appellate jurisdiction, or to be necessary to enable them to exercise appellate jurisdiction. . . .

It is the essential criterion of appellate jurisdiction, that it revises and corrects the proceedings in a cause already instituted, and does not create that cause. Although, therefore, a *mandamus* may be directed to courts, yet to issue such a writ to an officer for the delivery of a paper, is in effect the same as to sustain an original action for that paper, and, therefore, seems not to belong to appellate but to original jurisdiction. Neither is it necessary in such a case as this, to enable the Court to exercise its appellate jurisdiction.

The authority, therefore, given to the Supreme Court, by the act establishing the judicial courts of the United States, to issue writs of *mandamus* to public officers, appears not to be warranted by the Constitution; and it becomes necessary to inquire whether a jurisdiction so conferred can be exercised.

The question, whether an act, repugnant to the Constitution, can become the law of the land, is a question deeply interesting to the United States; but, happily, not of an intricacy proportioned to its interest. It seems only necessary to recognize certain principles, supposed to have been long and well established, to decide it.

That the people have an original right to establish, for their future government, such principles, as, in their opinion, shall most conduce to their own happiness is the basis on which the whole American fabric has been erected. The exercise of this original right is a very great exertion; nor can it, nor ought it, to be frequently repeated. The principles, therefore, so established, are deemed fundamental. And as the authority from which they proceed is supreme, and can seldom act, they are designed to be permanent.

This original and supreme will organizes the government, and assigns to different departments their respective powers. It may either stop here, or establish certain limits not to be transcended by those departments.

The government of the United States is of the latter description. The powers of the legislature are defined and limited; and that those limits may not be mistaken, or forgotten, the Constitution is written. To what purpose are powers limited, and to what purpose is that limitation committed to writing, if these limits may, at any time, be passed by those intended to be restrained? The distinction between a government with limited and unlimited powers is abolished, if those limits do not confine the persons on whom they are imposed, and if acts prohibited and acts allowed, are of equal obligation. It is a proposition too plain to be contested, that the Constitution controls any legislative act repugnant to it; or, that the legislature may alter the Constitution by an ordinary act.

Between these alternatives there is no middle ground. The Constitution is either a superior paramount law, unchangeable by ordinary means, or it is on a level with ordinary legislative acts, and, like other acts, is alterable when the legislature shall please to alter it.

If the former part of the alternative be true, then a legislative act contrary to the Constitution is not law: if the latter part be true, then written constitutions are absurd attempts, on the part of the people, to limit a power in its own nature illimitable.

Certainly all those who have framed written constitutions contemplate them as forming the fundamental and paramount law of the nation, and, consequently, the theory of every such government must be, that an act of the legislature, repugnant to the Constitution, is void.

This theory is essentially attached to a written Constitution, and is, consequently, to be considered, by this Court, as one of the fundamental principles of our society. It is not therefore to be lost sight of in the further consideration of this subject.

If an act of the legislature, repugnant to the Constitution, is void, does it, notwithstanding its invalidity, bind the courts, and oblige them to give it effect? Or, in other words, though it be not law, does it constitute a rule as operative as if it was a law? This would be to overthrow in fact what was established in theory; and would seem, at first view, an absurdity too gross to be insisted on. It shall, however, receive a more attentive consideration.

It is emphatically the province and duty of the judicial department to say what the law is. Those who apply the rule to particular cases, must of necessity expound and interpret that rule. If two laws conflict with each other, the courts must decide on the operation of each.

So if a law be in opposition to the Constitution; if both the law and the Constitution apply to a particular case, so that the court must either decide that case conformably to the law, disregarding the Constitution; or conformably to the Constitution, disregarding the law; the court must determine which of these conflicting rules governs the case. This is of the very essence of judicial duty.

If, then, the courts are to regard the Constitution, and the Constitution is superior to any ordinary act of the legislature, the Constitution, and not such ordinary act, must govern the case to which they both apply.

Those, then, who controvert the principle that the Constitution is to be considered, in court, as a paramount law, are reduced to the necessity of maintaining that courts must close their eyes on the Constitution, and see only the law.

This doctrine would subvert the very foundation of all written constitutions. It would declare that an act which, according to the principles and theory of our government, is entirely void, is yet, in practice, completely obligatory. It would declare that if the legislatures shall do what is expressly forbidden, such act, notwithstanding the express prohibition, is in reality effectual. It would be giving to the legislature a practical and real omnipotence, with the same breath which professes to restrict their powers within narrow limits. It is prescribing limits, and declaring that those limits may be passed at pleasure.

That it thus reduces to nothing what we have deemed the greatest improvement on political institutions, a written constitution, would of itself be sufficient, in America, where written constitutions have been viewed with so much reverence, for rejecting the construction. But the peculiar expressions of the Constitution of the United States furnish additional arguments in favour of its rejection.

The judicial power of the United States is extended to all cases arising under the Constitution.

Could it be the intention of those who gave this power, to say that in using it the Constitution should not be looked into? That a case arising under the Constitution should be decided without examining the instrument under which it arises?

This is too extravagant to be maintained.

In some cases, then, the Constitution must be looked into by the judges. And if they can open it at all, what part of it are they forbidden to read or to obey?

There are many other parts of the Constitution which serve to illustrate this subject.

It is declared that "no tax or duty shall be laid on articles exported from any state." Suppose a duty on the export of cotton, of tobacco, or of flour; and a suit instituted to recover it. Ought judgment to be rendered in such a case? Ought the judges to close their eyes on the Constitution, and only see the law?

The Constitution declares "that no bill of attainder or *ex post facto* law shall be passed."

If, however, such a bill should be passed, and a person should be prosecuted under it; must the Court condemn to death those victims whom the Constitution endeavors to preserve?

"No person," says the Constitution, "shall be convicted of treason unless on the testimony of two witnesses to the same overt act, or on confession in open court."

Here the language of the Constitution is addressed especially to the courts. It prescribes, directly for them, a rule of evidence not to be departed from. If the legislature should change that rule, and declare *one* witness, or a confession *out* of court, sufficient for conviction, must the constitutional principle yield to the legislative act?

From these, and many other selections which might be made, it is apparent, that the framers of the Constitution contemplated that instrument as a rule for the government of courts, as well as of the legislature.

Why otherwise does it direct the judges to take an oath to support it? This oath certainly applies in an especial manner, to their conduct in their official character. How immoral to impose it on them, if they were to be used as the instruments, and the knowing instruments, for violating what they swear to support! . . .

It is also not entirely unworthy of observation, that in declaring what shall be the *supreme* law of the land, the *Constitution* itself is first mentioned; and not the laws of the United States generally, but those only which shall be made in *pursuance* of the Constitution, have that rank.

Thus, the particular phraseology of the Constitution of the United States confirms and strengthens the principle, supposed to be essential to all written constitutions, that a law repugnant to the Constitution is void; and that courts, as well as other departments, are bound by that instrument.

The rule must be

Discharged.

39

McCulloch v. Maryland (1819)

Mr. Chief Justice Marshall delivered the opinion of the Court:

The first question . . . is: Has Congress power to incorporate a bank?

It has been truly said, that this can scarcely be considered as an open question, entirely unprejudiced by the former proceedings of the nation respecting it. The principle now contested was introduced at a very early period of our history, has been recognized by many successive legislatures, and has been acted upon by the judicial department, in cases of peculiar delicacy, as a law of undoubted obligation. . . .

The power now contested was exercised by the first Congress elected under the present Constitution. The bill for incorporating the Bank of the United States did not steal upon an unsuspecting legislature, and pass unobserved. Its principle was completely understood, and was opposed with equal zeal and ability. After being resisted, first in the fair and open field of debate, and afterwards in the executive cabinet, with as much persevering talent as any measure has ever experienced, and being supported by arguments which convinced minds as pure and as intelligent as this country can boast, it became a law. The original act was permitted to expire; but a short experience of the embarrassments to which the refusal to revive it exposed the government, convinced those who were most prejudiced against the measure of its necessity, and induced the passage of the present law. It would require no ordinary share of intrepidity to assert, that a measure adopted under these circumstances, was a bold and plain usurpation, to which the Constitution gave no countenance. . . .

In discussing this question, the counsel for the state of Maryland have deemed it of some importance, in the construction of the Constitution, to consider that instrument not as emanating from the people, but as the act of sovereign and independent states. The powers of the general government, it has been said, are delegated by the states, who alone are truly sovereign; and must be exercised in subordination to the states, who alone possess supreme dominion.

. . . It would be difficult to sustain this proposition. The convention which framed the Constitution was, indeed, elected by the state legislatures. But the

The question whether in the absence of specific constitutional authorization the federal government could establish a national bank had been an issue since the 1790s. In 1818 Maryland directly confronted the Bank of the United States, established by Congress in 1816, by requiring that all banks not chartered in that state pay a fee or tax for the issuance of bank notes. The cashier of the Baltimore branch of the Bank of the United States, James McCulloch, refused to pay the required tax and was convicted of violating the law by the Maryland courts. His case was appealed to the U.S. Supreme Court, where Chief Justice Marshall delivered a wide-ranging discourse on the nature of Congress's constitutional powers and the states' limited sovereignty.—Eds.

instrument, when it came from their hands, was a mere proposal, without obligation, or pretensions to it. It was reported to the then existing Congress of the United States, with a request that it might "be submitted to a convention of delegates, chosen in each state by the people thereof, under the recommendation of its legislature, for their assent and ratification." This mode of proceeding was adopted; and by the convention, by Congress, and by the state legislatures, the instrument was submitted to the *people*. They acted upon it, in the only manner in which they can act safely, effectively, and wisely, on such a subject by assembling in convention. It is true, they assembled in their several states; and where else should they have assembled? No political dreamer was ever wild enough to think of breaking down the lines which separate the states, and of compounding the American people into one common mass. Of consequence, when they act, they act in their states. But the measures they adopt do not, on that account, cease to be the measures of the people themselves, or become the measures of the state governments. . . .

It has been said that the people had already surrendered all their powers to the state sovereignties, and had nothing more to give. But, surely, the question whether they may resume and modify the powers granted to government, does not remain to be settled in this country. Much more might the legitimacy of the general government be doubted, had it been created by the states. The powers delegated to the state sovereignties were to be exercised by themselves, not by a distinct and independent sovereignty, created by themselves. To the formation of a league, such as was the confederation, the state sovereignties were certainly competent. But when, "in order to form a more perfect union," it was deemed necessary to change this alliance into an effective government, possessing great and sovereign powers, and acting directly on the people, the necessity of referring it to the people, and of deriving its powers directly from them, was felt and acknowledged by all.

The government of the Union, then (whatever may be the influence of this fact on the case), is emphatically and truly a government of the people. In form and in substance it emanates from them, its powers are granted by them, and are to be exercised directly on them, and for their benefit.

This government is acknowledged by all to be one of enumerated powers. . . . But the question respecting the extent of the powers actually granted, is perpetually arising, and will probably continue to rise, as long as our system shall exist. In discussing these questions, the conflicting powers of the general and state governments must be brought into view, and the supremacy of their respective laws, when they are in opposition, must be settled.

If any one proposition could command the universal assent of mankind, we might expect that it would be this—that the government of the Union, though limited in its powers, is supreme within its sphere of action. This would seem to result, necessarily, from its nature. It is the government of all; its powers are delegated by all; it represents all, and acts for all. Though any one state may be willing to control its operations, no state is willing to allow others to control them. The nation, on those subjects on which it can act, must necessarily bind its component parts. But this question is not left to mere reason: the people have, in express terms, decided it, by saying, "this Constitution, and the laws of the United States, which shall be made in pursuance thereof," "shall be the supreme law of the land," and by requiring that the members of the state legislatures, and the officers of the executive and judicial departments of the states, shall take the oath of fidelity to it.

The government of the United States, then, though limited in its powers, is supreme; and its laws, when made in pursuance of the Constitution, form the supreme law of the land, "anything in the constitution or laws of any state, to the contrary notwithstanding."

Among the enumerated powers, we do not find that of establishing a bank or creating a corporation. But there is no phrase in the instrument which, like the Articles of Confederation, excludes incidental or implied powers; and which requires that everything granted shall be expressly and minutely described. Even the Tenth Amendment, which was framed for the purpose of quieting the excessive jealousies which had been excited, omits the word "expressly," and declares only that the powers "not delegated to the United States, nor prohibited to the states, are reserved to the states or to the people"; thus leaving the question, whether the particular power which may become the subject of contest, has been delegated to the one government, or prohibited to the other, to depend on a fair construction of the whole instrument. The men who drew and adopted this amendment had experienced the embarrassments resulting from the insertion of this word in the Articles of Confederation, and probably omitted it, to avoid those embarrassments. A constitution, to contain an accurate detail of all the subdivisions of which its great powers will admit, and of all the means by which they may be carried into execution, would partake of the prolixity of a legal code, and could scarcely be embraced by the human mind. It would, probably, never be understood by the public. Its nature, therefore, requires, that only its great outlines should be marked, its important objects designated, and the minor ingredients which compose those objects, be deduced from the nature of the objects themselves. That this idea was entertained by the framers of the American Constitution, is not only to be inferred from the nature of the instrument, but from the language. Why else were some of the limitations, found in the ninth section of Article I, introduced? It is also, in some degree, warranted, by their having omitted to use any restrictive term which might prevent its receiving a fair and just interpretation. In considering this question, then, we must never forget, that it is a *constitution* we are expounding.

Although, among the enumerated powers of government, we do not find the word "bank," or "incorporation," we find the great powers, to lay and collect taxes; to borrow money; to regulate commerce; to declare and conduct war; and to raise and support armies and navies. The sword and the purse, all the external relations, and no inconsiderable portion of the industry of the nation, are intrusted to its government. It can never be pretended, that these vast powers draw after them others of inferior importance, merely because they are inferior. Such an idea can never be advanced. But it may with great reason be contended, that a government, intrusted with such ample powers, on the due execution of which the happiness and prosperity of the nation so vitally depends, must also be intrusted with ample means for their execution. The power being given, it is the interest of the nation to facilitate its execution. It can never be their interest, and cannot be presumed to have been their intention, to clog and embarrass its execution, by withholding the most appropriate means. Throughout this vast republic . . . , from the Atlantic to the Pacific, revenue is to be collected and expended, armies are to be marched and supported. The exigencies of the nation may require, that the treasure raised in the north should be transported to the south, that raised in the east, conveyed to the west, or that this order should be reversed. Is that construction of the Constitution to be preferred, which would render these operations difficult, hazardous, and expensive? Can we adopt that construction (unless the words imperiously require it), which would impute to the framers of that instrument, when granting these powers for the public good, the intention of impeding their exercise by withholding a choice of means? If, indeed, such be the mandate of the Constitution, we have only to obey; but that instrument does not profess to enumerate the means by which the powers it confers may be executed; nor does it prohibit the creation of a corporation, if the existence of such a being be essential to the beneficial exercise of those powers. It is, then, the subject of fair inquiry, how far such means may be employed. . . .

The creation of a corporation, it is said, appertains to sovereignty. This is admitted. But to what portion of sovereignty does it appertain? Does it belong to one more than to another? . . . The power of creating a corporation, though appertaining to sovereignty, is not, like the power of making war, or levying taxes, or of regulating commerce, a great substantive and independent power, which cannot be implied as incidental to other powers, or used as a means of executing them. It is never the end for which other powers are exercised, but a means by which other objects are accomplished. No contributions are made to charity for the sake of an incorporation, but a corporation is created to administer the charity; no seminary of learning is instituted in order to be incorporated, but the corporate character is conferred to subserve the purposes of education. . . . The power of creating a corporation is never used for its own sake, but for the purpose of effecting something else. No sufficient reason is, therefore, perceived, why it may not pass as incidental to those powers which are expressly given, if it be a direct mode of executing them.

But the Constitution of the United States has not left the right of Congress to employ the necessary means for the execution of the powers conferred on the government to general reasoning. To its enumeration of powers is added that of making "all laws which shall be necessary and proper, for carrying into execution the foregoing powers, and all other powers vested by this Constitution, in the government of the United States, or in any department thereof."

The counsel for the state of Maryland have urged . . . that this clause, though in terms a grant of power, is not so in effect; but is really restrictive of the general right, which might otherwise be implied, of selecting means for executing the enumerated powers. . . .

. . . [T]he argument on which most reliance is placed, is drawn from the peculiar language of this clause. Congress is not empowered by it to make all laws, which may have relation to the powers conferred on the government, but such only as may be "necessary and proper" for carrying them into execution. The word "necessary" is considered as controlling the whole sentence, and as limiting the right to pass laws for the execution of the granted powers, to such as are indispensable, and without which the power would be nugatory. That it excludes the choice of means, and leaves to Congress, in each case, that only which is most direct and simple.

Is it true, that this is the sense in which the word "necessary" is always used? Does it always import an absolute physical necessity, so strong, that one thing, to which another may be termed necessary, cannot exist without that other? We think it does not. If reference be had to its use, in the common affairs of the world, or in approved authors, we find that it frequently imports no more than that one thing is convenient, or useful, or essential to another. To employ the means necessary to an end, is generally understood as employing any means calculated to produce the end, and not as being confined to those single means, without which the end would be entirely unattainable. . . . A thing may be necessary, very necessary, absolutely or indispensably necessary. To no mind would the same idea be conveyed by these several phrases. This comment on the word is well illustrated by the passage cited at the bar, from the tenth section of Article I of the Constitution. It is, we think, impossible to compare the sentence which prohibits a state from laying "imposts, or duties on imports or exports, except what may be *absolutely* necessary for executing its inspection laws," with that which authorizes Congress "to make all laws which shall be necessary and proper for carrying into execution" the powers of the general government, without feeling a conviction, that the convention understood itself to change materially the meaning of the word "necessary" by prefixing the word "absolutely." This word, then, like others, is used in various senses; and, in its construction, the subject, the context, the intention of the person using them, are all to be taken into view.

Let this be done in the case under consideration. The subject is the execution of those great powers on which the welfare of a nation essentially depends. It must have been the intention of those who gave these powers, to insure, as far as human prudence could insure, their beneficial execution. This could not be done, by confining the choice of means to such narrow limits as not to leave it in the power of Congress to adopt any which might be appropriate, and which were conducive to the end. This provision is made in a constitution, intended to endure for ages to come, and consequently, to be adapted to the various *crises* of human affairs. To have prescribed the means by which government should, in all future time, execute its powers, would have been to change, entirely, the character of the instrument, and give it the properties of a legal code. It would have been an unwise attempt to provide, by immutable rules, for exigencies which, if foreseen at all, must have been seen dimly, and which can be best provided for as they occur. To have declared, that the best means shall not be used, but those alone, without which the power given would be nugatory, which have been to deprive the legislature of the capacity to avail itself of experience, to exercise its reason, and to accommodate its legislation to circumstances. . . .

Take, for example, the power "to establish post offices and post roads." This power is executed by the single act of making the establishment. But, from this has been inferred the power and duty of carrying the mail along the post road, from one post office to another. And, from this implied power, has again been inferred the right to punish those who steal letters from the post office, or rob the mail. It may be said, with some plausibility, that the right to carry the mail, and to punish those who rob it, is not indispensably necessary to the establishment of a post office and post road. This right is indeed essential to the beneficial exercise of the power, but not indispensably necessary to its existence. So, of the punishment of the crimes of stealing or falsifying a record or process of a court of the United States, or of perjury in such court. To punish these offences is certainly conducive to the due administration of justice. But courts may exist, and may decide the causes brought before them, though such crimes escape punishment. . . .

If this limited construction of the word "necessary" must be abandoned, in order to punish, whence is derived the rule which would reinstate it, when the government would carry its powers into execution, by means not vindictive in their nature? If the word "necessary" means "needful," "requisite," "essential," "conducive to," in order to let in the power of punishment for the infraction of law; why is it not equally comprehensive, when required to authorize the use of means which facilitate the execution of the powers of government, without the infliction of punishment?

In ascertaining the sense in which the word "necessary" is used in this clause of the Constitution, we may derive some aid from that with which it is associated. Congress shall have power "to make all laws which shall be necessary and proper to carry into execution" the powers of the government. If the word "necessary" was used in that strict and rigorous sense for which the counsel for the state of Maryland contend, it would be an extraordinary departure from the usual course of the human mind, as exhibited in composition, to add a word, the only possible effect of which is, to qualify that strict and rigorous meaning; to present to the mind the idea of some choice of means of legislation, not strained and compressed within the narrow limits for which gentlemen contend.

But the argument which most conclusively demonstrates the error of the construction contended for by the counsel for the state of Maryland, is founded on the intention of the convention, as manifested in the whole clause. . . .

We think so for the following reasons:

1st. The clause is placed among the powers of Congress, not among the limitations on those powers.

2d. Its terms purport to enlarge, not to diminish the powers vested in the government. It purports to be an additional power, not a restriction on those already granted. . . . The framers of the Constitution wished its adoption, and well knew that it would be endangered by its strength, not by its weakness. Had they been capable of using language which would convey to the eye one idea, and, after deep reflection, impress on the mind, another, they would rather have disguised the grant of power, than its limitation. If then, their intention had been, by this clause, to restrain the free use of means which might otherwise have been implied, that intention would have been inserted in another place, and would have been expressed in terms resembling these. "In carrying into execution the foregoing powers and all others," &c., "no laws shall be passed but such as are necessary and proper." Had the intention been to make this clause restrictive, it would unquestionably have been so in form as well as in effect.

The result of the most careful and attentive consideration bestowed upon this clause is, that if it does not enlarge, it cannot be construed to restrain the powers of Congress, or to impair the right of the legislature to exercise its best judgment in the selection of measures, to carry into execution the constitutional powers of the government. If no other motive for its insertion can be suggested, a sufficient one is found in the desire to remove all doubts respecting the right to legislate on that vast mass of incidental powers which must be involved in the Constitution, if that instrument be not a splendid bauble.

We admit, as all must admit, that the powers of the government are limited, and that its limits are not to be transcended. But we think the sound construction of the Constitution must allow to the national legislature that discretion, with respect to the means by which the powers it confers are to be carried into execution, which will enable that body to perform the high duties assigned to it, in the manner most beneficial to the people. Let the end be legitimate, let it be within the scope of the Constitution, and all means which are appropriate, which are plainly adapted to that end, which are not prohibited, but consistent with the letter and spirit of the Constitution, are constitutional. . . .

It being the opinion of the Court, that the act incorporating the bank is constitutional; and that the power of establishing a branch in the state of Maryland might be properly exercised by the bank itself, we proceed to inquire—

Whether the state of Maryland may, without violating the Constitution, tax that branch? . . .

The power of Congress to create, and of course, to continue, the bank, was the subject of the preceding part of this opinion; and is no longer to be considered as questionable.

That the power of taxing it by the states may be exercised so as to destroy it, is too obvious to be denied. But taxation is said to be an absolute power, which acknowledges no other limits than those expressly prescribed in the Constitution, and like sovereign power of every other description, is trusted to the discretion of those who use it. But the very terms of this argument admit, that the sovereignty of the state, in the article of taxation itself, is subordinate to, and may be controlled by, the Constitution of the United States. How far it has been controlled by that instrument must be a question of construction. In making this construction, no principle not declared, can be admissible, which would defeat the legitimate operations of a supreme government. It is of the very essence of supremacy, to remove all obstacles to its action within its own sphere, and so to modify every power vested in subordinate governments, as to exempt its own operations from their own influence. This effect need not be stated in terms. It is so involved in the declaration of supremacy, so necessarily implied in it, that the expression of it could not make it more certain. We must, therefore, keep it in view, while construing the Constitution. . . .

The sovereignty of a state extends to everything which exists by its own authority, or is introduced by its permission; but does it extend to those means which are employed by Congress to carry into execution—powers conferred on that body by the people of the United States? We think it demonstrable that it does not. Those powers are not given by the people of a single state. They are given by the people of the United States, to a government whose laws, made in pursuance of the Constitution, are declared to be supreme. Consequently, the people of a single state cannot confer a sovereignty which will extend over them.

If we measure the power of taxation residing in a state, by the extent of sovereignty which the people of a single state possess, and can confer on its government, we have an intelligible standard, applicable to every case to which the power may be applied. We have a principle which leaves the power of taxing the people and property of a state unimpaired; which leaves to a state the command of all its resources, and which places beyond its reach, all those powers which are conferred by the people of the United States on the government of the Union, and all those means which are given for the purpose of carrying those powers into execution. We have a principle which is safe for the states, and safe for the Union. We are relieved, as we ought to be, from clashing sovereignty; from interfering powers; from a repugnancy between a right in one government to pull down, what there is an acknowledged right in another to build up; from the incompatibility of a right in one government to destroy, what there is a right in another to preserve. We are not driven to the perplexing inquiry, so unfit for the judicial department, what degree of taxation is the legitimate use, and what degree may amount to the abuse of the power. . . .

. . . That the power to tax involves the power to destroy; that the power to destroy may defeat and render useless the power to create; that there is a plain repugnancy in conferring on one government a power to control the constitutional measures of another, which other, with respect to those very measures, is declared to be supreme over that which exerts the control, are propositions not to be denied. But all inconsistencies are to be reconciled by the magic of the word *confidence*. Taxation, it is said, does not necessarily and unavoidably destroy. To carry it to the excess of destruction, would be an abuse, to presume which, would banish that confidence which is essential to all government.

But is this a case of confidence? Would the people of any state trust those of another with a power to control the most significant operations of their state government? We know they would not. Why, then, should we suppose, that the people of any one state should be willing to trust those of another with a power to control the operations of a government to which they have confided their most important and most valuable interests? In the legislature of the Union alone, are all represented. The legislature of the Union alone, therefore, can be trusted by the people with the power of controlling measures which concern all, in the confidence that it will not be abused. . . .

If we apply the principle for which the state of Maryland contends, to the

Constitution generally, we shall find it capable of changing totally the character of that instrument. We shall find it capable of arresting all the measures of the government, and of prostrating it at the foot of the states. The American people have declared their Constitution and the laws made in pursuance thereof, to be supreme; but this principle would transfer the supremacy, in fact, to the states.

If the states may tax one instrument, employed by the government in the execution of its powers, they may tax any and every other instrument. They may tax the mail; they may tax the mint; they may tax patent rights; they may tax the papers of the custom-house; they may tax judicial process; they may tax all the means employed by the government, to an excess which would defeat all the ends of government. This was not intended by the American people. . . .

It has also been insisted, that, as the power of taxation in the general and state governments is acknowledged to be concurrent, every argument which would sustain the right of the general government to tax banks chartered by the states, will equally sustain the rights of the states to tax banks chartered by the general government.

But the two cases are not on the same reason. The people of all the states have created the general government, and have conferred upon it the general power of taxation. The people of all the states, and the states themselves, are represented in Congress, and, by their representatives, exercise this power. When they tax the chartered institutions of the states, they tax their constituents; and these taxes must be uniform. But when a state taxes the operations of the government of the United States, it acts upon institutions created, not by their own constituents, but by people over whom they claim no control. It acts upon the measures of a government created by others as well as themselves, for the benefit of others in common with themselves. The difference is that which always exists, and always must exist, between the action of the whole on a part, and the action of a part on the whole—between the laws of a government declared which, when in opposition to those laws, is not supreme.

But if the full application of this argument could be admitted, it might bring into question the right of Congress to tax the state banks, and could not prove the right of the states to tax the Bank of the United States.

The Court has bestowed on this subject its most deliberate consideration. The result is a conviction that the states have no power, by taxation or otherwise, to retard, impede, burden, or in any manner control, the operations of the constitutional laws enacted by Congress to carry into execution the powers vested in the general government. This is, we think, the unavoidable consequence of that supremacy which the Constitution had declared.

We are unanimously of opinion, that the law passed by the legislature of Maryland, imposing a tax on the Bank of the United States, is unconstitutional and void.

This opinion does not deprive the states of any resources which they originally possessed. It does not extend to a tax paid by the real property of the bank, in common with the other real property within the state, nor to a tax imposed on the interest which the citizens of Maryland may hold in this institution, in common with other property of the same description throughout the state. But this is a tax on the operations of the bank, and is, consequently, a tax on the operation of an instrument employed by the government of the Union to carry its powers into execution. Such a tax must be unconstitutional.

Reversed.

40

BROWN V. BOARD OF EDUCATION (1954)

Mr. Chief Justice Warren delivered the opinion of the Court:

These cases come to us from the states of Kansas, South Carolina, Virginia, and Delaware. They are premised on different facts and different local conditions, but a common legal question justifies their consideration together in this consolidated opinion.

In each of the cases, minors of the Negro race, through their legal representatives, seek the aid of the courts in obtaining admission to the public schools of their community on a nonsegregated basis. In each instance, they had been denied admission to schools attended by white children under laws requiring or permitting segregation according to race. This segregation was alleged to deprive the plaintiffs of the equal protection of the laws under the Fourteenth Amendment. . . .

The plaintiffs contend that segregated public schools are not "equal" and cannot be made "equal," and that hence they are deprived of the equal protection of the laws. Because of the obvious importance of the question presented, the Court took jurisdiction. Argument was heard in the 1952 term, and reargument was heard this term on certain questions propounded by the Court.

Reargument was largely devoted to the circumstances surrounding the adoption of the Fourteenth Amendment in 1868. It covered exhaustively consideration of the amendment in Congress, ratification by the states, then existing practices in racial segregation, and the views of proponents and opponents of the amendment. This discussion and our own investigation convince us that, although these sources cast some light, it is not enough to resolve the problem with which we are faced. At best, they are inconclusive. The most avid proponents of the post-War amendments undoubtedly intended them to remove all legal distinctions among "all persons born or naturalized in the United States." Their opponents, just as certainly, were antagonistic to both the letter and the spirit of the amendments and wished them to have the most limited effect. What others in Congress and the state legislatures had in mind cannot be determined with any degree of certainty.

Brown v. Board of Education is a landmark in the development of the contemporary interpretation of the "equal protection" clause of the Fourteenth Amendment. The decision declared that racial segregation, by law, in public schools is unconstitutional. The Supreme Court's unanimous holding placed considerable reliance on social science findings concerning the effect of racial segregation on blacks.—Eds.

In the first cases in this Court construing the Fourteenth Amendment, decided shortly after its adoption, the Court interpreted it as proscribing all state-imposed discriminations against the Negro race. The doctrine of "separate but equal" did not make its appearance in this Court until 1896 in the case of *Plessy v. Ferguson* involving not education but transportation. American courts have since labored with the doctrine for over half a century. In this Court, there have been six cases involving the "separate but equal" doctrine in the field of public education. In *Cumming v. County Board of Education* and *Gong Lum v. Rice* the validity of the doctrine itself was not challenged. In more recent cases, all on the graduate school level, inequality was found in that specific benefits enjoyed by white students were denied to Negro students of the same educational qualifications. *Missouri ex rel. Gaines v. Canada, Sipuel v. Oklahoma, Sweatt v. Painter, McLaurin v. Oklahoma State Regents.* In none of these cases was it necessary to reexamine the doctrine to grant relief to the Negro plaintiff. And in *Sweatt v. Painter* the Court expressly reserved decision on the question whether *Plessy* should be held inapplicable to public education.

In the instant cases, that question is directly presented. Here . . . there are findings below that the Negro and white schools involved have been equalized, or are being equalized, with respect to buildings, curricula, qualifications and salaries of teachers, and other "tangible" factors. Our decision, therefore, cannot turn on merely a comparison of these tangible factors in the Negro and white schools involved in each of the cases. We must look instead to the effect of segregation itself on public education.

In approaching this problem, we cannot turn the clock back to 1868 when the amendment was adopted, or even to 1896 when *Plessy* was written. We must consider public education in the light of its full development and its present place in American life throughout the nation. Only in this way can it be determined if segregation in public schools deprives these plaintiffs of the equal protection of the laws.

Today, education is perhaps the most important function of state and local governments. Compulsory school attendance laws and the great expenditures for education both demonstrate our recognition of the importance of education to our democratic society. It is required in the performance of our most basic public responsibilities, even service in the armed forces. It is the very foundation of good citizenship. Today it is a principal instrument in awakening the child to cultural values, in preparing him for later professional training, and in helping him to adjust normally to his environment. In these days, it is doubtful that any child may reasonably be expected to succeed in life if he is denied the opportunity of an education. Such an opportunity, where the state has undertaken to provide it, is a right which must be made available to all on equal terms.

We come then to the question presented: Does segregation of children in public schools solely on the basis of race, even though the physical facilities and other "tangible" factors may be equal, deprive the children of the minority group of equal educational opportunities? We believe that it does.

In *Sweatt, supra,* in finding that a segregated law school for Negroes could not provide them equal educational opportunities, this Court relied in large part on "those qualities which are incapable of objective measurement but which make for greatness in a law school." In *McLaurin* the Court, in requiring that a Negro admitted to a white graduate school be treated like all other students, again resorted to intangible considerations: ". . . his ability to study, to engage in discussions and exchange views with other students, and, in general, to learn his profession." Such considerations apply with added force to children in grade and high schools. To separate them from others of similar age and qualifications solely because of their race generates a feeling of inferiority as to their status in the community that may affect their hearts and minds in a way unlikely ever to be undone. The effect of this separation on their educational opportunities was well stated by a finding in the Kansas case by a court which nevertheless felt compelled to rule against the Negro plaintiffs: "Segregation of white and colored children in public schools has a detrimental effect upon the colored children. The impact is greater when it has the sanction of the law; for the policy of separating the races is usually interpreted as denoting the inferiority of the Negro group. A sense of inferiority affects the motivation of a child to learn. Segregation with the sanction of law, therefore, has a tendency to retard the educational and mental development of Negro children and to deprive them of some of the benefits they would receive in a racially integrated school system." Whatever may have been the extent of psychological knowledge at the time of *Plessy*, this finding is amply supported by modern authority. Any language in *Plessy* contrary to this finding is rejected.

We conclude that in the field of public education the doctrine of "separate but equal" has no place. Separate educational facilities are inherently unequal. Therefore, we hold that the plaintiffs and other similarly situated for whom the actions have been brought are, by reason of the segregation complained of, deprived of the equal protection of the laws guaranteed by the Fourteenth Amendment. . . .

PART TEN

THE POLICY PROCESS

Public policy is a governmental plan or course of action for dealing with an area of economic, political, or social concern. For instance, there are public policies on agriculture, labor relations, electoral campaign financing, social equality, the family, and so on. For decades critics have lamented the fact that government often seems unable to manage major policy problems *comprehensively*. In recent years, the critical outcry has become particularly shrill, as the political system struggles with complex new issues, such as energy crises, economic stagnation, and a burgeoning budgetary deficit. These and other complicated issues would seem to require integrated, long-term answers, instead of piecemeal and short-term adjustments.

Many reformers, often trained in private-sector management, have advocated a policy-making approach that would better approximate the following procedure: First, clear objectives would be set out; next, all possible techniques for achieving the objectives would be presented; then, an optimal course of action would be selected, after examining systematically all the possible results of each approach; finally, throughout the entire exercise, extant policies and precedents would not constrain the choice among alternatives (in other words, if necessary, even radical departures from past practices would be open for consideration).

In actuality, most public policy decisions are not formulated in anything like this fashion. At best, policymakers become adept at "muddling through," as Charles E. Lindblom put it. Past decisions usually restrict present choices. No one has either the capability or the inclination to consider carefully *all* possible means of attaining desired ends, much less to evaluate all their ramifications. In fact, the search for an optimal solution is quickly abandoned, once it becomes obvious that there is frequent disagreement about basic goals, or even about the existence of the problem to be solved. In short, policy is rarely informed by comprehensive analysis. Rather, it evolves through a series of incremental modifications (or, to use Lindblom's terminology, a succession of drastically limited comparisons among available alternatives).

Is disjointed incrementalism necessarily undesirable? The articles by Aaron Wildavsky and by Edward C. Banfield, as well as Lindblom, all sound a common theme, namely, that the answer is much more complicated than is generally understood. When policy seems to comprise little more than an assemblage of segmental decisions and marginal adjustments, it is because the actions of government in a pluralistic polity are seldom prescribed by a central decision maker with an explicit goal (or set of goals), but rather by the continual pulling and hauling of competing interests whose diverse preferences must be reconciled. As Wildavsky emphasizes, perhaps nowhere is this political reality more apparent than in the national budgetary process, which inevitably invites disputes over "who gets what." Try as reformers may to reorganize the operation (so as to encourage greater efficiency or facilitate review), the fact remains that virtually no reform would take the politics out of budgeting. It would only exchange one set of value-premises for another. Thus, whether the reform ultimately signifies a net gain to society depends very much on one's point of view—that is, on whether one stands among those who would gain or those who would lose.

Banfield, in the final chapter of his fascinating book on policy decisions in the Chicago city government, carries this general line of thought a step further. Legitimate public policy must weigh sensitively the disparate values of a variety of interested parties. Any comprehensive planner—even an enlightened and scrupulous one, supported by the most elaborate cost-benefit studies—risks weighting the competing values arbitrarily when he imposes his own judgment. Policies shaped not through "central decisions" but by spontaneous mutual accommodations among the affected interests are more likely to reflect just "social choices." As in an adversary proceeding, the process of negotiation and debate elicits the participation (and thus presumably takes into account the claims) of those groups in society whose stakes are greatest with respect to the issue at hand, while discounting the claims of indifferent, irrelevant, or frivolous groups. True, coherent policies often fail to emerge from pluralistic bargaining. But sometimes incoherent "resultants" are actually in the public interest.

To say that the policy process in the United States seldom resembles the rational-comprehensive model is not to say that it is *uniformly* incremental, haphazard, and given to interest-group haggling. Much seems to depend on the nature of the issue in question. In an influential paper that appeared in 1964, Theodore J. Lowi made one of the first serious attempts to classify the styles of politics related to differing types of policy issues. Lowi suggests that "distributive" policies (wherein the government is extending highly particularized benefits to specific groups) are characterized by the most intensely pluralistic pattern, as a multitude of small organized interests press for a share of the government pork barrel. "Regulatory" decisions (aimed at restricting or promoting interests within broader sectors, such as entire industries or occupations) also evoke pluralist politics, but of a higher order: coalitions are formed on the basis of shared desires to adopt, modify, or defeat governmental initiatives. Finally, "redistributive" programs (taking from some groups or individuals and giving to others) tend to involve a contest between the broadest associations, often representing social classes. Distributive and regulatory policies tend to be the more disaggregated and heavily bartered; redistributive schemes, which by definition necessitate a fairly clear-cut victory by one side over the other, are naturally less so.

41

CHARLES E. LINDBLOM

THE SCIENCE
OF "MUDDLING THROUGH"

Suppose an administrator is given responsibility for formulating policy with respect to inflation. He might start by trying to list all related values in order of importance, e.g., full employment, reasonable business profit, protection of small savings, prevention of a stock market crash. Then all possible policy outcomes could be rated as more or less efficient in attaining a maximum of these values. This would of course require a prodigious inquiry into values held by members of society and an equally prodigious set of calculations on how much of each value is equal to how much of each other value. He could then proceed to outline all possible policy alternatives. In a third step, he would undertake systematic comparison of his multitude of alternatives to determine which attains the greatest amount of values.

In comparing policies, he would take advantage of any theory available that generalized about classes of policies. In considering inflation, for example, he would compare all policies in the light of the theory of prices. Since no alternatives are beyond his investigation, he would consider strict central control and the abolition of all prices and markets on the one hand and elimination of all public controls with reliance completely on the free market on the other, both in the light of whatever theoretical generalizations he could find on such hypothetical economies.

Finally, he would try to make the choice that would in fact maximize his values.

An alternative line of attack would be to set as his principal objective, either explicitly or without conscious thought, the relatively simple goal of keeping prices level. This objective might be compromised or complicated by only a few other goals, such as full employment. He would in fact disregard most other social values as beyond his present interest, and he would for the moment not even attempt to rank the few values that he regarded as immediately relevant. Were he pressed, he would quickly admit that he was ignoring many related values and many possible important consequences of his policies.

As a second step, he would outline those relatively few policy alternatives that occurred to him. He would then compare them. In comparing his limited number of alternatives, most of them familiar from past controversies, he would not ordinarily find a body of theory precise enough to carry him through a comparison of their respective consequences. Instead he would rely heavily on the record of past experience with small policy steps to predict the consequences of similar steps extended into the future.

Moreover, he would find that the policy alternatives combined objectives or values in different ways. For example, one policy might offer price level stability at the cost of some risk of unemployment; another might offer less price stability but also less risk of unemployment. Hence, the next step in his approach—the final selection—would combine into one the choice among values and the choice among instruments for reaching values. It would not, as in the first method of policy-making, approximate a more mechanical process of choosing the means that best satisfied goals that were previously clarified and ranked. Because practitioners of the second approach expect to achieve their goals only partially, they would expect to repeat endlessly the sequence just described, as conditions and aspirations changed and as accuracy of prediction improved.

BY ROOT OR BY BRANCH

For complex problems, the first of these two approaches is of course impossible. Although such an approach can be described, it cannot be practiced except for relatively simple problems and even then only in a somewhat modified form. It assumes intellectual capacities and sources of information that men simply do not possess, and it is even more absurd as an approach to policy when the time and money that can be allocated to a policy problem is limited, as is always the case. Of particular importance to public administrators is the fact that public agencies are in effect usually instructed not to practice the first method. That is to say, their prescribed functions and constraints—the politically or legally possible—restrict their attention to relatively few values and relatively few alternative policies among the countless alternatives that might be imagined. It is the second method that is practiced.

Curiously, however, the literatures of decision-making, policy formulation, planning, and public administration formalize the first approach rather than the second, leaving public administrators who handle complex decisions in the position of practicing what few preach. For emphasis I run some risk of overstatement. True enough, the literature is well aware of limits on man's capacities and of the inevitability that policies will be approached in some such style as the second. But attempts to formalize rational policy formulation—to lay out explicitly the necessary steps in the process—usually describe the first approach and not the second.[1]

The common tendency to describe policy formulation even for complex problems as though it followed the first approach has been strengthened by the attention given to, and success enjoyed by, operations research, statistical decision theory, and systems analysis. The hallmarks of these procedures, typical of the first approach, are clarity of objective, explicitness of evaluation, a high degree of comprehensiveness of overview, and, wherever possible, quantification of values for mathematical analysis. But these advanced procedures remain largely the appropriate techniques of relatively small-scale problem-solving where the total number of variables to be considered is small and value problems restricted. Charles Hitch, head of the Economics Division of RAND Corporation, one of the leading centers for application of these techniques, has written:

> I would make the empirical generalization from my experience at RAND and elsewhere that operations research is the art of sub-optimizing, i.e., of solving some lower-level problems, and that difficulties increase and our special competence diminishes by an order of magnitude with every level of decision making we attempt to ascend. The sort of simple explicit model which operations researchers are so proficient in using can certainly reflect most of the significant factors influencing traffic control on the George Washington Bridge, but the proportion of the relevant reality which we can represent by any such model or models in studying, say, a major foreign-policy decision, appears to be almost trivial.[2]

Accordingly, I propose in this paper to clarify and formalize the second method, much neglected in the literature. This might be described as the method of *successive limited comparisons*. I will contrast it with the first approach, which might be called the rational-comprehensive method.[3] More impressionistically and briefly—and therefore generally used in this article—they could be characterized as the branch method and root method, the former continually building out from the current situation, step-by-step and by small degrees; the latter starting from fundamentals anew each time, building on the past only as experience is embodied in a theory, and always prepared to start completely from the ground up.

Let us put the characteristics of the two methods side by side in simplest terms.

Rational-Comprehensive (Root)

1a. Clarification of values or objectives distinct from and usually prerequisite to empirical analysis of alternative policies.

2a. Policy-formulation is therefore approached through means-end analysis: First the ends are isolated, then the means to achieve them are sought.

3a. The test of a "good" policy is that it can be shown to be the most appropriate means to desired ends.

4a. Analysis is comprehensive; every important relevant factor is taken into account.

5a. Theory is often heavily relied upon.

Assuming that the root method is familiar and understandable, we proceed directly to clarification of its alternative by contrast. In explaining the second, we shall be describing how most administrators do in fact approach complex questions, for the root method, the "best" way as a blueprint or model, is in fact not workable for complex policy questions, and administrators are forced to use the method of successive limited comparisons.

INTERTWINING EVALUATION AND EMPIRICAL ANALYSIS (1B)

The quickest way to understand how values are handled in the method of successive limited comparisons is to see how the root method often breaks down in *its* handling of values or objectives. The idea that values should be clarified, and in advance of the examination of alternative policies, is appealing. But what happens when we attempt it for complex social problems? The first difficulty is that on many critical values or objectives, citizens disagree, congressmen disagree, and public administrators disagree. Even where a fairly specific objective is prescribed for the administrator, there remains considerable room for disagreement on sub-objectives. Consider, for example, the conflict with respect to locating public housing, described in Meyerson and Banfield's study of the Chicago Housing Authority[4]—disagreement which occurred despite the clear objective of providing a certain number of public housing units in the city. Similarly conflicting are objectives in highway location, traffic control, minimum wage administration, development of tourist facilities in national parks, or insect control.

Successive Limited Comparisons (Branch)

1b. Selection of value goals and empirical analysis of the needed action are not distinct from one another but are closely intertwined.

2b. Since means and ends are not distinct, means-end analysis is often inappropriate or limited.

3b. The test of a "good" policy is typically that various analysts find themselves directly agreeing on a policy (without their agreeing that it is the most appropriate means to an agreed objective).

4b. Analysis is drastically limited:
   i) Important possible outcomes are neglected.
   ii) Important alternative potential policies are neglected.
   iii) Important affected values are neglected.

5b. A succession of comparisons greatly reduces or eliminates reliance on theory.

Administrators cannot escape these conflicts by ascertaining the majority's preference, for preferences have not been registered on most issues; indeed, there often *are* no preferences in the absence of public discussion sufficient to bring an issue to the attention of the electorate. Furthermore, there is a question of whether intensity of feeling should be considered as well as the number of persons preferring each alternative. By the impossibility of doing otherwise, administrators often are reduced to deciding policy without clarifying objectives first.

Even when an administrator resolves to follow his own values as a criterion for decisions, he often will not know how to rank them when they conflict with one another, as they usually do. Suppose, for example, that an administrator must relocate tenants living in tenements scheduled for destruction. One objective is to empty the buildings fairly promptly, another is to find suitable accommodation for persons displaced, another is to avoid friction with residents in other areas in which a large influx would be unwelcome, another is to deal with all concerned through persuasion if possible, and so on.

How does one state even to himself the relative importance of these partially conflicting values? A simple ranking of them is not enough; one needs ideally to know how much of one value is worth sacrificing for some of another value. The answer is that typically the administrator chooses—and must choose—directly among policies in which these values are combined in different ways. He cannot first clarify his values and then choose among policies.

A more subtle third point underlies both the first two. Social objectives do not always have the same relative values. One objective may be highly prized in one circumstance, another in another circumstance. If, for example, an administrator values highly both the dispatch with which his agency can carry through its projects *and* good public relations, it matters little which of the two possibly conflicting values he favors in some abstract or general sense. Policy questions arise in forms which put to administrators such a question as: Given the degree to which we are or are not already achieving the values of dispatch and the values of good public relations, is it worth sacrificing a little speed for a happier clientele, or is it better to risk offending the clientele so that we can get on with our work? The answer to such a question varies with circumstances.

The value problem is, as the example shows, always a problem of adjustments at a margin. But there is no practicable way to state marginal objectives or values except in terms of particular policies. That one value is preferred to another in one decision situation does not mean that it will be preferred in another decision situation in which it can be had only at great sacrifice of another value. Attempts to rank or order values in general and abstract terms so that they do not shift from decision to decision end up by ignoring the relevant marginal preferences. The significance of this third point thus goes very far. Even if all administrators had at hand an agreed set of values, objectives, and constraints, and an agreed ranking of these values, objectives, and constraints, their marginal values in actual choice situations would be impossible to formulate.

Unable consequently to formulate the relevant values first and then choose among policies to achieve them, administrators must choose directly among alternative policies that offer different marginal combinations of values. Somewhat paradoxically, the only practicable way to disclose one's relevant marginal values even to oneself is to describe the policy one chooses to achieve them. Except roughly and vaguely, I know of no way to describe—or even to understand—what my relative evaluations are for, say, freedom and security, speed and accuracy in governmental decisions, or low taxes and better schools than to describe my preferences among specific policy choices that might be made between the alternatives in each of the pairs.

In summary, two aspects of the process by which values are actually handled can be distinguished. The first is clear: evaluation and empirical analysis are intertwined; that is, one chooses among values and among policies at one and the same time. Put a little more elaborately, one simultaneously chooses a policy to attain certain objectives and chooses the objectives themselves. The second aspect is related but distinct: the administrator focuses his attention on marginal or incremental values. Whether he is aware of it or not, he does not find general formulations of objectives very helpful and in fact makes specific marginal or incremental comparisons. Two policies, X and Y, confront him. Both promise the same degree of attainment of objectives a, b, c, d, and e. But X promises him somewhat more of f than does Y, while Y promises him somewhat more of g than does X. In choosing between them, he is in fact offered the alternative of a marginal or incremental amount of f at the expense of a marginal or incremental amount of g. The only values that are relevant to his choice are these increments by which the two policies differ; and, when he finally chooses between the two marginal values, he does so by making a choice between policies.[5]

As to whether the attempt to clarify objectives in advance of policy selection is more or less rational than the close intertwining of marginal evaluation and empirical analysis, the principal difference established is that for complex problems the first is impossible and irrelevant, and the second is both possible and relevant. The second is possible because the administrator need not try to analyze any values except the values by which alternative policies differ and need not be concerned with them except as they differ marginally. His need for information on values or objectives is drastically reduced as compared with the root method; and his capacity for grasping, comprehending, and relating values to one another is not strained beyond the breaking point.

RELATIONS BETWEEN MEANS AND ENDS (2B)

Decision-making is ordinarily formalized as a means-ends relationship: means are conceived to be evaluated and chosen in the light of ends finally selected independently of and prior to the choice of means. This is the means-ends relationship of the root method. But it follows from all that has just been said that such a means-ends relationship is possible only to the extent that values are agreed upon, are reconcilable, and are stable at the margin. Typically, therefore, such a means-ends relationship is absent from the branch method, where means and ends are simultaneously chosen.

Yet any departure from the means-ends relationship of the root method will strike some readers as inconceivable. For it will appear to them that only in such a relationship is it possible to determine whether one policy choice is better or worse than another. How can an administrator know whether he has made a wise or foolish decision if he is without prior values or objectives by which to judge his decisions? The answer to this question calls up the third distinctive difference between root and branch methods: how to decide the best policy.

THE TEST OF "GOOD" POLICY (3B)

In the root method, a decision is "correct," "good," or "rational" if it can be shown to attain some specified objective, where the objective can be specified without simply describing the decision itself. Where objectives are defined only through the marginal or incremental approach to values described above, it is still sometimes possible to test whether a policy does in fact attain the desired objectives; but a precise statement of the objectives takes the form of a description of the policy chosen or some alternative to it. To show that a policy is mistaken one cannot offer an abstract argument that important objectives are not achieved; one must instead argue that another policy is more to be preferred.

So far, the departure from customary ways of looking at problem-solving is not troublesome, for many administrators will be quick to agree that the most effective discussion of the correctness of policy does take the form of comparison with other policies that might have been chosen. But what of the situation in which administrators cannot agree on values or objectives, either abstractly or in marginal terms? What then is the test of "good" policy? For the root method, there is no test. Agreement on objectives failing, there is no standard of "correctness." For the method of successive limited comparisons, the test is agreement on policy itself, which remains possible even when agreement on values is not.

It has been suggested that continuing agreement in Congress on the desirability of extending old age insurance stems from liberal desires to strengthen the welfare programs of the federal government and from conservative desires to reduce union demands for private pension plans. If so, this is an excellent demonstration of the ease with which individuals of different ideologies often can agree on concrete policy. Labor mediators report a similar phenomenon: the contestants cannot agree on criteria for settling their disputes but can agree on specific proposals. Similarly, when one administrator's objective turns out to be another's means, they often can agree on policy.

Agreement on policy thus becomes the only practicable test of the policy's correctness. And for one administrator to seek to win the other over to agreement on ends as well would accomplish nothing and create quite unnecessary controversy.

If agreement directly on policy as a test for "best" policy seems a poor substitute for testing the policy against its objectives, it ought to be remembered that objectives themselves have no ultimate validity other than they are agreed upon. Hence agreement is the test of "best" policy in both methods. But where the root method requires agreement on what elements in the decision constitute objectives and on which of these objectives should be sought, the branch method falls back on agreement wherever it can be found.

In an important sense, therefore, it is not irrational for an administrator to defend a policy as good without being able to specify what it is good for.

NON-COMPREHENSIVE ANALYSIS (4B)

Ideally, rational-comprehensive analysis leaves out nothing important. But it is impossible to take everything important into consideration unless "important" is so narrowly defined that analysis is in fact quite limited. Limits on human intellectual capacities and on available information set definite limits to man's capacity to be comprehensive. In actual fact, therefore, no one can practice the rational-comprehensive method for really complex problems, and every administrator faced with a sufficiently complex problem must find ways drastically to simplify.

An administrator assisting in the formulation of agricultural economic policy cannot in the first place be competent on all possible policies. He cannot even comprehend one policy entirely. In planning a soil bank program, he cannot successfully anticipate the impact of higher or lower farm income on, say, urbanization—the possible consequent loosening of family ties, possible consequent eventual need for revisions in social security and further implications for tax problems arising out of new federal responsibilities for social security and municipal responsibilities for urban services. Nor, to follow another line of repercussions, can he work through the soil bank program's effects on prices for agricultural products in foreign markets and consequent implications for foreign relations, including those arising out of economic rivalry between the United States and the U.S.S.R.

In the method of successive limited comparisons, simplification is systematically achieved in two principal ways. First, it is achieved through limitation of policy comparisons to those policies that differ in relatively small degree from policies presently in effect. Such a limitation immediately reduces the number of alternatives to be investigated and also drastically simplifies the character of the investigation of each. For it is not necessary to undertake fundamental inquiry into an alternative and its consequences; it is necessary only to study those respects in which the proposed alternative and its consequences differ from the status quo. The empirical comparison of marginal differences among alternative policies that differ only marginally is, of course, a counterpart to the incremental or marginal comparison of values discussed above.[6]

Relevance as Well as Realism

It is a matter of common observation that in Western democracies public administrators and policy analysts in general do largely limit their analyses to incremental or marginal differences in policies that are chosen to differ only incrementally. They do not do so, however, solely because they desperately need some way to simplify their problems; they also do so in order to be relevant. Democracies change their policies almost entirely through incremental adjustments. Policy does not move in leaps and bounds.

The incremental character of political change in the United States has often been remarked. The two major political parties agree on fundamentals; they offer alternative policies to the voters only on relatively small points of difference.

Both parties favor full employment, but they define it somewhat differently; both favor the development of water power resources, but in slightly different ways; and both favor unemployment compensation, but not the same level of benefits. Similarly, shifts of policy within a party take place largely through a series of relatively small changes, as can be seen in their only gradual acceptance of the idea of governmental responsibility for support of the unemployed, a change in party positions beginning in the early 30's and culminating in a sense in the Employment Act of 1946.

Party behavior is in turn rooted in public attitudes, and political theorists cannot conceive of democracy's surviving in the United States in the absence of fundamental agreement on potentially disruptive issues, with consequent limitation of policy debates to relatively small differences in policy.

Since the policies ignored by the administrator are politically impossible and so irrelevant, the simplification of analysis achieved by concentrating on policies that differ only incrementally is not a capricious kind of simplification. In addition, it can be argued that, given the limits on knowledge within which policy-makers are confined, simplifying by limiting the focus to small variations from present policy makes the most of available knowledge. Because policies being considered are like present and past policies, the administrator can obtain information and claim some insight. Non-incremental policy proposals are therefore typically not only politically irrelevant but also unpredictable in their consequences.

The second method of simplification of analysis is the practice of ignoring important possible consequences of possible policies, as well as the values attached to the neglected consequences. If this appears to disclose a shocking shortcoming of successive limited comparisons, it can be replied that, even if the exclusions are random, policies may nevertheless be more intelligently formulated than through futile attempts to achieve a comprehensiveness beyond human capacity. Actually, however, the exclusions, seeming arbitrary or random from one point of view, need be neither.

Achieving a Degree of Comprehensiveness

Suppose that each value neglected by one policy-making agency were a major concern of at least one other agency. In that case, a helpful division of labor would be achieved, and no agency need find its task beyond its capacities. The shortcomings of such a system would be that one agency might destroy a value either before another agency could be activated to safeguard it or in spite of another agency's efforts. But the possibility that important values may be lost is present in any form of organization, even where agencies attempt to comprehend in planning more than is humanly possible.

The virtue of such a hypothetical division of labor is that every important interest or value has its watchdog. And these watchdogs can protect the interests in their jurisdiction in two quite different ways: first, by redressing damages done by other agencies; and, second, by anticipating and heading off injury before it occurs.

In a society like that of the United States in which individuals are free to combine to pursue almost any possible common interest they might have and in which government agencies are sensitive to the pressures of these groups, the system described is approximated. Almost every interest has its watchdog. Without claiming that every interest has a sufficiently powerful watchdog, it can be argued that our system often can assure a more comprehensive regard for the values of the whole society than any attempt at intellectual comprehensiveness.

In the United States, for example, no part of government attempts a comprehensive overview of policy on income distribution. A policy nevertheless evolves, and one responding to a wide variety of interests. A process of mutual adjustment among farm groups, labor unions, municipalities and school boards, tax authorities, and government agencies with responsibilities in the fields of housing, health, highways, national parks, fire, and police accomplishes a distribution of income in which particular income problems neglected at one point in the decision processes become central at another point.

Mutual adjustment is more pervasive than the explicit forms it takes in negotiation between groups; it persists through the mutual impacts of groups upon each other even where they are not in communication. For all the imperfections and latent dangers in this ubiquitous process of mutual adjustment, it will often accomplish an adaptation of policies to a wider range of interests than could be done by one group centrally.

Note, too, how the incremental pattern of policy-making fits with the multiple pressure pattern. For when decisions are only incremental—closely related to known policies—it is easier for one group to anticipate the kind of moves another might make and easier too for it to make correction for injury already accomplished.[7]

Even partisanship and narrowness, to use pejorative terms, will sometimes be assets to rational decision-making, for they can doubly insure that what one agency neglects, another will not; they specialize personnel to distinct points of view. The claim is valid that effective rational coordination of the federal administration, if possible to achieve at all, would require an agreed set of values[8]—if "rational" is defined as the practice of the root method of decision-making. But a high degree of administrative coordination occurs as each agency adjusts its policies to the concerns of the other agencies in the process of fragmented decision-making I have just described.

For all the apparent shortcomings of the incremental approach to policy alternatives with its arbitrary exclusion coupled with fragmentation, when compared to the root method, the branch method often looks far superior. In the root method, the inevitable exclusion of factors is accidental, unsystematic, and not defensible by any argument so far developed, while in the branch method the exclusions are deliberate, systematic, and defensible. Ideally, of course, the root method does not exclude; in practice it must.

Nor does the branch method necessarily neglect long-run considerations and objectives. It is clear that important values must be omitted in considering policy, and sometimes the only way long-run objectives can be given adequate attention is through the neglect of short-run considerations. But the values omitted can be either long-run or short-run.

SUCCESSION OF COMPARISONS (5B)

The final distinctive element in the branch method is that the comparisons, together with the policy choice, proceed in a chronological series. Policy is not made once and for all; it is made and re-made endlessly. Policy-making is a process of successive approximation to some desired objectives in which what is desired itself continues to change under reconsideration.

Making policy is at best a very rough process. Neither social scientists, nor politicians, nor public administrators yet know enough about the social world to avoid repeated error in predicting the consequences of policy moves. A wise policy-maker consequently expects that his policies will achieve only part of what he hopes and at the same time will produce unanticipated consequences he would have preferred to avoid. If he proceeds through a *succession* of incremental changes, he avoids serious lasting mistakes in several ways.

In the first place, past sequences of policy steps have given him knowledge about the probable consequences of further similar steps. Second, he need not attempt big jumps toward his goals that would require predictions beyond his or anyone else's knowledge, because he never expects his policy to be a final resolution of a problem. His decision is only one step, one that if successful can quickly be followed by another. Third, he is in effect able to test his previous predictions as he moves on to each further step. Lastly, he often can remedy a past error fairly quickly—more quickly than if policy proceeded through more distinct steps widely spaced in time.

Compare this comparative analysis of incremental changes with the aspiration to employ theory in the root method. Man cannot think without classifying, without subsuming one experience under a more general category of experiences. The attempt to push categorization as far as possible and to find general propositions which can be applied to specific situations is what I refer to with the word "theory." Where root analysis often leans heavily on theory in this sense, the branch method does not.

The assumption of root analysts is that theory is the most systematic and economical way to bring relevant knowledge to bear on a specific problem. Granting the assumption, an unhappy fact is that we do not have adequate theory to apply to problems in any policy area, although theory is more adequate in some areas—monetary policy, for example—than in others. Comparative analysis, as in the branch method, is sometimes a systematic alternative to theory.

Suppose an administrator must choose among a small group of policies that differ only incrementally from each other and from present policy. He might aspire to "understand" each of the alternatives—for example, to know all the consequences of each aspect of each policy. If so, he would indeed require theory. In fact, however, he would usually decide that, *for policy-making purposes*, he need know, as explained above, only the consequences of each of those aspects of the policies in which they differed from one another. For this much more modest aspiration, he requires no theory (although it might be helpful, if available), for he can proceed to isolate probable differences by examining the differences in consequences associated with past differences in policies, a feasible program because he can take his observations from a long sequence of incremental changes.

For example, without a more comprehensive social theory about juvenile delinquency than scholars have yet produced, one cannot possibly understand the ways in which a variety of public policies—say on education, housing, recreation, employment, race relations, and policing—might encourage or discourage delinquency. And one needs such an understanding if he undertakes the comprehensive overview of the problem prescribed in the models of the root method. If, however, one merely wants to mobilize knowledge sufficient to assist in a choice among a small group of similar policies—alternative policies on juvenile court procedures, for example—he can do so by comparative analysis of the results of similar past policy moves.

THEORISTS AND PRACTITIONERS

This difference explains—in some cases at least—why the administrator often feels that the outside expert or academic problem-solver is sometimes not helpful and why they in turn often urge more theory on him. And it explains why an administrator often feels more confident when "flying by the seat of his pants" than when following the advice of theorists. Theorists often ask the administrator to go the long way round to the solution of his problems, in effect ask him to follow the best canons of the scientific method, when the administrator knows that the best available theory will work less well than more modest incremental comparisons. Theorists do not realize that the administrator is often in fact practicing a systematic method. It would be foolish to push this explanation too far, for sometimes practical decision-makers are pursuing neither a theoretical approach nor successive comparisons, nor any other systematic method.

It may be worth emphasizing that theory is sometimes of extremely limited helpfulness in policy-making for at least two rather different reasons. It is greedy for facts; it can be constructed only through a great collection of observations. And it is typically insufficiently precise for application to a policy process that moves through small changes. In contrast, the comparative method both economizes on the need for facts and directs the analyst's attention to just those facts that are relevant to the fine choices faced by the decision-maker.

With respect to precision of theory, economic theory serves as an example. It predicts that an economy without money or prices would in certain specified ways misallocate resources, but this finding pertains to an alternative far removed from the kind of policies on which administrators need help. On the other hand, it is not precise enough to predict the consequences of policies restricting business mergers, and this is the kind of issue on which the administrators need help. Only in relatively restricted areas does economic theory achieve sufficient precision to go far in resolving policy questions; its helpfulness in policy-making is always so limited that it requires supplementation through comparative analysis.

SUCCESSIVE COMPARISON AS A SYSTEM

Successive limited comparisons is, then, indeed a method or system; it is not a failure of method for which administrators ought to apologize. None the less, its imperfections, which have not been explored in this paper, are many. For example, the method is without a built-in safeguard for all relevant values, and it also may lead the decision-maker to overlook excellent policies for no other reason than that they are not suggested by the chain of successive policy steps leading up to the present. Hence, it ought to be said that under this method, as well as under some of the most sophisticated variants of the root method— operations research, for example—policies will continue to be as foolish as they are wise.

Why then bother to describe the method in all the above detail? Becuase it is in fact a common method of policy formulation, and is, for complex problems, the principal reliance of administrators as well as of other policy analysts.[9] And because it will be superior to any other decision-making method available for complex problems in many circumstances, certainly superior to a futile attempt at superhuman comprehensiveness. The reaction of the public administrator to the exposition of method doubtless will be less a discovery of a new method than a better acquaintance with an old. But by becoming more conscious of their practice of this method, administrators might practice it with more skill and know when to extend or constrict its use. (That they sometimes practice it effectively and sometimes not may explain the extremes of opinion on "muddling through," which is both praised as a highly sophisticated form of problem-solving and denounced as no method at all. For I suspect that in so far as there is a system in what is known as "muddling through," this method is it.)

One of the noteworthy incidental consequences of clarification of the method is the light it throws on the suspicion an administrator sometimes entertains that a consultant or adviser is not speaking relevantly and responsibly when in fact by all ordinary objective evidence he is. The trouble lies in the fact that most of us approach policy problems within a framework given by our view of a chain of successive policy choices made up to the present. One's thinking about appropriate policies with respect, say, to urban traffic control is greatly influenced by one's knowledge of the incremental steps taken up to the present. An administrator enjoys an intimate knowledge of his past sequences that "outsiders" do not share, and his thinking and that of the "outsider" will consequently be different in ways that may puzzle both. Both may appear to be talking intelligently, yet each may find the other unsatisfactory. The relevance of the policy chain of succession is even more clear when an American tries to discuss, say, antitrust policy with a Swiss, for the chains of policy in the two countries are strikingly different and the two individuals consequently have organized their knowledge in quite different ways.

If this phenomenon is a barrier to communication, an understanding of it promises an enrichment of intellectual interaction in policy formulation. Once the source of difference is understood, it will sometimes be stimulating for an administrator to seek out a policy analyst whose recent experience is with a policy chain different from his own.

This raises again a question only briefly discussed above on the merits of like-mindedness among government administrators. While much of organization theory argues the virtues of common values and agreed organizational objectives, for complex problems in which the root method is inapplicable, agencies will want among their own personnel two types of diversification: administrators whose thinking is organized by reference to policy chains other than those familiar to most members of the organization and, even more commonly, administrators whose professional or personal values or interests create diversity of view (perhaps coming from different specialties, social classes, geographical areas) so that, even within a single agency, decision-making can be fragmented and parts of the agency can serve as watchdogs for other parts.

NOTES

[1] James G. March and Herbert A. Simon similarly characterize the literature. They also take some important steps, as have Simon's recent articles, to describe a less heroic model of policy-making. See *Organizations* (John Wiley and Sons, 1958), p. 137.

[2] "Operations Research and National Planning—A Dissent," 5 *Operations Research* 718 (October, 1957). Hitch's dissent is from particular points made in the article to which his paper is a reply; his claim that operations research is for low-level problems is widely accepted.

For examples of the kind of problems to which operations research is applied, see C. W. Churchman, R. L. Ackoff and E. L. Arnoff, *Introduction to Operations Research* (John Wiley and Sons, 1957); and J. F. McCloskey and J. M. Coppinger (eds.), *Operations Research for Management*, Vol. II (The Johns Hopkins Press, 1956).

[3] I am assuming that administrators often make policy and advise in the making of policy and am treating decision-making and policy-making as synonymous for purposes of this paper.

[4] Martin Meyerson and Edward C. Banfield, *Politics, Planning, and the Public Interest* (The Free Press, 1955).

[5] The line of argument is, of course, an extension of the theory of market choice, especially the theory of consumer choice, to public policy choices.

[6] A more precise definition of incremental policies and a discussion of whether a change that appears "small" to one observer might be seen differently by another is to be found in my "Policy Analysis," 48 *American Economic Review* 298 (June, 1958).

[7] The link between the practice of the method of successive limited comparisons and mutual adjustment of interests in a highly fragmented decision-making process adds a new facet to pluralist theories of government and administration.

[8] Herbert Simon, Donald W. Smithburg, and Victor A. Thompson, *Public Administration* (Alfred A. Knopf, 1950), p. 434.

[9] Elsewhere I have explored this same method of policy formulation as practiced by academic analysts of policy ("Policy Analysis," 48 *American Economic Review* 298 [June 1958]). Although it has been here presented as a method for public administrators, it is no less necessary to analysts more removed from immediate policy questions, despite their tendencies to describe their own analytical efforts as though they were the rational-comprehensive method with an especially heavy use of

theory. Similarly, this same method is inevitably resorted to in personal problem-solving, where means and ends are sometimes impossible to separate, where aspirations or objectives undergo constant development, and where drastic simplification of the complexity of the real world is urgent if problems are to be solved in the time that can be given to them. To an economist accustomed to dealing with the marginal or incremental concept in market processes, the central idea in the method is that both evaluation and empirical analysis are incremental. Accordingly I have referred to the method elsewhere as "the incremental method."

42

AARON WILDAVSKY

POLITICAL IMPLICATIONS OF BUDGETARY REFORM

A large part of the literature on budgeting in the United States is concerned with reform. The goals of the proposed reforms are couched in similar language—economy, efficiency, improvement, or just better budgeting. The President, the Congress and its committees, administrative agencies, even the interested citizenry are all to gain by some change in the way the budget is formulated, presented, or evaluated. There is little or no realization among the reformers, however, that any effective change in budgetary relationships must necessarily alter the outcomes of the budgetary process. Otherwise, why bother? Far from being a neutral matter of "better budgeting," proposed reforms inevitably contain important implications for the political system, that is, for the "who gets what" of governmental decisions. What are some of the major political implications of budgetary reform and where should we look to increase our knowledge about how the budget is made? We begin with the noblest vision of reform: the development of a normative theory of budgeting that would provide the basis for allocating funds among competing activities.

A NORMATIVE THEORY OF BUDGETING?

In 1940, in what is still the best discussion of the subject, V. O. Key lamented "The Lack of a Budgetary Theory." He called for a theory which would help answer the basic question of budgeting on the expenditure side: "On what basis shall it be decided to allocate X dollars to Activity A instead of Activity B?"[1] Although several attempts have been made to meet this challenge,[2] not one has come close to succeeding. No progress has been made for the excellent reason that the task, as posed, is impossible to fulfill.[3] The search for an unrealizable goal indicates serious weaknesses in prevailing conceptions of the budget.

This research was begun on a Ford Foundation Grant for Research in Public Affairs awarded through Oberlin College which made it possible for the author and a student, Judd Kessler, to interview some fifty officials involved in budgeting in Washington, D. C. Further work is continuing under a grant from Resources for the Future. I would like to thank these organizations for their support. I am also grateful to V. O. Key, Jr., Chalres Lindblom, Nelson Polsby, and Allan Schick, for their useful criticisms. I would welcome comments from students and practitioners interested in studying the budgetary process.

If a normative theory of budgeting is to be more than an academic exercise, it must actually guide the making of governmental decisions. The items of expenditures which are passed by Congress, enacted into law, and spent must in large measure conform to the theory if it is to have any practical effect. This is tantamount to prescribing that virtually all the activities of government be carried on according to the theory. For whatever the government does must be paid for from public funds; it is difficult to think of any policy which can be carried out without money.

The budget is the life-blood of the government, the financial reflection of what the government does or intends to do. A theory which contains criteria for determining what ought to be in the budget is nothing less than a theory stating what the government ought to do. If we substitute the words "what the government ought to do" for the words "ought to be in the budget," it becomes clear that a normative theory of budgeting would be a comprehensive and specific political theory detailing what the government's activities ought to be at a particular time. A normative theory of budgeting, therefore, is utopian in the fullest sense of that word; its accomplishment and acceptance would mean the end of conflict over the government's role in society.

By suppressing dissent, totalitarian regimes enforce their normative theory of budgeting on others. Presumably, we reject this solution to the problem of conflict in society and insist on democratic procedures. How then arrive at a theory of budgeting which is something more than one man's preferences?

The crucial aspect of budgeting is whose preferences are to prevail in disputes about which activities are to be carried on and to what degree, in the light of limited resources. The problem is not only "how shall budgetary benefits be maximized?" as if it made no difference who received them, but also "who shall receive budgetary benefits and how much?" One may purport to solve the problem of budgeting by proposing a normative theory (or a welfare function or a hierarchy of values) which specifies a method for maximizing returns for budgetary expenditures. In the absence of ability to impose a set of preferred policies on others, however, this solution breaks down. It amounts to no more than saying that if you can persuade others to agree with you, than you will have achieved agreement. Or it begs the question of what kind of policies will be fed into the scheme by assuming that these are agreed upon. Yet we hardly need argue that a state of universal agreement has not yet arisen.

Another way of avoiding the problem of budgeting is to treat society as a single organism with a consistent set of desires and a life of its own, much as a single consumer might be assumed to have a stable demand and indifference schedule. Instead of revenue being raised and the budget being spent by and for many individuals who may have their own preferences and feelings, as is surely the case, these processes are treated, in effect, as if a single individual were the only one concerned. This approach avoids the central problems of social conflict, of somehow aggregating different preferences so that a decision may emerge. How can we compare the worth of expenditures for irrigation to certain farmers with the worth of widening a highway to motorists and the desirability of aiding old people to pay medical bills as against the degree of safety provided by an expanded defense program?

The process we have developed for dealing with interpersonal comparisons in Government is not economic but political. Conflicts are resolved (under agreed upon rules) by translating different preferences through the political system into units called votes or into types of authority like a veto power. There need not be (and there is not) full agreement on goals or the preferential weights to be accorded to different goals. Congressmen directly threaten, compromise, and trade favors in regard to policies in which values are implicitly weighted, and then agree to register the results according to the rules for tallying votes.

The burden of calculation is enormously reduced for three primary reasons: first, only the small number of alternatives which are politically feasible at any one time are considered; second, these policies in a democracy typically differ only in small increments from previous policies on which there is a store of relevant information; and, third, each participant may ordinarily assume that he need consider only his preferences and those of his powerful opponents since the American political system works to assure that every significant interest has representation at some key point. Since only a relatively few interest groups contend on any given issue and no single item is considered in conjunction with all others (because budgets are made in bits and pieces), a huge and confusing array of interests are not activated all at once.

In the American context, a typical result is that bargaining takes place among many dispersed centers of influence and that favors are swapped as in the case of log-rolling public works appropriations. Since there is no one group of men who can necessarily impose their preferences upon others within the American political system, special coalitions are formed to support or oppose specific policies. Support is sought in this system of fragmented power at numerous centers of influence—Congressional committees, the Congressional leadership, the President, the Budget Bureau, interdepartmental committees, departments, bureaus, private groups, and so on. Nowhere does a single authority have power to determine what is going to be in the budget.

THE POLITICS IN BUDGET REFORM

The seeming irrationalities[4] of a political system which does not provide for even formal consideration of the budget as a whole (except by the President who cannot control the final result) has led to many attacks and proposals for reform. The tradition of reform in America is a noble one, not easily to be denied. But in this case it is doomed to failure because it is aimed at the wrong target. If the present budgetary process is rightly or wrongly deemed unsatisfactory, then one must alter in some respect the political system of which the budget is but an expression. It makes no sense to speak as if one could make drastic changes in budgeting without also altering the distribution of influence. But this task is inevitably so formidable (though the reformers are not directly conscious of it) that most adversaries prefer to speak of changing the budgetary process, as if by some subtle alchemy the irrefractible political element could be transformed into a more malleable substance.

The reader who objects to being taken thus far only to be told the obvious truth that the budget is inextricably linked to the political system would have a just complaint if the implications of this remark were truly recognized in the literature on budgeting. But this is not so. One implication is that by far the most significant way of influencing the budget is to introduce basic political changes (or to wait for secular changes like the growing industrialization of the South). Provide the President with more powers enabling him to control the votes of his party in Congress; enable a small group of Congressmen to command a majority of votes on all occasions so that they can push their program through. Then you will have exerted a profound influence on the content of the budget.

A second implication is that no significant change can be made in the budgetary process without affecting the political process. There would be no point in tinkering with the budgetary machinery if, at the end, the pattern of budgetary decisions was precisely the same as before. On the contrary, reform has little justification unless it results in different kinds of decisions and, when and if this has been accomplished, the play of political forces has necessarily been altered. Enabling some political forces to gain at the expense of others requires the explicit introduction and defense of value premises which are ordinarily missing from proposals for budgetary reform.

Since the budget represents conflicts over whose preferences shall prevail, the third implication is that one cannot speak of "better budgeting" without considering who benefits and who loses or demonstrating that no one loses. Just as the supposedly objective criterion of "efficiency" has been shown to have normative implications,[5] so a "better budget" may well be a cloak for hidden policy preferences. To propose that the President be given an item veto, for example, means an attempt to increase the influence of the particular interests which gain superior access to the Chief Executive rather than, say, to the Congress. Only if one eliminates the element of conflict over expenditures, can it be assumed that a reform which enables an official to do a better job from his point of view is simply "good" without considering the policy implications for others.

Arthur Smithies may stand as a typical proponent of a typical reform. Identifying rationality with a comprehensive overview of the budget by a single person or group, Smithies despairs of the fragmented approach taken by Congress and proposes a remedy. He suggests that a Joint (Congressional) Budget Policy committee be formed and empowered to consider all proposals for revenue and expenditure in a single package and that their decisions be made binding by a concurrent resolution. And he presents his reform as a moderate proposal to improve the rationality of the budget process.[6] If the proposed Joint Committee were unable to secure the passage of its recommendations, as would surely be the case, it would have gone to enormous trouble without accomplishing anything but a public revelation of futility. The impotence of the Joint Committee on the Legislative Budget,[7] the breakdown of the single Congressional attempt to develop a comprehensive legislative budget,[8] and the failure of

Congressional attempts to control the Council of Economic Advisers[9] and the Budget Bureau,[10] all stem from the same cause. There is no cohesive group in Congress capable of using these devices to affect decison making by imposing its preferences on a majority of Congressmen. Smithies' budgetary reform presupposes a completely different political system from the one which exists in the United States. To be sure, there is a name for a committee which imposes its will on the legislature and tolerates no rival committees—it is called a Cabinet on the British model. In the guise of a procedural change in the preparation of the budget by Congress, Smithies is actually proposing a revolutionary move which would mean the virtual introduction of the British Parliamentary system if it were successful.

Smithies (pp. 188–225) suggests that his proposals would be helpful to the President. But the membership of the Joint Committee would be made up largely of conservatives from safe districts who are not dependent on the President, who come from a different constituency than he does, but with whom he must deal in order to get any money for his programs. Should the Joint Committee ever be able to command a two-thirds vote of the Congress, it could virtually ignore the president in matters of domestic policy and run the executive branch so that it is accountable only to them.

I do not mean to disparage in any way the important problem of efficiency, of finding ways to maximize budgetary benefits given a specified distribution of shares. In principle, there seems to be no reason why policy machinery could not be so arranged as to alter the ratio of inputs to outputs without changing the distribution of shares. One can imagine situations in which everyone benefits or where the losses suffered in one respect are made up by greater gains elsewhere. There may be cases where such losses as do exist are not felt by the participants and they may be happy to make changes which increase their felt benefits. The inevitable lack of full information and the disinclination of participants to utilize their political resources to the fullest extent undoubtedly leave broad areas of inertia and inattention open for change. Thus, the "slack" in the system may leave considerable room for ingenuity and innovation in such areas as benefit cost analysis and the comparability and interrelatedness of public works without running into outstanding political difficulties or involving large changes in the system. Most practical budgeting may take place in a twilight zone between politics and efficiency. Without presenting a final opinion on this matter, it does seem to me that the problem of distributing shares has either been neglected entirely or has been confused with the problem of efficiency to the detriment of both concerns. The statements in this paper should be understood to refer only to the question of determining shares in the budget.

WHAT DO WE KNOW ABOUT BUDGETING?

The overriding concern of the literature on budgeting with normative theory and reform has tended to obscure the fact that we know very little about it. Aside from the now classical articles on Congressional oversight of administration by Arthur MacMahon,[11] an excellent study of internal budgetary procedures in the

Army by Frederick C. Mosher,[12] and an interesting case history by Kathryn S. Arnow,[13] there is virtually nothing of substance about how or why budgetary decisions are actually made. Of course, the general literature on decision making in national government provides some valuable propositions, but it is not keyed-in to the budgetary process. Yet the opportunities for developing and testing important propositions about budgetary decisions are extraordinarily good and I would like to suggest a few of the many possible approaches here.

How do various agencies decide how much to ask for? Most agencies cannot simply ask for everything they would like to have. If they continually ask for much more than they can get, their opinions are automatically discounted and they risk a loss of confidence by the Budget Bureau and Appropriations subcommittees which damages the prospects of their highest priority items. The agencies cannot even ask for all that they are authorized to spend because their authorizations commonly run way ahead of any realistic expectation of achievement. At the same time, they do not wish to sell themselves short. The result is that the men who make this choice (an official title is no certain guide to whom they are) seek signals from the environment—supporting interests, their own personnel, current events, last year's actions, attitudes of Congressmen, and so on—to arrive at a composite estimate of "what will go." A combination of interviews, case studies, and direct observation should enable the researcher to determine what these signals are, to construct propositions accounting for the agencies' budgetary position, and to generally recreate the environment out of which these choices come.

Once having decided what they would like to get, how do agencies go about trying to achieve their objectives? Today, we do not even have a preliminary list of the most common strategies used by participants in trying to influence budgetary outcomes. Again, the techniques listed above should bring the necessary data to light.

Perhaps a few examples will demonstrate the importance of understanding budgetary strategies. There are times when an agency wishes to cut its own budget because it has lost faith in a program, for internal disciplinary reasons, or because it would like to use the money elsewhere. If the agency is particularly well endowed with effective clientele groups, however, it may not only fail in this purpose but may actually see the appropriation increased as this threat mobilizes the affected interests. One budget officer informed me that he tried to convince the Budget Bureau to undertake two projects which the agency did not want but which several influential Congressmen felt strongly about. Otherwise, the official argued, the Congressmen would secure their desires by offering additional projects to their colleagues. The Budget Bureau turned him down and the result was nine unwanted projects instead of two.

The appearance of a budget may take on considerable importance, a circumstance which is often neglected by proponents of program budgeting. Suppose that an agency has strong clientele backing for individual projects. It is likely to gain by presenting them separately so that any cut may be readily identified and support easily mobilized. Lumping a large number of items together may facilitate cuts on an across-the-board basis. Items lacking support, on the other hand, may do better by being placed in large categories so that it is more difficult to single them out for deeper slashes.

We might also inquire (through questionnaires, interviews, direct observation, documentary research) about the participants' perceptions of their roles and the reciprocal expectations they have about the behavior of others. In speaking to officials concerned with budgeting I was impressed with how often the behavior they described was predicated on a belief about what others would do, how they would react in turn, how a third participant would react to this result and so on. Budgetary items are commonly adjusted on the basis of mutual expectations or on a single participant's notion of the role he is expected to play. I strongly suspect, on the basis of some interviewing, that if we studied conceptions of role prevalent on the House Appropriations Committee, their transmittal to new members and staff, and the consequent resistance of members to seeing party as relevant to choice, we would understand a great deal more about the characteristic behavior of many members as budget cutters.

My interviews suggest that the administrator's perception of Congressional knowledge and motivation helps determine the kind of relationships he seeks to establish. The administrator who feels that the members of his appropriations subcommittees are not too well informed on specifics and that they evaluate the agency's program on the basis of feedback from constituents, stresses the role of supporting interests in maintaining good relations with Congressmen. He may not feel the need to be too careful with his estimates. The administrator who believes that the Congressmen are well informed and fairly autonomous is likely to stress personal relationships and demonstrations of good work as well as clientele support. Priority in research should be given to study of these perceptions and the ways in which they determine behavior.

Another approach would be to locate and segregate classes of administrative officials who are found by observation to have or not to have the confidence of the appropriations committees and to seek to explain the differences. For if there is any one thing which participants in budgeting are likely to stress, it is the importance of maintaining relations of confidence and they are highly conscious of what this requires. Since it appears from preliminary investigation that the difference is not accounted for by the popularity of the agency or its programs, it is possible that applications of some gross psychological and skill categories would reveal interesting results.

Many participants in budgeting (in the agencies, Congress, the Budget Bureau) speak of somehow having arrived at a total figure which represents an agency's or an activity's "fair share" of the budget. The fact that a fair share concept exists may go a long way toward explaining the degree of informal coordination that exists among the participants in budgeting. Investigation of how these figures are arrived at and communicated would help us understand how notions of limits (ceilings and floors) enter into budgetary decisions. A minimum effort in this direction would require the compilation of appropriations histories of various agencies and programs rather than just individual case histories which concentrate on some specific event or moment in time. Investigation of the Tennessee Valley Authority's experience in securing electric power appropriations, over a twenty-five-year period, for example, reveals patterns and presents explanatory possibilities which would not otherwise be available.[14]

By its very nature the budgetary process presents excellent opportunities for the use of quantitative data although these must be used with great caution and with special attention to their theoretical relevance. Richard Fenno has collected figures on thirty-seven bureaus dealing with domestic policies from 1947 to 1958 from their initial estimates to decisions by the Budget Bureau, appropriations committees in both houses, conference committees, and floor action. Using these figures he expects to go beyond the usual facile generalizations that the House cuts and the Senate raises bureau estimates, to the much more interesting question of determining the conditions under which the patterns that do exist actually obtain.[15] Although such data do not by any means tell the whole story, they can be used to check generalizations about patterns of floor action or conference committee action which would not otherwise be possible.

After giving the matter considerable thought, I have decided that it would not be fruitful to devise a measure which would ostensibly give an objective rank ordering of bureaus and departments according to their degree of success in securing appropriations. The first measure which might be used would be to compare an agency's initial requests with its actual appropriations. The difficulty here is that agency estimates are not merely a measure of their desire but also include a guess as to what they can reasonably expect to get. The agency which succeeds in getting most of what it desires, therefore, may be the one which is best at figuring out what it is likely to get. A better measure, perhaps, would be an agency's record in securing appropriations calculated as percentages above or below previous years' appropriations. But this standard also leads to serious problems. There are fortuitous events—sputnik, a drought, advances in scientific knowledge—which are beyond the control of an agency but which may have a vital bearing on its success in getting appropriations. Indeed, some "affluent agencies" like the National Institutes of Health may find that there is little they can do to stop vast amounts of money from coming in; they may not even be able to cut their own budgets when they want to do so. Furthermore, agencies generally carry on a wide variety of programs and the total figures may hide the fact that some are going very well and others quite poorly. Thus it would be necessary to validate the measure by an intensive study of each agency's appropriations history and this would appear to make the original computation unnecessary.

The purpose of this suggested research, much of which the author intends to pursue, is to formulate empirically valid propositions which will be useful in constructing theories (general explanations) accounting for the operation and outcomes of the budgetary process. A theory of influence would describe the power relationships among the participants, explain why some are more successful than others in achieving their budgetary goals, state the conditions under which various strategies are or are not efficacious, and in this way account for the pattern of budgetary decisions.

With such a theory, it would become possible to specify the advantages which some participants gain under the existing system, to predict the consequences of contemplated changes on the distribution of influence, and to anticipate sources of opposition. Possibly, those desiring change might then suggest a strategy to overcome the expected resistance. But they would not, in their scholarly role, accuse their opponents of irrationality in not wishing to have their throats cut.

It would also be desirable to construct a theory of budgetary calculation by specifying the series of related factors (including influence relationships) which affect the choice of competing alternatives by the decision makers. This kind of theory would describe how problems arise, how they are broken down, how information is fed into the system, how the participants are related to one another, and how a semblance of coordination is achieved. The kinds of calculations which actually guide the making of decisions would be emphasized. One would like to know, for example, whether long-range planning really exists or is merely engaged in for form's sake while decisions are really based on short-run indices like reactions to last year's appropriation requests. If changes in procedure lead to different kinds of calculations, one would like to be able to predict what the impact on decisions was likely to be.

THE GOALS OF KNOWLEDGE AND REFORM

Concentration on developing at least the rudiments of a descriptive theory is not meant to discourage concern with normative theory and reform. On the contrary, it is worthwhile studying budgeting from both standpoints. Surely, it is not asking too much to suggest that a lot of reform be preceded by a little knowledge. The point is that until we develop more adequate descriptive theory about budgeting, until we know something about the "existential situation" in which the participants find themselves under our political system, proposals for major reform must be based on woefully inadequate understanding. A proposal which alters established relationships, which does not permit an agency to show certain programs in the most favorable light, which does not tell influential Congressmen what they want to know, which changes prevailing expections about the behavior of key participants, or which leads to different calculations of an agency's fair share, would have many consequences no one is even able to guess at today. Of course, small, incremental changes proceeding in a pragmatic fashion of trial and error could proceed as before without benefit of theory; but this is not the kind of change with which the literature on budgeting is generally concerned.

Perhaps the "study of budgeting" is just another expression for the "study of politics"; yet one cannot study everything at once, and the vantage point offered by concentration on budgetary decisions offers a useful and much neglected perspective from which to analyze the making of policy. The opportunities for comparison are ample, the outcomes are specific and quantifiable, and a dynamic quality is assured by virtue of the comparative ease with which one can study the development of budgetary items over a period of years.

NOTES

[1] V. O. Key, Jr., "The Lack of a Budgetary Theory," 34 *American Political Science Review* 1137–44 (December 1940).

[2] Verne B. Lewis, "Toward a Theory of Budgeting," 12 *Public Administration Review* 42–54 (Winter 1952); "Symposium on Budgetary Theory," 10 *Public Administration Review* 20–31 (Spring 1954); Arthur Smithies, *The Budgetary Process in the United States* (McGraw-Hill, 1955).

[3] Key, in fact, shies away from the implications of his question and indicates keen awareness of the political problems involved. But the question has been posed by subsequent authors largely in the terms in which he framed it.

[4] See Charles E. Lindblom, "The Science of 'Muddling Through,'" 19 *Public Administration Review* 79–88 (Spring 1959), for a description and criticism of the comprehensive method. See also his "Decision-Making in Taxation and Expenditure" in National Bureau of Economic Research, *Public Finances: Needs, Sources, and Utilization* (Princeton University Press, 1961), pp. 295–327, and his "Policy Analysis," 48 *American Economic Review* 298–312 (June 1958).

[5] Dwight Waldo, *The Administrative State* (Ronald Press, 1948); Herbert A. Simon, "The Criterion of Efficiency," in *Administrative Behavior*, 2nd ed. (Macmillan, 1957), pp. 172–97.

[6] Smithies, *op. cit.*, pp. 192–93ff.

[7] Avery Leiserson, "Coordination of the Federal Budgetary and Appropriations Procedures Under the Legislative Reorganization Act of 1946," 1 *National Tax Journal* 118–26 (June 1948).

[8] Robert Ash Wallace, "Congressional Control of the Budget," 3 *Midwest Journal of Political Science* 160–62 (May 1959); Dalmas H. Nelson, "The Omnibus Appropriations Act of 1950," 15 *Journal of Politics* 274–88 (May 1953); Representative John Phillips, "The Hadacol of the Budget Makers," 4 *National Tax Journal* 255–68 (September 1951).

[9] Roy Blough, "The Role of the Economist in Federal Policy-Making," 51 *University of Illinois Bulletin* (November 1953); Lester Seligman, "Presidential Leadership: The Inner Circle and Institutionalization," 18 *Journal of Politics* 410–26 (August 1956); Edwin G. Nourse, *Economics in the Public Service: Admininstrative Aspects of the Employment Act* (Harcourt Brace, 1953); Ronald C. Hood, "Reorganizing the Council of Economic Advisors," 69 *Political Science Quarterly* 413–37 (September 1954).

[10] Fritz Morstein Marx, "The Bureau of the Budget: Its Evolution and Present Role II," 39 *American Political Science Review* 363–98 (October 1945); Richard Neustadt, "The Presidency and Legislation: The Growth of Central Clearance," 48 *Ibid.* 631–71 (September 1954); Seligman, *op. cit.*

[11] Arthur McMahon, "Congressional Oversight of Administration," 58 *Political Science Quarterly* 161–90, 380–414 (June, September 1943).

[12] Frederick C. Mosher, *Program Budgeting: Theory and Practice, with Particular Reference to the U.S. Department of the Army* (Public Administrative Service, 1954).

[13] *The Department of Commerce Field Offices*, Inter-University Case Series No. 21 (University of Alabama Press, 1954).

[14] See Aaron B. Wildavsky, "TVA and Power Politics," 55 *American Political Science Review* 576–90 (September 1961).

[15] From a research proposal kindly lent me by Richard Fenno. See also his excellent paper, "The House Appropriations Committee as a Political System: The Problem of Integration," delivered at the 1961 meeting of the American Political Science Association.

43

EDWARD C. BANFIELD

INFLUENCE AND THE PUBLIC INTEREST

Some will say that a political system such as has been described here can rarely produce outcomes that are in the public interest. If actions profoundly affecting the city's development are based not on comprehensive planning but on compromises patched up among competing parochial interests, if political heads are less concerned with the content of policy than with maintaining a voting alliance between the machine-controlled inner city and the suspicious suburbs and if the possessors of great private fortunes and the heads of big corporations cannot, despite all their talk of "civic responsibility," act concertedly for public ends—if all this be the case, the Chicago's future welfare depends (some will say) not so much upon the processes of government as upon that special providence that is reserved for fools and drunkards.

The great defect of the Chicago political system (those who take this view will say) is that it does not provide sufficient central direction. There are many special interests on the scene, each of which looks after itself and cares only incidentally, if at all, for the welfare of the community as a whole. Action in public matters is largely a by-product of the struggles of these special interests for their own advantage. What is needed (the critics will conclude) is a central public authority which will survey the entire metropolitan scene, form a comprehensive, internally consistent conception of what must be done for the good of the whole, and then carry that conception into effect without compromise. This is what the advocates of "planning" and "efficient metropolitan organization" have in mind.

It seems clear that there is a tension between the nature of the political system, on the one hand, and the requirements of planning—of comprehensiveness and consistency in policy—on the other. In part, this tension arises from the decentralization so characteristic of the Chicago political system; despite the trend of recent years toward formal centralization and despite the extensive informal arrangements for overcoming decentralization, no one is in a position to survey the city—much less the metropolitan area—as a whole and to

Banfield's study of policymaking in Chicago rests on six case studies of who actually makes decisions. The six cases concerned a hospital, a welfare merger, the Chicago Transit Authority, the Dearborn Project, the University of Chicago campus, and an exhibition hall.—Eds.

formulate and carry out a comprehensive policy. (Mayor Daley, despite his great power as boss, can do little even in the city proper without at least tacit support from the governor.) In part, too, the tension arises from a general premise of our political culture: the belief that self-government consists, not in giving or withholding consent at infrequent intervals on matters of general principle, but rather in making influence felt in the day-to-day conduct of the public business. So long as particular interests can prevent the executive from carrying out his policy, or so long as they can place hazards and delays in the way of his carrying it out, they can demand concessions from him as the price of allowing him to act. It is the necessity of constantly making such concessions—of giving everyone something so as to generate enough support to allow of any action at all—that makes government policy so lacking in comprehensiveness and consistency.

The tendency in the United States has long been towards strengthening the executive: in Chicago as elsewhere the formal centralization of executive power is much greater than it was a decade or two ago. It seems highly unlikely, however, that this strengthening will go far enough in the foreseeable future to change the essential character of the system. Chicagoans, like other Americans, want their city's policies to be comprehensive and consistent. But they also want to exercise influence in making and carrying out these policies; they want to be able to force the government to bargain with them when its policy threatens particular interests of theirs. It will be a long time, probably, before they will be willing to sacrifice as much of the second end as would be necessary to achieve the first. The tension between the nature of the system and the requirements of planning is, for all practical purposes, ineradicable.

This conclusion would be discouraging if it were perfectly clear that a comprehensive and consistent policy is necessarily better (i.e., more productive of "welfare" or "the public interest") than one which is not. We are apt to take for granted that this is the case. We are apt to suppose that a "correct" or "consistent" policy must be the product of a mind (or minds) which has addressed itself to a "problem," and, by a conscious search, "found" or "constructed" a "solution." Most of our study of political and administrative matters proceeds on the assumption that all of the elements of a problem must be brought together within the purview of some single mind (whether of a person or team) and that the task of organization is partly to assemble the elements of the problem. The more complicated the matter, the more obvious it seems that its solution must depend upon the effort of a mind which preceives a "problem" and deliberately seeks a "solution."

It will be convenient to make a fundamental distinction between "central decision" and "social choice." Both are processes by which selections are made among the action possibilities open to some group or public. A *central decision* is in some sense purposeful or deliberate: it is made by someone (leader, chairman, mayor, planning commission, council, committee of the whole, etc.) who, in making the selection, is trying (although perhaps ineffectually) to realize some intention for the group. From the standpoint of this decision-maker, the selection of an action, or course of action, for the group represents a "solution" to a "problem." A *social choice*, on the other hand, is the accidental by-product of the actions of two or more actors—"interested parties," they will be called—who have no common intention and who make their selections competitively or without regard to each other. In a social-choice process, each actor seeks to attain his own ends; the aggregate of all actions—the situation produced by all actions together—constitutes an outcome for the group, but it is an outcome which no one has planned as a "solution" to a "problem." It is a "resultant" rather than a "solution."

It may seem to common sense that because it is the product of intention, indeed of conscious and deliberate problem-solving, a central decision is much more likely to "work" than is a social choice. The social choice is, after all, an "accident": it was not designed to serve the needs or wishes of the group, whereas the central decision *was* so designed.

And yet, despite the presumptions of common sense, it may be that under certain circumstances the competition of forces which do not aim at a common interest produces outcomes which are more "workable," "satisfactory," or "efficient" than any that could be contrived by a central decision-maker consciously searching for solutions in the common interest. Charles E. Lindblom has observed that while it is customary to think of the analysis of a policy problem as going on in the mind of one man or of a small group of men, it can also be seen as a social process. "Fragmentation" of analysis (i.e., analysis that goes on among many individuals or groups, each of whom approaches the problem from his distinctive and limited point of view) may be an aid to the correct weighting of values in a choice.

> Just how does the weighting take place in fragmentation? Not, I have suggested, in any one analyst's mind, nor in the minds of members of a research team, nor in the mind of any policy-maker or policy-making group. The weighting does not take place until actual policy decisions are made. At that time, the conflicting views of individuals and groups, each of whom have been concerned with a limited set of values, are brought to bear upon policy formulation. Policies are set as a resultant of such conflict, not because some one policy-making individual or group achieves an integration but because the pulling and hauling of various views accomplishes finally some kind of decision, probably different from what any one advocate of the final solution intended and probably different from what any one advocate could comfortably defend by reference to his own limited values. The weighing or aggregation is a political process, not an intellectual process.

The evidence of the cases presented here makes it plausible to search for some such underlying logic not obvious to common sense. For if the outcomes alone of these cases are considered—that is, if the outcomes are considered apart from the seemingly "irrational" way in which they were reached—one might conclude that the political system is remarkably effective. It is impossible, of course, to come to any conclusion on this without making a large number of highly subjective judgments—not only judgments about values, but about facts and probabilities as well. Admitting this, the writer conjectures that most reasonable people who put themselves in the role of "statesman" and consider carefully all of the relevant circumstances will conclude that the outcomes are by no means indefensible. For himself, the writer can say that they are essentially what he would have favored had he been making "decisions." In every case, it seems to him "wrong" reasons (i.e., reasons which were irrelevant, illogical, or improper as a basis of a "decision" in the public interest) were controlling, but in every case these "wrong" reasons led to outcomes that were essentially "right" or "sound."

Others may not agree. But it is only necessary to establish that "obviously wrong" reasons led to outcomes that are "not obviously wrong" in order to raise the question: are such outcomes "lucky accidents" or is there some principle at work—an "invisible hand"—that leads a choice process to a result better than anyone intends?

The case for central decision rests upon the assumption that it is possible for a competent and disinterested decision-maker to find in any situation a value premise that uniquely determines the content of the public interest. If there existed several incompatible but equally desirable courses of action, a decision-maker would obviously have to employ some "arbitrary" procedure—e.g., flipping a coin, consulting his own or someone else's personal tastes, or assessing the relative influence of the interests having a stake in the matter—in order to arrive at the decision. But the assumption of administration-minded or planning-minded persons is that this embarrassing situation seldom arises. A competent and well-intentioned decision-maker, so they suppose, can usually find in the situation some premise that clearly ought to rule. The problem of good government, therefore, is to put into office men who will look for the proper premise and use it when they find it (i.e., who seek the public interest rather than private or party advantage) and who have the technical competence necessary to apply the premise correctly in the particular circumstances.

This assumption is wrong. No matter how competent and well-intentioned, a decision-maker can never make an important decision on grounds that are not in some degree arbitrary or non-logical. He must select from among incompatible alternatives each of which is preferable in terms of a different but defensible view of the public interest. If there is a single "ultimate" value premise to which all of the lesser ones are instrumental, if its meaning is unambiguous in the concrete circumstances, and if he can know for sure which lesser premise is most instrumental to the attainment of the ultimate one, he can, indeed, make his decision in an entirely technical and non-arbitrary way. But these conditions can seldom be met, and when they can be, the matter is not "important" and usually does not require "decision." Matters come before high officials for decision precisely when it is not clear which value premises ought to be invoked, what the premises imply concretely, or what is most instrumental to their achievement. If such questions do not arise, the matter does not present itself as a "problem" at all.

In the Branch Hospital case, for example, there were at least three defensible value premises, each of which implied an altogether different decision: (*a*) "relieve overcrowding expeditiously" implied expanding on the West Side where a site was available; (*b*) "improve service" implied building on the South Side in proximity to the service area; and (*c*) "eliminate racial discrimination" implied not building at all in order to put pressure on the private hospitals. There was no higher premise to which each of these stood in an instrumental relationship and by which they could be judged. (There were slogans, of course, like "the greatest good of the greatest number," but these meant nothing concretely.) Clearly, then, the decision could not be made on technical or non-arbitrary grounds.

In such cases, where the decision-maker must select among alternatives without having any "higher" value premise by which to judge their relative importance, he must, wittingly or unwittingly, employ a criterion which has nothing to recommend it except use and wont or professional acceptance (e.g., "this is the way it is done in standard professional practice") or which expresses only his own (or someone else's) tastes or advantage, or else he must enact in imagination a choice process, imputing preference scales to the interested parties and striking, on their behalf, that compromise which he thinks "fair," productive of the most satisfaction, or the best reflection of the distribution of influence.

Thus, for example, a city-planning technician faced with the competing value premises of the Branch Hospital dispute and seeing no "higher" premise by which to decide the claims of the "lesser" ones, would, following the usual professional practice, gather a great deal of factual information on the distribution of potential hospital users, travel time, the optimal size of hospitals, etc., and then in all likelihood "find in the data" some reason—e.g., economy of travel time—for putting the hospital on the South Side. The chances are that the planner would not be as sensitive to the value, "relieve overcrowding expeditiously," as to the professionally sanctioned one, "minimize cross traffic." And it is very likely that the value, "eliminate racial discrimination," would not occur to him at all or that, if it did, it would not seem to him to be an appropriate ultimate criterion. If it were expressly called to his attention, he might even say that it is a "political" factor which should not be allowed to influence the decision.

There is likely to be a systematic bias in a technician's choice of value premises. He will, it seems plausible to suppose, minimize the importance of those elements of the situation that are controversial, intangible, or problematic. He will favor those value premises upon the importance of which there is general agreement (e.g., travel time), and he will ignore or underrate those that are controversial or not conventionally defined (e.g., eliminating racial discrimination); he will favor those that can be measured, especially those that can be measured in money terms (e.g., the cost of transportation), and he will ignore or underrate those that are intangible and perhaps indefinable as well (e.g., the mood of a neighborhood); he will favor those that are associated with reliable predictions about the factual situation (e.g., the premise of accessibility is associated with relatively reliable predictions about population movements and consumer behavior), and he will ignore or underrate those that are associated with subjective judgments of probability (e.g., that it will be harder to get political approval for a South Side site).

In a social choice process, by contrast, there is a single ultimate criterion: the distribution of influence. The importance accorded to each alternative in a choice process depends, then, upon the relative amount of influence exercised on its behalf.

This may appear to be a highly inappropriate criterion in most situations. There are, however, a number of things that can be said in its favor:

1. The distribution of influence may be viewed as the outcome (as of a given moment) of a continuing "game" which has been going on under rules that a majority of the players have been free to change at any time. That the rules are as they are implies that they seem fair, over the long run, to most of the players. Accordingly, the outcome at any particular time is also fair, even though some players are losing. A player exerts himself to win only because winners receive rewards that are not given to losers. If, therefore, the winners have no more weight in a choice than do the losers—i.e., if the criterion does not reflect the distribution of influence—they will have that much less incentive to enter the game and to fight hard to win it. If the game is, on the whole, good for the society, it is foolish to reduce the incentive to play it. In other words, a society that wants people to exert themselves to get influence must not limit, unnecessarily, opportunities to exercise it once it has been obtained.

2. A criterion which reflects the distribution of influence also reflects, although roughly, the intensity with which the competing values are held. This is so because the choice process takes into account "real" influence, i.e., not the ability of each participant to modify the behavior of others, but the ability *which each sees fit to expend, out of his limited stock, for the sake of the particular value in question.* In the Fort Dearborn case, for example, the opponents had less influence than the Sponsors in the sense that if all had exerted themselves to the utmost, the Sponsors would have had their way. But the opponents were more intensely moved. Accordingly, they exercised a larger part of their influence potential than did the Sponsors. To the extent that the process was one of bargaining, it registered a compound of influence and intensity of interest. If it is considered appropriate to maximize "total satisfaction" of those whose views are taken into account, then it is essential to have some indication of how intensely each value is held. The choice mechanism forces each bargainer to give up something (the amount of influence he "spends"); this something can therefore be taken as a measure of the value to him of what he seeks. (If the influence distribution is "incorrect," the measure will of course be, to that extent, "wrong." But, as was maintained in the paragraph above, there is some reason to assume that the distribution is "correct.")

3. The character of the influence exercised may afford additional grounds for considering the distribution of influence to be an appropriate criterion. In one situation or set of situations, influence may consist of "forcing others to do one's will even when that will is anti-social." In another it may consist of "persuading others on reasonable grounds to accept a view of the common interest." There are circumstances in which one can exercise influence only by being (or seeming to be) intelligently concerned with the common good ("by main force of being right"). So far as this is the case in a given society or situation, the criterion of influence has further justification.

The appropriateness of the criterion of influence is, however, only one aspect of the larger question, namely, the appropriateness of the social-choice process as a whole. It would be a point in favor of the choice process and a point against the decision process if it could be shown that while neither is clearly undesirable as a procedure for selecting an ultimate criterion, the former is more likely to bring all relevant considerations to the fore and to give them the attention they deserve.

There is indeed much reason to think that this is the case. A decision-maker, even one of long experience and great capacity, is not likely, when an issue first arises, to be fully aware of all of the interests that are at stake in it or of the importance that is attached to each interest by those who hold it. He gets this information (except with regard to the most obvious matters) only as the interested parties themselves bring it to his attention. The effort an interested party makes to put its case before the decision-maker will be in proportion to *the advantage to be gained from a favorable outcome multiplied by the probability of influencing the decision*. Thus, no matter how high the stakes, an interested party will invest no effort at all in putting its case before a decision-maker who cannot be influenced. On the other hand, if there is a virtual certainty that the decision can be influenced, an interested party will have incentive to expend, in the effort to influence the decision, almost all of what may be gained from a favorable decision.

If the decision-maker is surely going to make the decision on purely public grounds, the possibilities of influencing him are relatively small. The interested party may present the facts of its case in the best possible light. It may argue that the public interest is to be understood in this way rather than that. But it cannot go much further than this. It cannot do more than try to persuade. In some cases the probability of success by persuasion may be sufficient to induce it to put forth a considerable effort. In others, however, its effort will be perfunctory because it knows that the decision-maker will pay little attention. In still others, it will make no effort at all because it knows that the decision-maker is not open to persuasion.

If, on the other hand, the official is open to influence by other means than persuasion, the probability of influencing the outcome may be vastly increased. If, indeed, it is possible, by a large enough expenditure of influence, virtually to compel him to select the favored alternative, then the incentive to make the effort is limited only by the advantage to be had from its success. In these circumstances, the affected interests will almost literally bring their cases "forcibly to the attention of" the official.

In a system of government in which the possibility of influencing outcomes is great, a vast amount of effort is spent by very able people in the attempt to do so. This expenditure of effort has some socially valuable results. It leads to the production of more information about the various alternatives and to a clarification of the values that are involved. Not only are the officials compelled to take into account more than they otherwise would, but the interests themselves are brought to examine their own and each other's positions with great care. Of course, in an instance where there exists some obviously appropriate and concretely meaningful value criterion upon which it is apparent, once the information is all at hand, that the official's decision ought to turn, the ability of an interested party to force the official to decide by some other criterion introduces error into the selection process. The argument here, however, is that such criteria almost never exist in matters of importance, and that when they do not exist, it is socially desirable that interested parties have incentive to vigorously assert value principles which will compete with those necessarily arbitrary ones (e.g., professional use and wont) which officials, wittingly or unwittingly, must fall back upon.

In a political system in which there exists no possibility whatever of influencing an outcome by an exercise of power (as distinguished from persuasion), it is unlikely that an interested party whose value position is not widely accepted as a plausible ultimate basis of decision will exert itself to put that position forward. Berry and Calloway, for example, would probably not have appeared upon the scene in the Branch Hospital dispute if the Chicago political system had been such as to make clear that the decision would be entirely in the hands of planners or technically-minded people; but had they not exerted themselves, it is likely that the "race" position would have been entirely overlooked or given little weight. (The Welfare Council's planners, it will be remembered, virtually ignored it.) A "decision" reached without the racial aspects of the matter having been taken fully into account would have been deficient, although it might well have *seemed* (the deficiency not being called to anyone's attention) more "rational" than the social choice that was actually made.

In summary, then, it has been maintained: (1) that when, as is the case in important matters, there exists no concretely unambiguous criterion which clearly ought to rule, the distribution of "real" influence, as revealed in competitive exercises of influence, may be the appropriate criterion; and (2) that a selection process (or political system) which allows of the exercise of power other than that of persuasion by affected interests produces a wider canvas of policy alternatives and a more thorough scrutiny of each alternative than does a process which allows the affected interests only the opportunity to persuade. A corollary of these propositions is that the "rationality" of the process in which only persuasion is possible (i.e., the decision process) is often a simplification secured by overlooking or radically undervaluing some alternatives.

The social-choice process, however, suffers from at least two inherent limitations of great importance:

1. It takes into account only such ends as actors of influence see fit to assert, and it weights these ends according to the amount of influence behind them and without regard to their intrinsic value. In many circumstances, the distribution of influence may be an entirely inappropriate criterion. There may be ends which are not asserted in the choice process at all or which are asserted only weakly (e.g., ends which pertain to the community "as a whole") but which nevertheless ought to determine the outcome, ought to enter into it along with the ends which are asserted by influentials, or ought to serve as criteria by which the appropriateness and relative value of these and other ends are established.

2. There may exist an outcome which represents the "greatest total benefit" of

the parties to the choice process but which is not likely to be found if each party seeks only his own advantage. There may, for example, be two ways in which A can attain his end equally well and between which he is indifferent. One of these ways may be advantageous to B and the other disadvantageous to him. A may not perceive the opportunity to increase total satisfaction by acting so as to benefit B; even if he does perceive it, he may have no incentive to act upon it.

It is a disadvantage of the choice process that no one has either an incentive to devise "greatest total benefit" solutions or the information about the preferences scales of the various interested parties that would be needed in order to do so.

In the Branch Hospital dispute, an arrangement whereby the county paid its clients' hospital bills in full, gave them freedom of choice in hospitals, and offered subsidies for expansion of those private hospitals which agreed not to discriminate might have represented a "greatest total benefit" solution. (It would presumably have suited both the left and the right wings of the Negro community, and the white hospitals as well.) But this solution was not likely to be devised by any of the parties to the struggle; each was too much committed to the solution implied by its own ends to look for one which would serve the ends of all.

The distribution of influence may be such as to paralyze action altogether. (In only two of the six cases described in the book—the Exhibition Hall and the Welfare Merger—was a course of action carried out as planned by its proponents; in the other cases, the outcomes were essentially the checking of action.) This tendency to paralyze action is sometimes regarded as a defect of the choice process. In certain circumstances it may be, of course. But from a general standpoint, there is no presumption that "inaction" represents a less desirable outcome than "action."

Certainly, a social-choice process is not always to be preferred to a central-decision process. Which is more appropriate will depend upon the circumstances of the case, especially the following: (a) the complexity of the policy problem to be solved, including especially the number of elements that must somehow be taken into account or weighted (and thus the amount of conflict in the situation) and the time and other resources that can be employed in looking for a solution; the more complicated the problem, the stronger the case for the choice mechanism; (b) the visibility of the factual and value elements that should be taken into account; where there is reason to believe that all relevant values (and their intensities) are not known, the play of influence should be allowed in order to assist their being made known; (c) the presence or absence of an appropriate "ultimate" criterion which is sufficiently definite in meaning to afford a basis for selection among the competing values that are instrumental to it; where such a criterion exists, a decision process is indicated, and the play of influence on the decision-maker is clearly undesirable; and (d) the appropriateness of one or another procedural criterion (e.g., that the settlement should reflect the distribution of influence, that it should accord with professional use and wont, that it should be "fair"); if the distribution of influence, or the bases upon which influence rests, are clearly undesirable, and if a decision-maker can be expected to employ procedural criteria which are *not* clearly undesirable, there is, of course, a presumption in favor of the decision process.

The discussion so far will have suggested the possibility of a selection process which combines features of both central decision and social choice and which therefore has some advantages (or, it could also be, disadvantages) of both. In a *mixed decision-choice* process, there are two or more interested parties each of whom seeks its own advantage without regard to any common intention. But there is also on the scene a central decision-maker who intervenes in the selection process to perform one or more of the following functions:

1. The central decision-maker may regulate the selection process so that "public values" are achieved or, negatively, not disregarded. He may, in the first place, decide whether the matter is one in which only the self-regarding ends of the interested parties should be taken into account (i.e., whether they are the only relevant value stuff) or whether there are corporate ends or "public values" that ought to be taken into account instead of, or along with, the self-regarding ends of the interested parties. He decides, in other words, whether selections ought to be made by social choice, central decision, or a mixed process. If he decides either that only "public values" or only "self-regarding ends" are relevant, the process then ceases to be "mixed": it becomes either central decision or social choice. But he may decide that what is appropriate is an aggregation of both public values *and* self-regarding ends—an aggregation in which certain public values and certain self-regarding ends are given greater or lesser weight. (He may, for example, decide that the matter is one in which a "qualified individualist" conception of the public interest is appropriate, and, accordingly, he may disregard "tastes" of "private-spirited" persons while giving great weight to the "settled convictions" of "public-spirited" persons.) Thus, the selection may be made through a social-choice process, but through a social-choice process *which operates within a limiting framework laid down by central direction.* The outcome of such a process is therefore both a "resultant" (from the standpoint of the interested parties) and a "solution" (from the standpoint of the central decision-maker, who decided which interested parties should be allowed to enter the process, how their ends should be weighted, and what importance should be accorded to "public values").

2. The central decision-maker may co-ordinate the activities of the interested parties in order to help them find positions optimal in terms of their (self-regarding) ends—i.e., positions such that no possible reallocation would make anyone better off without making others worse off. The central decision-maker keeps track of external economies and diseconomies, which are not visible to the interested parties, and he watches for "saddle-points." He may, for example, guide the interested parties to a greater total "welfare" merely by supplying information (e.g., he may know that A is indifferent as between states x and y, whereas B much prefers state y; by pointing out that someone will gain and no one will lose by choosing state y, he increases welfare), or he may be the agent through which interpersonal comparisons of welfare are made or other agreed-upon rules are applied (e.g., if state x would mean great gains to A and small losses to B, he may intervene to impose the loss on B).

3. The central decision-maker merely records the relative influence exercised by the competing interested parties. In this case, he is merely an environment which facilitates the working out of a social-choice process. The interested parties make their influence known by putting pressure upon him; his action is entirely in response to these pressures (he is a weathervane, responding equally to all the breezes that blow), and it constitutes the resultant of the selection process.

In the first two of these three roles—but not in the third—the central decision-maker may eliminate inconsistencies and anomalies from the outcome. Therefore, in these two types of mixed process the outcomes are both resultants (they are this insofar as they are the unintended product of competition among interested parties) and at the same time solutions (they are this insofar as they are the product of an intention—that of the central decision-maker).

It will be seen that the Chicago political system is of the type that has been called "mixed decision-choice." It has, therefore, in principle, and to a large extent in practice, the advantages of both polar types—social choice and central decision. In the writer's view, in its general features it is a reasonably close approximation of the logical model that is preferable.

One great advantage of social choice is that it involves a thorough canvas of all the elements—both the factual and the value elements—in a selection situation. The better their opportunities to influence an outcome, the more carefully will interested parties examine a situation for its effect on them, and the more vigorously will they assert their interests when they have identified them. In Chicago the opportunities to exercise influence are great enough to call into play the best abilities of many extremely able people. Nothing of importance is done in Chicago without its first being discovered what interests will be affected and how they will be affected and without the losses that will accrue to some being weighed carefully against the gains that will accrue to others. It is easy for Americans to take this kind of thing for granted, but there are cities—London, for example—where great decisions are made with little understanding of the consequences for those interests which are not plainly visible to the decision-makers.

Another great advantage of social choice is that, where there exists no concretely meaningful criterion of the public interest and where, accordingly (whether they realize it or not), central decision-makers must employ some standard (e.g., professional use and wont) that is essentially arbitrary, the competition of interested parties supplies a criterion—the distribution of "real" influence—which may be both generally acceptable and, since it puts a premium upon effort to acquire influence, serviceable to the society. In the cases reported here, there were not, in the writer's opinion, criteria from which central decision-makers could have obtained clear directions with regard to the main questions. (There was not, for example, any way by which a central decision-maker could have known whether "racial justice" or some other general end ought to be made decisive in the Branch Hospital dispute.) There being no "public values" which obviously ought to be decisive, the distribution of real influence was, it seems to the writer, as defensible a basis for decisions as any other. This judgment is strengthened by the character of the influence that is exercised in Chicago. For the most part, as previous chapters have shown, the interested parties in Chicago find it hard to take positions which cannot be defended in terms of some conception of the public interest.

The advantages of central decision are that the central decision-maker can assert the supremacy of "public values" and can find the outcome that is "best for all." On the Chicago scene there is, to be sure, no one central-decision-maker who can do this in all of the most important matters. The mayor and the governor, whose tacit collaboration is essential in anything of importance, are required by the logic of their positions to disagree. Antagonism between mayor and governor, Democrat and Republican, Cook County and downstate, is the very basis of the political system. (Even in the rare intervals when the governor is a Democrat, the antagonism is not removed, for even then the Senate is dominated by downstate and is almost sure to be Republican.) There is, nevertheless, an important element of central decision in the Chicago system. The governor, the mayor, and the president of the County Board are all in positions to assert the supremacy of "public values" and, in general, to regulate the workings of the social-choice process. Although their practice is to let the social-choice process work itself out with as little interference from them as possible, each of them has in some matters the power to impose a settlement when he thinks doing so is necessary. Sometimes, as in the Fort Dearborn Project case, a political head's intervention is a conspicuous feature of the situation. At other times, a political head merely registers the influence exerted by the competing interests. (In the Branch Hospital dispute, this seemed for a long while to be Ryan's main function; in the end, however, he intervened to patch up a last-minute compromise without which all parties would have been worse off. Some observers were left with the suspicion that the clash of interests in that affair was not as important as it seemed—that it was, in fact, nothing but a public show staged by Ryan to justify a decision he had reached long before on the basis of his view of "public values.")

That the mixed–decision-choice process, as it works in Chicago, takes more time to produce an outcome than, presumably, a central decision process would take and that the outcome, when reached, is likely to be a stalemate cannot, of course, be held against it. Time spent discovering and evaluating the probable consequences of a proposal is not necessarily wasted; and if in the end nothing is done, or not much is done, that may be because it is in the public interest to do little or nothing.

44

THEODORE J. LOWI

DISTRIBUTION, REGULATION, REDISTRIBUTION: THE FUNCTIONS OF GOVERNMENT

In the long run, all governmental policies may be considered redistributive, because in the long run some people pay in taxes more than they receive in services. Or, all may be thought regulatory because, in the long run, a governmental decision on the use of resources can only displace a private decision about the same resource or at least reduce private alternatives about the resource. But politics works in the short run, and in the short run certain kinds of government decisions can be made without regard to limited resources. Policies of this kind are called "distributive," a term first coined for nineteenth-century land policies, but easily extended to include most contemporary public land and resource policies; rivers and harbors ("pork barrel") programs; defense procurement and research and development programs; labor, business, and agricultural "clientele" services; and the traditional tariff. Distributive policies are characterized by the ease with which they can be disaggregated and dispensed unit by small unit, each unit more or less in isolation from other units and from any general rule. "Patronage" in the fullest meaning of the word can be taken as a synonym for "distributive." These are policies that are virtually not policies at all but are highly individualized decisions that only by accumulation can be called a policy. They are policies in which the indulged and the deprived, the loser and the recipient, need never come into direct confrontation. Indeed, in many instances of distributive policy, the deprived cannot as a class be identified, because the most influential among them can be accommodated by further disaggregation of the stakes.

Regulatory policies are also specific and individual in their impact, but they are not capable of the almost infinite amount of disaggregation typical of distributive policies. Although the laws are stated in general terms ("Arrange the transportation system artistically." "Thou shalt not show favoritism in pricing."), the impact of regulatory decisions is clearly one of directly raising costs and/or reducing or expanding the alternatives of private individuals ("Get off the grass!" "Produce kosher if you advertise kosher!"). Regulatory policies are distinguishable from distributive in that in the short run the regulatory decision involves a direct choice as to who will be indulged and who deprived. Not all applicants for a single television channel or an overseas air route can be propitiated. Enforcement of an unfair labor practice on the part of management weakens management in its dealings with labor. So, while implementation is firm-by-firm and case-by-case, policies cannot be disaggregated to the level of the individual or the single firm (as in distribution), because individual decisions must be made by application of a general rule and therefore become interrelated within the broader standards of law. Decisions cumulate among all individuals affected by the law in roughly the same way. Since the most stable lines of perceived common impact are the basic sectors of the economy, regulatory decisions are cumulative largely along sectoral lines; regulatory policies are usually disaggregable only down to the sector level.

Redistributive policies are like regulatory policies in the sense that relations among broad categories of private individuals are involved and, hence, individual decisions must be interrelated. But on all other counts there are great differences in the nature of impact. The categories of impact are much broader, approaching social classes. They are, crudely speaking, haves and have-nots, bigness and smallness, bourgeoisie and proletariat. The aim involved is not use of property but property itself, not equal treatment but equal possession, not behavior but being. The fact that our income tax is in reality only mildly redistributive does not alter the fact of the aims and the stakes involved in income tax policies. The same goes for our various "welfare state" programs, which are redistributive only for those who entered retirement or unemployment rolls without having contributed at all. The nature of a redistributive issue is not determined by the outcome of a battle over how redistributive a policy is going to be. Expectations about what it *can* be, what it threatens to be, are determinative.

ARENAS OF POWER

Once one posits the general tendency of these areas of policy or governmental activity to develop characteristic political structures, a number of hypotheses become compelling. And when the various hypotheses are accumulated, the general contours of each of the three arenas begin quickly to resemble, respectively, the three "general" theories of political process. The arena that develops around distributive policies is best characterized in the terms of E. E. Schattschneider's findings on the politics of tariff legislation in the nineteen-twenties. The regulatory arena corresponds to the pluralist school, and the school's general notions are found to be limited pretty much to this one arena. The redistributive arena most closely approximates, with some adaptation, an elitist view of the political process.

(1) The distributive arena can be identified in considerable detail from Schattschneider's case-study alone.[1] What he and his pluralist successors did not see was that the traditional structure of tariff politics is also in largest part the structure of politics of all those diverse policies identified earlier as distributive.

The arena is "pluralistic" only in the sense that a large number of small, intensely organized interests are operating. In fact, there is even greater multiplicity of participants here than the pressure-group model can account for, because essentially it is a politics of every man for himself. The single person and the single firm are the major activists.

Although a generation removed, Schattschneider's conclusions about the politics of the Smoot-Hawley Tariff are almost one-for-one applicable to rivers and harbors and land development policies, tax exemptions, defense procurement, area redevelopment, and government "services." Since there is no real basis for discriminating between those who should and those who should not be protected [indulged], says Schattschneider, Congress seeks political support by "giving a limited protection [indulgence] to all interests strong enough to furnish formidable resistance." Decision-makers become "responsive to considerations of equality, consistency, impartiality, uniformity, precedent, and moderation, however formal and insubstantial these may be." Furthermore, a "policy that is so hospitable and catholic . . . disorganizes the opposition."

When a billion-dollar issue can be disaggregated into many millions of nickel-dime items and each item can be dealt with without regard to the others, multiplication of interests and of access is inevitable, and so is reduction of conflict. All of this has the greatest bearing on the relations among participants and, therefore, the "power structure." Indeed, coalitions must be built to pass legislation and "make policy," but what of the nature and basis of the coalitions? In the distributive arena, political relationships approximate what Schattschneider called "mutual noninterference"—"a mutuality under which it is proper for each to seek duties [indulgences] for himself but improper and unfair to oppose duties [indulgences] sought by others." In the area of rivers and harbors, references are made to "pork barrel" and "log-rolling," but these colloquialisms have not been taken sufficiently seriously. A log-rolling coalition is not one forged of conflict, compromise, and tangential interest but, on the contrary, one composed of members who have absolutely nothing in common; and this is possible because the "pork barrel" is a container for unrelated items. This is the typical form of relationship in the distributive arena.

The structure of these log-rolling relationships leads typically, though not always, to Congress; and the structure is relatively stable because all who have access of any sort usually support whoever are the leaders. And there tend to be "elites" of a peculiar sort in the Congressional committees whose jurisdictions include the subject-matter in question. Until recently, for instance, on tariff matters the House Ways and Means Committee was virtually the government. Much the same can be said for Public Works on rivers and harbors. It is a broker leadership, but "policy" is best understood as cooptation rather than conflict and compromise.

Distributive issues individualize conflict and provide the basis for highly stable coalitions that are virtually irrelevant to the larger policy outcomes; thousands of obscure decisions are merely accumulated into a "policy" of protection or of natural-resources development or of defense subcontracting. Congress did not "give up" the tariff; as the tariff became a matter of regulation (see below), committee elites lost their power to contain the participants because obscure decisions became interrelated, therefore less obscure, and more controversy became built in and unavoidable.

(2) The regulatory arena could hardly be better identified than in the thousands of pages written for the whole polity by the pluralists. But, unfortunately, some translation is necessary to accommodate pluralism to its more limited universe. The regulatory arena appears to be composed of a multiplicity of groups organized around tangential relations or David Truman's "shared attitudes." Within this narrower context of regulatory decisions, one can even go so far as to accept the most extreme pluralist statement that policy tends to be a residue of the interplay of group conflict. This statement can be severely criticized only by use of examples drawn from non-regulatory decisions.

As I argued before, there is no way for regulatory policies to be disaggregated into very large numbers of unrelated items. Because individual regulatory decisions involve direct confrontations of indulged and deprived, the typical political coalition is born of conflict and compromise among tangential interests that usually involve a total sector of the economy. Thus, while the typical basis for coalition in distributive politics is uncommon interests (log-rolling), an entirely different basis is typical in regulatory politics.

Owing to the unrelatedness of issues in distributive politics, the activities of single participants need not be related but rather can be specialized as the situation warrants it. But the relatedness of regulatory issues, at least up to the sector level of the trade association, leads to the containment of all these within the association. When all the stakes are contained in one organization, constituents have no alternative but to fight against each other to shape the policies of that organization or actually to abandon it.

What this suggests is that the typical power structure in regulatory politics is far less stable than that in the distributive arena. Since coalitions form around shared interests, the coalitions will shift as the interests change or as conflicts of interest emerge. With such group-based and shifting patterns of conflict built into every regulatory issue, it is in most cases impossible for a Congressional committee, an administrative agency, a peak association governing board, or a social elite to contain all the participants long enough to establish a stable power elite. Policy outcomes seem inevitably to be the residue remaining after all the reductions of demands by all participants have been made in order to extend support to majority size. But a majority-sized coalition of shared interests on one issue could not possibly be entirely appropriate for some other issue. In regulatory decision-making, relationships among group leadership elements and between them on any one or more points of governmental access are too unstable to form a single policy-making elite. As a consequence, decision-making tends to pass from administrative agencies and Congressional committees to Congress, the place where uncertainties in the policy process have always been settled. Congress as an institution is the last resort for breakdowns in bargaining over policy, just as in the case of parties the primary is a last resort for breakdowns in bargaining over nominations. No one leadership group can contain the conflict by an almost infinite subdivision and distribution of the stakes. In the regulatory political process, Congress and the "balance of power" seem to play the classic role attributed to them by the pluralists.

Beginning with reciprocity in the 1930's, the tariff began to lose its capacity for infinite disaggregation because it slowly underwent redefinition, moving away from its purely domestic significance towards that of an instrument of international politics. In brief, the tariff, especially following World War II and our assumption of peacetime international leadership, became a means of regulating the domestic economy for international purposes. The significant feature here is not the international but the regulatory part of the redefinition. As the process of redefinition took place, a number of significant shifts in power relations took place as well, because it was no longer possible to deal with each dutiable item in isolation. Everything in Bauer, Pool, and Dexter points toward the expansion of relationships to the level of the sector. The political problem of the South was the concentration of textile industry there. Coal, oil, and rails came closer and closer to coalition. The final shift came with the 1962 Trade Expansion Act, which enabled the President for the first time to deal with broad categories (to the sector) rather than individual commodities.

Certain elements of distributive politics remain, for two obvious reasons. First, there are always efforts on the part of political leaders to disaggregate policies becuase this is the best way to spread the patronage and to avoid conflict. (Political actors, like economic actors, probably view open competition as a necessary evil or a last resort to be avoided at almost any cost.) Second, until 1962, the basic tariff law and schedules were still contained in the Smoot-Hawley Act. This act was amended by Reciprocal Trade but only to the extent of allowing negotiated reductions rather than reductions based on comparative costs. Until 1962, tariff politics continued to be based on commodity-by-commodity transactions, and thus until then tariff coalitions could be based upon individual firms (or even branches of large and diversified firms) and log-rolling, unrelated interests. The escape clause and peril point were maintained in the 1950's so that transactions could be made on individual items even within reciprocity. And the coalitions of strange bedfellows continued: "Offered the proper coalition, they both [New England textiles and Eastern railroads] might well have been persuaded that their interest was in the opposite direction."

But despite the persistence of certain distributive features, the true nature of tariff in the 1960's emerges as regulatory policy with a developing regulatory arena. Already we can see some changes in Congress even more clearly than the few already observed in the group structure. Out of a committee (House Ways and Means) elite, we can see the emergence of Congress in a pluralist setting. Even as early as 1954–1955, the compromises eventually ratified by Congress were worked out, not in committee through direct cooptation of interests, but in the Randall Commission, a collection of the major interests in conflict. Those issues that could not be thrashed out through the "group process" also could not be thrashed out in committee but had to pass on to Congress and the floor. After 1954 the battle centered on major categories of goods (even to the extent of a textile management-union entente) and the battle took place more or less openly on the floor. The weakening of the Ways and Means Committee as the tariff elite is seen in the fact that in 1955 Chairman Jere Cooper was unable to push a closed rule through. The Rules Committee, "in line with tradition," granted a closed rule but the House voted it down 207–178. Bauer, Pool, and Dexter saw this as a victory for protectionism, but it is also evidence of the emerging regulatory arena—arising from the difficulty of containing conflict and policy within the governing committee. The last effort to keep the tariff as a traditional instrument of distributive politics—a motion by Daniel Reed to recommit, with instructions to write in a provision that Tariff Commission rulings under the escape clause be final except where the President finds the national security to be involved—was voted down 206–199. After that, right up to 1962, it was clear that tariff decisions would not be made piecemeal. Tariff became a regulatory policy in 1962; all that remains of distributive politics now are quotas and subsidies for producers of specific commodities injured by general tariff reductions.

(3) Compared particularly with the regulatory area, very few case-studies of redistributive decisions have ever been published. This in itself is a significant datum—which C. Wright Mills attributes to the middle-level character of the issues that have gotten attention. But, whatever the reasons, it reduces the opportunities for elaborating upon and testing the scheme. Most of the propositions to follow are illustrated by a single case, the "welfare state" battle of the 1930's. But this case is a complex of many decisions that became one of the most important acts of policy ever achieved in the United States. A brief review of the facts of the case will be helpful. Other cases will be referred to in less detail from time to time.

As the 1934 mid-term elections approached, pressures for a federal social security system began to mount. The Townsend Plan and the Lundeen Bill had become nationally prominent and were gathering widespread support. Both schemes were severely redistributive, giving all citizens access to government-based insurance as a matter of right. In response, the President created in June of 1934 a Committee on Economic Security (CES) composed of top cabinet members with Secretary of Labor Perkins as chairman. In turn, they set up an Advisory Council and a Technical Board, which held hearings, conducted massive studies, and emerged on January 17, 1935, with a bill. The insiders around the CES were representatives of large industries, business associations, unions, and the most interested government bureaucracies. And the detailed legislative histories reveal that virtually all of the debate was contained within the CES and its committees until a mature bill emerged. Since not all of the major issues had been settled in the CES's bill, its members turned to Congress with far from a common front. But the role of Congress was still not what would have been expected. Except for a short fight over committee jurisdiction (won by the more conservative Finance and Ways and Means committees) the legislative process was extraordinarily quiet, despite the import of the issues. Hearings in both Houses brought forth very few witnesses, and these were primarily CES members supporting the bill, and Treasury Department officials, led by Morgenthau, opposing it with "constructive criticism."

The Congressional battle was quiet because the real struggle was taking place elsewhere, essentially between the Hopkins-Perkins bureaucracies and the Treasury. The changes made in the CES bill had all been proposed by Morgenthau (the most important one being the principle of contribution, which took away the redistributive sting). And the final victory for Treasury and mild redistribution came with the removal of administrative responsibility from both Labor and Hopkins's Federal Emergency Relief Administration. Throughout all of this some public expressions of opinion were to be heard from the peak associations, but their efforts were mainly expended in the quieter proceedings in the bureaucracies. The Congress's role seems largely to have been one of ratifying agreements that arose out of the bureaucracies and the class agents represented there. Revisions attributable to Congress concerned such matters as exceptions in coverage, which are part of the distributive game that Congress plays at every opportunity. The *principle* of the Act was set in an interplay involving (quietly) top executives and business and labor leaders.

With only slight changes in the left-right positions of the participants, the same pattern has been observed in income tax decisions. Professor Stanley S. Surrey notes: "The question, 'Who speaks for tax equity and tax fairness?,' is answered today largely in terms of only the Treasury Department." "Thus, in tax bouts . . . it is the Treasury versus percentage legislation, the Treasury versus capital gains, the Treasury versus this constituent, the Treasury versus that private group. . . . As a consequence, the congressman . . . [sees] a dispute . . . only as a contest between a private group and a government department." Congress, says Surrey, "occupies the role of mediator between the tax views of the executive and the demands of the pressure groups." And when the tax issues "are at a major political level, as are tax rates or personal exemptions, then pressure groups, labor organizations, the Chamber of Commerce, the National Association of Manufacturers, and the others, become concerned." The "average congressman does not basically believe in the present income tax in the upper brackets," but rather than touch the principle he deals in "special hardship" and "penalizing" and waits for decisions on principle to come from abroad. Amidst the 1954–1955 tax controversies, for example, Ways and Means members decided to allow each member one bill to be favorably reported if the bill met with unanimous agreement.

Issues that involve redistribution cut closer than any others along class lines and activate interests in what are roughly class terms. If there is ever any cohesion within the peak associations, it occurs on redistributive issues, and their rhetoric suggests that they occupy themselves most of the time with these. In a ten-year period just before and after, but not including, the war years, the Manufacturers' Association of Connecticut, for example, expressed itself overwhelmingly more often on redistributive than on any other types of issues. Table 44-1 summarizes the pattern, showing that expressions on generalized issues involving basic relations between bourgeoisie and proletariat outnumbered expressions on regulation of business practices by 870 to 418, despite the larger number of issues in the latter category. This pattern goes contrary to the one observed by Bauer, Pool, and Dexter in tariff politics, where they discovered, much to their surprise, that self-interest did not activate both "sides" equally.

TABLE 44-1. PUBLISHED EXPRESSIONS OF MANUFACTURERS' ASSOCIATION OF CONNECTICUT
ON SELECTED ISSUES

	Number of References in Ten-year Period (1934–40, 1946–48)	Per Cent of Favorable References
1. Unspecified regulation	378	7.7
2. Labor relations, general	297	0.0
3. Wages and hours	195	0.5
Total expressions, redistribution	870	
4. Trade practices	119	13.8
5. Robinson-Patman	103	18.4
6. Antitrust	72	26.4
7. Basing points	55	20.0
8. Fair-Trade (Miller-Tydings)	69	45.5
Total expressions, regulation	418	

Source: Lane, *The Regulation of Businessmen* (New Haven, 1953), 38ff. The figures are his; their arrangement is mine.

Rather, they found, the concreteness and specificity of protectionist interests activated them much more often and intensely than did the general, ideological position of the liberal-traders. This was true in tariff, as they say, because there the "structure of the communications system favored the propagation of particular demands." But there is also a structure of communications favoring generalized and ideological demands; this structure consists of the peak associations, and it is highly effective when the issues are generalizable. This is the case consistently for redistributive issues, almost never for distributive issues, and only seldom for regulatory issues.

As the pluralists would argue, there will be a vast array of organized interests for any item on the policy agenda. But the relations among the interests and between them and government vary, and the nature of and conditions for this variation are what our political analyses should be concerned with. Let us say, in brief, that on Monday night the big associations meet in agreement and considerable cohesion on "the problem of government," the income tax, the Welfare State. On Tuesday, facing regulatory issues, the big associations break up into their constituent trade and other specialized groups, each prepared to deal with special problems in its own special ways, usually along subject-matter lines. On Wednesday night still another fission takes place as the pork barrel and the other forms of subsidy and policy patronage come under consideration. The parent groups and "catalytic groups" still exist, but by Wednesday night they have little identity. As Bauer, Pool, and Dexter would say, they have preserved their unanimity through overlapping memberships. They gain identity to the extent that they can define the issues in redistributive terms. And when interests in issues are more salient in sectoral or geographic or individual terms, the common or generalized factor will be lost in abstractness and diffuseness. This is what happened to the liberal trade groups in the tariff battles of the 1950's, when "the protectionist positions was more firmly grounded in direct business considerations and . . . the liberal-trade position fitted better with the ideology of the times . . ."

Where the peak associations, led by elements of Mr. Mills's power elite, have reality, their resources and access are bound to affect power relations. Owing to their stability and the impasse (or equilibrium) in relations among broad classes of the entire society, the political structure of the redistributive arena seems to be highly stabilized, virtually institutionalized. Its stability, unlike that of the distributive arena, derives from shared interests. But in contrast to the regulatory arena, these shared interests are sufficiently stable and clear and consistent to provide the foundation for ideologies. Table 44-2 summarizes the hypothesized differences in political relationships drawn above.

Many of the other distinctive characteristics of this arena are related to, perhaps follow from, the special role of the peak associations. The cohesion of peak associations means that the special differences among related but competing groups are likely to be settled long before the policies reach the governmental agenda. In many respects the upperclass directors perform the functions in the redistributive arena that are performed by Congressional committees in the distributive arena and by committees and Congress in the regulatory arena. But the differences are crucial. In distributive policies there are as many "sides" as there are tariff items, bridges and damns to be built, parcels of public land to be given away or leased, and so on. And there are probably as many elites as there are Congressional committees and subcommittees which have jurisdiction over distributive policies. In redistribution, there will never be more than two sides and the sides are clear, stable, and consistent. Negotiation is possible, but only for the purpose of strengthening or softening the impact of redistribution. And there is probably one elite for each side. The elites do not correspond directly to bourgeoisie and proletariat; they are better understood under Wallace Sayre's designation of "money-providing" and "service-demanding" groups. Nonetheless, the basis for coalition is broad, and it centers around those individuals most respected and best known for worth and wealth. If the top leaders did not know each other and develop common perspectives as a result of common schooling, as Mills would argue, these commonalities could easily develop later in life because the kinds of stakes involved in redistributive issues are always the same. So institutionalized does the conflict become that governmental bureaucracies themselves begin to reflect them, as do national party leaders and Administrations. Finally, just as the nature of redistributive policies influences politics towards the centralization and stabilization of conflict, so does it further influence the removal of decision-making from Congress. A decentralized and bargaining Congress can cumulate but it cannot balance, and redistributive policies require complex balancing on a very large scale. What William H. Riker has said of budget-making applies here: ". . . legislative governments cannot endure a budget. Its finances must be totted up by party leaders in the legislature itself. In a complex fiscal system, however, haphazard legislative judgments cannot bring revenue into even rough alignment with supply. So budgeting is introduced—which transfers financial control to the budget maker. . . ." Congress can provide exceptions to principles and it can implement those principles

TABLE 44-2.   ARENAS AND POLITICAL RELATIONSHIPS: A DIAGRAMMATIC SURVEY

Arena	Primary Political Unit	Relation Among Units	Power Structure	Stability of Structure	Primary Decisional Locus	Implementation
Distribution	Individual, firm, corporation	Log-rolling, mutual non-interference, uncommon interests	Non-conflictual elite with support groups	Stable	Congressional committee and/or agency**	Agency centralized to primary functional unit ("bureau")
Regulation*	Group	"The coalition," shared subject-matter interest, bargaining	Pluralistic, multi-centered, "theory of balance"	Unstable	Congress, in classic role	Agency decentralized from center by "delegation," mixed control
Redistribution	Association	The "peak association," class, ideology	Conflictual elite, i.e., elite and counterelite	Stable	Executive and peak associations	Agency centralized toward top (above bureau"), elaborate standards

* Given the multiplicity of organized interests in the regulatory arena, there are obviously many cases of successful log-rolling coalitions that resemble the coalitions prevailing in distributive politics. In this respect, the difference between the regulatory and the distributive arenas is thus one of degree. The *predominant* form of coalition in regulatory politics is deemed to be that of common or tangential interest. Although the difference is only one of degree, it is significant because this prevailing type of coalition makes the regulatory arena so much more unstable, unpredictable, and non-elitist ("balance of power"). When we turn to the redistributive arena, however, we find differences of principle in every sense of the word.

** Distributive politics tends to stabilize around an institutional unit. In most cases, it is the Congressional committee (or subcommittee). But in others, particularly in the Department of Agriculture, the focus is the agency or the agency *and* the committee. In the cities, this is the arena where machine domination continues, if machines were in control in the first place.

with elaborate standards of implementation as a condition for the concessions that money-providers will make. But the makers of principles of redistribution seem to be the holders of the "command posts."

None of this suggests a power elite such as Mills would have had us believe existed, but it does suggest a type of stable and continual conflict that can only be understood in class terms. The foundation upon which the social-stratification and power-elite school rested, especially when dealing with national power, was so conceptually weak and empirically unsupported that its critics were led to err in the opposite direction by denying the direct relevance of social and institutional positions and the probability of stable decision-making elites. But the relevance of that approach becomes stronger as the scope of its application is reduced and as the standards for identifying the scope are clarified. But this is equally true of the pluralist school and of those approaches based on a "politics of this-or-that policy."

NOTE

[1] E. E. Schattschneider, *Politics, Pressures, and the Tariff* (Hamden, Conn.: Shoe String, 1935).

Charles A. Beard, "The Constitution as an Economic Document." Reprinted with permission of Macmillan Publishing Company from *An Economic Interpretation of the Constitution of the United States* by Charles A. Beard. Copyright 1913, 1935 Macmillan Publishing Company, renewed 1941 by Charles A. Beard. Renewed 1963 by William Beard and Miriam Beard Vagts.

Samuel H. Beer, "Federalism, Nationalism, and Democracy in America," *American Political Science Review* (March 1978), vol. 72, pp. 9–19. Reprinted by permission of the American Political Science Association and the author.

Alexander M. Bickel, "Establishment and General Justification of Judicial Review" from *The Least Dangerous Branch* by Alexander M. Bickel (1962: Bobbs-Merrill Publishing Co.). Copyright, Josephine Ann Bickel. Reprinted by permission.

James Bryce, "Why Great Men Are Not Chosen Presidents," from *The American Commonwealth.* Source: G. P. Putnam's Sons, 1959 edition. (Originally published 1888.)

Walter Dean Burnham, "The Changing Shape of the American Political Universe," *American Political Science Review* (March 1965), vol. 59, pp. 10–28. Reprinted by permission of the American Political Science Association and the author.

Angus Campbell, Philip E. Converse, Warren E. Miller, Donald E. Stokes, "The Development of Party Identification" from *The American Voter: An Abridgement* by Angus Campbell, Philip E. Converse, Warren E. Miller, and Donald E. Stokes. Copyright © 1964 John Wiley & Sons, Inc. Publishers. Reprinted by permission of John Wiley & Sons, Inc.

Edward S. Corwin, "The 'Higher Law' Background of American Constitutional Law," *Harvard Law Review*, vol. XLII (1928–1929), pp. 149–185; 365–409. Copyright © 1928, 1929 by the Harvard Law Review Association. Reprinted by permission.

Thomas E. Cronin, "The Swelling of the Presidency," *Saturday Review*, vol. 1 (February 1973), pp. 30–36. © 1973 Saturday Review Magazine. Reprinted by permission.

Robert A. Dahl, "On the Species *Homo Politicus*" from *Who Governs?* by Robert A. Dahl. Copyright 1961 by Yale University Press. Reprinted by permission of Yale University Press.

Martin Diamond, "The Federalist's View of Federalism" from *Essays in Federalism* published by Claremont Men's College, 1961. Reprinted by permission of The Henry Salvatori Center, Claremont McKenna College.

Richard F. Fenno, Jr., "Congressmen in Committees" from Richard F. Fenno, Jr., *Congressmen in Committees*, pp. 13–14, 43–45, 79–80, 137–138, and 276–279. Copyright © 1973 by Little, Brown and Company (Inc.). Reprinted by permission of the publisher and the author.

Morton Grodzins, "The Federal System," in The American Assembly, *Goals for Americans: The Report of the President's Commission on National Goals*, pp. 265–282. Englewood Cliffs, N.J., Prentice-Hall, Inc., 1960. Reprinted by permission.

Alexander Hamilton, James Madison, and John Jay, *The Federalist Papers*. Source: The New American Library, 1961 edition.

Louis Hartz from "The Concept of a Liberal Society" in *The Liberal Tradition in America*, copyright © 1955, 1983 by Louis Hartz. Reprinted by permission of Harcourt Brace Jovanovich, Inc.

Hugh Heclo, "Political Executives: A Government of Strangers" from *A Government of Strangers: Executive Politics in Washington*, The Brookings Institution, 1977. Reprinted by permission of The Brookings Institution.

Samuel P. Huntington, "Congressional Responses to the Twentieth Century," in The American Assembly, *The Congress and America's Future*, ed. David Truman, pp. 6–31, 2nd ed. Englewood Cliffs, N.J., Prentice-Hall, Inc., 1973. Reprinted by permission.

Charles E. Lindblom, "The Science of 'Muddling Through' " from *Public Administration Review*, vol. 19 (Spring 1959), pp. 79–88. Reprinted by permission of the author.

Seymour Martin Lipset, "Formulating a National Identity" from *The First New Nation: The United States in Historical and Comparative Perspective* by Seymour Martin Lipset. © 1963 by Seymour Martin Lipset. Reprinted by permission of Basic Books, Inc., Publishers.

Norton E. Long, "Power and Administration," *Public Administration Review*, vol. 9 (Autumn 1949), pp. 257–264. Reprinted with permission from *Public Administration Review*. © 1949 by The American Society of Public Administration, 1120 G St., N.W., Washington, D.C. All rights reserved.

Theodore J. Lowi, "The Public Philosophy: Interest-Group Liberalism," *American Political Science Review* (March 1967), vol. 61, pp. 5–24. Reprinted by permission of the American Political Science Association and the author. "Distribution, Regulation, Redistribution: The Functions of Government" from Theodore J. Lowi, "American Business, Public Policy, Case-Studies, and Political Theory," *World Politics*, vol. 16, no. 4 (July 1964). Copyright © 1964 by Princeton University Press. Reprinted by permission of Princeton University Press.

David R. Mayhew, "Congressional Elections: The Case of the Vanishing Marginals," *Polity*, vol. 6, no. 3 (Spring 1974), pp. 295–317. Reprinted by permission of *Polity* and the author.

C. Wright Mills, "The Structure of Power in American Society," *British Journal of Sociology*, vol. 9, no. 1 (May 1958), pp. 29–41. Reprinted by permission of Routledge & Kegan Paul PLC.

Richard E. Neustadt, "The Power to Persuade" from *Presidential Power: The Politics of Leadership with Reflections on Johnson and Nixon* by Richard E. Neustadt. Copyright © 1976 John Wiley & Sons, Inc. Reprinted by permission of John Wiley & Sons, Inc.

Norman H. Nie, Sidney Verba, and John R. Petrocik, "The Rise of Issue Voting." Reprinted by permission of the publishers from *The Changing American Voter*, enlarged edition, by Norman H. Nie, Sidney Verba, and John R. Petrocik, Cambridge, Mass.: Harvard University Press. Copyright © 1976, 1979 by The Twentieth Century Fund.

Mancur Olson, Jr., "Collective Action: The Logic" from *The Rise and Decline of Nations: Economic Growth, Stagflation, and Social Rigidities* (New Haven: Yale University Press). Copyright © 1982 Yale University Press. Reprinted by permission.

Nelson W. Polsby, "Strengthening Congress in National Policy-Making," *The Yale Review*, vol. LIX (June 1970), no. 4, pp. 481–497. Copyright 1970 Yale University. Reprinted by permission.

C. Herman Pritchett from "Libertarian Motivations on the Vinson Court," *American Political Science Review*, vol. 47 (1953), pp. 321–336. Reprinted by permission of the American Political Science Association and the author.

William H. Riker, "Federalism: Origin, Operation, Significance" from Aaron Wildavsky, ed., *American Federalism in Perspective* published by Little, Brown & Co., 1967. Reprinted by permission of William H. Riker.

E. E. Schattschneider, "The Scope and Bias of the Pressure System" from *The Semisovereign People* by E. E. Schattschneider. Copyright © 1975 by E. E. Schattschneider and The Dryden Press. Reprinted by permission of CBS College Publishing.

James L. Sundquist, "Missing Capabilities: Political Leadership and Policy Integration" from *The Decline and Resurgence of Congress*. Copyright 1981 by The Brookings Institution. Reprinted by permission of The Brookings Institution.

Aaron Wildavsky, "Political Implications of Budgetary Reform," *Public Administration Review*, vol. 21 (Autumn 1961), pp. 183–190. Reprinted with permission from *Public Administration Review*, © 1961 by The American Society for Public Administration, 1120 G. St., N.W., Washington, D.C. All rights reserved.

James Q. Wilson, "The Rise of the Bureaucratic State." Reprinted with permission of the author from *The Public Interest*, no. 41 (Fall 1975), pp. 77–103. © 1975 by National Affairs, Inc.

Woodrow Wilson, "Congressional Government" from Woodrow Wilson, *Congressional Government*, pp. 193–215 (Gloucester, Mass.: Peter Smith Publisher, 1973). Reprinted by permission of the publisher.